# Real Estate Investing

## ALL-IN-ONE

by Ray Brown; Peter Conti;
Robert S. Griswold, MSBA;
Laurence C. Harmon; Peter Harris;
Symon He; Joe Kraynak; Kyle Roberts;
Ralph R. Roberts; James Svetec;
Eric Tyson, MBA; and Nicholas Wallwork

for
dummies®
A Wiley Brand

# Real Estate Investing All-in-One For Dummies®

Published by: **John Wiley & Sons, Inc.,** 111 River Street, Hoboken, NJ 07030-5774, www.wiley.com

Copyright © 2023 by John Wiley & Sons, Inc., Hoboken, New Jersey

Published simultaneously in Canada

For general information on our other products and services, please contact our Customer Care Department within the U.S. at 877-762-2974, outside the U.S. at 317-572-3993, or fax 317-572-4002. For technical support, please visit https://hub.wiley.com/community/support/dummies.

Wiley publishes in a variety of print and electronic formats and by print-on-demand. Some material included with standard print versions of this book may not be included in e-books or in print-on-demand. If this book refers to media such as a CD or DVD that is not included in the version you purchased, you may download this material at http://booksupport.wiley.com. For more information about Wiley products, visit www.wiley.com.

Library of Congress Control Number: 2022948311

ISBN 978-1-394-15284-1 (pbk); ISBN 978-1-394-15289-6 (ebk); ISBN 978-1-394-15288-9 (ebk)

SKY10038284_111022

# Contents at a Glance

# Table of Contents

## BOOK 7: GONE GLOBAL: INVESTING IN INTERNATIONAL REAL ESTATE

# Introduction

S uccessful real estate investing requires smart decisions. *Real Estate Investing All-in-One For Dummies* presents basic real estate investing topics — such as buying and selling houses, investing in foreclosures, and flipping properties — but also introduces advanced subjects, like international and commercial real estate investing, that can help you build even more wealth. You even get the ins and outs of short-term rentals like Airbnb, so all your passive income options are covered.

This book can help you start investing in real estate quickly and easily, thanks to expert tips and information that will help you avoid costly mistakes. It's your one-stop resource for all things real estate. Explore the pages of this book and find the topics that most interest you within the world of real estate investing.

## About This Book

You don't need a fancy degree to invest in real estate. What you *do* need is a desire to read, absorb, and practice the simple yet effective strategies in this book. *Real Estate Investing All-in-One For Dummies* is designed to give you a realistic approach to investing in real estate. It provides sound, practical lessons and insights. You're not expected to read it from cover to cover. Instead, this book is designed as a reference tool. Feel free to read the chapters in whatever order you choose. You can flip to the sections and chapters that interest you or those that include topics that you need to know more about.

A quick note: Sidebars (shaded boxes of text) dig into the details of a given topic, but they aren't crucial to understanding it. Feel free to read them or skip them. You can pass over the text accompanied by the Technical Stuff icon, too. The text marked with this icon gives some interesting but nonessential information about the subject of real estate investing.

One last thing: Within this book, you may note that some web addresses break across two lines of text. If you're reading this book in print and want to visit one of these web pages, simply key in the web address exactly as it's noted in the text, pretending as though the line break doesn't exist. If you're reading this as an e-book, you've got it easy — just click the web address to be taken directly to the web page.

# Foolish Assumptions

No matter your skill or experience level with real estate investing, you can get something out of this book. Here are some assumptions we made about you as we wrote this book:

>> You're new to investing in real estate and don't know what properties and strategies will work for you.

>> Your real estate experience is limited to renting an apartment or owning your own home, and you're interested in finding out more about foreclosures, flipping, and other investment options.

>> You may already be a seasoned real estate investor, but you're ready to go to the next level with commercial and international properties.

>> You want to diversify your investment portfolio.

# Icons Used in This Book

Throughout this book, icons help guide you through suggestions, solutions, and cautions. Here's what they mean.

The name says it all! This icon indicates something *really* important to take away from this book.

Information marked with this icon is interesting but not crucial to understanding real estate investing. Skip it or read it; the choice is yours.

This icon highlights helpful strategies that can enable you to build your real estate portfolio (and your wealth) faster.

This icon indicates treacherous territory in real estate investing. Skip this information at your own peril.

# Beyond the Book

In addition to the material in the print or e-book you're reading right now, this product comes with a free access-anywhere Cheat Sheet that can put you on the road to successful real estate investing. To get this Cheat Sheet, simply go to www.dummies.com and search for "Real Estate Investing All-in-One For Dummies Cheat Sheet" in the Search box.

# Where to Go from Here

If you're a new real estate investor, you may want to consider starting from the beginning; head to Book 1 on getting started. That way, you'll be ready for some of the more advanced topics introduced later. But you don't have to read this book from cover to cover. *Real Estate Investing All-in-One For Dummies* makes it easy to find answers to specific questions. Just turn to the table of contents or index to locate the information you need. You can get in and get out, just like that. Good luck!

# 1
# Getting Started with Real Estate Investing

# Contents at a Glance

Chapter **1**

# Evaluating Real Estate as an Investment

I t's never too early or too late to formulate your own plan for a comprehensive wealth-building strategy. For many, such a strategy can help with the goals of funding future education for children and ensuring a comfortable retirement.

The challenge involved with real estate is that it takes some real planning to get started. Contacting an investment company and purchasing some shares of your favorite mutual fund or stock is a lot easier than acquiring your first rental property. Buying property need not be too difficult, though. With a financial and real estate investment plan, a lot of patience, and the willingness to do some hard work, you can be on your way to building your own real estate empire!

This chapter gives you information that can help you decide whether you have what it takes to make money *and* be comfortable with investing in real estate. You compare real estate investments to other investments. You find some questions you should ask yourself before making any decisions. And finally, you get guidance on how real estate investments can fit into your overall personal financial plans. Along the way, you find insights and thoughts on a long-term strategy for building wealth through real estate that virtually everyone can understand and actually achieve.

# Understanding Real Estate's Income- and Wealth-Producing Potential

Compared with most other investments, good real estate can excel at producing periodic or monthly cash flow for property owners. So in addition to the longer-term appreciation potential, you can also earn investment income year in and year out. Real estate is a true growth *and* income investment.

**REMEMBER**

The vast majority of people who don't make money in real estate make easily avoidable mistakes, which this book helps you avoid.

The following list highlights the major benefits of investing in real estate:

>> **Tax-deferred compounding of value:** In real estate investing, the appreciation of your properties compounds *tax-deferred* during your years of ownership. You don't pay tax on this profit until you sell your property — and even then, you can roll over your gain into another investment property and avoid paying taxes. (See the later section "Being aware of the tax advantages.")

>> **Regular cash flow:** If you have property that you rent out, you have money coming in every month in the form of rents. Some properties, particularly larger multi-unit complexes, may have some additional cash flow sources, such as from parking, storage, or washers and dryers.

**REMEMBER**

When you own investment real estate, you should also expect to incur expenses that include your mortgage payment, property taxes, insurance, and maintenance. The interaction of the revenues coming in and the expenses going out tells you whether you realize a positive operating profit each month.

>> **Reduced income tax bills:** For income tax purposes, you also get to claim an expense that isn't really an out-of-pocket cost — depreciation. Depreciation enables you to reduce your current income tax bill and hence increase your cash flow from a property. (Find out about this tax advantage and others in the later section "Being aware of the tax advantages.")

>> **Rate of increase of rental income versus overall expenses:** Over time, your operating profit, which is subject to ordinary income tax, should rise as you increase your rental prices faster than the rate of increase for your property's overall expenses. The following simple example shows why even modest rental increases are magnified into larger operating profits and healthy returns on investment over time.

Suppose that you're in the market to purchase a single-family home that you want to rent out and that such properties are selling for about $200,000 in the area you've deemed to be a good investment. (*Note:* Housing prices vary widely across different areas, but the following example should give you a relative sense of how a rental property's expenses and revenues change over time.) You expect to make a 20 percent down payment and take out a 30-year fixed rate mortgage at 6 percent for the remainder of the purchase price — $160,000. Here are the details:

| | |
|---|---|
| Monthly mortgage payment | $960 |
| Monthly property tax | $200 |
| Other monthly expenses (maintenance, insurance) | $200 |
| Monthly rent | $1,400 |

Table 1-1 shows you what happens with your investment over time. Assume that your rent and expenses (except for your mortgage payment, which is fixed) increase 3 percent annually and that your property appreciates a conservative 4 percent per year. (For simplification purposes, depreciation is ignored in this example. If the benefit of depreciation had been included, it would further enhance the calculated investment returns.)

**TABLE 1-1    How a Rental Property's Income and Wealth Build over Time**

| Year | Monthly Rent | Monthly Expenses | Property Value | Mortgage Balance |
|---|---|---|---|---|
| 0 | $1,400 | $1,360 | $200,000 | $160,000 |
| 5 | $1,623 | $1,424 | $243,330 | $148,960 |
| 10 | $1,881 | $1,498 | $296,050 | $133,920 |
| 20 | $2,529 | $1,682 | $438,225 | $86,400 |
| 30 | $3,398 | $1,931 | $648,680 | $0 |
| 31 | $3,500 | $1,000 | $674,625 | $0 |

Now, notice what happens over time. When you first buy the property, the monthly rent and the monthly expenses are about equal. By year five, the monthly income exceeds the expenses by about $200 per month. Consider why this happens — your largest monthly expense, the mortgage payment, doesn't increase. So, even though you can assume that the rent increases just 3 percent per year, which is the same rate of increase assumed for your nonmortgage expenses, the compounding of rental inflation begins to produce larger and larger cash flows to you, the property owner. Cash flow of $200 per month may not sound like much, but consider that this $2,400 annual income is from an original $40,000 investment. Thus, by year five, your rental property is producing a 6 percent return on your down payment investment. (And remember, if you factor in the tax deduction for depreciation, your cash flow and return are even higher.)

In addition to the monthly cash flow from the amount that the rent exceeds the property's expenses, also look at the last two columns in Table 1-1 to see what has happened by year five to your *equity* (the difference between market value and mortgage balance owed) in the property. With just a 4 percent annual increase in market value, your $40,000 in equity (the down payment) has more than doubled to $94,370 ($243,330 – $148,960).

By years 10 and 20, you can see the further increases in your monthly cash flow and significant expansion in your property's equity. By year 30, the property is producing more than $1,400 per month cash flow and you're now the proud owner of a mortgage-free property worth more than triple what you paid for it!

After you get the mortgage paid off in year 30, take a look at what happens in year 31 and beyond to your monthly expenses (big drop as your monthly mortgage payment disappears!) and therefore your cash flow (big increase).

# Recognizing the Caveats of Real Estate Investing

Despite all its potential, real estate investing isn't lucrative at all times and for all people — here's a quick outline of the biggest caveats that accompany investing in real estate:

>> **Few home runs:** Your likely returns from real estate won't approach the biggest home runs that the most accomplished entrepreneurs achieve in the business world. That said, by doing your homework, improving properties, and practicing good management (and sometimes enjoying a bit of luck), you can do extremely well!

>> **Upfront operating profit challenges:** Unless you make a large down payment, your monthly operating profit may be small, nonexistent, or negative in the early years of rental property ownership. During soft periods in the local economy, rents may rise more slowly than your expenses or they may even fall. That's why you must ensure that you can weather financially tough times. In the worst cases, rental property owners lose both their investment property and their homes. See the later section "Fitting Real Estate into Your Plans."

>> **Ups and downs:** You're not going to earn an 8 to 10 percent return every year. Although you have the potential for significant profits, owning real estate isn't like owning a printing press at the U.S. Treasury. Like stocks and other types of ownership investments, real estate goes through down periods as well as up periods. Most people who make money investing in real estate do so because they invest and hold property over many years.

>> **Relatively high transaction costs:** If you buy a property and then want out a year or two later, you may find that even though it has appreciated in value, much (if not all) of your profit has been wiped away by the high transaction costs. Typically, the costs of buying and selling — which include real estate agent commissions, loan fees, title insurance, and other closing costs — amount to about 8 to 12 percent of the purchase price of a property. So, although you may be elated if, in the short term, your property appreciates 10 percent in value, you must consider the overall financial picture. You may not be so thrilled when you realize that selling the property may not have any greater return than stashing your money in a lowly bank account.

>> **Tax implications:** Last, but not least, when you make a positive net return or profit on your real estate investment, the federal and state governments are waiting with open hands for their shares. Throughout this book, you discover ways to improve your after-tax returns. Keep in mind that the profit you have left after government entities take their bites (not your pretax income) is what really matters.

These drawbacks shouldn't keep you from exploring real estate investing as an option; rather, they simply reinforce the need to really know what you're getting into with this type of investing and whether it's a good match for you. The rest of this chapter takes you deeper into an assessment of real estate as an investment as well as introspection about your goals, interests, and abilities.

# Comparing Real Estate to Other Investments

Surely, you've considered or heard about many different investments over the years. To help you grasp and understand the unique characteristics of real estate, the following sections compare and contrast real estate's attributes with those of other wealth-building investments like stocks and small business.

# Returns

Clearly, a major reason that many people invest in real estate is for the healthy total *returns* (which include ongoing cash flow and the appreciation of the property). Real estate often generates robust long-term returns because, like stocks and small business, it's an *ownership investment.* This means that real estate is an asset that has the ability to produce periodic income *and* gains or profits upon refinancing or sale.

Research and experience suggest that total real estate investment returns are comparable to those from stocks — about 8 to 9 percent on average, annually. Over recent decades, the average annual return on real estate investment trusts (REITs), publicly traded companies that invest in income-producing real estate such as apartment buildings, office complexes, and shopping centers, has appreciated at about this pace as well.

And you can earn long-term returns that average much better than 10 percent per year if you select excellent properties in the best areas, hold them for several years, and manage them well.

# Risk

Real estate doesn't always rise in value — witness the decline occurring in most parts of the U.S. during the late 2000s and early 2010s. That said, market values for real estate generally don't suffer from as much volatility as stock prices do. You may recall how the excitement surrounding the rapid sustained increase of technology and internet stock prices in the late 1990s turned into the dismay and agony of those same sectors' stock prices crashing in the early 2000s. Many stocks in this industry, including those of leaders in their niches, saw their stock prices plummet by 80 percent, 90 percent, or more. Generally, you don't see those kinds of dramatic roller-coaster shifts in values over the short run with the residential income property real estate market.

However, keep in mind (especially if you tend to be concerned about shorter-term risks) that real estate can suffer from declines of 10 percent, 20 percent, or more. If you make a down payment of, say, 20 percent and want to sell your property after a 10 to 15 percent price decline, you may find that all (as in 100 percent) of your invested dollars (down payment) are wiped out after you factor in transaction costs. So you can lose everything.

REMEMBER

You can greatly reduce and minimize your risk investing in real estate through buying and holding property for many years (seven to ten or more). Note that many of these fantastic success stories about amazing profits on "flipping" single-family homes and small rental properties are just like gamblers who only tell you about their biggest winnings or forget to tell you that they turned around and lost much of what they won. While there is a lot of hype on cable television and the internet about "flipping properties" for short-term profits (get the scoop in Book 4), think of real estate as a long-term investment.

# Liquidity

*Liquidity* — the ease and cost with which you can sell and get your money out of an investment — is one of real estate's shortcomings. Real estate is relatively *illiquid:* You can't sell a piece of property with the same speed with which you can whip out your ATM card and withdraw money from your bank account or sell a stock or an exchange-traded fund with a click of your computer's mouse or by tapping on your cellphone.

**REMEMBER**

You can actually view real estate's relative illiquidity as a strength, certainly compared with stocks that people often trade in and out of because doing so is so easy and seemingly cheap. As a result, some stock market investors tend to lose sight of the long term and miss out on the bigger gains that accrue to patient, buy-and-stick-with-it investors. Because you can't track the value of investment real estate daily on your computer and because real estate takes considerable time, energy, and money to sell, you're far more likely to buy and hold onto your properties for the longer term.

Although real estate investments are generally less liquid than stocks, they're generally more liquid than investments made in your own or someone else's small business. People need a place to live and businesses need a place to operate, so there's always demand for real estate (although the supply of such available properties can greatly exceed the demand in some areas during certain time periods).

# Capital requirements

Although you can easily get started with traditional investments such as stocks and mutual funds with a few hundred or thousand dollars, the vast majority of quality real estate investments require far greater investments — usually on the order of tens of thousands of dollars.

**TIP**

If you're one of the many people who don't have that kind of money, don't despair. Among the simplest low-cost real estate investment options are real estate investment trusts (REITs). You can buy these as exchange-traded stocks or invest in a portfolio of REITs through a REIT mutual fund.

# Diversification value

An advantage of holding investment real estate is that its value doesn't necessarily move in tandem with other investments, such as stocks or small-business investments that you hold. You may recall, for example, the massive stock market decline in the early 2000s. In most communities around the United States, real estate values were either steady or actually rising during this horrendous period for stock prices.

However, real estate prices and stock prices, for example, *can* move down together in value (witness the severe recession and stock market drop that took hold in 2008). Sluggish business conditions and lower corporate profits can depress stock *and* real estate prices.

# Opportunities to add value

Although you may not know much about investing in the stock market, you may have some good ideas about how to improve a property and make it more valuable. You can fix up a property or develop it further and raise the rental income accordingly. Perhaps through legwork, persistence, and good negotiating skills, you can purchase a property below its fair market value.

Relative to investing in the stock market, tenacious and savvy real estate investors can more easily buy property in the private real estate market at below fair market value because the real estate market is somewhat less efficient and some owners don't realize the value of their income property or they need to sell quickly. Theoretically, you can do the same in the stock market, but the scores of professional, full-time money managers who analyze the public market for stocks make finding bargains more difficult.

# Being aware of the tax advantages

Real estate investment offers numerous tax advantages. The following sections compare and contrast investment property tax issues with those of other investments.

### Deductible expenses (including depreciation)

Owning a property has much in common with owning your own small business. Every year, you account for your income and expenses on a tax return. Be sure to keep good records of your expenses in purchasing and operating rental real estate. One expense that you get to deduct for rental real estate on your tax return — depreciation — doesn't actually involve spending or outlaying money. *Depreciation* is an allowable tax deduction for buildings because structures wear out over time. Under current tax laws, residential real estate is depreciated over 27½ years (commercial buildings are less favored in the tax code and can be depreciated over 39 years). Residential real estate is depreciated over shorter time periods because it has traditionally been a favored investment in U.S. tax laws.

## Tax-free rollovers of rental property profits

When you sell a stock, mutual fund, or exchange-traded investment that you hold outside a retirement account, you must pay tax on your profits. By contrast, you can avoid paying tax on your profit when you sell a rental property if you roll over your gain into another like-kind investment real estate property.

**REMEMBER**

The rules for properly making one of these 1031 exchanges are complex and involve third parties. Make sure that you find an attorney and/or tax advisor who is an expert at these transactions to ensure that you meet the technical and strict timing requirements so everything goes smoothly (and legally).

If you don't roll over your gain, you may owe significant taxes because of how the IRS defines your gain. For example, if you buy a property for $200,000 and sell it for $550,000, you not only owe tax on the gain from the increased property value, but you also owe tax on an additional amount, the property's depreciation you used during your ownership. The amount of depreciation that you deduct on your tax returns reduces the original $200,000 purchase price, making the taxable difference that much larger. For example, if you deducted $125,000 for depreciation over the years that you owned the property, you owe tax on the difference between the sale price of $550,000 and $75,000 ($200,000 purchase price − $125,000 depreciation).

## Deferred taxes with installment sales

*Installment sales* are a complex method that can be used to defer your tax bill when you sell an investment property at a profit and you don't buy another rental property. With such a sale, you play the role of banker and provide financing to the buyer. In addition to often collecting a competitive interest rate from the buyer, you only have to pay capital gains tax as you receive proceeds over time from the sale that are applied toward the principal or price the buyer agreed to pay for the property. Because of the complexity of this method, consider consulting with a tax attorney.

## Special tax credits for low-income housing and old buildings

If you invest in and upgrade low-income housing or certified historic buildings, you can gain special tax credits. The credits represent a direct reduction in your tax bill from expenditures to rehabilitate and improve such properties. These tax credits exist to encourage investors to invest in and fix up old or run-down buildings that likely would continue to deteriorate otherwise. The IRS has strict rules governing what types of properties qualify. See IRS Form 3468 to discover more about these credits.

The 2017 Tax Cuts and Jobs Act bill created "qualified opportunity zones" to provide tax incentives to invest in "low-income communities," which are defined by each state's governor and may comprise up to 25 percent of designated "low-income communities" in each state. (States can also designate census tracts contiguous with "low-income communities" so long as the median family income in those tracts doesn't exceed 125 percent of the qualifying contiguous "low-income community.")

The new qualified opportunity zone tax incentive allows real estate investors the following potential benefits:

>> The capital gains tax due upon a sale of the property is deferred if the capital gain from the sale is reinvested within 180 days in a qualified opportunity fund.

>> For investments in the qualified opportunity fund of at least five years, investors will receive a step-up in tax basis of 10 percent of the original gain.

>> For investments in the qualified opportunity fund of at least seven years, investors will receive an additional 5 percent step-up in tax basis.

>> For investments of ten or more years or earlier than December 31, 2026, investors can exclude all capital gains of the investment.

## 20% Qualified Business Income (QBI) deduction for "pass-through entities"

The 2017 Tax Cuts and Jobs Act includes lower across-the-board federal income tax rates, which benefit all wage earners and investors, including real estate investors. If you spend at least 250 hours per year on certain activities (defined in a moment) related to your real estate investments, you may also be able to utilize an additional tax break targeted to certain small business entities.

In redesigning the tax code, Congress realized that the many small businesses that operate as so-called pass-through entities would be subjected to higher federal income tax rates compared with the 21 percent corporate income tax rate (reduced from 35 percent). Pass-through entities are small businesses such as sole proprietorships, LLCs, partnerships, and S corporations and are so named because the profits of the business *pass through* to the owners and their personal income tax returns.

To address the concern that individual business owners who operated their business as a pass-through entity could end up paying a higher tax rate than the 21 percent rate levied on C corporations, Congress provided a 20 percent Qualified Business Income (QBI) deduction for those businesses. So, for example, if your sole proprietorship netted you $60,000 in 2019 as a single taxpayer, that would push you into the 22 percent federal income tax bracket. But you get to deduct 20 percent of that $60,000 of income (or $12,000) so you would only owe federal income tax on the remaining $48,000 ($60,000 − $12,000).

Another way to look at this is that the business would only pay taxes on 80 percent of its profits and would be in the 22 percent federal income tax bracket. This deduction effectively reduces the 22 percent tax bracket to 17.6 percent.

**REMEMBER**

For tax year 2022, this 20 percent pass-through QBI deduction gets phased out for service business owners (for example, lawyers, doctors, real estate agents, consultants, and so on) at single taxpayer incomes above $170,050 (up to $220,050) and for married couples filing jointly incomes over $340,100 (up to $440,100). For other types of businesses above these income thresholds, this deduction may be limited, so consult with your tax advisor.

The Internal Revenue Service has clarified that certain rental real estate investor entities are eligible for the QBI 20 percent pass-through deduction in a given tax year if the following conditions are met:

>> Separate books and records are maintained to reflect income and expenses for each rental real estate enterprise.

>> For tax years 2022 and earlier, 250 or more hours of rental services are performed (as described in this revenue procedure) per year with respect to the rental enterprise. For tax 2023 and beyond, in any three of the five consecutive taxable years that end with the taxable year (or in each year for an enterprise held for less than five years), 250 or more hours of rental services are performed (as described in this revenue procedure) per year with respect to the rental real estate enterprise.

>> The taxpayer maintains contemporaneous records, including time reports, logs, or similar documents, regarding the following:

- Hours of all services performed

- Description of all services performed

- Dates on which such services were performed

- Who performed the services

Such records are to be made available for inspection at the request of the IRS. The contemporaneous records requirement will not apply to taxable years prior to 2019.

Per the Internal Revenue Service, rental services include the following:

>> Advertising to rent or lease the real estate

>> Negotiating and executing leases

>> Verifying information contained in prospective tenant applications; collection of rent

>> Daily operation, maintenance, and repair of the property

>> Management of the real estate

>> Purchase of materials

>> Supervision of employees and independent contractors

Rental services may be performed by owners or by employees, agents, and/or independent contractors of the owners. The term rental services does not include financial or investment management activities, such as arranging financing; procuring property; studying and reviewing financial statements or reports on operations; planning, managing, or constructing long-term capital improvements; or time spent traveling to and from the real estate.

Real estate used by the taxpayer (including an owner or beneficiary of a relevant pass-through entity) as a residence for any part of the year is not eligible for this tax break. Real estate rented or leased under a triple-net lease is also not eligible for the QBI deduction.

TIP

Tax advisor Vern Hoven suggests that you can easily avoid the triple-net lease exclusion by changing the terms of the lease to a "net lease" in which the landlord makes the payments for both the real estate property taxes and insurance. So that the financial terms of the original lease remain the same, the landlord then increases the amount of the rent paid by the tenant to offset that full amount of taxes and insurance now paid by the landlord. Thus, your "triple-net lease" becomes a "net lease" with the same net effective financial terms but qualifies for the 20 percent QBI deduction.

# Determining Whether You Should Invest in Real Estate

Most people can succeed at investing in real estate if they're willing to do their homework, which includes selecting top real estate professionals. The following sections ask several important questions to help you decide whether you have what it takes to succeed and be happy with real estate investments that involve managing property. Income-producing real estate isn't a passive investment.

## Do you have sufficient time?

Purchasing and owning investment real estate and being a landlord are time consuming. The same way an uninformed owner can sell property for less than what it's worth, if you fail to do your homework before purchasing property, you can end up overpaying or buying real estate with a slew of problems. Finding competent and ethical real estate professionals takes time. (Chapter 3 in Book 1 guides you through the process.) Investigating communities, neighborhoods, and zoning also soaks up plenty of hours as does examining tenant issues with potential properties.

As for managing a property, you can hire a property manager to interview tenants, collect the rent, and solve problems such as leaky faucets and broken appliances, but doing so costs money and still requires some of your time. Of course, if you hire a competent and experienced property manager, you will be rewarded with less time required for oversight.

TIP

If you're stretched too thin due to work and family responsibilities, real estate investing may not be for you. So, unless you want to locate, interview, hire, and pay for a qualified property manager, then you may want to look into less time-intensive real estate investments such as real estate investment trusts.

## Can you deal with problems?

Challenges and problems inevitably occur when you try to buy a property. Purchase negotiations can be stressful and frustrating. You can also count on some problems coming up when you own and manage investment real estate. Most tenants won't care for a property the way property owners do.

REMEMBER

If every little problem (especially those that you think may have been caused by your tenants — think "bed bugs"!) causes you distress, at a minimum, you should only own rental property with the assistance of a property manager. You should also question whether you're really going to be satisfied owning investment property. The financial rewards come well down the road, but you live the day-to-day ownership headaches (including the risk of litigation) immediately.

## Does real estate interest you?

Some of the best real estate investors have a curiosity and interest in real estate. If you don't already possess it, such an interest and curiosity *can* be cultivated — and this book may just do the trick.

On the other hand, some people simply aren't comfortable investing in rental property. For example, if you've had experience and success with stock market investing, you may be uncomfortable venturing into real estate investments. Some people are on a mission to start their own business and may prefer to channel the time and money into that outlet.

## Can you handle market downturns?

Real estate investing isn't for the faint of heart. Buying and holding real estate is a whole lot of fun when prices and rents are rising. But market downturns happen, and they test you emotionally as well as financially.

### HOW LEVERAGE AFFECTS YOUR REAL ESTATE RETURNS

Real estate is different from most other investments in that you can typically borrow (finance) up to 70 to 80 percent or more of the value of the property. Thus, you can use your small down payment of 20 to 30 percent of the purchase price to buy, own, and control a much larger investment. (During market downturns, lenders tighten requirements and may require larger down payments than they do during good times.) So when your real estate increases in value (which is what you hope and expect), you make money on your investment as well as on the money that you borrowed. That's what we mean when we say that the investment returns from real estate are enhanced due to *leverage.*

Take a look at this simple example. Suppose you purchase a property for $150,000 and make a $30,000 down payment. Over the next three years, imagine that the property appreciates 10 percent to $165,000. Thus, you have a profit (on paper) of $15,000 ($165,000 – $150,000) on an investment of just $30,000. In other words, you've made a 50 percent return on your investment. (**Note:** This example ignores *cash flow* — whether your rental income that you collect from the property exceeds the expenses that you pay or vice versa, and the tax benefits associated with rental real estate.)

Keep in mind that leverage magnifies all of your returns, and those returns aren't always positive! If your $150,000 property decreases in value to $135,000, even though it has only dropped 10 percent in value, you actually lose (on paper) 50 percent of your original $30,000 investment. (In case you care, and it's okay if you don't, some wonks apply the terms *positive leverage* and *negative leverage.*) See the earlier section "Understanding Real Estate's Income- and Wealth-Producing Potential" for a more detailed example of investment property profit and return.

Consider the real estate market price declines that happened in most communities and types of property surrounding the 2008 financial crisis. In many parts of the United States, the impact was still a reality several years later. Such drops can present attractive buying opportunities for those with courage, a good credit score, and cash for the down payment.

**REMEMBER**

No one has a crystal ball, though, so don't expect to be able to buy at the precise bottom of prices and sell at an exact peak of your local market. Even if you make a smart buy now, you'll inevitably end up holding some of your investment property during a difficult market (recessions where you have trouble finding and retaining quality tenants or when rents and property values may fall rather than rise). Do you have the financial (and emotional) wherewithal to handle such a downturn? How have you handled other investments when their values have fallen?

# Fitting Real Estate into Your Plans

For most non-wealthy people, purchasing investment real estate has a major impact on their overall personal financial situation. So, before you go out to buy property, you should inventory your money life and be sure your fiscal house is in order. This section explains how you can do just that.

## Ensuring your best personal financial health

If you're trying to improve your physical fitness by exercising, you may find that not eating healthfully and smoking are barriers to your goal. Likewise, investing in real estate or other growth investments such as stocks while you're carrying high-cost consumer debt (credit cards, auto loans, and so on) and spending more than you earn impedes your financial goals.

**REMEMBER**

Before you set out to invest in real estate, pay off all your consumer debt. Not only will you be financially healthier for doing so, but you'll also enhance your future mortgage applications.

Eliminate wasteful and unnecessary spending; analyze your monthly spending to identify target areas for reduction. This practice enables you to save more and better afford making investments, including real estate. The importance of living below your means is also important. However, this takes a lot of discipline and self-control in the face of our consumer-driven "must have" world in which having the latest technology or keeping up with the "influencers" is how some people define their success. As Charles Dickens said, "Annual income twenty pounds; annual expenditures nineteen pounds; result, happiness. Annual income twenty pounds; annual expenditure twenty pounds; result, misery."

## Protecting yourself with insurance

Regardless of your real estate investment desires and decisions, you absolutely must have comprehensive insurance for yourself and your major assets, including:

>> **Health insurance:** Major medical coverage protects you from financial ruin if you have a major accident or illness that requires significant hospital and other medical care.

>> **Disability insurance:** For most working people, their biggest asset is their future income-earning ability. Disability insurance replaces a portion of your employment earnings if you're unable to work for an extended period of time due to an incapacitating illness or injury.

>> **Life insurance:** If loved ones are financially dependent upon you, term life insurance, which provides a lump sum death benefit, can help to replace your employment earnings if you pass away.

>> **Homeowner's insurance:** Not only do you want homeowner's insurance to protect you against the financial cost due to a fire or other home-damaging catastrophe, but such coverage also provides you with liability protection. (After you buy and operate a rental property with tenants, you should obtain rental owner's insurance.)

>> **Auto insurance:** This coverage is similar to homeowner's coverage in that it insures a valuable asset and also provides liability insurance should you be involved in an accident.

>> **Excess liability (umbrella) insurance:** This relatively inexpensive coverage, available in million-dollar increments, adds on to the modest liability protection offered on your basic home and auto policies, which is inadequate for more-affluent people.

Nobody enjoys spending hard-earned money on insurance. However, having proper protection gives you peace of mind and financial security, so don't put off reviewing and securing needed policies. For assistance, see the latest edition of *Personal Finance For Dummies* by Eric Tyson, MBA (Wiley).

# Considering retirement account funding

If you're not taking advantage of your retirement accounts — such as 401(k)s, 403(b)s, SEP-IRAs, and so on — you may be missing out on some terrific tax benefits. Funding retirement accounts gives you an immediate tax deduction when you contribute to them. And some employer accounts offer "free" matching money — but you've got to contribute to earn the matching money.

In comparison, you derive no tax benefits while you accumulate your down payment for an real estate investment purchase (or other investments such as for a small business). Furthermore, the operating positive cash flow or income from your real estate investment is subject to ordinary income taxes as you earn it. To be fair and balanced, we must mention here that investment real estate offers numerous tax benefits, which are detailed in the earlier section "Being aware of the tax advantages."

# Thinking about asset allocation

With money that you invest for the long term, you should have an overall game plan in mind. Fancy-talking financial advisors like to use buzzwords such as *asset allocation,* a term that indicates what portion of your money you have invested in different types of investment vehicles, such as stocks and real estate (for appreciation or growth), versus lending vehicles, such as bonds and certificates of deposit, also known as CDs (which produce current income).

**TIP**

Here's a simple way to calculate asset allocation for long-term investments: Subtract your age from 110. The result is the percentage of your long-term money that you should invest in ownership investments for appreciation. So, for example, a 40-year-old would take 110 minus 40, which equals 70 percent in growth investments such as stocks and real estate. If you want to be more aggressive, subtract your age from 120; a 40-year-old would then have 80 percent in growth investments.

As you gain more knowledge, assets, and diversification of growth assets, you're in a better position to take on more risk. Just be sure you're properly covered with insurance as discussed earlier in the section "Protecting yourself with insurance."

**REMEMBER**

These are simply guidelines, not hard-and-fast rules or mandates. If you want to be more aggressive and are comfortable taking on greater risk, you can invest higher portions in ownership investments.

As you consider asset allocation, when classifying your investments, determine and use your *equity* in your real estate holdings, which is the market value of property less outstanding mortgages. For example, suppose that prior to buying an investment property, your long-term investments consist of the following:

| | |
|---|---|
| Stocks | $150,000 |
| Bonds | $50,000 |
| CDs | $50,000 |
| Total | $250,000 |

So, you have 60 percent in ownership investments ($150,000) and 40 percent in lending investments ($50,000 + $50,000). Now, suppose you plan to purchase a $300,000 income property, making a $75,000 down payment. Because you've decided to bump up your ownership investment portion to make your money grow more over the years, you plan to use your maturing CD balance and sell some of your bonds for the down payment. After your real estate purchase, here's how your investment portfolio looks:

| | |
|---|---|
| Stocks | $150,000 |
| Real estate | $75,000 ($300,000 property – $225,000 mortgage) |
| Bonds | $25,000 |
| Total | $250,000 |

Thus, after the real estate purchase, you've got 90 percent in ownership investments ($150,000 + $75,000) and just 10 percent in lending investments ($25,000). Such a mix may be appropriate for someone under the age of 50 who desires an aggressive investment portfolio positioned for long-term growth potential.

## BECOME YOUR OWN LANDLORD

Many real estate investors are actually involved in other activities as their primary source of income. Ironically, many of these business owners come to realize the benefits of real estate investing but miss the single greatest opportunity that is right before their eyes — the prospect of being their own landlord. Many business owners purchase the buildings occupied by their own businesses and essentially pay the rent to themselves. If you own a business that rents, do yourself a favor — consider becoming your own landlord!

Chapter **2**

# Covering Common Real Estate Investments

I f you lack substantial experience investing in real estate, you should avoid more esoteric and complicated properties and strategies. This chapter discusses the more accessible and easy-to-master income-producing property options. In particular, *residential income property* can be an attractive real estate investment for many people.

Residential housing is easier to understand, purchase, and manage than most other types of income property, such as office, industrial, and retail property. If you're a homeowner, you already have experience locating, purchasing, and maintaining residential property.

In addition to discussing the pros and cons of investing in residential income property, this chapter includes insights as to which may be the most appropriate and profitable for you, and touches on the topics of investing in commercial property as well as undeveloped land.

# Identifying the Various Ways to Invest in Residential Income Property

The first (and one of the best) real estate investments for many people is a home in which to live. The following sections cover the investment possibilities inherent in buying a home for your own use, including potential profit to be had from converting your home to a rental or fixing it up and selling it. These sections also give you some pointers on how to profit from owning your own vacation home.

## Buying a place of your own

During your adult life, you're going to need a roof over your head for many decades. And real estate is the only investment that you can live in or rent out to produce income. A stock, bond, or mutual fund doesn't work too well as a roof over your head!

**REMEMBER**

Unless you expect to move within the next few years, buying a place may make good long-term financial sense. (Even if you need to relocate, you may decide to continue owning the property and use it as a rental property.) In most real estate markets, owning usually costs less than renting over the long haul and allows you to build *equity* (the dollar difference between market value and the current balance of the mortgage loans against the property) in an asset.

Under current tax law, you can also pocket substantial tax-free profits when you sell your home for more than you originally paid plus the money you sunk into improvements during your ownership. Specifically, single taxpayers can realize up to a $250,000 tax-free capital gain; married couples filing jointly get up to $500,000. In order to qualify for this homeowner's *gains tax exemption,* you (or your spouse if you're married) must have owned the home and used it as your primary residence for a minimum of 24 months out of the past 60 months. The 24 months don't have to be continuous. Additionally, this tax break allows for pro-rata (proportionate) credit based on hardship or change of employment. Also note that the full exemption amounts are reduced proportionately for the length of time you rented out your home over the five-year period referenced above.

Some commentators have stated that your home isn't an investment because you're not renting it out. But consider the fact that some people move to a less costly home when they retire (because it's smaller and/or because it's in a lower-cost area). Trading down to a lower-priced property in retirement frees up equity that has built up over many years of homeownership. This money can be used to supplement your retirement income and for any other purpose your heart desires. Your home is an investment because it can appreciate in value over the years, and you can use that money toward your financial or personal goals. The latest edition of *Home Buying Kit For Dummies* by Eric Tyson, MBA, and Ray Brown (Wiley) can help you make terrific home buying decisions. You can also flip to Book 2 for a primer on buying a house.

## Converting your home to a rental

Turning your current home into a rental property when you move is a simple way to buy and own more properties. You can do this multiple times (as you move out of homes you own over the years), and you can do this strategy of acquiring rental properties not only with a house, but also with a duplex or another small multi-unit rental property where you reside in one of the units. This approach is an option if you're already considering investing in real estate (either now or in the future), and you can afford to own two or more properties. Holding onto your current home when you're buying a new one is more advisable if you're moving within the same area so that you're close by to manage the property. This approach presents a number of positives:

>> You save the time and cost of finding a separate rental property, not to mention the associated transaction costs.

>> You know the property and have probably taken good care of it and perhaps made some improvements.

>> You know the target market because the home appealed to you.

**WARNING**

Some people unfortunately make the mistake of holding onto their current home for the wrong reasons when they buy another. This situation typically occurs when a homeowner must sell their home in a depressed market. Nobody likes to lose money and sell their home for less than they paid for it or sell for a good deal less than it was worth several years ago. Thus, some owners hold onto their homes until prices recover. If you plan to move and want to keep your current home as a long-term investment (rental) property, you can. If you fully convert your home to rental property and use it that way for years before selling it, after you do sell you can either take advantage of the lower long-term capital gains rates or do a tax-deferred exchange. For tax purposes, you get to deduct depreciation and all the write-offs during the ownership and you can shelter up to $25,000 in income from active sources subject to income eligibility requirements. (Or even more if you or your spouse happen to qualify as a real estate professional.)

**WARNING**

Turning your home into a *short-term* rental, however, is usually a bad move because

>> You may not want the responsibilities of being a landlord, yet you force yourself into the landlord business when you convert your home into a rental.

> » You owe tax on the sale's profit (and recaptured depreciation) if your property is classified for tax purposes as a rental when you sell it and you don't buy another rental property. (You can purchase another rental property through a 1031 exchange to defer paying taxes on your profit.)

You lose some of the capital gains tax exclusion if you sell your home and you had rented it out for a portion of the five-year period prior to selling it. For example, if you rented your home for two of the last five years, you may only exclude 60 percent of your gain (up to the maximums of $250,000 for single taxpayers and $500,000 for married couples filing jointly), whereas the other 40 percent is taxed as a long-term capital gain. Also be aware that when you sell a home previously rented and are accounting for the sale on your tax return, you must recapture the depreciation taken during the rental period.

## Investing and living in well-situated fixer-uppers

*Serial home selling* is a variation on the tried-and-true real estate investment strategy of investing in well-located fixer-upper homes where you can invest your time, sweat equity, and materials to make improvements that add more value than they cost. The only catch is that you must actually move into the fixer-upper for at least 24 months to earn the full homeowner's capital gains exemption of up to $250,000 for single taxpayers and $500,000 for married couples filing jointly (as covered in the earlier section "Buying a place of your own").

REMEMBER

Be sure to buy a home in need of that special TLC in a great neighborhood where you're willing to live for 24 months or more! But if you're a savvy investor, you would've invested in a great neighborhood anyway.

Here's a simple example to illustrate the potentially significant benefits of this strategy. You purchase a fixer-upper for $275,000 that becomes your principal residence, and then over the next 24 months you invest $25,000 in improvements (paint, repairs, landscaping, appliances, decorator items, and so on), and you also invest the amount of sweat equity that suits your skills and wallet. You now have one of the nicer homes in the neighborhood, and you can sell this home for a net price of $400,000 after your transaction costs. With your total investment of $300,000 ($275,000 plus $25,000), your efforts have earned you a $100,000 profit completely tax-free. Thus, you've earned an average of $50,000 per year, which isn't bad for a tax-exempt second income without strict office hours. (Note that many states also allow you to avoid state income taxes on the sale of your personal residence, using many of the same requirements as the federal tax laws.)

Now, some cautions are in order here. This strategy is clearly not for everyone interested in making money from real estate investments. This strategy is not likely to work well for you if any of the following apply:

>> You're unwilling or reluctant to live through redecorating, minor remodeling, or major construction.

>> You dislike having to move every few years.

>> You're not experienced or comfortable with identifying undervalued property and improving it.

>> You lack a financial cushion to withstand a significant downturn in your local real estate market as happened in numerous parts of the country during the late 2000s and early 2010s.

>> You don't have the budget to hire a professional licensed and insured contractor to do the work, and you don't have the free time or the home improvement skills needed to enhance the value of a home.

One final caution: Beware of transaction costs. The expenses involved with buying and selling property — such as real estate agent commissions, loan fees, title insurance, escrow or closing costs, and so forth — can gobble up a large portion of your profits. With most properties, the long-term appreciation is what drives your returns. Consider keeping homes you buy and improve as long-term investment properties.

## Purchasing a vacation home

Many people of means expand their real estate holdings by purchasing a *vacation home* — a home in an area where they enjoy taking pleasure trips. For most people, buying a vacation home is more of a consumption decision than it is an investment decision. That's not to say that you can't make a profit from owning a second home. However, potential investment returns shouldn't be the main reason you buy a second home.

For example, one family lived in Pennsylvania and didn't particularly like the hot and humid summer weather. They enjoyed taking trips and staying in various spots in northern New England and eventually bought a small home in New Hampshire. Their situation highlights the pros and cons that many people face with vacation or second homes. The obvious advantage this family enjoyed in having a vacation home is that they no longer had the hassle of securing accommodations when they wanted to enjoy some downtime. Also, after they arrived at their home away from home, they were, well, home! Things were just as they expected — with no surprises, unless squirrels had taken up residence on their porch.

The downsides to vacation homes can be numerous, including:

>> **Expenses:** With a second home, you have the range of nearly all the costs of a primary home — mortgage interest, property taxes, insurance, repairs and maintenance, utilities, and so on.

>> **Property management:** When you're not at your vacation home, things can go wrong. A pipe can burst, for example, and the mess may not be found for days or weeks. Unless the property is close to a good neighbor or other kind person willing to keep an eye on it for you, you may incur the additional expense of paying a property manager to watch the property for you.

>> **Lack of rental income:** Most people don't rent out their vacation homes, thus negating the investment property income stream that contributes to the returns real estate investors enjoy (see Chapter 1 in Book 1). If your second home is in a vacation area where you have access to plenty of short-term renters, you or your designated property manager can rent out the property. (Note that using a service like Airbnb assists with finding people to rent your property but doesn't help with the arrival/departure and security deposit issues, applicant screening, keeping your property maintained, and many other similar services a property manager performs. See Book 5 for details on using your home as an Airbnb.) However, this entails all the headaches and hassles of having many short-term renters. (But you do gain the tax advantages of depreciation and all expenses as with other rental properties.)

>> **Obligation to use:** Some second homeowners complain about feeling obliged to use their vacation homes. Oftentimes in marriages, one spouse likes the vacation home much more than the other spouse (or one spouse enjoys working on the second home rather than enjoying the home itself).

Before this section on vacation homes closes out, here are a few tax tips, as found in the current tax code:

>> If you retain your vacation home or secondary home as personal property, forgoing the large income streams and tax write-offs for depreciation and operating expenses associated with rental properties, you can still make a nice little chunk of tax-free cash on the side. The current tax code permits you to rent the property for up to 14 days a year — and that income is *tax-free!* You don't have to claim it. Yes, you read that right. And you can still deduct the costs of ownership, including mortgage interest and property taxes, as you do for all other personal properties.

>> If you decide to maintain the property as a rental (you rent it out for more than 14 days a year), you, as the property owner, can still use the rental property as a vacation home for up to 14 days a year, or a maximum of

10 percent of the days gainfully rented, whichever is greater, and the property still qualifies as a rental. Also, all days spent cleaning or repairing the rental home don't count as personal use days — so that's why you paint for a couple of hours every afternoon and spend the morning fishing!

**REMEMBER**

Before you buy a second home, weigh all the pros and cons. If you have a partner with whom you're buying the property, have a candid discussion. Also consult with your tax advisor for other tax-saving strategies for your second home or vacation home.

## Paying for timeshares and condo hotels

*Timeshares,* a concept created in the 1960s, are a form of ownership or right to use a property. A more recent trend in real estate investing is condo hotels, which in many ways are simply a new angle on the old concept of timeshares. A condo hotel looks and operates just like any other first-class hotel, with the difference that each room is separately owned. The hotel guests (renters) have no idea who owns their room.

Both timeshares and condo hotels typically involve luxury resort locations with amenities such as golf or spas. The difference between the traditional timeshare and condo hotel is the interval that the unit is available — condo hotels are operated on a day-to-day availability, and timeshares typically rent in fixed intervals such as weeks.

Some of the most popular projects have been the branded condo hotels such as Ritz Carlton, Four Seasons, Trump, W, Westin, and Hilton located in high-profile vacation destinations like Hawaii, Las Vegas, New York, Chicago, and Miami. You can also find many foreign condo hotel properties in the Caribbean and Mexico, and the concept is expanding to Europe, the Middle East, and Asia.

Two types of individuals are attracted to investing in condo hotels and timeshares. One group is investors who believe that the property will appreciate like any other investment. The other group is people who use the condo hotel or timeshare for personal use and offset some of their costs.

Timeshares and condo hotels aren't worthy real estate investments as they don't appreciate and they don't generate income. But they are often presented as a viable alternative real estate investment, and millions have been purchased. You will likely be solicited to consider this opportunity during an upcoming vacation, so the following sections share some concerns.

## Taming timeshares

Timeshares are offered as deeded and non-deeded timeshares. With deeded time-shares you own a permanent or fee simple interest, and with non-deeded time-shares you have a right to use the property, but there is an expiration date. (See the sidebar "Still interested in a timeshare?" later in this chapter for more info on the types of timeshare ownership.) The most popular timeshares are deeded, and they can be sold or transferred just like any other interest in real estate, assuming there is demand.

Many investors' first experiences with timeshares are tempting offers of a free meal, a great discount offer to a theme park, or even a free one- or two-night stay at the resort, with the catch that they have to spend some time listening to an informational presentation. These offers usually come from individuals contact-ing you in known tourist locations or when you check into a hotel that just hap-pens to offer condos as well.

From an investment standpoint, the fundamental problem with timeshares is that they're overpriced, and like a condominium, you own no land (which is what gen-erally appreciates well over time). For example, suppose that a particular unit would cost $150,000 to buy. When this unit is carved up into weekly ownership units, the total cost of all those units can easily approach four to five times that amount! (Now you understand why timeshare developers and promoters can give you "free stuff" if you will listen to their sales pitch — their profit margins are very high on every sale!)

To add insult to injury, investors find that another problem with timeshares is the high management fees or service fees and almost guaranteed rising annual main-tenance fees over time. As the property gets older, the annual maintenance costs, which you are required to pay to retain ownership of your timeshare interval, continue to increase and can even exceed what you would pay for a comparable stay at a nearby non-timeshare. Is it worth buying a slice of real estate at a 400 to 500 percent premium to its fair market value and paying high ongoing mainte-nance fees on top of that? Nope.

Many owners of timeshares find that they want to vacation at a different location or time of year than what they originally purchased. To meet this need, several companies offer to broker or sell or "trade" timeshare slots for a fee. However, timeshare availability and desirability have so many variables — including loca-tion, time of year, amenities, and quality of the particular resort — that it has been difficult to fairly value and trade timeshares. For a given resort, it can be difficult online to determine which of two identical floorplan units has the prime location, versus a less desirable one. As a result, resort rating systems have been developed to compare resort location, amenities, and quality. Resorts Condominiums Inter-national (RCI) and Interval International are two of the most well known.

Timeshares may make sense for you if you like to vacation at the same resort around the same time every year and if the annual service or maintenance fees compare favorably to the cost of simply staying in a comparable resort. Keep in mind, though, that if the deal seems too good to be true, it *is* too good to be true. The only folks who generally make money with timeshares and condo hotels are the developers, not the folks who buy specific days of ownership.

A cottage industry for timeshare cancellations has sprouted up, and undoubtedly you have seen or will soon see or hear an ad for a company that is offering to assist you in canceling or getting rid of your timeshare. The demand for these services is increasing as many timeshare properties are aging and the maintenance fees are rising, often to the point that it is more expensive to stay at your own timeshare than to simply pay for a comparable rental, possibly at a much newer and more luxurious resort property in the same area.

The timeshare cancellation strategies often involve either selling your timeshare (almost always at a significant or even a complete loss), attempting to rescind the timeshare (virtually impossible unless you just bought it while on vacation early this week and are still within the "cooling off" or rescission period!), asking the developer to just take it back (most won't, but rarely one actually will), renting out or gifting your interval, or hiring an attorney who may be able to find a legitimate way to challenge the disclosures or the validity of the timeshare contract.

Timeshare laws vary greatly from state to state, so you want to find a timeshare cancellation company or attorney that specializes in canceling timeshares in the state where your timeshare is located. While you will take a large financial hit when you sell or cancel your timeshare, you need to consider that the benefits of cutting your future losses (maintenance fees) may make such a tough decision the right one.

## Coping with condo hotels

The developers and operators of condo hotels love the concept because one of the most consistently successful principles of real estate is increasing value by fractionalizing interests in real estate. As with timeshares, the developers are able to sell each individual hotel room for much more than they could get for the entire project.

Condo hotel operators are able to generate additional revenue from service and maintenance fees to cover their costs of operations. Often the owners' use of their own rooms doesn't negatively impact the overall revenues of the property because the rooms would have sometimes been vacant anyway. Condo hotels allow their owners to stay in their units but often impose limits on the amount of personal usage. There may also be resort fees, parking fees, or other amenity costs as well.

# STILL INTERESTED IN A TIMESHARE?

Timeshares are packaged in a multitude of ways — some resorts offer fixed units where you vacation at the exact same unit every year either on set dates or set numbered weeks (though the actual calendar date may vary). Other timeshares are available *biennially* (every other year) so you can have some variety. Some offer fixed weeks, where you have the same week every year but may be in a different unit.

Timeshares aren't just a one-time purchase; they also have monthly or annual service or maintenance fees. These funds are established each year by the homeowners' association or resort management company. There are different types of ownership for timeshare interests, with fee simple, right of use, and leasehold being the primary options:

- **Fee simple** (or deeded) ownership is a fee simple estate in real estate that provides the absolute ownership subject to state and local laws and government powers such as taxation, eminent domain, police power, and so on.

- **Right-to-use** (or non-deeded) ownership provides occupancy rights for a given number of years but no actual ownership interest in the property. Some states and many foreign countries don't allow the fee simple ownership of timeshares, so they offer long-term lease or right-to-use agreements that can be from 20 to 99 years. The actual fee simple title of the real estate remains with the resort developer or management company. A homeowners' association or a resort management company typically handles the day-to-day operations of timeshares, and you have the same type of service or annual management and maintenance fees.

- **Leasehold** is an agreement between the lessee (tenant) and lessor (owner or landlord) specifying the lessee's right to use the leased property for a given purpose and given time at a specified rental payment.

If you're interested in buying a timeshare, know that timeshare owners are required by law to disclose their full, audited financials. Read them carefully. You can talk with the developer directly; this method may make sense if you're looking for a particular time of the year in the high season. The timeshare industry typically uses a color-coded pricing system to denote the seasonal demand for a particular timeshare property. Although the concept is pretty consistent, the designation of dates for each particular color can vary from one resort to another. In general, the demand is broken down into three categories:

- Red for the prime or high demand

- Yellow or white for intermediate or medium season

- Green or blue for off-season or low demand

The purchaser of the condo hotel unit sees this type of investment as an option to direct ownership of a second home and likes the ability to generate income. The professional management is another one of the attractions to investors. The owners don't pay a management fee to the hotel operator unless their room is rented, and then the collected revenue is split, typically in the 50-50 range, and the operator has complete control over the rental rate as well as which units are rented each day.

REMEMBER

These properties are often hyped, and the expectations of the condo hotel investor are often much greater than the reality. Investors are lured to condo hotels by the potential for appreciation and cash flow as well as professional management. Many investors find themselves being pressured into presale offering presentations even before the units are built. These events can be tempting, but savvy investors need to do their own due diligence. So when you hear a sales pitch indicating that your proposed investment in a condo hotel unit will provide significant income from hotel rentals and cover most or all of your mortgage and carrying costs, that's the time to grab your wallet and find the nearest exit.

# Surveying the Types of Residential Properties You Can Buy

If you've been in the market for a home, you know that in addition to single-family homes, you can choose from numerous types of attached or shared housing including duplexes, triplexes, apartment buildings, condominiums, townhomes, and co-operatives. The following sections provide an overview of each of these properties and show how they may make an attractive real estate investment for you.

TIP

From an investment perspective, the top recommendations are apartment buildings and single-family homes. Attached-housing units generally aren't recommended; they have associations and shared common areas. If you can afford a smaller single-family home or apartment building rather than a shared-housing unit, buy the single-family home or apartments.

Unless you can afford a large down payment (25 percent or more), the early years of rental property ownership may financially challenge you: With all properties, as time goes on, generating a positive cash flow gets easier because your mortgage expense stays fixed (if you use fixed rate financing), while your rents increase faster than your expenses (unless you are in a rent controlled area). Regardless of what you choose to buy, make sure that you run the numbers on your rental income and expenses to see whether you can afford the negative cash flow that often occurs in the early years of ownership, and always allow for unexpected vacancy or capital improvements like flooring and window coverings, appliances, and/or the water heater.

## Single-family homes

As an investment, single-family, detached homes generally perform better in the long run than attached or shared housing. In a good real estate market, most housing appreciates, but single-family homes tend to outperform other housing types for the following reasons:

>> Single-family homes tend to attract more potential buyers — most people, when they can afford it, prefer a detached or stand-alone home, especially for the increased privacy and less noise from neighbors.

>> Attached or shared housing is less expensive and easier to build *and to overbuild;* because of this surplus potential, such property tends to appreciate more moderately in price.

Because so many people prefer to live in detached, single-family homes, market prices for such dwellings can often become inflated beyond what's justified by the rental income these homes can produce. That's exactly what happened in some parts of the United States in the mid-2000s and led in part to a significant price correction in the subsequent years. To discover whether you're buying in such a market, compare the monthly cost (after tax) of owning a home to the monthly rent for that same property. Focus on markets where the rent exceeds or comes close to equaling the cost of owning and shun areas where the ownership costs exceed rents.

Single-family homes that require just one tenant are simpler to deal with than a multi-unit apartment building that requires the management and maintenance of multiple renters and units. The downside, though, is that a vacancy means you have no income coming in. Look at the effect of 0 percent occupancy for a couple of months on your projected income and expense statement! By contrast, one vacancy in a four-unit apartment building (each with the same rents) means that you're still taking in 75 percent of the gross potential (maximum total) rent.

With a single-family home, you're responsible for all repairs and maintenance. You can hire someone to do the work, but you still have to find the contractors and coordinate and oversee the work. Also recognize that if you purchase a single-family home with many fine features and amenities, you may find it more stressful and difficult to have tenants living in your property who don't treat it with the same tender loving care that you may yourself.

TIP

The first rule of being a successful landlord is to let go of any emotional attachment to a home. But that sort of attachment on the tenant's part is favorable: The more they make your rental property their home, the more likely they are to stay and return it to you in good condition — except for the expected normal wear and tear of day-to-day living.

REMEMBER

Making a profit in the early years of ownership from the monthly cash flow with a single-family home is generally the hardest stage. The reason: Such properties usually sell at a premium price relative to the rent that they can command (you pay extra for the land, which you can't rent). Also note that with just one tenant, you have no rental income when you have a vacancy.

# Attached housing

As the cost of land has climbed over the decades in many areas, packing more housing units that are attached into a given plot of land keeps housing somewhat more affordable. Shared housing makes more sense for investors who don't want to deal with building maintenance and security issues.

The following sections discuss the investment merits of three forms of attached housing: condominiums, townhomes, and co-ops.

## Condos

*Condominiums* are typically apartment-style units stacked on top of and/or beside one another and sold to individual owners. When you purchase a condominium, you're actually purchasing the interior of a specific unit as well as a proportionate, undivided (meaning, you don't directly own a portion) interest in the common areas — the pool, tennis courts, grounds, hallways, laundry room, and so on. Although you (and your tenants) have full use and enjoyment of the common areas, the homeowners' association actually owns and maintains the common areas as well as the building structures themselves (which typically include the foundation, exterior walls, roof, plumbing, electrical, and other major building systems).

One advantage to a condo as an investment property is that of all the attached housing options, condos are generally the lowest-maintenance properties (from the perspective of unit owners) because most condominium or homeowners' associations deal with issues such as roofing, landscaping, and so on for the entire building and receive the benefits of quantity purchasing. Note that you're still responsible for necessary maintenance inside your unit, such as servicing appliances, floor and window coverings, interior painting, and so on.

Although condos may be somewhat easier to keep up, they tend to appreciate less than single-family homes or apartment buildings unless the condo is located in a desirable urban area.

Condominium buildings may start out in life as condos or as apartment complexes that are then converted into condominiums.

**WARNING**

Be wary of apartments that have been converted to condominiums. They're often the most affordable housing options in many areas of the country and may also be blessed with an excellent urban location that can't easily be re-created. But you may be buying into some not-so-obvious problems. These converted apartments are typically older properties with a cosmetic makeover (new floors, new appliances, solid surface countertops, new landscaping, and a fresh coat of paint). However, be forewarned: The cosmetic makeover may look good at first glance, but the property probably still boasts 40-year-old plumbing, heating/cooling, and electrical systems; poor soundproofing; and a host of economic and functional obsolescence.

Within a few years, most of the owner-occupants move on to the traditional single-family home and rent out their condos. You may then find the property is predominantly renter-occupied and has a volunteer board of directors unwilling to levy the monthly assessments necessary to properly maintain the aging structure. Within 10 to 15 years of the conversion, these properties may well be the worst in the neighborhood.

## Townhomes

*Townhomes* are essentially attached or row homes — a hybrid between a typical airspace-only condominium and a single-family house. Like condominiums, townhomes are generally attached, typically sharing walls and a continuous roof. But townhomes are often two-story buildings that come with a small yard and offer more privacy than a condominium because you don't have someone living on top of your unit.

**REMEMBER**

As with condominiums, you absolutely must review the governing documents before you purchase the property to see exactly what you legally own. Generally, townhomes are organized as *planned unit developments* (PUDs) in which each owner has a *fee simple* ownership (no limitations as to transferability of ownership — the most complete ownership rights one can have) of the individual lot that encompasses the owner's dwelling unit and often a small area of immediately adjacent land for a patio or balcony. The common areas are all part of a larger single lot, and each owner holds title to an undivided, proportionate share of the common area.

## Co-ops

Co-operatives are a type of shared housing that has elements in common with apartments and condos. When you buy a co-operative, you own a stock certificate that represents your share of the entire building, including usage rights to a specific living space per a separate written occupancy agreement. Unlike a condo, you generally need to get approval from the co-operative association if you want to remodel or rent your unit to a tenant. In some co-ops, you must even gain approval from the association for the sale of your unit to a proposed buyer.

**WARNING**

Turning a co-op into a rental unit is often severely restricted or even forbidden and, if allowed, is usually a major headache because you must satisfy not only your tenant but also the other owners in the building. Co-ops are also generally much harder to finance, and a sale requires the approval of the typically finicky association board. Therefore, it's highly recommended that you avoid co-ops for investment purposes.

# Apartments

Not only do apartment buildings generally enjoy healthy long-term appreciation potential, but they also often produce positive *cash flow* (rental income – expenses) in the early years of ownership. But as with a single-family home, the buck stops with you for maintenance of an apartment building. You may hire a property manager to assist you, but you still have oversight responsibilities (and additional expenses).

**REMEMBER**

In the real estate financing world, apartment buildings are divided into two groups based on the number of units:

>> **Four or fewer units:** You can obtain more favorable financing options and terms for apartment buildings that have four or fewer units because they're treated as residential property.

>> **Five or more units:** Complexes with five or more units are treated as commercial property and don't enjoy the extremely favorable loan terms of the one- to four-unit properties. Check out Book 8 for details on commercial real estate.

Apartment buildings, particularly those with more units, generally produce a small positive cash flow, even in the early years of rental ownership (unless you're in an overpriced market where it may take two to four years before you break even on a before-tax basis).

**WARNING**

One way to add value, if zoning allows, is to convert an apartment building into condominiums. Keep in mind, however, that this metamorphosis requires significant research on the zoning front and with estimating remodeling and construction costs. You also may be exposed to litigation brought by your individual unit buyers who within a few years become disenchanted with their investments and find an experienced attorney and a team of experts to make claims of construction defects or allege that you failed to have adequate reserves at the time of the conversion.

## EASY FIXES CAN YIELD BIG BUCKS

Avoid shared housing units in suburban areas with substantial undeveloped land that enables the building of many more units. Attached housing prices tend to perform best in fully developed or built-out urban environments.

For higher returns, look for property where relatively simple cosmetic and other fixes may allow you to increase rents and, therefore, the market value of the property. Examples of such improvements may include but not be limited to

- Adding fresh paint and flooring

- Improving the landscaping, including trees and seasonal color

- Upgrading the kitchen with solid surface (also known as "granite") countertops, new designer-colored appliances, and new cabinet/drawer hardware that can totally change the look

- Converting five-unit apartment buildings into four-unit buildings (for example, by converting two one-bedroom units into a two-bedroom, two-bath unit) to qualify for more favorable mortgage terms (see the earlier section "Apartments")

Look for property with a great location and good physical condition but some minor deferred maintenance. Then you can develop the punch list of items with maximum results for minimum dollars — for example, a property with a large yard but dead grass or completely overgrown and dated landscaping, or a two- or three-car garage but peeling paint or a broken garage door. You can also add a garage door opener to jazz up the property for minimum cost. You can also really add value to a property with a burnt-out, absentee, or totally disinterested owner who is tired of the property, or a property that is simply poorly managed.

# Considering Commercial Real Estate

*Commercial real estate* is a generic term that includes properties used for office, retail, and industrial purposes. You can also include self-storage and hospitality (hotels and motels) properties in this category as well as special purpose properties (for example, mobile home parks, amusement parks, and so on). If you're a knowledgeable real estate investor and you like a challenge, you need to know two good reasons to invest in commercial real estate:

>> You can use some of the space if you own your own small business. Just as it's generally more cost-effective to own your home rather than rent over the years, so it is with commercial real estate if — and this is a big *if* — you buy at a reasonably good time and hold the property for many years.

>> You're a more sophisticated investor who understands the more complicated aspects of commercial leases and has a higher tolerance for risk because these properties can have longer intervals of vacancy or increased tenant improvement costs plus rent concessions. Of course, just like with residential income property, only invest when your analysis of your local market suggests that it's a good time to buy.

**WARNING**

Commercial real estate shouldn't be high on your priority list, especially for inexperienced investors. Residential real estate is generally easier to understand and also usually carries lower investment and tenant risks.

With commercial real estate, when tenants move out, new tenants nearly always require extensive and costly improvements to customize the space to meet their particular planned usage of the property. And you usually have to pay for the majority of the associated costs in order to compete with other building owners. Fortunes can quickly change — small companies can go under, get too big for a space, and so on. Change is the order of the day in commercial real estate, and especially in the small business world where you're most likely to find your tenants.

So how do you evaluate the state of your local commercial real estate market? You must check out the supply and demand statistics for recent years. How much total space (sublease and vacant space) is available for rent, and how has that changed in recent months or years? What's the vacancy rate for comparable space, and how has that changed over time? Also, examine the rental rates, usually quoted as a price per square foot. Check out Book 8 for an introduction to commercial real estate investing.

One danger sign that purchasing a commercial property in an area is likely to produce disappointing investment returns is a market where the supply of available space has increased faster than demand, leading to higher vacancies and falling rental rates. (This is called *negative absorption*. What you want instead is a track record and projections showing *positive absorption* — when the supply of space isn't keeping up with the demand.) A slowing local economy and a higher unemployment rate also spell trouble for commercial real estate prices. You not only have to consider vacant space, but also space available for subleasing (the current tenant isn't using the space and will rent it to someone else, often at favorable terms) when evaluating the overall supply and demand for commercial income properties. Each market is different, so make sure you check out the details of your area.

# Buying Undeveloped or Raw Land

For prospective real estate investors who feel tenants and building maintenance are ongoing headaches, buying undeveloped land may appear attractive. If you buy land in an area that's expected to experience expanding demand in the years ahead, you should be able to make a tidy return on your investment. This is called *buying in the path of progress*, but of course the trick is to buy before everybody realizes that new development is moving in your direction.

You may even hit a home run if you can identify land that others don't currently see the future value in holding. However, identifying many years in advance which communities will experience rapid population and job growth isn't easy. Land prices in areas that people believe will be the next hot spot likely already sell at a premium price. That's what happened in most major cities with new sports facilities or transportation corridors (especially because these decisions often are disclosed well in advance of the municipality leadership vote or the ballot initiative). You don't have much opportunity to get ahead of the curve — or if you guess wrong, you may own land that falls in value!

Investing in land certainly has other drawbacks and risks:

>> **Care and feeding:** Land requires ongoing cash to pay the property taxes and liability insurance, and to keep the land clear and free of debris while it most likely produces little or no income. Although land doesn't require much upkeep compared with tenant-occupied property, it almost always does require financial feeding.

>> **Opportunity costs:** Investing in land is a cash drain, and of course, purchasing the land in the first place costs money. If you buy the land with cash, you

have the opportunity cost of tying up your valuable capital (which could be invested elsewhere), but most likely you will put down 30 to 40 percent in cash and finance the balance of the purchase price instead. Although you can often buy residential income property with much lower down payments, the fact that there is typically no periodic rental income with vacant undeveloped land means down payments are higher. Many times you can only acquire these properties with cash.

>> **Costly mortgages:** Mortgage lenders require much higher down payments and charge higher loan fees and interest rates on loans to purchase land because they see it as a more speculative investment. Obtaining a loan for buying and holding raw land, or for buying land that you will develop and receive entitlements for future building, is challenging and more expensive than obtaining a loan for a developed property.

>> **Lack of depreciation:** You don't get depreciation tax write-offs because undeveloped or raw land isn't depreciable.

On the income side, some properties may be able to be used for parking, storage income, or maybe even growing Christmas trees in the Northwest or grain in the Midwest! (After you make sure you've complied with local zoning restrictions and have the proper insurance in place, that is.)

REMEMBER

Although large-scale land investment isn't for the entry-level real estate investor, savvy real estate investors have made fortunes taking raw land and getting the proper entitlements and then selling (or better yet, subdividing and then selling) the parcels to developers of commercial and residential properties (primarily home builders). If you decide to invest in land, be sure that you

>> **Do your homework.** Ideally, you want to buy land in an area that's attracting rapidly expanding companies with increased employment demand and that has a shortage of housing and developable land. Take your time to really know the area. This isn't a situation in which you should take a hot tip from someone to invest in faraway property in another state. Nor should you buy raw land just because you heard that irresistible opening bid price advertised on the radio for the government excess land auction down at the convention center this Saturday (lately, these are online auctions).

>> **Know all the costs.** Tally up your annual *carrying costs* (ongoing ownership expenses such as property taxes, insurance, and keeping the land clear of debris) so that you can see what your annual cash drain may be. What are the financial consequences of this cash outflow — for example, will you be able to fully fund your tax-advantaged retirement accounts? If you can't, count the lost tax benefits as another cost of owning land.

» **Determine what improvements the land may need.** Engineering fees; subdivision map and permit costs; environmental studies; stormwater control; running utility, water, and sewer lines; building roads; curbs and gutters; landscaping; and so on all cost money. If you plan to develop and build on the land that you purchase, research these costs. Make sure you don't make these estimates with your rose-tinted glasses on — improvements almost always cost more than you expect them to. (You need to check with the planning or building department for their list of requirements.)

Also make sure that you have access to the land or the right to enter and leave through a public right-of-way or another's property (known as *ingress* and *egress*). Some people foolishly invest in landlocked properties. When they discover the fact later, they think that they can easily get an *easement* (legal permission to use someone else's property). Wrong!

» **Understand the zoning and environmental issues.** The value of land is heavily dependent on what you can develop on it. Never purchase land without thoroughly understanding its zoning status and what you can and can't build on it. This advice also applies to environmental limitations that may be in place or that may come into effect without warning, diminishing the potential of your property (with no compensation).

This potential for surprise is why you must research the disposition of the planning department and nearby communities. Attend the meetings of local planning groups, if any, because some areas that are antigrowth and antidevelopment are less likely to be good places for you to buy land, especially if you need permission to do the type of project that you have in mind. Through the empowerment of local residents who sit on community boards and can influence local government officials, zoning can suddenly change for the worse — sometimes you may find that your property has been *downzoned* — a zoning alteration that can significantly reduce what you can develop on a property and therefore the property's value.

IN THIS CHAPTER

» **Assembling your team from the get-go**

» **Hiring tax and financial advisors**

» **Seeking lending professionals**

» **Finding top real estate agents and brokers**

» **Adding appraisers and attorneys**

Chapter **3**

# Building Your Team

With some investments — called *passive investments* — you simply turn your money over to professional money managers or financial advisors who then act on your behalf and make the day-to-day investment decisions, buying and selling investment assets within the portfolio. Mutual funds and exchange-traded funds are examples of this type of passive investment. You send your money to your favorite fund firm and periodically evaluate how your fund's managers are doing.

Investments in real estate that you're directly involved in managing are the norm, because passive investments in real estate aren't readily available (except for real estate investment trusts and tenants in common real estate investments). And for most real estate investors, real estate investing is hands-on and complicated enough to require the services and knowledge of a team of professionals. Although you may be skilled in your chosen field, it's unlikely that you possess all the varied and detailed skills and knowledge necessary to initiate and close a good real estate transaction.

Evaluate proposed real estate investments carefully and methodically before you make the ultimate purchase decision. The uniqueness of each potential real estate opportunity requires the investor to patiently critique the pending investment. You should understand the economic climate and potential for growth, the current physical condition of the property, the tenants, and the value of the property in the marketplace. Then you should ensure that you've got a solid negotiating strategy to orchestrate a deal, that the financing comes through, and that the transfer of real estate is handled properly. This requires a team approach.

This chapter discusses the different real estate professionals and service providers you should consider teaming up with as you search for real estate investment opportunities and proceed with the purchase of property.

# Knowing When to Establish Your Team

REMEMBER

Some real estate investors make the mistake of looking for a property to buy without spending enough time upfront thinking about and identifying the pros whose help should be retained. You should have your team in place before you begin your serious property searching, for two reasons:

>> **You can move quickly.** The speed at which you can close a transaction is an advantage in any type of market.

- In a rising or seller's market, sellers typically won't tolerate having their property tied up for a long time until closing with a buyer who doesn't understand the current market conditions or how to properly evaluate the property. Sellers may be missing out on a better deal with a buyer willing to close quicker and/or pay more.

- In a soft or buyer's market, some sellers are desperate for cash and need to close quickly. In a buyer's market, although less property may be selling overall, there is always demand for the most appealing properties that are priced right and well located. These properties often attract multiple offers, so being organized and efficient can make the difference between securing and losing a desirable property.

>> **You can effectively research the property before making an offer.** Prudent investors conduct research and gather information before they even make an offer, so they know which property or properties are worth seriously pursuing. Typically, the real estate industry describes *due diligence* as the period of time after you place a property under contract. But you really need to perform due diligence even before making an offer. You don't want to waste time or money on a property that can't meet your goals.

Some real estate investors like to make an offer and get a property under contract before they begin due diligence. This is a mistake and can lead to a reputation with sellers (and agents) that you're not a serious buyer (see the later section "Working with Brokers and Agents"). You should make offers only when you have done enough due diligence to feel comfortable that your further, thorough review of the property interiors and financials probably won't reveal any surprises that will lead to canceling the purchase.

The most effective research is done with the assistance of real estate professionals to give you the advice and information you need to make an intelligent decision. This pre-offer period is critical; it's the one real opportunity for a prospective buyer to investigate a property while retaining the ability to terminate the transaction without a significant monetary loss. You may invest time and several hundreds to several thousands of dollars to perform the necessary due diligence, but this is a small amount compared to the potential losses from the purchase of a bad property.

# Adding a Tax Advisor

A tax advisor may not be the first person that you think to consult before making a real estate transaction. However, a good tax advisor can highlight potential benefits and pitfalls of different real estate investment strategies. Of course, make sure that your tax person has experience with real estate investing and understands your needs and specific goals in regard to your property investments.

**REMEMBER**

Although you may pick up a lot of information about real estate and discover some of the advantages of property investing speaking with some tax people, don't rely on generic information ("investing in real estate offers a terrific tax shelter," for example). You need specific feedback and ideas from a tax expert regarding your unique financial situation and which types of real estate investments work best for you.

Based on your age, income, and other important factors, the benefits you seek from real estate may be entirely different from those of other investors. Many real estate investors are looking for immediate cash flow from their properties. But others have sufficient income currently from other sources and prefer to look at real estate as a wealth builder for their retirement years. And almost all real estate investors are looking for tax benefits.

The role of your accountant is to evaluate and recommend investments and tax strategies that maximize your financial position. Keep in mind the old adage that says, "It's not what you make that matters but what you keep."

A good tax advisor with property investment experience can tell you whether your best real estate investment is the direct ownership of properties or perhaps owning triple-net leased properties with lower returns but fewer management headaches. An accountant can inform clients as to whether they can (or how to) meet the active participation required for certain tax benefits while hiring a property management company to handle the bulk of the day-to-day tenant/landlord issues. (See Chapter 5 in Book 1 for an introduction to managing rentals.)

You may also want to find out whether you qualify for the added tax benefits that are available for some investors who qualify as real estate professionals. Achieving such qualification isn't easy, and the IRS may someday audit you, so be sure to implement a reliable method to document and ensure that you meet the requirements. Meet with your tax advisor and get to know the benefits and pitfalls of your proposed real estate investments before you start making offers.

# Finding a Financial Advisor

In theory, everyone entering into major investments like real estate should seek holistic financial advice from a financial advisor who charges an hourly fee.

**WARNING**

In reality, many financial consultants sell investment and insurance products that provide them with commissions or manage money for an ongoing percentage in stocks, bonds, mutual and exchange-traded funds, and the like. Such salespeople and money managers can't provide objective, holistic advice, especially on real estate transactions. When you buy property, you spend money these people want to manage. Check out the nearby sidebar "Avoiding financial conflicts of interest" for more information.

**TIP**

If you've worked with or can locate financial advisors who sells their time and nothing else, just as a good tax advisor does, consider hiring one of them. A true financial advisor can help you understand how real estate investment property purchases fit with your overall financial situation and goals. (Chapter 1 in Book 1 discusses all the variables that affect the way your investments mesh with your situation and goals.)

# AVOIDING FINANCIAL CONFLICTS OF INTEREST

Here are a couple of stories that highlight the conflicts of interest you may be subjected to when working with a financial advisor.

- While serving as an expert real estate witness, coauthor Robert had a case where a retired couple was given some self-serving advice by their financial planner. This couple owned their principal residence plus three other rental homes valued at $1 million. All of their real estate was owned free and clear, and the rentals were in great condition with good long-term tenants. The properties provided a nice monthly income stream that was mostly tax-free due to their depreciation deduction. Although the real estate was clearly their largest asset and completely debt-free, they also had nearly $500,000 in liquid assets such as stocks, bonds, and individual retirement accounts, and seemed to be fairly set. That was, until their new financial advisor told them that their retirement was at risk because they had too much invested in real estate. The planner's recommendation was to keep their own home as their real estate investment, but sell the three highly appreciated rental properties and invest the proceeds in mutual funds and other financial products from companies affiliated with the planner.

  The planner failed to disclose his relationship with the sponsors of the new investments and also failed to warn them about the significant capital gains taxes that would be due upon sale. By the time they met with their accountant, it was too late — two of the three rental properties had been sold and more than $200,000 in taxes was due. The accountant advised the couple to contact an attorney and file a lawsuit against the financial advisor. Although the couple prevailed, they recovered only a small portion of what they paid in taxes. Even worse, they lost the benefits of cash flow and appreciation on their real estate while now owning fully taxable investments.

- In coauthor Eric's previous work as an hourly-based financial advisor, he often had clients come to him who were disappointed with the biased and confusing advice they got from various so-called financial planners. In one typical case, a widow had been told by an advisor to sell her two investment properties because he believed that the stock market would produce better returns. She set the wheels in motion to unload the properties but put the brakes on at the last minute after deciding she needed a second opinion. She met with Eric. The first thing that she noticed working with him was that he was far more thorough in examining her overall financial situation, including *all* of her investments, insurance, and resources for retirement. She also realized that she was happy with her real estate holdings and really didn't

*(continued)*

*(continued)*

have any motivation to sell them. Furthermore, she found out from Eric that over the long term, the returns from stocks and real estate were quite comparable. She thus decided to keep her life simple and stable and hold onto her nicely performing rental properties.

It's true that selling real estate can make sense at times. However, you must ask a lot of questions and run any proposed investment strategies by good independent advisors before you make the decision to liquidate your real estate and shift your investments to other opportunities.

# Lining Up a Lender or Mortgage Broker

Before looking at specific real estate opportunities, you need a budget. And because your budget for real estate purchases is largely a function of how much you can borrow (in addition to your cash available for a down payment), you need to determine the limits on your borrowing power. If you can't afford a property, it doesn't matter what a great deal it is.

**REMEMBER**

Postpone making an appointment to look at investment properties until after you examine the loans available. You have two resources to consult:

>> **A lender** is any firm, public or private, that directly loans you the cash you need to purchase your property. This type of lender is often referred to as a *direct lender*. Most often, your list of possible lenders includes banks, credit unions, and private lenders (including property sellers). Lenders tend to specialize in certain types of loans.

>> **A mortgage broker** is a service provider who presents your request for a loan to a variety of different lenders in order to find the best financing for your particular needs. Just like real estate or insurance brokers, a good mortgage broker can be a real asset to your team (mortgages are covered in detail in Chapter 4 of Book 1).

## Understanding lending nuances

Lenders and mortgage brokers are in the business of making loans. That's how they make money. Their product is cash, and they make money by renting it to people and businesses that pay them the money back plus *interest*, which is the cost of renting the money. Money is a commodity just like anything else, and its availability and pricing are subject to an assortment of variables.

Lenders and mortgage brokers want to find you money for your next real estate purchase, but they're not objective advisors to provide counsel for how much you should borrow. They're trained to calculate the maximum that you *may borrow*. Don't confuse this figure with the amount that you *can truly afford* or that fits best with your overall financial and personal situation. Because they only are paid when they make loans, many borrowers have learned the hard lesson that some lenders and mortgage brokers are willing to make any loan.

So why is getting a loan so difficult at times? Because lenders want to make loans to those investors who are a good credit risk and who they think have a high probability of repaying the loan in full plus the interest. This concern became more pronounced in the late 2000s and early 2010s as real estate prices fell and defaults and foreclosures escalated. The lender has costs of doing business and needs to make a profit. Because the money they lend often belongs to their depositors, lenders need to be careful and selective about the loans they make.

On the upside, lenders can also serve a valuable role by preventing you from making serious mistakes. Particularly in overheated seller's markets where prices are irrationally climbing with insufficient fundamental economic support, your lender and the required appraisal from a competent professional appraiser can keep you from getting caught up in a buy-at-any-price frenzy. (Of course, this isn't always the case; look no further than the subprime loan debacle that came to light in the late 2000s.) In these markets, lenders tend to be a little more conservative, limiting loan amounts and requiring larger down payments. These factors provide the lender with additional protection should market prices fall, but they're also a signal that the lender feels the loan exceeds the intrinsic value of the property that they'll be stuck with if you default. Smaller loan offers with higher down payment requirements are a clue that you may be paying more than a property is worth or buying at the market's peak.

Lenders require collateral to protect them if the borrower doesn't make the debt service payments as required. *Collateral* is the real or personal property that's pledged to secure a loan or mortgage. If the debt isn't paid as agreed, the lender has the right to force the sale of the collateral to recover the outstanding principal and interest on the loan. Typically, the property being purchased is the pledged collateral for real estate loans or mortgages.

## Building relationships with lenders

Relationships with lenders can take time to build, so begin looking for lenders that specialize in the types of properties within the geographic area that you have targeted. They can help you understand your financial qualifications or how much you can borrow before you begin your search for an investment property. Although lenders only make money by making loans and some lenders seem to be

Building Your Team

willing to lend money on any property at any price, the type of lender you should associate with is one who understands real estate cycles and your local real estate market. Not all lenders and mortgage brokers were hit by the subprime lending mess, and it does matter that you develop a relationship with a lender that's likely to be there when you want to acquire additional properties.

When you get together with your lender or mortgage broker, provide your latest personal financial statement, which includes your income and expenses as well as your assets and liabilities and net worth. For the most part, the days of "no documentation" or "stated income" loans are over, but be wary if you see these loans being marketed again.

REMEMBER

Always be truthful with your lender. One way to sabotage a relationship with a lender is to exaggerate or stretch the truth about your current financial situation or about the potential for your proposed property acquisition. Lenders require supporting documents for your income and assets and will obtain a current credit report. When you don't oversell yourself or your proposed property, lenders are often more willing to work with you and even offer better terms.

# Working with Brokers and Agents

REMEMBER

Your investment team should include a sharp and energetic real estate broker or agent. All real estate brokers and agents are licensed by the state in which they perform their services. A real estate *broker* is the highest level of licensed real estate professional, and a licensed real estate sales *agent* is qualified to handle real estate listings and transactions under the supervision of a broker. The vast majority of real estate licensees are sales agents. This chapter refers to both real estate brokers and agents simply as agents.

Real estate agents must have their licenses placed under a supervising broker who's ultimately responsible for the actions of those sales agents. Real estate brokers often begin their careers as real estate agents, but it's possible to meet the more stringent qualifications and immediately qualify as a broker. Brokers and agents can perform the same functions; many real estate agents actually have more practical experience and hands-on market knowledge than the brokers they work for. Brokers who have many agents reporting to them often spend most of their time educating, supervising, and reviewing the transactions presented by their agents. So, if you have a problem with an agent, contact the broker — the buck stops there!

Generally, you deal with real estate agents, but the added experience and dedication of a broker can be beneficial to you if you're involved in larger and/or more complicated transactions. Real estate agents are fine to handle the majority of real estate transactions, including the typical purchase or sale of an owner-occupied single-family home or condo. However, many owners of investment real estate don't want the disruption that can occur with openly listing the property. The management company and onsite employees begin to worry about their jobs, and tenants become concerned that rents will be raised. These problems can be avoided by quietly talking to one or two top brokers in an area with the understanding that the potential transaction is to be kept confidential. This leads to some great opportunities for the top brokers and their clients.

TIP

Whether you use a broker or an agent, make sure that this person has a solid track record with investment property transactions in your area. And although having a real estate agent on your team is an excellent strategy that gives you a competitive edge, don't completely ignore the various online listing services; the Multiple Listing Service (MLS), which is still popular in some areas; or in-house listings of brokers. Such sources often include properties that other investors overlooked because they didn't have the vision or the right team members to see a potential opportunity.

## Seeing the value of working with an agent

In many metropolitan areas, looking at the properties on a Multiple Listing Service (MLS), in the newspaper, or online listings isn't enough. The best deals are often the ones that don't make it into these sources. This is where the "insider information" from real estate sales agents can make you the bride and not the bridesmaid. (Of course, many brokers are themselves interested in investing in income producing properties, and they have the first chance at the best deals.)

You want to be the first one contacted about the best properties coming on the market rather than one of many when everyone knows about the property as it is plastered across a dozen online listing services or the MLS. The *MLS* is a service created and maintained by real estate professionals per guidelines established by the National Association of Realtors (NAR). This service gathers all the local property listings into a single place so that purchasers may review all available properties from one source. The MLS also deals with commission splitting and other relations between agents.

For many years the MLS dominated the markets, but the Department of Justice filed an antitrust lawsuit that was settled with NAR in 2008, agreeing that other listing services would be given access to the same listings. Now there are several investment real estate listing services that are gaining market share and offering instant access to an incredible database of information on all types of properties, from single-family homes and condos to large commercial, industrial, and retail properties. Several of the most popular listing services for investment properties are Loopnet (`www.loopnet.com`), the Commercial Investment Multiple Listing Service (CIMLS; `www.cimls.com`), and CoStar (`www.costar.com`).

## Grasping the implications of agency

When you deal with a real estate agent, you need to know whom that agent represents. Real estate investors need to understand the concepts of dual agency and single agency and the implications of each:

>> **Single agency:** This is when an agent only represents the buyer or the seller. The other party either uses self-representation or is represented by an agent who doesn't work for the same broker as the other agent. For example, a buyer's agent only has a fiduciary relationship with the buyer. The buyer's agent has a duty to promote the interests of the buyer and keep all information confidential unless legally required to disclose. The buyer's interest should be first and foremost, and no information is passed to the seller without the agent's knowledge other than that information that directly affects the agent's ability to perform on the contract as written.

REMEMBER

You should work with an agent who operates as a single agency representative. A lot of money is involved in income property transactions, and you want to have someone looking out for your interests, whether you're buying or selling an investment property.

>> **Dual agency:** A situation in which the same individual agent represents both the seller and the buyer *or* when two different agents representing the seller and buyer are from the same firm (with the same broker). With any transaction, each agent involved owes a fiduciary duty of loyalty to each client the agent represents, but this is nearly impossible for one agent who is representing both the buyer and seller in the same transaction (and difficult as well if two agents work for the same broker).

WARNING

Avoid the inherent conflict of interest found with dual agency and establish a relationship with a single agency agent who represents only *your* interests. Dual agency makes it extremely challenging for one agent, or two agents working for the same broker, to be loyal to clients with opposing interests. For example, an agent may hear confidential information from sellers about what their minimum acceptable price is, and the same agent or another agent from the same firm hears from buyers that they're willing to pay more than what they first offered.

Agents, and especially their brokers, prefer dual agency — they generate more commissions by representing both sides of the transaction. That's why many agents start out showing their clients only properties that are listed by their firms.

However, this desire to capture a bigger share of the real estate commission has led to some serious conflicts of interest. Now most states either prohibit dual agency or at least require the agent to disclose the exact nature of the agency relationship prior to commencing the representation of a client by taking a listing, showing a property, or making an offer.

## Getting a feel for compensation

Real estate agents are generally motivated to see the transaction go through because they're compensated when a sale is made. Compensation for agents is typically calculated as a percentage of the sales price paid for a property. So the agents actually have an interest in the property going for a higher price. Commissions vary based on the property and the size of the transaction:

>> Individual residential properties, such as single-family homes and condos, have commissions of 5 to 6 percent of the sales price.

>> Small multifamily and commercial properties are often in the 3 to 5 percent range.

>> Larger investment properties have commissions of 1 to 3 percent.

>> Raw land (in its natural state with no grading, construction, or improvements) is usually at 10 percent, unless the acreage is large. Subdivided or finished developable lots in suburban areas typically draw a lower commission.

These commissions are typically split between the firm listing the property for sale and working with the seller and the agent representing the buyer. The actual proportion of the split varies, with the listing agent sometimes taking a smaller percentage than the buyer's agent if the commissions aren't evenly split. The commission actually is paid to the broker, and the agent receives a share based on the employment or commission agreement, which also often calls for the agent to cover some of the agent's own expenses and overhead.

Real estate commissions can be a significant cost factor for real estate investors. Most listing agreements acknowledge that commissions aren't fixed by law and are negotiable. Traditionally, the seller "pays" the commission to the real estate agents involved in the transaction, although because the buyer is the one paying for the property, both the buyer and seller ultimately pay for the agent's commissions.

Real estate agents do add to the cost of purchasing property, but a good agent, like a good property manager, can justify the cost of services by introducing you to properties that you would not otherwise have considered. A good agent earns commissions in other ways as well — as a good negotiator and through offering other marketplace knowledge.

Some real estate investors get a real estate license so that they can eliminate paying at least one-half of the real estate commission to agents. Be sure to disclose immediately to all parties in writing prior to entering into any transaction that you're a licensed real estate agent. And at times, you'll be able to use your sale's or broker's license to effectively reduce your transaction expenses and investment requirement by representing yourself in a transaction. This is particularly helpful when you're looking to sell a property in a strong seller's market.

But as a licensee you need to be very careful to follow all real estate disclosure laws about your licensing status to all parties in the transaction. Generally, a real estate agent is expected to have more knowledge in a real estate transaction than others without such credentials. Thus, you must be very careful when you act as an agent and a principal in a purchase or sale transaction.

Although you may often have superior knowledge of market values and opportunities in the marketplace, you need to make sure that you're not self-dealing or taking advantage of insider information that would have a material impact on the value of the property. Real estate agents who buy properties for the long term for their own account are not likely to be challenged, but such agents who uses their knowledge to flip properties for a quick profit may be subject to claims by sellers that they withheld information. For example, you may find yourself named in a lawsuit if you bought a property at a low price when you knew that a new road was going to be built that would greatly enhance the property value in the next year or so.

WARNING

Many allegations of self-dealing or failing to act properly in real estate transactions have been made against licensed real estate professionals when they buy the property for an entity that they have a financial interest in or have a straw man or secret partner. This situation can happen even if you disclose your real estate license status and your financial interest in the buyer entity, but it is illegal and likely to be considered more egregious if you conceal this information from the seller. Agents have also been accused of illegal activity when they sell their own property (for example, as a tenants in common or triple-net investment opportunity) at a much higher price than market value.

One example involved a real estate agent who advised an elderly owner to sell a residential rental fourplex where the apartments were contiguous but each rental unit was on a separate lot. The agent advised this unsophisticated owner to sell all four units as a single property to a business associate of the agent. Then the new owner turned around and within less than 12 months had sold each of the four individual properties separately at a gross profit of over $1 million. The agent clearly knew that real estate sold in smaller increments generates a higher overall value. The aggrieved elderly owner filed suit against the agent. The case settled, after both parties incurred significant legal costs. The agent paid the elderly owner a significant sum with the understanding that the owner wouldn't file a complaint against the agent with the state real estate commission. But the lawsuit is a public record and certainly had a negative impact on the agent's reputation.

## Finding a good broker or agent

REMEMBER

The key to finding a good broker or agent to assist you in the purchase of investment real estate is to narrow the field down to those individuals who are the best. Look for folks with the following qualifications:

>> **Full-time professional:** Because the commissions earned on the sale of a large income property can be so great, you'll find that almost all brokers or agents you contact will claim that they can represent you. But you want to eliminate those brokers or agents who are greedy, incompetent, or simply mediocre. Although many part-time real estate professionals sell single-family homes and condos, you'll quickly find that the most qualified real estate investment property agents are full-time.

>> **Expert in the geographic market and specific property type:** Find someone who knows your market and the specific property type you're seeking. This knowledge is especially important if you don't live nearby. Avoid brokers who aren't experts in your specific property type. For example, don't use a broker who specializes in single-family homes and condominiums unless that's your target market. Likewise, a commercial property broker is unlikely to have the best investment opportunities for your consideration with single-family investment property.

TIP

Some real estate investment books advise you to contact every broker or real estate agent who targets your preferred geographic area. Although casting a bigger net has some inherent attraction, you should only work with one broker or agent at a time in a given market area.

Real estate agents can be a key source for new investment opportunities and general market information. These agents know buyers and sellers and also possess contacts for other services and products that you need as your real estate investment portfolio expands.

TIP

After narrowing down the candidates, you can apply many standard screening techniques to pinpoint the top three that you should interview:

>> **Verify the professional's license status:** Nearly every state has an online broker and agent database. Confirm that their real estate license is current with no citations or disciplinary action for past or pending violations. Note that

not all states will post pending violations but only adjudicated or resolved matters, so ask agents directly in writing and have them respond in writing. If you're using a real estate agent, check both the license status of the agent and supervising broker. If the broker or agent has been disciplined by the state, inquire further to understand the relevance to your transaction. A suspension or temporary revocation of a license can be a serious issue — even if it was reinstated. The facts of the case may be material to your choice of a real estate professional.

>> **Check references:** Get the names and phone numbers for at least three clients (in the geographical area where you're seeking property) that the broker or agent has worked with in the past year. Investment real estate transactions tend to be fewer than owner-occupied property transactions, so speaking with three or more clients from the last year maximizes your chances of speaking with clients other than the agent's all-time favorites.

Don't just ask for the references; you must call them. And don't just ask generic questions about whether the client was happy with the broker or agent. Dig deeper — find an agent whom you can work with on investments that are critical to your long-term wealth-building goals. Ask questions about the types of properties and the geographic locations involved. Ask questions like, "Did the broker or agent assertively represent you and take charge of the transaction, or did you have to initiate conversations?"

Consider these traits when investigating potential brokers and agents as well:

>> **Willingness to communicate with you:** The number-one complaint about real estate professionals is that they don't keep their clients informed during transactions. You're looking for someone with experience who isn't necessarily the top producer, because you want someone who can take the time to communicate regularly with you.

>> **Interpersonal skills:** A broker or agent needs to get along with you and with a whole host of others involved in a typical real estate deal: other agents, property sellers, inspectors, escrow officers or attorneys, lenders, and so on. An agent needs to know how to put your interests first without upsetting others.

>> **Negotiation skills:** Putting a real estate deal together involves negotiation, so you want a broker or agent with negotiating skills and lots of experience in larger transactions. Is your agent going to exhaust all avenues to get you the best deal possible? Be sure to ask the agent's former clients how the agent negotiated for them. (Flip to Chapter 3 in Book 2 for more information on negotiating deals.)

>> **Reputation for honesty, integrity, and patience:** When it comes to the brokering of investment properties, the reputation of your representative can be critical. Just as you asked in writing about licensing violations, ask about any litigation. Most brokers with years of experience will get sued on occasion, but you want to know about the details so you can determine the validity of the claims. Brokers or agents with a track record of dealing fairly with their clients and their peers can greatly assist in gaining the cooperation of an adversarial seller. And gaining such cooperation is often needed to close a complicated transaction. Some strife is almost guaranteed when buying investment real estate — there are several opportunities where the transaction can unravel and only the trustworthiness, perseverance, and patience of the real estate professionals involved can keep the transaction on course.

## Making the most of your agent's services

To get the best deals, timing is critical. You want your broker or agent to think of you first. To do this, you need to build a solid rapport with your agent, which you can do by building a track record of not wasting the time of your professional team. Because agents only get paid for deals they close, they're not interested in investing time and energy with numerous potential buyers. They want serious buyers who will close the deal. Plus, if you garner a reputation of tying up properties and then renegotiating the deal or canceling the escrow, you'll find that your offers won't be accepted in the future. Sellers and their brokers don't want to waste time with phantom buyers.

TIP

If you're not interested in or not able to purchase a property at the time, let your agent know at once and explain your situation and thank the agent for thinking of you. A handwritten thank-you note or simple gift also lets your agent know that you appreciate the effort — and keeps you at the top of the list for the next opportunity.

# Considering an Appraiser

Many real estate investors know appraisers solely in the role of providing the property valuation report required by lenders. And it's generally in this role that investors can find appraisers to be a source of aggravation rather than a potential resource. However, an appraiser can be an effective team member if your real estate investment strategy involves buying and selling properties with somewhat-hidden opportunities to add value. Appraisers see many properties over their career and thus often possess insight into real estate opportunities that others miss.

REMEMBER

Appraisers can help you by telling you the current value of a property, but they bring real value as part of your real estate investment team by

>> Providing insight into the factors that can lead to an increase in the market value of a property

>> Assisting you in maximizing the return on your investment by suggesting cost-effective and high-demand upgrades to distressed or fixer-upper properties

>> Giving you useful information on the demographics of the area and helping to identify those properties that are distressed but have plenty of upside potential (properties requiring work in good neighborhoods)

>> Identifying areas that are in the path of progress based on important influencers that impact and create the best potential for appreciation, often based on transportation improvements, new businesses with jobs, better schools, and other factors that will increase demand as the neighborhood becomes more desirable

One highly successful real estate investor in foreclosure properties has even hired an appraiser as an in-house member of his real estate investment team. Virtually every property that appears on the weekly Notice of Default list from the title company is reviewed first by the appraiser, who looks for properties that are located in the path of progress and with some real upside potential if brought to marketable condition physically and aesthetically.

The appraiser is also able to assist in determining the as-is value and the cost of making the necessary repairs and upgrades to the property. This information helps the investor establish the maximum price she should pay for the property, based on comparable sales in the market.

TIP

As many have learned from the debacles of the real estate collapse in the early 1990s and the late-2000s and early-2010s subprime disaster, appraisals are often an art and can be very subjective. You need to make sure you find an appraiser who has a comprehensive education and training in proper appraisal techniques and complies with the Uniform Standards of Professional Appraisal Practice (USPAP) set out by the Appraisal Foundation. The appraiser you use should have extensive product knowledge of your target property type (residential, commercial, retail, and so on), along with significant experience and market knowledge in your area. Contact the local American Society of Appraisers and the Appraisal Institute for referrals. The most competent and experienced appraisers are often members of The Counselors of Real Estate (CRE®). Like many of the top professionals you seek for your team, you should not simply look for the lowest price because you may end up with an inferior appraisal.

# Finding an Attorney

You may think that adding an attorney to your real estate investment team seems like an expensive luxury that you can't afford. Indeed, you may be able to purchase properties when you're just starting out as a real estate investor without consulting an attorney because buying a small rental property is often not much different from purchasing your own home. The process is relatively simple with preprinted forms that seem so easy to complete. And you usually have an experienced real estate agent to guide you through the process.

For simple transactions, the retention of an attorney is strictly a function of whether attorneys are traditionally involved as the intermediary or closing agent. If you live in an area where attorneys aren't usually involved in real estate transactions, an attorney may not be necessary. In some states, having an attorney is essential to handle the transaction and closing.

TIP

You should consult with an experienced real estate attorney as your investments increase in size and complexity. With more complicated transactions, have the attorney review the documents — even in states where the title or escrow company handles the paperwork and serves as the independent intermediary or closing agent. A good real estate attorney can help you structure proposed transactions. Particularly if you're looking into a large transaction where you assume loans or you're attempting to secure special financing, a competent real estate attorney can be invaluable.

REMEMBER

The best time to consult with an attorney is *before* you finalize the proposed transaction. Your attorney can't do as much to avoid legal snafus and expensive litigation if you don't hire your attorney to draft, review, and negotiate the terms of your proposed transaction in advance. Although such a review may cost you some money upfront, it's definitely much more economical than having to hire an attorney to get you out of a bind.

IN THIS CHAPTER

» **Understanding lender financing options and fees**

» **Selecting the best mortgage for your situation**

» **Looking at home equity loans**

» **Seeking seller financing**

» **Knowing which mortgages to avoid**

# Chapter **4**

# Financing Your Property Purchases

Some property investors have spent dozens to hundreds of hours finding the best properties in great locations only to have their deals unravel when they were unable to gain approval for needed financing. You can't play if you can't pay.

This chapter covers the financing options you should consider (and highlights those that you should avoid). You find out how to select the mortgage that is most appropriate for the property you're buying and your overall personal and financial situation.

## Taking a Look at Mortgage Options

Although you can find thousands of different types of mortgages (thanks to all the various bells and whistles available), only two major categories of mortgages exist: fixed interest rate and adjustable rate. Technically speaking, some mortgages combine elements of both — they may remain fixed for a number of years and then have a variable interest rate after that. The following sections discuss these major loan types, what features they typically have, and how you can intelligently compare them with each other and select the one that best fits with your investment property purchases.

# Fixed-rate mortgages

**REMEMBER**

*Fixed-rate mortgages,* which are typically for a 15- or 30-year term for single-family properties, condos, and one- to four-unit apartments, have interest rates that remain constant over the entire life of the loan. Because the interest rate stays the same, your monthly mortgage payment stays the same.

## Examining the pros and cons

For purposes of making future estimates of your property's cash flow, fixed-rate mortgages offer you certainty and some peace of mind because you know precisely the size of your mortgage payment next month, next year, and ten plus years from now. (Of course, the other costs of owning investment property — such as property taxes, insurance, maintenance, capital expenses, and so on — still escalate over the years.)

**WARNING**

Peace of mind, however, comes at a price:

>> You generally pay a premium, in the form of a higher interest rate, compared with loans that have an adjustable interest rate over time. If you're buying a property and planning to improve it and sell it within five to ten years, you may be throwing money away by taking out a fixed-rate loan to lock in an interest rate for decades.

>> If, like most investment property buyers, you're facing a tough time generating a healthy positive cash flow in the early years of owning a particular investment property, a fixed-rate mortgage is going to make it even more financially challenging. An adjustable-rate mortgage, by contrast, can lower your property's carrying costs in those early years. (Find out about adjustable-rate mortgages later in this chapter.)

>> You run the risk of needing to refinance if you need or want to:

   • Fixed-rate loans carry the risk that if interest rates fall significantly after you obtain your mortgage and you're unable to refinance, you're stuck with a relatively higher-cost mortgage. For example, you may be unable to refinance if you lose your job, your employment income declines, the value of your property decreases, or the property's rental income slides. Also note that even if you're able to refinance, you'll probably have to spend significant time and money to get it done.

- Fixed-rate loans on larger investment properties can also have prepayment penalties that effectively eliminate your ability to refinance the loan when rates fall. The lenders want to lock in a certain interest rate for these loans as they are sold to investors who are counting on that level of return for a long period of time. These loans often have *yield maintenance* or *defeasance,* which are both formulas for calculating the prepayment penalty that you would have to pay to refinance.

## Making a point of comparing fixed rates

In addition to the ongoing, constant interest rate charged on a fixed-rate mortgage, lenders also typically levy an upfront fee, called points, which can be considered prepaid interest. *Points* are generally a percentage of the amount borrowed. To illustrate, 1.5 points are equal to 1.5 percent of the loan amount. So, for example, on a $200,000 mortgage, 1.5 points translate into $3,000 upfront (also known as prepaid) interest. Points can add significantly to the cost of borrowing money, particularly if you don't plan to keep the loan for long.

REMEMBER

Generally speaking, the more points you pay on a given loan, the lower the ongoing interest rate the lender charges on that loan. That's why you can't compare various lenders' fixed-rate loans to one another unless you know the exact points on each specific mortgage, in addition to that loan's ongoing interest rate.

The following are two approaches to dealing with points, given your financial situation and investment goals:

>> **Minimize the points:** When you're running low on cash to close on a mortgage, or if you don't plan to hold the loan or property for long, you probably want to keep your points (and other loan fees discussed in the next section) to a minimum. You may want to take a higher interest rate on your mortgage.

>> **Pay more points:** If you're more concerned with keeping your ongoing costs low, plan to hold the property for many years, and aren't cash constrained to close on the loan now, consider paying more points to lower your interest rate. This is known as *buying down the loan rate* and can be an excellent strategy to lower your overall costs of borrowing and increase the property's cash flow and equity buildup.

TIP

To make an easier apples-to-apples comparison of mortgages from different lenders, get interest rate quotes at the same point level. For example, ask each lender for the interest rate on a particular fixed-rate mortgage for which you pay one point or two points. You may also compare the *annual percentage rate* (APR), which is a summary loan cost measure that includes all of a loan's fees and costs.

However, keep in mind that the APR assumes that you hold the mortgage for its entire term — such as 15 or 30 years. If you end up keeping the loan for a shorter time period, either because you refinance or pay off the mortgage early, the APR isn't valid and accurate (unless you recalculate based on the changed term and payoff).

# Adjustable-rate mortgages (ARMs)

**REMEMBER**

*Adjustable-rate mortgages* (ARMs) carry an interest rate that varies over time. An ARM starts with a particular interest rate, usually a good deal lower than the going rate on comparable length (15- or 30-year) fixed-rate mortgages, and then you pay different rates for every six months or every year, possibly even every month, during a 30-year mortgage. Because the interest rate on an ARM changes over time, so too does the size of the loan's monthly payment. (You shouldn't use an adjustable-rate mortgage with a monthly adjustment period as you need some certainty in your cash flow.)

ARMs are often attractive for a number of reasons:

>> You can start paying your mortgage with a relatively low initial interest rate compared with fixed-rate loans. Given the economics of a typical investment property purchase, ARMs better enable an investor to achieve a positive cash flow in the early years of property ownership.

>> Should interest rates decline, you can realize most, if not all, of the benefits of lower rates without the cost and hassle of refinancing. With a fixed-rate mortgage, the only way to benefit from an overall decline in the market level of interest rates is to refinance.

ARMs come with many more features and options than do fixed-rate mortgages, including caps, indexes, margins, and adjustment periods. The following sections help you understand these important ARM features and how to avoid surprises.

## Start rate

The *start rate* on an ARM is the interest rate the mortgage begins with. Don't be fooled though: You don't pay this often tantalizingly low rate for too long. That is why it's often called a *teaser rate*. The start rate on most ARMs is set artificially low to entice you. In other words, even if the market level of interest rates doesn't change, your ARM is destined to increase as soon as the terms of the loan allow (more on this topic in a minute). An increase of one or two percentage points is common.

The start rate won't last long, so the formula for determining the future interest rates on an ARM and rate caps is far more important in determining what a mortgage is going to cost you in the long run. Keep reading.

## Future interest rate

REMEMBER

The first important thing to ask a mortgage lender or broker about an ARM you're contemplating is the formula for determining the future interest rate on your loan. ARMs are based on the following formula:

Future Interest Rate = Index + Margin

The *index* is a designated measure of the market interest rate that the lender chooses to calculate the specific interest rate for your loan. Indexes are generally (but not always) widely quoted in the financial press. The *margin* is the amount added to the index to determine the interest rate that you pay on your mortgage.

For example, suppose that the loan you're considering uses a 1-year Treasury bill index, which, say, is at about 2 percent, and the loan you're considering has a margin of 2.75 percent (also often referred to as 275 *basis points*; 100 basis points equals 1 percent). Thus, the following formula would drive the rate of this mortgage:

1-Year Treasury Bill Rate (2 percent) + Margin (2.75 percent)

Do the math and you get 4.75 percent. This figure is known as the *fully indexed rate* (the rate the loan has after the initial rate expires and if the index stays constant). If this loan starts out at just 2 percent, you know that if the one-year Treasury bill index remains at the same level, your loan can increase to 4.75 percent. If this index rises one percent to 3 percent during the period that you're covered by the ARM's start rate, that means the loan's fully indexed rate goes to 5.75 percent (3.00 + 2.75), which is nearly 3 percent higher than the loan's start rate.

TIP

Compare the fully indexed rate on an ARM you're considering to the current rate for a comparable term fixed-rate loan. You may see that the fixed-rate loan is at about the same interest rate, which may lead you to reconsider your choice of an ARM that carries the risk of rising to a higher future level.

## Understanding ARM indexes

The different indexes used on ARMs vary mainly in how rapidly they respond to changes in interest rates. If you select an adjustable-rate mortgage tied to one of the faster-moving indexes, you take on more of a risk that the next adjustment may reflect interest rate increases. When you take on more of the risk that rates may increase, lenders cut you breaks in other ways, such as through lower *caps* (the maximum rate increase possible over a given time period; see the next section), lower margins, or lower points.

Should you want the security of an ARM tied to a slower-moving index, you pay for that security in one form or another, such as a higher start rate, caps, margin, or points. You may also pay in other, less-obvious ways. A slower-moving index, such as the 11th District Cost of Funds Index (COFI), lags behind general changes in market interest rates, so it continues to rise after interest rates peak and goes down slower after rates have turned down. The following list covers some of these indexes:

>> **Treasury bills (T-bills)** are IOUs that the U.S. government issues. Most ARMs are tied to the interest rate on 6-month or 12-month T-bills (also referred to as the 1-year constant maturity Treasury index). This is a relatively rapidly moving index. Some investment property mortgages are tied to the rate on 10-year Treasury Notes. Being a somewhat longer-term bond, a 10-year index doesn't generally move as rapidly as the shorter-term indexes.

>> **Certificates of deposit (CDs)** are interest-bearing bank deposits that lock the depositor in at a set interest rate for a specific period of time. ARMs are usually tied to the average interest rate that banks are paying on 6-month CDs. Like T-bills, CDs tend to respond quickly to changes in the market's level of interest rates.

>> **London Interbank Offered Rate Index (LIBOR)** is an average of the rate of interest that major international banks charge each other to borrow large sums of U.S. dollars, which is commonly referred to by real estate lenders as an index for their adjustable loans. LIBOR tends to move and adjust quite rapidly to changes in interest rates and is at times even more volatile than the U.S. Treasury or CD index rates.

>> **Eleventh District Cost of Funds Index (COFI)** is a relatively slow-moving index. Adjustable-rate mortgages tied to the 11th District Cost of Funds Index tend to start out at a higher interest rate. A slower-moving index has the advantage of moving up less quickly when rates are on the rise. On the other hand, you have to be patient to benefit from falling interest rates.

In a relatively low-interest rate environment, fewer lenders tend to offer COFI loans. This illustrates the point that lenders don't always offer the same choice of indexes. Rather, each lender offers one or typically no more than two indexes, and borrowers should specifically look at the index as part of their overall decision on choosing a lender.

## Future interest rate adjustments

After the initial interest rate ends, the interest rate on an ARM fluctuates based on the loan formula. Typically, ARM interest rates change every 6 or 12 months, but some adjust every month. In advance of each adjustment, the lender sends you a notice telling you your new rate. Be sure to check these notices because on rare occasions, lenders make mistakes.

Almost all ARMs come with a rate cap, which limits the maximum rate change (up or down) allowed at each adjustment. This limit is usually referred to as the *adjustment cap.* On most loans that adjust every six months, the adjustment cap is 1 percent; the interest rate charged on the mortgage can move up or down no more than one percentage point in an adjustment period.

Loans that adjust more than once per year usually limit the maximum rate change that's allowed over the entire year as well — known as the *annual rate cap.* On the vast majority of such loans, 2 percent is the annual rate cap. Likewise, almost all ARMs come with *lifetime caps,* which represent the highest rate allowed over the entire life of the loan. Lifetime caps of 5 to 6 percent higher than the initial start rate are common for adjustables.

Many ARMs also have a *rate floor* that is the minimum interest rate that will apply to the loan. Often the *rate floor* is equal to the *start rate,* which means that your loan can adjust up or down over the life of the loan, but never lower than the *start rate.* Coauthor Robert had an ARM loan for many years that adjusted annually up or down based on the COFI index. During the low interest rate years, this loan actually adjusted down, but it could go no lower than the *rate floor,* which was specified in the loan documents. For several years in a row, Robert received an annual adjustment that led to a reduction in his monthly mortgage payment for the following year, until it did reach the rate floor. Since Robert plans to own this property for a long time, he then refinanced to a fixed rate that was actually lower than the adjustable rate loan would have been at the next rate adjustment period.

WARNING

Taking an ARM without rate caps is like heading out for a weeklong outdoor trek without appropriate rain gear and clothing for varying temperatures. When you consider an adjustable-rate mortgage, you must identify the maximum payment that you can handle. If you can't handle the payment that comes with a 10 or 11 percent interest rate, for example, don't look at ARMs that may go that high. As you crunch the numbers to see what your property's cash flow looks like under different circumstances, consider calculating how your mortgage payment changes based on various higher interest rates.

### Avoiding negative amortization ARMs

As you make mortgage payments over time, the loan balance you still owe is gradually reduced or *amortized*. *Negative amortization* (when your loan balance increases) is the reverse of this process. It occurs when the monthly loan payments are less than the amount of interest that is accruing during that time. Some ARMs allow negative amortization. How can your outstanding loan balance grow when you continue to make mortgage payments? This phenomenon occurs when your mortgage payment is less than it really should be.

**REMEMBER**

Some loans cap the increase of your monthly payment amount but don't cap the interest rate. Thus, the size of your mortgage payment may not reflect all the interest that you currently owe on your loan. So, rather than paying the interest that you owe and paying off some of your loan balance (or *principal*) every month, you end up paying off some, but not all, of the interest that you owe. Thus, lenders add the extra, unpaid interest that you still owe to your outstanding debt.

Negative amortization is similar to paying only the minimum payment that your credit card bill requires. You continue to rack up finance charges (in this case, greater interest) on the unpaid balance as long as you only make the artificially low payment. Taking a mortgage with negative amortization defeats the whole purpose of borrowing an amount that fits your overall financial goals.

**WARNING**

Avoid ARMs with negative amortization. The only way to know whether a loan includes negative amortization is to ask explicitly. Some lenders and mortgage brokers aren't forthcoming about telling you. If you have trouble finding lenders that will deal with your financial situation, make sure that you're especially careful — you find negative amortization more frequently on loans that lenders consider risky, which should be taken as a sign that maybe you're overreaching for a property that isn't an ideal investment. You're likely only to be considering such a mortgage because your cash flow won't allow you to have a fully amortized loan. Therefore, you would need to achieve significant appreciation in the property to cover this negative cash flow plus your desired rate of return in order for this investment to make sense.

# Reviewing Other Common Fees

Whether the loan is fixed or adjustable, mortgage lenders typically assess other upfront fees and charges. The lender must disclose these ancillary fees. You may have to search carefully to find them in the paperwork, so make sure that you do because they can significantly add up to quite a bundle with some lenders. Here are some typical extra charges you're likely to encounter:

» **Application fee:** Most lenders charge several hundred dollars to work with you to complete your paperwork and see it through their loan evaluation process. Should your loan be rejected, or if it's approved and you decide not to take it, the lender wants to cover its costs. Some lenders credit or return this fee to you upon closing with their loan, but you need to verify it upfront in writing.

» **Credit report charge:** Most lenders charge you for the cost of obtaining your credit report, which tells the lender whether you've filed bankruptcy in the last seven years, plus repaid other loans, including *consumer debt* (such as credit cards, auto loans, and so on), on time. A credit report also allows the lender to verify your employment and personal residence and business addresses. Your credit report should cost about $50 for each individual or entity that will be a borrower.

» **Appraisal fee:** The property for which you borrow money needs to be valued. If you default on your mortgage, a lender doesn't want to get stuck with a property that's worth less than you owe. The cost for standard form appraisal typically ranges from several hundred dollars for most residential properties of one to four units to as much as $1,000 or more for larger investment properties. (On particularly large properties, this fee can be more significant — on a 30,000-square-foot office building, an appraisal may run around $4,000; on a 300-plus-unit apartment building, it is more in the $7,000 to $8,000 range.) You may be able to save some money if the property has been appraised recently and you contact the appraiser who's willing and able to provide you with an updated appraisal.

» **Environmental assessment or phase I:** Virtually all lenders making loans on residential properties with five or more units or, especially, commercial property, require a qualified engineering company to perform a site assessment and overview of the entire area in which the property is located to identify possible environmental issues. This type of report is commonly referred to as a *phase I environmental report,* and the cost directly correlates to the location, type of property, size, and even the prior use of the property and the surrounding area. Phase I reports can run from $300 to as much as tens of thousands of dollars.

» **Third-party physical inspection:** Depending on the property being financed, lenders often require third-party inspections by competent professionals. For example, an inspection report from a licensed pest control firm documenting the property condition and specifically the presence of termites and/or wood-destroying organisms is required in virtually all transactions, including single-family homes and commercial properties. For loans on larger properties, a property condition assessment (PCA) report is typically required. Again, the cost of these reports varies depending on the property.

**REMEMBER**

Request a detailing of other fees and charges in writing from all lenders that you're seriously considering. You need to know the total of all lender fees so that you can accurately compare different lenders' loans and determine how much closing on your loan will cost you. For residential and commercial income proper-ties, the lender usually asks for a deposit that the lender uses to cover the types of fees and charges outlined here.

**TIP**

To reduce the possibility of wasting your time and money applying for a mortgage that you may not qualify for, ask the lender for any reasons it may not approve you. Disclose any problems on your credit report or with the property.

# Making Some Mortgage Decisions

You can't (or at least shouldn't) spend months deciding which mortgage may be right for your situation. The following sections help you zero in on which type is best for you.

## Choosing between fixed and adjustable

Choosing between a fixed-rate or adjustable-rate loan is an important decision in the real estate investment process. Consider the advantages and disadvantages of each mortgage type and decide what's best for your situation prior to going out to refinance or purchase real estate. The following sections cover the key factors to consider.

## Your ability and desire to accept financial risk

How much risk can you handle in regard to the size of your property's monthly mortgage payment? If you can take the financial risks that come with an ARM, you have a better chance of saving money and maximizing your property's cash flow with an adjustable-rate rather than a fixed-rate loan. Your interest rate starts lower and stays lower with an ARM, if the overall level of interest rates stays unchanged. Even if rates go up, they'll likely come back down over the life of your loan. If you can stick with your ARM for better and for worse, you should come out ahead in the long run.

ARMs make more sense if you borrow less than you're qualified for. If your income (and applicable investment property cash flow) significantly exceeds your spending, you may feel less anxiety about the fluctuating interest rate on an ARM. If you do choose an adjustable loan, you may feel more financially secure if you have a hefty financial cushion (at least six months' to as much as a year's worth of expenses reserved) that you can access if rates go up.

Some people take ARMs when they can't really afford them. When rates rise, property owners who can't afford higher payments face a financial crisis. If you don't have emergency savings that you can tap into to make the higher payments, how can you afford the monthly payments and the other expenses of your property?

**WARNING**

If you can't afford the highest-allowed payment on an ARM, don't take one. You shouldn't take the chance that the rate may not rise that high — it can, and you can lose the property.

**TIP**

Ask your lender to calculate the highest possible monthly payment that your loan allows. The number the lender comes up with is the payment that you face if the interest rate on your loan goes to the highest level allowed, or the *lifetime cap*. (For more on caps, see the earlier section "Future interest rate adjustments.")

**REMEMBER**

Don't take an adjustable mortgage because the lower initial interest rate allows you to afford the property that you want to buy (unless you're absolutely certain that your income and property cash flow will enable you to meet future payment increases). Try setting your sights on a property that you can afford to buy with a fixed-rate mortgage.

## Length of time you expect to keep the mortgage

Saving interest on most ARMs is usually a certainty in the first two or three years. An adjustable-rate mortgage starts at a lower interest rate than a fixed one. But if rates rise, you can end up repaying the savings that you achieve in the early years of the mortgage.

If you aren't going to keep your mortgage for more than five to seven years, you pay more interest to carry a fixed-rate mortgage. A mortgage lender takes extra risk in committing to a fixed-interest rate for 15 to 30 years. Lenders don't know what may happen in the intervening years, so they charge you a premium in case interest rates move significantly higher in future years.

**TIP**

You may also consider a hybrid loan, which combines features of fixed- and adjustable-rate mortgages. For example, the initial rate may hold constant for three, five, seven, or ten years and then adjust once a year or every six months thereafter. Such loans may make sense for you if you foresee a high probability of keeping your loan seven to ten years or less but want some stability in your future monthly payments. The longer the initial rate stays locked in, the higher the interest rate. Don't confuse these loans with the often-unadvisable balloon mortgage (which is discussed in the later section "Mortgages That Should Make You Think Twice").

# Selecting short-term or long-term

Most mortgage lenders offer you the option of 15-year or 30-year mortgages. You can also find 10-year, 20-year, and 40-year options, but they're unusual. Some lenders are even allowing you to select *customized* or *other length amortization terms* that allow you to personalize the number of years of your mortgage. Personalizing your mortgage may make sense if you have a specific goal in mind, such as completing your mortgage payments before tackling college tuition bills or a particular retirement date. So how do you decide whether a shorter- or longer-term mortgage is best for your investment property purchase?

To afford the monthly payments and have a positive cash flow, many investment property buyers need to spread their mortgage loan payments over a longer period of time, and a 30-year mortgage is the way to do it. A 15-year mortgage has higher monthly payments because you pay it off quicker. At a fixed-rate mortgage interest rate of 7 percent, for example, a 15-year mortgage comes with payments that are about 35 percent higher than those for a 30-year mortgage.

**WARNING**

Locking yourself into higher monthly payments with a 15-year mortgage may actually put you at greater financial risk. If your finances worsen or your property declines in value, odds are you'll have trouble qualifying for a refinance. You *may* be able to refinance your way out of the predicament, but you can't count on it.

Don't consider a 15-year mortgage unless you're sure that you can afford the higher payments that come with it. Even if you can afford these higher payments, taking the 15-year option isn't necessarily better. You may be able to find better uses for the money. If you can earn a higher rate of return investing your extra cash versus paying the interest on your mortgage, for instance, you may come out ahead investing your money rather than paying down your mortgage faster. Some real estate investors are attracted to 15-year mortgages to get their loans paid off by or even before retirement age.

TIP

If you decide on a 30-year mortgage, you still maintain the flexibility to pay the mortgage off faster if you choose to. You can choose to make larger-than-necessary payments and create your own 15-year mortgage. However, you can fall back to making only the payments required on your 30-year schedule when the need arises. One situation when you shouldn't pay off your 30-year mortgage faster is if the loan has a *prepayment penalty* (a penalty for paying off your loan before you're supposed to). Normally, prepayment penalties don't apply if you pay off a loan because you sell the property, but when you refinance a loan with prepayment penalties, you typically have to pay the penalty. (Prepay penalties are negotiable with the lender to the extent that the lender has the ability to waive or reduce the penalty. However, this typically happens only when prevailing current interest rates are above the contract rate. If current market rates are below the contract rate, you can pretty much forget it.)

Typically, the interest rate will be lower for a 15-year loan than a 30-year loan, but if they're the same or very close, then you gain flexibility with a 30-year loan with no prepayment penalty at zero cost. You can then adjust your payments over the life of the loan to customize your loan to exactly the term you desire. Many years ago, coauthor Robert started making extra principal payments each month to turn a 15-year loan on an income property into a 10-year loan that would coincide with his oldest daughter going off to college. With the loan paid in full, the "loan payment" could then be used toward the ever-increasing cost of college tuition!

# Borrowing Against Home Equity

*Home equity loans* (or a derivative called a *HELOC* — home equity line of credit) enable you to borrow against the equity in your home. Because such loans are in addition to the mortgage that you already have (known as the *first mortgage*), home equity loans are also known as *second mortgages.*

A home equity loan may provide a relatively low-cost source of funds for an investment property purchase, especially if you're seeking money for just a few years. You can refinance your first mortgage and pull cash out for an investment property purchase, but you shouldn't do that if your first mortgage is at a lower interest rate than you can obtain on a refinance.

Home equity loans generally have higher interest rates than comparable first mortgages because they're riskier to a lender. The reason: In the event that you default on the first mortgage or file for bankruptcy protection, the first mortgage lender gets first claim on your home.

Interest paid of up to $750,000 on home mortgages for primary or secondary residences is tax deductible ($1 million for mortgage loans, plus up to $100,000 in home equity, taken out before December 17, 2017).

# Getting a Seller-Financed Loan

Not every seller needs or even wants to receive all cash as payment for the property, so you may be able to finance part or even all of an investment property purchase thanks to the property seller's financing. The use of seller financing is the cornerstone of most no-money-down strategies.

*Seller financing* is a transaction in which the seller accepts anything less than all cash at closing. One form of an all-cash transaction to the seller is the buyer literally paying all cash, but typically it's a transaction in which the buyer uses a *conventional loan* (money to purchase the property from a lender other than the seller) so that the seller effectively receives all cash at closing.

Some sellers are financially well off enough that they don't need all the sales proceeds immediately for their next purchase or are buying a property for less money — or maybe not buying a replacement property at all — and prefer to receive payments over time. They may be looking for the payments to replace their income in retirement, or they may prefer to receive the funds over time so they can reduce their taxable income.

TIP

Any seller with equity can offer seller financing, but usually private individuals are the best sources. The best candidates for seller financing are sellers with significant equity or, best of all, folks who own their property free-and-clear (without any debt on the property at all). Many seniors have owned their properties for years and may be more willing to extend a loan.

Sometimes sellers offer this option, but in other cases, you need to pop the question. Here are two good reasons to ask for the seller to help finance an investment property purchase:

>> **Better terms:** Mortgage lenders, which are typically banks or large monolithic financial institutions, aren't the most flexible businesses in the world. You may well be able to obtain a lower interest rate, lower or waived fees, and more flexible repayment conditions from a property seller. There are also many expenses with conventional loans that a property seller may not require: loan points, origination fees, and an appraisal. Some sellers may not even require a loan application or credit report, but they'd be wise to go through due diligence (including a personal financial statement) on the buyer.

>> **Loan approval:** Perhaps you've had prior financial problems that have caused mortgage lenders to routinely deny your mortgage application. Some property sellers may be more flexible, especially in a slow real estate market or with a property that's challenging to sell. A seller can also make a decision in a few days, whereas a conventional lender often takes weeks.

**WARNING**

Be careful when considering a property where a seller is offering financing as part of the deal; this act may be a sign of a hard-to-sell property. Investigate how long the property has been on the market and what specific flaws and problems it may have.

Some of the reasons why sellers may offer their own financing include the following:

>> **They're attracted to the potential returns of being a mortgage lender.** This reason shouldn't concern the buyer as long as the terms of the seller financing are reasonable and avoid the issues raised elsewhere in this chapter about balloon payment and negative amortization or interest-only loans.

>> **The seller has significant equity.** This situation creates another win-win opportunity for both the buyer and seller to use seller financing.

>> **The current financing has prepayment issues.** This road can be a problem for the buyer; if the underlying financing has a due-on-sale clause and the lender becomes aware of the sale, it can demand the full payment of the outstanding loan balance on short notice. The seller is responsible for any prepayment penalties for their current financing when they pay it off.

>> **They're seeking a price that exceeds the normal conventional loan parameters, or the property doesn't qualify for a conventional loan for some reason.** Examples of qualification issues include a cracked slab, environmental issues (including drug manufacturing like methamphetamine), improvements done without permits, and so on. This scenario is risky for the buyer and may be an indication that the seller is over-reaching or pursuing a property that's not a good investment.

>> **The income property is owned with partners, and per a buy-sell agreement, one of the partners needs to sell.** If you own income properties with others, you should have a buy-sell agreement as the goals and needs for each partner can vary over time. If one partner needs to sell, and another partner is the buyer, it can make good sense for all parties to use seller financing. The seller certainly knows the property and likely knows the buyer, so getting paid over time also allows the seller to minimize the tax hit.

TIP

Be sure that your seller financing agreement is nonrecourse (as discussed later in this chapter) and doesn't contain a *due-on-sale clause* prohibiting you from selling the property without paying off the loan in full. If the seller requires a due-on-sale clause, you have to pay off the full balance owed to the seller when you sell the property. Most sellers wisely ask for the due-on-sale clause so that the property can't be sold to another owner.

# Mortgages That Should Make You Think Twice

You may come across other loans such as balloon loans and interest-only mortgages. You should also know the potential risks associated with recourse loans and loan guarantees. The following section presents some thoughts on these options.

## Balloon loans

One type of loan that is sometimes confused with a hybrid loan is a balloon loan. *Balloon loans* start off just like traditional fixed-rate mortgages. You make level payments based on a long-term payment schedule, over 15 or 30 years, for example. But at a predetermined time, usually 3 to 15 years after the loan's inception, the remaining loan balance becomes fully due.

Balloon loans may save you money because they have a lower interest rate than a longer-term fixed-rate mortgage. Sometimes, balloon loans may be the only option for the buyer (or so the buyer thinks). Buyers are more commonly backed into these loans during periods of high interest rates. When a buyer can't afford the payments on a conventional mortgage and really wants a particular property, a seller may offer a balloon loan.

WARNING

Balloon loans are dangerous for the simple reason that your financial situation can change, and you may not be able to refinance when your balloon loan is due. What if you lose your job or your income drops? What if the value of your property drops and the appraisal comes in too low to qualify you for a new loan? What if interest rates rise and you can't qualify at the higher rate on a new loan? Many of these loans also have onerous prepayment penalties and are also known as "bullet loans." Balloon loans are recommended *only* when the following conditions apply:

>> Such a loan is your sole financing option.

>> You've really done your homework to exhaust other financing options.

>> You're certain that you can refinance when the balloon comes due.

**TIP**

If you take a balloon loan, get one with as much time as possible, preferably 7, 10, or even 15 years, before it becomes due.

## Interest-only loans

In the early years of interest-only mortgages, your monthly mortgage payment is used only to pay interest that is owed. Although this helps keep your payments relatively low (because no money is going toward repaying principal), the downside is that you're not making any headway to pay down your loan balance. Before the economic downturn in the late 2000s and early 2010s, interest-only loans were becoming more prevalent.

However, a pure interest-only loan for 10 or 15 years is still not the norm. Usually, after a preset time period paying only interest, such as five or seven years, your loan converts to an amortizing loan and your mortgage payment jumps substantially so that you can begin to pay down or amortize your loan balance. Many people don't really understand or investigate how this increased payment affects them, which is why you shouldn't take these types of loans.

The main attraction for interest-only mortgages for investment property purchases is that the low initial payments help you achieve more positive cash flow early on. A concern, however, is seeing some property buyers attracted to interest-only loans to afford purchasing high-cost property that is difficult to realize positive cash flow from.

**WARNING**

If the only way for you to invest in an income property is to use an interest-only loan, perhaps you shouldn't invest. Investing in rental real estate is risky, and you can lose your entire investment if the market turns and you don't have the staying power to ride through the real estate cycles. The margin of safety that you have with a decent down payment and an amortizing loan (where each payment reduces your loan balance) can be very positive if your rental property hits a rough patch.

If you consider an interest-only mortgage, be sure that you understand upfront exactly how high your payment will be after the loan moves out of the interest-only payment phase. And be sure that you've surveyed the mortgage marketplace and understand how the terms and conditions of interest-only loans stack up versus other types of mortgages. Interest-only loans are also for a finite period and thus are essentially balloon loans. While you may think that interest-only loans are for investors who can't afford a loan that amortizes principal, the reality is that interest-only loans are often used by institutional buyers or very wealthy individuals, as the risk can be very high unless you have substantial liquid assets. Billionaires may use interest-only loans; the rest of us don't.

## Recourse financing

The goal of most real estate investors is to accumulate wealth over time while not taking any unreasonable risks. That's why using interest-only loans or loans with balloon payments is discouraged. But there is another factor to explore before agreeing to any loan: Is the loan nonrecourse or recourse?

>> **Nonrecourse financing:** In the event you fail to fulfill the terms of your loan, this type of loan limits the lender to only foreclosing on the underlying property. *Foreclosure* is the full and complete satisfaction of the loan, and the lender can't seek a deficiency judgment or go after your other assets. Agreeing only to loans with nonrecourse financing is extremely important because you increase your overall net worth through real estate investing. You don't want one bad investment to jeopardize your successful properties or, even worse, the equity in your primary residence or a business.

>> **Recourse loans:** These loans lower the lender's risk because they offer additional protection. The lender has the legal right to seek a deficiency judgment against you personally or pursue other assets to cover any shortfall should the property value not fully cover the lender's outstanding debt balance. Note that after a loan is in default, the interest penalties and legal fees can add up quickly. If you're already in default on the loan for your rental property, the last challenge you need is to have a lender looking to take your home or other viable rental properties to satisfy its deficiency judgment.

As long as you're not too aggressive and don't overleverage your rental properties, real estate investing can be relatively safe, and the chances are you won't be faced with losing your property by defaulting on your loan. But there are limits to your ability to control all the diverse factors that can affect your property. For example, your cash flow will definitely suffer if the major employer in your area suddenly leaves.

Nonrecourse financing has more stringent qualification standards, such as higher debt coverage ratios, and generally results in a lower loan amount. But just as with borrowers who utilize interest-only loans so that they can borrow as much money as possible, the closer you live to the edge, the more likely you'll regret it.

Many of the loans you consider will be nonrecourse, but if you're seeking financing for an *unstabilized property* (a property whose cash flow is uncertain due to vacancy or unusually high expenses) or a property requiring major renovation, you may find that lenders are willing to provide the funds you need only with a full recourse loan.

WARNING

Typically you're evaluating different loan proposals with either full recourse or full nonrecourse financing. But lenders can also offer a partial recourse loan. A *partial recourse loan* allows the lender to seek a deficiency judgment up to a certain limit if you default. Again, there may be great real estate investment options where such a loan makes sense, but be very careful before agreeing to such terms, and include the consequences to your overall financial status in a worst-case scenario in your overall analysis.

REMEMBER

No matter what type of loan you use, you should only use nonrecourse financing. You'll sleep better at night!

## Loan guarantees

Another way that lenders reduce their risk of a loan defaulting is by requiring a loan guarantee. A *loan guarantee* is a promise by the guarantor (the person or entity subject to the loan guarantee and legally responsible for repayment of any shortfall) to assume the debt obligation of the borrower if the borrower defaults on the loan. Investment real estate is often purchased in the name of a legal entity that may not have other assets than the real property subject to the loan. In these instances, a *personal loan guarantee* will be required from an individual, which is usually the person who is the owner or one of the owners of the legal entity that owns the real property.

Particularly if the loan is nonrecourse, the lender will want a loan guarantee to be included. The loan guarantee can be limited or unlimited, which controls whether the guarantor is responsible for some or all of the debt. You may have seen or heard about guarantors for leases, such as a parent serving as the guarantor of their child's college apartment.

Chapter **5**

# Grasping the Legal Fundamentals of Managing Residential Rentals

Whenever you approach a subject for the first time, you probably try to wrap your brain around it before getting into the specifics. This chapter helps you gain the big-picture perspective by highlighting the key legal aspects of being a landlord and managing all types of residential rentals, including single-family homes; condominiums; and small, medium, and large multi-family apartments.

The first section stresses the importance of running your business as a legal entity in order to protect your personal assets, mitigate risk, minimize taxes, and maximize profits. The second section touches on important steps to follow when taking ownership of the property. The third and longest section in this chapter introduces your legal obligations as a landlord; here you find out how to fulfill your obligations while protecting your rights and avoiding legal problems.

# Running Your Operation as a Corporation or LLC

**REMEMBER**

Unless you take steps to give your business the status of a corporation or limited liability company (LLC), you're operating as a sole proprietorship and, for legal purposes, placing your personal assets at risk. If you can't pay what you owe to a creditor, such as a contractor, a utility company, or the lender that holds the mortgage on your property, they can pursue your personal assets to collect what you owe. Operating your business as a corporation or LLC insulates your personal assets from your business assets, thus protecting your personal assets from such claims. In addition, operating your business as a corporation or LLC potentially reduces your taxes, increasing your net profit.

Most landlords choose to operate as an LLC because it provides the protection of a corporation without the costs and complexities of forming and managing a corporation. Any claims by creditors against the LLC are limited to the LLC's assets, protecting your home, personal financial accounts, and other personal or unrelated business assets from those claims.

**WARNING**

An LLC *doesn't* provide complete protection. If a court finds that your carelessness or negligence contributed to a tenant's injury, for example, you could be held personally liable. You should purchase a landlord insurance policy that covers such scenarios.

Structuring your business and operating it as a corporation is much more complicated and expensive than forming an LLC. You need to register a name for your corporation with your state's Secretary of State, write and file articles of incorporation and bylaws, issue stock (at least one share), have regular corporate meetings, prepare and file minutes from those meetings, and comply with regulations for recording and reporting financial transactions. In addition, to take full advantage of tax savings, you may need to pay a portion of your profits from the rental property to yourself as a salary, which requires payroll processing.

# Taking Ownership of a Rental Property

Assuming you've completed the closing on your rental property, you realize that transferring ownership of any real estate is a somewhat complicated endeavor. The process is even more complicated when transferring ownership of a rental property. When you buy a rental property, make sure you get the following items from the seller:

>> A list of personal property included in the sale

>> All leases or rental agreements and all documents in each of the tenant files

>> Seller-verified rent roll, including a list of all security deposits

>> Building blueprints and site plans

>> All required governmental licenses and permits

>> Recent utility bills with all account numbers and due date

>> Every service agreement or contract

>> Copy of the seller's current insurance policy, including five-year loss history

**REMEMBER**

Meet with a reputable insurance provider and purchase a policy for the property with an effective date prior to taking possession so that there's no lapse in insurance coverage when you take possession. If the property burns down before closing, it's the seller's problem. If an uninsured property burns down or floods after closing, it's your problem.

After you become the proud owner of the residential rental property, you have a few tasks to attend to as soon as possible, including the following:

>> Meet with the tenants in person, introduce yourself as the new owner, and answer any questions they may have.

>> Inspect the outside of the rental property carefully and make a list of any maintenance and repair issues. Address these issues as soon as possible.

>> Evaluate the current rent. You can't raise the rent for current tenants until their lease expires or at the end of the month (for month-to-month renters), but you can analyze how much rent your tenants are paying now. Also consider how much you need to charge new tenants to cover your higher expenses as the new owner and turn a decent profit, so you know how much to raise the rent for existing tenants when that time comes.

>> Use current professional forms from your local affiliate of the National Apartment Association (NAA) or landlord-tenant legal advisor to prepare rental contracts (either a fixed-term lease or a month-to-month rental agreement) so that they're ready for new applicants and for current tenants who decide to remain after their rental contract expires.

# Avoiding the Legal Pitfalls of Managing Residential Rental Properties

Owning residential rental property comes with legal obligations and risks. You're legally responsible to comply with fair housing laws, keep your property in "habitable" condition, ensure your tenants' rights to "quiet enjoyment" of the property, comply with laws for handling and refunding security deposits, take reasonable steps to prevent crime, and eliminate any known dangerous or hazardous conditions. If you have employees, you may be liable for their legal actions as well. And tenants can file a claim against you for any number of reasons, regardless of whether those claims have legal merit.

The following sections highlight many of the most common legal issues you need to be aware of and be prepared to resolve. They also guide you in best practices that help you avoid legal problems in the first place, such as screening applicants carefully and legally, as well as always honoring your tenants' legal rights.

## Obeying fair housing laws

**REMEMBER**

Fair housing laws prohibit landlords from using certain criteria, such as race or sex, to target tenants in advertising or to refuse housing to applicants. When screening applicants, for example, you're permitted to consider only factors that are likely to indicate whether the person will pay their rent on time, take care of the property, get along with the neighbors, and comply with your other policies. You may use criteria such as income, credit history, past evictions, criminal history, and similar factors to determine the prospect's qualifications. You can't use race; color; national origin or ancestry; religion or creed (belief system); sex (including gender, pregnancy, sexual orientation, and gender identity); familial status; or physical or mental handicap; plus certain other state or local municipality criteria.

The following sections explain the federal Fair Housing Act and look at how some states expand coverage of that Act. They also stress the importance of considering fair housing laws when advertising your rental property.

### Federal law: The Fair Housing Act

**REMEMBER**

The Fair Housing Act prohibits you, as landlord, from discriminating against or giving preferential treatment to people based on their *protected class* status — a characteristic that can't be used to discriminate against or in favor of an individual or group. The Fair Housing Act specifies the following seven protected classes:

>> **Race:** Ethnicity or culture, such as African American, Caucasian, Hispanic, Asian, American Indian, and so on

>> **Color:** Skin color or shade, which may seem to be the same thing as race, but people of the same race sometimes discriminate against one another based on lightness or darkness of skin

>> **Religion or creed:** Christianity, Islam, Judaism, Hinduism, and so on

>> **Sex:** Male or female, but also relates to pregnancy, sexual orientation, and gender identity

>> **Handicap:** Physical or mental handicaps or disabilities, including mobility, hearing, or visual impairments; chronic alcoholism; and HIV/AIDS

>> **Familial status:** Whether a person or couple has a minor or is expecting or adopting or gaining custody of a minor/minors; it also makes no difference if the adult members of the household are single, related, married or civil-union status, separated, divorced, or widowed

>> **National origin or ancestry:** The country or area a person was born in, such as Canada, Mexico, the Middle East, or Nigeria

**REMEMBER**

Consider only those characteristics that reflect the likelihood that the person will pay their rent in full and on time, treat your rental property with care, and get along with their neighbors. As a landlord, you should consider nothing else.

## State and local laws

Some states and municipalities have extended the Fair Housing Act to other protected classes, including the following:

>> Age

>> Occupation

>> Educational or student status

>> Medical status

>> Broader definitions of HIV/AIDS status

>> Broader definitions of sexual orientation

>> Source of income

>> Victim of domestic violence, stalking, or sexual assault

>> Military/veteran status

>> Political affiliation

>> Genetic information

>> Personal appearance, including physical size

Although several states do not have laws prohibiting discrimination against unmarried couples who live together, many prohibit any distinction in access to housing based on marital status. The majority of states have very broad fair housing laws forbidding all arbitrary discrimination on the basis of a person's characteristics or traits. Such laws can prohibit the use of appearance as a basis for housing decisions. If an applicant has tattoos or piercings, for example, or wears clothing that could be construed as being typical of a gang member, you can't legally use that information as a reason to deny their application.

REMEMBER

Always be sure to fully understand the fair housing requirements and limitations that apply to your rental property.

Fair housing laws also are a consideration when you're marketing and advertising your property. To comply with fair housing laws in advertising, follow these four general guidelines:

>> Avoid any obviously discriminating words and phrases that state or imply that certain protected classes are unwelcome or that you prefer a certain type of clientele, such as singles, married couples, or affluent individuals.

>> If you use photographs or pictures of people in your advertisements, make sure they convey diversity in race, sex, familial status, and so on.

>> Don't use location, place names, directions, and other factors that may suggest exclusion or preference for a prospect who may be a member of a certain protected class. For example, stating that the property is near a certain country club or religious facility may be construed as a preference for some prospects while discriminating against others.

>> Include the U.S. Department of Housing and Urban Development's (HUD's) Equal Housing Opportunity logo or statement on all advertising to invite people of all protected classes to apply.

Most landlords avoid blatantly discriminatory language and images in their advertisements. They're more likely to inadvertently commit a violation by showing a picture of a young couple, for example, or mentioning that the property is "perfect" for certain classes of prospects.

TIP

Have someone who's well versed in federal, state, and local fair housing laws review all of your advertisements before you start running them.

# Setting rents and payment policies

Sometime prior to renting out a property, you need to set your rents and payment policies to address the following aspects of rent payments:

>> **Amount:** You want to charge enough rent to cover your operating expenses, earn a decent profit, and remain competitive. In a few cities in a handful of states, you also may need to consider rental rate regulation or *rent control* as well.

>> **Due date:** We recommend that your lease requires that all tenants pay the rent in full on the first of the month. If the tenant moves in on a day other than the first, you collect the first month's rent in full and then prorate the second rent payment. This way you collect more money up-front and minimize the risk that your tenant will gain possession of your rental property by just paying you a nominal amount of rent.

>> **Payment form:** This may be cash, check, money order, cashier's check, online/electronic payment, or even the latest cryptocurrency, depending on what you're willing to accept.

>> **Late payments and penalties:** Specify when payments are considered late; for example, "Payments received more than five (5) days after the first of the month are considered late payments." Also specify a penalty, perhaps a certain dollar amount or a specific percentage late fee when the payment is past due.

>> **Penalties for returned checks:** Penalties may include a flat fee to cover the fee your financial institution charges you plus a little extra for your time, inconvenience, and aggravation. You may also want to specify that if a certain number of checks are returned unpaid, the tenant will be required to pay rent only with a secure, electronic payment method (of which there are more every day).

>> **Penalties for missed payments:** The penalty for missed payments is usually that the tenant is in violation of the lease provisions and is subject to being evicted.

# Screening applicants

Carefully screening applicants is essential to keep your rental units occupied with tenants who pay on time, take care of the property, and get along with their neighbors. Careful screening can help you avoid legal issues, because you have less need to take legal action against good tenants, and they're less likely to file legal claims against you. To screen applicants, take the following steps:

1. **Have the individual complete and submit an application that includes their name, current address, Social Security number, employment history, rental history, income, financial resources, and so on.**

2. **Order a credit and background check for the prospective tenant.**

   You can find several services online that perform credit and background checks. Your application should include language specifying that the applicant agrees to a credit and background check. Note that California has unique requirements for the legally required disclosure language, including a very specific "check box." Be sure to only use the latest application forms from the Institute of Real Estate Management (IREM), your local affiliate of the National Apartment Association (NAA), or your landlord-tenant legal advisor.

3. **Contact the applicant's employer to verify the applicant's employment and income and find out how long the applicant has been employed there.**

   You may also want to require copies of pay stubs, recent W-2s and 1099s, the previous year's tax return, and a recent financial institution statement.

4. **Contact the applicant's personal references.**

5. **Contact any landlords the applicant rented from in the past and ask about payment history, the condition the applicant left the property in, and whether the applicant caused problems with their neighbors.**

6. **Interview the applicant in person.**

   Ask why the person is moving and why they chose your property. Ask questions related to information you gathered previously to determine whether what the applicant tells you is consistent with what you already know. Inconsistencies can be a red flag.

REMEMBER

When screening prospective renters, you must comply with fair housing laws, so certain questions are off-limits. You can gather information about a prospect's employment status, income or financial resources, credit history, housing history, and certain aspects of their criminal past, but you're prohibited from asking an applicant whether they have minors, what country they're from, their religion, and so forth.

## Drafting a lease or rental agreement

Your rental contract (either the lease or month-to-month rental agreement) establishes the legal contract that you have with the tenant, including who's going to be living in the unit and paying rent and for how long, the rent amount and when it's due, the security deposit amount and what it can be used for, your obligations, the tenant's obligations, whether pets are allowed and under what conditions (not to be confused with service or companion animals, which are considered "durable medical equipment"), and so on.

**TIP**

We recommend that you start with an existing lease and modify it to suit your specific needs. You can obtain a sample lease by doing any of the following:

>> Search the web for your state, followed by "lease" or "rental agreement." Sometimes attorneys or property management companies post the lease or rental agreement they use.

>> Ask a reputable local attorney who specializes in landlord-tenant law or real estate for a copy of a residential lease and a residential rental agreement. You may be able to obtain the lease for free or for a modest fee.

>> Use an online legal service such as www.rocketlawyer.com to obtain a state-specific lease or rental agreement. (Many of these services advertise "free lease." The hook is that they lead you through a long process of creating a rental contract and then require that you sign up for the service and provide credit card information. You may be able to sign up for a free week or month of the service to get the contracts you need and then cancel the service.)

>> Contact your local affiliate of the National Apartment Association (NAA), the Institute of Real Estate Management (IREM), the National Association of Residential Property Managers (NARPM), or a similar rental industry group about membership. They often have comprehensive, up-to-date legal forms that comply with all applicable laws for your area available for their members at a reasonable cost.

## Managing security deposits

Prior to when a tenant moves in, you need to collect the first month's rent (or prorated rent) along with a *security deposit* — a lump sum that you hold until the tenant moves out in order to cover the cost of any unpaid rent and damages (beyond ordinary wear and tear). You should have a security deposit policy in place that specifies the following:

>> **Amount:** Usually no more than the equivalent of one month's or two months' rent. Some states and municipalities have specific limits.

>> **Due date:** Usually due at the signing of the rental contract.

>> **Allowed uses:** State and local laws usually allow landlords to use security deposits only to cover unpaid rent, damages to the unit beyond ordinary wear and tear, cleaning expenses (only to make the unit as clean as it was when the tenant moved in), and to restore or replace damaged or missing property, including keys and appliances furnished with the unit.

>> **Where the deposit will be held:** We recommend depositing all security deposits into a separate interest-bearing account and passing along any interest earned (unless nominal) to the tenant when you return any unused portion of the deposit.

>> **Return of the unused portion:** Specify the maximum number of days you're allowed to hold any unused portion of the security deposit before returning it to the former tenant. State law may establish a limitation.

# Moving tenants in and out

Two very important days in the course of a tenant's stay are the first and the last — the day they move in and the day they move out. The following sections cover the essential tasks you need to perform on these two days.

## Moving a tenant in

How well you manage the process of getting a new tenant moved in can affect your relationship over the entire term of their occupancy. Get started by performing the following steps leading up to and including move-in day:

1. **Agree on a move-in date with the tenant.**

2. **Make sure any utilities the tenant is responsible for paying are transferred to the tenant's name and are turned on by the move-in date.**

3. **Review important terms of your rental contract and any addenda to the contract, and answer any questions the tenant may have.**

4. **Collect the rent and full security deposit, if you haven't done so already.**

5. **Inspect the property with the tenant, complete a written or electronic checklist to record the property's condition, and make sure you and the tenant sign the checklist.**

    Take photos or a video so you have a visual record of the property's condition as well.

    **TIP**

6. **Orient the tenant to the rental unit and any appliances in the unit, utility shutoffs, and common areas, such as parking, clubhouse, fitness facilities, business center, laundry, pool, and hot tub.**

7. **Present a move-in letter and a copy of your policies and guidelines (aka rules and regulations).**

    These documents may include instructions for requesting maintenance and repairs, taking on a roommate, replacing lost keys, paying rent, and so on. You may also include policies for guests, parking, wall hangings, ceiling hooks, pets, and so on.

8. **Give the tenant time to read the move-in letter and the policies and guidelines and then have them sign and date two copies of each document — one for their records and one for yours.**

9. **Give the tenant keys or instructions for entry devices to the rental unit and their mailbox.**

## Moving a tenant out

To avoid disputes and litigation after a tenant moves out, manage the process appropriately. Here's how:

1. **Require that tenants notify you in writing a certain number of days (30 days is common) prior to the date they intend to move out or the lease expires.**

2. **Present the tenant with a move-out letter with instructions on how to prepare the rental unit for the move-out inspection.**

   Include a reminder of your policies and guidelines for returning the security deposit after any lawful deductions for unpaid rent or damages beyond ordinary wear and tear.

3. **Sign and have the tenant sign a termination agreement, so you have documentation that the tenant officially moved out.**

4. **Inspect the unit carefully for any damages or missing items that were furnished with the rental unit, and record your observations on a written or electronic move-out checklist.**

   TIP

   Take photos or video to document any deductions for damages or missing items, or a failure to return the rental unit to the same level of cleanliness as it was upon their move-in.

5. **As soon as possible, perform the repairs/replacements, maintenance, and cleaning required to bring the rental unit back to the condition it was in before the departing tenant lived in it.**

   TIP

   Keep receipts for all materials and labor.

6. **Deduct the costs of any repairs/replacements, maintenance, or cleaning that qualify as beyond ordinary wear and tear, and return the remainder of the security deposit (with interest, if required by state or local law), along with an itemized list of expenses deducted with an explanation and/or photos/video.**

   Some jurisdictions require you to provide the former tenant with receipts for work done upon request.

**WARNING**

Of course, not all tenants move out this smoothly. Sometimes, tenants simply skip town, abandoning the property without notifying you. In other situations, such as when a tenant fails to pay rent or breaches the contract in other ways, you may need to either get the tenant to leave voluntarily or evict the tenant. These exceptions to the standard move-out scenario have particular legal procedures you must follow according to state or local law.

# Fulfilling your maintenance and safety obligations

Your rights as a landlord are based on your rental contract and your state's landlord-tenant laws. Your obligations, however, are primarily in the form of written laws or implied warranties and *covenants* (agreements). The following sections summarize your legal obligations to your tenants, whether they're in writing or not.

## Recognizing your duty to maintain habitable living conditions

According to the *implied warranty of habitability,* you must provide tenants with dwellings that are fit to live in. For example, the unit's plumbing and electrical must be in working condition, tenants must have running water and reasonable amounts of hot water, and the unit must be heated in the winter.

**REMEMBER**

If you fail to maintain habitable living conditions, tenants may be permitted by law to withhold rent, have the repairs done and bill you for them, sue for damages, take legal action to force you to solve the problems, or move and terminate the lease.

## Addressing potentially dangerous conditions

Accidents happen regardless of how careful people are, but if anyone is injured on your property as a result of something you did or failed to do, you could be held liable for the person's medical bills and lost pay and may even be subject to punitive damages (for any reckless or intentional acts that cause injury). Here are a few areas to consider focusing your safety program on:

>> **Fire safety:** Educate tenants on the most common fire hazards, provide and maintain working fire extinguishers and smoke alarms, and provide tenants with a copy of your evacuation procedures. Your local fire department can help you comply with the fire-safety codes in your area. Carbon monoxide alarms are also important if you have gas appliances and are now required in most jurisdictions.

>> **Pool and hot tub safety:** If you have a pool and/or hot tub, enclose it with fencing and gates that comply with your local building codes, and post required signage to inform tenants and their guests of your rules, such as no diving allowed and adult supervision required for minors.

>> **Exterior lighting:** Make sure parking lots, stairways, walkways, and entryways that are all routinely used have adequate lighting to keep people from tripping or bumping into things.

>> **Safety within units:** Use safety or tempered glass in shower stalls or tub surrounds, use window coverings with safe or no cords, make sure all openable windows have working locks and screens, and use outlets with ground fault protection near water (in bathrooms and near the kitchen sink).

>> **General maintenance issues:** Fix any loose railings, stairs, or handrails; repair uneven pavement on sidewalks and parking lots; replace burnt-out exterior lights; and so on. Shovel and de-ice walkways in the winter as needed. Make sure that you immediately mop up any spills and that you place signs to warn tenants when floors are wet/slippery.

>> **Set and enforce pet policies:** If you allow pets, make sure your tenants comply with local leash laws, as well as licensing, spay or neutering, or any other requirement.

>> **Construction site safety:** Make sure contractors secure their construction sites to prevent injuries to curious minors and adults.

TIP

Team up with tenants to improve safety. Encourage them to report any safety concerns to you, respond immediately to their concerns, and thank them for their efforts.

## Disclosing and responding to environmental hazards

We define *environmental hazard* as anything that may adversely affect a person's health, including the following:

>> Asbestos

>> Carbon monoxide

>> Formaldehyde

>> Radon

>> Lead-based paint

>> Visible mold

>> Hazardous wastes, including chemical residue from meth labs

>> Pests, including rats, mice, cockroaches, silverfish, and bedbugs

Each of these hazards has specific laws regarding the landlord's obligation to disclose and address.

**WARNING**

The best course of action isn't always to remove an environmental hazard. In fact, if not done properly, attempts to remove harmful substances, such as asbestos, lead paint, and visible mold, may increase the danger.

## Protecting tenants and workers from criminal activity

Landlords are legally obligated to take reasonable steps to prevent crime on their property, which is a job that's more challenging than most landlords realize. If a crime occurs on your property and the courts find that you could have, should have, or didn't take measures to prevent it, you may be held liable for any injuries or property losses that result. Here are several of your primary responsibilities for protecting tenants and workers from criminal acts:

>> **Provide and maintain basic security features,** including doors with deadbolt locks and peepholes for rental units, key locks, or keyless (smart key or entry device systems) for external doors, windows with working latches and insect screens (and in some jurisdictions, locking devices), and sufficient visibility lighting.

>> **Report suspected criminal activity to local law enforcement** and inform tenants of any significant criminal activity in the area that comes to your attention.

>> **With proper legal advice, take steps to evict tenants who commit serious crimes,** within a certain number of days of being notified by local law enforcement.

>> **Safeguard sensitive tenant information** to prevent identity theft and other crimes.

>> **Secure master and duplicate keys, or entry device systems,** to prevent unauthorized entry to rental units. This also applies to common areas if they're access controlled and to the extent that it's reasonably feasible.

>> **As permitted by law, seek criminal background checks on prospective employees of the rental property** and monitor employee activity for any signs of criminal activity.

**TIP**

Team up with local law enforcement agencies. Many law enforcement agencies have pamphlets or booklets (some available online), with valuable guidance on how to secure rental properties.

## Knowing the limitations on your right to enter the premises

Landlords frequently believe that because they own the rental property, they can enter rental units whenever they want. You do have a right to enter rental units you own, but your right of entry is balanced against the *covenant of quiet enjoyment* that gives a tenant the right to undisturbed use of the property. In most states, a landlord can enter a residence only under certain conditions, some of which require the landlord to give reasonable advanced notice, and some that don't:

>> You can legally enter a rental unit without notice to respond to an emergency that threatens health, safety, life, or property; when a tenant has abandoned the property; when responding to a court order; or when you ask for and a tenant gives you permission to enter.

>> You can legally enter a rental unit with reasonable notice to check smoke alarms and carbon monoxide alarms; inspect for and make necessary repairs; check for problems during a tenant's extended absence; or show the property to a prospective renter, buyer, or lender.

# Dealing with cotenants, sublets, and assignments

Every landlord recognizes the importance of screening applicants before permitting them to move into a unit. Unfortunately, tenants often try to move others into their unit without your permission by taking on a roommate, subletting the unit to someone else, or assigning their lease to someone you don't know. Such practices significantly increase your exposure to risk because it opens your doors to people who have no contractual obligation to you. You're not given the opportunity to screen the person, and you don't have the power of a legal contract to enforce your rules.

**REMEMBER**

Screen everyone prior to allowing them to live in one of your rental units. Have the person complete an application, and then follow your standard screening procedure, including performing background checks. If you give approval, make sure the person signs a rental contract. A roommate may simply sign the existing rental contract. Instead of subletting and assignments, we recommend terminating the previous tenant's lease and creating a new one for the new tenant.

# Terminating rental contracts

All good things (and bad things) must come to an end, and the same is true of rental contracts. The process differs depending on whether you're terminating a lease or a rental agreement and on the circumstances surrounding the termination:

» **Lease:** A *lease* is a rental contract for a fixed term, usually one or two years. You can terminate a lease in any of the following three ways:

- Let it expire and don't renew it. In this case, you should serve your tenant a Notice of Nonrenewal 30 or 60 days prior to the date on which the lease expires.

- Mutually agree with your tenant to end the lease, in which case you should both sign a Mutual Termination of Lease Agreement.

- Require that the tenant move out for breach of contract. In this situation, you must serve the tenant a termination notice giving them a certain number of days to move out.

» **Rental agreement:** A *rental agreement* is a month-to-month contract. You typically can terminate a rental agreement with or without cause:

- **With cause:** If the tenant breaches the contract, you may be able to require that the tenant move out in as little as a few days.

- **Without cause:** In most states, you can end a rental agreement without cause, as long as you give the tenant sufficient notice, typically 30 to 60 days prior to the termination date.

# 2

# Welcome Home: Buying a House

# Contents at a Glance

# Chapter **1**

# Knowing Where and What to Buy

What's your idea of the perfect car, the perfect job, and the perfect way to spend a day? Would you have said the same things ten years ago? Probably not. Perfection is a moving target — it changes as you change.

Where *the* perfect home is concerned, there's no such thing. For one thing, few people have the financial resources to afford what they think is the perfect home. Even if you're among the fortunate few with bucks to burn, it's still highly unlikely that one home will be perfect for you from birth to earth. The home that's great in your 20s when you're footloose and fancy-free probably won't cut it when you're in your 40s if you're married or raising a family. Fast-forward another 20 years to when you're nearing retirement. You may want or need to move to a smaller home that's easier to maintain.

Don't fret. Even though no single home stays perfect forever, this chapter shows you how to profitably achieve sequential perfection in your homes. And because moving is expensive, you also find out how to minimize the number of times you buy and sell.

# A Crash Course on Factors Affecting a Home's Value

You probably know someone who's lost money on a house sale. Surely you don't plan to be the next victim of a capricious real estate market such as the one that hit during the late 2000s. Getting a bargain when you buy a home is a fine objective, but don't stop there. Don't you also want your home to appreciate in value while you own it?

**REMEMBER**

The best time to think about how much you'll get for your house when you sell it is before you buy it. Never let your enthusiasm for a house blind you to its flaws. Before you buy, try to look at the property through the eyes of the *next* potential buyer. Anything that disturbs you about the house or neighborhood will probably also bother the next buyer.

This isn't to say that you should plan to sell your house immediately after buying it. Perhaps you'll live happily ever after in the home you're about to purchase. Then again, an unforeseen life change, such as a job transfer or family expansion, may force you to sell. If that happens, making a profit can take some of the sting out of moving day.

Appreciation is handy for a lot more than just increasing your net worth. Given that your home increases in value over time, you may someday find that this *equity* (the difference between market value and the mortgage you owe) can help you accomplish a multitude of important financial and personal goals. You can use the money any way you want — add to your retirement, help pay your kids' college education, start your own business, or take the Orient Express from London to Venice to celebrate your 25th wedding anniversary. Nest eggs are extremely versatile financial tools — and they're cholesterol free!

In a world filled with uncertainties, no one can guarantee that your home will increase in value. However, buying a good property in a desirable neighborhood tremendously increases your odds of making money. This maxim holds true whether the real estate market is strong or weak when you sell.

**REMEMBER**

Property prices aren't static. They rise and fall because of such factors as the local job market, the supply of and demand for available housing and rental units, interest rates, and annual cycles of strong versus weak market activity. Most of these things are beyond your control and ability to predict. But this doesn't mean that your financial destiny as a homeowner is a total fluke of fate. On the contrary, you control three important factors that greatly affect your home's value:

>> How much you pay for your home

>> Where your home is located

>> What home you buy

**WARNING**

The number-one controllable factor is how much you pay for your home. If you grossly overpay for your house when you buy it, you'll be extremely lucky to make a profit when you sell. That's why Chapter 2 in Book 2 is devoted to making sure you know exactly how to spot well-priced properties and avoid overpriced turkeys.

The rest of this chapter focuses on the other two crucial factors under your control: where and what you buy.

# Location, Location, Value

If you're wildly wealthy, you can afford to live anywhere you darn well please. The rest of us, however, have somewhat more limited budgets. Even so, unless you're foraging at the bottom of the housing food chain, you have many choices on places to spend your money. Where you ultimately decide to buy is up to you.

You've probably already heard that the three most important things you should look for when buying a home are "location, location, location." That axiom is largely true. People buy neighborhoods every bit as much as houses. In good times and bad, folks pay a premium to live in better neighborhoods. Conversely, rotten neighborhoods ravage home values. You'd have trouble selling the Taj Mahal if it were surrounded by junkyards and chicken farms.

But simply stating that the secret of making money in real estate when you buy is "location, location, location" is akin to saying you'll make a fortune in the stock market if you buy low and sell high. It takes more than glittering generalities to make money. You need specifics.

First off, don't agree that the three most important factors are location, location, location. *Value* — what you get for your money — is important too. If, for example, everyone knows that Elegant Estates is the *best* neighborhood in town, you'll pay a hefty premium to live there. And although Elegant Estates is currently king of the hill and may stay that way forever, keep in mind that this particular neighborhood has no place to go except downhill.

Other neighborhoods, ones that aren't held in such high esteem right now, may eventually improve what they offer home buyers and ultimately experience far greater property-value appreciation. Buying a home in a good location, though important, shouldn't be your sole home-shopping criterion. If you want to buy a home that is a good investment, you must look for good value.

## Checking out the characteristics of good neighborhoods

Good neighborhoods, like beauty, are in the eyes of the beholder. For example, being near excellent schools is important if you have young children. If, conversely, you're ready to retire, buying in a peaceful area with outdoor activities may appeal to you, and being next to a noisy junior high school is your nightmare! Neither neighborhood may suit you if you're the footloose and fancy-free type. Your ideal neighborhood is probably a singles' condo complex downtown so you can be near the action day or night.

Personal preferences aside, all good neighborhoods have the following characteristics:

» **Economic health:** Nothing kills property values faster than a forest of "For Sale" signs precipitated by layoffs, foreclosures, or short sales where mortgage lenders agree to accept less money than is owed on properties to avoid going through the lengthy and costly foreclosure process.

» **Amenities:** Amenities are special features of a neighborhood that make it an attractive, desirable place to live. Wide streets bordered by stately oak trees, lush green parks, ocean views, quiet cul-de-sacs, parking, and proximity to schools, shopping, restaurants, transportation, playgrounds, tennis courts, and beaches are prime examples of amenities that add value to a neighborhood. Of course, few people can afford to buy in a neighborhood that has all these amenities, but the more of these perks a neighborhood has, the better.

» **Quality schools:** You may not care how good or bad the local schools are if you don't have school-age children. However, unless you're buying in a remote, retirement, or vacation-type community, you had better believe that when you're ready to sell your house, most prospective buyers with kids will be deeply concerned about the school system.

TIP

Don't rely on test scores or someone's opinion when assessing school quality; visit the schools and speak with parents and teachers to get a handle on the schools in an area.

» **Low crime rates:** Most folks today are concerned with crime — and well they should be, given that crime rates in many parts of America are too high. As with schools, don't rely on hearsay or isolated news reports. Communities compile crime statistics, generally by neighborhood. Call the local police department, visit its website, or check the town's reference library to get the facts.

>> **Stability:** Some communities are in a constant state of flux. "Out with the old and in with the new" is their motto. Imagine what would happen to property values if a junkyard were replaced by a beautiful park. How about the reverse — an ugly, multistory, concrete parking garage appears where there was once a beautiful park? Check with the local planning department and a good real estate agent for the inside scoop on proposed developments in neighborhoods that you're considering.

>> **Pride of ownership:** A home's cost has no bearing on the amount of pride its owners take in it. Drive through any neighborhood, posh or modest, and you see in a flash whether the folks who live there are proud of their homes. A neighborhood filled with beautifully maintained homes and manicured lawns shouts pride of ownership.

**WARNING**

Property values sag when homeowners no longer take pride in their property. Avoid declining neighborhoods that display the red flags of dispirited owners — poorly kept houses, junk-filled yards, abandoned cars on the street, many absentee owners renting houses, and high rates of vandalism, crime, short sales, and foreclosures. Neighborhood deterioration is a blight that spreads from one house to another.

## Selecting your best neighborhood

You may get lucky and find the neighborhood of your dreams right away. You're far more likely, however, to end up evaluating the strengths and weaknesses of several neighborhoods while trying to decide which one to favor with your purchase. If you're on a budget — and most people are — you may have to compromise and make tradeoffs.

Suppose that one neighborhood has the schools you like, the second is closest to your office (which would save you an hour a day commuting), and the third neighborhood is in a town with a delightful beach. They're all good neighborhoods, so your decision isn't easy.

The following sections offer ways to research and select the best neighborhood *for you.*

### Prioritize your needs

**REMEMBER**

Buying a home when you have budgetary constraints involves making tradeoffs. For example, if you want to live in the town with great schools and parks, you'll probably have to settle for a smaller home than you would if you bought in a more average community. When push comes to shove and you have to choose a place to live, you must decide what is most important to you.

# Research

As noted in the earlier section "Checking out characteristics of good neighborhoods," you should examine the health of the local economy, area amenities such as parks and entertainment, school quality, and crime rates before you buy a home. So where can you find this wealth of information?

>> **Tap local resources.** Check the local library. The local chamber of commerce is another excellent source of information.

>> **Talk to people who live in the neighborhoods.** Who knows more about a neighborhood than folks who live in it? In addition to asking how they feel about their neighborhood, see what residents say about the other neighborhoods you're considering. If you can spark some neighborhood rivalry, you'll get the dirt about the other neighborhoods' parking problems, unfriendly or snobby owners, and so on.

TIP

Renters are a great source of information. Because they don't have a wad of cash invested in a home, renters are generally candid about the shortcomings of a neighborhood. Also, drive or walk through the neighborhoods at various times of the day and evening to make sure that their charm stays on 24 hours a day.

>> **Get days-on-market (DOM) statistics from your real estate agent.** DOM statistics indicate how long the average house in an area takes to sell after it goes on the market. As a rule, the faster property sells, the more likely it is to sell close to full asking price. Quick sales indicate strong buyer demand, which is nice to have when you're ready to sell.

>> **Get help from a professional.** Ask a real estate agent, lender, or appraiser to compare the upside potential of home values in each neighborhood. As Chapter 3 in Book 1 explains, home buying is a team sport. Get an analysis of each neighborhood's present and future property values from full-time real estate people.

TIP

Neither real estate agents nor lenders charge for opinions of value. They both, however, have a vested interest in selling you something. Appraisers, on the other hand, have no ax to grind. True, appraisers charge to analyze neighborhood property values and pricing trends. But if you're going to spend hundreds of thousands of dollars for a home, paying an additional few hundred dollars to get an unbiased, professional analysis of a neighborhood's property values may be money well spent.

TIP

>> **Go online.** Several real estate websites provide local community data and information. Good resources include the following:

- The National Association of Realtors (www.realtor.com)

- The Federal Emergency Management Agency (www.fema.gov)

- The American Society of Home Inspectors (www.ashi.org)

- The U.S. Department of Housing and Urban Development (www.hud.gov)

- The U.S. Department of Commerce's Bureau of Economic Analysis (www.bea.gov)

# Fundamental Principles for Selecting Your Home

Good news. It doesn't matter whether you buy a log cabin, Cape Cod colonial, French provincial, Queen Anne Victorian, or California ranch-style house. You can make money on any property by following three fundamental principles to select the home you buy. As you read the following guidelines, keep in mind that they're not hard-and-fast rules — exceptions do exist.

## The principle of progression: Why to buy one of the cheaper homes on the block

An appraiser can tell you that the *principle of progression* states that property of lesser value is enhanced by proximity to better properties. English translation, please? Buy one of the cheaper homes on the block because the more expensive houses all around yours pull up the value of your home.

For instance, suppose that your agent shows you a house that just came on the market in a neighborhood you like. At $225,000, it's one of the least expensive homes you've seen in the area. The agent says that the other homes around it sell for anywhere from $275,000 to $300,000. You start to salivate.

**REMEMBER**

Don't whip out your checkbook yet. Do a little homework first. Find out why this house is so cheap. If the right things are wrong with it, write up the offer. If the wrong things are wrong with it, move on to the next property.

### Curable defects

If a house is a bargain because it has defects that aren't too difficult or expensive to correct, go for it. For example, maybe the house is an ugly duckling that just needs a paint job, landscaping, and some other minor cosmetic touches in order to be transformed into a swan. Perhaps it's the only two-bedroom house on the block, but it has a large storage area that you can convert into a third bedroom for not more than $15,000. For $240,000 ($225,000 for the house plus $15,000 to add the bedroom), you're living in a $275,000 to $300,000 neighborhood. Such a deal!

Problems like these are *curable defects* — property deficiencies you can cure by upgrading, repairing, or replacing the defects relatively inexpensively. Painting, modernizing a bathroom, installing new counters and cabinets in the kitchen, and upgrading an electrical system are some examples of curable defects.

Depressed property values are another type of curable defect. A high number of short sales or foreclosures in a neighborhood drives property values down. One person's misfortune is another's opportunity. Some investors specialize in purchasing distressed properties at rock-bottom prices. These investors then rehab the houses and rent them out with an eye toward selling them for a profit when property values improve.

## Incurable defects

**WARNING**

If a house has major problems, it's not a bargain at any price. Who'd want a house located next to a garbage dump? Or what about a *really* ugly home? Just because the seller made a fortune in the sausage business doesn't mean that you (or anyone else) would want to live in a house built in the shape of a giant hot dog. Maybe the house is cheap because a contractor says it's a wreck about ready to fall down, and you'd have to spend at least $125,000 on a new roof, a new foundation, new plumbing, and complete rewiring.

Enormous deficiencies like these are called *incurable defects*. They aren't economically feasible to correct. You can't fix the fact that a house is poorly located. Nor does it typically make sense to pay $225,000 for the hot-dog house so you can tear it down and build a new home (unless that's what comparable vacant lots sell for). By the same token, if you pay $225,000 for the wreck and then pour in another $125,000 on corrective work, you'll have the dubious honor of owning the most expensive house in the neighborhood.

All rehabs aren't bad, though. Find out more about fixer-uppers later in this chapter.

## The benefits of renovating cheaper homes

The less-expensive houses on the block are also the least risky ones to renovate, thanks to the principle of progression. For example, suppose that you just paid $225,000 for a house that needs a major rehab. Your construction project is located smack-dab in the middle of a neighborhood of $300,000 homes.

The difference between your purchase price and the value of the surrounding homes approximately defines the most you should consider spending on a rehab.

In the preceding example, you should spend no more than $75,000 to bring your home up to the prevailing standard set by the other houses. Of course, this is assuming that you can afford to spend that kind of money and that you have the time and patience to coordinate the rehab work or do it yourself. As long as you improve the property wisely and stay within your budget, you'll probably get most or all the rehab money back when you sell the property.

Use the principle of progression in conjunction with location, location, value (covered earlier in this chapter). Buying one of the better less-expensive homes in a good neighborhood enhances your likelihood of property appreciation in the years ahead.

## The principle of regression: Why not to buy the most expensive house on the block

You guessed it. The *principle of regression* is the economic opposite of the principle of progression in the previous section. If you buy the most expensive house on the block, the principle of regression punishes you when you sell. The lower value of all the other homes around you brings down your home's value.

If an evil spirit whispers in your ear that you should buy the most expensive house on the block to flaunt your high status in life, go to an exorcist immediately. Don't succumb to the blandishments of the evil spirit unless the probability of losing money when you sell fills you with joy. Satisfy your ego — and make a wiser investment — by purchasing one of the less-expensive homes in a better neighborhood.

The most expensive house on the block is also the worst candidate for remodeling. Suppose that you buy a $300,000 home in a neighborhood of $200,000 houses. From an appraiser's perspective, the home already sticks out like a financial sore thumb. Spending another $50,000 to add a fancy new kitchen to what is already the most expensive house on the block further compounds your problem.

That new kitchen almost certainly won't increase your home's value to $350,000. No one can dispute the fact that you spent $50,000 on the kitchen if you have the receipts to prove your expenditures. But folks who buy $350,000 homes generally want to be surrounded by other homes worth as much as, or more than, the one they're buying.

Homes are like cups. When you fill a cup too full, it overflows. By the same token, when you make excessive improvements to your house (based on sale prices of comparable homes in the neighborhood), the money you spend on the rehab goes down the financial drain. This phenomenon is called *overimproving a property*.

Even if you buy the least expensive house in the neighborhood, you can overimprove it if you spend too much fixing it up. The best time to guard against over-improving your house is *before* you do the work.

REMEMBER

If you'll end up with the most expensive house on the block when you finish a project, don't do the project.

## The principle of conformity: Why unusual is usually costly

The principles of progression and regression deal with economic conformity. If you want to maximize your chances for future appreciation of the home you buy, your home should also conform in size, age, condition, and style to the other homes in your neighborhood. That's the *principle of conformity*.

This principle doesn't mean that your home has to be an identical clone of every other house on the block. It should, however, stay within the prevailing standards of your neighborhood. For example:

>> **Size:** Your home shouldn't dwarf the other houses on the block, or vice versa. If your home is smaller than surrounding houses, use the principle of progression as a guide to bring it into size-conformity with the other houses and increase your home's value. If, conversely, you have a three-bedroom home in a neighborhood of two- and three-bedroom homes, adding a large fourth bedroom to your house would violate the principle of regression.

>> **Age:** You almost never see an older home in the midst of a tract of modern new homes. However, every now and then you find a brand-new home incongruously plunked in the midst of older homes. A modern home typically looks out of place in a neighborhood of gracious, older homes. Even if you get a terrific deal on the price, the modern home's lack of conformity with other homes on the block will probably come back to haunt you when you attempt to sell it.

>> **Condition:** The physical condition of your house has a tremendous impact on its value. Not surprisingly, your home loses value if it's a dilapidated dump compared with the rest of the houses on the block.

Ironically, having your home in far nicer condition than other houses in the neighborhood isn't wise either. Even if your home conforms to all the other houses in size, age, and style, you still overimprove your home if the quality of materials, workmanship, and appliances in your home greatly exceeds the prevailing neighborhood quality standards.

» **Style:** The architectural style of the house you buy isn't critical — as long as it conforms to the prevailing architectural style of other homes in the neighborhood. From an investment standpoint, for example, you don't want to buy the only Queen Anne Victorian in a block filled with Pennsylvania Dutch Colonial houses, or vice versa. Nor should you buy a three-story home when all the surrounding houses are one story high.

TIP

Your home doesn't have to be a bland, boring replica of every other house on the block. You can follow the principle of conformity and still express your individuality by the way you landscape, paint, and furnish your home. You know you've done well when people use words like "tasteful" and "exquisite" to describe your home. On the other hand, your decorating motif is a problem if folks refer to your house as "weird" or "eccentric."

# Defining Home Sweet Home

What exactly is a home? When you come right down to it, home is an elusive concept. Everyone knows, for example, that home is where the heart is. That's fine and good if you're a romantic but not too helpful if you're a home buyer.

Up until now, we've loosely used the terms "home" and "house" to mean any place where you live or want to live. Under that definition, everything from a studio apartment in Manhattan to a grass hut on a Hawaiian beach qualifies as a home. Now, however, precision matters. The following sections focus on the specific types of property you're most likely to buy: detached homes, condominiums, and co-operative apartments. Each of these options offers homeowners distinct financial and personal advantages and disadvantages that you must understand to make a wise buying decision.

## Detached residences

If you were raised in a big city, your mental image of home is probably an apartment in a multistory steel-and-concrete building, an attached brownstone, or some other type of row house. If, on the other hand, you grew up in a small town, when someone says "home" you most likely visualize a brick or wood-frame residence with a white picket fence, a garden, and a swingset in the yard.

**TECHNICAL STUFF**

To distinguish the kind of home you see in areas of abundantly cheap land from condos, co-ops, and other types of property that folks call home, the correct terminology for the white-picket-fence type property is *detached single-family dwelling*. The operative word is "detached," because such homes aren't attached to any of the surrounding properties. Now that you're properly dazzled by the depth and breadth of knowledge, just call these "homes" or "houses" like everyone else does.

Detached homes, like cars, come in two basic types: *new* and *used*.

## New homes

If you're the type of person who'd never think of buying a used car because you like the new-car smell and don't like buying someone else's problems, you may feel the same way about new homes. They have some very appealing advantages:

» **A properly constructed new home is built to satisfy today's buyers.** Choosing a new home produced by a reputable builder of high-quality properties gives you the peace of mind of knowing that your home doesn't contain asbestos, lead-based paints, formaldehyde, or other hazardous or toxic substances. Furthermore, you can rest assured that your new home complies with current (and more stringent) federal, state, and local building, fire, safety, and environmental codes. Of course, you have no guarantee that future years won't uncover more hazards!

» **A properly constructed new home should be cheaper than a used home to operate and maintain.** Operating expenses are minimal because a new home should incorporate the latest technology in energy-efficient heating and cooling systems, modern plumbing and electrical service, energy-efficient appliances, and proper insulation levels. And with a quality new home, your initial maintenance expenses are practically nonexistent because everything is new — roof, appliances, interior and exterior paint, carpets, and so on. Other than changing the light bulbs, what's to fix?

» **A properly designed new home won't force you to adjust your lifestyle to its limitations.** On the contrary, new homes have enough wall and floor outlets to accommodate all your high-tech goodies — microwave oven; espresso machine; satellite TV and cable outlets; hair dryers; electric razors; electric toothbrushes; and home-office gear such as computers, monitors, printers, broadband internet connections, and so on. No unsightly, hazardous tangle of extension cords for you.

**TIP**

New homes are only as good as the developers who build them. Visit several of the developer's older projects. See with your own eyes how well the developments have weathered over the years. Ask homeowners in older developments whether they'd buy another new home from the same developer. See what kinds of problems, if any, they've had with their homes over the years. Inquire whether the builder closed the sale on time and honored all contractual commitments, including the completion of any unfinished construction work, on time. Also find out whether the developer amicably fixed defects that occurred or whether home-owners had to take legal action to get problems corrected. Ask real estate agents how much homes in the developments have appreciated in value over time and how that compares with other homes in the general area.

As you may expect, new homes also have some disadvantages. To wit:

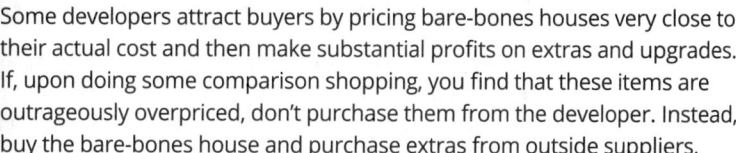
>> **What you see usually isn't what you get.** You see a professionally deco-rated, exquisitely furnished, beautifully landscaped model home. You buy a bare-bones, unfinished house where nearly everything — appliances, carpets, window coverings, painting, fireplace finishes, landscaping, and so on — is an extra that isn't included in the base price. Developers often spend tens of thousands of dollars lavishly decorating model homes. Unwary new home buyers can spend small fortunes trying to duplicate the look of model homes. When touring a model home, ask the salesperson to explain exactly what is and isn't included in the no-frills base price.

>> **Prices are less negotiable.** Developers maintain price integrity to protect the value of their unsold inventory of homes and to sustain appraised values for loan purposes. In fact, a developer who cuts prices is warning you that the project is floundering. Rather than reduce their asking prices, developers bargain with you by throwing in free extras or giving you upgrades (for instance, more expensive grades of carpet, better appliances, or granite kitchen counters rather than Formica) in lieu of a price reduction.

**WARNING**

Some developers attract buyers by pricing bare-bones houses very close to their actual cost and then make substantial profits on extras and upgrades. If, upon doing some comparison shopping, you find that these items are outrageously overpriced, don't purchase them from the developer. Instead, buy the bare-bones house and purchase extras from outside suppliers.

>> **On a price-per-square-foot basis, new homes are usually more expensive than used ones.** No surprise. Land, labor, and material costs are higher today than they were years ago, when the used homes were built. And don't forget that you're buying a home without any wear and tear.

>> **New homes in more developed areas are generally built in spots previously considered undesirable or unbuildable.** It's the old "first-come, first-served" principle. Earlier developments got better sites. Today's develop-ers take whatever land is available — steep hillsides, flood plains, and land located far away from the central business area. Ten or twenty years from now, today's so-called lousy sites will be considered prime areas for new building — it's all relative.

>> **New homes may have hidden operating costs.** Developments with extensive amenities usually charge the homeowners dues to cover operating and maintenance expenses of common areas such as swimming pools, tennis courts, exercise facilities, clubhouses, and the like. Some homeowners associations charge each owner the same annual fee. Others prorate dues based on the home's size or purchase price — the larger or more expensive your home, the higher your dues. If the development has a homeowners association, find out how its dues are structured and what your dues would be.

Also find out what rules (called *covenants*) govern what you can do with your home as part of the development. Some covenants limit the colors you can use when painting the house, what additions you can make to the property, whether you can rent the property, and so on. Although meant to maintain high property values, some of these rules can create problems later as you seek to adapt your property to your changing lifestyle. For more detailed information about the important documents associated with homeowners associations and covenants, be sure to see the later section on condominiums.

**WARNING**

Sometimes, homeowners-association dues are set artificially low to camouflage the true cost of living in the development. When that happens, sooner or later homeowners get slugged with a special assessment to repaint the clubhouse, resurface the tennis courts, or whatever. Make sure that the homeowners association in the neighborhood you're considering has adequate reserves and that its dues accurately reflect actual operating and maintenance costs. Also check to see whether the historic rate of increase in dues has been reasonable and is in line with the current overall inflation rate, which you can probably determine by asking your lender.

>> **You may have to use the developer's real estate agent to represent you.** Developers always have their own sales staff and their own purchase contracts. Some developers, however, let you be represented by an outside real estate agent, which is called *broker cooperation*. Others insist that you use their agent. This isn't a negotiable item. If you don't like it, your option is to walk away without buying a home.

If you've fallen in love with a new home but the developer won't cooperate with outside agents, you should pay for an independent appraisal to get an unbiased opinion of the home's value. You also want to have a real estate lawyer of your own choosing review your contract. (See Chapter 3 in Book 1 for how to find one and what they can do for you.)

**REMEMBER**

Just because a home is brand-spanking new doesn't mean that it's flawless. People build homes. People are human. To err is human. Moreover, builders work for profit and may be tempted to cut corners to maximize their short-term profits, not to mention that some builders simply aren't very good. Also keep in mind that a completed new home is only as good as the sum of its parts. If construction took place during the rainy season, damp wood may develop mildew or even mold before being nailed into place and covered with sheetrock. Thus, even a brand-new, never-been-lived-in home should be *thoroughly* inspected from foundation to roof by a professional property inspector to discover possible human errors before you purchase it.

## Used homes

Perhaps you're wondering why this chapter classifies all homes as being either new or used. Why not "new and old" rather than "new and used"? Because *old* isn't a precise term. How old is old? Is a home built more than 25 years ago old? Or should the cutoff be homes constructed over 50 years ago? If homes built more than 50 years ago are old, what should you call homes built 100 or 200 years ago — decrepit? *Used*, on the other hand, merely means that someone owned the home before you did. (Considering how expensive homes are, you may prefer to call the place you purchase a "previously owned" home. If that makes you feel better, go right ahead.)

Regardless of what you choose to call them, used homes have many commendable features:

>> **Used homes are generally less expensive than new homes.** As a rule, folks who bought houses years ago paid less for their homes than developers charge to build comparable new homes today. Furthermore, at any given time, more used homes are on the market than new homes. Good old competition holds down the price of used homes.

>> **Asking prices of used homes are generally much more negotiable than asking prices of new homes.** Sellers of used homes don't have to protect the property values of an entire development. They typically just want to get their money and move on to life's next great adventure.

>> **Used homes are usually located in well-established, proven neighborhoods.** With a used home, you don't have to wonder what the neighborhood will be like in a few years when it's fully developed. Just look around, and you can see exactly what kind of schools, transportation, shopping, entertainment, and other amenities you have.

>> **Used homes have been field tested.** By the time you buy a used home, its previous owners have usually discovered and corrected most of the problems that developed over time due to settling, structural defects, and construction flaws. You won't have to guess how well the home will age over the years — you can see it with your own eyes.

No matter how well a home ages, you should still have it thoroughly inspected (inside and out) by qualified professionals before you buy it. The last owners may not have had the time, desire, or money to fix problems. They may also not have been aware of hidden problems. Be sure that the home meets today's building codes; doesn't have environmental, health, or safety hazards; is well insulated; and so on. Never try to save money on home inspections just because the house looks fine to you. The only exception to this stern admonishment is if you happen to be a professional property inspector.

>> **Used homes are "done" properties.** When you buy a used home, you generally don't have to go through the hassle and expense of buying and installing carpets, window coverings, and light fixtures; finishing off the fireplace; planting a lawn; landscaping the grounds; building fences and patios; installing sprinkler systems; and the like. The work is already done (unless the used home is a major rehab project), and everything is generally included in the purchase price.

>> **Buying a used home may be the only way to get the architectural style, craftsmanship, or construction materials you want.** What if your heart is set on owning an authentic 1800s New England farmhouse or a Queen Anne Victorian? Perhaps you want plaster walls, parquet floors, stained-glass windows, or some other kind of materials or craftsmanship that is unaffordable, if not impossible to find, in new homes. If that's the case, buy a used home.

Like new homes, used homes have some disadvantages:

>> **Used homes are generally more expensive than new homes to operate and maintain.** Some used homes have been retrofitted with energy-efficient heating and cooling systems. Even so, a used home with 12-foot-high ceilings will always be more expensive to heat than a new home with 9-foot-high ceilings. By the same token, the older a used home's roof, gutters, plumbing system, furnace, water heater, appliances, and so on, the sooner you'll need to repair or replace them.

Before buying a used home, ask the seller for copies of the past two years' utility bills (gas, electric, water, and sewer) so you can see for yourself exactly how much it costs to operate the house. If the utility bills are horrendous, ask your property inspector about the cost of making the house more energy efficient.

>> **Used homes generally have some degree of functional obsolescence.** Examples of functional obsolescence due to outdated floor plans or design features are things like the lack of a master bedroom, one bathroom in a three-bedroom house, no garage, inadequate electrical service, and no central

heating or air conditioning. How much functional obsolescence is too much? That depends on you. What one person thinks is charming, you may consider an uninhabitable disaster. Find out about extreme functional obsolescence in the later section on fixer-uppers.

>> **Wonderful used homes are sometimes located in less-than-wonderful neighborhoods.** You may be attracted to an utterly charming older home in a lousy neighborhood. Despite how much you think you'd love living in it, don't forget that you'll have to travel through the undesirable surrounding area every time you want to get in and out of your dream house.

**WARNING**

Even though you may be able to ignore vacant lots and overgrown lawns, will prospective buyers be equally tolerant when you're ready to sell? Remember: "location, location, value." No matter how stunning the property or how great the deal you're offered on it, don't buy someone else's problem.

# Condominiums

If you can't accept the rules and regulations that would, of necessity, be imposed on you by communal living, don't read any further. You're much too free a spirit to be happy owning an attached residence like a condominium or a co-operative apartment (covered later in this chapter). But if you're willing to put up with the constraints of communal living to get the economic and lifestyle goodies associated with it, read on. You may be pleasantly surprised.

## THE INVESTMENT VALUE OF DETACHED HOMES

Americans have always had a deep-seated love for detached homes. Like spawning salmon returning to the stream where they were born, many people are inexorably drawn to the same kind of house they grew up in when it's their turn to buy a home. Even if you didn't grow up in a detached home, you may covet one because TV shows and advertisements have drilled into your head that such homes are desirable and a sign of success.

Buyer demand for detached homes makes them good investments. Compared with attached residences, such as condominiums and co-operative apartments, detached homes tend to hold their value better in weak markets and appreciate more rapidly in strong markets. Ask a local real estate agent for a comparison of property-value appreciation in detached versus attached residences, and you can see what we mean.

What type of property offers first-time buyers their most affordable housing option and gives empty-nesters who own detached homes an ideal lifestyle alternative for their golden years? If you said "condominiums," go to the head of the class.

Some folks think that a *condominium* is a type of building. They're wrong. The kind of building in which a condo is located doesn't matter. Condos can be apartments in a Chicago high-rise or split-level townhouses in Dallas or Victorian flats in San Francisco. What makes a condo a condo is the way its *ownership* is structured.

**TECHNICAL STUFF**

First, a quick break for today's foreign-language lesson. In Latin, *con* means "with," and *dominium* means "ownership." Put the two words together, and you get *condominium,* which translates to "ownership with others." You'll definitely dazzle your pals "con" that etymology trivia tidbit.

## Defining the term "condominium"

Suppose you buy a condo in a Chicago high-rise. You have a mortgage, property taxes, and a fancy deed suitable for framing to prove that you own unit 603, one of 100 condos in that building. So far, owning a condominium is pretty much like owning a detached home that floats in the sky.

When you buy a detached home, an invisible line runs along the border of your property to separate what belongs to you from what belongs to your neighbors. When you purchase a condo, on the other hand, generally your property line is the interior surfaces (walls, floors, ceilings, windows, and doors) of your unit. In other words, with a condo, you get a deed to the air inside your unit and everything filling it — carpeting, window coverings, and all.

Air and interior improvements aren't all you own. You and the other condo owners in the condominium complex share ownership of the *land* on which the project is located and the high-rise *building* that contains your individual units. Thus, all of you own a portion of the roof, exterior building walls, and foundation — as well as a chunk of the garage, elevators, lobby, hallways, swimming pool, tennis courts, exercise facilities, and so on. All the parts of the complex beyond the individual units are known as *common areas* because you own them *in common* with all the other condo owners.

If you buy a condo, you automatically become a member of the project's homeowners association. You don't have to attend the meetings unless you want to, but you must pay homeowners' association dues. The dues cover common-area operating and maintenance expenses for everything from staff salaries, chlorinating the pool, lighting the lobby, and garbage collection to fire insurance for the building. In most places, a portion of your dues goes into a reserve fund to cover inevitable repairs and replacements, such as painting the building occasionally and replacing the roof.

**TIP**

Before buying a condo, find out exactly what percentage of joint ownership you'd have in the entire condominium complex. That amount establishes how much you'll be assessed for monthly homeowners' association dues and what percentage you'll pay of a special assessment that may be imposed on owners to cover unforeseen common-area expenses. It also determines how many votes you'd have in earthshaking matters affecting the complex, such as whether to paint the building aqua or tangerine, whether to repair the existing treadmill in the health club or buy a new one, and so on.

Condominiums use several different methods to establish the ownership percentages:

>> The simplest method is to give each owner an equal share of ownership in the entire development. Thus, each owner has one vote and pays an equal amount of the monthly dues and any special assessments.

>> If the ownership percentage is based on the size or market value of the condo, people who own the larger or more expensive units have more say in what happens in the complex than do owners of the smaller or less-expensive condos. However, the heavy hitters also have accordingly higher monthly homeowners' association dues and pay a larger percentage of special assessments.

## Why a condo?

Given their complexity, why do folks buy condominiums? Why doesn't everyone stick to simple, straightforward detached homes? Here's why:

>> **Attached residences increase your buying power.** Compare the price of a two-bedroom condo with a two-bedroom detached single-family dwelling in the same neighborhood. On the basis of livable square footage, condos generally sell for at least 20 to 30 percent less than comparable detached homes. Owning your very own roof, foundation, and plot of land is much more expensive than sharing these costs with a bunch of other owners.

For some would-be buyers, the choice is either buying a condo that meets their living-space needs or continuing to rent. Economic necessity explains why the path to the American dream for nearly one out of five first-time real estate buyers is condominium ownership. There's buying power in numbers.

» **Attached residences generally cost less to maintain than detached homes.**
Suppose that you're one of 100 condo owners in a Chicago high-rise. Unlike the owner of a detached home, who has to pay the entire cost of maintenance expenses such as installing a new roof or getting an exterior paint job, you can split these maintenance expenses with the other 99 owners. Although replacing the high-rise's roof, for example, costs more in absolute terms than replacing the roof of a detached single-family home, the cost per owner should be less. There's economy in numbers.

» **Attached residences have amenities that you can't otherwise afford.**
How many people do you know who own detached single-family homes with tennis courts, swimming pools, and fancy exercise clubs? Most homeowners can't afford expensive goodies like these. But when the cost is shared among all the owners in a large condo complex, the impossible dream is suddenly your hedonistic reality. There's luxury in numbers.

» **Attached residences are ideal homes for some empty-nesters.** As you near retirement, you may find yourself rattling around in a detached single-family home like a little ol' pea in a great big empty pod. Perhaps a two-bedroom condo in a building with no maintenance hassles and a doorman who'll forward your mail while you're off on one of your frequent vacations would solve all your problems. There's lifestyle in numbers.

# CONDOS NEED TO BE INSPECTED, TOO

When you buy a condo, you must inspect the entire building — not just your unit. You need a professional property inspector on your real estate team because the structural and mechanical condition of a property greatly affects its value. (See Chapter 3 in Book 1 for more about building a team.)

What's the condition of expensive common-area components such as the roof, heating and cooling systems, plumbing and electrical systems, elevators, foundation, and the like? Are amenities such as tennis courts, swimming pool, and health facilities in good shape? Because you're buying part of all the common areas in addition to your individual unit, you need a professional's opinion of the entire complex's condition.

Check the building's soundproofing by asking other owners whether they're bothered by noises emanating from units above, below, or beside their unit. The building has a ventilation problem if you can smell other people's cooking odors in your unit or the hallways. If you discover that expensive repairs or replacements are necessary and the condominium's reserve fund doesn't have anywhere near enough money to cover the anticipated costs, don't buy a unit in this complex. Sooner or later, the owners can expect a special assessment and/or a big dues increase.

# Condo drawbacks

Like detached homes, condos aren't for everyone. Judge for yourself how much the following drawbacks may affect you:

>> **Condominiums offer less privacy.** Shared walls mean you can hear others more easily. Noise pollution is one of the biggest problems with condos and the one area that prospective condo buyers frequently overlook. Visit the unit at different times of the day and different days of the week to listen for noise. Talk to owners of condominiums in the complex to see whether they're bothered by noise pollution. If possible, spend a few hours or an evening in a unit. Be sure to turn off the easy-listening music that real estate agents may have playing during your tour of the unit.

**TIP**

As a rule, the fewer common walls you share with neighbors, the more privacy you have in your unit. That's one reason corner units sell for a premium. And if your unit is on the top floor, you won't have people walking on your ceiling (unless there's a roof deck, of course). The ultimate in condo privacy, if you can afford it, is a top-floor corner unit.

>> **Condominiums are legally complex.** Prior to buying your condo, you should receive copies of three extremely important documents: a Master Deed or Declaration of Covenants, Conditions, and Restrictions (CC&Rs); the home-owners' association bylaws; and the homeowners' association budget. (See the nearby sidebar "Condominium documents" for more details.) Read these documents from cover to cover.

**WARNING**

The CC&Rs, bylaws, and budget are legally binding on all condo owners. Even though they're bulky, bloated, and boring, you must read them very, very, very carefully. If you have questions about what these documents mean, or if you don't understand how they affect you, consult a real estate lawyer. And find out from your agent or the homeowners' association whether the condominium is either currently involved in litigation or plans to be in the foreseeable future. Lawsuits are expensive.

>> **Condominiums are financially complex.** As a prospective owner, check the current operating budget. Be sure that it realistically covers building mainte-nance costs, staff salaries, utilities, garbage collection, insurance premiums, and other normal operating expenses. If the budget is too low, prepare to get slugged with a massive dues increase sooner or later. By the same token, make sure that the budget includes adequate reserve funds to provide for predictable major expenses such as occasional exterior paint jobs and new roofs. How much is adequate? Three to five percent of the condominium's gross operating budget is generally considered a minimally acceptable reserve. If the reserve fund is too low, you're in danger of getting a special assessment in the event of a financial emergency.

Review the past several years' operating budgets and financial statements for indicators of poor fiscal management. Here are some red flags to look out for:

- **Frequent, large homeowners' association dues increases:** Dues shouldn't be increasing annually much faster than the current rate of inflation.

- **Special assessments that wouldn't have been necessary if the association had an adequate reserve fund:** When discussing the budget and reserve fund, find out whether any dues increases or special assessments are anticipated in the near future to make up operating deficits or to cover the cost of a major project.

- **Too many homeowners who are delinquent in paying their dues:** Operating expenses continue unabated regardless of whether all the owners pay their dues. You can bet that homeowners in foreclosure or mired in a short sale probably aren't paying their dues. Too many distressed properties in a condo complex are the fiscal equivalent of a field of red flags flying.

>> **Some condominium rules are overly restrictive.** People who live in proximity to one another need a smattering of rules to maintain order and keep life blissful. Too many rules, however, can turn your condo into a prison. For example, the condominium may have rules specifying what kind of floor and window coverings you must have in your unit, rules regulating the type or number of pets you can have in your unit, rules limiting your ability to rent your unit to someone else, rules forbidding you to make any alterations or improvements to your unit, rules limiting when or how often you can entertain in your unit, and so on. Before you buy, read the CC&Rs and bylaws carefully to find out exactly what kind of usage restrictions they contain. Some of these same restrictions can apply in new detached housing developments, as discussed in the earlier section "New homes."

If you discover that the condominium (or the new housing development) has restrictions you don't like, don't buy the unit. Trying to modify CC&Rs or bylaws to eliminate restrictions after you've bought a unit is usually an expensive exercise in frustration and futility. You have far better things to do with your life than waste a big chunk of it haggling with condominium associations and their lawyers.

Prudent rental restrictions are good. Ideally, all units in the complex will be owner-occupied. If some owners *occasionally* let friends use their units or rent the units for a week or two while they're on vacation, no big deal. However, if most of the units are owned by absentee investors who rent them to an endless parade of partying strangers, that's bad if you happen to have difficulty sleeping with loud music blaring late at night. You may also have trouble getting a mortgage in a complex with too many renters.

>> **Brand-new condominium developments have the same advantages and disadvantages as new detached homes, compounded by a condo's added legal and economic complexity.** If you haven't yet read the earlier section about new detached homes, now's the time to do so. All the cautionary statements about new detached homes also apply to new condominiums. Like new detached homes, new condo projects are as good or bad as the developers who build them and the lawyers who create them. Because any new project, by definition, doesn't have a track record yet, you must visit earlier projects done by the same developer to see how well they've aged and how satisfied the condo owners are.

**WARNING**

Some unscrupulous developers of new condominium projects purposely lowball monthly operating costs to deceive prospective purchasers into thinking that living there costs less than it really does. These developers pay a portion of the monthly expenses out of their own pockets to keep project costs artificially low. The economic ax falls when the developer turns the project over to the homeowners' association, which is soon forced to jack up the dues to cover actual operating expenses. When projected operating costs look too good to be true, they probably are. Compare the new project's projected operating expenses with the actual operating expenses of a comparable established project.

>> **Where condominium parking and storage are concerned, things can be unclear.** For example, does your condo deed include a deeded garage or parking space that only you can use, or is parking on a first-come, first-served basis? Do parking privileges cost extra, or is parking part of the monthly dues? What about provisions for guest parking or a parking area for boats or trailers? Do you have a deeded storage area located outside your unit? If so, where is it? If you need even more storage, is any available, and how much does it cost? You're much better off getting answers to these questions before, rather than after, you buy.

>> **Some older buildings that have been converted from apartments into condominiums have functional obsolescence problems.** Older buildings frequently have excellent detailing and craftsmanship. However, they also often have outdated heating and cooling systems, and may lack elevators, which are mighty handy if, for instance, you're carrying groceries or suitcases up several flights of stairs. If you're buying a condo in an older building, find out whether utilities are individually metered or lumped into the monthly homeowners' association dues. Does your unit have a thermostat to control its heating and air-conditioning, or is the heating and cooling system centrally controlled?

**WARNING**

If utilities are part of the monthly dues, other condo owners have no incentive to economize by moderating their use of heat or air-conditioning. If you're frugal, you just end up subsidizing owners who aren't. By the same token, in a building with central heating and cooling, your climate choices may be limited to roasting in the winter and freezing in the summer. Even if you can live with utility overcharges and personal discomfort, these factors may deter future buyers from purchasing when you try to sell your unit.

>> **Size can be a problem.** Large condo complexes usually have a cold, impersonal, hotel-like feeling. And as a rule, people who live in large complexes tend not to pay much attention to finances and day-to-day operating details because the homeowners' association hires professional property managers to run things for the owners. There are, however, a couple of offsetting advantages to owning a condo in a large complex. If, for instance, several owners in a 100-unit complex fail to pay their monthly dues, it's not the end of the world financially. What's more, socially speaking, the odds of regularly running into an owner you detest diminish as the complex increases in size.

WARNING

Don't buy into a small condominium complex unless you enjoy intimate relations with your neighbors. Carefully size up the other owners. Be sure that they're the kind of folks you can trust to carry their fair share of the load financially and operationally. In a small condo, you actively participate in the homeowners' association because you must. Every vote has an immediate impact on your finances and the quality of your life. You don't have to love the other owners. BUT (note the big "but") if some or all of them are the type of people you'll be unable to get along with, don't buy the unit.

After reading the disadvantages of condo ownership, you may think that only a fool would buy a condo. Not true. Plenty of content condo owners would never consider buying a detached dwelling.

TIP

Condominiums make the most sense for folks who don't want operating and maintenance hassles (remembering that you'll still have the *expense*), who want to maximize their bang for the buck spent on living space, and who don't need a private yard. Buying a condo for a few years while you save enough money to purchase a detached home usually doesn't make economic sense. Given the expenses of buying and selling a condo, combined with its probable lack of decent appreciation, you're probably better off waiting to buy a detached home if you think you can do so within five years.

## Co-operative apartments

The two most common types of attached residences are condominiums and co-operative apartments, which are usually called co-ops. You can't tell which is which by looking at the building or individual units. Like condominiums, what makes a co-op a co-op is its legal status.

# CONDOMINIUM DOCUMENTS

A condo project is born when the project developer records a map and a condominium plan along with a Declaration of Covenants, Conditions, and Restrictions (CC&Rs) in the county recorder's office, which officially makes this information a matter of public record for all the world to see. CC&Rs establish the condominium by creating a homeowners' association, stipulating how the condominiums' maintenance and repairs will be handled, and regulating what can and can't be done to individual units and the condominiums' common areas. A similar procedure is sometimes used with new developments for detached housing.

Bylaws keep the condominium functioning smoothly. They describe in minute detail the homeowners' association's powers, duties, and operation. The bylaws also cover such nitty-gritty items as how the homeowners' association officers are elected and grant the association the right to levy assessments on individual condo owners.

Last, but far from least, the developer creates a budget. Unlike the government, the condominium's budget can't (theoretically, at least) operate in the red. The current budget establishes how much the condominium expects to spend this year to operate and maintain itself. Condo owners also receive an annual statement of income and expenses showing precisely how last year's dues were spent and spelling out the condominium's current financial condition.

You'll be delighted to know that most of the pros and cons of condominium ownership also apply to co-ops, so you don't have to read a ton of new stuff. (If you haven't read the previous section on condos, do so now.) The following sections focus on the three ways in which condos and co-ops differ: the definition of legal ownership, management, and your financing options.

## The definition of legal ownership: Deed versus stock

When you buy a condo, you get a deed to your unit. When you buy a co-op, you get a stock certificate (to prove that you own a certain number of shares of stock in the cooperative corporation) and a *proprietary lease*, which entitles you to occupy the apartment you bought. The corporation owns the building and has the deed in its name as, for example, the 10 West Eighty-Sixth Street Corporation. Thus, you're simultaneously a co-owner of the building (via your stock ownership) and a tenant in the building you co-own.

In most co-operatives, shares are allocated based on how big a unit is and what floor it's on. Thus, a top-floor apartment usually has more shares than a ground-floor unit of the same size. The more shares you have, the greater your influence in the co-op because each share gives you one vote. Unfortunately, power has a price. Your proportionate share of the co-operative's total maintenance expenses is based on the number of shares you own in the corporation. If you own a great many shares, your monthly expenses will be disproportionately high. And when you're ready to sell, your unusually high monthly expenses may reduce your unit's value.

## Management: Homeowners' association versus board of directors

If you've always fantasized about being the chairman of the board, here's your chance: Buy a co-op apartment, and work your way up the corporate ladder. Because your unit is in a building owned by a corporation, it's governed by a board of directors elected by you and the other owners. Nomenclature aside, just like the homeowners' association in a condominium, the board of directors is responsible for the co-operative's day-to-day operations and finances.

## Financing your purchase

Securing a mortgage to purchase your co-op may be difficult. Many lenders flat-out refuse to accept shares of stock in a co-operative corporation as security for a mortgage. Conversely, some co-ops absolutely won't permit any individual financing over and above the mortgage the corporation has on the building as a whole. These co-ops believe that one proof of creditworthiness is your ability to pay all cash for your unit.

Unless you're richer than Midas, don't buy a co-op if only one or two lenders in your area make co-operative-apartment loans. Odds are you'll pay a higher interest rate because of the lack of lender competition and lender concerns about the greater risks of co-ops. Worse yet, what if these lenders stop making co-op mortgages and no other lenders take their place? You won't be able to sell your unit until you find an all-cash buyer (and they're few and far between) or until you have the financial resources to lend the money yourself to the next buyer.

## BUYING AND SELLING CO-OPS IS OFTEN CHALLENGING

Buying and selling co-ops is usually a lot more difficult than buying and selling condos. Most co-operatives stipulate that individual owners can't sell or otherwise transfer their stock or proprietary leases without the express consent of either the board of directors or a majority of owners.

Prospective buyers generally must provide several letters of reference regarding their sterling character and Rock of Gibraltar creditworthiness. In addition, they may have to submit to a personal grilling by the board of directors. Given that the owners live in close proximity to one another and depend on one another financially, having the ability to screen out party animals, deadbeats, and the like is reasonable as long as that power isn't misused to unfairly discriminate against buyers.

Even so, some buyers find the approval process extremely intrusive and strenuously object to giving strangers their financial statements. The approval process also tends to slow the sale of co-op units on the market.

Owning a co-op is a two-edged sword. As a co-op owner, you have much more control over who your neighbors will (or won't) be than do condo owners. Unfortunately, that control cuts both ways. When you try to sell your unit, people you consider perfect buyers may be turned down by the co-op because your neighbors think that the prospective buyers would entertain too much or can't carry the load financially. Giving up the right to sell your co-op to the highest bidder may be too high a price to pay for the right to choose your neighbors.

# Finding a Great Deal

If you're like most people, you're cursed with champagne taste and a beer budget. The homes you hunger for cost far more than you can afford. To buy one of these dream homes, you'd either have to get a really, really good deal or win the lottery.

Good deals *are* out there. The trick is knowing where to find them and how to evaluate them. Don't waste time looking at perfect houses if you're searching for a deal. People pay premium prices for perfection. The houses you find great deals on are imperfect properties — houses with either physical or financial problems. The deal you're offered is an inducement to tackle the problem. Whether the deal is ultimately better for you or for the seller is the question.

The following sections cover special property situations that may be good deals or pigs in a poke.

# Finding a fixer-upper

*Fixer-uppers* are run-down houses with physical problems. Real estate agents generally refer to fixer-uppers euphemistically as "needing work," "having great potential," or being a "handyman's special."

Fixer-uppers aren't very popular in sluggish real estate markets. Most buyers in such markets don't want to put up with the hassle or financial uncertainties associated with doing a major rehab. They prefer to buy houses in move-in condition. Such a house is a safe but passive investment. Because its potential has already been fully realized, the new owner can't do anything to significantly increase its value.

A fixer-upper, on the other hand, offers potentially larger rewards to folks who have the vision to see beyond the mess that is to the wonderful home that can be. A fixer-upper buyer must also have the financial resources and courage to tackle the risks. If you fit that profile, here's what you may be able to look forward to after you've transformed your ugly duckling into a swan:

>> You'll be living in a nicer home and a better neighborhood than you'd otherwise have been able to afford.

>> Instead of buying a home decorated in someone else's idea of good taste, your home will be done the way you like it.

>> You may have increased your home's fair-market value in excess of your out-of-pocket expenses for improvements you made.

For example, if you're handy, you can add thousands of dollars of value to a fixer-upper by doing labor-intensive jobs such as painting, wallpapering, and landscaping yourself. Sweat equity can pay big dividends.

**REMEMBER**

If you're mechanically challenged, forget sweat equity. It's less frustrating and cheaper in the long run to earn money doing what you do best and then using some of that money to hire competent contractors to do what *they* do best. Poor workmanship is a false economy; it looks awful and reduces property values. Doing the project well the first time is easier, faster, and ultimately less expensive than doing it badly yourself and then paying someone else to fix your mess. If you're one of those rare people who can do quality work yourself, by all means try your hand at it — just be realistic about the required time and costs.

Some fixer-uppers are easy to spot. They look like classic haunted houses — peeling paint, shutters falling off, overgrown yard, and so on. Things don't get any better on the inside. These houses may need everything from a good cleaning to electrical system and plumbing overhauls.

# STRUCTURAL REPAIRS VERSUS RENOVATIONS

Work done on fixer-uppers falls into two broad categories: structural repairs and renovations.

- *Structural repairs* are changes you make to a property to bring it up to local health and safety standards. Such work can include foundation repairs, roof replacements, new electrical and plumbing-system installations, and so on — things that cost big bucks but add relatively little value to property. Ideally, you can get a credit from the seller to do some, if not all, of the necessary structural repairs. The less you have to take out of your pocket for corrective work, the more you have to spend on renovations.

- *Renovations* increase a fixer-upper's value by modernizing the home. Remodeling an old kitchen, installing a second bathroom, and adding a garage are a few examples of major structural renovations that make your home more functional, more pleasant to live in, and more valuable when you sell it.

  *Cosmetic renovations* (painting, carpeting, landscaping, and the like) also add value with far less expense and aggravation. The ideal fixer-uppers to buy are ones that look awful but simply need cosmetic fixes to look their best.

Other fixer-uppers, however, are much more subtle. Some older houses, condos, and co-ops, for example, may look fine at first glance but have functional obsolescence. They're livable, but they need improvements, such as adding master bedrooms, bathrooms, or garages, and upgrading their electrical systems to bring them up to today's more rigorous housing standards.

## Digging for a diamond among the dumps

Finding the right fixer-upper isn't a matter of luck. On the contrary, it takes persistence, skill, and plain hard work. You spend lots of time tromping through properties; invest more precious time evaluating promising fixer-uppers that ultimately don't make sense economically; and then, just when you're ready to give up, you finally discover a diamond in the rough that you end up buying.

Here's how to separate diamonds from dumps:

>> **Read this book.** Everything you need to know is here. Pay special attention to the topics covered in this chapter (good neighborhoods; principles of progression, regression, and conformity; and used homes and condos) and Chapter 2

of Book 2 (accurately determining fair-market value so you don't overpay). Also, be sure that you can financially afford all the necessary expenditures after the purchase for the fix-up work.

REMEMBER

>> **Inspect the heck out of the fixer-upper before you buy it.** Every property should be carefully inspected prior to purchase. Fixer-uppers need even more scrutiny so you know precisely what you're getting yourself into. Make your purchase offer conditional upon your approval of the property inspections and satisfactory resolution of corrective-work issues you discover.

>> **Get contractors' bids for structural repairs and renovations.** You can use contractors' bids as a negotiating tool to get a corrective-work credit or lower sales price from the sellers for structural repairs such as termite-damage repairs and a new roof. You should also get cost estimates for renovations such as bathroom modernization, new kitchen appliances and cabinets, central heating, and anything else required to bring the property up to date.

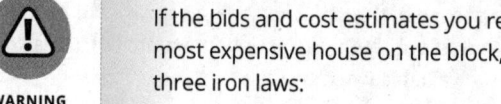

If the bids and cost estimates you receive indicate that you'd end up with the most expensive house on the block, don't do the project. Fix-up work has three iron laws:

WARNING

● It's always more disruptive than you expected.

● It always takes longer to finish than you planned.

● It always costs more than you estimated.

So if estimated fix-up costs would make the property the most expensive house on the block, by the time the work is finally completed, the actual costs will make it the most expensive house in the state!

TIP

Getting a loan is usually difficult if the cost of anticipated corrective-work repairs exceeds 3 percent of the property value, which is always the case with major fixer-uppers. However, a good real estate agent should know which lenders in your area specialize in fixer-upper loans. Given that one such lender finds you creditworthy and your project feasible, that lender may give you a mortgage to buy the property *and* a construction loan to make the improvements.

## Final thoughts on fixer-uppers

Feeling somewhat overwhelmed by the risks associated with fixer-uppers is normal. Now you understand why most home buyers avoid them — they fear being sucked into a bottomless bog that utterly disrupts their lives and totally devours their savings.

Most novice home buyers, especially first-time buyers, woefully underestimate the time and cost required to fix up homes. When all is said and done, nearly all people find that it would have cost them the same or less to buy a more finished home and avoid the headaches of doing or coordinating the renovations. Some folks have ended up in financial ruin and even divorced over the stresses of such renovations.

TIP

If you like challenges and are willing to do a ton of extra detective work, follow these tips to maximize your chances of succeeding with a fixer-upper:

>> Buy in the best neighborhood you can afford.

>> Buy one of the cheaper houses on the best block.

>> Make sure that the renovations will more than pay for themselves in increased property value. There are online resources that can help with this, like the Cost vs. Value Report by Remodeling Magazine (check out the latest data at www.remodeling.hw.net/cost-vs-value/2022/). Here you will find cost estimates for many remodeling projects as well as the value those projects are likely to retain at resale.

>> Make sure that the purchase price is low enough to allow you to do the corrective work and renovations without turning your property into the most expensive house on the block.

REMEMBER

If the real estate gods play fair and square, whoever buys the exquisitely *finished* home you transformed from a dump will pay a bonus for your farsightedness to see the fixer-upper's potential, for your audacity to tackle the financial risk, and for your stamina to put up with the chaos and filth of a rehab. If (and only if) you select wisely, negotiate the price wisely, and renovate wisely, you'll enjoy years of blissful living in the wonderful home you created — and ideally make a fine profit to boot when you sell it.

## Taking over a foreclosure

To get a mortgage, you give the lender the right to take your home away from you and sell it to pay the balance due on the mortgage if you

>> Don't make your loan payments

>> Don't pay your property taxes

>> Let your homeowner's insurance policy lapse

>> Do anything else that financially endangers your home

# BACK-ON-THE-MARKET PROPERTIES

When a house listed for sale receives an acceptable offer, the sellers usually tell their agent not to actively market the property or solicit other offers while they work with the buyers to satisfy the contract's terms and conditions of sale, such as property inspections and financing. If such a property comes back on the market (*BOM*, in real estate lingo), it means that the deal fell apart.

Property comes back on the market for many reasons. Perhaps the buyers couldn't qualify for a loan or got cold feet. Maybe the lender didn't think the house was worth as much money as the buyers were willing to pay for it and wouldn't approve their request for a loan. The far and away most common reason deals fall through, however, is that the buyers and sellers couldn't agree on how to handle the corrective work discovered during the inspections.

Ironically, the castle that all the buyers coveted when it was the newest listing on the market may turn into a "that old thing" pumpkin when it returns. Suddenly, suspicious buyers wonder what's wrong with the house. Real or imagined, that stigma of being a problem property repels a lot of people. They don't want to buy a house that someone else rejected. As a result of reduced buyer enthusiasm, BOM homes often sell for a lower price the second time around.

Don't categorically reject a house that comes back on the market. Find out why it's BOM. If the problem is related to property defects, ask the sellers to show you copies of the inspection reports. Given that the problems are correctable and that you can negotiate a good deal, the sellers' misfortune may be your good fortune. Sellers who've had a deal implode are frequently more willing to realistically negotiate on price and terms with the next buyer. If you apply the principles covered in the fixer-upper section of this chapter, you can turn a BOM into a great deal.

The legal action to repossess a home and sell it is called a *foreclosure.* Every year, hundreds of thousands of homes end up in foreclosure. Foreclosures in the late 2000s hit a high not seen in decades. Most foreclosures result from people over-extended on debt, including mortgages whose payments ratchet higher than the borrowers are prepared to handle. In other cases, however, people fall on hard times — they lose a job, experience unexpected healthcare costs, suffer a death in the family, or go through a divorce. Finally, some borrowers who have little invested choose to walk away from properties that have declined in value.

You may have heard stories about people who got good deals buying foreclo-sures far below the property's appraised value. And in fact, some people who buy foreclosed property luck out. But for every lucky winner, many more people don't profit or, worse, actually lose money buying foreclosures.

**WARNING**

Buyer beware — foreclosures are generally legal and financial cesspools. Unless you have an expert on your team who can guide you through the entire foreclosure process from beginning to end, don't even think about buying a foreclosure at an auction.

If you buy a foreclosed home, you most likely also buy the previous owner's problems. Here's a list of risks to ponder:

>> **Physical:** Some homeowners react to the emotional devastation of a foreclosure with a scorched-earth attitude of "if we can't have it, we'll make darn sure that nobody else wants it." Before leaving, they take appliances, light fixtures, cabinets, sinks, toilets, and anything else of value. In extreme cases, they break windows, pour concrete down kitchen and bathroom drains, rip wiring out of walls, uproot shrubs, cut down trees, and do anything else they can think of to trash the property. What if you're the high bidder for a sabotaged house at an auction of foreclosed properties? Lucky you.

**WARNING**

Lenders usually won't let you inspect foreclosed properties prior to their auction. Nor can you make your offer to purchase subject to getting a loan. Lenders don't guarantee clear title to these properties, nor can you get title insurance to protect against undisclosed or undiscovered flaws in the chain of title or liens against the properties. The risk of buying a property at a foreclosure auction greatly exceeds the possible reward.

>> **Financial:** Depending on which state the house is located in, a foreclosure can take anywhere from four months to over a year to complete. Suppose that you get what appears to be a good deal from people who are actually selling partway through the foreclosure process to avoid the stigma of foreclosure. What if these people lie about how much they owe on their mortgage and property taxes? What if they don't tell you about unpaid homeowners' association fees, unrecorded mortgages, court judgments, or federal and state tax liens (outstanding tax bills) hanging over the house? One guess who's liable for debts secured by the property. Lucky you.

>> **Possession:** Suppose that after buying a foreclosure at an auction, you visit your new home and discover that the previous owners are still living in it with their last remaining possession — a shotgun. They have no intention of leaving peacefully. Who do you think will have the pleasure of evicting them? Lucky you.

**TIP**

Given possible sabotage by the previous owner, buying a foreclosure is never *entirely* safe. The least risky way to purchase a foreclosure is to buy a real estate owned (REO) property directly from a lender, government loan insurer, or other government agency that holds the title to the property because no one bought it at the foreclosure auction. Here's why:

>> Any recorded or undisclosed mortgages, court judgments, or tax liens on the house are either removed from the property or at least revealed to you prior to your purchase.

>> You can — absolutely must, in fact — have the house minutely scrutinized by professional property inspectors. Where foreclosures are concerned, you have to find out whether the previous owner left any hidden surprises for you.

>> The price and terms of sale are negotiable. Even though foreclosures are normally listed at their appraised value, lenders may make allowances for corrective work by either reducing the price or giving you a credit to do the work. They'll also, as a rule, offer attractive loan terms (low cash down payments, no loan fees, and below-market interest rates) to get rid of these blighted properties quickly. After all, they're in the loan business — not property management.

**WARNING**

Think long and hard before buying a foreclosure. Even if you purchase the REO property directly from a lender, loan insurer, or government agency, you may be buying a house permeated from foundation to roof by shattered dreams. Such a house probably hasn't been given the best of care. Do your homework carefully, have the property thoroughly inspected, and understand *fully* what you're getting yourself into before you buy. If you're still interested in this option, check out Book 3 on investing in a foreclosure property.

## Seeking a short sale

Compared to acrimonious foreclosures where in the worst cases spiteful owners strip everything of any value from their house before maliciously trashing it, short sales are downright cordial. Short-sale owners may be *underwater* (owe more on the loan than their house is worth), but they're doing whatever they can to limit further damage to their credit rating by cooperating with the lender to maximize the property's sale price.

To that end, short-sale owners live in their house and continue to maintain it so it shows well. Depending on the severity of their financial problems, the owners may even make token loan payments. The lender, in turn, agrees to eat the loss by accepting the sale proceeds as full satisfaction of the debt. By working together, both parties avoid a far more odious foreclosure.

Here are critical issues you should consider before beginning the process of buying a short–sale property:

>> **Short sales aren't screaming bargains.** Lenders typically price short-sale properties based on the sale prices of nondistressed property. They want to get as close as possible to fair-market value to minimize the loss on their mortgage. You may get a purchase price 5 to 10 percent below market because short sales are considerably more time consuming, risky, and complex than a nondistressed property sale. However, don't count on getting an extraordinary deal.

>> **Short sales aren't short.** If you must complete your purchase quickly, forget doing a short sale. Even with knowledgeable, cooperative folks on both ends of the deal, short sales usually take at least 30 days for approval plus at least another 30 days to close the sale. If there's more than one lender and/or loan insurer involved, the process takes even longer. Worst of all, your offer remains contingent during that lengthy lender approval process. If the lenders receive a better offer before your offer has been approved, they'll drop yours like a hot potato. It doesn't matter that you made the first offer. It's not fair, but that's how the short-sale game is played.

>> **You can't do a short sale if you're related to or have a financial arrangement with the seller.** Buyer, seller, and agents must sign a form ensuring there are no pre-existing relationships or financial agreements. Lenders want to prevent secret deals where a buyer and seller agree to sell the house below its fair-market price and then kick back money to the seller under the table after close of escrow. This is collusion. This is fraud. You can go to jail. Enough said.

>> **Don't buy a short-sale property if you need financial help with closing costs or want a credit for repairs or corrective work.** By definition, short-sale sellers are short of cash, so don't expect financial help from them. And, whereas lenders infrequently offer to make minor repairs or throw a few bucks your way for closing costs, lenders aren't as willing or flexible in this area as traditional sellers.

>> **You can't make an offer contingent upon the sale of your home.** It's extremely unlikely that any lender will accept your offer if it hinges on selling your house to get the money to buy the short-sale property. This constraint limits the field of perspective short-sale purchasers to first-time buyers, folks who don't have to pull equity out of their present home to buy a property, and real estate investors.

>> **Short sales are sometimes "as is."** Include an inspection contingency in your offer. Be advised that some lenders won't accept an offer subject to a property inspection. That means you must either spend hundreds of dollars having the property inspected before making your offer on the outside chance it will be accepted or forego an inspection.

>> **Don't make offers on multiple short-sale properties.** Unscrupulous get-rich-quick seminars recommend making offers on several short-sale properties at the same time. They encourage buyers to tie up multiple properties, see which one works out best, and then cancel the other deals. Terrible idea! Real estate purchase agreements are binding contracts. They should never be entered into lightly. Such a practice is unfair to fiscally challenged short-sale sellers and can lead to severe financial penalties for capricious buyers.

REMEMBER

If you're not scared off yet, here are questions you must have answered by the short-sale sellers or their agent prior to writing an offer:

>> **How many loans are on the property and who are the lenders?** This tips you off regarding the short sale's complexity. The more lenders involved, the more potential problems. How quickly (or slowly) a bank bureaucracy digests the short sale and internal corporate negotiating strategies vary widely from lender to lender. Savvy real estate agents know which lenders are relatively easy to work with and, conversely, which ones are awful.

>> **Where are the sellers in the short-sale process?** Have the sellers just begun discussing a short sale with the lender? Has the lender notified the homeowners they've started the foreclosure process? If so, when? As noted in the foreclosure section, this sets a date when the property may be sold to the highest bidder or revert to the foreclosing lender. Is time your friend or your enemy? You must know.

>> **Who is negotiating the short sale with the lender — the seller, the seller's real estate agent, or a short-sale facilitator?** If a facilitator is involved, who pays for the facilitator's service? In some cases, the buyer is asked to pay that fee. This isn't illegal if properly disclosed in writing to all lenders involved. How much the facilitator charges and whether you want to pay the fee is another issue.

>> **Are there other liens on the property in addition to the mortgage?** As noted in the earlier foreclosure section, there may be liens on the property for unpaid federal and state income taxes, unpaid property taxes, unpaid homeowners' association dues, mechanic's liens, and court judgments. You need to know what debts are on the property and who is responsible for paying them off prior to close of escrow.

TIP

Ah, the moment of truth. If a short sale seems feasible based on what you learned during your information–gathering phase, here are things you can do to improve the odds of having a successful transaction:

>> **Work with a real estate agent who understands the complexities of short sales.** You need an agent on your team with specialized training such as SFR (Short Sales and Foreclosures) or CDPE (Certified Distressed Property Expert). Ideally, your agent will also have hands-on practical expertise gained by representing other buyers of short-sale properties.

>> **Get a letter from your lender specifying that you have been preapproved for a mortgage.** Not prequalified for a loan, *preapproved*. Short-sale lenders insist upon this.

>> **If possible, attach a short-sale addendum to your offer.** Standard purchase agreements don't have provisions for the unusual terms and conditions involved in a short sale. To correct that oversight, many states have addendums specifically written to deal with the nuances of short sales.

>> **Be realistic in your timing.** The short-sale lender will probably need 30 days or more to approve the contract. When it has been approved, you'll need at least another 30 days to close the sale.

>> **Don't be surprised if you get a counteroffer from the lender.** The lender isn't trying to dump the short-sale property. On the contrary, the lender is trying to obtain market value for it to limit its loss.

# Chapter **2**

# Determining a House's Worth

You see a home for sale. The asking price is $249,500. Is that charming cottage a steal or an overpriced turkey?

If you don't have the faintest idea, don't worry — that's normal. Most buyers don't know property values when they start hunting for a home. To become an educated buyer, you need to take time to familiarize yourself with property values. This chapter helps you understand property values so you can get your dream home for the best price.

## Preparing to Tour an Endless Parade of Homes

The best way to learn property values is to eyeball as many houses as possible and then monitor them until they sell. That's how agents educate themselves.

You don't need to see every house in town to get educated. A good agent can accelerate your learning curve by playing the real estate version of show and tell. You have to tour only houses that meet your specific wish list for budget, style, size, and neighborhood. After seeing no more than a dozen houses comparable to your dream home, you should be an educated buyer.

**TIP**

Don't be surprised if you're utterly confused after a day spent looking at property for sale. When you see six or seven houses in rapid succession, it's challenging to remember which one had the wonderful kitchen and which one had the huge backyard with a swing set. To make your property tours productive, follow these tips:

>> **Take notes.** You'll probably get a listing statement (those one-page, house-for-sale advertisements/marketing pieces), brochure, or Multiple Listing Service fact sheet describing each property you visit. To help you remember the house, make notes directly on your information sheet regarding distinguishing features such as a sunken living room, a crazy floor plan, or a location near a commuter rail stop.

>> **Review the tour.** After you finish for the day, discuss the houses you saw with your real estate agent (if you have one). If your memory is fuzzy about a property or two that you visited, your agent can probably fill in the details.

>> **Save the info sheets.** As you see when you read the later section "Figuring Out Fair Market Value: Comparable Market Analysis," sale prices are mighty important negotiating tools. Ask your agent (or the listing agent, if you don't have an agent) to tell you when a house you toured sells and how much it sold for. Mark the sale price and date of sale on your info sheet for future reference.

# The Three Elusive Components of Worth

Oscar Wilde said a cynic is someone who knows the price of everything and the value of nothing. In the real estate game, neither *cost* nor *price* is the same as *value*. When you understand what these words mean and how they differ, you can replace emotion with objectivity when looking at houses and during price negotiations after you finally make an offer. Out-facting people usually beats trying to out-argue them.

# Value is a moving target

*Value* is your opinion of what a particular home is worth to you, based on how you intend to use it now and in the future. Value isn't carved in stone; on the contrary, it's pretty darn elusive.

For one thing, opinions are subjective. We, your humble authors, may think that we resemble George Clooney and Brad Pitt. You, on the other hand, are of the opinion that we look like Boris Karloff and Bela Lugosi — in full monster makeup. No harm done, as long as we all realize that a big difference exists between subjective opinions and objective facts.

Furthermore, *internal factors* — things related to your personal situation — have a sneaky way of changing over time. Suppose that you currently place great value on a home with four bedrooms and a large, fenced-in backyard. The home must be located in a town with a good school system. Why? Because you have young children.

Twenty years from now, when the kids are grown and have moved out (you hope!), you may decide to sell the house. Why? Because you no longer need such a big home. Neither the house nor the school system changed — what changed were internal factors regarding your use for the property, and thus its value to you.

*External factors* are things outside your control that affect property values. If your commute time is cut in half because mass-transit rail service is extended into your neighborhood after you buy your home, your home's value may increase. If a garbage dump is built next door to you, you'll have a big problem getting top dollar for your house when you sell it.

The law of supply and demand is another external factor that affects value. If more people want to buy than sell, buyer competition drives home prices up. Conversely, if more people want to sell than buy, home prices drop. A high number of distressed property sales (foreclosures or short sales) in a neighborhood also drag down property values.

# Cost is yesterday

*Cost* measures past expenditures — for example, what the sellers paid when they bought their house. What the sellers originally paid or how much they spent fixing up the house after they bought it doesn't mean diddlypoo as far as a house's present or future value is concerned. That was then; this is now.

For example, when home prices skyrocketed in most parts of both coasts during the latter half of the 1990s and into the mid-2000s, some buyers accused sellers of being greedy. "You paid $400,000 seven years ago. Now you're asking $850,000," they said. "If you get your price, you'll make an obscenely large profit."

"So what?" sellers replied compassionately. "If you don't want to pay our modest asking price, move out of the way so those nice buyers standing behind you can present their offer." In a hot seller's market, people who base their offering price on what sellers originally paid for property waste everyone's time.

However, the market doesn't always go in the same direction forever. In the early 1990s and again in the late 2000s, for example, prices declined in many areas. Sellers would've been ecstatic to find buyers willing to pay them what they'd paid five years earlier, when home prices peaked.

## Price is what it's worth today

Sellers have *asking prices* on their houses. Buyers put *offering prices* in their contracts. Buyers and sellers negotiate back and forth to establish *purchase prices.* Today's purchase price is tomorrow's cost. Is the purchase price a good value? That depends.

You may get a bargain if you find a house owned by people who don't know property values or who must sell quickly because of an adverse life change such as divorce, job loss, or a death in the family. Folks who don't have time to sit around waiting for buyers willing to pay top dollar usually take a hit when they sell. Time is the seller's enemy and the buyer's pal.

If, however, you must buy quickly to relocate for a new job or to get your kids settled before school starts, watch out. You can overpay because you don't have enough time to search for a good deal.

REMEMBER

Cost is the past, price is the present, and value (like beauty) is in the eye of the beholder. What the sellers paid for their house years ago, or what they'd like to get for it today, doesn't matter. Don't squander your hard-earned money on an overpriced house to satisfy a seller's unrealistic fantasy.

# Explaining Fair Market Value

Natural disasters aside, every home will sell at the right price. That price is defined as its *fair market value* (FMV) — the price a buyer will pay and a seller will accept for the house, given that neither buyer nor seller is under *duress*. Duress can come from life changes such as major health problems, divorce, or a sudden job transfer, which put either the buyers or sellers under pressure to perform quickly. Distressed property sales are an extreme example of financial duress. If appraisers know that a sale is made under duress, they raise or lower the sale price accordingly to more accurately reflect the house's true fair market value.

*Fair market value* is more powerful than plain old *value*. As a buyer, you have an opinion of what the house is worth to you. The sellers have a separate, not necessarily equal (and probably higher) opinion of their home's value. These values are opinions, not facts. You can't bank opinions.

## "CAN'T SELL" VERSUS "WON'T SELL"

Two weeks of extraordinarily heavy winter rain years ago undermined the soil of a subdivision in the Anaheim Hills area of Los Angeles. After this drenching, homes in the 25-acre development began slipping downhill at the rate of about 1 inch a day.

Home foundations and swimming pools cracked. Streets and sidewalks buckled. Local authorities finally ordered everyone in the subdivision to evacuate their homes until the ground stabilized.

Unlike most frustrated sellers, these folks really *couldn't* sell their homes. Forces of nature beyond their control reduced their houses' value to zero. Other than salvage value, no market exists for unintentionally mobile homes.

Fortunately, most homeowners who claim that they "can't" sell their houses don't have this problem. They aren't disaster victims whose homes are suddenly rendered valueless by an act of God. On the contrary, they have buyers galore for their houses, as well as scads of lenders who'd make loans to those buyers.

If nothing is wrong with their houses, what's the problem? The homeowners. The problem isn't that they *can't* sell. These homeowners *won't* sell.

As long as homeowners choose not to accept what buyers are willing to pay for their houses, they won't sell — and those houses will remain on the market at their inflated asking prices. It's a self-fulfilling prophecy. As a prospective home buyer, beware of such greedy, unrealistic sellers.

Unlike value, fair market value is fact. It becomes a fact when buyers and sellers agree upon a *mutually acceptable price.* Just as it takes two to tango, it takes a buyer and a seller to make fair market value. Facts are bankable.

## When fair market value isn't fair: Need-based pricing

Whenever the real estate market gets all soft and mushy, many would-be sellers feel that fair market value isn't fair at all. "Why doesn't our house sell?" they ask. "Why can't we get our asking price? It's not fair."

Don't let your highly developed sense of fair play make a sucker out of you. Sellers frequently confuse "fair" with "impartial." Despite its friendly name, fair market value isn't a warm, cuddly fairy godmother. On the contrary, it can be heartless and cruel. Need isn't a component of fair market value. Fair market value doesn't care about any of the following:

>> How much the sellers *need* because they overpaid for their house when they bought it

>> How much the sellers *need* to recover the money they spent fixing up their house after they bought it

>> How much money the sellers *need* to pay off their loan

>> How much money the sellers *need* from the sale to buy their next humble abode: Buckingham Palace

Here's why a seller's *need-based pricing* doesn't enter into fair market value. Suppose that two identical houses next door to each other are listed for sale. One house was purchased for $32,000 three decades ago. The other house sold a couple of years ago for $320,000, soon after home prices peaked in the area. The first home has no outstanding loan on it. The other still has a big mortgage.

Bill and Mary, who own the house purchased 2 years ago, *need* more money than Ed, owner of the house purchased 30 years ago. After all, they paid ten times as much as Ed for their house, and they owe the bank big bucks to pay off their mortgage.

Because the houses are basically identical in size, age, condition, and location, they have the same fair market value. Not surprisingly, they both sell for $275,000. That gives Ed a nice nest egg for retirement but barely pays off Mary and Bill's mortgage. Fair? Ed thinks so. Bill and Mary don't.

Fair market value is brutally impartial. It is what it is — not what buyers or sellers want it to be.

## Median home prices versus fair market value

Some folks think that median sale prices for homes indicate fair market values. They don't.

Organizations such as the National Association of Realtors, the Chamber of Commerce, and private research firms generate *median sale-price statistics* by monitoring home sales in a specific geographic region such as a city, county, or state. One function of these organization is to gather market-research data on home-sales activity.

There's nothing magical about the *median sale price.* It's simply the midpoint in a range of all the home sales for a reporting period. Half the sales during the reporting period fall above the median, and half fall below it. The median-price home, in other words, is the one exactly in the middle of the prices of all the houses that sold.

In the first quarter of 2022, the median sale price of a home in the United States was about $428,700, which tells you that half the homes in the United States sold for more than $428,700, and half sold for less than $428,700. Unfortunately, all you know about this hypothetical median-price home is its price.

You don't know how many bedrooms or baths the median-price home has. Nor do you know how many square feet of interior living space the house has, how old it is, or whether it has a garage or a yard. You don't even know where this elusive median-price house is located, other than that it's somewhere in the United States.

If median-price information is so vague, why bother with it? Because it tells you two important things:

>> **Price trends:** If the median price of a home in America was $238,400 ten years ago and is $428,700 now, you know home prices in general are rising. You don't know why median prices are going up, just that they are.

>> **Price relativity:** If the median-price home in Yakima, Washington, sells for $230,500 versus $661,300 for the median-price Honolulu home, you know that you'll get a much bigger bang for your housing buck in Yakima. Honolulu has many excellent qualities, but cheap housing isn't one of them.

Median-home-price statistics make interesting reading, but they aren't any more accurate for determining specific home values than median-income statistics are for determining how much you'll earn from your next employer. You need much more precise property-value information before you invest a major chunk of your life's savings in a home.

**TECHNICAL STUFF**

U.S. median home prices declined during the late 2000s because of a weak housing market and a large increase in foreclosures. Foreclosures distort regional statistics if counties with a large number of foreclosures are lumped together with other counties that have relatively few foreclosures but are in the same statistical market area. No single report gives a truly comprehensive snapshot of any market.

**TIP**

When median-price statistics indicate that home prices are rising or falling sharply in an area, find out why by reading and talking to players on your real estate team, such as your agent.

# Figuring Out Fair Market Value: Comparable Market Analysis

Believe it or not, houses are like Red Delicious apples. Most houses are green and need more time on the real estate tree before they're ready to pick. A few are ripe for picking right now. The trick is knowing which is which, because houses don't turn red as they ripen.

That's one reason you must understand fair market value and know the asking prices and sale prices of houses comparable to the one you want to buy. Smart home buyers know which houses are green and which are ripe.

## The basics of a helpful CMA

The best way to accurately determine a home's fair market value is to prepare a written *comparable market analysis* (CMA). A competent real estate agent can and should prepare a CMA for a home that you're interested in before you make your purchase offer. Every residential real estate office has its own CMA format. No matter how the information is presented to you, Tables 2-1 and 2-2 show you what good CMAs contain.

**TABLE 2-1**   Sample CMA — "Recent Sales" Section

| Address | Date Sold | Sale Price | Bedrm/Bath | Parking | Condition | Remarks |
|---|---|---|---|---|---|---|
| 210 Oak | 04/30/22 | $390,000 | 3/3 | 2 car | Very good | Best comp. Approx. same size and cond. as dream home (DH), slightly smaller lot. 1,867 sq. ft. $209/S.F. |
| 335 Elm | 02/14/22 | $368,500 | 3/2 | 2 car | Fair | Busy street. Older baths. 1,805 sq. ft. $204/S.F. |
| 307 Ash | 03/15/22 | $385,000 | 3/3 | 2 car | Good | Slightly larger than DH, but nearly same size and condition. Good comp. 1,850 sq. ft. $208/S.F. |
| 555 Ash | 01/12/22 | $382,500 | 3/2.5 | 2 car | Excellent | Smaller than DH, but knockout renovation. 1,740 sq. ft. $220/S.F. |
| 75 Birch | 04/20/22 | $393,000 | 3/3 | 3 car | Very good | Larger than DH, but location isn't as good. Superb landscaping. 1,910 sq. ft. $206/S.F. |

**TABLE 2-2**   Sample CMA — "Currently for Sale" Section

| Address | Date Listed | Asking Price | Bedrm/Bath | Parking | Condition | Remarks |
|---|---|---|---|---|---|---|
| 220 Oak (Dream Home) | 04/25/22 | $395,000 | 3/3 | 2 car | Very good | Quieter location than 123 Oak, good detailing, older kitchen. 1,880 sq. ft. $210/S.F. |
| 123 Oak | 05/01/22 | $399,500 | 3/2 | 2 car | Excellent | High-end rehab. & priced accordingly. Done, done, done. 1,855 sq. ft. $215/S.F. |
| 360 Oak | 02/10/22 | $375,000 | 3/2 | 1 car | Fair | Kitchen & baths need work, no fireplace. 1,695 sq. ft. $221/S.F. |

*(continued)*

**TABLE 2-2** *(continued)*

| Address | Date Listed | Asking Price | Bedrm/Bath | Parking | Condition | Remarks |
|---------|-------------|--------------|------------|---------|-----------|---------|
| 140 Elm | 04/01/22 | $379,500 | 3/3 | 2 car | Good | Busy street, small rooms, small yard. 1,725 sq. ft. $220/S.F. |
| 505 Elm | 10/31/21 | $425,000 | 2/2 | 1 car | Fair | Delusions of grandeur. Grossly overpriced! 1,580 sq. ft. $269/S.F. |
| 104 Ash | 04/17/22 | $389,500 | 3/2.5 | 2 car | Very good | Great comp! Good floor plan, large rooms. Surprised it hasn't sold. 1,860 sq. ft. $209/S.F. |
| 222 Ash | 02/01/22 | $419,500 | 3/2 | 1 car | Fair | Must have used 505 Elm as comp. Will never sell at this price. 1,610 sq. ft. $261/S.F. |
| 47 Birch | 03/15/22 | $409,000 | 4/3.5 | 2 car | Good | Nice house, but over-improved for neighborhood. 2,005 sq. ft. $204/S.F. |
| 111 Birch | 04/25/22 | $389,500 | 3/3 | 2 car | Very good | Gorgeous kitchen, no fireplace. 1,870 sq. ft. $208/S.F. |

These are facts. The CMA's "Recent Sales" section helps establish the fair market value of 220 Oak — your *dream home* that's currently on the market — by comparing it with *all* the other houses that:

>> Are located in the same neighborhood

>> Are approximately the same age, size, and condition

>> Have sold in the past six months

These houses are called *comps,* which is short for *comparables.* Depending on when you began your house hunt, you probably haven't actually toured all the sold comps. No problem. A good real estate agent can show you listing statements for the houses you haven't seen, take you on a verbal tour of the properties, and explain how each one compares with your dream home.

TIP

Communicating well with your agent about subjective terms such as *large, lots of light, close to school,* and so on is critically important. You must understand precisely what the agent means when using such terms. Conversely, your agent must understand precisely what you want, need, and can afford.

TIP

If you and your agent were to analyze the sale comps in the example, you would find that houses comparable to the home you want to buy — 220 Oak, in Table 2-2 — are selling for slightly over $200 per square foot. Putting the sale prices into a price-per-square-foot basis makes comparisons much easier. As you can see in Table 2-2, anything that's way above or below the norm really leaps out at you.

The "Currently for Sale" section of the CMA compares your dream home (in this case, 220 Oak) with neighborhood comps that are *currently on the market.* These comps are included in the analysis to check price trends:

>> **If prices are falling:** Asking prices of houses on the market today will be lower than sale prices of comparable houses. This may be due to an increase of distressed property sales.

>> **If prices are rising:** You'll see higher asking prices today than for comps sold three to six months ago.

If you've been looking at houses in a specific area for a while, you've probably been in all the comps currently on the market in that area. You don't need anyone to tell you what you've seen with your own eyes. However, you do need an agent's help to compare the comps you've seen with comps you haven't seen, because some houses sold before you began your house hunt.

As Table 2-2 shows, your dream house appears to be priced very close to its fair market value based on the actual sale price of 210 Oak (in Table 2-1). Given that 220 Oak has 1,880 square feet, it's worth $392,920 at $209 per square foot. Factually establishing property value is easy when you know how.

**REMEMBER**

Your CMA must be comprehensive. It should include *all* comp sales in the past six months and *all* comps currently on the market. Getting an accurate picture of fair market values is more difficult if some parts of the puzzle are missing, especially in a neighborhood where homes don't sell frequently.

## DISTRESSED PROPERTY SALES

The CMA should also include any distressed property sales. If foreclosures and short sales dominate the area, property values of all houses in the neighborhood are dragged lower. If, however, there have been only one or two distressed property sales in the neighborhood in the past six months, that's probably an aberration that shouldn't affect property values.

Comparing sale prices of owner-occupied, non-distressed properties to sales of bank-owned properties and short-sale properties can be difficult. When a bank takes a house back through foreclosure, the property is very often in poor condition. If that bank-owned property is sold as is, the sale price will be significantly lower than the sale price of an owner-occupied house that is the same age and size but in pristine condition. When doing an appraisal, appraisers adjust prices up or down to reflect the subject property's condition.

*Short sales,* in which a lender agrees to accept less than the outstanding loan balance to satisfy the debt to avoid going through the foreclosure process, present a different challenge. If, for example, you make an offer to purchase a non-distressed property, the seller usually responds to your offer within a few hours or, at worst, a couple of days. In a short sale, however, the seller doesn't have power to approve the sale. The lender must approve the sale. Accordingly, although the seller enters into contract with the buyer, the sale is conditioned upon the lender's approval of price and terms.

Banks generally move much, much more slowly because their representatives are overloaded with cases. It's not unusual to wait 30 to 60 days for a response to your offer on a short-sale property — longer if more than one mortgage lender and private mortgage insurance are involved. The entire short-sale process from start to finish can take six months or, gasp, more. Appraisers make an adjustment if the buyer waited an inordinately long time before closing the sale.

Like milk in your refrigerator, comps have expiration dates. Lenders usually won't accept houses that sold more than six months ago as comps. Their sale prices don't reflect current consumer confidence, business conditions, or mortgage rates. As a general rule, the older the comp, the less likely it is to represent today's fair market value.

Six months is generally accepted as long enough to have a good cross section of comp sales but short enough to have fairly consistent market conditions. But six months isn't carved in stone. If a major economic calamity occurred three months ago, for example, then six months is too long for a valid comparison. Conversely, if homes in a certain area rarely sell, you may need to examine comparable sales that occurred more than six months ago.

REMEMBER

Sale prices are always given far more weight than asking prices when determining fair market value. Sellers can ask whatever they want for their houses; asking prices are sometimes fantasy. Sale prices are always facts — they indicate fair market value. The best proof of what a house is worth is its sale price. Don't guess — analyze the sale of comparable homes. Be sure that the comparable sales information factors in price reductions or large credits given for corrective work repairs (for example, a $5,000 credit from the sellers to the buyers to replace a broken furnace).

## The flaws of CMAs

CMAs beat the heck out of median-price statistics for establishing fair market values, but even CMAs aren't perfect. People can use exactly the same comps and arrive at very different opinions of fair market value. Discrepancies creep into the CMA process if you blindly compare comps without knowing all the following details of the subject properties:

>> **Wear and tear:** No two homes are the same after they've been lived in. Suppose that two identical tract homes are located next door to each other. One, owned by an older couple with no children or pets, is in pristine condition. The other, owned by a family with several small kids and several large dogs, resembles a federal disaster area. Your guess is as good as ours when figuring out how much it'll cost to repair the wear-and-tear damage in the second house. A good comparable analysis adjusts for this difference between the two homes.

>> **Site differences within a neighborhood:** Even though all the comps are in the same neighborhood, they aren't located on precisely the same plot of ground. How much is being located next to the beautiful park worth? How much will you pay to be seven minutes closer to the commuter-train stop? These value adjustments are a smidge less precise than brain surgery.

>> **Out-of-neighborhood comps:** Suppose that in the past six months, no homes were sold in the neighborhood where you want to live. Going into another neighborhood to find comps means that you and your agent must make value adjustments between two different neighborhoods' amenities (schools, shopping, transportation, and so on). Comparing different neighborhoods is far more difficult than making value adjustments within the same neighborhood.

>> **Distressed property sales:** Foreclosures are easy to spot; short sales aren't. A house, for example, may come on the market as a normal owner-occupied property sale. However, sometime while it was being marketed or after an offer had been accepted but before the sale was completed, the house became a short sale because the owners didn't keep up their loan payments. A good agent continually checks the Multiple Listing Service to determine whether any properties you're using as comps became short sales or bank-owned properties. If so, they may not be good comps because they sold under duress. (See the nearby sidebar "Distressed property sales" for more details.)

>> **Non-comp home sales:** What if five houses sold in the neighborhood in the past six months, but none of them were even remotely comparable in age, size, style, or condition to the house you want to buy? You and your agent must estimate value differences for three- versus four-bedroom homes, old versus new kitchens, small versus large yards, garage versus carport, and so on. If the home you want has a panoramic view and none of the other houses has any view at all, how much does the view increase the home's value? Guesstimates like these don't put astronauts on the moon.

These variables aren't insurmountable obstacles to establishing your dream home's fair market value. They do, however, greatly increase the margin of error when trying to determine a realistic offering price. You can minimize pricing problems created by these variables if you and/or your agent actually tour comparable homes inside and out.

**WARNING**

A valid comparison of your dream home to the other houses is impossible if you and your agent have only read about the comps in listing statements (brief data sheets about houses offered for sale) or seen the properties on a website. Here's why:

>> **Most listing statements are overblown to greater or lesser degrees.** You don't know how exaggerated the statement is if you haven't seen the house for yourself. You may consider the "large" master bedroom tiny. That "gourmet" kitchen's only distinction may be an especially fancy hot plate. The "sweeping" view from the living room may exist only if you're as tall as LeBron James. Of course, you won't know any of these things if you only read the houses' puff sheets instead of visiting them in person.

>> **Floor plans greatly affect a home's value.** Two houses, for example, may be approximately the same size, age, and condition, yet vary wildly in value. One house's floor plan flows beautifully from room to room; the rooms themselves are well proportioned with high ceilings. The other house doesn't work well because its floor plan is choppy and the ceilings are low. You can't tell which is which just by reading the two listing statements.

>> **Whoever controls the camera controls what you see.** Keep in mind that when you're viewing those stunning color photos or the video footage of a house advertised on a website, you're permitted to see only what the person who took the pictures wants you to see. You certainly won't get a peek at less desirable things, such as worn areas on the living room carpet or graffiti sprayed on the garage door of the house next door.

REMEMBER

Eyeball. Eyeball. Eyeball. *Eyeballing* — personally touring houses and noting important details both inside and out with your own eyes — is the best way to decide which houses are true comps for your dream home.

# Getting a Second Opinion: Appraisals versus CMAs

If you're in no rush to submit an offer and you're the suspicious type, you can double-check the opinion of value that you and your agent arrive at before making an offer on your dream home. You can pay several hundred dollars to get a professional appraisal of the house.

Getting an *unbiased* second opinion of value is always reassuring. An appraiser won't tell you what you want to hear just to make a sale. The appraiser isn't trying to sell you anything. Whether you buy the house or not, the appraiser gets paid.

WARNING

Unfortunately, the fact that the appraiser charges a fee regardless of whether you buy the house cuts both ways. Suppose that you and the sellers can't reach an agreement on price and terms of sale because the sellers are deluded. Even if your offer isn't accepted, you still get a bill from the appraiser. Paying for appraisals or property inspections before your offer is accepted generally isn't wise.

If you think a professional appraisal is vastly superior to your agent's opinion of value, think again. A good agent's CMA is usually as creditable as an appraisal. Conversely, if a professional appraisal is vastly superior because your agent is a lousy judge of property values, you should get a better agent (find out how to build a team in Chapter 3 of Book 1).

In any given geographical area, appraisers usually don't eyeball nearly as many houses as agents who concentrate on that area. Appraisers aren't lazy; they use their time in other ways.

Formal appraisals are time-consuming. An appraiser inspects the property from foundation to attic, measures its square footage, makes detailed notes regarding everything from the quality of construction to the amount of wear and tear, photographs the house inside and out, photographs comps for the house being appraised, writes up the appraisal, and so on. Agents can tour 15 to 20 houses in the time it takes an appraiser to complete one appraisal.

**REMEMBER**

Because touring properties is so time-consuming, because good agents are already doing the legwork, and because it's usually impossible to tour a home after the sale has been completed, appraisers frequently call agents to get information about houses the agents have listed or sold that may be comps. No matter how good an agent's description of the house is, however, personally touring the property is still best. Any appraisal's accuracy is reduced somewhat whenever the appraisal is based on comps the appraiser hasn't seen.

Agents also call one another about houses they haven't seen, so don't think that appraisers are the only ones who dial for info. However, you're relying on your agent's local market knowledge to help you determine what a home is worth. If your agent hasn't seen most of the comps used in your CMA, get an agent who knows the market.

**TIP**

Unless you're pretty darn unsure about a property's value and willing to spend the money whether or not the deal goes through, don't waste money on a precontract appraisal.

# Why Buyers and Sellers Often Start Far Apart

The average buyer may be brighter than the average seller. How else can you explain why buyers are generally so much more realistic about property prices?

It's not as though there are two different real estate markets: an expensive one for sellers and a cheap one for buyers. Sellers have access to exactly the same comps that buyers do. Yet buyers' initial offering prices tend to be far more realistic than sellers' initial asking prices. Why? Figure 2-1 may offer some insight into that question.

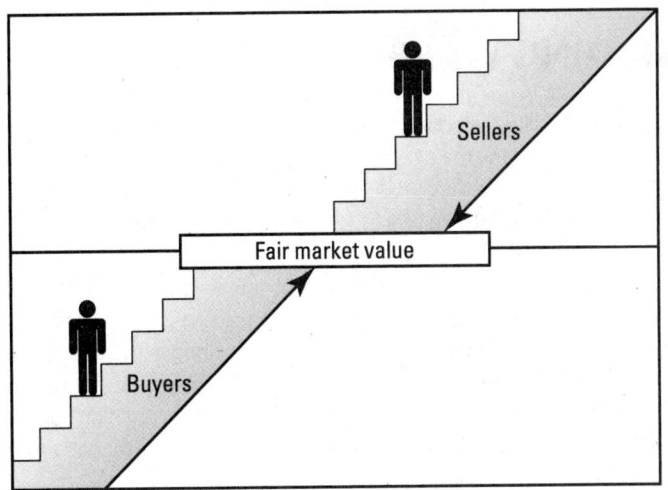

FIGURE 2-1:
How buyers and
sellers approach
fair market value.

Sellers

Fair market value

Buyers

Some people believe that the selfish interests of buyers and sellers force them to approach a house's fair market value from opposite directions. Buyers bring their offering price *up* to fair market value because they don't want to overpay. Sellers ratchet their price *down* to fair market value because they hate the thought of leaving any money on the table.

That's logical but simplistic. This reasoning still doesn't explain why many sellers initially tend to be so much more unrealistic than buyers.

The better you understand the warped thought processes of these sellers, the better you can handle their unreasonable objections to your eminently fair offer. To that end, here are the common causes of absurdly high asking prices.

## Inept agents

Just because *you* use the information in Chapter 3 of Book 1 to select a great agent doesn't mean that everyone will. In fact, many people do a rotten job of picking an agent.

Perhaps the sellers' agent is an incompetent boob who doesn't know anything about property values. Those poor misguided sellers didn't put a smart asking price on their house because their agent gave them lousy advice.

When your agent discovers that the other agent is inept — either by the poor quality of the comps that the sellers' agent used to establish the asking price or by reputation (these things get around in the real estate brokerage community) — what can you do? That depends.

# BIDDING WARS

When house sellers select an agent, the interviewing process may go awry. Bidding wars often develop among the agents competing to list a seller's house for sale. The concept of fair market value is the bidding war's first victim. If you try to buy such a house, you could be the second victim. Here's what happens when a seller interviews agents:

"Thanks for giving me an opportunity to list your lovely house, Mr. and Mrs. Seller," the first agent says. "As you can see by reviewing the CMA, my fair market value analysis indicates that eight houses sold in your neighborhood in the past six months. Three of them were significantly larger than yours, so they can't be used as comps. The five houses comparable to yours in size, age, location, and condition sold in the range of $350,000 to $370,000. Based on their sale prices, I recommend an asking price of $375,000."

Now the second agent strikes. "Who cares what the comps indicate? Your house is painted a particularly attractive shade of turquoise, and your lawn is greener than the lawns of any of those other houses. I suggest starting with a nice, round asking price of $400,000."

Agent three knows that he probably won't get the listing unless he outbids the other two agents. "Our firm's internet marketing program is incredibly successful," he says, oozing confidence. "Through our relocation service and internet referrals, we'll undoubtedly be able to find a buyer willing to pay $425,000."

This technique of successive agents giving ever-higher property valuations is known as *buying a listing*. Sellers, when confronted by the choice of market reality versus fantasy, often succumb to fantasy. They rationalize their decision by telling themselves that the highest bidding agent has the most faith in their house.

That's horse-hockey. If the sellers in this example select the highest bidder, it's because that agent dazzled them with the extra $50,000 they'd get by selecting that agent to sell their house. The agent told them what they wanted to hear. Greed triumphed over reason.

So who wins the bidding war? Not the folks who own the house. If their asking price has no basis in the real world, you won't purchase it. Neither will any other educated buyer.

How can you avoid becoming the victim of a bidding war? You know what we're going to say. Trust the comps to tell you what the house is worth. If the sellers won't listen to reason, move on. Comps don't fantasize. Neither should you.

If the house has been on the market for a month or two and the sellers are open to reason, your agent's brilliant comps will prevail over their agent's fantasy pricing. The sellers will grasp the concept of fair market value and either gratefully accept your offer or make a modest counteroffer because your offering price is so logical, realistic, and fair.

You have a problem, however, if their house just came on the market. The sellers probably won't believe anything you and your agent say about the asking price being too high. They'll discount your opinion of their house's fair market value because they suspect that you're trying to steal their home. They'll be nearly as suspicious of a formal appraisal done by your hand-picked appraiser.

Time cures overpricing by inept agents. The longer the house stays on the market without selling, the more the sellers will doubt their own and their agent's opinion of value.

TIP

If the sellers' house isn't priced to sell and they won't listen to reason, move on to the next house on your list. No telling how long the sellers will take to get smart. Don't put your life on hold waiting for them to wise up. They may be very slow learners.

## Unrealistic sellers

Some sellers get excellent pricing advice from agents — and choose to ignore it. Sellers attempting to sell without an agent often make the same mistake — they opt for the ever-popular need-based pricing method (which is described earlier in this chapter) to set their asking price.

Sellers need time to accept that buyers don't care how much they paid for their house, how much they spent fixing it up, or how much they need to buy their next home. The sellers are stuck with these problems. The buyer isn't.

REMEMBER

Unless an overpriced house has been on the market long enough to bring the sellers back to reality, move on. Most sellers aren't open to reason until they've tried their price for a couple of months or feel external pressure to sell. Trying to reason with such sellers prematurely is like trying to teach a pig how to whistle. Your time is wasted, and the pig gets upset.

## SPOTTING OVERPRICED TURKEYS

Many agents show buyers overpriced houses, but their intention isn't to sell these houses. One of the tactics that smart agents adopt early in their careers is using OPTs (overpriced turkeys) to graphically demonstrate the value of well-priced homes.

Suppose an agent shows you a three-bedroom, two-bath house with a price tag of $299,500 and then takes you to an even more attractive four-bedroom, three-bath home in the same neighborhood *with the same asking price.* The agent doesn't have to say another word — the difference between price and value is glaringly obvious. The OPT makes the sale.

Here's another way to spot OPTs: They get lots of showings but no offers.

# Chapter **3**

# Negotiating Your Best Deal

W hen it comes to buying things, most Americans are lousy negotiators. Negotiation isn't part of our culture. We've been conditioned for generations to be docile buyers who pay whatever price is marked on a can of beans or a TV. Instead of negotiating with someone eyeball-to-eyeball to drive down the price, at best we comparison shop to find the store with the lowest price. (And many time-starved people don't even do that.)

Sure, we can negotiate when our back is to the wall. We haggle over expensive things like cars and dicker with the boss for a raise, but doing so makes us uncomfortable. We walk away from these encounters with the nagging suspicion that we came out on the short end of the deal — that someone else could've done better.

Realizing our nation's discomfort with negotiating, some car dealers have taken the haggling out of buying a car. Instead of using high-pressure sales tactics, these dealers post a sales price on the car — the *no-dicker sticker.* That's their price; take it or leave it. If you take it, you probably won't get the lowest price, but some people think that's a fair trade-off to avoid the unpleasantness of negotiating.

You won't find no-dicker stickers on homes. On the contrary, generally everything from the purchase price to the date that escrow closes is negotiable. Given today's high home prices in most of the densely populated parts of the United

States, buying a home is the ultimate in high-stakes negotiating. Good negotiators come out of a home purchase smiling. Bad negotiators take it in the wallet.

Following the tips in this chapter will give you the negotiating advantage you so richly deserve throughout the home-buying process. And of course, these tips make getting the keys to your dream home faster, easier, and less expensive.

# Understanding and Coping with Your Emotions

Emotion is an integral part of home buying. Real estate transactions are emotional roller coaster rides for everyone involved.

Sometimes, like San Francisco fog, emotion drifts into transactions so quietly that you hardly notice it. More often, however, it thunders into deals like a herd of elephants.

## Examining the forces at work

Consider the forces acting on you during the home-buying process:

>> **You're dealing with people at their most primal level.** Shelter, food, and security are the three most basic necessities of life. Home is where the heart is. Your home is your castle. People become vicious when their homes are threatened. Speaking of primal urges, now you know why looking for a home is called house hunting.

>> **You're playing for large amounts of real money.** Whether this is your first home or your last, it's probably the largest purchase you've ever made. How much you pay for a home isn't the issue. When significant amounts of real money are at risk, the emotional intensity for you and the seller is just as great, whether the house you buy costs $250,000 or $2.5 million.

>> **You're probably going through a life change.** Buying a home would be plenty stressful if you only had to deal with seeking shelter and spending tons of money. Throw in a life change (such as marriage, divorce, birth, death, job change, or retirement), which is often the motivation to purchase a home, and you've created an emotional minefield.

Because eliminating emotions from a home purchase is impossible, the next-best thing to do is recognize and manage them. By all means, share your concerns and frustrations in a productive way with your spouse or a friend who has purchased a home or, better yet, with a good therapist! Bottling up emotions isn't healthy or possible — the longer you stew, the worse the likely explosion is going to be. But the worst thing you can do is vent your frustrations and fears at other people in the transaction — especially the sellers. The folks who do the best job of controlling and properly directing their emotions generally end up getting the best deals.

## Controlling yourself

You can try using these five techniques to control your emotions during the home-buying negotiations:

>> **Put the transaction in perspective.** Which is worse: a failed home purchase or failed open-heart surgery? No matter how badly things go with your real estate transaction, keep reminding yourself that this isn't a life-or-death situation. Tomorrow is another day. The sun will rise again, roses will bloom again, birds will sing again, and children will laugh again. Life goes on. If worse comes to worst, the deal may die, but you'll live on to find another place that you can call home.

>> **Don't let time bully you.** Most life changes have predictable time frames. You have plenty of advance notice on marriages, births, retirements, and the like. Don't put yourself under needless pressure by procrastinating or by creating unnecessary, self-imposed deadlines. Allow yourself enough time to buy a home. Allocate time properly, and it will be your friend rather than your enemy.

>> **Maintain an emotional arm's length.** Keep your options open. Be ready to walk away from a potential house purchase if you can't reach a satisfactory agreement with the sellers on price and terms. Mentally condition yourself to the prospect that the deal may fall through. Houses are like buses: If you miss one, another will come along sooner or later.

>> **Accept uncertainty as a part of your transaction.** Much as you'd like to know everything about a property before making an offer on it, the game is played with incomplete information. You always have far more questions than answers at the beginning of a transaction. Don't worry; you'll be fine as long as you know what things you need to find out and get the answers in a timely manner during your transaction.

» **Stay objective.** Use a comparable market analysis (CMA) to factually establish the fair market value of the home you want to buy (see Chapter 2 in Book 2). A good real estate agent can help you use this information to prepare an equitable offer. If you don't plan to use an agent, consider working with a real estate lawyer. Having someone to buffer you from your unavoidable emotional involvement is helpful if your composure starts to slip. Just make sure you work with professionals who are patient, not pushy, and who are committed to getting you the best deal. (Flip to Chapter 3 in Book 1 for tips on assembling a great real estate team.)

## FIRST THINGS FIRST

Early in coauthor Ray's career, he worked with a buyer who insisted on having every question about a house answered before he'd submit an offer to purchase it. He wanted to structure a flawless offer. Because Ray didn't know any better, he went along with the plan. They spent several weeks fine-tuning the offering price by checking comparable home sales and getting quotes from contractors to do the necessary corrective work that had been discovered during the inspections ordered by a previous prospective buyer.

Unfortunately, Ray and the buyer got a hard lesson in accepting uncertainty because they overlooked one tiny detail; Ray's "buyer" didn't have a signed offer on the house. The seller got tired of their dithering around, endlessly gathering information, and sold the property to someone else.

If you're smart, you'll do what the successful buyer of this home did: Make a deal first. Condition your offer on getting all your questions answered while you have the house "tied up" with a contract.

That way, if everything goes well, you end up the proud owner of a wonderful home. If, however, you can't get a loan, or you don't like the findings of the inspection reports, you can either renegotiate the deal or bail out of the transaction and move on to a more promising home. In the meantime, however, you remove the property from the competition by getting your offer accepted.

Don't waste time getting answers to secondary questions until you answer the primary question: Can you and the seller agree on price and terms of sale? Failure to go for the commitment wastes time and money and may cause you to lose the property.

# The Art of Negotiating

Is negotiating like water or ice? If you said "water," go directly to the head of the class.

**REMEMBER**

Negotiating is fluid, not rigid. There's no one-size-fits-all *best* negotiating strategy that you can use in every home-buying situation. Good negotiators adjust their strategy based on a variety of factors, such as the following:

>> How well-priced a property is

>> How long it's been on the market

>> How motivated the sellers are

>> How motivated you are

>> Whether you're dealing from a position of strength (a buyer's market) or weakness (a seller's market)

## "GOOD" DEPENDS ON YOUR PERSPECTIVE

Brace yourself. You may be shocked by the sellers' response to your offer to buy their home. From your perspective, you made a really good offer. They, on the other hand, may think your offer stinks.

Here, for example, is the perspective of first-time buyers who just blew their budget to smithereens making a $210,000 offer for a home listed at $239,000: "Honey, I'm so nervous. Do you think the sellers will accept our offer? I know their home costs a lot more than we planned to spend, but you know as well as I do that it's the best place we've seen in four months of looking. What's taking them so long to get back to us? The suspense is killing me."

And here's the perspective of the retired couple who got their $210,000 offer: "Calm down, dear. Your face is beet red. Remember your blood pressure. I'm sure that nice young couple didn't mean to insult us. And no matter what you say, I can't believe that they think we're doddering old fools who don't know how much our house is worth. They probably made the best offer they could. Please don't throw it away."

Two entirely different takes on the exact same offer. Buyers generally think that they're paying too much. Sellers usually think that they're giving their house away. When you're playing for real money, these conflicting perceptions fuel emotional fires that heat up the negotiating process.

Negotiating Your Best Deal

Good negotiators, however, apply a few basic principles to every situation. If you understand these principles, you can greatly increase the odds of getting what you want.

# Being realistic

Good negotiators understand that facts are the foundation of successful negotiation. If you want to become a good negotiator, you must see things as they are, rather than as you want them to be. Wishful thinking makes bad negotiation.

What's wishful thinking? A common wish in a rising real estate market, for example, is that you can pay yesteryear's price for today's home. Perhaps you saw a similar house offered for sale at a much lower price six months ago. You ignore the fact that prices have increased since then, which eliminates your chance of buying a home today at the old price. Another common (and generally unrealistic) wish is that you can afford to buy a home similar to the one that you were reared in.

How do you eliminate wishful thinking? By replacing fantasy with facts. Unfortunately, that's easier said than done, because we all inevitably get emotionally involved when we negotiate for something that we intensely desire. Even though that emotional involvement is part of human nature, allowing emotion to seep into a negotiation can cost you dearly.

## The importance of objectivity

Unlike you and the seller, good real estate agents don't take things personally. The seller's agent, for example, won't be offended if your agent reports that you hate the emerald-green paint in the kitchen and the red flocked wallpaper in the den. Your agent, by the same token, won't blow a cork if the seller's agent says that your offer is ridiculously low.

Agents find it easy to be objective. After all, they're not the ones who spent three long weekends painting the kitchen or months looking for just the right wallpaper to put in the den. Neither is it their life's savings on the negotiating table.

Good agents listen to what the market says a house is worth. They don't allow distracting details (such as how much the seller paid for the house ten years ago, or how little you can afford to spend for it today) to confuse negotiations. As you know if you've read Chapter 2 in Book 2, no correlation exists between these need-based issues and the current fair market value of a home.

Some folks think that agents have calculators for hearts. Not true. The good agents know that if they aren't coldly realistic about property values, the home won't sell, and they won't get paid.

## The red flags in agent negotiations

**WARNING**

Doing a lousy job of selecting an agent can cost you big bucks. Bad agents don't know how to determine fair market values; as a result, you may pay too much for your home. And why should the bad agent care? After all, the more you pay, the more your agent makes because agents' commissions are typically a percentage of the purchase price. If your agent pushes you to buy and can't justify the offering price by using comparable home sales, fire your agent and get a good one.

Good negotiators avoid making moral judgments. As long as the seller's position isn't illegal, it's neither immoral nor unfair. It's simply a negotiating position. Of course, agents are human. Sometimes, even the best agents *temporarily* lose their objectivity in the heat of battle. You know this has happened if your agent gets red in the face and starts accusing the other side of being unfair.

If your agent snaps out of the funk quickly, no problem. On the other hand, if your agent can't calm down, you've lost your emotional buffer. Agents who lose their professional detachment are incapable of negotiating well on your behalf.

**TIP**

No matter how satisfying it may be to go on an emotional rampage with your agent about the seller's utter lack of good taste, market knowledge, or scruples, getting angry won't get you the house. If your agent can't maintain a level head, ask your agent's broker (see Chapter 3 in Book 1) to negotiate for you, or get another agent.

## Examining your negotiating style

Finding two people who have exactly the same negotiating style is as unlikely as finding two identical 200-year-old houses. All negotiating styles, however, boil down to variations on one of these two basic themes:

- » **Combative (I win, you lose):** These negotiators view winning only in the context of beating the other side. To them, negotiation is war. They take no prisoners.
- » **Cooperative (we both win):** These negotiators focus on solving problems rather than defeating opponents. Everyone involved in the transaction works together to find solutions that are satisfactory to both sides.

Which negotiating style is better? That depends on the kind of person you are, what your objectives are, and how much time you have.

Most folks opt for cooperation because they know that the world is round — what goes around nearly always comes back either to haunt you or to help you. Why fight battles in some weird game of mutually assured destruction if you can peacefully work together as allies to solve your common problems?

Combative negotiation is tolerated in a strong buyer's or seller's market. The operative word is *tolerated*. People grudgingly play an "I win, you lose" game when they have no alternative. However, in a balanced market that favors neither buyers nor sellers, combative negotiators are usually told, "I won't play your stupid game because I don't like your style."

## FACT VERSUS OPINION

You and the sellers can use exactly the same facts (that is, recent sale prices of comparable houses) and yet reach entirely different opinions of fair market value. As Chapter 2 in Book 2 points out, although houses may be comparable in terms of age, size, and condition, no two homes are identical after they've been lived in.

Furthermore, even though all the houses used in the comparable market analysis are in the same neighborhood, *site differences* (that is, proximity to schools, better view, bigger yard, and the like) usually affect individual property values. Last but not least, even though all the comparable houses were sold during the previous six months, property values can be affected by changes in mortgage rates and consumer confidence.

For example, your agent thinks that 123 Main Street, which sold two months ago for $280,000, is the best comparable *(comp)* for the house that you're trying to buy. The seller's agent agrees that it's a good comp but points out that this house has a two-car garage, whereas 123 Main Street has only a one-car garage. Your agent says that 123 Main Street has a larger kitchen with a breakfast nook and is two blocks closer to the park. The seller's agent says that the property you're considering has higher-quality kitchen cabinets and a new refrigerator, and is three blocks closer to the bus stop.

And so it goes. Everyone agrees on 123 Main Street's sale price and date of sale. These are *facts.* They're the same no matter who looks at them.

But how much value does a second garage space add to the home that you want to buy? Is being closer to the bus stop worth more to you than proximity to the park? Is an eat-in kitchen more or less valuable to you than fancy kitchen cabinets and a new refrigerator? The answers to these questions are *opinions* that are based on your value judgments. Another person would probably value the amenities somewhat differently.

Pricing isn't 100 percent scientific at this level of scrutiny. No two buyers are alike. Each buyer has different needs and, due to those differing needs, will reach different conclusions regarding opinions of value.

Cooperative negotiation, on the other hand, works well under all market conditions because its goal is to scratch everyone's itch. We all enjoy winning and hate losing. People sometimes cry when they're defeated. Problems, on the other hand, never cry when they're solved.

TIP

Unfortunately, some people are born competitors. The only cooperation they understand is the cooperation of a team that's working together to defeat its opponents. If you're a cooperative negotiator, here are two ways to protect yourself from combative negotiators:

>> **Try switching them from combative to cooperative by finding ways you both can win.** Shift their emphasis from beating you to solving the problem. "You want to sell. I want to buy. How can we do it?"

>> **If that fails, deep-six the deal.** If you keep negotiating, born competitors will strip the money from your bank account and the flesh from your bones. They confuse concessions with weakness. If, for example, you offer to split the difference, they'll take the 50 percent you give them as their just due and then go for the rest. They won't be happy until they thrill to a victory that's enhanced by your unconditional defeat. Life's too short to subject yourself to this kind of punishment. No matter how strong a seller's market you must contend with, you can find sellers who are cooperative negotiators — if you try.

## Negotiating with finesse

TIP

Skillful negotiators get what they want through mutual agreement — not brute force. Brute force is crude, rude, ugly, and decidedly unfriendly. Here are some concepts that you may find useful for negotiating with finesse:

>> **Use phones only for making appointments.** Never, never, never let your agent or lawyer present an offer or attempt to negotiate significant issues over the phone. Saying no over the phone is too easy for the sellers. Even if they agree with everything you want, they may change their minds by the time they actually have to sign the contract.

>> **Remember that oral agreements are useless.** In U.S. society, we have *written* contracts because people have notoriously selective memories. If you want your deal to be enforceable in a court of law, put everything about it in writing. Get into the habit of writing short, *dated* MFRs (Memos for Record) of important conversations (such as "June 2 — lender said we'd get 6.0 percent mortgage rate," "June 12 — sellers want to extend close of escrow a week," and so on). Put these notes into your transaction file, just in case you need to refresh your memory. Heed the immortal words of Samuel Goldwyn: "A verbal agreement isn't worth the paper it's written on."

>> **Manage deadlines.** Real estate contracts are filled with deadlines for things like contingency removals, deposit increases, and (of course) the close of escrow. Failure to meet deadlines can have dreadful consequences. Your deal can fall apart — you can even get sued. Most deadlines, however, are flexible — if you handle them correctly. Suppose that you just found out that completing the property inspections will take longer than anticipated. *Immediately* contact the sellers to explain the reason for the delay and then get a *written* extension of the deadline. Reasonable delays can usually be accommodated if properly explained and promptly handled.

## BRUTE FORCE VERSUS STYLE

One particular real estate agent is a superb technician. He's brilliant at determining a home's fair market value; writes flawless contracts; understands financing; and stays current on real estate laws, rules, and regulations. Technically, he's impeccable.

Unfortunately, he has no compassion. He's coldly perfect himself and expects equal perfection from everyone else. He's an ultra-hardball negotiator who neither gives nor expects mercy from his opponents. Some of his own clients don't even like him, but they all respect him because they know that he'll fight ruthlessly on their behalf.

Other agents hate working with this agent *because* he's such a brutal negotiator. They deal with him only when they have absolutely no alternative. If he represents a buyer in a multiple-offer situation, for example, his buyer's offer won't be selected if the selling agent can find any way to work with another buyer whose agent is less combative.

Ray Jones, a San Francisco agent who died several years ago, was this agent's exact opposite. Jones lacked technical polish, but he was kind, fair, and generous, and made folks smile with their hearts. His clients and other agents adored him. In a multiple-offer situation, his buyer's offer was either accepted or at least counteroffered, if possible. He made buying a home fun.

Think carefully when selecting an agent to represent you. People do business with you for only two reasons: because they have to or because they want to. The right agent can give you a negotiating advantage. The ruthless negotiator may make sense for buyers who are in no hurry to buy and who desire to get a good deal on a property. For others, such a piranha can be bad news.

# The Negotiating Process

Negotiation is an ongoing process — a series of steps without a neatly defined beginning and end. Think of water flowing.

Each step in the negotiating process begins by gathering information. After you read this book, you'll understand the various aspects of buying a home (not to mention other types of real estate investing). Then you can translate your information into action that generates more information that in turn leads to further action. And so it goes, until you're the proud owner of your dream home.

One way to begin the first action phase is to get your finances in order, get preapproved for a loan, and select an agent to work with you through the next information-gathering phase. You and your agent then investigate various neighborhoods and tour houses so you know what's on the market. You also figure out the difference between asking prices and fair market values. After you know what houses are really worth, you're ready to focus on the specific neighborhood you want to live in and begin seriously searching for your dream home.

## Making an offer to purchase

After you find your dream home, you're ready for the next action step in the negotiating process: making an offer to purchase. No standard, universally accepted real estate purchase contract is used throughout the United States. On the contrary, purchase contracts vary in length and terms from state to state and, within a state, from one locality to another. When you're ready to write an offer, your real estate agent or lawyer should provide a suitable contract for your area.

Real estate contracts are revised quite often because of such things as changes in real estate law and mandated seller disclosure requirements. A good agent or lawyer will use the most current version of the contract. Check the contract's revision date (usually noted in the bottom-left or -right corner of each page) to make sure you're not using a form just slightly newer than the Declaration of Independence.

**WARNING**

A carelessly worded, poorly thought-out offer can turn what should be a productive negotiation into an adversarial struggle between you and the sellers. Instead of working together to solve your common problem (that is, "you want to buy, and they want to sell — how can *we* each get what *we* want?"), you get sidetracked by issues that can't be resolved so early in the negotiating process.

Although buying a home can be a highly emotional experience, good offers defuse this potentially explosive situation by replacing emotion with facts. Buyers and sellers have feelings that can be hurt. Facts don't. That's why facts are the basis of successful negotiations.

All good offers have three things in common:

>> **Good offers are based on the sellers' most important concern: a realistic offering price.** You shouldn't pull the offering price out of thin air. Instead, base your offering price on houses (comparable to the seller's house in age, size, condition, and location) that have sold within the past six months. As Chapter 2 in Book 2 explains, sellers' asking prices are often fantasy. Actual sale prices of comparable houses are facts. *Focus on facts.*

>> **Good offers have realistic financing terms.** Your mortgage's interest rate, loan origination fee, and time allowed to obtain financing (explained in the next section) must be based on current lending conditions. Some offers get blown out of the water because a buyer's loan terms are unrealistic. *Focus on facts.*

TIP

If you've been prequalified or, better yet, preapproved for a loan, you or your agent should stress that advantage when you present your offer. This proves to the sellers that you're a creditworthy buyer who's ready, willing, and financially able to purchase their house. Flip to Chapter 4 in Book 1 for an introduction to financing a property purchase.

>> **Good offers don't expect a blank check from the sellers.** Unless property defects are glaringly obvious, neither you nor the sellers will know whether any corrective work is needed at the time that your offer is initially submitted. Under these circumstances, it's smart to use property-inspection clauses (explained in the next section) that enable you to reopen negotiations regarding any necessary corrective work *after* you've received the inspection reports.

REMEMBER

Keep in mind that negotiation is an ongoing process. After the *action* of having your offer accepted, your property inspectors gather *information*. After they've determined what's actually required in the way of corrective work, you and the sellers can renew your negotiations *(action)* armed with hard facts *(information)*. This sequence beats wasting time and energy by arguing with the sellers about the cost to complete corrective work before any of you know the precise number of dollars needed to do the repairs. *Focus on facts.*

If the sellers agree with the price and terms contained in your offer, they'll sign it. Their agent should give you a signed copy of the offer immediately. When you actually receive a copy of the offer signed by the sellers, you have what's called a *ratified offer* (that is, a signed or accepted offer). This doesn't mean you own the house or it has been sold. All you can say for now is that a sale is pending.

# Leaving an escape hatch: Contingencies

Even though the sellers have accepted your offer, it should contain extremely important escape clauses known as contingencies, which you cleverly built into the contract to protect yourself. A *contingency* is some specific future event that must be satisfied in order for the sale to go through. It gives you the right to pull out of the deal if that event fails to happen. If you don't remove a contingency, the sale falls apart, and your deposit money is usually returned.

These two contingencies appear in nearly every offer:

>> **Financing:** You can pull out of the deal if the loan specified in your contract isn't approved. Some contracts also have separate property appraisal contingencies that allow you to cancel the deal if a qualified appraiser does not think the home is worth what you've agreed to pay. As noted in Chapter 1 of Book 2, short sales require a special financing addendum.

>> **Property inspections:** You can pull out of the deal if you don't approve the inspection reports or can't reach an agreement with the sellers about how to handle any necessary repairs.

Other standard contingencies give you the right to review and approve such things as a condominium's master deed, bylaws, and budget, as well as a property's title report. You can, if you want, make the deal contingent on events such as your lawyer's approval of the contract, or your parents' inspection of the house. As a rule, no *reasonable* contingency will be refused by the seller.

Don't go overboard with contingencies if you're competing for the property with several other buyers. Sellers, especially in strong real estate markets, don't like offers with lots of contingencies. From their perspective, the more contingencies in an offer, the more likely the deal is to fall apart. You must delicately balance the need to protect yourself with the compelling need to have your offer accepted. Keep your contingency time frames realistic but short. Resolve as many simple questions as possible before submitting the offer. For instance, if your parents insist on seeing the property you want to buy before they'll loan you money for a down payment, take them through the home before making your offer to eliminate that contingency.

If you're considering making your offer subject to the sale of another house (such as the one you're living in now), don't do so if you're in a bidding war with other buyers. Check out the later section "Negotiating from a position of weakness" for reasons why including this type of contingency can cost you the house you're bidding on.

Negotiating Your
Best Deal

Here's a typical loan contingency:

> Conditioned [the magic word] upon buyer getting a 30-year, fixed-rate mortgage secured by the property in the amount of 80 percent of the purchase price. Said loan's interest rate shall not exceed 5.0 percent. Loan fees/points shall not exceed 2 percent of loan amount. If buyer can't obtain such financing within 30 days from acceptance of this offer, buyer must notify seller in writing of buyer's election to cancel this contract and have buyer's deposits returned.

**TIP**

The purchase agreement you sign is meant to be a legally binding contract. As Chapter 3 in Book 1 says, it's wise to put a lawyer on your team immediately if you have *any* concerns about the legality of your contract. Even if you don't have a lawyer when you sign the contract, including the following clause in your offer may be prudent if you have legal questions:

> Conditioned upon my lawyer's review and approval of this contract within five days from acceptance.

Using this clause doesn't mean you actually have to hire a lawyer. It does, however, give you the option of having the contract reviewed later by a lawyer if you want. By the way, good contracts provide space to write in additional terms and conditions.

Include a provision in your contract that specifically states that contingencies must be removed in writing. Doing so should eliminate confusion between you and the sellers regarding whether a contingency has been satisfied.

What good is a ratified offer filled with escape clauses? Well, a ratified offer (riddled with escape clauses or not) ties up the property. You don't have to worry about the owners selling the property to someone else while you're spending time and money inspecting it.

**REMEMBER**

*First* get an agreement on the price and terms of sale — *then* get answers to all your other questions.

## Getting a counteroffer

It's highly unlikely that the sellers will accept your offer as it's originally written. Even if they love your offering price, they'll probably tweak your offer here and there to make it acceptable to them. Sellers use *counteroffers* to fine-tune the price, terms, and conditions of offers they receive.

Suppose you offer $275,000 for a home you like, and you ask to close escrow 30 days after the sellers accept your offer. Because they had the house listed at $289,500, the sellers think that your offering price is a mite low. Furthermore, they need six weeks to relocate.

Instead of rewriting your entire offer, they give you a counteroffer. It states that they're willing to accept all the terms and conditions of your offer except that they want $285,000 and six weeks after acceptance to close escrow.

The ball's in your court once again. You don't mind a six-week close of escrow, but you don't want to pay more than $280,000, so you give the sellers a *counter-counteroffer* to that effect.

Now only one bone of contention remains: the price. The sellers come back to you with a *firm* $284,000. You grudgingly respond at $281,000 and instruct your agent to make it clear to the sellers that you won't go any higher. Two can play the *firm* game. Negotiations now resemble the trench warfare of World War I.

If you really want the home, this phase of the game can be nerve-racking. You worry about another buyer making the sellers a better offer and stealing the house away while you're trying to get the price down that last $3,000. The sellers are equally concerned that they'll lose you by pushing too hard for the final $3,000. You don't want to pay a penny more than you have to. The sellers don't want to leave any money on the table.

You and the sellers are tantalizingly close to agreement on price. Your offering price and the sellers' asking price are both factually based on recent sales of comparable houses in the neighborhood. So why the deadlock? Because sometimes the same facts can lead to different conclusions (see the earlier sidebar "Fact versus opinion").

An equitable way to resolve this type of impasse is to split the difference fifty-fifty. If the sellers in the example use this technique, they'll come back to you with a $282,500 offer — down $1,500 from their *firm* asking price of $284,000 and up $1,500 from your *firm* offering price of $281,000. The mutual $1,500 concession equals less than 1 percent of the home's fair market value based on a $282,500 sale price. That's pinpoint accuracy in a real estate transaction.

**REMEMBER**

Splitting the difference won't work in all situations. It is, however, a fair way to quickly resolve relatively small differences of opinion (a few percent or less of the home's price) so you can make a deal and get on with your life.

# The Finer Points of Negotiating

A perfectly balanced market that favors neither buyer nor seller is rare. The market is almost always in a state of flux. As a result, the playing field usually tilts toward the buyer or seller.

## Negotiating when the playing field isn't level

President Lyndon Johnson was a consummate politician. He'd cajole, promise, arm-twist, flatter, pressure, sweet-talk, threaten, jawbone, wheedle, bully, or horse-trade other politicians into supporting his legislation.

The late president's negotiating skills were legendary. Once, when accused of using somewhat unethical tactics to get the votes required to pass one of his Great Society programs, LBJ just shrugged. "Sorry you feel that way, son," he supposedly said. *"All I ever wanted was my unfair advantage."*

In a perfect world, you'd always have an unfair advantage. Unfortunately, the world is imperfect. No matter how good you are as a negotiator, sooner or later you'll have to negotiate from a position of weakness. The trick in these circumstances is to give yourself every possible advantage.

### Buyer's and seller's markets

In the early 2000s, many home buyers complained bitterly about sellers taking unfair advantage of them. Given the seller's market at that time in many parts of the country, it wasn't unusual for owners of a well-priced house to receive multiple offers on it while their agent was still nailing up the For Sale sign. (Slight exaggeration, but you get the point.) Five years later, the hobnailed boot was on the other foot. Instead of a supply-demand imbalance, there was a demand-supply imbalance. The anguished screams now came from sellers who were complaining about buyers taking unfair advantage of *them*.

REMEMBER

The party in the weaker position always characterizes the market as "bad." Because you're a seeker of wisdom and truth, don't kid yourself. The market is, in reality, neither good nor bad. The market is impersonal. The market is the market. Moaning and groaning about unfair market dynamics won't help you if you're caught in a seller's market any more than complaining helps sellers caught in the viselike grip of a buyer's market.

# Negotiating from a position of weakness

Newly listed homes that are priced to sell often generate multiple offers in a seller's market. But even when the market isn't a seller's market, a well-priced, attractive new listing may draw multiple offers.

**WARNING**

Unless you absolutely *must* have a particular home and price is no object, be careful about entering a bidding war. Such auctions can drive the price of a home above its fair market value. That situation is great for the seller, but it is financially deadly for you.

If you really want a home and you know that other offers will be made, here's how to improve your chances of winning in a multiple-offer situation:

» **Use comparable sales data to predetermine the upper limit of what you'll pay.** Don't get caught up by the excitement of a bidding war and let your emotions override your common sense. Be sure you read Chapter 2 in Book 2 and you know how to determine fair market value. Set no-matter-what limits on the amount you'll bid. Otherwise, you can grossly overpay.

» **Put yourself in the sellers' position.** The sellers don't care how long you've been looking for a home or how little you can afford to pay. Faced with several offers, sellers select the offer that gives them the best combination of price, terms, and contingencies of sale. Find out what the sellers' needs are before making your offer. Their self-interest invariably prevails.

**TIP**

A high purchase price isn't the only way to sweeten a deal. If you have the money, make an extra-large (25 or 30 percent or more of the purchase price) down payment so the sellers know that your loan will surely be approved. Or you can offer to let the sellers rent back their house for a month or two after the close of escrow, or give the sellers an extra-long close of escrow so they have plenty of time to find another home. You can also offer to buy the home "as is" so the sellers won't have to pay for any corrective work. If you do this, however, make your offer contingent on your approval of inspection reports so you can get out of the deal if the house needs too much work.

» **Make your best offer initially.** Buyers who win bidding contests, in the words of Civil War General Nathan Bedford Forrest, get there "firstest with the mostest." If you want the house, don't hold back in a multiple-offer situation: You may never get a second chance to make your best offer.

» **Get preapproved for a loan.** Informed sellers worry about the financial strength of prospective buyers. They don't want to waste their time on buyers who can't qualify for a loan. All other things being equal, if you're preapproved for a loan, you should prevail over buyers whose financial status is in doubt. And if you've been preapproved for a loan, you'll know *you* aren't wasting your time and money on a house that you may not qualify to buy.

>> **Don't make your offer subject to the sale of another house.** As discussed in the earlier section on contingencies, if you own a house that you *must* sell in order to get the down payment for your new home, you're in trouble. You'll most likely be competing with other buyers who don't have that limitation. The sellers have enough problems selling their house without worrying about whether you can sell yours. Why should they take your offer if they can accept one without a subject-to-sale contingency in it? Offers made subject to the sale of another house get no respect in a multiple-offer situation.

TIP

>> **If you must sell in order to buy, put your old house on the market before seriously looking for a new home.** Ideally, you'll have a ratified offer on your old house before making an offer to buy a new place. Then, even with a subject-to-sale clause, your negotiating position will be much stronger. And you won't waste time worrying about how much money you'll have when and if your house sells. Stipulate a long close of escrow on the old house and the right to rent it back for several months after the sale so you'll have adequate lead time to buy your new home.

# Spotting fake sellers

Why would anyone want to be a fake seller? That some people would knowingly waste their time and money on an exercise in futility is absurd.

The key word is *knowingly*. All sellers start out thinking that they're sincere. As the quest for a buyer continues, however, circumstances ultimately prove that some sellers are phony.

Fake sellers cleverly mimic genuine sellers. Like real sellers, counterfeit sellers sign listing agreements, have For Sale signs in their yards, advertise in news-papers, and have open houses on Sundays. They outwardly appear to be the real McCoy. If you don't know how to detect fake sellers, you'll waste your precious time, energy, and money by fruitlessly negotiating to buy a house that isn't really for sale.

Identifying bogus sellers is ridiculously easy once you know how. Here are five simple tests you can use to spot the fakes.

## Are the sellers realistic?

The number-one reason that houses don't sell is that they have unrealistic asking prices. When people categorically state that they "can't" sell a grossly overpriced house, they expose themselves as fakes. What they're actually saying is that they refuse to accept the market's opinion of what their house is worth. People who won't listen to reason aren't sellers — they're property owners masquerading as sellers.

Real sellers may *inadvertently* overprice their homes initially. Unlike fake sellers, however, they eventually wise up. They know they have a problem if they get no offers (or only lowball offers). Authentic sellers accept the relevance of using recent sales of comparable houses in the neighborhood to establish their house's fair market value. Genuine sellers are realistic.

## Are the sellers motivated?

Most folks don't sell their homes to generate commissions for real estate agents. Sellers are usually motivated by a life change, such as wedding bells, a job transfer, family expansion, retirement, or a death in the family. Perhaps the sellers are in contract to buy another home but can't complete the purchase until their house sells. Or their house may be in foreclosure (covered in Book 3). Real sellers always have a motive for selling.

In dire situations, such as an impending foreclosure or divorce, sellers often instruct their agents not to tell anyone why they're selling. If possible, however, find out why the house is being sold *before* making your offer. Knowing the sellers' motivation allows you to shape your offer's terms (that is, quick close of escrow, letting the sellers rent back the house after the sale, and the like) to fit the sellers' circumstances.

Lack of motivation is a gigantic red flag. If the sellers or their agent say that they're testing the market, run as fast as you can in the opposite direction.

## Do the sellers have a time frame?

Deadlines make things happen. Seller deadlines are often established by such things as when the twins are due, when school starts, when they have to begin new jobs in another city, when the escrow is due to close on the new home they're buying, and so on. Authentic sellers always have a deadline by which they must complete their sale.

Time is a powerful negotiating tool. If you aren't under pressure to buy and the sellers must sell immediately (if not sooner), time is your pal and their enemy. Conversely, if you have less than four weeks to find a place to live before the kids start school, the watch is on the other wrist. Ideally, you know the sellers' deadline, but they don't know yours. Most real negotiation occurs at the 11th hour, 59th minute, and 59th second of a 12-hour deadline.

# SOMETIMES, HOMES SELL FOR MORE THAN THE ASKING PRICE

Amy was a buyer who knew precisely what she wanted. Her dream home didn't have to be large. It did, however, need a light and airy feeling, a gourmet kitchen, nice views, a beautiful garden, and a garage. She'd been house hunting a long time because she refused to settle for anything less than her dream home.

Amy had a good agent. When a house that met all of Amy's specifications was listed at $295,000, Amy and her agent were waiting at the front door on the first day the house was opened for inspection.

They weren't alone. The home was mobbed with drooling buyers and agents. Everything about the property, including its finely honed price, was flawless. The house was definitely priced to sell.

The listing agent told everyone that offers would be accepted in two days. Given the high level of buyer interest, Amy's agent knew there would be multiple offers. She suggested that Amy could probably beat the competition by offering $5,000 over the asking price. Based on the sale price of comparable houses in the neighborhood, the agent said the home was priced at (or perhaps slightly below) its fair market value. If all the other offers came in right at full asking price, Amy's $300,000 offer would stand out from the crowd.

Amy refused. Why, she reasoned, spend an extra $5,000 if she didn't have to? A full-price offer certainly wouldn't insult the sellers. If that wasn't enough money, Amy was sure that the sellers would give her a counteroffer.

She was wrong. The sellers didn't counter any of the many offers they received. Instead, they simply accepted the highest offer, which wasn't Amy's.

Amy took a calculated risk. She could've been right. In fact, there have been multiple-offer situations in which not one of the offers was close to full asking price. Multiple offers are no guarantee that a house will sell at or over its asking price.

Each situation is different and must be evaluated on its own merits. And don't forget to look at the comparable sales data.

**WARNING**

You can be in deep trouble if you have a deadline and the sellers don't. If you reveal this information to the sellers, they may use your deadline to beat you to a pulp. Beware of procrastination. Don't let time bully you — and keep your deadlines to yourself.

## Are the sellers forthright?

Genuine sellers are disarmingly candid about their house's physical, financial, and legal status. They know that withholding vital information endangers the sale and may lead to a lawsuit. Early disclosure of possible problems, on the other hand, gives everyone the lead time required to solve them. Real sellers don't have a "buyer beware" mindset.

REMEMBER

If you keep getting nasty surprises, you're working with fake sellers. Straight-forward folks have only one defense against devious sellers who are playing an expensive, and possibly even devastating, game of "I've Got a Secret": Terminate the transaction.

## Are the sellers cooperative?

Real sellers look for ways to make transactions go more smoothly. They work with you to solve problems rather than waste time trying to figure out who's to blame if something goes wrong. Genuine sellers have a let's-make-it-happen attitude. They're deal makers, not deal breakers.

WARNING

Inconsistent behavior is a red flag. If the sellers suddenly start missing contract deadlines or become strangely uncooperative, they may have lost their motivation to sell. Perhaps the wedding was postponed or the new job fell through. What-ever the reason, people sometimes switch from being real sellers to being fakes in mid-transaction. Find out why the sellers are acting strangely as soon as you notice the change, and you may be able to head off the problem. If you ignore the danger signs, you'll never know what hit you when the deal blows up in your face.

# Lowballing

A *lowball* offer is one that's far below a property's actual fair market value. An example of a lowball offer is a $200,000 offer on a house that's worth every penny of $250,000.

Who makes lowball offers? Sometimes, it's a graduate from one of those scuzzy, get-rich-quick real estate seminars. Another lowball offer may come from some-body who's bottom-fishing for sellers in dire financial distress. More often, how-ever, lowballing is a negotiating tactic used by people who state categorically, "No one ever pays full asking price. You always have to start low to end up with a fair price."

Those statements aren't true, of course. When you do your homework, you know the difference between well-priced properties and overpriced turkeys. (See Chap-ter 2 in Book 2 for a brush-up.)

## Why lowballing is usually a bad idea

As discussed earlier in this chapter, lowballing a well-priced house breaks the first rule of a good offer: Make a realistic offering price based on the sale price of comparable houses. Because skillful negotiators understand both sides of the issue, imagine that you're the seller of a house that's priced as close as humanly possible to its fair market value.

Several days after your house goes on the market, you receive an offer with an absurdly low purchase price. After the vein in your neck stops pounding, what conclusions can you form about the lowballing buyers?

>> **Taken in the best possible light, the buyers obviously haven't done their homework regarding comparable home sales.** Because they're grossly ignorant about fair market value, why should you try to educate them?

>> **Maybe the buyers think you don't know what your house is really worth and are trying to exploit your ignorance.** (That vein starts throbbing again.)

>> **Perhaps the buyers are trying to steal your house based on a mistaken impression that you're desperate to sell.** There's a name for critters that prey on misfortune: *vultures.*

None of these conclusions is at all favorable. As a seller, you'd probably make one of the following responses to buyers who lowballed your well-priced house:

>> **Let the buyers know their offer is totally unacceptable by having your agent return it with a message that you wouldn't sell your house to them if they were the last buyers on earth.** Why make a counteroffer to people who are either idiots or scoundrels?

>> **Make a full-price counteroffer.** To show your contempt for the buyers, you'll hardball them on each and every term and condition in their offer. (Two can play this game.)

REMEMBER

Buyers who lowball a well-priced property listed by sellers who can wait for a better offer destroy any chance of developing the mutual trust and sense of fair play on which cooperative negotiation is based. Bargaining is fine, but you must find a motivated seller and not aim too low. Starting at 25 percent below what the home is worth generally won't work unless the seller is desperate.

## When low offers are justified

There's a huge difference between submitting an offer that's at the low end of a house's fair market value and lowballing. Suppose you offer $280,000 for a home listed at $299,500. You base your offering price on the fact that comparable houses in the neighborhood recently sold in the $280,000-to-$295,000 price range. You're at the low end of the range of fair market values. The sellers are at the high end. You're both being realistic.

If your offer is based on actual sales of comparable houses, it won't insult the seller. Such a low offer will, however, spark lively debate as both of you attempt to defend your respective prices. Coming in on the low side of a property's fair market value is fine as long as you have plenty of time to negotiate and reason to believe that the seller is motivated.

TIP

In situations like the preceding one, your best bet is to have an encyclopedic comparable market analysis and an agent who has *personally* eyeballed all the comps. Follow the guidelines discussed in Chapter 2 of Book 2.

A low offer is justified only when it isn't a *lowball* offer. Ironically, some sellers provoke low offers by their unwise pricing. These sellers insist on leaving room to negotiate in their price because they "know" that buyers never pay full asking price.

Sound familiar? This practice, unfortunately, becomes a self-fulfilling prophecy. When buyers who know property values make an offer on an overpriced house, their initial offering price is usually on the low side to give themselves room to negotiate. What goes around comes around.

Suppose that a house's fair market value is $300,000. If the sellers put this house on the market at $360,000 so they'll have a 20-percent negotiating cushion, and you offer $240,000 for the same reason, you and the sellers start out $120,000 apart. It takes a heap of extra negotiating to bridge a gap that big.

TIP

Don't play their silly game unless you have time to squander. Make your initial offer at the low end of the house's fair market value and see how the sellers respond to it. If they refuse to accept the hard evidence of recent comparable home sales in the neighborhood, don't waste valuable time trying to educate them. They aren't sellers yet — they're property owners masquerading as sellers. If you want the house, bide your time. Don't make your move until they wise up and lower their price, or their agent puts the word out that they're motivated sellers who won't turn down any reasonable offer.

## Negotiating credits in escrow

Putting a "let's sell it" price on a house isn't always enough to get the house sold, especially in a buyer's (weak) market. Sellers often find that they have to give buyers money in the form of seller-paid financial concessions in order to close the deal. The two most common concessions are for nonrecurring closing costs and corrective work.

## Nonrecurring closing costs

Some sellers come right out and tell you that they'll pay your nonrecurring closing costs if doing so will help put a deal together. *Nonrecurring closing costs* are one-time charges for such things as your appraisal, loan points, credit report, title insurance, and property inspections. Closing costs can amount to 3 to 5 percent of the purchase price.

TIP

Even if the sellers don't offer to pay your nonrecurring closing costs, asking for this concession as one of the terms in your offer *usually* won't hurt. Two general exceptions to this rule are when it's a seller's (strong) market or when you're in a multiple-offer situation.

Here's how the credit works. Say you've signed a contract to buy a $250,000 house. You have $55,000 in cash, and the escrow officer has just told you that you'll have nonrecurring closing costs totaling 4 percent ($10,000) of the purchase price.

About now, you may be wondering, "Why not just reduce the purchase price to $240,000 instead of asking the sellers for a $10,000 credit?" After all, the sellers' net proceeds of the sale are the same either way, and simply reducing the purchase price is less complicated. Not to mention that because property taxes are often based on the purchase price, a lower purchase price will probably cut your annual tax bite.

The reason: If you're short of cash, as most buyers are, a credit is more helpful than a price reduction. If you have to pay $10,000 in closing costs, you won't have enough cash left to make a 20 percent ($48,000) down payment on your $240,000 home. With less than 20 percent down, your monthly loan costs increase because you have to pay a higher interest rate on your mortgage plus private mortgage insurance (PMI) costs. Neither will you have any cash left over for emergencies. Under these circumstances, you'd probably decide to buy a less expensive house.

Contrast that scenario with paying $250,000 for the house and getting a credit from the sellers for nonrecurring closing costs. After putting 20 percent ($50,000) cash down to get the loan with the lowest interest rate, you still have $5,000 in the bank thanks to the $10,000 credit. The credit makes the deal happen.

TIP

If you have plenty of cash, get a price reduction rather than a credit. In most areas, the lower your purchase price, the lower your annual property taxes. Just be aware that some less-than-scrupulous agents will lobby for the credit because a price reduction cuts into their commissions.

## Corrective work

Typically, neither you nor the sellers know how much, if any, corrective work is needed when you submit your offer. Therefore, purchase contracts have provisions for additional negotiations regarding corrective-work credits *after* all the necessary inspections have been completed.

If the property inspectors find that little or no corrective work is required, you have little or nothing to negotiate. Suppose, however, that your inspectors discover the $250,000 house you want to buy needs $25,000 of corrective work for termite and dry-rot damage, foundation repairs, and a new roof. Big corrective-work bills can be deal killers.

**TIP**

Seeing is believing. It's strongly recommended that you and the seller's agent be present, if possible, during property inspections so you both actually see the damage. And when you receive the inspection reports, use them as negotiating tools. Give the sellers copies of the reports for them to review before you meet with them to negotiate a corrective-work credit.

This is the moment of truth in most home sales. Sellers usually don't want to pay for the corrective work. Neither do you. The deal *will* fall through if this impasse can't be resolved.

At this point in the negotiations, it's critical that the sellers realize that the value of their house has just been reduced by the cost required to repair it. If comparable houses with no termite or dry-rot damage, with solid foundations, and with good roofs are selling for $250,000, the sellers' house is worth only $225,000 in its present condition. Given its reduced value, an 80 percent loan is $180,000 — not $200,000 based on a $250,000 fair market value. If you can borrow only $180,000 and the sellers refuse to reduce the selling price from $250,000 to $225,000, you have to drop out of the deal.

The sellers may refuse to pay for repairs found by inspectors that you've hired. The sellers may question the impartiality or validity of your inspection reports and order their own inspections to verify or refute yours. The sellers may even threaten to pull out of the contract if you don't back off on your demands.

Sellers who try to punish the messenger are usually making a big mistake. You didn't bring the damage with you when you came, and (luckily for you) you won't take it with you when you go. Like it or not, the sellers are stuck with it. If they drive you away, they may still have a legal obligation to tell other buyers what you've discovered. That disclosure will probably lower the price that any future buyer will pay for their house. All things considered, working things out with you will probably be faster (and no more expensive) than waiting for another buyer.

Lenders also participate in corrective-work problems. They get copies of inspection reports when borrowers tell them that a serious repair problem exists, when their appraisal indicates a property obviously needs major repairs, or when the purchase contract contains a credit for extensive repairs. Whenever the property's loan-to-value ratio exceeds 80 percent, lenders actively help buyers and sellers resolve corrective-work problems.

You can solve repair problems in a variety of ways:

>> **Ideally, the sellers leave enough money in escrow to cover the required corrective work with instructions for the escrow officer to pay the contractors as their work is completed.** This strategy has several advantages. You can supervise the work to be sure that it's done properly by contractors of your choice. The sellers don't have to suffer through having the work done while they're living in the house, and they don't have to incur any liability for the workmanship. Last but not least, the lender knows the work will be done.

>> **Alternatively, the lender withholds a portion of the full loan amount in a passbook savings account until the corrective work has been completed.** In cases involving major corrective work, the lender may refuse to fund the loan until the problems have been corrected.

>> **The sellers may give a credit for corrective work directly to buyers at the close of escrow.** Lenders usually don't approve of this approach, because it raises uncertainties about whether the corrective work will actually be completed. If it isn't, the security of the lender's loan is impaired.

You can make the sellers feel better by offering to get competitive bids on the work from several reputable, licensed contractors. As long as the lowest bidder will do a quality job in a timely fashion, you and the sellers benefit. This additional effort on your part shows the sellers that you don't want to get rich off their misfortune. All you want is what you thought you were buying in the first place: a well-maintained home with a good foundation and a roof that doesn't leak. Empathy is an excellent negotiating tactic.

# 3

# Investing in a Foreclosure Property

# Contents at a Glance

**IN THIS CHAPTER**

» **Brushing up on the differences in how foreclosures are handled**

» **Investigating the early missed-payment pre-foreclosure period**

» **Finding opportunities in the Notice of Default stage**

» **Arriving at the foreclosure auction stage**

» **Waiting out post-foreclosure, from redemption to eviction**

Chapter **1**

# Getting Up to Speed on the Foreclosure Process

A common foreclosure myth is that it's a one-time event. Homeowners miss a mortgage payment or two, and the lender swoops in and scoops up the property. The fact is that foreclosure is typically a long, drawn-out legal process that begins with missed payments, proceeds through some sort of legal system, and often results in homeowners losing their homes.

An understanding of the foreclosure process reveals the various stages at which you can purchase properties. By knowing what to expect, you can often maximize your opportunities while minimizing costly mistakes.

This chapter provides a road map of the foreclosure process, beginning with a notice to the homeowners and the public of missed mortgage payments and ending with the homeowners relinquishing possession of the property. Anywhere along the way, the homeowners have options to interrupt the process and regain control of the property. This chapter points out these opportunities to help you better assist homeowners in making choices and to warn you about what homeowners can do to derail your plans.

**REMEMBER**

Homeowners find themselves facing foreclosure for any number of reasons, including long-term illness or disability, overspending, substance abuse, divorce, and gambling, to mention only a few. As a real estate investor, you gain nothing by judging people in foreclosure. The best way to approach homeowners in foreclosure is with respect and empathy, offering solutions that enable them to leave the past behind and build a more solid financial future.

# Identifying the Foreclosure Process in Your Area

The end result of foreclosure is that the homeowners lose ownership and ultimately lose possession of their property. That's true no matter where you're buying foreclosure properties. But different states and counties follow different foreclosure procedures. The two main procedures are

>> Foreclosure by trustee sale, also referred to as *foreclosure by advertisement*

>> Foreclosure by judicial sale, also referred to as *judicial foreclosure*

The following sections describe these two types of foreclosure. Counties may also have their own local rules for how the sale is carried out, so visit your county courthouse (the Register of Deeds office), and ask for an explanation of the rules and regulations. You should also sit in on a few auctions before bidding on anything.

## Foreclosure by trustee sale

A few more than half of the states follow the trustee-sale route. When the homeowners purchase a property in one of these states, the county issues a sheriff's deed that the trustee (which may be the sheriff in some areas) holds in trust until the mortgage is paid in full. After paying off the mortgage, the trustee releases the deed to the homeowners.

If the homeowners default on the payment, the lender can notify the trustee to initiate foreclosure proceedings. Then the trustee can sell the property and transfer the proceeds to the lender as payment of the loan. Because the foreclosure doesn't need to progress through the courts, foreclosure by trustee sale is typically much faster than foreclosure by judicial sale.

## Foreclosure by judicial sale

Fewer than half the states follow a judicial foreclosure process. As the name implies, judicial foreclosure passes through the justice system: the state (circuit) or district court. When the homeowners default on their mortgage, the lender files a claim to recover the unpaid balance of the loan from the borrowers. The courts decide the case, which usually takes a long time to resolve — typically four to six months, but sometimes up to a year. During this time, unless the homeowners work out a payment plan or some other solution with the lender, they're almost guaranteed to lose their home.

# Exploring the Missed-Payment Notice Stage

Some lenders initiate foreclosure proceedings as soon as the homeowners miss one or two payments. Other lenders start sending reminder notices, often following a predictable timeline:

>> **Two-week notice:** Some lenders give homeowners a two-week grace period, after which they begin to start calling the homeowners or sending them letters.

>> **30-day notice:** When a payment is so late that it's time for the next payment, the lender gets a little jittery and ramps up its efforts. The lender may even begin levying late-payment fees.

>> **45-to-60 days' notice:** Unless the homeowners contact the lender and work out some new payment agreement, the lender typically sends out a certified letter insisting that the homeowners pay up.

>> **90-day limit:** If the homeowners still haven't contacted the lender or shown any commitment to make good on the loan, the lender typically initiates formal foreclosure proceedings. At this point, the lender transfers the matter to outside legal counsel (an attorney), and the attorney in charge posts a foreclosure notice, sometimes referred to as a Notice of Default (NOD). As soon as the attorney starts foreclosure by advertisement, these legal notices or advertisements begin to attract investors.

**REMEMBER**

The missed-payment notice stage, before the start of foreclosure proceedings, is the best time for homeowners to act and the best time for you to step in to assist them. Usually the homeowners' best option is to sell the property, cut their losses, and find more-affordable housing. With your assistance, the homeowners still have time at this stage to take advantage of this option.

# Getting Serious: The Notice of Default

For investors, the foreclosure process officially kicks off with the posting of the NOD or foreclosure notice in the county's legal newspaper or the local newspaper — private, for-profit publications that get the word out to prospective bidders. At this point, distressed homeowners usually realize the inevitability of losing their property. Some remain in denial; others become resigned to the fact, even though they may have several options to abort the foreclosure process and regain control of their property . . . and their finances.

TIP

If you plan on purchasing properties before the foreclosure sale, your best chance is to contact the homeowners before the NOD is posted. After the NOD appears in the papers or in legal publications, competition for the property begins to heat up. The only way to find distressed homeowners before the NOD is posted is through word-of-mouth networking. See Chapter 2 in Book 3 for additional guidance on choosing the stage of the foreclosure process that's right for you.

# Proceeding to the Foreclosure Sale

Before the foreclosure sale, the homeowners can work with the lender or their attorney to delay or cancel the foreclosure sale. In other words, just because you see a foreclosure notice in the local paper doesn't mean that if you show up for the sale, that property is going to be auctioned off.

TIP

Calling the attorney who's in charge of the foreclosure before the sale is a great way to find out whether the property is going to be offered at the sale. The attorney's name is usually listed on the foreclosure notice.

REMEMBER

At the foreclosure sale, you have an opportunity to bid against other investors for any properties that are being auctioned off. Some auctions have open bidding; others use a sealed bid system. However your county chooses to hold its auctions, a few words of advice can assist you in acquiring properties and not losing your shirt:

>> Sit in on at least five auctions before bidding to get a feel for the process and to gather information.

>> Research the property thoroughly before you bid.

>> Buy only senior liens (first mortgages). You can really get burned buying junior liens because foreclosure typically wipes them off the books. When you have more experience and knowledge, you can start working the junior-lien circuit and tax liens.

» Set a maximum bid, and never ever exceed that amount, no matter how juiced up you get at the auction.

» When you plan to bid, show up with a cashier's check. Most auctions require payment at time of purchase or within an hour.

# Halting the Foreclosure Process

Distressed homeowners are plagued by a swarm of emotions, ranging from disbelief and resentment to shame and guilt. They may have several options to stop the foreclosure process, but they're too upset and confused to think clearly or explore their options, and they're so angry or fearful that they hesitate to contact the lender to work out a solution.

The following sections introduce various ways that homeowners in foreclosure can stop or delay the foreclosure process. Use this information not only to better assist distressed homeowners, but also to prepare yourself for the possibility that the homeowners may choose to cut you out of a promising deal by successfully negotiating with the lender or another investor.

**REMEMBER**

Encourage the homeowners to contact their lender, even if this action results in your losing a prospective property. Never supply misleading information to discourage homeowners from taking the action that's best for them. Be a real estate investor, not a con artist. In addition to keeping you out of legal trouble, acting with integrity establishes goodwill with the homeowners and leads to future referrals.

## Reinstating the mortgage

Before the foreclosure auction, homeowners who can get their hands on enough cash may have the option to *reinstate the mortgage,* which consists of making up for all missed payments and paying any late fees or other penalties.

To reinstate the mortgage, the homeowners must contact the lender before the auction date to verify that reinstatement is an option. If the option is available, the homeowners must work out a payment schedule with their lender.

**TIP**

If you're trying to assist distressed homeowners in finding a solution and you're running out of time, the homeowners can file for bankruptcy to buy more time. See the later section "Filing for bankruptcy" for details.

## A SMOOTH OPERATOR

A real estate investor once purchased a property at a sheriff sale and did everything he could to contact the homeowner. He even tried to drop in for a personal visit, but she slammed the door in his face as though she knew who he was and had been expecting him.

Later, the investor discovered that a con artist named Brian had gotten to her during the redemption period. He established some sort of emotional connection with the homeowner, took her to the county building to pick up the overbid (the money the investor paid for the property at auction in excess of what was owed on it), and convinced her that he could save her house for her.

Brian bought her a vacuum cleaner and a few groceries in exchange for her signature on a *quitclaim deed* — a document signing away her rights to the property. He videotaped her making statements that he thought would protect him legally.

With quitclaim deed in hand, Brian redeemed the property, and the investor got his money back. Then Brian sold the property to an investor named Ray. Ray came to the original investor's office. Without knowing what had transpired, the original investor bought the property and sold it to another investor. When that investor showed up at the homeowner's house to work out a rental agreement with her, he learned about the con job and wanted nothing to do with the property.

Eventually, the matter wound up in court. The original investor bought the property back from the other investor and gave the homeowner some money so that she could move to a more-affordable home. While in court, the investor got a $100,000 judgment against Brian. Last the investor heard, Brian was scheduled for a creditors' hearing.

Never take advantage of homeowners for your own benefit. After all, this property is their home, and any equity they have in that home is theirs. Commit to becoming a champion of the homeowners. If you can help them and earn some compensation for your assistance, everybody wins. Quick money never lasts. By acting with integrity and in the best interest of the homeowners, you provide a much-needed service to a suffering portion of your community.

## Requesting and receiving a forbearance

When homeowners have a temporary loss of income with the promise of regaining their financial footing, the lender may agree to a *forbearance*, in which the homeowners can delay payment for a short period or negotiate a payment plan to make up for missed payments over the course of several months, as explained in the following section.

The lender may also offer some sort of combination between a forbearance and reinstatement, enabling homeowners to delay payment for a short period and then bring their payments current by a specific date.

TIP

The phone number on the mortgage payment coupons may put you in contact with the loan servicer that processes the payments instead of the lender that actually owns the loan. The loan servicer may not offer much assistance, so ask the loan servicer who the lender is and contact the lender directly.

## Making a mortgage modification or repayment plan

To enable financially strapped homeowners to make up missed payments slowly, a lender may agree to a mortgage modification or repayment plan:

>> A *mortgage modification* consists of adding the past-due payments and penalties to the remaining principal, so the homeowners pay off the past-due amounts and penalties over the life of the loan. This arrangement is commonly known as adding amounts due to the back of the loan.

>> A repayment plan enables the homeowners to submit payment of a portion of their past-due amount and penalties with future payments until the past-due amount and penalties are paid off.

WARNING

When homeowners are already having trouble making their monthly mortgage payments and don't have the resources to cover higher payments, mortgage modification and repayment plans are rarely ideal solutions. Often, these options simply delay the inevitable.

## Filing for bankruptcy

WARNING

Filing for bankruptcy sounds like a permanent solution to a significant financial predicament like foreclosure, but it's not the ideal solution. It destroys the homeowner's credit rating for seven years or so and doesn't exactly wipe all debt off the books. Bankruptcy simply relieves some of the debt burden and provides homeowners some extra time to restructure their remaining debt.

Bankruptcy is one more option for distressed homeowners, however, and it's certainly something you should know about as a foreclosure investor. By filing for bankruptcy at least a couple of days before the auction date, a homeowner can delay the foreclosure process and leave a property that you've already purchased in limbo — at least until the foreclosure trustee and the courts sort out all the legal issues.

Bankruptcy is another opportunity for real estate investors. As the trustee or courts decide how to liquidate the property, you may be able to step in and work with the lawyers and trustee to purchase the property and make their lives a little easier.

## Agreeing to a deed in lieu of foreclosure

When homeowners have very little to no equity or even negative equity built up in their property, and they have no hope of turning the financial tide, they may offer the lender a *deed in lieu of foreclosure.* The homeowners agree to sign their deed over to the lender and give them the keys to the property without having to go through a messy public foreclosure process.

Although this approach may give the homeowners a less-embarrassing escape route, it often leaves the lender with a property that it doesn't want, along with the expense of repairing and rehabbing the property and then selling it. As an investor, you may be able to step in as the ultimate middleman, negotiate with the lender, getting it to accept less than the full loan amount due (what real estate insiders call a *short sale*), and still provide the homeowner a clear escape route.

Some investors around the country make a really good living just working short sales. If you can't purchase a foreclosure property for a low-enough price to make a profit, negotiating a short sale can make the deal more profitable. Keep in mind, however, that lenders won't agree to short sales if they foresee the homeowners walking away with money, and you shouldn't negotiate a lower payoff to put money in the pockets of the homeowners.

## Getting one last chance during the redemption period

Reasonable people would assume that when they buy a property at a foreclosure sale, it's automatically their property, but that's not always the case. Many areas of the country have a mandatory redemption period, which can last from a few months to an entire year.

During the redemption period, the person who purchased the property at the sale is responsible for insuring the property and paying the property taxes, but the foreclosed-upon homeowners have the right to redeem the property. To do so, the homeowners must come up with enough cash to pay off the mortgage in full, along with any interest and penalties and, in some cases, the investor's expenses.

**WARNING**

Depending on the rules that govern redemption in your area, the buyer may or may not have the right to recover expenses (including property taxes and insurance) from the homeowners. Consult your real estate attorney to find out exactly what you're allowed to recover if the homeowners redeem the property. (See Chapter 3 in Book 1 for details on finding an attorney and other members of your real estate team.)

**REMEMBER**

If you purchase a property at a foreclosure sale in an area that has a mandatory redemption period, you end up with the property about 50 percent of the time. The only sure way to end up with the property is to buy in markets that don't have redemption periods. To protect your investment in areas that have a redemption period, take the following precautions:

» If possible, repair any defects in the house that may be considered to be unsafe or lead to further deterioration of the property. If the property is vacant and unsafe, and you don't take care of the problem immediately, the property is likely to lose value. Avoid investing any more money in repairs than is absolutely necessary; if someone redeems the property, you stand to lose that money.

» Insure the house and file an affidavit of payment so that if the homeowners redeem the property, you have a better chance of recouping your expenses. Consult your real estate attorney to determine your rights to recover expenses.

» Pay the property taxes, and file an affidavit proving payment.

» Don't invest in any renovations. If the homeowners redeem the property, you could lose all the money you invested in the renovations. Generally, you perform repairs only to protect your investment if the house is vacant or if you've worked out an arrangement with the occupants to ensure that you won't lose any money you invest in the property. Different states may have different abandonment laws that may restrict you from doing anything. Your real estate attorney can provide guidance here.

» Keep an eye on the property to protect it from vandalism and theft. Some disgruntled homeowners may strip the property before vacating it.

All sales aren't final in areas with redemption periods. If you miss out on an opportunity during the foreclosure sale, you haven't necessarily lost the property for good. The homeowners still control the property, and you can work with them to bump the investor who purchased the property out of the deal. The knife cuts both ways, of course: You could end up getting bumped. You get your money back, but you lose out on the property.

## LOSING OUT ON A JUNIOR LIEN

One real estate investor bought a first mortgage (senior lien) at the first foreclosure sale on a property for $25,000. Another investor bought the second mortgage (junior lien) for $25,000. Thinking that he had the property in the bag, the second invenstor spent another $25,000 during the redemption period renovating the house, so now he had $50,000 invested in a property that was worth about $100,000.

That sounds like a good deal, but the second investor made a huge mistake: He failed to pay off the senior lien, which the first investor held. The second investor could have redeemed the $25,000 senior lien that the first investor held, sold the property for $100,000, and made a $25,000 profit, but he forgot to redeem the senior lien.

The first investor took possession of the house and put it up for sale. The other investor called, understandably upset because he was convinced that the house was his. The first investor had to explain that due to the second investor's oversight, the house was not in fact his.

The moral of the story is that if you buy a junior lien attempting to control the senior lien, be sure that you redeem that senior lien.

# Finalizing the Foreclosure: Ushering the Previous Owners out the Door

Eviction is an unpleasant experience for both the evictor and the evictee, so you want to do everything you can, within reason, to encourage the previous home-owners to vacate voluntarily. Offer them an incentive package — a free dumpster, use of a moving van, relocation expenses, or whatever else they need — to put this problem behind them and move on to a potentially rosier future.

If that approach doesn't work, you have no option but to file a request with the district court to have the homeowners evicted. After you file your request, assuming that it's approved, the sheriff's office delivers the homeowners an eviction notice stating the date on which the eviction will occur. On that date, if the home-owners haven't vacated the premises, the sheriff shows up to forcibly remove them and their belongings, and you formally take possession of the property.

# PUTTING SOME EMPATHY IN EVICTION

There once was an investor who reveled in evictions. He would drive to the eviction site, park his red Porsche in front of the house, and make fun of the people being evicted. He even went so far as to take photographs and hang them on his office wall. The company he worked for was doing a billion dollars' worth of business annually, so maybe that fact made this cold-hearted investor feel justified, but the only real justice was what finally happened to him and all the senior management at his company: The U.S. Securities and Exchange Commission investigated its business practices and found the company guilty of several counts of mortgage fraud. The investor received a four-year sentence in a federal prison.

When you have to evict homeowners, do it with heart. Put yourself in their shoes and try to appreciate how you'd feel in a similar situation or how you'd feel if one of your family members was being evicted. If possible, rent a moving truck for the homeowners, and help them pack and load their possessions. Whatever you do, don't cause additional pain while you're getting your gain.

Chapter **2**

# Picking Your Point of Entry in the Foreclosure Process

**F**oreclosure investing encompasses much more than simply buying properties for pennies on the dollar at a foreclosure auction. The foreclosure process often takes three months to a year to run its course, and investors can step in at any time to scoop up a property. In fact, investors can even step in before official foreclosure proceedings begin and (in some areas) months after they wrap up.

TIP

Although you can buy properties at numerous stages in the foreclosure process, you should become a specialist in one area first. Focus on pre-auction properties, auctions, or post-auctions so you can become an expert in one area. You can branch out later, as you become more experienced, develop better connections, and strengthen your investment team and your financial position.

This chapter reveals the various entry points in the foreclosure process, covering everything from pre-auction to post-redemption, also known as Real Estate Owned (REO) opportunities. It points out the pros and cons of investing at each stage so that you can make a well-informed decision about where you'd like to begin your journey in foreclosure investing.

# Dipping In at the Pre-Auction Stage

Homeowners often feel reluctant to take action when they first get an inkling of financial foreboding. Instead of contacting their lenders, an attorney, or a real estate agent who specializes in foreclosures to seek advice and try to work out a solution, they often stick their heads in the sand and hope the problem goes away. By the time they act, they're usually too late. Behind on their house payments, drowning in credit card debt, and unable to pay back taxes, they sealed their fate months before the bank initiated foreclosure proceedings.

When the bank finally moves forward to foreclose, the homeowners are often in a panic. They don't know what to do or where to go for reliable information. As a foreclosure investor, you can step into the process, provide homeowners options to cut their losses, and perhaps even help them retain possession of their property.

TIP

You may think that doing everything you can to enable homeowners to retain possession of their property is contrary to the idea of profiting from foreclosures. In about 90 percent of pre-auction foreclosures, however, the homeowners are too deep in debt and must sell their home. By acting with integrity, you give yourself a much better chance of obtaining the property — and doing some good at the same time.

## Exploring the pros and cons of pre-auction foreclosures

Although you can certainly wait for the foreclosure auction to roll around, the pre-auction stage offers several benefits to foreclosure investors:

>> Less competition from other investors

>> More options for negotiating deals with homeowners and their lenders

>> More time to put together a deal and close on the house

>> Increased opportunity to inspect the condition of the house, inside and out

>> No redemption period or other legal issues at the end that can sink the deal: When you close on the property, it's yours. You may have to wait a week or two to take possession, depending on your agreement with the homeowners, but you don't have to wait three months to a year for the redemption period to expire. For more about redemption, skip to the later section "Waiting Out the Redemption Period — If Necessary."

**WARNING**

At this point, you're probably ready to dive into the pre-auction stage and start scooping up properties from homeowners who are eager to shed the financial burden. But before you leap, consider some of the following drawbacks of buying directly from homeowners:

>> Emotional fallout, including anger and resentment, from the loss of a home

>> Complications of dealing with other people's financial messes

>> Misleading information or outright lies from homeowners who are desperate or still in denial

>> Indecisiveness of homeowners who change their minds at the last minute because they really don't know what they want

>> Legal issues concerning just how far you can go to persuade homeowners to sell their property at less than market value without committing fraud

**REMEMBER**

Carefully consider the pros and cons before investing in anything, and honestly assess your ability to deal with the negative aspects of certain investment options. Buying foreclosure properties in the pre-auction stage isn't for everyone.

## Guiding homeowners to good decisions

When helping homeowners, you can't try to pass yourself off as an attorney, accountant, financial adviser, or therapist unless you really *are* one. But you're often called on to play some of these roles. Like a therapist, you have to be able to listen to the homeowners. Like an accountant, you need to be able to look at the homeowners' finances to assess their options. And, like an attorney, you need to know the foreclosure and redemption laws in your area.

**WARNING**

Make it very clear to the homeowners that you're not an attorney, real estate agent, or accountant unless you are one. State up front that you're an investor representing *yourself.* Full disclosure is the best policy. Passing yourself off as something you're not is fraud.

## A TYPICAL DAY IN THE FORECLOSURE OFFICE

One real estate broker once met with a couple facing foreclosure. The husband worked two jobs and the wife took care of the bills. Though the husband was working hard to make ends meet, the couple had fallen behind in their mortgage payments and were receiving notices from their lender. The broker and the couple set up a meeting at the broker's office to do a conference call with the lender to negotiate a solution.

When the couple arrived at the broker's office, the broker immediately saw the nature of the problem. The wife was decked out in designer clothes and adorned in jewelry that would have made the queen of England jealous. After looking over their finances, the broker explained that to avoid foreclosure, the couple would need to slash expenses and sell some of their more valuable assets.

Upon hearing the broker's words, the wife was visibly upset. Angry and near tears, she stood up and asked, "What do you want me to do — take the clothes off my back and the rings off my fingers?"

The broker said, "You can leave your clothes on, but let's take a closer look at those rings." The couple were $10,000 behind on their mortgage payments. The broker agreed to take the jewelry and give them $10,000 in return so they could sell the house and move on. The next day, the broker took the jewelry to a friend of his who owned a jewelry store. He appraised the rings at $5,000. So the broker took a $5,000 loss but scored a great Valentine's Day gift for his wife!

**REMEMBER**

You can't offer legal advice if you're not a licensed lawyer, but you can inform homeowners of their options and recommend professionals who can help. If the homeowners can refinance their way out of a foreclosure, you may be able to steer them to a loan officer or financial adviser who can provide additional assistance. Chapter 3 in Book 1 explains how to assemble a team of experts who can help you buy and sell foreclosure properties so that you'll have plenty of experts on hand to recommend to the homeowners.

## Dealing with anger and angst

Understandably, when people are in a financial bind, they're often upset, anxious, and angry. Parents have the daunting task of facing their kids and telling them, "We can no longer afford to live here." They're embarrassed about what their neighbors, friends, and family may think. They may be angry at their boss for laying them off or firing them. In many cases, the husband or wife has just found out about the pending foreclosure from their significant other who spent the family into the poorhouse. During the COVID-19 pandemic, many homeowners struggled with the financial fallout from family illness, job loss, business closures, and mandatory shutdowns.

When you show up at the home of a couple or person facing foreclosure, and you tell the homeowners that you want to help them by buying their property, all that fear, frustration, and anger is likely to get unleashed on you. Even if you can manage to avoid direct conflict, you may be recruited into refereeing a domestic dispute or witnessing emotional outpourings that you're just not used to seeing.

Distressed homeowners are often most upset about something that happened in the past — something they can't go back in time and fix. One of your first jobs when dealing directly with homeowners is encouraging them to put the past behind them and address the current situation. Shifting focus to the present can reduced the emotional energy significantly.

TIP

You can often relieve some of the pain of foreclosure by letting the homeowners know that they're not alone. Know the foreclosure statistics for your area, share this information with them, and let them know about their options. This information can often defuse a tense situation and remove some of the anger that may be causing a rift in a couple's relationship. Ask at your county's Register of Deeds office; sometimes, the office tracks foreclosure numbers for the county and may be able to provide city, county, and state statistics.

## Assessing your ability to deal with pre-auction scenarios

The most successful pre-auction investors are people who are well versed in local foreclosure laws and procedures and who can quickly and accurately assess the average homeowner's financial predicament. To determine whether you have the qualities to invest successfully in properties in the pre-auction stage, place a check mark next to any of the following statements that you feel are true:

>> ❑ People generally like me and trust me right off the bat.

>> ❑ I feel comfortable talking with people I've never met.

>> ❑ I'm a good listener.

>> ❑ I'm diplomatic, often acting as the mediator when friends, family members, or co-workers have issues with one another.

» ❏ I never met a problem I couldn't solve.

» ❏ I'm good with math, especially dollars and cents.

» ❏ I can tell people the truth even when they don't really want to hear it.

» ❏ I can handle disappointment. Even if I've invested a great deal of time and effort in helping a homeowner, I won't get terribly upset if I don't get the house.

» ❏ I can let people fail even after I offer them outstanding advice on how to avoid a catastrophe.

REMEMBER

Having every single one of these qualities isn't essential for success in investing in pre-auction properties, but if you checked only two or three items, you may want to consider stepping into the foreclosure process at the auction or post-auction stage. The more of these qualities you have, the more successful you're likely to be in dealing directly with homeowners.

# Pursuing Foreclosure Notices

Whether you buy properties directly from homeowners before auction or wait until the auction, the weekly foreclosure notices in your area are required reading. In almost all areas of the United States, the lender must post a weekly foreclosure notice or Notice of Default (NOD) in a publicly accessible publication several weeks before the auction.

The posting of the foreclosure notice is almost an entirely separate stage of the foreclosure process — after negotiations between the homeowners and lender break down, but before the property is sold at auction. At this stage, every foreclosure investor in your area probably knows about the property, and any investors who are interested in buying the property before auction are likely in the process of trying to contact the homeowners.

The investor who arrives first and whom the homeowners trust most is typically the investor who stands to get the property.

TIP

You can find foreclosure properties even before the foreclosure notice is posted by keeping your ears open, networking effectively, and getting the word out that you buy properties.

## Knowing the benefits of waiting for the foreclosure notice

Many foreclosure investors don't like dealing with distressed homeowners until the official foreclosure notice is posted because until that point, homeowners may be unwilling to accept the fact that foreclosure is imminent. The posting of the foreclosure notice removes most of the lingering doubt and acts as a wake-up call, spurring the homeowners to take action.

The foreclosure notice offers several additional benefits:

>> Contains the location of the property (usually a legal address, not a street address, but you can use the legal address to obtain the street address, as discussed in Chapter 3 of Book 3)

>> Lists the names of the homeowners being foreclosed on so you can refer to them personally by name instead of addressing them with general terms

>> Specifies the name of the lender foreclosing on the property, so you have the information you need to gather more information from the lender

>> Provides the name of the attorney or trustee in charge of liquidating the property, so you have someone to call for additional details

As you'll discover throughout your experience as a foreclosure investor, every bit of information you have about a property is a valuable puzzle piece that clarifies the situation and enables you to put together an attractive deal that benefits all those involved.

REMEMBER

Just because the lender posts a foreclosure notice doesn't mean that the property is destined for the auction block. Any time before the sale, the homeowners can strike a deal with the lender, refinance with another lender, or sell the property. As soon as the foreclosure notice is posted, the clock starts ticking for any investor who's looking to buy the property before auction.

TIP

Keep track of properties from the day they're advertised to the time they're sold. Very often, a particular foreclosure sale is adjourned, so the property doesn't go up for auction on the scheduled day. By following the adjournments, you often find that the property goes up for sale later. If you're prepared, you may be able to grab the property without facing any competing bids.

## Weighing the drawbacks of waiting for the foreclosure notice

Although the posting of the foreclosure notice delivers some valuable benefits to foreclosure investors, it also heats up competition among investors, all of whom are looking for the best deal. As soon as that foreclosure notice is published, every foreclosure investor working the pre-auction circuit catches the scent and heads out to research the property and contact the homeowners.

REMEMBER

When you're buying properties from distressed homeowners pre-auction, finding out about prospective foreclosure properties before the posting of the notice often gives you a competitive edge. Networking provides the earliest leads. Reading the notices as soon as they're posted and acting quickly to contact the homeowners is the next-best option.

## Wrapping up your deal before the sale

Buying a property from the homeowners before the sale is a standard seller-to-buyer transaction. If you've ever bought a house (and you should be a homeowner if you're investing in real estate), you know the drill:

1. **Present your offer to the homeowners in the form of a purchase agreement.**

   You may need to work through a series of counteroffers to agree on a price and terms.

2. **Have the property professionally inspected.**

3. **Order title insurance to protect yourself if the title has any hidden claims against it.**

4. **Sign the papers at closing.**

5. **Take possession of the property on the agreed-upon date.**

REMEMBER

Because you purchased the property directly from the homeowners, they have no right of redemption, so you don't have to wait around for several months. You can move into the property immediately, renovate and sell it, or turn it into a rental unit. See Chapter 4 in Book 3 for details on profiting from a property after you take possession of it.

# Bidding for a Property at a Foreclosure Auction

Foreclosure investors often choose to do their bidding at auctions. A common misconception about foreclosure auctions is that investors bid on properties. The truth is that investors bid on mortgages (also called *liens*). What's the difference?

>> When you buy a property from homeowners, you own the property.

>> When you buy a lien at a foreclosure sale, you may or may not eventually take possession of the property; if your area has a redemption period, the homeowners or someone else who has a legal claim to the property can redeem it. Consult your county's Register of Deeds office to find out more about the redemption period in your state.

For a better understanding of what you're actually buying at a foreclosure auction, brush up on the following types of liens:

>> **Senior lien:** The *senior lien,* or *first mortgage,* is the loan that the homeowners took out to purchase the property. Novice investors should always buy first mortgages because owning the senior lien gives you the best opportunity to take possession of the property eventually.

>> **Junior lien:** The *junior lien* is any other loan the homeowners took out, using their home as collateral. A junior lien is usually a second mortgage, but it can be a home-equity loan, line of credit, or contractor financing provided for home improvements. Junior liens are often wiped off the books during the foreclosure process, so they can be very risky investments.

>> **Tax lien:** A *tax lien* is a claim against the property for unpaid tax bills. Unlike junior liens, which foreclosure typically erases, a tax lien remains in place after foreclosure. If the tax lien is for overdue property taxes, the buyer must pay the taxes. If the lien is for income taxes, the Internal Revenue Service or other taxing agency may choose to forgive the taxes, but make sure that the foreclosing attorney notifies the IRS. Buying a property tax lien is usually a safe investment, because if someone else purchases the property, you stand to get your money back and perhaps even earn a small profit.

**WARNING**

Don't bid at auctions until you fully understand the process and know what you're buying. Whenever a foreclosure guru stages a local foreclosure seminar, one real estate broker's office begins receiving calls from angry novice investors who purchased junior liens, thinking that they were buying senior liens. One investor purchased more than $100,000 in junior liens only to find out later that those liens were useless pieces of paper.

## Weighing the pros and cons of buying at auctions

The foreclosure auction provides you an opportunity to purchase a controlling interest in a property without having to deal directly with the homeowners in often-uncomfortable situations. In a way, the auction simplifies the process of acquiring properties. You show up, submit the winning bid, and walk away with the sheriff's deed.

**WARNING**

Buying at auction, however, presents several additional challenges, including the following:

>> You may not have the opportunity to inspect the property thoroughly, although you should at least inspect the property from the outside, as Chapter 3 in Book 3 advises.

>> Properties are often sold as is, so you're more likely to take possession of a property that requires costly repairs.

>> Cash payment is usually required at the time of purchase, so you need to show up with a cashier's check. In some cases, you have a few hours or days to come up with the cash, but you still need ready access to cash to close on the deal.

>> Depending on the number of investors at the auction who actually bid on properties, you may face some stiff competition.

>> When you buy a property at an auction in an area that has a mandatory redemption period, you may need sufficient funds to hold the property for several months to a year until you see your profit. (If you're using your own money, you need just enough cash to insure the house and pay the property taxes. If you borrowed the money, you may need additional cash to cover the monthly payments. For more about financing a real estate purchase, see Chapter 4 in Book 1.)

REMEMBER

Chapter 3 in Book 3 reveals tips and techniques for meeting these challenges and minimizing the risks of bidding at auctions. Only by being thoroughly prepared going into an auction can you confidently purchase properties that are almost sure to turn a profit.

## Setting a maximum bid well in advance

One big mistake to avoid at an auction is getting caught up in the excitement of the bidding experience. (Coauthor Ralph knows the risks of overbidding firsthand. He hates to lose, so if someone's bidding against him, he always wins — the bid, that is. Only later does he realize that his obsession with winning made him the big loser for having spent too much for a property.)

TIP

The trick to effective bidding is to research the property thoroughly and set the highest price you can afford to pay for the property and still make a profit of 20 percent or more. That's your ceiling. You can bump your head on it, but don't crash your head through it; if you do, you'll have serious headaches in the future.

## Putting on your poker face

Bidding on a property at foreclosure is a bit like sitting around a poker table and trying to figure out why a particular investor is bidding on a specific property for a certain amount of money. In some cases, the other investor may know more about the property than you do. In other cases, the investor knows less. The person may be bidding on instinct to drive up bidding or simply to toy with other investors.

The comparison of bidding on foreclosure properties with playing poker ends there, however. Bidding on properties is a high-stakes game in which you stand to lose as much as you stand to gain — or more. You may never know why a particular investor bids a specific amount on the property, but you always need to know why *you're* bidding a specific amount, what you're bidding on, and how high you're willing to bid.

**REMEMBER**

With a fully fleshed-out property dossier, which Chapter 3 in Book 3 shows you how to assemble, you hold all the cards in the deck. This dossier enables you to put on the dispassionate poker face required to win the bidding game. You know exactly how much you can afford to bid to earn the desired profit. Not everyone who's bidding against you will have the same advantage.

# Acquiring Properties after the Auction

The auction close doesn't signal the end of your opportunity to acquire foreclosure properties. For investors who choose to focus on post-auction properties, an auction's close signals the beginning. These investors don't want to deal directly with homeowners, and they prefer to avoid the sometimes-messy auction process. They'd rather buy properties from the new owners.

The following sections list various opportunities and resources for tracking down post-auction properties, from bank-owned and government-owned repos to properties that have been seized because they were paid for with ill-gotten gains. You can make a good profit by focusing on any one of the categories described here.

**REMEMBER**

The opening bid at an auction is typically the amount owed on the property, plus attorney fees, plus a dollar. Contrary to what many people think, banks don't want to be in the real estate business, so they rarely bid up a property to take possession of it. A bank holding a second lien, however, may bid on the first lien to protect the bank's interest.

## Scoping out REO properties

Auctions typically start with a minimum bid. If nobody in the room bids high enough, a representative for the bank that's foreclosing offers a bid and takes possession of the deed. The bank transfers the property to its REO or Other Real Estate Owned (OREO) department, which prepares the property for sale.

Because preparing properties for sale and selling them costs banks additional money, they're often willing to negotiate sales with investors rather than place the properties on the market.

**WARNING**

Admittedly, the process sounds pretty easy, but it can be very challenging for any or all of the following reasons:

>> Banks don't like to sell properties at bargain-basement prices just to unload them.

>> REO managers often pass the best deals on to their closest contacts and to investors with proven track records, so you may need to invest some time in building fruitful relationships.

>> REO managers may require you to buy two or more properties as a package deal. You must agree to take one not-so-promising property along with another that has more potential.

>> Properties are sold as is, so you can get stuck with a lemon, especially if you don't do your homework.

# Finding and buying government properties

The U.S. government sponsors several programs to encourage home ownership, including Department of Housing and Urban Development (HUD) and Department of Veterans Affairs (VA) financing. Often, borrowers default on these loans, and the government ends up with a property that it doesn't need or want. In addition, state and local governments may seize properties for infrastructure improvements or as a result of unpaid taxes or criminal activities.

As a citizen, you have the right to purchase these government properties, and you can often pick them up at deep discounts. Following is a list of common resources for government-owned properties:

>> **HUD and VA repos:** When homeowners default on a HUD or VA home loan, like any lender, the government can choose to foreclose on the property. These deals aren't always best for investors because HUD and VA homes are commonly listed at or just below market value, but by being persistent, you can often find some pretty good deals.

>> **State department of transportation:** The department of transportation commonly buys up property for road improvements and disposes of the property after completing the project.

>> **State or county drug enforcement agency:** If a homeowner is paying for a property with illicit funds, or if the house is home to criminal activity, the government may step in, take possession of the property, evict the homeowners, and sell the house.

>> **County sheriff's office:** When your county sheriff's office seizes a property, perhaps because it was purchased with proceeds from criminal activity, it may offer the property for sale through a broker or at auction.

A condominium association can also foreclose on a property to collect unpaid condominium fees. Note, however, that a condo lien is just another lien. The senior lien (first mortgage) takes precedence.

## Buying properties from other investors

Some foreclosure investors are more interested in discovering and acquiring foreclosure properties than they are in fixing them up and reselling them. These investors consider themselves to be *foreclosure wholesalers* who find and buy properties and then sell them to other investors.

**WARNING**

Generally, you shouldn't buy properties from foreclosure wholesalers (or whatever they call themselves). Whenever someone tries to sell you on some great investment opportunity, ask yourself this question: "If the property were as profitable as they want me to think, why don't *they* fix it up and sell it?" Another reason not to buy from other investors is that by doing so, you're usually paying a markup or finder's fee. Plenty of foreclosure properties are available, and they're not that difficult to track down, so pocket the markup, and use that money for renovations or the purchase of your next property. But if you've done your research (as explained in Chapter 3 of Book 3), and the price is right, you certainly don't have to pass on the deal.

Don't become a foreclosure wholesaler yourself, either. You can make more money by working the foreclosure from start to finish: buy, renovate, and sell. For details about renovating and selling a house for more than you paid for it, check out Book 4 as well as the latest edition of *Flipping Houses For Dummies* by Ralph R. Roberts with Joe Kraynak and Kyle Roberts (Wiley).

# Waiting Out the Redemption Period — If Necessary

Many areas of the United States give foreclosed-upon homeowners one last chance to get their homes back — through redemption. If the homeowners can come up with enough money to pay off the balance of their loans and all penalties and back taxes, they get to keep the property. In some cases, homeowners have up to a year to redeem their property before the high bidder at the auction takes possession.

Surviving the redemption period can be tricky, especially if other investors take interest in the property. The redemption period can affect you in any of several ways:

>> If you purchased the property at auction, you must wait to do anything to the property until the redemption period expires. Otherwise, you may invest heavily in renovations only to see the homeowners or another investor redeem the mortgage that you bought and cut you out of the deal. You may need to secure the home (particularly if it's vacant) and perform repairs to make the property safe and prevent deterioration, such as from a leaky roof, but invest as little as possible during this period.

>> The homeowners may still be able to file for bankruptcy during the redemption period to buy themselves some additional time, which can throw your plans for renovating and selling the property for a loop.

>> If another investor purchased a property and is waiting for the redemption period to expire, you still have an opportunity to purchase the property. You can work with the homeowners to bump the other investor out of the deal, redeem the property, and buy it directly from the homeowners.

# Chapter **3**

# Performing Your Due Diligence

A large part of foreclosure *investing* consists of *investigating* — knowing what you're about to buy before you lay your cash on the line. You need to know how much the property is worth, how much is owed on it, whether it has any additional liens or encumbrances, whether the property is in violation of any building codes, and whether the person selling the house is really the legal owner.

TIP

For each property you consider buying, create a separate folder (paper or digital) with a photo of the property, its address, and all publicly accessible information available for it. This chapter shows you the type of information you need and provides instructions on how to dig it up and organize it to create your very own custom property dossier.

In addition to helping you determine whether the property is worth your time pursuing, this information is critical for assisting homeowners, negotiating with homeowners and lenders, and bidding on a property at auction.

# Collecting Essential Information about the Property

Every property has some vital statistics that must find their way into your property dossier. You can collect most of the data you need through the Notice of Default (NOD) or foreclosure notice (if one has been posted) and from your county's courthouse and city or town offices. Later in this chapter, you find out how to get essential details from the foreclosure notice and dig up additional information at the county courthouse.

If you're working with the homeowners in pre-foreclosure, gather as much information as you can from them first. You need to know as much as possible about their situation to be of assistance and minimize your risk as an investor.

The following sections point you to the sources of key information and provide a couple of forms for recording the essential data in a format you can quickly reference later.

## Honing your title acquisition and reading skills

TIP

To hone your skills at gathering data related to foreclosure properties, consider practicing on your own home first. Unless you're currently in foreclosure, of course, you won't have access to a foreclosure notice (lucky you), but you can practice researching your title, mortgage, and other documentation relating to your property. You may have several of the documents you need to practice on in the closing packet you received when you purchased your home, but don't cheat by referring to those documents. Go out in the field to see what sorts of publicly accessible data you can gather on your own:

1. **Head down to your local title company.**

   You can find a list of title companies online (or in your phone book, if you're old-school that way).

2. **Meet with one of the representatives.**

   Explain that you're reading this book called *Real Estate Investing All-in-One For Dummies,* and you want to know everything they can teach you about titles.

3. **Request a title commitment on your own property.**

   The title company may take a couple of days to prepare the title commitment. Offer to pick it up when it's ready so that the company won't have to pay postage.

4. **Visit your county courthouse and track down the Register of Deeds office.**

5. **Ask nicely to see everything recorded against your house in the past 24 months.**

   In some cases, the records may not go that far back, but you should be able to obtain the last two recorded documents — perhaps the deed and the mortgage showing when you purchased the property.

6. **Compare the title commitment you received from the title company with the documents you picked up through your own detective work.**

## GETTING BURNED BY BAD DECISIONS

A doctor, highly educated and very successful in her field, attended a seminar on foreclosure investing. She purchased the books and CDs for sale at the seminar, studied them carefully, and decided to begin purchasing foreclosure properties.

The system seemed straightforward enough, so she began attending auctions and purchasing properties right out of the chute. Well, she *thought* she was purchasing properties. At foreclosure auctions, you actually purchase foreclosed-on mortgages. If you buy a first mortgage, you're likely to take possession of the property after the redemption period. Second mortgages and other liens against the property are usually wiped out by the foreclosure process; in most cases, they're worthless.

The doctor bought about seven or eight second mortgages thinking that she would own the properties when the redemption periods expired.

Paul (coauthor Ralph's buyer at foreclosure auctions) observed the doctor over the course of a couple of weeks. One week, he approached her and asked whether she understood what she was doing. During the conversation, Paul realized that the doctor was following some bad advice. He brought her back to the office to meet Ralph.

They researched the properties for her and helped her understand what she'd done. She had purchased several second mortgages that were destined to become worthless pieces of paper because the foreclosure would wipe them off the books. She had invested about $100,000 and was going to lose all of it. That lesson was a tough one to learn, but with her newfound understanding, the doctor went on to become a successful real estate investor.

The moral of the story is this: Do your homework before you start investing. Know what you're buying before you put your money on the line.

You should notice a big difference in the documents. The title commitment won't include all the information from the documents you picked up at the county courthouse. Instead, it extracts the essential details and presents them in a more easily accessible format, showing the following:

>> Homeowners' names

>> First mortgage

>> Any second mortgage or other liens against the property

>> Property taxes paid or due

>> Delinquent water bills or bills for other services supplied by the municipality

## Picking up details from the foreclosure notice

When a NOD or foreclosure notice is published, like the one shown in Figure 3-1, you have a wealth of information at your fingertips. The NOD or foreclosure notice presents the following details, which you can record on your foreclosure information sheet, like the one shown in Figure 3-2:

>> **Case or reference number[1]:** Some attorneys include a case or reference number in the foreclosure notice to simplify the process of searching for information in their database.

>> **Insertion date[2]:** The date may appear in the notice itself, but if it doesn't, use the date of the publication in which the notice is posted. In the legal news, the advertisements are listed under subtitles to indicate the order of the posting: first, second, third, and so on.

>> **County[3]:** The county in which the property is located is your key to unlocking other details about the property. Using this bit of information, you know which county's Register of Deeds office to visit to research the title and mortgage and find the property's address. (Start with your county.) This issue may not arise if the paper you're using is county-specific, in which case pay attention to the city with a special focus on the city where you live or the cities that are most familiar.

>> **Legal lot, subdivision, and city[4]:** The legal description of the property doesn't provide the property's mailing address, but from the legal description, you can find the mailing address. See the later section "Finding the property" for details.

- >> **Name of the mortgagor[5]:** The *mortgagor* is the borrower, typically the homeowners — the person or people who owe the money, even if they're not in possession of the property.

- >> **Name of the mortgagee[6]:** The *mortgagee* is the lender that is foreclosing on the property.

- >> **Amount owed on the mortgage[7]:** The NOD or foreclosure notice always states the exact amount the homeowners currently owe on this mortgage. They may owe additional sums on other loans. The amount owed changes between the times when the notice is published and the sale occurs, so call the foreclosing attorney closer to the date of sale to determine the actual opening bid amount.

- >> **Interest rate of loan[8]:** The longer the amount owed on the mortgage remains unpaid, the more it increases by the specified interest rate. You can use the interest rate to monitor the amount owed as it increases over time. In addition, you are charged this interest rate if you purchase the mortgage and someone buys it back from you during the redemption period.

- >> **The mortgage company's attorney[9]:** The mortgage company attorney's name and contact information are useful for double-checking the sale date and the opening bid and then contacting the mortgage company to work out a deal.

- >> **Mortgage sale date[10]:** This date is when the attorney for the lender expects the mortgage to be auctioned. The date can change, but jot it down so that you can keep track of it.

- >> **Length of the property's redemption period, if applicable[11]:** If your area has a mandatory redemption period, it should appear in the NOD or foreclosure notice. Using the date of sale and redemption period, you can determine the last day the homeowners can redeem the property. Verify the redemption period with your own research; occasionally, the wrong redemption period is published.

- >> **Liber (the legal book in which the deed is recorded at the county courthouse) and page number of the recorded mortgage that is in foreclosure[12]:** This information tells you where to find the mortgage document and which mortgage is being foreclosed on if the homeowners have more than one mortgage on the property.

**TIP**

If you're buying properties directly from homeowners who contacted you before the beginning of foreclosure proceedings, you can gather most of the information you need to complete the foreclosure information sheet from the homeowners. Just be sure to verify the information by inspecting the title and other records, as explained in the following sections.

ROBERTS & KRAYNAK, P.C.
Attorneys and Counselors
1313 Mockingbird Ln., Ste. 200
Dellingham Farms, MI 48025

THIS FIRM IS A DEBT COLLECTOR ATTEMPTING TO COLLECT A DEBT. ANY INFORMATION WE OBTAIN WILL BE USED FOR THAT PURPOSE.

ATTN PURCHASERS: This sale may be rescinded by the foreclosing mortgagee. In that event, your damages, if any, shall be limited solely to the return of the bid amount tendered at sale, plus interest.

MORTGAGE SALE - Default has been made in the conditions of a mortgage made by **JOHN Q PUBLIC** and **JANE Q PUBLIC**[5], husband and wife, original mortgagor(s), to Federal City Mortgage Co D/B/A Commonwealth United Mortgage Company[6], Mortgagee, dated March 4, 2017, and recorded on April 10, 2017 in Liber 55555 on Page 617[12], in Oakland county[3] records, Michigan, on which mortgage there is claimed to be due at the date hereof the sum of Four Hundred Seventy-Two Thousand Seven Hundred Fifty-Eight And 23/100 Dollars ($472,758.23)[7], including interest at 5.625% per annum[8].

Under the power of sale contained in said mortgage and the statute in such case made and provided, notice is hereby given that said mortgage will be foreclosed by a sale of the mortgaged premises, or some part of them, at public venue, at the Main entrance to the Court House in Pontiac at 10:00 AM, on **JANUARY 31, 2023**[10].

Said premises are situated in Charter Township of West Bloomfield, Oakland County, Michigan, and are described as:

Homesite No. 55, Amberleigh Condominium, according to the Master Deed recorded in Liber 55555, Pages 665 through 730, Oakland County Records, as amended, and designated as Oakland County Subdivision Plan No. 1555[4] together with rights in the general common elements and the limited common elements as shown on the Master Deed and as described in Act 59 of the Public Acts of 1978, as amended

The redemption period shall be 6 months from the date of such sale[11], unless determined abandoned in accordance with MCLA 600.3241a, in which case the redemption period shall be 30 days from the date of such sale.

Dated: December 30, 2022[2]

For more information, please call:

FC F 555.555.5555

Roberts & Kraynak, P.C.[9]

Attorneys For Servicer

1313 Mockingbird Ln., Ste. 200

Dellingham Farms, MI 48025

File #055000F05[1]

**FIGURE 3-1:**
Collect important details about the foreclosure property from the NOD or foreclosure notice.

# Foreclosure Information Sheet

Date: _____

**Foreclosure Notice**

Case or Reference Number: _____

Insertion Date: _____ Thru: _____

County: _____

Legal Lot: _____

Subdivision: _____

City: _____

Mortgagor (Homeowners): _____

Mortgagee (Lender): _____

Mortgage Amount: _____

Interest Rate: _____

Mortgage Company's Attorney: _____

Mortgage Company's Attorney Phone Number: _____

Mortgage Sale Date: _____

Redemption Period: _____

Last Day to Redeem: _____

**Register of Deeds (Title)**

Property Address (Ask Clerk): _____

Mortgagor Names: _____

Price Paid for Property: _____

Deed Warranty Names: _____

Previous Mortgagor (Previous Title): _____

Price Paid for Property (Previous Title): _____

Current 1st Mortgage Mortgagee (Lender): _____

Original Mortgagee (Lender): _____

**Register of Deeds (1st Mortgage and Note)**

1st Mortgage Loan Amount: _____

Interest Rate: _____

Date Recorded: _____ Liber: _____ Page: _____

Mortgagee (Lender): _____

Address: _____

© John Wiley & Sons, Inc.

FIGURE 3-2:
Record information from the foreclosure notice and public records on your foreclosure information sheet.

Mortgage Assumable? ☐ Yes ☐ No

**Register of Deeds (Second Mortgage and Note)**

2nd Mortgage Loan Amount: _____

Interest Rate: _____

Date Recorded: _____ Liber: _____ Page: _____

Mortgagee (Lender): _____

Address: _____

Mortgage Assumable? ☐ Yes ☐ No

**Register of Deeds (Additional Mortgages or Liens)**

Junior Lien Holder 1: _____

Address: _____

Junior Lien Holder 2: _____

Address: _____

Tax Lien: _____

Address: _____

**County Tax Assessor**

Sidwell (Tax ID #): _____

Taxable Value (SEV): _____

Property Tax Formula: _____

Unpaid Property Taxes: _____

Property Tax Lien? ☐ Yes, Amount: _____ ☐ No

**State, County, City or Town Property Worksheet**

Building Permits: _____

Code Violations: _____

Other: _____

**Other Information**

Opening Bid: _____

Homeowner's Phone: _____

Estimated Property Value: _____

Total Owed on Property: _____

**FIGURE 3-2:**
(Continued)

Estimated Equity in Property: _____

# Digging up details at the Register of Deeds office

Whether you're planning to bid on a property at auction or purchase the property directly from homeowners, a trip to your county's Register of Deeds office is a necessity. The Register of Deeds or county clerk is the one who records most of the legal paperwork for a property, including the title work, deed, and mortgage. The following sections point out the essential information you need to scrounge up from this most important source.

**TIP**

The records you need to research can be recorded on any of several types of media. You may be pulling out folders, flipping through pages in a book, or looking for records on microfilm.

## Finding the property

The NOD or foreclosure notice describes the location of the property through a legal description rather than simply providing a mailing address. Isn't that just like lawyers? Fortunately, you can use the property description to track down the mailing address by employing one of the following strategies:

>> Ask the clerk at your county's Register of Deeds office.

>> Ask your real estate attorney.

>> Contact your title company. If you have a good relationship with the company, someone there may be willing to look up the address for you.

>> Use a land data software program to search a database of property information. These programs are available in some areas and on the web.

## THE CHICKEN MAN

One of the most successful foreclosure investors in coauthor Ralph's area is dubbed "The Chicken Man" because he delivers buckets of chicken to the staff members in the Register of Deeds office. By catering lunch on a regular basis, The Chicken Man has established an outstanding relationship with the clerks. He can walk in through the back door of the Register of Deeds office and help himself to the records. When he can't find a record he needs, the clerks are more than willing to lend a hand. You might say that The Chicken Man has a leg up (and a wing and a thigh and a breast) on the competition.

Before you step into the Register of Deeds or county clerk's office, turn on your charm, and brush up on your manners. Ask politely for assistance and say "Thank you" when the people behind the desk provide that assistance. The office staff stands between you and the information you need, and they're usually as helpful as you are polite.

Some companies, such as HomeInfoMax (`www.homeinfomax.com`), provide online search tools that can help you find a property's address based on its legal description. Most online tools don't cover all counties, however, and typically charge per search. You can get the information for free by doing a little legwork or contacting the Register of Deeds office.

When you have the address, plug it into an online mapping program you use, and print a map of the property's location. You can also use Google Earth to print a satellite image of the property. Keep in mind, however, that satellite images are often months or even years old; they're no substitute for driving to the property and inspecting it with your own two eyes. See the later section "Doing Your Field-work: Inspecting the Property."

## Obtaining the property's title and other key documents

When most homeowners buy a property, they agree to buy it from the seller before any mention of the title occurs. Before closing on the transaction, they hire a title company that inspects and insures the title to protect the buyer from any messy legal battles over who owns the property.

When buying foreclosure properties, however, inspect the title *before* you decide to pursue a property. If anything about the title smells fishy, you may want to do a little extra research or simply cross the property off your list.

You can do your preliminary title research yourself by heading down to your county's Register of Deeds office and asking the clerk to provide you the information of what's recorded on title for a particular property. At the bare minimum, obtain a copy of the deed and any other recorded documents for the current and previous owner. If possible, obtain copies of all documents recorded in the past 24 months.

Although you can do this research yourself (and you really should do it yourself to learn about title research), when you're starting out, you should consult your title company for a second opinion and order a title commitment. When you feel comfortable doing your own research, you can take on more of the burden.

## Researching the property's title

Inspect the title work and deed for the following critical pieces of data, and record them in the corresponding spaces of the foreclosure information sheet (refer to Figure 3-2):

- >> **Mortgagor (homeowners') names:** Note whether the mortgagor's name matches the name of the property's title holder. Differing names raise a red flag; make a note of any.

- >> **Price paid for the property:** Depending on how long ago the current homeowners purchased the property, this information can provide some indication of the property's current value.

- >> **Deed warranty names:** The names on the deed should match the homeowners' names on the title. If they don't match, the difference raises a red flag; again, make a note of it.

- >> **Previous mortgagor:** Check the previous title, and jot down the names on it. Note any chinks in the chain of ownership. If the title work shows that Johnson sold the property to Davis and then Howard sold it to Pinkerton, who did Davis sell the house to? This gap indicates a problem in the chain of ownership. Consult with your title company whenever you notice any irregularities in the chain of title. Take note of maiden-name changes (changes in names after divorce). A name change may result in what only appears to be a gap in the chain of ownership.

- >> **Previous price paid for the property:** This piece of data isn't crucial, but it can point to a pattern of an increasing or decreasing property value.

- >> **Current first mortgage mortgagee (lender):** The *first mortgage mortgagee* is the bank or other lending institution that holds the first (senior) lien on the property. By obtaining the lender's name from the title, you can begin the process of tracking down the lender. Their information should be on the actual mortgage document, a copy of which you can obtain at the Register of Deeds office. For more about liens, including which liens take precedence, see the later section "Uncovering facts about any additional liens."

- >> **Original first mortgage mortgagee (lender):** In many cases, a lending institution loans the homeowners money to buy the property and then sells the mortgage to another lending institution almost immediately. The title typically includes the name of the original lender. When you start making calls, having this information at your fingertips helps convince the person you contact that you know what you're talking about.

If the property has a second mortgage on it, record the same information for the second mortgage. You may be able to work with the second-mortgage lender to shore up your position.

# PROTECTING YOURSELF AGAINST MORTGAGE FRAUD

By carefully researching the properties that interest you — particularly the legal documents associated with them — you protect yourself not only from inadvertent errors, but also from con artists who are trying to fleece you. Con artists often manipulate the legal documents and file false documents as part of their scams. Sometimes, they can even sell a house they don't own or sell a house several times to different buyers. To protect yourself from falling victim to a real estate scam, take the following precautions:

- Check the records to see whether the mortgage on the property was paid off recently. Sellers rarely pay off mortgages right before they sell, so any document that shows the mortgage as having been recently paid off is likely to be phony.

- Be wary of an investor who's pitching you a great deal on a property. Con artists often target novice investors in double-sales scams.

- Analyze the title commitment for suspicious transactions.

- Ask your title company for a 24-month property history, including mortgages.

- Purchase title insurance as soon as possible, and pay for it upfront. Sometimes, this insurance is your only protection.

## Gathering information from the mortgage and note

The mortgage and note are recorded along with the title when someone purchases a property. These documents include important details about the senior lien, so be sure to record these details on your foreclosure information sheet:

- » **First-mortgage loan amount:** How much did the homeowners borrow to finance the purchase of the property?

- » **Interest rate:** Knowing the interest rate on the first mortgage helps you calculate the homeowners' current monthly payments and provide them refinance options.

- » **Date recorded, liber, and page number:** With the date recorded, liber, and page number, you can access the information much more quickly.

- » **Mortgagee (lender):** You may have already obtained the mortgagee's name from the title, but check the mortgage for any discrepancies. Also, jot down the mortgagee's address for future reference.

## Uncovering facts about any additional liens

Although the first (senior) lien is the most important, the property may have other liens from second or third mortgages or construction liens that you should know about. Unless the homeowners very recently took out another loan using the property as collateral, or the Register of Deeds is way behind in recording documents, records of these liens should be accessible.

**REMEMBER**

Some liens take precedence over others. Buying liens with a higher precedence gives you more power. Property tax liens almost always take precedence over other liens. Then the pecking order usually follows the dates on which the loan agreements were executed and recorded, typically giving the first mortgage the most power. If you order a title commitment, it lists the liens in order of precedence.

**TIP**

On your foreclosure information sheet, record the names and addresses of any additional lien holders. The date on which a lien was recorded should alert you to the fact that a particular lien is a junior lien. The liber and page number on which the junior lien was recorded should also be higher than that of the senior lien, because the junior lien was recorded later.

## Uncovering unpaid property taxes and other tax liens

When homeowners get behind on their taxes, government agencies at the federal, state, or county level can place additional liens on the property. While researching the title, inspect it for any of the following additional liens:

>> Internal Revenue Service federal income tax liens

>> State income tax liens

>> Property tax liens

>> Record of deceased owner (if the death certificate is on the title)

**TIP**

If you see a death certificate, and the property is in foreclosure, try to locate the probate attorney who's in charge of liquidating the property. To locate the attorney, head down to the county building, visit the probate office, and ask whether anyone has opened a probate case in the name of the deceased party. If the case is in probate, ask to see the file, which will contain the name and contact information of the person who's handling the case.

**TIP**

Additional liens — most important, liens for overdue property taxes and IRS tax liens — are a good sign that the homeowners will be unable to redeem the property. They're probably too deeply in debt to catch up on their payments.

# Gathering tax information at the assessor's office

In addition to checking the title for any property tax liens, visit the county treasurer's or assessor's office, and ask for the following:

» **The property's tax ID number (often called a *property identification number,* or PIN):** The city or county taxing authority assigns this number to the property for reference and tracking. Some cities, such as Detroit, have ward numbers that serve the same function. Regardless of what the number is called, it identifies a specific parcel of land. As soon as you have a feel for the identification system, you can almost tell just by the number where the property is located.

» **The taxable value of the property:** You may have to visit the county assessor's office for this tidbit. Knowing the taxable value of a property may assist you in guesstimating the property's market value, but it's no substitute for an accurate current appraisal or your own research on market values of comparable properties. In some cases, the taxable value may be expressed as state equalized value (SEV). SEV may represent a fraction of the actual assessed value of the property; in some areas, for example, the SEV is calculated as half the previous sales price.

» **The property tax formula:** At the time of writing in Michigan, a house is generally worth 2 to 2.2 times the SEV, so a house with an SEV of $200,000 is worth $400,000 to $440,000. Ask the assessor what formula your area uses. This information can often give you a rough estimate of the property's market value.

» **Property tax status:** Find out whether property taxes are currently paid up and whether the assessor's office has a property tax lien on the property.

# Getting your hands on the property worksheet

Every town, city, or county in the United States keeps a worksheet on every property, showing when it was built, any building permits issued on the property, code violations, inspection reports, and so on. Find out who keeps the property worksheets and obtain a copy of the worksheet for any home you're considering buying. On your foreclosure information sheet, record the following data from the property worksheet:

» **Building permits:** Building permits provide a record of all approved property improvements. If you inspect the property later and discover an improvement that was performed without a permit, this information may be a warning that the improvement doesn't conform to building codes.

>> **Code violations:** If the property has any code violations recorded against it that haven't been resolved, you want to know so that you don't unknowingly take possession of a property that you'll be responsible for bringing up to code later.

>> **Other interesting tidbits:** The property worksheet may include additional information about health code violations that warn you to inspect the property more closely before purchasing it. For tips on physically inspecting a foreclosure property, see the later section "Doing Your Fieldwork: Inspecting the Property."

**WARNING**

A permit showing that the work passed final inspection is best. That permit shows that no matter who pulled (obtained) the permit (the homeowner or a licensed contractor), the work was completed and was at least up to code. Open permits — those that don't indicate that the work passed final inspection — may indicate that the work was completed to code or that you're going to be in for some costly repairs. In any event, knowing what's been recorded with the city concerning work begun or completed on the property is beneficial.

## Gathering additional information

**TIP**

To complete the foreclosure information sheet, do a little extra detective work to gather the following additional details:

>> **Opening bid:** If you found out about the property through a NOD or foreclosure notice, call the attorney listed in the notice to find out the opening bid.

>> **Homeowner's telephone number:** Finding the homeowners' phone number can be challenging, especially if their account has been canceled or the number is unlisted. Using the homeowners' names and the property address, try looking up the phone number on a site such as www.whitepages.com.

>> **Estimated property value:** The property's current value is how much the homeowners could get for the property if they sold it today. You can obtain a ballpark estimate by checking the prices of comparable homes that have sold in the past month or so. A real estate agent can come in handy here.

>> **Total owed on the property:** Add up the balance on all liens against the property. You can come up with a pretty accurate figure by adding the original balances and deducting estimated payments. If the loans are less than ten years old, chances are pretty good that the balances haven't been paid down very much, because a good chunk of each payment in the early years is applied to interest, not principal.

# Doing Your Fieldwork: Inspecting the Property

An investment property may seem like a steal on paper when it's actually a gutted shell of a home in the center of the low-rent district. Until you see the property for yourself, you have no idea what it is, what kind of homes surround it, or what condition it's in.

**REMEMBER**

Before you plop down your money or borrowed money on a property, always inspect it as closely as possible with your own two eyes, carefully record your observations, and add the details you gather to your growing property dossier. The following sections provide an exterior home inspection form to complete and lead you through the process of performing your due diligence in the field.

## Doing a drive-by, walk-around inspection

The least you should do (and the most you can do in some situations) to inspect a property is to drive over and walk around the property — at a safe distance, of course; we're not suggesting that you trespass. Even if you can't get inside to take a closer peek, the drive-by, walk-around inspection provides you enough preliminary information to develop a ballpark estimate of the property's value and rule out any really bad properties.

**WARNING**

Whenever you visit a property in person, you're at some risk. The homeowners, and sometimes their dog, may not appreciate uninvited guests, especially if you trespass. Keep your distance. Knocking on the front door is usually okay, but if the homeowners ask you to leave, respect their wishes and follow up with a letter.

As you perform your drive-by, walk-around inspection, complete the exterior inspection form provided in Figure 3-3. You can use your smartphone to take photos and video clips and to record notes. If you decide to use your smartphone, refer to Figure 3-3 as a checklist for the information you need to gather on your phone. You may be unable to collect all the information listed on the form but collect as much information as possible without becoming too pushy if the homeowners confront you.

**TIP**

If the home is currently listed for sale, call the agent, and take a tour of the inside of the house. You don't need to tell the agent that you know the homeowners are facing foreclosure. Figure 3-4 is an inspection form for the interior of the property; take the form with you and fill it out.

## Exterior Property Evaluation

Owner: _____

Home Phone: _____Work Phone: _____Pager/Mobile: _____

Address: _____

Distinguishing Feature of Property: _____

Property is:  ❑ Vacant          ❑ Owner Occupied          ❑ Tenant Occupied

**Tenant Info:**          How Long at Home? _____Monthly Rent: _____

---

**Neighborhood Details:**          ❑ Brick  ❑ Frame    ❑ Mix

Block Club?              ❑ Yes    ❑ No

# of burn-outs: ____#of board-ups:_____#of vacant lots:_____%ownership:_____

Neighborhood Rating:   ❑ Poor        ❑ Fair          ❑ Good         ❑ Excellent

Neighborhood Listings:

    Address:_____Phone:_____Asking Price: _____

    Address:_____Phone:_____Asking Price: _____

    Address:_____Phone:_____Asking Price: _____

---

**House Details:**

Garage: ❑ Yes ❑ No  # of Cars: ____      Condition: ❑ Poor ❑ Fair ❑ Good

Driveway:   ❑ None    ❑ Solid   ❑ Ribbon    ❑ Asphalt    ❑ Alley

          Condition:  ❑ Poor   ❑ Fair       ❑ Good

Roof Type: _____Age:_____      Condition: ❑ Poor ❑ Fair ❑ Good

Type of Construction:   ❑ Brick      ❑ Frame     ❑ Aluminum   ❑ Block

                  ❑ Asbestos   ❑ Vinyl      ❑ Brickote    ❑ Stucco

      Condition:     ❑ Poor      ❑ Fair       ❑ Good

Year Built: _____Square Footage:_____Number of Bedrooms: ___

House Style:       ❑ Tudor      ❑ Bungalow  ❑ Ranch       ❑ Split-Level

              ❑ Colonial   ❑ Cape Cod  ❑ Multi-Family: _____

Foundation:        ❑ Basement  ❑ Slab      ❑ Crawl      ❑ Piers

Storm Doors/Storm Windows/Screens Condition:    ❑ Poor        ❑ Fair       ❑ Good

Window Condition:        ❑ Poor ❑ Fair   ❑ Good          Lot Size: _____

Fence: ❑ Chain  ❑ Wood ❑ Wire     Landscape: ❑ Poor ❑ Fair  ❑ Good

Porch: ❑ Cement ❑ Wood ❑ Brick      Condition:  ❑ Poor ❑ Fair  ❑ Good

Steps: ❑ Cement ❑ Wood ❑ Brick      Condition:  ❑ Poor ❑ Fair  ❑ Good

Door: ❑ Wood  ❑ Steel            Condition:  ❑ Poor ❑ Fair  ❑ Good

Recommendation: ❑ Cash Buy   ❑ Re-Fi ❑ Listing   ❑ Short Sale    ❑ Pass

          ❑ Other:_____

Reasoning/Notes:_____

_____

_____

© John Wiley & Sons, Inc.

**FIGURE 3-3:** Personally inspect the neighborhood and the exterior of the property and record your observations.

**TIP**

Never pass up the opportunity to talk to a neighbor. If a neighbor wanders out to ask what you're doing, strike up a conversation and try to find out more about the homeowners and the condition of the property. What if the neighbors aren't nosy? Then consider becoming a little nosy yourself and knocking on doors. A neighbor may have been inside the house recently. If you can't get in to inspect the property, a secondhand report from a neighbor is the next-best thing. In some cases, you may even stumble across a neighbor whom the homeowner has anointed to be caretaker; if they have keys or are willing to show you around, you've struck gold!

### *Interior Property Evaluation*

Owner: _____

Home Phone: _____ Work Phone: _____ Pager/Mobile: _____

Address: _____

Cross Streets: _____

**Occupant reported problems:**

❑ Electrical  ❑ Plumbing  ❑ Heating  ❑ Leaks  ❑ Others: _____

                       Details: _____

**KITCHEN**

Check:  ❑ Water Pressure  ❑ Lights  ❑ Floor  ❑ Cabinets  ❑ Counter Tops  ❑ Sink

Overall Condition:  ❑ Poor  ❑ Fair  ❑ Good  ❑ Excellent

Kitchen Notes: _____

_____

**BATHROOM**

Check:  ❑ Water Pressure  ❑ Lights  ❑ Floor  ❑ Sink  ❑ Tub/Shower

            ❑ Mirror  ❑ Vanity

Overall Condition:  ❑ Poor  ❑ Fair  ❑ Good  ❑ Excellent

Bathroom Notes: _____

_____

**OTHER ROOMS (Living Room / Bedrooms / Family Room / Den / Library / etc.)**

Check:  ❑ Floor Covering  ❑ Paint/Wallpaper  ❑ Ceiling

Overall Condition:  ❑ Poor  ❑ Fair  ❑ Good  ❑ Excellent

Other Rooms Notes: _____

_____

Interior Extras: _____

**BASEMENT**

Check:  ❑ Cracks in Walls & Floor  ❑ Windows  ❑ Watertight?  ❑ Stairs/Handrail
          ❑ Lights

Overall Condition:  ❑ Poor  ❑ Fair  ❑ Good  ❑ Excellent

Basement Notes: _____

_____

Recommendation:  ❑ Cash Buy  ❑ Re-Fi  ❑ Listing  ❑ Short Sale  ❑ Pass
                   ❑ Other: _____

Reasoning/Notes: _____

_____

**FIGURE 3-4:**
Inspect the home's interior if possible.

© *John Wiley & Sons, Inc.*

## Snapping some photos

As you walk around the property, take a couple of photos of every side of the house, the landscape, and surrounding houses. The photo documentary you create is priceless. If you inspect dozens of properties, you're not likely to remember a specific house. A few photos can take you right back to the day when you inspected the property.

**TIP**

If possible, take your photos in late morning or early afternoon, when the home-owners are more likely to be at work and the kids to be in school. Then you can likely avoid any confrontation with the homeowners and keep the kids from asking their parents embarrassing questions like "Why is that person taking pictures of our house?" You can also keep a low profile by snapping photos from inside your car. Whatever you do, just make sure you're on public property — the sidewalk or street rather than in someone's yard.

In addition to photographing the property itself, photograph the neighborhood:

>> Take a photo of the street view (both ways).

>> Take a picture of the houses across the street.

>> Photograph any eyesores.

If you're using old-school folders for your property dossiers, as soon as possible after snapping the photos, print them or upload them to your favorite photo processing service to have them printed. Stick the photos in your property dossier for later reference. If you prefer a more modern approach, upload all your data to the cloud so that you can access it from anywhere with any digital device. Create a separate folder for each property.

# Assembling Your Property Dossier: A Checklist

For every property coauthor Ralph investigates, he creates a separate folder for all the documents pertaining to that property. He uses different-colored folders to keep data for his top prospects separate. You can use a similar strategy, but feel free to be creative; just make sure that your system keeps all the data on each house separate and easily accessible. You can even store the information in separate folders on your computer or in the cloud.

**REMEMBER**

However you choose to organize your property information, make sure that each folder contains the following items:

>> An 8-by-10-inch photograph of the property that you can tape to the front of the folder for quick reference

>> The foreclosure notice

>> The foreclosure information sheet you completed

- » The exterior inspection form you completed

- » Neighborhood inspection, complete with photos

- » Information on any other properties that are listed for sale in the area so you can track their sale prices and how long they took to sell

- » A map showing the location of the property

- » The title commitment and 24-month history in the chain of title or (at minimum) the last two recorded documents

- » The last recorded first mortgage so that you know how much the homeowners currently owe on the property

- » Records of other liens on the property, such as second mortgages, construction liens, and tax liens — property tax liens are especially important, because if you buy the property, you're responsible for paying any back property taxes.

- » A copy of the deed with the current homeowners' names which should match the names on the title

- » The city worksheet on the property showing its history

- » The SEV

- » Multiple Listing Service (MLS) listings of comparable properties that have recently sold or are currently for sale

TIP

If you gathered information to bid for properties at an auction, bring all your folders with you. You may have researched 20 properties and narrowed your prospects to the top three, but take all 20 folders with you, because you never know what will happen come auction day. You may have ruled out a $250,000 house that had a $260,000 mortgage on it, but when the auction rolls around, it may open with a bid for $170,000. By referencing your property dossier and doing some basic math, you realize that you can pick up $80,000 in equity. Because you've done your homework and have your property dossier with you, you may be the only person in the room who knows what that house is worth. When that happens, you're like a fox in the henhouse.

# Recognizing the Most Common and Serious Red Flags and Big Mistakes

WARNING

Part of performing your due diligence involves spotting red flags and avoiding big mistakes. Here are a few of the most common and serious red flags and big mistakes to avoid:

>> **Right address, wrong street:** When inspecting a property, be sure that you're at the right address on the right street, not one or two streets over. Take a photo of the address from the front of the property or its mailbox; then go to the corner and take a photo of the street signs at the nearest intersection. Check the address in your research notes to be sure you're inspecting the right property. (This issue is less common in newer neighborhoods.)

>> **Overlooked lien:** If a property has a tax lien against it and the foreclosing bank or its attorney failed to give proper notice to the IRS, the state, or the county, the lien may not get wiped out in the foreclosure process. You're not legally liable to pay other people's income taxes, but the taxing authorities could make your life uncomfortable.

>> **Condemned home:** If you're looking at an older home that needs work, check with the municipality to ensure that it's not condemned and subject to being torn down.

TIP

When you're buying a bank-owned property or a property at a foreclosure sale, using the title company that's owned by the law firm representing the bank can save you a lot of time. Large law firms across the country that represent banks frequently own their own title company, which provides them another revenue source.

Performing Your Due Diligence

IN THIS CHAPTER

» Selling quick and for top dollar through an agent

» Prepping your property for a showing

» Marketing your property to spark interest

» Negotiating offers and closing the deal

» Investigating other cash-out options

# Chapter 4

# Cashing Out on Your Foreclosure Property

Most investors who deal in foreclosures flip properties; they buy the property at a bargain price, repair or renovate it if necessary to maximize their return on investment, and then turn around and place the property back on the market. Some investors, however, prefer the buy-and-hold strategy, leasing the property for a steady cash flow. This chapter covers both strategies.

## Selling Through a Qualified Real Estate Agent

You can boost your bottom line on a property in two ways: increase the price or cut expenses. Increasing the price is often counterproductive, as discussed in the later section "Generating Interest Through Savvy Marketing." Cutting expenses within reason may be a possibility, but steer clear of any temptation to cut costs by trying to sell the house yourself. Why? The following sections answer that question and then provide tips on how to select an agent who's best qualified to sell your property.

## SELL IT YOURSELF?

Sellers often try to sell their homes on their own to avoid paying an agent's commission, but doing so rarely saves them enough to justify the hassle. What usually happens is that when prospective buyers place an offer on the house, they know that the seller is saving about 6 percent by self-listing, so they deduct 6 percent from their offer. If the sellers accept that offer, they essentially give the buyer as much as they would have paid the agent, and they had to do all the work without the additional benefits of professional assistance and advice!

Most people choose to sell without a real estate agent because they had a bad experience with an agent or felt that the agent didn't do enough to justify their 6 percent commission. This point is very valid, but it simply means that the seller didn't pick the right agent.

When you're selling a house, don't look only at the cost of hiring an agent. Look also at the cost of *not* hiring an agent and consider the benefits an agent brings to the table — particularly the closing table.

## Selling faster for a higher price

Sure, a 6 to 8 percent agent commission can take a sizable bite out of your net profit, but consider the advantages of having an agent:

» On average, an agent sells a home in half the time it takes a homeowner working alone. If you ballpark your holding costs at $100 per day, you lose about $3,000 every month your property sits on the market.

» According to the National Association of Realtors (NAR), the average home sells for 16 percent more when sold by a Realtor. (A Realtor is a real estate agent who's certified by the NAR and is required to receive additional training and adhere to a strict code of ethics.)

» An agent can market to other agents through Multiple Listing Services (MLSes) and network with other agents, relocation firms, and other services to increase interest in your property, ideally triggering a bidding war that can boost the sale price.

» An agent can prescreen buyers so that you don't waste time showing the home to people who don't have the cash and can't obtain the financing to buy it. You want qualified buyers, not lookie-loos.

>> An agent takes on the burden of fielding phone calls from interested buyers, scheduling tours, showing the house, and handling the paperwork. That's time you can spend working on other investment properties.

>> Having an agent during negotiations is like putting on a poker face when playing cards. The agent can negotiate with a buyer without giving away any secrets concerning what you may be willing to accept.

**TIP**

You should sell the property yourself *only* if the conditions are right:

>> Someone walks through while you're rehabbing and is willing to sign a purchase agreement on the spot, and you completely understand the purchase agreement and are confident in executing the agreement without the assistance of a professional.

>> You're in a seller's market — an area where you have significantly more buyers than sellers. Try this approach for only a short period of time, however. If the house doesn't sell, call an agent.

>> The house is on a street that already has plenty of buyer traffic and you have the best house with the best price.

>> You have the time and desire to show the house at any time of day or night when a buyer calls to see it.

>> You have the computer skills required to produce slick marketing materials and advertise on the Internet.

>> You're able to show the house without tipping your hand.

>> You intend to hire an attorney to approve all the documentation and attend the closing.

The next section offers guidance on finding an agent who's best qualified to sell the property.

**TIP**

If you're trying to sell the home yourself, plant a for sale by owner (FSBO) sign in the front yard along with a note saying something like "Buyer's Agents Welcome" or "Commission Paid to Broker." This message lets buyer's agents know that if they show the home to someone who purchases it, you're willing to pay them something, which may increase traffic.

## Choosing a top-notch seller's agent

Real estate agents generally fall into two camps: buyer's agents and seller's agents (also called *listing agents*). Think of the difference in terms of prosecuting and defense attorneys. Each type of attorney specializes in serving a different type of client with very different needs:

>> In real estate, a buyer's agent is typically much more skilled at looking out for the interests of the buyer — finding the right house for the buyer at the right price and negotiating for a lower price and more attractive terms.

>> A seller's agent has a skill set that leans more toward marketing and sales. (Some top-producing firms have both buyer's and seller's agents.)

For a seller like you, a seller's agent offers the following unique benefits:

>> Prices your house to sell for top dollar without lingering on the market

>> Markets your property more effectively — a buyer's agent may be less skilled at marketing

>> Ensures that you properly disclose any defects in the property

>> Passes along any information about the buyer that may assist you in negotiating for a higher price

REMEMBER

To choose a qualified real estate agent, make sure that the agent has the following:

>> **Credentials:** Look for a designation or certification proving that the agent received proper training, such as Certified Residential Specialist (CRI), Graduate Realtor Institute (GRI), StarPower Star or member, or Golden R-Top 1% Club.

>> **Experience:** Consider someone with ten years or more of experience. You may find an inexperienced agent who's very well qualified, but an experienced agent with a solid track record is more of a sure thing.

>> **Drive:** Choose an agent dedicated to research who can provide you market analysis and listings of comparable properties. The agent should be willing to hold open houses, show the house on a moment's notice, and be attentive to your questions and needs.

# Staging Your House for a Successful Showing

Staging a property consists of making it look as pretty as possible. Studies by the staging industry (yes, it's an entire industry) prove that a properly staged home sells in half the time for 7 to 10 percent more than a comparable unstaged home.

Given those numbers, a home that normally would take three months to sell at a price of $250,000 would sell in six weeks for $267,500 tp $275,000 with professional staging!

You're free to hire a professional stager, of course, but if your budget is already strained, you can probably do a pretty good job staging the home yourself. The latest edition of *Flipping Houses For Dummies* (Wiley) devotes an entire chapter to the basics. The following sections provide a brief overview of the areas to focus on when you're staging the house you're selling.

## Jazzing up the front entrance

TIP

During your renovations, you improve the appearance of the house so much that minor imperfections stick out. Carefully inspect the outside of the house for anything that sticks out and attend to it immediately. Here are some tips for perking up the curb appeal:

>> **Spruce up the landscaping.** Mow and edge the lawn, pull weeds, fix any cracks in the pavement, and sweep up after yourself. Lay fresh mulch, plant fresh flowers (in season), and keep the plantings watered. While you're at it, put the garden hose away and hide the garden gnomes.

>> **Freshen the entryways.** Sweep the porch and stairs, lay down an attractive new doormat, fix the screens, wash the windows, polish the doorknobs, and clear the clutter out of the entryways. Make sure that the doors open and close with ease.

>> **Check the outside lights.** Make sure that the porch and security lights are working.

## Decluttering the inside

TIP

Clutter makes a house feel cramped and makes buyers nervous. Investment properties usually don't have a problem with clutter. You probably dejunked the place before you started repairs and renovations, but if you can't walk through the house without tripping over something, take the following steps to remove nonessential items:

>> **Dejunk the place.** Remove all nonessential items. You can sell the stuff, dump it, or give it away. Just make sure that it doesn't appear on the premises.

>> **Clear the counters.** Counter space is pure gold. In the kitchen, remove everything from the counters, including coffeepots, electric can openers,

blenders, toasters, flour tins, cookie jars, and especially knife racks and dish drainers. In the bathroom, hide the toothbrush holder, hairbrushes, lotions, creams, and other glamour paraphernalia.

>> **Empty the closets.** Storage space is prime real estate.

>> **Ditch politically incorrect décor.** A house showing is an emotional event. Any decor that may stir negative emotions in potential buyers has to go, including religious icons, political paraphernalia, and zodiac signs.

## Adding a few tasteful furnishings

When showing a house, your goal is to create a blank canvas on which buyers can paint their dreams and visions. Less is more, but a vacant house can be just as unappealing. Homeowners want to be able to envision themselves living in the house, so make it look livable with a few tasteful furnishings:

>> **A small kitchen or dining room table with matching chairs:** Dress the table with an attractive tablecloth (not plastic), a bouquet of fresh-cut flowers, or some other attractive centerpiece. Better yet, opt for a table with a glass top; it can make the kitchen look a little roomier.

>> **An attractive sofa and a coffee table in the living room or den:** Accent the room with a few small lamps and a bit of greenery. Hanging one or more stylish mirrors that reflect the windows can also create the illusion of wide-open space.

>> **A standard-size bed and small dresser in the master bedroom**

>> **A few neutral paintings or other artwork on the walls**

TIP

Seasoned investors often have some surplus furniture left behind in other homes they've sold. To keep costs down, consider moving furniture from your permanent residence to the house you're selling or borrow surplus furniture from friends or family members.

TIP

To gather some ideas about how to stage a home professionally, visit a few model homes in newly constructed subdivisions. You'll quickly notice that these model homes are clean, tastefully furnished, and attractively decorated; they're never vacant. Also, check out the window dressings. In models, instead of heavy curtains or blinds, you typically see something more airy such as valances.

## Appealing to the senses

**TIP**

When you go out to eat at a fine restaurant, the quality of your dining experience relies on much more than the quality of the food and service. The lighting, aromas, and background music all contribute to the ambience. When staging a home, you want to create a pleasant sensory experience for the buyer. The following are some tips to assist you:

>> **Light it up.** Turn on all the lights to make the house appear warmer and roomier and to prove that you're not trying to hide something.

>> **Bring the outside in.** If the weather's nice, open the house to air it out. Place fresh-cut flowers in the kitchen, living room, and den to add a fresh, natural aroma. Most professional stagers recommend against using potpourri, scented candles, and air fresheners. If the home has a fireplace, consider lighting it — only in season, of course. Another nice touch is to arrange cut and uncut citrus fruit in a glass bowl on the kitchen counter or dining room table; the natural aroma of fresh citrus is pleasant without being overpowering and the arrangement is both attractive and inexpensive.

>> **Play some relaxing background music.** Classical music is often a good choice. Rock, rap, and heavy metal are usually bad choices.

**WARNING**

If you're living in the house you're selling, you may be tempted to hang out while your agent shows the prospective buyers around. Avoid the temptation. Your presence can make the buyers nervous and make the house feel crowded. Step out until everyone leaves. You can contact your agent after the showing to find out how it went.

# Generating Interest Through Savvy Marketing

**TIP**

If you took our advice and hired a top-notch seller's agent to list your property, your agent can handle the marketing for you, primarily by creating an MLS listing. If you decide to sell the home on your own, the marketing job falls on your shoulders, and without access to the MLS, you need to ramp up your marketing efforts. Here are some ideas for creating your own effective marketing campaign:

>> **Set a competitive asking price.** Shoppers look for value. Set the right asking price and you attract more buyers. Set your asking price too high and the property is likely to linger on the market while holding costs chip away at your

profit. Set the price too low and prospective buyers may think something is wrong with the house. Starting a little high is preferable to starting a little low; you can adjust down, but adjusting up can raise some eyebrows. Smart agents and buyers ask for a listing history. See Chapter 3 in Book 6 for more about pricing a house to sell.

>> **Plant a "For Sale" sign on the front lawn.** The sign taps into "the power of 20"; the 5 neighbors on either side of you and the 10 neighbors across the street notice the sign immediately and start telling people about it. Use a professional sign, not one of those cheap, wire-frame jobs you can buy at the local hardware store.

>> **List the property online.** Several companies list homes for sale by owner, and buyers can search for homes without going through an agent. Before you sign up with one of these services, make sure that it's legitimate, that it lists plenty of homes in your area, and that it's used by many buyers in your area.

>> **Advertise in the classifieds.** Post an ad in the classifieds section of your local newspaper and on any classifieds websites such as Craigslist (https://craigslist.org).

>> **Design, print, and distribute flashy flyers.** Include full-color photos of the property, highlighting its most attractive features. Also include the address of the property, the asking price, a description of the property, your name, and your phone number. Print the flyers on high-quality paper and post them wherever you can legally do so — grocery stores, gas stations, restaurants, and apartment complexes, to name a few.

>> **Design, print, and distribute business cards.** Create a business card for the house and pass it out to everyone you meet.

>> **Generate some word-of-mouth buzz.** Soon after placing the house on the market, host an open house and invite the neighbors. Post some "Open House" signs around the neighborhood and provide food and beverages. Sunday afternoons are usually the best times to schedule an open house because many people have nothing better to do.

TIP

To market any product effectively, determine who's likely to buy it. When you're marketing a house to a first-time homeowner, for example, you might highlight the affordability of the house and provide a lead on where to go for financing. When you're marketing to movin'-on-up buyers, you may want to pitch the house as being spacious beyond belief. Empty-nesters and downsizers are often looking for something smaller that's in move-in condition. Consider sending flyers to the residents of local apartment complexes. Modify your marketing materials to appeal to your target buyers.

# Negotiating Offers and Counteroffers

When prospective buyers deem your house to be worthy of purchase, they present an offer in writing. The high-profile part of the offer is the purchase price, but savvy sellers don't focus on price alone; they also consider the price and terms of the offer. In many cases, a lower offer is superior if the buyer has the cash or financing in place and doesn't demand a lot of extras, such as closing costs and repairs.

The following sections provide some guidance on how to pick the best offer when you have two or more competing offers and show you how to negotiate to get more of what you want.

## Comparing offers

**REMEMBER**

When you're buying and selling houses, you need to be able to evaluate offers based on the following factors:

>> **Price:** An obvious lowball offer may cause some concern, but if you set your asking price in line with comparable properties, the offer should include a price that's close to your asking price. Coauthor Ralph usually considers a cash offer of 5 percent below his asking price to be pretty good, and he expects a higher offer if the buyer needs to finance the purchase.

>> **Buyer's financing:** Cash is king, preapproved financing is queen, and prequalification is a jack. An offer that proves the ability of the buyer to close on the sale is much better than an offer from buyers who plan on applying for a loan after they find the house they want. If you have any doubts about a buyer's financing, ask them to contact your mortgage specialist (loan officer), who can advise you on their ability to qualify for financing.

>> **Earnest money:** The more earnest money a buyer includes with the purchase offer, the more likely they are to be willing and able to purchase the property. An earnest-money deposit of at least 1 percent of the purchase price shows a fairly strong buyer commitment.

>> **Conditional clauses:** Standard conditions include that the property must appraise at the sales price or higher, title must be clear, and the house must pass inspection. Watch out for anything that can undermine the closing, including conditions that the buyer's existing home must sell first. Contingencies that allow the buyer to back out of the deal without just cause (commonly called *weasel clauses*) also raise red flags, such as "Buyer's attorney must review and approve the offer."

>> **Closing date:** A faster closing reduces your holding costs, so if one buyer offers $2,000 less than another buyer but can close a month earlier, the lower offer may be the better offer.

Accept offers only from serious buyers who are at least prequalified for a loan that's sufficient for purchasing your house. Have your mortgage specialist on call to check up on a prospective buyer's qualifications before you sign the purchase agreement. Your mortgage specialist can contact the buyer's lender and perform background checks to ensure that the buyer has sufficient financing in place.

**TIP**

If you're not 100 percent confident in a buyer's offer, consider countering the offer with a 72-hour contingency that allows you to accept the buyer's offer while continuing to market the property. Your agent should be well versed in this strategy.

## Mastering the art of counteroffers

Some offers are so low that all you can do is laugh and shrug them off, but in most cases, no offer is too low to reject outright. When you receive an offer that appears to be irrational, don't take it personally. If you're not ready to say either yes or no, simply reply with your counteroffer.

### STEERING CLEAR OF "CASH BACK AT CLOSING" DEALS

More and more buyers are looking to get a little cash back at the closing table. They may even offer to pay more than your asking price with the agreement that you'll hand the excess cash back to them at closing. "Cash back at closing" deals are illegal, no matter what the buyer claims to need the money for — repairs, renovations, credit card or medical bills, or whatever.

Why are these deals illegal? Because the lender is never in the know. To obtain cash back at closing, the buyer must fool the lender into thinking that the house is worth as much as the buyer is asking to borrow. The lender approves the loan, thinking that the home's value is sufficient to cover the loan amount. If the borrower can't pay the mortgage, the bank can foreclose and sell the house to cover the loss. "Cash back at closing" deals trick lenders into approving riskier loans.

If someone approaches you with one of these deals, call the lender. The lender's phone number is usually listed on the mortgage note or the closing instruction letter included in the closing papers.

To navigate counteroffer negotiations more effectively, employ the following strategies:

>> Pitch the counteroffer through your agent. Otherwise, you risk tipping your hand.

>> Make yourself readily available to your agent during the negotiation process so that you can respond quickly to counteroffers.

>> Don't bid against yourself. Wait for the buyer's counteroffer before offering any additional concessions.

>> Don't give ultimatums. Ultimatums or take-it-or-leave-it offers shut down communications. Successful negotiations require an open forum.

>> Don't let a personality clash get in the way of making the deal.

>> Keep a lid on it. If you talk too much, you're liable to tip your hand or upset the buyer, neither of which is productive.

>> Respond only in writing. If the buyers or their agent contact you over the phone with a proposed offer, request that they present it in writing to keep it legal. In real estate, everything has to be in writing to be legal.

If you receive an offer that's close to what you want, you don't have to counter. If you can live with the offer, countering a couple thousand dollars higher may be a bad idea (and generally is) because it lets the buyer off the hook and free to pursue the search for another house. If you're receiving lots of offers, you may want to counter, but in a buyer's market, an offer that's close to what you want with acceptable terms may be a great offer.

Consider countering a lowball offer with a highball offer. If the prospective buyers offer $100,000 on a house you listed for $143,000, consider countering with $142,500. This offer lets the buyers know that you'll deal, but they must be serious. Have your agent contact the buyers' agent and try to find out why the offer was so low. Have your agent play the game; your agent tells the buyers' agent that you have some wiggle room, but not much and that you were ready to walk away but after some convincing decided to try to work with the buyers. This approach may build some goodwill with the buyers that may result in a more reasonable offer. Your other option is to simply write *Rejected* across the offer and send it back.

# Closing the Deal

After you and the buyers reach an agreement on price and terms, and assuming that nothing happens to sabotage the deal, the sale proceeds to the closing, at which you receive your money and sign over the deed to the buyer. At this point, you have two goals: to make the closing proceed as smoothly as possible and to ensure that your back end is covered.

**REMEMBER**

As soon as you and the buyer agree on price and terms, return the documents to the buyer's mortgage company and to your title company or real estate attorney and schedule a closing date. Closings typically occur 30 to 45 days from the day you sell the property, so you don't want to waste any time. As soon as you sell the property, you must order the title policy. Neither the buyer nor the seller needs to worry about this process; your real estate agent keeps it moving forward and can recommend a title company or attorney to handle the paperwork.

To ensure that the closing proceeds as smoothly as possible, supply your closing agent any documents necessary for preparing the closing packets. Documents typically include the following:

>> Termite inspection report: If the buyer is receiving Federal Housing Administration (FHA) financing to purchase the house, immediately schedule a termite inspection and send the report to the closing agent or attorney who's handling the closing.

>> Purchase agreement and any addendums.

>> Mortgage-payoff information and any second mortgages or other liens.

**WARNING**

Even if you sell the house yourself, you should have professional representation at the closing — a qualified Realtor or a real estate attorney. Keep in mind that Realtors aren't lawyers and can't give legal advice. Obtain the closing packet two or three days before closing, review the papers with the assistance of your attorney or Realtor, and clear up any issues and concerns before the scheduled closing. Get your attorney involved before you sign on the dotted line. After you sign, your attorney has much less power to protect you.

# Checking Out Other Cash-Out Strategies

Buying a foreclosure property, fixing it up (or not), and then placing it back on the market is the most common way to profit from a foreclosure, but it's not the only way. For those of you who are practicing the buy-and-hold strategy, this section suggests some of the pros and cons of leasing the property and taking on the role of landlord, which many investors simply aren't cut out to do. You can also profit from your property instantly by refinancing your loan for more than you invested in the property, or you can sell or lease the property back to the previous owners or even sell the senior mortgage you bought at auction to another lienholder. Here, you find several strategies for pulling the equity out of an investment property, along with other novel ways to profit from your foreclosure investment.

## Becoming a landlord

Most people who invest in real estate are looking for a quick score. They buy, sell, and then sit back and count the money. Others prefer the buy-and-hold strategy, leasing the property for some period before selling it. The buy-and hold strategy offers several valuable benefits:

>> **By holding the property for one year and a day, you pay long-term rather than short-term capital gains on your profit.** During the writing of this book, the feds were charging up to 37 percent in short-term capital gains and only up to 20 percent in long-term capital gains.

>> **You can claim depreciation of the property as a tax deduction.** This approach is a rare tax situation in which you can claim depreciation as the property appreciates.

>> **You profit in three ways.** You profit when you buy the property below market value, the property appreciates over time, and the rent from your tenants pays down the principal on the loan.

>> **You can deduct any expenses that you incur for maintenance and management of the property.**

REMEMBER

These tips are simply suggestions on strategies to discuss with your accountant.

Keep in mind that not everyone is landlord material. You need to find renters, collect the rent, maintain the property, and be able to handle calls from tenants at any time of day or night. You may be able to hire a property management company to take care of all these tasks for you, but that expense cuts into your profits. If you're considering the leasing option, you should read the latest edition of *Property Management Kit For Dummies* by Robert S. Griswold (Wiley). You can also check out Chapter 5 in Book 1 for basics on managing residential rentals.

## Refinancing to cash out the equity

Homeowners commonly refinance their homes to cash out equity. Refinancing consists of taking out a new mortgage for more than you currently owe on the property and paying off the old mortgage. Assuming that you purchased the property for significantly below market value and your credit is in pretty good shape, you may be able to turn right around after the purchase and refinance to cash out that equity.

We say "may" because some lenders won't refinance a mortgage until after you've owned a home for six months and a day or a year and a day. The reason is that a house is worth only what you actually paid for it or what it appraises for, whichever is lower. A home-equity loan to cover repairs and renovations, however, is often easier to obtain.

TIP

You don't have to cash out all the equity in a property. You can cash out a portion of it to cover repairs and renovations, and cash out the rest when you sell the property.

REMEMBER

When you're refinancing to cash out the equity in a home, be as careful shopping for mortgages as you were when you borrowed the money to purchase the property. Avoid high-cost loans and any loans that have prepayment penalties, especially if you're planning to place the house back on the market soon. See Chapter 4 in Book 1 for guidance on financing property purchases.

## Reselling the property to the previous owners or their family

After you officially own a property it's yours to sell, and the previous homeowners must move out if they haven't moved out already. Sometimes after foreclosure, however, the homeowners break the news to other family members who are in a position to bail them out by loaning or giving them some money or buying the house and letting them live in it. In such cases, you may be able to sell the property back to the original owners or their relatives.

The following sections reveal some do's and don'ts that apply to these situations, along with some of the positive aspects of selling a foreclosure back to the previous owners.

### Reselling to the previous owners

WARNING

The previous owners are likely to do whatever it takes to remain in their home. If their financial situation has improved since the foreclosure, or if friends and family members have offered them a good chunk of cash, they may be in a position to buy back the property. The opportunity, however, is not always available or attractive for you as an investor. Keep the following caveats in mind:

>> If the property has any liens against it that were wiped off the books by the foreclosure, those liens reattach themselves to the property if the previous homeowners buy it back. This situation can drive the homeowners back into foreclosure, which isn't something that you or they really want.

>> Legally, you're prohibited from stripping the homeowners of all the equity they have in the property. Suppose that you purchased a property worth $300,000 for $175,000. If you sell it back to the previous homeowners for $300,000, you've taken all the equity out of the house. You have two options: Sell the house to someone else for $300,000 or sell it back to the previous owners at a discount of, say, $225,000. Whatever you do, you don't want to be an equity-stripper. See the nearby sidebar "Equity stripping: Don't do it!" for details.

Why would you agree to accept less than full market value for the house? Whenever coauthor Ralph can earn a quick, tidy profit on a house and do the right thing for the homeowners, he jumps at the chance. Usually, he develops a close relationship with the homeowners during the foreclosure process and doesn't want to destroy their trust by taking them to the cleaners. In addition, he doesn't want to ruin his reputation in the community; he's in it for the long term. If Ralph treats the homeowners fairly, they're likely to recommend him to others they know who find themselves in similar situations. If you can earn a fair profit while helping your fellow humans, you're strongly encouraged to do so. Otherwise, simply have them move out and sell to someone who can afford to pay the full price.

Another reason why you may want to consider selling the property back to the previous owners comes down to simple economics. Suppose that you're facing the likelihood of holding the property for six months. If you're paying $100 per day in holding costs, you're looking at a total bill of $18,000. On top of that, figure closing costs of 7 percent on $200,000 (a total of $14,000), and your bill is up to $32,000. Now figure in your time and effort plus the costs of repairs and renovations. Sure, the homeowners get a break, but you also save yourself some money.

WARNING

If you took out a traditional loan to purchase the property, your mortgage probably has a due-on-sale clause, which means that you're prohibited from selling the property back to the previous homeowners without the lender's approval.

TIP

If selling the home back to the previous homeowners isn't an option due to the possibility of having other liens reattach to the property, you may be able to sell to a family member who agrees to let the homeowners remain in the house.

# EQUITY STRIPPING: DON'T DO IT!

Homeowners who are facing foreclosure are often unaware of their options and of just how much equity they've built up in their property. They may have been making their monthly mortgage payments for 10 or 15 years while housing values in their neighborhood have been rising at a rate of 5 to 10 percent annually. They're completely unaware that the house they bought for $100,000 ten years ago is now worth $150,000, and they've paid off about $14,000 of the principal, so they have $64,000 worth of equity. All they see are the monthly bills coming in that they can't pay.

The homeowners' ignorance of the amount of equity they have in their home can make them vulnerable to predatory lenders and other crooks who want to cash out that equity for themselves. These equity-strippers employ a variety of schemes to bleed this money out of the homeowners, including these:

- Mortgage brokers attempt to persuade the homeowners to refinance their way out of a financial setback by taking out a loan with higher monthly mortgage payments than the homeowners can afford. The mortgage broker rakes in the payments until the homeowners run out of money, then they foreclose on the property.

- Crooked investors persuade homeowners who have a substantial amount of equity built up in their property to sell the property to them for significantly less than the property is worth. The "investor" may promise the homeowners that they can continue living in the home indefinitely, and then, as soon as the homeowners sign the papers, the con artist evicts them.

- Con artists offer to save the homeowners from foreclosure. All the homeowners are required to do is sign a quitclaim deed over to the con artists, who promise to "take care of everything." The con artists slither over to the county courthouse and have the deed recorded in their names, making them the owners. Yes, it's that easy.

- A con artist may offer to buy the home from the homeowners and lease it back to them. The con artist collects the monthly rent and never pays off the underlying mortgage, so the homeowners lose their rent money and also lose the house in foreclosure.

If you buy a property directly from homeowners who are facing foreclosure or at auction for a bargain-basement price and then sell the property back to the homeowners at full market value, you're practicing yet another form of equity stripping, which the courts frown upon. Regardless of whether you get caught, it's still wrong, and if you do get caught, you can look forward to a hefty fine and perhaps some jail time. At the very least, you'll be ordered to undo the transaction and put the homeowners back in the position they were in before they met you.

### Financing the buyback through insurance-policy proceeds and other means

Homeowners are often unaware of assets and other collateral they have to secure financing, or they come into some quick money after the foreclosure is a done deal. In such cases, you may be able to help the homeowners obtain the funds needed to buy back the property simply by making them aware of their options. Following are two options that may be available:

>> **Life insurance policies:** If the home ended up in foreclosure because one of the homeowners passed away, and the deceased had a life insurance policy, cashing out that policy may provide sufficient funds for the surviving home-owner to repurchase the property. In some cases, a serious illness drives a couple into foreclosure, and then the spouse who was seriously ill passes away, leaving behind a life insurance policy that can cover the purchase price. See the nearby sidebar "Life-saving life insurance."

>> **Retirement savings:** You can borrow against some retirement plans for the purchase of a house. If the homeowners have sufficient retirement savings, they may be able to borrow against it to buy the house back from you.

## Leasing the property to the foreclosed-on homeowners

Families are often reluctant to move out of their home because they have kids in school. They really need to sell the house and find more-affordable accommodations, but they don't want to force their kids to change schools. In such cases, you may want to consider purchasing the property and then leasing it back to the family until the kids move out or the family has more time to plan.

**WARNING**

Don't jump into a lease agreement with the previous homeowners before you've performed some serious number-crunching. If the homeowners couldn't afford the monthly mortgage payments, don't sign them up for a lease that has them paying monthly rent they can't afford. You'll end up with deadbeat renters and set the family up for another failure. Before offering them the option to rent, make sure that they've resolved the issues that sent them into foreclosure and that they can afford the rent.

If you decide to lease the property to the previous homeowners, consult your real estate attorney to prepare a lease agreement for you. Keep in mind that not everyone is cut out to be a landlord. See the earlier section "Becoming a landlord" for details and recommendations on additional resources that can assist you in managing a rental property effectively.

## LIFE-SAVING LIFE INSURANCE

Coauthor Ralph once had a very positive experience with a man who lost his wife and had substantial life insurance policy proceeds coming to him. He had suffered with his wife's illness on and off for the several years, struggling to keep things together both at home and at work.

Ralph bought the house in foreclosure, not knowing the situation beforehand. The man's wife was still alive when the foreclosure happened. About a month or so before the end of the redemption period, she passed away. The man was now facing the loss of his home on top of everything else.

He told Ralph that he wanted to buy the house back and that he would do so with cash from the life insurance, but the check wouldn't arrive until after the expiration of redemption. Ralph spoke with him and his family quite extensively, and what he ultimately decided was to use the money to buy a different property. The man made the right decision. The house he was losing needed some work, and he didn't feel that he was up to the challenge.

He decided to buy a condo, pay cash, and let someone else worry about the upkeep. Ralph worked with him and gave him plenty of time — first to mourn and then to close on his new condo and move. They worked together, and the man left the house he lost nearly spotless.

Sometimes, doing the right thing results in having to wait a little longer for your profits. Ralph sold that house and made money, the man got a fresh start without the burden of the house, and Ralph knows that the time he waited will pay off tenfold with positive word of mouth. The man and his family couldn't stop thanking Ralph for what he had done.

## Offering a lease-option agreement

When a buyer really wants to purchase a property but isn't currently in the financial position to do so (whether they're the previous owners or some other buyers), you may consider offering them a lease-option agreement. Perhaps the buyers need more time to secure financing or fix something on their credit report, or they're waiting for an insurance check or some other payment. With a lease option, the buyers agree to rent the property from you for a fixed period, with the option to purchase the property at the end of that period.

Lease options aren't always viable, but if the homeowners can come up with a down payment and provide some assurance that they'll be receiving money or be able to qualify for financing in the specified time, a lease option enables you to establish some revenue flow while you're waiting to sell the property. Consider structuring lease-option deals as follows:

>> **Down payment:** Require 5 to 10 percent down. You may want more money down when dealing with buyers who've just been through foreclosure. You credit them for the down payment by taking it off the purchase price, but a substantial down payment assures you that they're serious. If they can't afford it, they can't afford it; let them move on.

>> **Rent:** Specify that rent is due on the first of the month and set the rent at about 1 percent of the purchase price or as close to that amount as is affordable. You don't want to be too flexible, but you don't want to break the bank, either. You can offer a bonus for paying on time and add the monthly payments to the down payment.

>> **Terms and conditions:** The agreement should spell out the lease term and conditions. Your lease-option agreement should contain a forfeiture clause stating that nonpayment results in the forfeiture of the option and the down payment. The agreement should also contain a statement that the option is exercisable at any time, with no prepayment penalty or anything like that. (What coauthor Ralph tells people is that if they win the lottery and want to pay the balance owed on the house tomorrow, that's fine by him. He wants them to succeed, and he wants to realize his profit — the faster the better.)

REMEMBER

Make sure the renters understand that they're renting with an option to buy. If they don't exercise their option during the option period, they may forfeit it. If they don't pay rent, they may forfeit it. Make the terms clear. Follow up with them throughout the lease-option period, ask how their mortgage hunt is coming along, and refer them to mortgage lenders you may know.

TIP

During the paper-signing stage, you can open the recording app on your smartphone and ask permission to record the transaction from beginning to end. You can say that this recording is protection for everyone, ensuring that everyone lives up to their parts of the agreement. Make sure to be thorough and to allow the renters to ask questions, and encourage them to seek legal counsel.

# REPEATING THE SAME MISTAKE

Whenever you're working with homeowners who have a less-than-stellar track record, be careful. People tend to follow the same patterns and repeat the same mistakes.

Coauthor Ralph once purchased a foreclosure property at auction for $245,000. The house was worth about $550,000. The couple who owned the property were fairly affluent, but the wife, who was in charge of making the monthly mortgage payments, wasn't much of a money manager. She failed to make the payments and failed to tell her husband about it. The property ended up on the auction block and Ralph bought it. He actually won the auction with an overbid of $50,000 — that is, he bid $50,000 more than what was owed on the mortgage. That $50,000 was placed in escrow. The couple was entitled to it.

Ralph could have sold the property for $550,000 and walked away with nearly $300,000 in profit, but when he heard the husband tell the story, he figured that he would give the couple a break and sell it back to them for about $300,000 — about $50,000 more than he paid for it. Ralph knew that they had access to the $50,000 in overbid money, so that amount was a pretty good down payment, and the husband earned a good income, so the couple certainly had the means to regain their financial footing and could afford the house. The husband was going to take over the job of paying the bills. Ralph's attorney happened to be in the office that day and sat in on the interview. He advised Ralph to have the couple move and sell the house at full value. Ralph went against his advice because of the husband.

Ralph offered the couple a lease-option agreement that gave them 12 months to buy back the house. They paid him the $50,000 down payment, and he gave them back $10,000 to help them cover their monthly bills. They managed to make their monthly payments for about five months. Then they stopped making payments. What happened? After about five months, the wife insisted on reassuming responsibility for paying the bills and the husband let her. As soon as he stopped managing the finances, the payments stopped. He didn't realize what was happening until Ralph called and told him that they had forfeited the lease option.

During those first five months, they easily could have sold the house themselves for $550,000, paid Ralph the balance of $250,000, and walked away with more than $200,000, but they chose to stiff him. Ralph took possession of the property, and they lost everything — the $50,000 overbid, their house, and the opportunity to make $200,000 free and clear. He didn't feel any sympathy for them. He had given them a break and they returned to the same old patterns that got them into trouble in the first place.

The moral of the story: When you're working with distressed homeowners, be careful. People often develop expensive habits and destructive patterns that are tough to break.

# Assigning your position to a junior lienholder

Suppose that you buy the first mortgage. Do you have to take possession of the property to make a buck? Nope. You can sell your position to a junior lienholder and avoid the ugliness of eviction and the hassles of repairing and renovating the property. Here's how the process works, assuming that you're working in an area with a redemption period (see Chapter 2 in Book 3):

**1.** **Buy the first mortgage, either at auction or by negotiating a short sale with the lender.**

Now you have controlling interest. Just make sure to pay any property taxes owed on the property.

**2.** **Wait out the redemption period.**

If the property has other liens against it, and the lienholders decide to foreclose, another investor may buy one of the junior liens at a sheriff's sale. If another investor buys a junior lien on the property, the clock on that redemption period begins to start ticking while you're already partially through the redemption period on your investment.

**3.** **Approach the holder of the junior lien and say something like "Look, if you buy my interest, I'll sign over my position to you."**

**TIP**

Make your offer worthwhile for the junior lienholder; otherwise, redeeming your lien and waiting a little longer may be the better option. One big advantage of buying your interest is that the junior lienholder then assumes your position in the redemption period instead of having to start from scratch.

# TAKING ADVANTAGE OF YOUR POSITION

Knowing the lienholder positions can often open your eyes to win–win situations with other parties who have a financial interest in the property.

Coauthor Ralph purchased a first mortgage on a property at auction. The house had a second mortgage on it — a lien by the local police department and the county prosecutor. The owner pleaded guilty to drug dealing and had to pay a fine of about $50,000, which was taken as a lien against the house. About one week remained in the redemption period, and the county was going to redeem Ralph's first mortgage, meaning that he stood to get his money back, and that was about all.

Ralph knew from experience that the county didn't want to pay him off and then take possession of the property and have to sell it, so he called the county prosecutor in charge of drug seizures and explained the situation to her. He told her that if she would agree not to redeem his first mortgage, he would split his profits with the county 50/50. It took him less than an hour to work out an agreement. She came back with a counteroffer. She wanted a guaranteed minimum of $20,000, which was a smart move on her part. He agreed.

Ralph ended up taking possession of the property and selling it for a $37,000 profit. The county received the first $20,000, and he received $17,000. He sold the house pretty quickly and got what he wanted out of it, and the county was able to acquire $20,000 without the hassle of dealing with the property.

Had they not struck a deal, Ralph would have walked away with next to nothing.

The take-home message is that you must remain vigilant throughout the process and be prepared to deal with the other lienholders. Remain flexible, and be on the lookout for win–win opportunities; otherwise, you may find yourself the big loser.

# 4

# Flipping a House

# Contents at a Glance

Chapter **1**

# Devising an Effective Flipping Strategy

B efore making an offer on a house, know how you'll profit from it. Will you buy it at a bargain and resell it immediately at market value (or for less, to sell it faster), do a quick makeup job and resell it, perform a few major renovations, or fix it up and use it as a rental? Each of these strategies has benefits and drawbacks, but each strategy gives you a perfectly legitimate way to flip property for a profit.

This chapter explores several house flipping strategies and encourages you to develop your own strategy based on your neighborhood, the resources you have at your disposal, and your preferred approach.

# Deciding on the Role You Want to Play

Flipping a house generally involves buying it, fixing it, and then selling it, but you can profit from this overall process in various ways — depending on how involved you want to be in each of these three progressive steps:

>> **Do it all yourself.** Casual flippers often do it all (or mostly) by themselves — buying the property with their own money (or a conventional loan), completing most of the repairs (and hiring professionals to do anything beyond their level of expertise), and listing the home. Maybe these flippers have a real estate agent help them navigate the buying-and-selling process. This approach may be the most profitable, especially if you live in the home you're flipping.

**WARNING**

Making all the repairs yourself isn't necessarily the most profitable approach. If you take a long time to complete the repairs, holding costs (interest, insurance, utilities, maintenance, and so on) can eat away your profits.

>> **Delegate the heavy lifting.** Experienced flippers often delegate most or all of the work, buying and selling properties through an agent and hiring a contractor to coordinate the repairs and renovations. Sometimes, experienced flippers play the role of contractor, hiring subcontractors (electricians, plumbers, painters, and others) to do the work. Hiring out the work increases repair and renovation expenses, but it can speed the process and reduce holding costs.

>> **Put up the money.** If you have money to invest and don't want to get your hands dirty, you can loan money to people who are willing to do all the work and charge them interest. Or, you can partner with a flipper for a percentage of the profits (assuming that the flip generates a profit).

>> **Bird-dog it.** *Bird-dogging* (also referred to as *wholesaling*) involves buying and selling contracts. You're a treasure hunter, finding properties and contracting with sellers to buy the properties for an agreed-on price. Then you sell the contract to a house flipper for a finder's fee. You never take possession of the property or make any repairs — you're just a go-between. See the later section "Flip contracts (or do it all on paper)" for details.

# Surveying Different Strategies

When developing a game plan, you try to maximize your strengths, minimize your weaknesses, and fully exploit the opportunities that surround you. Many flippers have already developed their own strategies that achieve these three goals. By becoming more aware of these existing strategies, you can choose the one that fits you best and perhaps even improvise to develop your own, unique strategy.

The following sections reveal house flipping strategies that many flippers practice with varying levels of success.

**REMEMBER**

Always buy low. If you can't get a house for at least 20 percent less than what you estimate it will cost to buy, repair, hold, and sell it, keep looking. Chapter 3 in Book 4 explains how to calculate the maximum purchase price to improve your chances of earning a decent profit.

## Buy into a hot market

In a sizzling real estate market, you can turn a profit fairly quickly by buying a house, moving in, and then sitting back and watching the real estate values soar. This approach works only if you have time on your hands, are speculative by nature, and have a knack for purchasing houses in a hot market at just the right time. This strategy offers several benefits:

>> If the market remains strong, your property value rises and you don't have to lift a finger.

>> Your equity in the property rises, boosting your borrowing power for other investments.

>> When you live in the home for two years or more, up to $250,000 of your profit ($500,000 for a couple filing jointly) may be tax free, at least according to the tax laws in place at the time of writing.

**WARNING**

Buying into a hot market also carries some significant risks:

>> Soaring property values often create a housing bubble, which can burst, leaving you with a home that's worth less than the amount you paid for it.

>> Stuff happens. You can have a great house at a great price in a hot market with the top agent working to sell it and the house *still* may not sell. Prepare yourself for all contingencies.

## Buy low, do nothing, sell quick

Occasionally, you stumble on a house that's priced significantly below market value and requires few or no repairs. The property may be in foreclosure (see Book 3) or perhaps is part of an estate that's being liquidated, making the owner highly motivated to sell. By being at the right place at the right time with ready cash, a solid plan, and a friendly, approachable demeanor, you can pounce on the deal and put the house back on the market the very same day!

Sounds great, huh? Well, getting a house that's far below market value is ideal when it happens, but being in the right place at the right time requires time, effort, and luck. You need to build a solid team (see Chapter 3 in Book 1 for details), do plenty of research, secure some solid investment capital (see Chapter 4 in Book 1 for tips on financing), and be properly equipped to execute this strategy.

**WARNING**

Beware of deals that are *too* sweet. A stranger who approaches you at an investment seminar with a hot tip on a piece of real estate, for example, may just be looking for a sucker to buy a property they got stuck with. Unless you know the market values in the area, see the house with your own eyes, research the title, and don't take the bait.

## Buy low, apply makeup, sell quick

You can learn a lot from used car dealers. The first thing they do when they take possession of a vehicle is clean and polish it and vacuum and deodorize the interior. Looking and smelling its best, that used car can sell for a handsome profit.

Even a good home, if not clean and well maintained, can look disheveled and smell stale. Many homeowners place their homes on the market with no proper *staging* (showcasing). They don't mow the lawn, trim the bushes, touch up the paint, or even tidy up the house during showings. Unknowingly, they turn away prospective buyers and lower the profit potential of their property.

This kind of home gives you a perfect opportunity to swoop in and snag a great deal. You buy the home for significantly less than market value, add elbow grease, and then resell the home for thousands of dollars more than you invested in it. Chapter 4 in Book 3 notes some basics on how to properly market and stage a home to attract top dollar.

**REMEMBER**

Buying low, applying makeup, and selling quickly is an excellent strategy for the first-time flipper. By purchasing a property that's an easy rehab job, you can focus on the process of flipping rather than on the complexities of rehabbing. After you master this strategy, you're better prepared to move up to more distressed properties.

# Buy low, renovate, sell high

Some homes are undervalued because they're missing an essential feature — a livable living room, a third bedroom, a deck, or a laundry room on the main floor. Other homes may have major eyesores, such as an outdated kitchen or bathroom. In either case, moderate to major renovations may improve the marketability of the house and its profit potential in two ways:

>> **Increasing the home's actual value:** Wear-and-tear depreciate a home over time. Updates restore value, and added living space can boost the house into a higher price bracket.

>> **Expanding the pool of interested house hunters:** A two-bedroom house, for example, appeals only to people who are looking for a one- to two-bedroom house. Adding a third bedroom attracts anyone looking for a one- to three-bedroom house or a house with office space.

REMEMBER

Adding to the real value of a home is a useful way to maximize your profit — but don't take on more than you can handle or build a mansion among bungalows. If you're a weekend warrior or you have contractors on your team, consider this strategy. If not, you may want to hold off until you get to know some local contractors.

# Buy low, move in, renovate, sell high

To maximize your profit, reduce expenses, and take a more hands-on role in rehabbing a home, consider moving into the home and renovating it at your own pace. If you and your family don't mind living in the chronic chaos of a construction zone, this approach is appealing, for several reasons:

>> By living in the home you're flipping, you avoid making a second mortgage payment or paying a tax bill and utility costs.

>> Because you're living in the home, you develop a better feel for the types of renovations that can make it more attractive to future buyers.

>> If you live in the home for at least two years, up to $250,000 of the profit ($500,000 for a couple filing jointly) may be tax free, as discussed previously. (This is according to the tax laws in place at the time of writing.)

>> You're onsite for any repairs or renovations you have to hire out. And you're around more often to prevent thieves from walking off with your tools and materials.

If you're single or married with no kids, this strategy is an excellent choice. If you have children in school, however, you should avoid this approach, unless you intend to remain in the same school system after selling. Your children begin to form relationships, and big moves disrupt their lives.

**WARNING**

If you're planning major renovations such as gutting the house or completely rehabbing the kitchen, consider performing that renovation *before* you move in, or plan to reside elsewhere during the renovation — especially if you have kids and pets. The persistent noise, dust, and inconvenience can rattle nerves and strain relationships.

## Buy, hold, lease

You don't have to sell a house to profit from it. Many real estate investors opt to buy a house and lease it out for at least enough to cover the monthly expenses of holding it — mortgage, insurance, taxes, maintenance, and utilities. Here's a rundown of how this strategy works:

>> You buy the house at less than market value so that you earn equity at the time of purchase. In other words, if you buy a $100,000 house for $80,000, you immediately earn $20,000 in equity. You don't realize your profit until you sell the house, but you can borrow against the equity.

>> Assuming that the rent you charge covers your mortgage and other expenses, the rent pays down the principal of the loan, so your equity in the home gradually rises. (Your renters are paying off your debt.)

>> As real estate values rise, your equity in the home rises accordingly, so the house is worth more when you sell it — assuming, of course, that your tenants don't trash it.

**REMEMBER**

In short, you're making money in three ways: when you buy the house, when you hold the house, and when you sell the house. If you perform some value-added updates and renovations while you own the property, you may increase your profit even more. Of course, with this strategy you don't see the immediate influx of cash that accompanies a quick flip, but your net worth (the value of your assets minus the amount you owe on those assets) gradually rises until you cash out your chips at the end of the game.

## Invest in new construction

A home doesn't have to be old and dilapidated for you to flip it. Many real estate investors profit from flipping new homes or condos. Unless you're focusing on a niche market that rules out new construction (see the next section), don't over-look newly constructed homes.

The best time to hit newly constructed homes is at the beginning, when the builder first starts to sell units. After 60 months of construction, the cost to build may have risen substantially, so if you bought at the beginning, five years later you have that extra equity built up in the property compared to the other homes in the division.

In October 2020, coauthor Ralph and his wife to downsize. They signed a purchase agreement to buy a detached condo to live out their retirement days in a space that worked for them. Within six months, the value of the property increased over $200,000!

TIP

When a new subdivision is opening, ask to buy the model from the builder. The builder can then rent it from you for a few years. It'll be well taken care of because it's for showing to prospective purchasers.

WARNING

When purchasing a newly constructed home or condo, read the purchase agree-ment *carefully*. Here's what you're looking for:

>> **Conditional clauses:** Make sure that the purchase is conditional on the satisfactory completion of the building and on your ability to secure financing for the purchase. If you sign a purchase agreement and then are denied financing, the builder may keep your earnest money and perhaps even sue you for breach of contract.

>> **Inflated profit estimates:** Beware. You've probably heard stories of people who invested in a development and made $100,000 in short order. What you don't hear are the stories of people who *lose* money, and those stories are much more common.

>> **Variable building costs:** Some contracts include language that allows builders to charge a variable amount — for the price of materials, for exam-ple. That variable amount could end up costing you double your investment (or more) if the cost of materials rises substantially, as it did during the COVID-19 pandemic.

TIP

If, after doing your research, you're convinced of the benefits of investing in a new construction project, make sure you're among the first 10 percent of buy-ers. These buyers make the lion's share of the profit because, as construction proceeds, building costs rise. To find out whether you'd be in the first 10 percent group, ask the salesperson, who's usually camped out in the model home, the number of total units planned and the number sold, and then divide the number sold by the total number of units planned.

# Focus on a niche market

When you're looking for properties to flip, the first impulse is to cast a wide net in the search for the best deals, but sometimes you can find better deals by fishing deeper in one spot, such as one of these:

>> **Foreclosures:** You can find more homes in foreclosure than you can possibly flip, and by focusing your efforts on these properties, you quickly discover the ins and outs of locating them and effectively negotiating the price and terms you want. See Book 3 for details about foreclosures.

>> **VA foreclosures:** To narrow your scope even further, consider focusing on Veterans Affairs (VA) foreclosures.

>> **Probate:** You can find leads from probate lawyers and the neighborhood grapevine to locate families who need to unload a house in order to settle an estate.

>> **Divorces:** When couples divorce, they're often stuck with a home that neither of them can afford. By keeping your ears open and letting people know that you buy houses, you can often score first dibs on these homes.

>> **HUD homes:** Working with an agent who specializes in US Department of Housing and Urban Development (HUD) homes, you can build a career by purchasing these homes at a discount and rehabbing them for quick, profitable sales.

>> **For Sale By Owner (FSBO):** The Multiple Listing Service (or MLS) is an organization that maintains a database of houses and other real estate for sale or rent all over the country. When everyone else is searching the MLS for deals, you may prefer driving around the neighborhood and looking for homes with a For Sale By Owner sign on the front lawn or searching for the ugly duckling on the street and then visiting your county's register of deeds to see who owns it.

>> **Seized homes:** Law enforcement agencies commonly seize property and then need to unload it. By focusing your energy in this area, you can corner the market on seized homes.

>> **Teardowns:** Homes that are beyond hope may still hold opportunities if the price and location are right. Some investors earn a sizable return by tearing down old homes and building new ones in their place.

**TIP**

Don't try to be a high roller and master everything all at once. Select a niche (foreclosures, probate, divorce — whatever), and work that niche until you achieve success. After you establish yourself in that area, you can add another to expand your operation. Your niche market can also be a specific area that you farm by becoming an expert in the area and establishing a strong network.

# Flip contracts (or do it all on paper)

*Flipping contracts* (sometimes called *wholesaling*) consists of locating a distressed property, contracting with the homeowner to buy the property, and then selling the contract to an investor who wants to flip the property. In essence, you earn a finder's fee by serving as an investor's bird dog, and you don't even have to lift a hammer.

Here's how it works: You pay the homeowner a deposit, typically $1,000 or 5 percent to 10 percent of the estimated purchase price. In return, you receive a purchase contract giving you the right to sell the property to an investor. You then find an investor who's willing to purchase the property and pay you a fee in excess of the amount you have tied up in the property.

**WARNING**

This strategy may sound rosy, but we strongly discourage you from flipping contracts. We include the strategy here only because you're going to hear about it elsewhere, and you should be aware of the high risk, especially the risk of buying from a bird dog. If someone ties up a $200,000 house and wants to sell you their purchase agreement for $10,000, you're purchasing the house for $200,000 *and* paying a fee of $10,000. You're taking all the risk and giving that person $10,000. If it's such a good deal, you need to analyze it and ask yourself why the bird dog isn't the one flipping the house.

# Cook up your own strategy

Successful investors, whether they invest in real estate or stocks, devise unique strategies based on their personalities, their abilities, and the resources they have at their disposal. If you like to help people and you're good at dealing with uncomfortable situations, for example, you may want to focus on foreclosures or divorces. If you're good at primping a house but not so good at rehabbing, consider focusing on homes that require only a little makeup.

You can even mix-and-match strategies to develop a custom strategy. You may, for example, choose to buy a quick flip in a hot market or buy only duplexes, move into one half, and rent out the other half while renovating the half you're living in. The variations are limited only by your imagination.

**REMEMBER**

Reevaluate your situation and be ready to shift your strategy as your skills, knowledge, resources, and market change. At this point, you may not feel confident taking on major renovations, but in a year or two, it could well become your area of expertise.

# Drawing Up a Detailed Plan in Advance

REMEMBER

Every day that you own a property, holding costs chip away at your profit, unless of course the property is a rental. *Holding costs* are the daily expenses — interest payments, property taxes, utility bills, homeowners' association fees, and maintenance costs. The trick to reducing these costs is to flip the property as quickly as possible, and that means planning well in advance. Make sure that your plan covers all five stages of the flipping process:

1. **Secure cash or financing.**

   With financing (or, preferably, cash in hand), you can move on the deal much more quickly than other buyers and negotiate from a position of power if other prospective buyers have no cash. See Chapter 4 in Book 1 for more about financing, and see Chapter 3 in Book 4 to determine how much you can pay for a property to earn a decent profit from it.

2. **Search and research.**

   The fun, exciting step in the process of flipping houses is searching for and finding diamonds in the rough. To limit your exposure to risk, however, you need to follow up your search with research, particularly if you're buying a home in foreclosure. See Book 2 for more about finding properties.

3. **Purchase.**

   Buying the property is probably the easiest step in the process, but you want to be sure to negotiate (or bid) a price that's at least 20 percent less than the cost of buying, renovating, holding, and selling the property. You also need to negotiate other terms, including the closing date and the date on which the previous owners move out.

4. **Rehab.**

   Jot down a list of improvements you want to make to the property when you first see the house, and schedule the work before you close on the purchase. Ideally, you should start renovating the property the same day or the day after closing. Chapter 2 in Book 4 walks you through the process of inspecting a property for the first time; Chapter 4 in Book 4 is devoted to prioritizing and planning your renovations.

5. **Sell or lease.**

   As soon as you know the closing date for purchasing the property, set the date on which you want to put the house back on the market or have it available for tenants. If you're selling the house, also decide whether you want to sell it yourself or work with an agent. You don't have to wait to market the house until renovations are complete — the activity that surrounds the house during renovations can be an excellent marketing tool. It gets the neighbors talking. See Chapter 5 in Book 4 for more about selling your rehabbed property.

Mark Workens, owner of Mortgage 1 (http://mortgageone.com) and a good friend of coauthor Ralph, offers some other FHA-related mortgage input that every house flipper should know. As you develop a flipping strategy, keep these rules in mind:

>> **HUD/FHA 90-day rule:** According to the Department of Housing and Urban Development's (HUD's) 90-day rule, you must own the home for longer than 90 days before you can transfer the title to a buyer who's using a Federal Housing Authority (FHA) loan to finance the purchase. If you're planning to sell to first-time buyers, this rule can reduce your pool of prospective buyers and you may need to hold the property for longer than you had planned. Owning the home for fewer than 90 days voids your eligibility for an FHA-insured mortgage.

>> **HUD/FHA 91-to-180-day rule:** If you resell a home between 91 and 180 days after you buy it and the resale price is 100 percent or more than what you paid for the property, a second appraisal is required if the buyer is using an FHA loan to finance the purchase. If the second appraisal is 5 percent or more higher than the first appraisal, the lesser of the two appraisals is used for FHA loan approval.

>> **The 24-month history rule:** Banks require title reports to determine chain of title dating back 24 months. If any more than one person has owned the property in that 24-month window, fraud might have played a factor. As an investor, always be careful about how many sales occurred in the past 24 months. Anything more than one and there might be a problem.

TIP

Simply strolling into your county's register of deeds and asking for all details recorded on a particular property within the past 24 months alleviates all doubts about the chain of title.

Keep in mind that most buyers (except cash buyers) require financing and that certain types of financing, such as FHA loans, come with rules that can eat into your profits. When coauthor Ralph puts real estate on the market, he targets cash and conventional loan offers first. If he's not getting offers, he considers buyers with government financing. When a buyer is receiving an FHA loan, the government essentially sets the rules of engagement.

TIP

For more information on FHA mortgage related questions, visit http://portal.hud.gov/hudportal/HUD.

# Plan B: Surviving a Flip That Flops

This book provides tips, tricks, and warnings to enable you to maximize your profit and minimize your risks, but that doesn't guarantee a successful flip every time. Flips sometimes flop, even for experienced investors. The following tips can help you avoid some of the more serious situations and recover your composure when something goes wrong:

>> If your flip flops because of a dip in the housing market, skip to Chapter 4 in Book 3 to explore other ways to profit from your investment.

>> As soon as you see that a property is a money pit, cut your losses. Don't throw good money after bad. You may need to sell the house now at a small loss instead of later at a bigger loss. On the other hand, you can go to plan C and rent out the property for 12 to 36 months until the market perks back up and you can comfortably sell the home at or above cost.

>> Keep in touch with your team, especially your financial backers and agent. Communication is paramount, especially when times are bad. Good team members can help you out of a jam and help you recover.

REMEMBER

Don't give up just because a single flip doesn't turn out as well as you had expected. Failure is an excellent educator, and if you can work through it, it can be a true confidence builder. Flip three or four houses before throwing in the towel. Your plan, however, must include an exit strategy for all contingencies; otherwise, your flop will take you by total surprise and you won't know what to do.

Chapter **2**

# Inspecting the Property and Estimating Rehab Costs

Befo e you even consider making an offer on a property, examine the property inside and out to evaluate its potential, and then draw up a preliminary list of improvements that would make the property marketable at an attractive yet profitable price. You can inspect the property during an open house or showing or during a private visit with your agent, who can assist you in determining which renovations could add the most value to the home and help you decide whether the property is a good investment.

This chapter takes you through a preliminary inspection and points out the features of the landscape and house that should draw your focus. It highlights the types of defects you should avoid at all costs, areas of a home that are often packed with potential, and the types of renovations that truly boost a property's resale value. By the end of this chapter, you should be able to walk through a house in 15 to 30 minutes, give it the thumbs up or thumbs down, and walk away with a list of repairs and renovations and an estimate of their costs.

No problem is a real deal breaker if you know about it. You can calculate the cost of fixing a problem into your offer so that you prevent the loss of any money and you have a good chance of earning a decent profit. The situation to avoid is buying a house when you don't know about an issue or the cost to fix it. A thorough inspection of the premises and estimates for repairs and renovations are critical in determining how much to offer for a house.

# Packing for Your Inspection Mission

A house inspection isn't just a pleasure trip — you're on an information-gathering mission to find the property with the most potential and to estimate the cost of making the property marketable in order to maximize your profit. To complete your mission successfully, plan ahead and pack the following essential tools:

>> Pen or pencil

>> Clipboard

>> Smartphone (mostly for its camera and flashlight features)

>> Circuit tester to check the outlets (a circuit tester has a three-pronged plug on one end and indicator lights on the other end that show whether the outlet works and is wired properly)

>> Stepladder

>> One copy of the home inspection checklist in Figure 2-1 for each house you plan to visit (or a checklist you created with more space for comments)

>> Screwdrivers (Philips and flathead)

>> Tape measure or (the pricier) laser distance measurer for measuring rooms, doorways, ceilings, and other items

Figure 2-1 shows an example of a home inspection checklist.

If you don't like the idea of writing everything down, record comments during the walk-through using your smartphone's audio or video recording apps. A house inspection trip typically brings you in contact with at least three or four properties, and when you're done looking, you're too exhausted and overwhelmed to remember important details. Don't rely on your memory alone. Consider walking through the house once to get a general idea of what needs to be done and then a second time to record your observations for future reference.

# Home Inspection Checklist

**Property Address:** _____

| Area | Comments | Estimated Costs | Estimated Time |
|---|---|---|---|
| **EXTERIOR** | | | |
| **Roof** | | | |
| ☐ Shingles & Underlayment | | | |
| ☐ Underlayment | | | |
| **Gutters & Siding** | | | |
| ☐ Missing or Damaged Gutters | | | |
| ☐ Aluminum Siding | | | |
| ☐ Vinyl Siding | | | |
| ☐ Brick | | | |
| ☐ Other | | | |
| **Windows** | | | |
| ☐ Glass | | | |
| ☐ Screens | | | |
| ☐ Frames & Sills | | | |
| **Driveway** | | | |
| ☐ Trip Hazards | | | |
| ☐ Gravel | | | |
| ☐ Asphalt | | | |
| ☐ Concrete | | | |
| **Landscaping** | | | |
| ☐ Backyard | | | |
| ☐ Front & Side Yards | | | |
| **Doors** | | | |
| ☐ Screens | | | |
| ☐ Storms | | | |
| ☐ Entry Doors & Frames | | | |
| **Porch** | | | |
| ☐ Front Porch & Stairs | | | |
| ☐ Back Porch & Stairs | | | |
| **Garage** | | | |
| ☐ Roof, Siding, & Gutters | | | |
| ☐ Doors & Windows | | | |
| ☐ Foundation & Floor | | | |
| ☐ Electric | | | |
| **INTERIOR** | | | |
| **Electrical** | | | |
| ☐ Fuses/Circuit Breakers | | | |
| ☐ Wiring | | | |
| ☐ Switches | | | |
| ☐ Junction Box Covers | | | |
| ☐ Faceplate Covers | | | |
| **Plumbing** | | | |
| ☐ Water Pipes | | | |
| ☐ Wastewater Pipes | | | |
| ☐ Hot Water Heater | | | |
| ☐ Floor Drains/Sump Pump (Basement) | | | |

© *John Wiley & Sons, Inc.*

**FIGURE 2-1:** A home inspection checklist is an essential inspection tool.

| Heating & Cooling | | | |
|---|---|---|---|
| ☐ Furnace/Radiators/Boilers | | | |
| ☐ Duct Work & Vents | | | |
| ☐ Filters | | | |
| ☐ Air Conditioning | | | |
| ☐ Humidifier/Dehumidifier | | | |
| **Living Room/Family Room** | | | |
| ☐ Floor/Carpet | | | |
| ☐ Walls | | | |
| ☐ Ceiling | | | |
| **Laundry Room** | | | |
| ☐ Floor/Carpet | | | |
| ☐ Walls | | | |
| ☐ Ceiling | | | |
| ☐ Washing Machine Connect | | | |
| ☐ Laundry Tub | | | |
| **Kitchen** | | | |
| ☐ Floor | | | |
| ☐ Walls | | | |
| ☐ Ceiling | | | |
| ☐ Light Fixtures | | | |
| ☐ Cabinets/Countertops | | | |
| ☐ Sink | | | |
| ☐ Stove | | | |
| ☐ Refrigerator | | | |
| ☐ Dishwasher | | | |
| **Bedrooms** | | | |
| ☐ Floor/Carpet | | | |
| ☐ Walls | | | |
| ☐ Ceiling | | | |
| **Bathrooms** | | | |
| ☐ Floor | | | |
| ☐ Ceiling | | | |
| ☐ Walls | | | |
| ☐ Tile | | | |
| ☐ Cabinets | | | |
| ☐ Countertop | | | |
| ☐ Lights | | | |
| ☐ Tub/Shower/Enclosure | | | |
| ☐ Toilet | | | |
| ☐ Sink & Vanity | | | |
| ☐ GFIs (Ground Fault Interrupters) | | | |
| **Basement** | | | |
| ☐ Stairs & Handrail | | | |
| ☐ Watertight Foundation | | | |
| ☐ Windows & Lighting | | | |
| ☐ Finished | | | |
| **Attic** | | | |
| ☐ Insulation | | | |
| ☐ Vents | | | |
| **Other** | | | |
| **Total Estimated Costs** | | | |
| **Total Estimated Time** | | | |
| **Additional Comments** | | | |

**FIGURE 2-1:**
(Continued)

# Finding the Perfect Candidate for a Quick Makeover

When you're flipping your first or second property, look for the easy score — a property that looks a lot worse than it is. These houses are typically sold below market value because nobody wants them and the owners aren't motivated enough to do what's necessary to make somebody want to buy them. In short, look for a good, solid house that looks ugly and requires no major repairs. The following sections help you spot the signs of an ideal candidate.

**TIP**

Coauthor Ralph's team does a lot of *whiteboxing* — they buy houses that are cosmetically challenged but in pretty good shape and give them a quick makeover. They paint the walls white, install new light switch and electrical outlet covers, lay new carpeting, spruce up the landscaping, and complete other quick tasks to give the property a nice, clean, well-manicured look.

## Poor-but-promising curb appeal

**REMEMBER**

If you go to look at a property and your first impulse is to drive past, that's a good sign that curb appeal is lacking. Either the house looks ugly from the street or you simply don't see it. The house has no pop. Assuming that the shell of the house is sound — you don't need to replace the roof, gutters, windows, or siding — you can often improve the curbside appeal with a few quick and affordable do-it-yourself improvements.

Figure 2-2 shows a potentially perfect candidate, although a closer inspection could prove otherwise. The house appears to be in good shape, but it doesn't stand out from the street. However, some landscaping and light touches on the exterior can change that situation.

## Cosmetically challenged, inside and out

Often, homeowners' poor taste is enough to turn away prospective buyers. The owners paint their house with colors that shouldn't be legal. They install carpeting that clashes and tile that can turn your stomach. They install a pink bathtub and paint the walls yellow.

**FIGURE 2-2:**
This house is
a potentially
perfect candidate
for a quick
makeover.

© Luke Roberts

**TIP**

Fortunately for you, cosmetically challenged houses are often a good buy, assuming that they're in decent condition. Simply by decking out the house in a new, neutral color scheme, you can raise the resale price by thousands of dollars and attract a steady stream of house hunters who previously couldn't stomach looking at the property.

## A second-rate showing

Homeowners often lack the energy, motivation, and expertise required to properly *stage* their home for a showing. Staging, as discussed in Chapter 4 of Book 3, is the process of beautifying your home for prospective buyers. Think of it as primping yourself for a hot date. A properly staged home draws more interested buyers and commands a higher sales price.

**TIP**

When looking for a property to quickly flip for a profit, keep an eye out for poorly staged homes. The poor staging reduces your competition as a buyer, enables you to make a lowball offer, and provides you with the opportunity to raise the resale price just by doing a little clean-up and redecorating.

# Assessing Potential Curbside Appeal

Poor curbside appeal isn't necessarily a bad thing. It's often one of the main reasons you can purchase a property below market value. What you're looking for at this point is potential. When you pull up to the curb, don't scramble out of the car and sprint to the front door. Linger for a few moments, observe the outside of the house, and ask yourself these questions:

>> **Is the house visible from the street?** If it's visible, good. If you can do something relatively easy and inexpensive to increase its visibility, that's good, too. If the house is hopelessly hidden, that's bad.

>> **Is the house on a busy thoroughfare?** If it is, that can be a good thing if the location provides convenient access to stores, schools, and work. It can also be a drawback because people may worry about the noise and traffic.

>> **Is the house near a park, school, or golf course?** Each of these places can be a big draw.

>> **Is the exterior of the house inviting?** Can you make it more inviting without spending too much money? A little landscaping, including trimming trees and shrubs, mowing, and edging, can do wonders and doesn't cost a lot of money.

>> **Are the sidewalks and driveway structurally sound?** Sidewalks and driveways can be solid and still look awful. Pulling weeds, patching cracks, and resealing an asphalt drive are easy, inexpensive fixes. If you need to install a new concrete drive or sidewalks, that can become costly.

>> **What does the garage look like?** If the house has no garage, you may be able to add one, depending on how much land you have to work with. If the garage looks worse than it is, some minor improvements can give it the pop it needs.

>> **How does this house stack up to neighboring homes?** Can you make affordable adjustments to make it the prettiest peacock on the block?

**REMEMBER**

>> **Does the house look as though it requires a greater investment than you can afford, in both time and money?** Bottom line: If the house strikes you as a money pit, walk away. Don't play the hero and try to salvage a hopeless home.

**TIP**

A home's entryway is the bridge to an oasis, so include it in your curb appeal assessment. Visitors entering the home at the front door should feel as though they're entering a new and better world. If the front porch is cluttered, the doors are ugly, and you feel as though you're being shoved into a closet as you enter, consider options for making the entryway more inviting.

**TIP**

Don't forget the backyard! Homeowners often treat the backyard like a pristine nature preserve. This undeveloped space often provides you with the pure potential you need to unleash your creativity, add living space, and significantly boost the property value. You may want to consider adding or improving a patio, a deck, or an attached garage.

# Taking a Big Whiff, Inside and Out

Nothing turns away a prospective buyer like a foul odor, so when you start looking at properties, get your sniffer up to snuff. Take a big whiff inside and out to check for any of these foul smells:

>> **Gas smells may indicate a leaking gas line.** Contact the gas company to report a possible gas leak.

>> **Sewage odors outside may point to problems with a septic tank or nearby sewer line.** Indoor sewer odors may indicate a plumbing problem.

>> **Doggy doo is a common fragrance in backyards populated with one or more dogs.** A little scooping can fix this problem. In addition, watch out for indoor pet odors from cats, dogs, or other animals and for decaying flesh from dead animals somewhere in the house — perhaps in a crawlspace or in a duct or between the exterior and interior walls.

>> **Cigarette smoke is a turnoff for many buyers.** If the homeowners were heavy smokers, the walls and ceilings may be stained brown with tar and nicotine.

>> **Mold and mildew may be in damp areas in the house.** The notorious black mold isn't always black, but usually you can smell it.

None of these malodorous problems is a deal breaker, assuming that you can locate the source of the smell and remove it without too much expense. Don't dismiss a bad smell, however, until you know what's causing it. If the seller is trying to mask bad smells by burning candles and incense or by using an assortment of air fresheners, try to smell past the cover-ups and pick up the scent in other rooms of the house. Any bad smells can be good for your profit margin, enabling you to negotiate a lower price.

**TIP**

When you run into a pet odor, replace the carpet, but before laying the new carpet, sand and stain the flooring below the carpet to kill the odor. If you lay new carpet over the odor, eventually the odor rises up through the carpet.

**TIP**

Lots of companies specialize in treating odors; they are quick and inexpensive and do a thorough job of eliminating offensive smells.

# Inspecting the House for Big-Ticket Items

Almost every property that's flippable can use a fresh coat of paint, new carpeting, and some tender loving care. You expect that, and you budget it into the cost of fixing the property. Unexpected defects in big ticket items, however, can quickly bust your budget and drastically cut into your potential profit. Many of these items are costly to repair or replace, and unfortunately, the repairs don't increase the value of the property.

Although you should have the property professionally inspected before you close on the deal, you can often save yourself the time and money by catching any major problems on your first visit. The following sections point out the most common and expensive problem areas.

## Focusing on the foundation

Every house rests on a foundation — typically, a basement or concrete slab. Inspect the foundation, inside and out, for any of the following symptoms of a sick foundation:

>> **Cracked foundation or walls:** Almost all foundations have cracks, but large cracks that run down the entire length of the basement wall or along the floor are symptoms of costly structural problems. Check inside the house for cracked walls that may also point to foundation problems.

>> **Bowed walls:** Check basement walls for any signs of bowing, indicating that water and dirt are pushing the foundation in from the outside.

>> **Warped floors:** Uneven floors may be a sign of underlying structural problems. If a floor is sinking, you may see the tops of the walls separating from the ceiling or cabinets pulling away from walls.

>> **Spongy floors, particularly under wall-to-wall carpeting:** Be mindful while you walk to discover any spongy areas that may point to trouble. If the house has a basement or crawlspace, check the joists and the condition of the floor from the underbelly of the house. If you can poke a hole through the floor joists with a screwdriver, they need to be replaced, which can be a very expensive endeavor.

>> **Mold/mildew:** Mold and mildew on basement walls is often a sign of a leaky basement. The basement may appear to be dry now, but when the rain starts pouring down, you may have an indoor pool in your basement.

>> **Recently installed paneling:** Recently installed paneling or drywall may indicate a foundation problem that the owner is trying to conceal.

**TIP**

Dampness in a basement isn't always a sign of a serious problem. Clogged gutters or downspouts that fail to direct the water away from the house are common causes of dampness too — problems that are much easier and cheaper to correct. Note the problem and be sure to mention it when you have the home inspected.

## Checking out walls and floors

Walls and floors are particularly susceptible to water damage in bathrooms. To check for water damage in the floor, press your foot near the base of the toilet or try rocking the toilet back and forth. If the toilet moves, the subfloor it's anchored to is rotting.

If the bathroom is tiled, press lightly on the tiles around the bathtub, shower, and sink. In homes with drywall, moisture often softens the drywall and causes it to crumble. Note any serious damage you find, but don't rule out the house just yet.

**WARNING**

Nine-by-nine-inch vinyl-looking tile is usually asbestos and needs to be removed by professionals in hazmat suits, which can get expensive. Again, it's not a deal-breaker. Just be sure to account for it.

## Examining the siding

Visually inspect the outside of the house and note the type of facing — aluminum, brick, stucco, vinyl, or wood. Compare it to the neighboring properties. Inspect the facing and note any damage or signs of aging:

>> **Aluminum:** Dented or peeling siding

>> **Brick:** Worn or missing mortar

>> **Stucco:** Cracked, bowed, or peeling stucco

>> **Vinyl:** Cracked, warped, or peeling siding

>> **Wood:** Rotted, cracked, or missing boards

# Giving the roof and gutters the once-over

As you inspect the home's facing, let your eyes wander up a little higher to check out the roof and gutters. Note any of the following potential problems:

>> **Bowed or damaged roof:** These signs may indicate a problem with the underlying structure of the roof.

>> **Damaged or aging shingles:** Shingles curling at the edges are often a sign that the house needs to be reroofed.

>> **Obvious patches:** An obvious patch or an area with shingles that don't match the color of surrounding shingles may indicate that the roof leaked in the past and may be damaged beneath the shingles.

>> **Two or more layers of shingles:** You can usually lay one layer of shingles over another, but if the home needs a new roof and it already has two or more layers of shingles, the roofers will need to strip off the old layers first, which can nearly double the cost of roofing the house.

>> **Gutters pulling away from the house:** You may be able to reattach the gutters, unless the facing board they're anchored to is rotten.

**TIP**

Listen to your contractors. Coauthor Ralph's team once flipped a house that needed a new roof, to the tune of $8,500. The contractor noted that only the front side of the roof needed to be replaced; the back had about ten years of life left. They spent $4,400 on the front roof and saved a bunch of money.

# Glancing at the windows, inside and out

Windows are not only a functional part of every house, letting in light while insulating the house and acting as a barrier against the natural elements, but they also play an aesthetic role — accenting both the interior and exterior. Inspect windows for both function and appearance, and note the following:

>> Any broken panes

>> Torn or missing screens

>> Windows painted shut

>> Rotted wood, especially window sills

# Evaluating the plumbing

As you walk through a house, turn the faucets on and off, flush the toilets, and check for the following common plumbing problems:

>> **Clogged drains:** Leave the faucets running for several seconds to see whether the water backs up.

>> **Leaking drains or pipes:** Check under the cabinets for any signs of leaking drains or pipes. Water stains on the ceilings and walls are often a sign of leaking pipes that can sink your flip if gone unchecked.

>> **Dripping faucets:** Drips are relatively easy and inexpensive to fix, but note them anyway.

>> **Leaking toilets:** Try rocking the toilet or press your foot near its base to make sure that the floor isn't rotted.

>> **Low water pressure:** Water should flow faster than a trickle, especially if the house has an upstairs bathroom.

>> **Broken water heater:** Make sure that you're getting hot water, and visually inspect the water heater for rust, leaks, and other signs of damage.

# Exploring the electrical system

A home's electrical system delivers power to every light, appliance, and gadget in the house. Fortunately, most homes built in the past 30 years or so have reliable electrical systems built to code. If the outlets function, the lights don't flicker, and the home was built in the past 30 years, you can be fairly confident that the electrical system is acceptable. Even so, you should always check for the following:

>> **The condition of the electrical box:** An old electrical box with fuses rather than breaker switches may need to be replaced.

>> **The type of wiring used:** The best wiring is installed in conduit (metal tubes that completely insulate the wire). Many homes use flexible cables insulated in white plastic, which are also acceptable. Older knob-and-tube wiring strings the wires around porcelain knobs and usually doesn't meet modern building codes. Aluminum wire (silver rather than copper) may also be a problem in some areas.

>> **The use of lots of extension cords:** This indicates that the house has too few outlets or outlets that aren't working.

>> **The functionality of the outlets inside and out:** Use your handy-dandy circuit tester, described earlier in this chapter, to determine whether the outlets work and whether they're properly grounded.

>> **The functionality of the lights:** Turn on all the lights to make sure that they work. (Of course, nonfunctioning lights typically just need new lightbulbs — a cheap and easy fix.)

## Checking out the furnace and air conditioner

REMEMBER

When examining a house for investment purposes, compare what the house has to what it needs to bring it up to neighborhood standards. If most homes in the area have forced-air heat and central air conditioning, and the house you're looking at has radiant heat with no ductwork, adding central air conditioning can be costly, but it can also add true value to the property.

Visually inspect the furnace and air conditioning unit to determine their approximate age and any obvious damage. You may not be able to test the air conditioning if you're looking at a house in the winter, but you can check the furnace year-round by turning it on and cranking up the thermostat.

TIP

Check the seller's disclosure for the approximate age and condition of the furnace and air conditioning system. (Ten years is considered old, but some furnaces can last up to 30 years if they're good and well-maintained.) Also, turn on the furnace fan at the thermostat and check the vents around the house to make sure the furnace fan is working.

## Adjusting your eyes to the lighting

Some houses feel more like caves than homes. Even on a bright, sunny day, little light penetrates, and the house has insufficient lighting to compensate. As your eyes adjust to the lighting in various houses, observe what well-lit houses have that ill-illuminated houses lack. Focus on the following items:

>> **Windows:** Compare the number, size, and positions of the windows.

>> **Window dressings:** Some drapes and blinds are more translucent than others. What styles of window dressings are used in well-lit houses?

>> **Colors:** Dark walls, trim, carpet, and furnishings absorb light, often making a house seem darker than it really is.

>> **Floor plan:** A house that's chopped into tiny rooms often prevents outside light from penetrating into the inner recesses.

>> **Landscaping:** Trees and shrubs can filter out just enough light while shading the house and improving privacy, or they can blanket the house in gloomy darkness.

>> **Skylights:** Modern homes often incorporate skylights to draw daytime lighting into a room and make it appear more open. Skylights don't necessarily add value to a home; if you're inspecting a home that has skylights, look for signs of leaks around the skylights, such as a patched or discolored ceiling. Skylights may also be a source of heat loss in the winter.

>> **Light fixtures:** Well-lit homes typically have plenty of overhead light fixtures, track lighting, or recessed lights. Poorly lit homes rely on lamps, which tend to cast shadows and consume living space.

# Discovering Some Promising Features

Some houses are like army barracks. They're neat and clean and well suited for sheltering a family, but they're no work of art. A handful of homes are more inspired. They have a couple of features that take your breath away (in a good way) — perhaps a lush garden in the backyard, a master bedroom with a fireplace and built-in entertainment system, or a huge kitchen that opens into a living and dining room area complete with a fireplace. Keep an eye out for the following special features:

>> **Rooms with character and class:** Real estate agents often use the word *character* to mean *old,* and they're typically justified in doing so. Older homes tend to have more character, such as interior walls of brick, tin ceilings, hardwood floors, and sculpted plaster ceilings that are ten feet high. But some newer homes have their own classy features as well, such as fine woodwork, an open-concept floor plan, or built-in shelves. Look for features that have marketing potential — that will draw prospective buyers to see the home.

TIP

Also note any rooms that fall short of the standard. These are the rooms that you can improve to make the house more attractive to potential buyers.

>> **Hardwood floors:** Valuable hardwood floors are often concealed beneath wall-to-wall carpeting, especially in older homes. You may be able to peel up a corner of the carpet in a closet to see what's underneath without damaging the carpet. If you find a hardwood floor, you're in luck. Hardwood flooring costs two to three times as much as carpeting laid over plywood, so it's definitely a bonus in terms of the property's value.

>> **Large, open kitchen:** A large, open kitchen is better than a cramped one. A large, open kitchen that opens to a living room and dining room is even better. Best, perhaps, is a large kitchen that's closed off from the rest of the house but has the potential of being opened up with the removal of one or two walls. If you can buy the house at a bargain price, removing those walls can significantly improve its marketability.

>> **Large bathroom:** People don't generally hang out in the bathroom as much as they do in the kitchen, but they like to have at least one large bathroom to relax in. The minimum size for a bathroom is about 5 by 7 feet; no matter how you arrange the toilet, shower, and sink, that feels a little cramped. An extra foot (5 by 8) significantly increases your choice of tub or shower. Any additional space makes the bathroom a more marketable feature.

>> **Two or more bathrooms:** An extra bathroom or even a half bath is a bonus, making the home more attractive to more people.

>> **Room to add a bathroom:** If a home has only one bathroom, look for possible spaces you can convert into a bathroom or half bath — for example, one corner of the basement.

**TIP**

You can usually improve the marketability of a home by cleaning the bathrooms. A thorough cleaning, some fresh caulk, and a coat of paint may be enough to transform a vile health hazard into a sparkling, nearly new bathroom. With a little extra money, you can retile the floor and walls, resurface the tub, or install a new shower stall.

>> **At least one large bedroom:** Consider a 10-by-10-foot bedroom the bare minimum. When you consider that a queen-size bed hogs about 35 square feet of floor space and a small dresser consumes another 5 or 6 square feet, a 100-square-foot bedroom quickly fills up. Of course, the larger the better.

**TIP**

A master suite, complete with a walk-in closet and an attached bathroom, is attractive because it appeals to married couples who have or are planning to have children. In homes that don't include a master suite, consider ways of converting existing spaces into a master suite; for example, you may be able to combine two neighboring bedrooms and a bathroom. However, you need to weigh the trade-offs of having more bedrooms versus more room in a master bedroom.

>> **At least two bedrooms:** A two- or three-bedroom house is much more marketable than a one-bedroom house. Even if a prospective buyer doesn't need the second bedroom, most appreciate having an extra room for a home office or study or for overnight guests.

>> **Lots of closet space:** Although some people barely notice the closet space (or lack thereof) in a home until they move in, others quickly rule out homes that are lacking in closet space. Some buyers won't even consider a home that

doesn't contain at least one walk-in closet. When checking out homes to buy, opt for homes with plenty of closet space.

Hallway closets are also helpful for storing linens, cleaning supplies, and other items. Again, the bigger, the better.

>> **Laundry room:** A main-floor laundry room is appealing. Most buyers don't want to have to run up and down the stairs to do their laundry. In some cases, converting an extra small room on the main floor into a laundry room is a smart move. The room should be large enough to hold a washer, a dryer, a shelf for storing clothes, and one or two people to fold the laundry.

Step into the laundry room and perform the usual inspections of the ceiling, walls, and floor to look for any damage or water stains that might indicate plumbing problems. Make sure that the water pipe connections for the washing machine are present and that the threads on the connectors aren't stripped. If the room has a laundry tub, note its condition and whether it needs to be replaced. Also note the size of the room.

>> **Attic:** If the house has an accessible attic, climb up there and note whether it has a floor (yes or no), adequate insulation (which you may not see if the attic has a floor), and sufficient venting for the roof. Is the attic large enough to convert into another room? Also inspect the underside of the roof for any damage and note it on the roof section of your inspection sheet.

>> **Basement:** Head to the cellar to inspect the stairway and handrail. Carefully check the outside walls for water or structural damage (walls bowed in or covered with mold or mildew). Is the basement finished or partially finished? Note the types of improvements you can make to the basement to enhance its appearance and functionality.

>> **Bonus rooms:** *Bonus rooms* are family rooms and dens — any attractive, spacious, and comfortable area that's conducive for friends and family members to hang out and enjoy one another's company or some peace and quiet. A fireplace is appealing, as long as it's in working order. Be sure to have the chimney inspected and get an estimate of any required repairs before you close on the house.

A single overpowering feature can often sell a home, so as you tour homes, look for these hidden gems. When comparing houses, give more weight to a house with character than a house that's simply neat and tidy.

Some houses are begging for reconstruction. They're either too chopped up to allow smooth movement or they have too few rooms to make them marketable. Always look for houses with great floor plans (spacious with a natural, efficient flow) so that you don't have to invest in any major surgery. But if you can't find a house with a good floor plan, look for one that has a floor plan you can reconfigure affordably. If you're debating between two houses — one with three bedrooms and one with two bedrooms that you can convert into a three-bedroom house — all other conditions being equal, go with the three-bedroom house.

# Arriving at a Ballpark Figure for Repair and Renovation Costs

As you inspect a property and figure out what needs to be done before placing it on the market, you need to come up with a ballpark figure for the costs of repairs and renovations. After you gain some experience, you'll know the approximate costs of most repairs and renovations. For example, coauthor Ralph knows that a 1,500-square-foot house costs about $2,250 to 3,000 to paint because where he flips houses in Michigan, painters charge about $1.50 to $2.00 per square foot. Some offer better deals. Kitchen rehabs cost between $5,000 and $10,000, furnaces/air conditioners cost about $2,000 and $5,000, and so on.

TIP

When you're starting out in the flipping biz, however, you may have no idea how much different repairs and renovations cost. Until you get up to speed, consider having a contractor walk through your properties and inspect them with you. A contractor who knows that you're interested in flipping properties and that you will hire them to perform the repairs and renovations, assuming that you purchase the property, may see their time as a small investment that will lead to a steady stream of work.

Some flippers estimate rehab costs using fixed price-per-square-foot calculations depending on the level of repairs/renovations needed. For example, their rehab brackets may look something like this:

>> **Light rehab at $20 per square foot:** This is what coauthor Ralph's team refers to as *whiteboxing* — deep cleaning, fresh paint, new carpet, new light-switch and electrical-outlet covers, new carpeting, newish appliances, and basic landscaping.

>> **Medium rehab at $25 per square foot:** At this level, the property may need a new roof, new front door, new flooring (carpet and hard flooring), new bath or shower, resurfaced cabinets, and new countertops.

>> **Heavy rehab at $30 per square foot:** At this level, the property has some extensive damage. Mechanicals (plumbing, sewer/septic, electrical, or HVAC) may be dysfunctional or missing; drywall, siding, floors, or doors may be damaged; floors may need replaced.

>> **Designer rehab at $40 per square foot:** Here, you're bringing a property up to another level; for example, replacing a Formica countertop with a granite one, replacing tile flooring with ceramic, installing all new hardwood kitchen cabinets, and adding crown molding.

The problem with this approach is that rehab costs vary from one location to another and the dollar figures don't account for inflation. Thanks to the COVID-19 pandemic, for example, lumber prices shot up 300 percent in 2021. As of this writing, they've dropped considerably, but they're still 50 percent higher than in 2020. Also, as material costs rise, so do labor costs. Contractors generally charge a markup for materials, so if materials cost $1,000, they might charge $1,500 (a 50 percent markup). Use the price-per-square-foot approach for estimating rehab costs only after you have some experience under your belt or are in close consultation with an experienced contractor. Then be ready to make adjustments as construction costs change.

Chapter **3**

# Calculating Your Profit and Best Offer

Real estate investors follow this credo: "You make your profit when you buy; you realize it when you sell." In other words, if you purchase a property for a low enough price, you ensure yourself a profit at the time of purchase. Pay too much for a property, and you have a tough time turning a profit, if you ever do.

This chapter offers the guidance you need to answer the big question you face every time you're about to make an offer or bid on a property: What's the most I can pay for this property to earn a profit of at least 20 percent after all is said and done?

## Doing the Math to Ensure a Profitable Flip

Although late night TV real estate gurus dangle the promise of easy money in front of investor wannabes, a 50 percent profit from a flip is rare — although it does sometimes happen. Investors who consistently see 50 percent or higher profits are either very good or are involved in a dishonest scheme.

A good rule of thumb is to shoot for a 20 percent profit over and above your total investment in the property, including all closing costs. If, at the end of the project, you invested $200,000 and walked away with a net profit of $40,000, you've done well. By total investment, I mean every penny you paid to purchase, repair, renovate, hold, and sell the property:

>> The purchase price plus any closing costs or other fees you pay when you buy the property

>> Holding costs from the time you buy the property until the time you sell it, including monthly interest payments on the loan plus property taxes, homeowner's insurance, and utilities

>> Repair and renovation costs

>> Commissions you pay a real estate agent to market and sell the property

>> Any costs or fees you pay at closing when you sell the property

## Adjusting for market conditions

Shooting for a 20 percent profit in real estate is like trying to hit a moving target: Housing values in your area may be going up, going down, or holding steady. To give yourself a better chance of hitting the 20 percent mark, adjust the percentage to your market conditions:

>> 20 percent in a market where homes values are rising

>> 25 percent in a market where home values are steady

>> 30 percent or more in a market where home values are declining

This doesn't mean you'll make 10 percent *more* in a declining market than in a rising market; it means that you set your goal 10 percent higher in a declining market so that you can hit your target of making a 20 percent profit. In other words, you figure in more of a profit buffer when property values are falling.

Don't even think of buying into an area where the market is in a steep decline and shows no signs of recovering. Wait for the market to bottom out and exhibit signs of improvement before you dive in.

# Crunching the numbers

When you have a pretty good idea of the cost of renovations, holding costs, real estate commissions, and other expenses (read the rest of this chapter for details), you're ready to calculate a maximum price to offer for the property:

1. **Start with the future sale price of the home after improvements.**

   Base your estimate on recent sale prices of comparable homes in the same area, as explained in the later section "Estimating a Realistic Resale Value."

2. **For an estimated profit of at least 20 percent, divide the amount from Step 1 by one of the following:**

   - 1.20 in a market where home values are rising (to shoot for a 20 percent return on your investment)

   - 1.25 in a market where home values are steady (to shoot for a 25 percent return and likely see a 20 percent profit)

   - 1.30 in a market where home values are declining (to shoot for a 30 percent return and likely see a 20 percent profit)

3. **Subtract any closing fees, including loan origination fee, points, appraisal fee, and recording fees.**

   See the later section "Closing costs" for details.

4. **Subtract any unpaid property taxes and utility bills you'll be responsible for paying when you purchase the property.**

5. **Multiply the estimated costs for repairs and renovations by 1.2 (to account for unforeseen expenses) and subtract that amount from the total determined in Step 3.**

6. **Multiply monthly holding costs by the expected duration of the project and subtract that amount from Step 3.**

   For example, if monthly holding costs are $3,000 and you expect to spend six months renovating and selling the property, $3,000 multiplied by 6 equals $18,000.

7. **Subtract agent commissions and/or marketing and advertising costs for selling the property.**

   If you plan to stage (furnish) the property for showings, be sure to include the cost as part of your marketing costs. (See Chapter 4 in Book 3 for an introduction to staging.)

8. **Subtract any additional closing costs you expect to pay when you sell the property.**

   See the later section "Closing costs" for details. The resulting amount is the maximum you can afford to pay for the property.

Suppose that you're looking at a property in a flat market with an after repair value (ARV) of $350,000, back taxes of $10,000, and repairs and renovations of $20,000. Monthly holding costs are $3,000, and you plan to fix and sell the property within four months, paying an agent commission of 6 percent:

1. Divide $350,000 by 1.25 to get $280,000.

2. Subtract closing costs of $5,000 to get $275,000.

3. Subtract back taxes of $10,000 from $275,000 to get $265,000.

4. Multiply $20,000 for repairs and renovations by 1.2 to get $24,000, and subtract that amount from $265,000 to get $241,000.

5. Multiply $3,000 in holding costs by four months to get $12,000, and then subtract that amount from $241,000 to get $229,000.

6. Multiply the expected sales price of $350,000 by a 6 percent agent commission to get $21,000, and subtract that amount from $229,000 to get $208,000.

7. Subtract an estimated $5,000 in closing costs from $208,000 to get $203,000, which is the most you can pay for the property.

REMEMBER

The maximum purchase price isn't necessarily the price you want to offer for the property. This is simply a fairly safe amount to offer to be relatively certain you'll earn a 20 percent return on your investment. Of course, the less you pay for a property, the better.

## Estimating a Realistic Resale Value

You start house hunting by looking at neighborhoods and houses in your price range (see Book 2 for the scoop on buying a house). When you're guesstimating profits, though, you start your journey at the end by determining a realistic ballpark figure for the home's resale value after improvements. The key term here is *realistic*. Overestimating the resale value of the house can be as devastating as discovering termites in the floorboards: It can cause you to overpay for a house and almost guarantee low or no profit, or even a loss.

To estimate a realistic resale value for a house, imagine the house all fixed up and then research the actual sale prices of comparable homes that have recently sold in the same neighborhood. Assuming that you're comparing apples to apples — this house to comparable homes in the same area with the same amenities — you should come away with an accurate estimate. What if the market takes a nosedive? By following the guidelines in the earlier section "Crunching the numbers," you're already taking into account potential market fluctuations.

**REMEMBER**

Your goal as a house flipper is to purchase the worst house on the street for the lowest price possible and convert it into the best-looking house on the street at the highest price the market can bear. Anything you can do to add *wow* to the home, especially in terms of curbside appeal, can boost your bottom line. However, don't invest so much in renovations that you spend yourself out of a profit. Nobody's likely to pay $350,000 for a home in a neighborhood where the next-best property sold for $300,000 regardless of what that $350,000 home has to offer.

# Accounting for Expenses

The tough part of deciding how much to pay for a property is accounting for all the costs involved in buying, fixing up, holding, and selling the property. Many beginners don't account for all the costs and often overlook holding costs — loan payments, homeowner's insurance, utilities, property taxes, homeowners' association fees, and so on — from when you take ownership of the property until you sell it.

The following sections serve as a checklist to make sure you account for all the costs associated with buying, renovating, holding, and selling the property.

## Unpaid property taxes and water bills

**REMEMBER**

If you purchase a property at a tax sale or in foreclosure (covered in Book 3), you're responsible for paying any property taxes or water bills that are past due — an amount of money that may be significant. Before making an offer or bidding on a property, you should know of any past-due property taxes and other claims against the property, such as the water bill, that stay with the property even after foreclosure.

## Closing costs

You may face closing costs when you buy the property and when you sell it. Generally, the seller is responsible for the lion's share of the closing costs, which include the agents' commissions. Your real estate agent, lending institution, or title company can provide a detailed estimate of closing costs, which, if you're taking out a traditional loan to finance the purchase, typically include the following items for the buyer:

>> **Loan origination fee:** If you finance the purchase through a bank or another lending institution, you may be subject to a fee for establishing the loan. (See Chapter 4 in Book 1 for details about financing your purchase.)

>> **Discount points:** Some lending institutions charge discount points — a percentage of the total amount borrowed — to provide you with a lower interest rate or wring another few hundred (or thousand) bucks out of you.

Avoid loans with discount points. You usually have to hold a property for several years to justify the monthly savings, and when you're flipping houses, holding a property for several years isn't your goal.

>> **Appraisal fee:** The lending institution charges you this fee to have an appraiser ensure that the property is worth at least the amount you're borrowing to purchase it.

>> **Title insurance:** Even if you researched the title or hired a title company to do it for you, the bank may require you to pay for title insurance or a mortgage policy (sometimes called a *mortgagee* policy). If your lender doesn't require title insurance, buy a title insurance policy yourself; title insurance is essential for protecting your investment.

>> **Insurance and taxes:** If you take out a loan that requires you to pay taxes and insurance from an escrow account, you may need to pay a prorated share of insurance and taxes upfront.

>> **Deed recording fee:** Whenever a property changes hands, the name on the deed changes and must be recorded. Yes, you're charged for this task, too.

>> **Credit report charge:** The lending institution does a financial background check on you called a *credit report* and then charges you for the privilege.

>> **Closing fee:** The title company typically charges a closing fee.

Most closing costs originate with the bank or lending institution. By financing the purchase with your own money — through the seller or with money from private investors, partners, friends, or family members — you can trim closing costs considerably.

## Cost of repairs and renovations

Eager house flippers often underestimate the cost of repairs and renovations. They're so enthusiastic about purchasing the house, selling it, and counting their money that they forget how much a carpenter or plumber charges per hour and the cost of materials at the local hardware store. Repairs and renovations are costly, and if you wait until you take possession of the house before obtaining estimates, you're already too late.

**REMEMBER**

If you're still interested in a house after you take a quick tour of it, complete a second, more thorough inspection of the premises to determine the repairs and renovations you want to make. (See Chapter 2 in Book 4 for details on the process of inspecting a potential flip.) List all the repairs and improvements needed to bring the property in line with your projected resale price (see the earlier section "Estimating a Realistic Resale Value"). Estimate the cost of repairs by completing these tasks:

>> **Flag any repairs you can do yourself.** These are zero-labor repairs, but you may need to visit your local hardware store to check out prices for materials.

>> **Complete a walk-through with a member of your team.** This person should have experience with construction projects and offer estimates and advice. (See Chapter 3 in Book 1 for details on building your team.) To prevent the naysayers from undermining your vision, keep in mind that you're taking the risk and making the final decisions.

>> **Call one or two local contractors to obtain ballpark estimates for any repairs or improvements you can't do yourself.** You may be able to hire a general contractor to walk through the house with you and provide a professional opinion.

**REMEMBER**

If you can't look at the wiring in a house and come up with a pretty good guess at the cost to bring it up to code, you'd better consult somebody who can.

>> **Research estimated costs online.** Contractors.com (`www.contractors.com/`; registration required) features a tool for estimating the costs of bathroom and kitchen renovations, room additions, decks, roofs, and other improvements. LetsRenovate.com (`www.letsrenovate.com/`) offers a toolbox packed with calculators for estimating the costs of repairs and renovations and the return you can expect on your investment.

Tally the estimated costs of repairs and renovations, and multiply the total by 1.2 to add 20 percent for unexpected expenses.

**TIP**

You can trim the costs of repairs and renovations in several ways:

>> Trade your services for free labor. Bartering (or trading services) may have tax consequences, so check with your accountant.

>> Do some of the labor-intensive work yourself.

>> Negotiate with the property owner to share the costs.

Chapter 4 in Book 4 has more details on planning and prioritizing your renovations, including tips on tagging do-it-yourself projects and knowing when to hire professionals for certain tasks.

# Holding costs

As a homeowner, you're well aware of the monthly costs of owning a home, but when you first begin flipping properties, you tend to overlook the monthly expenses, such as your house payment, homeowner's insurance, and property taxes. Reality hits after you've owned the property for four or five months and begin running out of cash. By then, your 20/20 hindsight leads only to panic and despair.

To keep the property, you need money to pay the mortgage, property taxes, and insurance. And if you plan on using any power tools on the premises and keeping the pipes from freezing in the winter, you'd better pay your electric and gas bills, too (in addition to other utilities).

If you're using the home you're flipping as your primary residence, you can safely skip this section. For you, holding costs are actually *living expenses* — the normal amounts you pay to have a roof over your head.

**TIP**

One way to project holding costs for a house you're flipping with borrowed money is to assume, on average, an amount of $100 per day. This amount works for most houses and provides for any surprises along the way. If it takes you a total of six months to flip a property (including rehab and resale time), total holding costs break down this way:

>> Start with $100 per day.

>> Six months multiplied by 30 days per month equals 180 days.

>> Multiply 180 days by $100 per day to total $18,000 (in other words, $3,000 per month).

Of course, holding costs vary depending on several factors, including whether you paid cash for the property or financed it. To establish a more accurate estimate of monthly holding costs, add the total estimated monthly bills for each of the following items:

>> **Loan interest:** Mortgage interest and interest on any home equity loans you use to finance renovations make up a significant chunk of your monthly holding costs.

>> **Homeowner's insurance:** Ask your insurance agent for a quote and explain your plans, including whether you plan to live in the house, to properly insure the property. (A typical homeowner's policy allows for a home to be vacant only a certain number of days.)

>> **Property taxes:** Set aside enough money per month to pay the property taxes when they're due. If you pay property taxes from an escrow account, this amount may already be part of your mortgage payment.

>> **Utilities:** Gas, electric, water, sewer, and trash bills are all part of your monthly holding costs. The seller should be able to provide averages for last year's bills, or you can contact the various utility companies to gather the information you need. (If nobody is living in the house, certain utility bills will be lower than normal.)

>> **Homeowners' association fees (if applicable):** You may prepay these fees at closing and chalk them up as part of your closing fees, but if that's not the case, be sure to include them (if applicable) as part of your monthly fees.

>> **Maintenance:** If you pay somebody for mowing the lawn, watching the house, and letting real estate agents inside to show the home, include these amounts as part of your holding costs.

REMEMBER

Err on the safe side. Budget sufficient funds to hold the house for three to six months beyond the date on which you expect to place the house back on the market. Few experiences are more demoralizing than renovating a house and then losing it in foreclosure because you underestimated your holding costs and can't make the monthly loan payments (or cash calls, if you're working with hard money borrowed from a private lender).

TIP

Holding costs can be a great motivator for completing the project on schedule. The faster you flip, the less you pay in holding costs, and the sooner you can redeploy your funds on another venture.

## Marketing and selling costs

When you place your rehabbed house back on the market, you incur additional expenses for marketing the house before you sell it and selling the house when you close the deal. These costs vary depending on whether you sell the home yourself or with a real estate agent:

>> **Agent fees:** Attempting to sell your home without the help of a real estate agent can backfire, drastically restricting your number of potential buyers. Even if you choose not to use an agent, the agents hired by prospective buyers may not show your home unless they can collect their 3 percent cut at the time of sale. Count on paying from 3 to 7 percent of the sale price in agent fees. If you don't use an agent, add $250 to $1,000 for attorney fees.

- » **Marketing fees:** If you choose to sell the home yourself, you can count on investing 1 to 2 percent of the list price in marketing fees. Whether you list your home in the classifieds or on a For Sale By Owner (FSBO) website, you pay for advertising. You also need a few bucks for a For Sale sign and for finger foods for your open house. (See Chapter 4 in Book 6 for more about marketing a property.)

- » **Home warranty:** Supplying a warranty for the house can make it an attractive deal while protecting you against any lawsuits in the event that some undiscovered defect in the property rears its ugly head after the sale. If you decide to offer a warranty, budget enough to cover its cost. The cost of a typical home warranty ranges from $400 to well over $600, depending on the add-ons.

- » **Closing fees:** A title company typically manages the closing and charges $300 or more for the service. Ask your title company for a more specific estimate.

- » **Title insurance:** Insuring the title ensures that you're not liable for any hidden liens against the property. Title insurance can cost hundreds of dollars, so shop around for the best price and service. You can trim this cost by asking the seller to pay for the policy.

- » **Deed preparation:** The cost of preparing the deed usually goes to the seller and is typically about 50 bucks.

- » **Transfer tax:** Your state, city, or town may levy a transfer tax on the exchange of property. The amount varies depending on your location, so consult your accountant.

- » **Delinquent water or sewer bills:** At closing, you must pay any water or sewer bills that are in *arrears* (overdue or unpaid).

- » **Other charges and fees:** You may be charged other fees depending on local requirements and on the closing company you're using. These fees may include a Title Insurance Enforcement Fund Fee (TIEFF) and a Closing Protection Letter (CPL) fee.

TIP

Don't list your house while you're rehabbing it, but feel free to talk to people during this time and pass out your business cards. If a buyer falls into your lap by way of your neighborhood contacts, get hold of a real estate agent or an attorney to complete the transaction. Check out Chapter 5 in Book 4 for more details about negotiating the sale of your rehabbed house.

# Income tax

When calculating the profit of any business venture or investment, you don't subtract income tax. For example, if you buy stock that earns you a 10 percent return, that return represents a pretax amount. The same is true for any profit you earn by flipping a house. However, for two reasons, you need to consider how your profit from flipping is taxed:

>> Your house flipping strategy may determine how your profit is taxed (for example, whether it's taxed as employment or investment income) and the rate at which it's taxed.

>> The amount you get to keep after taxes will help you decide whether house flipping is worth the time, effort, and risk.

How your profit is taxed varies depending on your situation and on how you choose to flip:

>> If you flip the primary residence in which you lived for two of the past five years and you earn $250,000 or less ($500,000 or less for a couple), you walk away with your entire profit scot-free, at least according to the tax laws that were in effect at the time of writing.

>> Owning the investment property for at least one year and one day qualifies your profit as a *long-term capital gain,* taxable at a rate of 0 to 20 percent, depending on your tax bracket (plus a 3.8 percent Medicare surcharge if your ordinary income places you in one of the top two tax brackets). *Long-term* is longer than one year plus one day. *Capital gain* is whatever you make on the sale of an asset that has increased in value.

>> Owning the investment property for less than one year and one day qualifies your profit as a *short-term capital gain,* taxable at the same rate as the rest of your income from work-related activities (plus a 3.8 percent Medicare surcharge if your ordinary income places you in one of the top two tax brackets); the tax rate on your net profit could be as high as 43.4 percent.

>> If flipping is your main line of business, the IRS considers you to be a dealer, so you can't treat your profits as long-term capital gains. The IRS treats your profits as income, subject to income tax and self-employment tax. You may find yourself paying 35 percent or more in taxes! This may be reason enough to keep your day job and flip houses in your spare time.

>> If you lease the property, any income you receive from the rental, minus the cost of owning and maintaining the property, is considered ordinary income and is taxed at the same rate as your work-related income.

**REMEMBER**

The tax figures provided here are accurate during the writing of this book, but tax rules can change at any time. Consult your accountant for accurate estimates on the amount of taxes you can expect to owe on your profits.

Though house flippers often boast about how much they earn flipping properties, the real measure of success is not your gross profit but rather your net profit — how much you get to keep *after taxes*. To determine your net profit, simply subtract your taxes from your gross profit.

**IN THIS CHAPTER**

» **Looking for local trends in home renovations**

» **Ranking the importance of your renovations**

» **Assigning renovation duties**

» **Coming up with a tentative budget**

» **Scheduling renovations and keeping them on track**

# Chapter **4**

# Prioritizing and Planning Your Renovations

P rioritizing and planning renovations is like planning for a vacation: You have a limited amount of time to complete the trip, a list of activities you want to accomplish during that time, and a certain amount of money set aside to pay for it. With a vacation, you need to schedule flights and car rentals well in advance, plot your journey from Point A to Point B, and pack sufficient clothing, necessities, and accessories for a comfortable journey. Repairing and renovating a property requires the same foresight and attention to detail. You need to prioritize your list of projects, order materials well in advance, schedule the work, hire workers, and make sure that everything gets completed on time and on budget.

This chapter steers you toward valuable resources that can help you train your tastes and choose the renovations that are most appealing to most house hunters in your area. Then you go through the process of prioritizing and planning your renovations to complete your projects in a reasonable amount of time without spending too much money.

**REMEMBER**

Before you even buy a property, you should carefully inspect it and have a solid idea of the work you need to do. See Chapter 2 in Book 4 for guidance on how to inspect a property *before* buying it.

# Developing an Eye for Home Improvements

House flippers are like talent scouts: They can gauge a home's potential instantly and envision it as a final, finished product on the first walk-through. Experienced flippers can envision the kitchen with new cabinets, countertops, and appliances and new tile — and, of course, a new sink — and then turn around and imagine the barely functional restroom converted into a luxurious new bathroom. They can close their eyes and visualize the outside of the home completely revamped to entice passersby into taking a look inside.

Some people have it, and some people don't. If you're one who doesn't have it, don't despair — you can develop the required sensibilities by engaging in the following activities:

**TIP**

>> **Visit open houses.** Search the classifieds for open house dates and times — they're often held on Sunday afternoons — and plan to attend two or three this weekend. Look for open houses in your target neighborhood and price range to form a better idea of the types and styles of renovations that are optimum for your market.

Attend several open houses and complete a comparative analysis to gauge the hottest home fashions in your market. They vary depending on your location, price range, and current styles. Become a trend spotter.

>> **Attend home-and-garden shows.** These shows typically feature model homes, the latest in building supplies and gadgetry, and renovation ideas and demonstrations, along with plenty of catalogs and brochures you can tote home for reference.

>> **Check out magazines, TV shows, and websites.** These media resources are helpful for getting up to speed on what's hot and what's not in home decor:

- Better Homes and Gardens at www.bhg.com

- HGTV at www.hgtv.com

- Magnolia Network at https://magnolia.com/DIYNetwork/

- This Old House at www.thisoldhouse.com

- » **Flip through home remodeling books.** Many home remodeling books feature both remodeling ideas and how-to instruction. Here are a couple of titles to get you started:

  - *Bathroom Remodeling For Dummies* by Gene Hamilton and Katie Hamilton (Wiley)

  - *Home Improvement For Dummies* by James Carey and Morris Carey Jr. (Wiley)

- » **Pay attention to landscaping.** Whether you're out for a morning drive, visiting open houses, or simply taking a stroll around the neighborhood, examine the landscaping. Note the features of the landscape and try to imagine how you could landscape the front of the house to improve its curbside appeal. You may not want to chop down any 50-year-old trees, but a careful trim can freshen up a house, much as a new hairstyle can make you look years younger.

  Landscaping books, magazines, and websites are about as plentiful as plants, and most are packed with copious collections of color photos. When you need some landscaping ideas and advice, check out these offerings:

  - *Landscaping For Dummies* by Teri Chace and the National Gardening Association (Wiley)

  - Landscape Architect at `https://landscapearchitect.com`

  - HGTV's landscaping page at `www.hgtv.com/design/topics/landscaping`

**TIP**

- » **Recruit a renovation mentor.** If you don't have a knack or a passion for remodeling, find someone who does and ask that person to accompany you on your walk-throughs and offer advice. The final decisions are still up to you, but a gifted pair of eyes can help you make superior choices.

**REMEMBER**

Knowing your renovation options (and their costs) before you start looking at properties is the key to buying a property that you're sure can turn a profit.

# Prioritizing Your Projects

**REMEMBER**

Unless you have a bottomless bank account and an infinite amount of time to flip a specific house, you have to prioritize your renovation projects. Here's the overall strategy for prioritizing projects:

1.  **Fix any underlying structural problems and *mechanicals* first, such as plumbing, electric, heating, and air conditioning.**

2. **Make any essential repairs that aren't structural or mechanical, such as dangling gutters, cracked windows, or rickety doors.**

   If something is broken, repair, replace, or remove it. If it ain't broke and it doesn't look bad, don't fix it.

3. **Concentrate on renovations that promise to deliver the highest return on your investment, such as laying new carpeting, replacing the bathroom vanity, or installing a new kitchen countertop.**

   Renovate only if it makes financial sense to do so.

4. **If time allows, do anything you can do yourself for little or no money that makes the house more attractive, such as adding decorative shutters and replacing blinds.**

   Save for last any items that won't sink your sale.

**REMEMBER**

All home buyers want a nice, clean house that's in move-in condition, in the price range they can afford, in the best neighborhood possible, and with good schools for their children. When you buy and renovate houses, let these factors direct your decisions regarding which renovations make sense.

I following sections guide you through the process of prioritizing your renovation projects. When you finish, you should have a list of projects ranked by importance along with projects that promise the most bang for your buck. Check out the later section "Coming Up with a Game Plan" for the full scoop on making sure that you complete your projects with minimal fuss.

**REMEMBER**

Start planning renovations and lining up contractors as soon as you're fairly certain you're going to buy the property, especially for larger projects — roofing, heating and cooling, foundation repairs, and the like. Don't spend any money before you close, but be prepared to start your renovations the next day. If you wait until closing, you may find that all the contractors in your area are already backed up with projects. Get things moving right away.

## Tackling essential repairs

Making a ramshackle house look pretty is like putting lipstick on a pig — and that's not something we recommend. You want a good, solid home devoid of any problems that may crop up later during your buyer's home inspection. The best way to purge a house of problems is to review your home inspection report and address every item on the list. (Chapter 2 in Book 4 covers home inspections in detail.) Focus on the big stuff first, such as these potential problems:

>> Foundation problems

>> Worn or damaged roof

>> Furnace that needs to be repaired or replaced

>> Electrical system that's not up to code or doesn't work

>> Plumbing that's not up to code or doesn't work

>> Air conditioning that's nonexistent or inoperable

>> Insulation that's absent, insufficient, or ugly

After listing the major repairs required, you can address any minor problems that crop up during the inspection and are essential to fix, such as light fixtures that don't work, leaky faucets, broken doors, or peeling paint.

## Gauging renovations to get the most bang for your buck

When you're planning renovations, always aim to make your return on investment (ROI) exceed 100 percent. Otherwise, you become a real estate philanthropist — giving the buyer something for nothing. So, whenever you see claims online that you can expect only an 80 percent return on a new kitchen or a 75 percent return on a bathroom remodel, you may wonder why any flipper in their right mind would consider rehabbing the kitchen or bath. They do it for these three reasons:

>> **The renovation is paid for.** As a flipper, you already covered the cost of the renovation by purchasing the property below market value (see Chapter 3 in Book 4).

>> **With a little DIY work, the ROI can be boosted to well over 100 percent.** When you look at those 75 or 80 percent ROI numbers, keep in mind that the person punching numbers into the calculator is usually assuming that you're having a professional do all the work.

>> **The property needs to be in move-in condition for first-time home buyers.** Few buyers can afford to renovate the kitchen or bathroom after paying a boatload of money for a house. They'd rather borrow a little more and pay for a house that's finished. To avoid excluding these first-time home buyers from your market, some renovations are essential (even though on the surface they may not appear to be cost effective).

The fact that renovations boost your ROI doesn't mean that you should redo every room in the house. When you have a limited budget and time frame, you may find that you need to make some trade-offs. When debating which trade-offs to make, keep your eye on the bottom line (see the later section "Drawing Up a Tentative Budget" for more about money matters) and let the following considerations guide your decisions:

>> **Enhance curb appeal.** In flipping, curb appeal rules, and you usually get more bang for your buck from landscaping and exterior renovations. A fresh coat of paint coupled with some basic landscaping is often much less expensive than the cost of remodeling a kitchen or bath.

>> **Add fresh paint and carpeting.** For a few thousand dollars, you can carpet most houses and add a fresh coat of paint. It's a quick, inexpensive way to make the house look newish.

>> **Consider the competition.** After touring comparable homes in the neighborhood, you know what your house needs to make it slightly more attractive than comparable homes. Making the property as attractive or slightly more attractive is good enough.

>> **Weigh the expense.** Invest no more than it takes to bring your house up to neighborhood standards. If the kitchen is good enough for the neighbors, it should be good enough for you.

>> **Target popular demand.** By knowing what most house hunters in your target area find attractive (see the earlier section "Developing an Eye for Home Improvements" for details), you can more effectively base your renovation decisions on what sells rather than on what you like.

## Adding inexpensive, last-minute touches

After you've completed the major remodeling and examined your bank account to see how much money remains, take a step back to see whether any final touches can further enhance the property's appearance. You may want to add decorative shutters to the windows, light up the landscaping with exterior lamps, or spring for some new throw rugs. Look for inexpensive items that won't blow your budget and easy updates that won't take more than a few hours.

After you remodel the house, don't get carried away with sprucing it up even more. Keep your budget in mind or else you'll end up blowing all the profit on minor changes that may end up becoming major expenses.

# Delegating Duties

After you have a detailed to-do list, it's time to delegate — to determine which jobs you can do yourself, which jobs you can rope your friends into doing, and which jobs you need to hire a professional to complete. The following sections provide some guidance on how to pick the people on your team who are best qualified for various duties.

REMEMBER

The first rule in house flipping is to do the job right, so as you assign duties, be honest about each person's abilities and inabilities. If you don't know a screwdriver from a scuba diver, maybe you should stick to the money end of the deal and leave the repairs to someone who's more qualified. You may save a little money by doing it yourself, but you'll pay later for any shoddy workmanship.

## Identifying do-it-yourself projects

The most obvious way to cut costs is to do the work yourself. You may not be able to install a new furnace or hot water heater, but most people can push a broom, mow the lawn, scrub a toilet, or tear out old carpeting. The following list points out the chores that most house flippers who are just starting out choose to do themselves:

>> Scheduling of subcontractors

>> Basic cleaning

>> Yard work

>> Tearing out old material

>> Odd jobs for the weekend warrior

REMEMBER

When considering whether to do a job yourself or hire a professional, ask yourself this question: "Can I do the job as well and as quickly as a professional?" If doing it yourself jeopardizes the quality of work or the schedule, hire a professional. The $100 per day rule (see Chapter 3 in Book 4) applies here. If a project takes you seven days to complete, it costs you about $700 in holding costs (assuming that you're working with borrowed money). If you can hire someone to do the same project in two days for $500, you save $200 and cut five days off the schedule.

## Getting a little help from your friends

Consider asking friends, family members, and neighbors to help with the cleanup and renovation and assign tasks based on your helpers' skills and experience. Of course, you then have to pitch in whenever they need a hand, but you can pick up additional skills and knowledge by working alongside people with expertise in a variety of areas. You can work as a group on landscaping renovations, work alone, or team up with one other person to perform a task, such as wallpapering, that's a little easier to do with four hands.

**WARNING**

When you're bartering with friends, family, and neighbors, the value of the item or service you're trading may be subject to taxes. Consult your accountant. (See Chapter 3 in Book 1 for more about building your real estate investing team.)

## Flagging jobs that require professional expertise

**REMEMBER**

Licensed, insured contractors and subcontractors have four advantages that many do-it-yourselfers lack: time, tools, know-how, and good insurance. When faced with the decision of whether to do the job yourself or hire a professional, consider these four factors:

>> **Time:** Do you personally have the time to complete the job yourself, or would your time be better invested in other pursuits, such as your day job? Can you complete the job on schedule?

>> **Tools:** Do you own the tools required to do the job? How much do the required tools cost to buy or rent? Do you have the means to haul large, heavy materials, such as rolls of carpet or sheets of drywall, to the worksite? How much would it cost to have materials delivered?

>> **Know-how:** Do you have the expertise to do the job well? Be honest. Materials can cost a lot of dough. If you tear up fancy wood paneling in the process of installing it or ruin a roll of vinyl flooring by making the wrong cuts, these missteps add to the cost of the job.

>> **Insurance:** Is the job dangerous? If you or someone who's helping you is injured in the process, will your insurance cover the doctor bills and any income lost from missed work?

Unless you have the basic qualifications to do the job right, consider hiring a professional to do the following work:

>> Structural repairs, including the foundation

>> Major renovations that require knocking down or building walls

>> Roof replacement or repairs

>> Siding or tuck-pointing (replacing the mortar between bricks)

>> Window replacement

- » Furnace and air conditioning installation or repairs

- » Electrical upgrades

- » Major plumbing repairs, including septic system

- » Removal or treatment of toxic substances

- » Installation of new carpet, tile, or vinyl flooring

**WARNING**

For major projects, such as remodeling a kitchen or bathroom, tell the contractor, in writing, exactly what you want done, the deadline, and the budget amount. If you leave decisions to the contractor, you're likely to experience cost overruns, in both time and money.

# Drawing Up a Tentative Budget

How much you profit from the sale of the house often hinges on the cost of repairs and renovations. Overzealous flippers get burned when their visions for improving a house exceed their ability to pay for them. Whether you have $10,000 or $100,000 budgeted for repairs and renovations, decide early on, preferably before closing, how much of that money to set aside for each project.

To establish a budget, follow these steps:

1. **List the projects you plan on hiring a professional to complete (covered earlier in this chapter).**

2. **Obtain estimates for these jobs.**

   Estimates should break out the cost of materials and labor.

3. **Jot down the projects you plan to complete yourself (covered earlier in this chapter).**

4. **For each of these projects, list the required materials.**

   If you're remodeling a bathroom, for example, you may need a new toilet, sink, and cabinet; tile (for the walls); flooring (vinyl or ceramic); paint; and caulk. Visit your local hardware store (or its website) to research the cost of materials.

**TIP**

   Many hardware stores display two prices for materials — an uninstalled price and an installed price. Use these comparisons to determine how much you're saving by doing the work yourself.

5. **Tally all the estimated costs and add 20 percent to cover sales tax and unexpected expenses.**

   The cost of most projects exceeds estimates.

Use the renovation planner shown in Figure 4-1 to estimate costs and keep all your notes in one place. It features space for listing each project, its start and completion dates, and its costs for materials and labor. See Chapter 2 in Book 4 for more about estimating the cost of renovations.

| Renovation Planner | | | | | |
|---|---|---|---|---|---|
| Project | Start Date | Completion Date | Materials Cost | Labor Cost | Total Cost |
| | | | | | |
| | | | | | |
| | | | | | |
| | | | | | |
| | | | | | |
| | | | | | |
| | | | | | |
| | | | | | |
| | | | | | |
| | | | | | |
| | | | | | |
| | | | | | |
| | | | | | |
| | | | | | |
| | | | | | |
| | | | | | |
| | | | | | |
| | | | | | |
| | | | | | |
| | | | | | |
| | | | | | |
| | | | | | |
| | | | | | |
| | | | | | |
| | | | | | |
| | | | | | |
| | | | | | |
| | | | | | |
| | | | | | |
| | | | | | |
| | | | | | |
| | | | | | |

| | | |
|---|---|---|
| Total Materials Costs | $ | |
| Total Labor Costs | + $ | |
| Total Materials and Labor Costs | $ | |
| 20 Percent for Sales Tax and Unexpected Costs | x | 1.2 |
| Grand Total | $ | |

FIGURE 4-1: A renovation planner is a handy tool for estimating costs.

**WARNING**

If you're working with money from an investor, don't let that person talk you into taking on a project in which you assume most of the risk while they stand to gain most of the profit. When budgeting, make sure that you're the one making the decisions on how to spend the money. Remember that it's *your* money. It's important to keep your investor(s) happy because they're helping finance the venture, but use your own discretion in deciding what's best for *your* long-term gain.

# Coming Up with a Game Plan

Without proper planning, you can literally paint yourself into a corner when you're renovating a house. If you refinish the hardwood floors first, subsequent construction traffic ruins the finish. If you install new drywall before the plumbers show up, you may find them hacking chunks out of it later to get at the pipes. Before scheduling the work, sit down with your project list and arrange your renovations in a logical sequence so that the work flows smoothly and you don't end up dribbling paint all over your new carpeting. The following sections lead you through the process of drawing up an overall renovation plan.

**TIP**

When coauthor Ralph schedules renovations, he tries to reserve as much energy as possible going into the project to maximize the synergies of the workers and crews. Nobody wants to look like a slacker in the midst of fellow workers. This strategy also helps draw more attention to the house from neighbors and potential buyers.

## Switching on utilities and ordering materials and a dumpster

Few things are more discouraging to a flipper than having workers show up at the house only to find that the electricity is turned off and they don't have the materials they need to get started. This lack of foresight not only undermines your schedule but also saps the enthusiasm of your team at a time when that enthusiasm is at its peak. The following sections explain how to make sure your project launches on the scheduled date and time.

### Utilities

Before you begin scheduling the work, you must have the power (gas and electric), water, and materials you need to get started. Contact the utility companies as soon as possible to have them turn on the gas, electricity, and water. Otherwise, you can't work on the gas or electric furnace, repair the lights or outlets, or work on the plumbing. Call the utility companies immediately after closing to have the utilities switched to your name and to specify a date on which you want them turned on.

If you forget to have the utilities turned on, don't use this misstep as an excuse to postpone renovations. You can buy or rent a generator, obtain water and electricity from the neighbors, and use portable heaters to remain toasty in cold weather. Time is money! Get to work and keep working so that you can realize that profit.

WARNING

When the utilities are turned on, you should be at the house to check for any leaks and be prepared to turn off the water or gas at the main shutoff if you notice any leaks. If the temperature is below freezing, turn on utilities in the following order: electricity, gas, water. Always have the water turned off at the meter, and then slowly turn it on so that you can catch any leaks quickly, before the pipes hit full pressure.

## Materials

List all the materials you need for repairs and for your home improvement projects, order the materials as soon as you know what you need (but not before closing on the house), so that you have time to make substitutions or find another supplier if something is out of stock.

TIP

Some stores are willing to hold the materials for you until you're ready to start and then deliver them right to your door or schedule a curbside pickup. If the property has a secure garage, empty out as much space as possible before delivery day rolls around.

## Dumpster

Now is the time to order a dumpster for any major cleanup and demolition, and a portable potty for your workers — it's essential if you are doing a lot of construction outdoors and don't want workers traipsing through the house and leaving footprints.

## Combination key lockbox

TIP

Don't forget to provide easy access to the inside of the home for any contractors or subcontractors who need to get inside to work. A combination key lockbox is a great solution. You put the housekey in the box, attach the box to an exterior doorknob, and lock it. Anyone who has the combination can unlock the box to access the key and use it to unlock the house. Most hardware stores carry these lockboxes.

# Tackling underlying problems first

If you're scheduled for liposuction, you don't run out and buy a whole new wardrobe. You don't even know whether the new clothes will fit. The same is true when you're renovating a house. If the house isn't level, you level the house before installing a new kitchen. If pipes need to be replaced, you complete that job before you paint the walls or install new flooring.

**REMEMBER**

For most renovations, follow the same sequence as the one used for new construction:

1. **Repair or replace the underlying structure.**

   Correct any problems with the foundation and have the carpenters first rough out the walls, ceilings, and entryways.

2. **Install new ductwork, if needed, for heating and central air conditioning.**

3. **Replace any water pipes or sewage lines that need to be replaced.**

4. **Run new electrical lines, if needed.**

5. **Drywall or plaster the walls and ceilings, install flooring and cabinets, and perform any other final renovations.**

# Working from the top down

When it comes to home repairs and renovations, gravity rules, water seeks its level, and traffic runs across the floor — so schedule your work from the top down. If the roof is leaking, fix it first. Otherwise, the water can damage the drywall or the new carpeting. If the house has more than one floor, consider starting at the top and working your way downstairs. In a room, paint the ceiling first, and then the trim, and then the walls, and, finally, lay the carpet or flooring. If you're doing major renovations in a room, save the painting, carpeting, and new-fixture installation for last.

**TIP**

If you plan to live in the house during renovation, consider renovating one bathroom, one bedroom, and the kitchen (in that order) before you move in. These changes make the house livable so that you can take your time with the other renovations.

## Working from the outside in, or vice versa

Weather permitting, work on the outside of the house first to generate some neighborhood buzz. By working on the outside of the house first, you immediately put the wheels of your marketing machine in motion and have a much better chance of selling the house when you put it on the market.

**REMEMBER**

Plan ahead to take advantage of the weather, and keep in mind that house hunting season generally starts to heat up in early spring and cool off in the late fall. You don't want to get stuck with a house over the long winter months, when heating bills peak.

If the weather is frigid or searing, or if you plan to spend a year or more renovating the inside, you may want to reverse this strategy: Begin inside and then complete the outside renovations when you're closer to the date on which you plan to plant the For Sale sign on the front lawn. Keep in mind, however, that if something on the outside, such as a leaky roof, is likely to cause additional damage, you need to take care of that first.

**TIP**

If you need to kick it up a notch to meet deadlines or prepare the house for closing, work indoors and outdoors at the same time and consider scheduling crews in shifts. Keep in mind, however, that *the neighbors may not welcome or appreciate any noise that's created during the graveyard shift.* Check with your neighbors first, invite them over to witness your progress, and ask them whether multiple shifts for a limited period is acceptable. Becoming friendly with the neighbors is always (well, usually) a good idea.

## Allotting sufficient time for your projects

At this point, you may be wondering just how long it will take to renovate your house and put it back on the market. The best answer we can offer is this: It depends. Specifically, it depends on the following:

>> The condition of the house

>> The extent of the planned renovations

>> How much work you plan to do yourself

>> The number of waking hours you can reasonably commit to the project

>> How well you plan the renovations

>> How much help you have

>> How long you plan to hold on to the house, especially if you're living in the house you flip

If you're doing a cosmetic job, and you have plenty of hired hands working in unison, you can expect to complete your renovations in one to two weeks and place the house right back on the market. On the other hand, if you're gutting the house and doing most of the work yourself on nights and weekends, the project can easily stretch out over months and years rather than weeks.

**TIP**

Consult with your contractors to set reasonable dates for completing the work, and plan, based on the information you gather, to place the house on the market the day after the work and final cleanup are scheduled to be completed. Then let everyone know the date. You can bump it out later, if necessary, but having a completion date in place is an effective motivator.

# Chapter **5**

# Negotiating the Sale to Maximize Your Profit

So you've devised your flipping strategy, bought a property, and made all the renovations you deemed necessary to maximize your profit. You followed our advice and hired an agent to sell your house. That's an excellent decision, but it's not the last decision you need to make. Your agent can find prospective buyers, show them the house, and encourage them to submit an offer, but the sale price and terms are up to you. And although your agent can help guide you through the often-sensitive negotiation process, you can always benefit from a few extra strategies and techniques. You need to know for yourself how to haggle with buyers in a way that gives them what they want without giving away too much of what you need.

This chapter assists you in evaluating various offers as they come in and show you how to use multiple offers to your advantage. Finally, you go through the process of closing the deal, and you're introduced to the paperwork you need to shuffle to make everything legal.

If you do decide, against our advice, to sell the house without using an agent, check out the latest edition of *Selling Your House For Dummies* by Eric Tyson, MBA, and Ray Brown (Wiley).

Think twice about flying solo when you put your house on the market. According to the National Association of Realtors (NAR), the average seller receives 16 percent more for a house when using a Realtor (a real estate agent who is a NAR member). The reason the seller gets so much less by not using an agent is that both the buyer and the seller try to save the commission. When nobody comes looking at the house, the seller subtracts the commission to make the house a more attractive purchase. The buyer, who knows that the seller isn't paying a commission, also subtracts the commission when making an offer. See Chapter 3 in Book 1 for information on hiring an agent.

# Comparing Seemingly Similar Offers

When homeowners sell a property, they often act as auctioneers looking for the high bid, but price is only one component of an offer (or purchase agreement). In many cases, a lower offer is superior if the buyer can close quickly and doesn't demand a lot of extras, such as closing costs and repairs.

When you're flipping houses, you need to be able to evaluate offers and see beyond price to weigh all factors. The following sections reveal the major factors you should consider so that you can compare offers as you receive them. Consult with your agent for specific advice on issues that concern you.

Your first offer is usually the best offer, so don't reject it outright, thinking that better offers are soon to follow. If you receive an offer soon after you put the house up for sale, you may be tempted to assume that you priced the house too low and try to sabotage the deal so that you can raise your asking price. This tactic is often a costly mistake. That first offer may be the only one you receive. Remember: Pigs get fat; hogs get slaughtered.

## Does the buyer have financing?

Buyers don't have to be able to afford your house in order to bid on it. They can have a dollar in their pocket and ten dollars in a bank account and still submit an offer. If you accept the offer by signing the purchase agreement, they can tie up your house for several days of negotiations until you discover that they can't get financing.

When fielding offers, don't sign a purchase agreement unless the bidder provides proof of one of the following types of financing (see Chapter 4 in Book 1 for general information on financing):

>> **Cash:** Cash offers are tops, but you should verify that the buyer has the cash to close the deal. Verification can be in the form of a letter from the buyer's bank or credit union or from Grandma Rowland, who's putting up the money. Or, you can ask for a copy of the buyers' recent bank statements — advise the buyers to black out their account numbers so that the account numbers don't fall into the wrong hands. If you can't locate the actual statements or if the buyers prefer not to provide copies, the bank can provide an official letter stating that sufficient funds are available in the buyers' accounts.

>> **Preapproval:** *Preapproval* means that a lender has already okayed the loan. This offer is the next best thing to a cash offer, but preapproval letters are worth only as much as the paper they're printed on. Ask the buyers to talk with your mortgage person (a loan officer you trust or one your agent recommends). Don't trust the word of the buyer's loan officer because that person may not be the most reliable source of accurate information. If the buyers balk at this suggestion, tell them that buying and financing a home is important business and they wouldn't have major surgery without getting a second opinion, so they should consider getting some additional input from your loan officer. More than likely, your mortgage specialist will be of a higher caliber than the one they may have just stumbled on.

>> **Prequalification:** If the buyer has prequalification, a lender has researched the buyer's financial records and decided that the buyer can probably secure a loan. Prequalification is one rung down from preapproval.

All things being equal, a cash offer is best, but if the cash offer is more than 5 percent lower than a noncash offer, you need to weigh the benefits against the lower purchase price.

**REMEMBER**

Accept offers only from serious buyers who are at least preapproved for a loan that's sufficient for purchasing the property. Have your mortgage specialist on call to examine a prospective buyer's qualifications before you sign the purchase agreement. You should always receive a letter from the buyer's lender with the offer, and this letter should contain the lender's contact information. Your mortgage specialist can contact the buyer's lender and perform background checks to ensure that the buyer has secured sufficient financing.

## How "earnest" is the buyer?

Most offers have an earnest-money deposit attached to them that shows how committed the buyer is to purchasing the property. A buyer who backs out of the deal without due cause forfeits the earnest-money deposit — and you get to keep it. Needless to say, an offer with a large earnest-money deposit is less likely to fall apart at the last minute than an offer with a smaller deposit. To the seller, having that assurance carries a lot of weight.

A reasonable amount to offer as an earnest-money deposit depends on the nature of the financing: 20 percent deposit on a conventional loan, 10 percent on a cash offer, and 3.5 percent on an FHA (Federal Housing Administration) loan. Any lesser amount shows a weakness in the buyer's financing or commitment. Any more shows that the buyer is in a stronger position to purchase the property and more committed to closing the deal.

When buyers offer a low deposit, explain that by putting down more money now, they have to come up with less money at closing. You can also consider adding an incentive for putting down a higher deposit by saying something like this: "I'd be much more comfortable with a deposit of $5,000 than with the $1,000 you're offering. In fact, I'd be willing to drop the price of the house by $500 in exchange for a larger deposit." If you figure that each day you hold the property costs you $100, then $500 is a small investment for ensuring that the deal goes through.

Don't hold the earnest-money deposit yourself. Ask your agent, attorney, or title company to hold on to the cash. That way, you won't be tempted to dip into the cookie jar before the deal is done.

## What else is the buyer asking for?

Buyers ask for all sorts of stuff when they submit offers. They may ask you to remove that pool you just installed because they won't use it and don't want to maintain it. They can ask for the sports car you have stored in your garage. They can request that you pay as much as 6 percent of their closing costs, pay for a home warranty, or immediately vacate the property at closing. When evaluating an offer, take all these requests into consideration. The following suggestions can help you handle common requests:

>> **Possession at closing:** Buyers often want to take immediate possession of a property. When you're flipping, this situation is ideal, assuming that you don't reside in the house. If you're living in the house you flip, draw up a contingency plan and try your best to accommodate this request. It may inconvenience you, but as a flipper, you want to sell your house as quickly as possible to cut your holding costs and have cash to finance your next flip.

>> **Payment of closing costs:** Many first-time homeowners request that the seller pay a portion of the closing costs so that they don't have to pay these costs upfront. If buyers ask for closing costs, consider offering to pay the closing costs upfront if the buyer is willing to pay a little more for the house to cover the closing costs. Many first-time buyers would rather roll the closing costs into their mortgage than pay the fees upfront. Of course, this is an

option only if the property appraises for the amount the buyers are willing to pay. If the appraisal comes in too low, you can challenge it, but if you lose that battle, you need to lower the price.

>> **No tax proration:** At closing, you normally get back any taxes you paid for the months that the new owner will live in the house. When buyers request no tax proration, they're asking you to pay their property taxes. Ask your title company to calculate the amount you would be getting back at closing. If the amount is small — only a few hundred bucks — you may want to agree to this request. If you recently paid the tax bill and the sale closes in the first month after paying, that money should be reimbursed to you. For example, if the taxes are $6,000 for the year, which equals $500 per month, you lose $5,500 at closing if you give up tax proration.

TIP

In some states, homeowners pay taxes in arrears rather than in advance. In other words, the homeowner pays this year to cover last year's property taxes. In states in which taxes are paid in arrears, the seller customarily credits the buyer at closing for as much as one year of taxes. The theory is that, because the seller used the property in the previous year and those taxes are being paid this year, they are the seller's responsibility. In such cases, you're better off if the buyer doesn't ask for the taxes to be prorated. Consider offering to pay the next installment due after the closing — it can save you approximately six months in taxes versus a full year's proration. But again, if the buyer won't budge on this term and is presenting a sweet offer, you may want to give in.

WARNING

Beware of the red herring move: Buyers often request something they know you won't agree to in an attempt to focus your attention on that lone request and give in on everything else. If the buyer requests something odd, such as the Oriental rug in the living room, it should raise a red flag. Unless giving away that rug eats up your profit, giving in may be your best option.

WARNING

Under no circumstances should you offer a buyer cash back at closing. Con artists often use *cash-back-at-closing* deals to trick lenders out of money: In this scheme, the buyer agrees to pay more for the house (often, much more than the asking price), and the seller kicks back a portion of the extra money (or all of it) to the buyer after closing. These deals are fraudulent; if you become involved in one, you may find yourself on the wrong end of a judge's bench.

## What conditions has the buyer included?

Conditional statements (weasel clauses) accompany every offer. Some are built into the offer, but the buyer can jot down additional conditions. If you're smart, you probably did the same thing when you bought the house. This list describes the most common conditions that buyers stipulate:

>> **Financing must be approved:** Every purchase agreement has this condition, and if you're already screening out anyone who's not prequalified for a loan, this clause should pose no problem. (See the earlier section "Does the buyer have financing?" for more information.)

>> **Property must appraise at the sale price or higher:** If you've done your homework and priced your property competitively, this condition should pose no problem.

>> **House must pass inspection:** You had the house inspected when you bought it, and you repaired everything, so this point is another non-issue.

>> **Title must be clear:** Before you purchased the house, you researched the title and purchased title insurance, so you're safe here, too.

>> **My existing home must sell first:** You don't want the sale of your house hanging in limbo because the buyers can't sell their house. If you like the offer, consider countering with an offer that gives the prospective buyers *first right of refusal,* which keeps the house on the market but provides the buyers with notice (often 72 hours) before you sell to someone else. The buyers then have that much time (72 hours, for example) to match any offer you receive. If you don't like the offer, give your other offers a higher priority.

**WARNING**

Beware of any conditions the buyer adds to gain an unfair advantage or saddle you with all the financial risk. Anything that enables the buyer to easily back out of the deal with no financial loss should raise a red flag, including interest rate contingencies (the offer is removed if the buyer can't secure a loan at a certain interest rate), a clause saying the buyer's attorney must review and approve the offer, or a clause giving the buyer the right to back out of the deal without cause.

## How soon does the buyer want to close?

**TIP**

As a flipper, you're well aware of holding costs. Every day you own your property costs you money, so the sooner you close, the less money you're out. When comparing offers, check the date on which the buyer wants to close. If one buyer who wants to close immediately is offering $2,000 less than another buyer who wants to close a month from now, the lower offer may be the better offer, assuming all other conditions are equal.

## AVOIDING THE DOMINO EFFECT

Having the sale of your house conditional upon the sale of another house is known as the *domino effect*. (Coauthor Ralph has seen this arrangement go seven deep.) Each house is dependent on another one selling. If something happens anywhere along the line, your deal is dead. Our advice is to sign a 72-hour contingency that allows you to keep your house on the market. This contingency gives you two opportunities to sell the house: You can sell the house to the first buyer, or, if another buyer comes along, you can sign an agreement with the second buyer contingent upon the first deal not going through. You then give the first buyer notice that they can lift their 72-hour contingency or else you will act on the second offer at the 73rd hour. Top-producer agents are well trained in this method, and you should be, too.

Keep in mind that each offer stands on its own terms. The first buyer is under no obligation to match a higher offer. Price has nothing to do with the contingency.

# Mastering the Art of Counteroffers

Some offers are so low that all you can do is laugh and shrug them off, but in most cases, no offer is too low to reject outright. When you receive an offer that appears to be a little irrational, don't take it personally. If you're not ready to say either yes or no, simply reply with your counteroffer.

**REMEMBER**

Take-it-or-leave-it ultimatums have no place in negotiations. Defuse your emotions. Depressurize your passions. Proceed with logic and always treat buyers with respect, even if you think they're off their rockers.

The following sections explore counteroffers in greater depth and show you some techniques for turning the tables on buyers without insulting or confronting them.

**WARNING**

Never counter yourself. Suppose you're asking $200,000 for a property and you receive an offer of $180,000, so you counter with $195,000, and the buyer hesitates. You begin thinking about it. Maybe you should have countered with $190,000. You have bills to pay. Baby needs new shoes. You want to call back with a new counteroffer. Don't do it. Your baby doesn't need new shoes that badly. Wait for the next counteroffer to come in before you decide on your next move; otherwise, you're essentially bidding against yourself.

# Submitting a counteroffer

After you receive and evaluate a reasonable offer, you have two choices: Accept the offer as is or submit a counteroffer in writing. If the buyer offers the full price and attractive terms (as covered in the earlier section "What conditions has the buyer included?"), accept the offer immediately. Don't start to second-guess yourself or wonder whether you sold yourself short. Lady Fortune has smiled down upon you, so smile back and sign the agreement.

If the offer isn't stellar but shows some promise for negotiation, craft a counteroffer. The following sections show you the basics.

## Coming up with a savvy counteroffer

Offering and counteroffering is like a game of chess, in which buyer and seller attempt to anticipate one another's next move. You never know what a buyer will request or state as a condition, so you need to tread carefully and think creatively. The following list presents some examples of counteroffers that have worked in the past:

>> **Buyer offers $5,000 less than asking price and no tax proration:** Knowing that the loss of tax proration will cost you $1,000 at closing, you counter that you agree to pay the tax proration if the buyer pays the full asking price.

>> **Buyer offers $10,000 less than asking price:** Knowing that your home is priced competitively with comparable homes in the area and that you're in a sellers' market, you counter with your original asking price but provide a comparison chart showing that your house is well worth that price.

>> **Buyer makes a firm offer for less than you can accept:** Return the offer with a note that says, "Sorry, but I can't accept less than [a specific amount]."

>> **Buyer requests that you provide a home warranty:** The average home warranty costs around $425, so it's usually not a deal breaker. A home warranty is a reasonable request, and if it doesn't break the bank, accept it. Besides, having a home warranty may protect you from a future lawsuit if the property has a defect that went unnoticed during the inspection.

## Putting your counteroffer in writing

If you decide to counter, write your counteroffer on the copy of the purchase agreement you received from the buyers or the buyers' agent, initial your changes, and then scan and email, photograph and text, or hand-deliver your counteroffer to the buyers' agent or directly to the buyers if they aren't working through an agent. (Some agents prefer to submit counteroffers on a separate form rather than mark up the original offer; they number the counteroffers along the lines of Seller 1, Buyer 2, Seller 3, and so on.) If you're using an agent, have your agent present the counteroffer. Be sure to stipulate the deadline for a response to your counteroffer.

**WARNING**

Don't make verbal agreements — they won't stand up in court. Only what's written on an offer counts, so make sure that all offers and counteroffers are in writing.

## Leveraging the power of multiple offers

When you receive an outstanding offer, jump on it. If the offer falls short of outstanding, call your other prospects and let them know that you've received an offer and will pursue it if you don't receive an offer from them by a certain deadline (in one or two days). This tactic applies pressure to all interested parties, encouraging them to get off their duffs and act quickly or lose the house for good. Keep the details about the offer you received a mystery so that new bidders don't have an unfair advantage.

If additional offers arrive, you can then compare offers, as explained earlier in this chapter, and accept the best offer or counter it. Keep a copy of those other offers on hand, however, just in case what you consider to be the best offer falls through.

**TIP**

If you receive competing offers, let both buyers know that you'll be looking at their best and final offer. If you have an agent, let the agent do the talking. After both offers come in, you can then pick the best offer and start negotiating.

## THINKING LIKE AN AGENT

Agents are master negotiators, so when you're selling a house, it pays to think like an agent or work with an agent. Skilled agents know how to break down the numbers into minimums. For example, if a buyer offers $5,000 less than the asking price, the seller is out $5,000 over a single transaction. But for a buyer with a mortgage interest rate of 6.5 percent, that $5,000 represents about $30 a month or less than $1 a day! Presenting these numbers in this way to the buyer puts the offer in perspective. This strategy can be highly effective in convincing buyers to up the ante when the seller won't budge.

Another strategy we use in our office is to place the buyers and sellers in separate conference rooms — we have several of them. The buyers and sellers exchange letters. They each jot down bullet points specifying what they like and dislike about the offer, and we eliminate their differences, one by one. After everyone has agreed, we join together in one room and sign documents.

Countering two offers with signed counteroffers is fraud. You can legally respond to more than one offer by submitting unsigned counteroffers and stipulating that none of the counteroffers is legal and binding until you sign it. However, it's preferable to ask all interested parties to submit their best offer so that you know who's most serious.

# Shuffling Papers and Other Legal Stuff at Closing

After you and the buyers reach an agreement on price and terms, and assuming that nothing happens to sabotage the deal, the sale proceeds to closing, where you receive your money and sign over the deed to the buyer. At this point, you have two goals: to make the closing proceed as smoothly as possible and to ensure that your back end is covered. The following sections show you how to proceed with a closing from start to finish.

In real estate, everything must be in writing. All pertinent details must be disclosed. You can't hide anything or make deals on the side.

## Having the right folks represent you

Even if you sell the house yourself, you should never try to fly solo during the closing. Closings are complicated legal and financial transactions accompanied by mounds of paperwork. You need to make sure that your interests are protected at closing by hiring a closing agent and a real estate attorney to represent you and ensure that all paperwork is properly completed. Your agent can attend the closing but usually advises you to have your attorney present; whether you choose to have your attorney present is up to you.

In most cases, your title company supplies the closing agent, but in some cases, the buyer's lender insists on handling the buyer's end of the closing. However the closing is handled, you should supply your attorney with copies of the paperwork to review before the closing date to avoid any nasty surprises at closing.

As soon as you and the buyer agree on price and terms, call your title company or real estate attorney and schedule a closing date. Closings typically occur 30 to 45 days from the day you sell the property, so don't waste time. As soon as you sell the property, you must order the title policy. Neither the buyer nor seller needs to worry about this task — your real estate agent keeps the process moving forward and can recommend a title company or attorney to handle the paperwork.

# Prepping for closing

To ensure that the closing proceeds as smoothly as possible, supply your closing agent with any documents necessary to assemble the closing packets. Documents typically include these items:

>> **Termite inspection report**

   If the buyer is financing the purchase with a Veterans Affairs (VA) loan, immediately schedule a termite inspection, if it hasn't already been done, and send the report to the closing agent or attorney who's handling the closing. (Typically, the buyer orders the termite inspection and has it done before closing, and the seller pays for it at closing.)

>> **Purchase agreement and any addendums**

>> **Mortgage payoff information and any second mortgages or other liens**

>> **Buyer's financial information**

TIP

If you use the same title company at closing that you used when you purchased the property, the title company often discounts the fee it charges for title work. Even if you're using a different title company, turn in your old policy. You can usually receive a credit for it.

# Sealing the deal with paperwork

At the closing, the closing agent or attorney in charge supplies you and the buyer with separate closing packages. The buyers' package is typically much thicker than yours because they're the ones borrowing money. Your package should include the following items:

>> **Settlement statement:** Both you and the buyer receive a settlement statement that breaks down the charges and credits for the buyer and seller and shows the net amount each of you receives or must pay at closing.

>> **Deed:** The deed is the document that transfers ownership of the property from you (the seller) to the buyer.

>> **Bill of sale:** If you included any appliances in the sale of the property, your closing package may include a bill of sale that transfers ownership of these items to the buyer.

>> **Mortgage payoff statement:** If you took out a loan to purchase the property, your lender supplies you with a letter indicating the full amount due on the closing date to pay off the mortgage. After the closing is final, the lender receives full payment.

- >> **Escrow statement:** If your monthly mortgage payments included escrow payments to cover bills, such as water and sewer, homeowner's insurance, or property taxes, some of the money held in escrow may be returned to you at closing. The escrow statement shows you how much you can expect to get back.

- >> **1099-S report:** The federal government requires that the 1099-S be filed to report the exact sale price of the house.

- >> **Estoppel certificate:** Some title companies require the buyer and the seller to sign an estoppel certificate that verifies they are of legal age to enter into a legally binding agreement, that the deed has no hidden liens, and that nobody is disputing the title.

- >> **Homestead exemption update:** Some properties qualify for a homestead tax exemption. At closing, you may be asked to rescind the exemption that's in place so that the buyers can claim the exemption, if they qualify for it.

Often, the buyers sign their closing paperwork first because they have so many more documents to sign. Buyers and sellers may sign together, separately, electronically, or via traditional mail. No way is wrong so long as all parties sign the required documents.

REMEMBER

After you and the buyer sign the required documents, the deal is done. Hand over the keys and the garage door openers to the new owner along with any manuals for appliances you're leaving with the property. At this point, you should also inform the buyers of the date on which utilities will be turned off. Bring the phone numbers of the various utility companies to the closing. After closing, you and the new owners can call the companies and have the utilities transferred to the new owners. Because your name is on the utility bills, you may need to verify with the utility company that you approve the transfer. Overlooking a minor detail like switching over the utilities can inconvenience the new owners and result in your receiving unexpected bills later.

# 5
# Using Your House as an Airbnb

Contents at a Glance

# Contents at a Glance

# Chapter **1**

# Hosting on Airbnb: What It Really Means

Becoming an Airbnb host isn't for everyone, and even though you may want to start immediately, holding off for a bit may be in your best interest. Having the right type of hosting mindset is important if you want to host successfully on Airbnb. This chapter walks you through some important things to consider prior to hosting and helps you determine whether you're currently ready to start hosting on Airbnb.

## Having a Hospitality Mindset: What It Takes to Be a Host

An Airbnb host and a landlord are two different positions. Many people think nothing will change when switching from acting as the landlord of a long-term rental property to the host of a short-term Airbnb rental. You may think that the only changes will concern money and overall operations. However, when you decide to host on Airbnb, you're signing up for a much different experience.

As an Airbnb host, you're inviting someone into your home and space. You're actually in the hospitality industry rather than the real estate industry. With this change comes a new way of thinking. After all, you're opening your home and welcoming guests into it. Hosting family or friends is a more similar experience to what hosting on Airbnb entails rather than renting a space to someone for 6 or 12 months at a time.

As an Airbnb host, you need to set your expectations clearly on your listing and then reliably deliver on those expectations. Most importantly, you need to maintain a guest-focused mindset. Your main focus should be on making your guests' stay as great as possible. Ensure you have the following in place to effectively deliver on all those expectations.

## THE HOSPITALITY MINDSET: HOW HOSTING ON AIRBNB DIFFERS FROM BEING A LANDLORD

Being an Airbnb host versus being a landlord differs more than you may think. The alternative to hosting on Airbnb is renting your space long term to a tenant. When you make that choice, you leave the hospitality industry and enter the real estate industry. Essentially, within the real estate space you're providing someone a space — anything from a room to an apartment or house — and it's that tenant's choice where to go from there.

The tenant must deal with everything from the furniture to decorations and any other amenities. Responsibilities such as cleaning and maintenance of the property is the tenant's responsibility, although there's a small degree of the service element in real estate. If there's an electrical issue or structural damage, you tend to that. However, to a certain extent, you're just offering a space.

With Airbnb you go further: You're providing an overall experience. You're making sure your guest's stay is perfect. You aren't just giving them a room with four walls. Rather, you're offering all the amenities and services. You're not only tending to the property maintenance and service, but you're also communicating with guests and offering recommendations of where to go, where to eat, and what to do in the area. You're part of a different industry, and realizing that difference is important.

# Opening your heart and your home to guests

**REMEMBER**

If you're offering your personal space to guests, you're letting people right into your life. You must be ready to welcome them into your home and not just on the good days. Some days you may be stressed and not want to talk to people. Even though other things are going on in your life, as an Airbnb host you're still welcoming people into your home whenever your calendar is open. You really have to be ready for that reality. You can't let any of your day-to-day life impact your guests' stay.

On the flip side, being a great host doesn't mean you have to spend all your time with your guests. Be mindful of what sharing your space looks like and the extent to which you're letting guests into your life. The most involved way to host is by offering your spare bedroom or living room in the place where you're living. Doing so can be challenging at times but also rewarding because you can meet and get to know your guests and build relationships.

However, pursuing that arrangement means going in with your eyes wide open because more than likely you won't want to interact and help guests every day (or however many days you set your listing available). Essentially, be prepared to be there for your guests whether you want to or not.

If you have a vacation home that you're welcoming people into and you're not living there with them, you still need to remember the "mi casa es su casa" mentality. You want to avoid thinking "Hey, you're in my home for this set amount of time." Instead, you're setting an expectation that "While you're here, make yourself at home." Be prepared for that type of hospitality. You want your guests to feel comfortable and be able to enjoy themselves. They shouldn't be walking on eggshells worried about upsetting you or messing up your space.

**TIP**

To avoid having your guests feel that way, consider putting away anything that carries extreme sentimental value to you that may risk being damaged by guests. Doing so can put you at ease with having guests in your space.

Also be sure to clearly communicate anything that you're particular about, such as how certain things get organized or put away. If you don't communicate clearly, then you risk becoming frustrated with your guests, which is the opposite of what you want.

You have to be comfortable with your guests during their stay. Physically and mentally prepare yourself. Doing so can be tough. If you're not ready to welcome people and have your home be their home, then being an Airbnb host may not be the best fit. Ultimately, as soon as you can fully welcome guests into your space, you'll be able to offer the best experience.

REMEMBER

Make known any concerns about your space so your guests can meet those expectations and enjoy a stress-free stay.

## Establishing trust through transparency and dependability

Because you're essentially operating in the hospitality industry as an Airbnb host, a high degree of customer service comes into play. Unmet expectations can frustrate your guests. As a result, you want to establish your guests' trust by being transparent and dependable.

Keeping an eye on the big picture and remembering that each individual guest stay adds up to create an overall level of guest satisfaction is important. No single guest can be looked at as being insignificant or unimportant. If you don't consistently offer transparency and dependability, you're going to lose trust and credibility in your reviews. When you aren't meeting the expectations you set, your guests are going to let you know.

REMEMBER

Clear and fast communication is a good example of what shows up in the reviews. People won't trust you to get back to them when they have questions in the future if they see a high number of past guests complaining about the time it took for you to respond to their messages. This applies to any expectation you're setting for your listing as well as the baseline expectations for staying in any Airbnb accommodation. Essentially, ensure that you're thinking in the long term and that you maintain trust by always meeting and exceeding guests' expectations.

## Keeping your place clean and well equipped

From your own standpoint as the owner of your listing, you may be perfectly content with some weeds in the front lawn or some dust on the baseboards. However, when you become a host, you need to consider these different elements from a different mindset. Keeping your place clean and well maintained is an important part of being a great host.

Similarly, you may not often cook for yourself and you may therefore have a relatively limited supply of cooking utensils. Though that amount may be entirely acceptable for you, as a host you have to consider things from your guests' perspective. If there's something that your guests would reasonably want or expect, then it's in your best interest to equip your property with it.

# Delivering on (rising) expectations

Airbnb is continually raising the bar on the guest experience, and the bar is already set high. Airbnb started as a simple air bed and breakfast. Guests had the expectation that they would be staying on an air mattress on the floor of an apartment. Back then, it was closer to an upgraded version of couch surfing. Today, many guests view Airbnb as an alternative to a hotel, and the expectations are clearly higher.

REMEMBER

In addition to what you've promised as their host in your listing, your guests will have certain baseline expectations. Meeting those expectations is a great place to start. As Airbnb grows and expands as a company, these expectations continue to rise.

REMEMBER

Here are some baseline expectations your guests will have:

>> Your property is clean.

>> Your Wi-Fi Internet is reliable (check out Chapter 3 in Book 5).

>> Your property is safe and secure.

>> Your property has adequate heating and cooling.

>> You quickly and reliably communicate with your guests. If you take hours or even days to respond to them, you can expect unhappy guests and negative reviews.

As a new host or a host who wants to do better at hosting, you have to understand those expectations and be prepared to meet them. Even if you aren't in an Airbnb Plus/Airbnb Luxe space or aiming to reach Superhost status, you should still aim to offer the great customer service and unique experience Airbnb promises its guests.

## Setting up systems so your guests have a unique stay

Most hosts want to share their city with other people, and as a host that opportunity should excite you. If you set up systems to lighten your hosting load and delegate certain responsibilities, then you're much more likely to enjoy the hosting experience.

One of the most common examples is hosts putting a system in place around cleaning. Most hosts don't want another part-time job as a house cleaner, and needing to add that to your plate can be stressful. After you start hosting, you can set up systems around tasks like cleaning so you won't get burnt out in the long term and can consistently deliver that personal touch as a host.

## Adding a touch of personal magic

What sets Airbnb apart most and the reason guests consistently choose Airbnb over hotels is the experience of living like a local. Guests have already experienced the same corporate hotel experience in different places around the world. With Airbnb they're getting the unique experience of living in a home or apartment.

Your touch of personal magic is about making sure you have the bandwidth to enjoy hosting, and that shows up in small and big ways. You communicate with your guests and answer their questions, which demonstrates you're excited about their arrival. This excitement can materialize both in person and through your messages.

You're passionate about hosting and really love what you're doing. Perhaps you give a small gift basket and are eager to hear how your guests are doing. You share tips about event and activities in the area with your guests. You may even leave something special for your guests during their stay. Compared to the burnt-out host who is just going through the motions about their guests being there, you're excited and do what you can to make their stay memorable and relaxing.

# Before You Become an Airbnb Host: What to Consider

This section focuses on what to think about before you make the decision to host. You may have reservations in the back of your mind that you aren't aware of but need to bring to the forefront. Ask the questions in this section to make sure you're ready to be a host. This is your chance to consider whether hosting is the right fit for you.

## Being aware of your hidden expectations

To realize your hidden expectations, first ask yourself what your expectations are for each aspect of hosting. How much money do you expect to make? What is your expectation for how much time you're willing to put into hosting? What are your expectations for which parts of hosting you will and won't participate in? What do you believe a reasonable guest will be like?

Jot down any expectations you have and what you think hosting is going to look like for you. Then critically go through that list and ask how realistic each expectation is. For example, expecting your property to bring in $10,000 per month may be realistic for you or it may be completely unrealistic. (Chapter 2 in Book 5 helps you determine what is realistic for you to earn.)

Be aware of some of the most common host misconceptions:

>> **Money:** People typically have a number in their head for how much money they'll bring in and a number for how much time it'll take to reach that amount.

>> **Time:** People often assume that they can just set up their listing on Airbnb and forget about it while the money rolls in. This isn't the case, and the truth is, hosting requires a fair bit of ongoing work to do well. You can put systems in place to reduce your workload, but hosting will always take more than a few minutes a month unless you decide to hire a property manager.

>> **Effort:** This expectation is similar to how much time hosting will require. Oftentimes people believe that hosting doesn't require much effort and will be an easy way to pass the time while bringing in large amounts of money.

>> **How the guest will act and behave:** Some people expect certain guest behaviors such as whether or not guests will use the kitchen or the common space and how tidy guests will keep the bathroom.

>> **How the guests will interact with the host:** People have different expectations for the engagement of guests and interactions they'll have.

>> **What hosting a guest actually looks like:** People usually have an expectation or idea of what the experience of hosting will entail. They usually have a vision of what a typical guest stay will look like. For some people, they think, "Oh it's horrible. They'll burn down my property." That's quite extreme on one side of the spectrum, but on the other extreme are the people who expect that hosting will be a breeze. They may think, "I'll send their check-in instructions and never hear from them again. It'll be no work for me."

When you're aware of your own expectations, you can cross-reference them with the common misconceptions listed here to be sure that you don't have the wrong idea of what it takes to be a host. As long as your expectations are realistic, you'll be able to make the right call when deciding whether or not hosting is for you.

## Inviting strangers into your home

An important thing to remember when considering being an Airbnb host is you don't get to control the personalities of the people staying in your home. Ultimately those people are strangers. All types of people with all kinds of backgrounds will be able to make a reservation in your home.

That's a tough reality for some people. You have to be nondiscriminatory and ready to welcome all guests regardless of their background or who they are as individual persons. As a baseline, be ready to be accepting of people from all walks of life because that's what you're going to get. You're going to have every type of person you can imagine.

REMEMBER

Essentially, be ready to go in with an open mind and an open heart. You don't get to control the types of people coming into your space so plan on welcoming everyone the same way and appreciating everyone for who they are. If you're hung up on this point, then Airbnb isn't the right platform for you.

REMEMBER

Airbnb is serious about antidiscrimination. The platform is 100 percent inclusive for both guests and hosts. It's absolutely against Airbnb's rules and policies to deny a guest based on race, religion, sexual orientation, and so on. Every host must formally agree before hosting to never discriminate against any guest.

## Making the commitment

Consider that by choosing to host you're planning to make a commitment that can affect your time, money, and energy, which are discussed in the following sections.

REMEMBER

The following money-related commitments especially apply if you're interested in hosting an entire apartment or home on Airbnb. Some people may have an apartment or home that's their vacation home or their former residence so it's already furnished. However, many other people are converting their long-term rental to a short-term rental and renting it on Airbnb. A huge deciding factor for those people is the return on investment (ROI) for hosting. Although you can make more money on Airbnb than through a 12-month tenant, ask yourself whether it's worth the additional time and cost.

### Time commitment

Ask yourself whether you have the time to devote to hosting. Do you actually have the time? Is your lifestyle set up for hosting? For instance, if you know you're going to be partying Friday and Saturday nights, then you may need to choose not to host at your home those weekend nights. If you aren't able to message guests during the day or throughout the week, then you may need to consider getting someone to help you with communications.

**REMEMBER**

Consider your own lifestyle and figure out how much time hosting requires. Be realistic about whether you can actually host and do so in a way that aligns with how much time and energy you have.

## Money commitment

Although you can control how much money goes into hosting, be aware that a portion of your Airbnb income is going to cover expenses like the extra toilet paper, hand soap, and dish soap you'll need. If you do it yourself or hire an outside cleaner, you're also going to spend money (and time) cleaning your property and doing the laundry. You need to invest in your hosting so consider to what extent you're comfortable doing that. Then get realistic about what your hosting will look like.

These expenses range from buying the day-to-day items like paper towels and hand soap to fully stocking your kitchen with cooking supplies to the larger and more costly requirements like furniture. For example, if you have a spare bedroom that you need to furnish or an entire property that you need to furnish, it'll cost money. Consider what kind of financial investment you need to put into your property before you decide to host (check out Chapter 3 in Book 5 for more guidance on what you'll need to have or add to your property to make it ready for guests).

## Energy commitment

When you make the decision to become a host, you're essentially making the commitment to put your best foot forward even when you don't necessarily feel like it. Your guests are going to have needs and you need to be ready to meet those needs with a positive attitude.

**REMEMBER**

Especially when hosting space in your own home, make sure you're ready to make the commitment to be positive and energetic when guests are around. Having a bad day at work isn't going to be an acceptable excuse for being rude or short with guests.

# Looking at how technologically savvy you are

Although Airbnb is an easy and user-friendly platform, when getting started you still need to make sure you're comfortable with technology. Two technology-related considerations for host are as follows:

>> **Consider whether you have access to technology.** You'll need a computer and ideally a smartphone. You'll use your smartphone to respond to guests

and complete tasks on the go rather than needing to constantly be near a computer.

>> **Make sure you're comfortable with technology.** Generally, anyone can host because the platform is user friendly. The best way to get accustomed to technology is by going on the Airbnb site and setting up a listing without making it live.

**REMEMBER**

Familiarize yourself with the back end of the platform, including how everything works in terms of setting your pricing, responding to guests, and seeing how your listing performs. Don't overlook the technology, but also don't be overwhelmed by it. Fortunately, the technology is fairly easy to pick up. Essentially, the more you understand and integrate this technology as a host, the better the results for you and your guests.

## Being aware of how your decision to host affects others in your life

You don't live on an island. Your decision to host can affect others as well. Consider the following two factors when deciding to host on Airbnb.

### How your hosting will impact others

When you decide to host, you're taking on a commitment that will potentially impact those around you. The most extreme impact will be on other people who are living with you when you decide to host guests in your personal home. Suddenly, you'll have people living in that space, making noise in that space, and using the amenities of that space such as the bathroom. Bringing another person or people into your space will have a definite impact on your family or roommates, and you need to be mindful of that reality.

In a less direct way, hosting means that you're giving your guests the space that you list. You won't be able to offer it to your sister or parents or friends when they come to town. Unless you plan in advance, your family or friends can't come last minute and crash at your place. Your decision to host will potentially change that expectation for them.

This doesn't mean that if you experience any of these situations you can't host, but it's important to be mindful and consider to what extent hosting will change your lifestyle. You may need to say no to your friends about going out or have them plan on crashing somewhere else.

### How your decisions in life affect your guests

You must be mindful of how your everyday decisions as a host impact your guests. For example, going out late at night and returning early in the morning, hanging out until midnight with friends in the living room, or being noisy isn't going to be acceptable when you're hosting guests and they're trying to sleep. Doing so is going to have a huge negative impact on your guests. For example, your sleeping guests who may be on vacation aren't going to appreciate your decision to use the blender at 5 a.m. to make a smoothie. Suddenly, your decision to take a long shower, or leave your hair in the sink or shower is impacting the people staying with you.

These decisions all impact the guests who are staying in your home. However, even if they're staying in your vacation home or an additional property you have, you're still going to be impacted. You can't have a family vacation at the last minute if your extra space is already booked with guests.

## Determining the type of host you want to become

You need to figure out what type of host you want to be. Fortunately there is no one set way. If you do want to be an Airbnb host, you now can figure out what makes you unique and offer that personal touch to your guests.

**REMEMBER**

When figuring out who you are as a host, the good news is you have so much flexibility. You can really make hosting whatever you want it to be. You have the freedom to decide how you host, when you host, what space you host in, and what space you don't host in. You can map out what best suits your current goals and lifestyle and what you want to get out of hosting.

For example, maybe you have spare bedrooms in your own home as well as a vacation home. After examining what you want from your Airbnb experience, you find you don't want people in your own home because it's not conducive to your lifestyle, but you still want to host your second property. On the other hand, you may decide that you want guests during the week, but on weekends you like having more privacy and keeping your space to yourself. You can choose to host for just one week a month or just when you leave town for the weekend. You may work a seasonal job and don't want people there in the summers, but in the wintertime when everything is a bit quieter you do want guests there.

No matter when you decide to host, you need understand what the baseline requirement for hosting is. Choosing to host for the additional income and not realizing the rest of the expectations and requirements — in other words hosting for the wrong reasons — is when you can run into issues.

IN THIS CHAPTER

» **Determining your revenue potential on Airbnb**

» **Conducting property market research**

» **Estimating your true profit potential**

» **Comparing city and rural markets**

» **Researching and following local Airbnb regulations**

# Chapter **2**

# Determining Your Profit Potential

Before you invest significant resources and energy into becoming an Airbnb host, you first need to determine the profit potential for your future Airbnb listing to make sure all that effort will be worth it — in other words, you want to make sure you make money hosting. Far too many aspiring hosts jump into hosting with blindfolds on and don't understand whether their expectations are realistic and achievable. When reality and expectations don't match, disappointment results.

Not all properties and markets can perform well on Airbnb as short-term rentals. By doing a bit of research and analysis before you host, you can set realistic expectations and ultimately decide whether hosting on Airbnb still makes sense for you, with your property, in your market.

This chapter provides guidance on how to determine the profit potential of your future Airbnb listing before you host. You can conduct proper market research and analysis to determine the "size of your pie"— how much you can reasonably expect to make as a host on Airbnb.

# Decoding How Much You Can Really Make on Airbnb

Aspiring hosts quickly discover, when attempting to estimate their Airbnb profit potential, that *where* they gather the relevant information can have a big impact on their calculations.

Looking at broad national averages can give you a rough sense of how an average host is performing, but it may tell you very little about what you could expect in your specific market with your property. To get an accurate gauge of your listing may perform, you need to gather the right kind of information and make sure those numbers are directly applicable to your situation. The following sections explain the basics.

## Starting with national averages

Earnest.com, a student and private loan refinance provider, analyzed tens of thousands of loan applications from applicants who reported earnings from working on sharing economy platforms like Airbnb. They found the average Airbnb host earned approximately $924 per month from hosting.

However, because a small fraction of hosts earned disproportionately higher income than their peers, the median earning for hosts was much lower. Figure 2-1 shows that only half of Airbnb hosts earned more than $440 per month (approximately $5,280 per year).

According to Earnest.com, about one in two Airbnb hosts earns less than $500 per month and nearly three in every four earns less than $1,000 per month. Only one in ten hosts will earn $2,000 or more per month.

## Recognizing that your location mostly determines your profit potential

**REMEMBER**

The profit potential of your Airbnb listing is primarily determined by the property's exact location. That is, how much you could expect to make from your Airbnb is mostly out of your control and can't be changed after your listing goes live on the platform.

So, asking yourself questions like: "How much should my one-bedroom Airbnb listing earn?" doesn't help. Even if you're asking within the boundaries of your specific city, listings that are a minute walk from each other can experience significantly different levels of Airbnb travel demand.

Airbnb Income Distribution

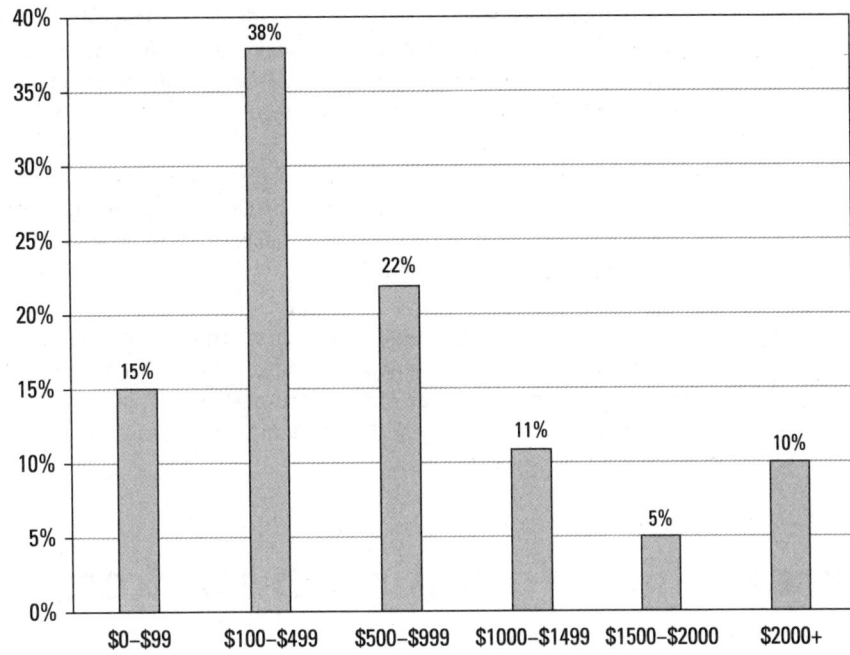

**FIGURE 2-1:**
How much Airbnb hosts earn.

Some markets have very high Airbnb travel demand with a limited supply leading to high occupancy rates and high nightly rates. For example, a one-bedroom entire apartment listing in downtown Los Angeles, located immediately across the street from the Los Angeles convention center and walking distance to the Staples Center where the L.A. Lakers and Clippers basketball teams play their home games, will significantly outperform an identical listing only two blocks away. Figure 2-2 compares two properties and looks at how a three-minute walk could potentially impact your earning potential.

| | Listing A | Listing B | Difference | |
|---|---|---|---|---|
| Avg Occupancy Rate % | 86.7% | 73% | | 13.4% |
| Avg Occupancy Rate (days/mo) | 26 | 22 | | 4 |
| Avg Nightly Rate | $126 | $105 | $ | 21 |
| Avg Monthly Revenue | $3,276 | $2,309 | $ | 967 |
| Avg Annual Revenue | $39,312 | $27,707 | $ | 11,605 |

**FIGURE 2-2:**
Two blocks away, a world of difference.

Just two blocks away, these two nearly identical Airbnb listings could see about a $1,000 difference per month (or almost $12,000 for the full year). Airbnb travel can become hyper local in some markets, especially if travelers care about immediate walking distance to points of interest.

In other words, the performance of Airbnb listings can vary drastically even across a short distance because of the high variability of demand across markets, which is more pronounced in dense urban markets. In more spread-out rural markets, the radius of a local market is larger.

**REMEMBER**

The demand for Airbnb rentals in your specific market, whether it's a one-block radius in a downtown area or a five-mile radius in an open rural area, determines the profit potential of your Airbnb listing. However, just because you could expect to earn a certain profit doesn't mean you'll automatically achieve it. You still must earn it by being a great host.

# Researching Your Airbnb Market: Earning Statistics

Picture yourself running a nice one-bedroom Airbnb listing in your city. After all the operating expenses that include supplies, utilities, and cleaning, say you're able to pocket a tidy $1,000 per month in profits. Should you be happy with your performance? Are you doing well as a host?

What if you found out that the other one-bedroom Airbnb listings in your market are making only $500 per month in profits on average? That would mean you're earning twice as much as your competition! You should feel good about that because that means you're executing well as a host.

But what if, instead, your competition is earning $4,000 per month in profits on average? You wouldn't be feeling too good about that information. If hosts with similar listings in the same market are earning three times as much as you are, you're doing some things wrong as a host.

**REMEMBER**

The best way to estimate your profit potential on Airbnb is to find out what similar listings in your neighborhood are already earning on the platform. But how do you find out? You gather *performance statistics* — the occupancy rates and nightly rates — for existing listings in your market that you'll be competing with.

In the early years, you would have to gather and estimate these statistics manually, a painfully laborious and inaccurate exercise that took hours to complete only to be outdated immediately. However, the growth and maturation of short-term rental data providers in recent years have provided fast, accurate, and up-to-date statistics to aspiring hosts for a nominal starting at just $20 to access local market reports. Some providers offer free limited reports or free trials occasionally, so make sure to search online for a recent offer before making a purchase.

TIP

For a list of currently recommended data providers, go to the online resources at www.learnbnb.com/airbnbfordummies.

TIP

Get the free reports and trials to see which one you like and then get a one-month subscription for full access to the market data in your market. You can't get the statistics on your own, and even if you tried, doing so would take you many painful hours to days only to put together an inaccurate data set. Don't waste your time! You can always cancel your subscription after the first month. However, we recommend ordering the reports at least once a year to keep a pulse on your market and to gauge how your listing is faring against your competition in the market.

You need to look beyond the published asking nightly rates of similar properties on Airbnb — just because a few listings ask for $250 per night doesn't mean guests are paying that much nor does it mean that these listings are able to fill their availabilities at this rate.

And what the performance is like during one part of the calendar may look entirely different during other parts of the calendar. So, in addition to understanding the nightly rates, you need to look at other market metrics and considerations to access your profit potential accurately.

## Finding the crucial market statistics

Regardless of which data provider you ultimately go with, you want to pay attention to a few key statistics when assessing the viability of hosting your property in your market. Here are the statistics you should get and why you need to pay attention to each:

>> **Daily rates:** The best way to know what you can charge is to find out what identical or similar listings in your market can currently charge guests. Although obtaining market averages is better than having nothing, getting a range of daily rates is more useful because a few very high-performing or very low-performing listings can artificially inflate or deflate the average figures in the market. For example, AirDNA market reports will also give you the 25th,

50th, 75th, and 90th percentile figures (see Figure 2-3 for an example of this data). Most hosts should use the 50th percentile figure (median) for their initial estimate unless they have reason to place their listing as more or less attractive than competitors to use the 75th or 25th percentile figures instead.

These numbers are the average monthly rental revenue for one-bedroom listings in a select area of Los Angeles, shown at the 25th, 50th, 75th, and 90th percentiles. For example, to achieve rental revenue rates at the 90th percentile line, your listing would need to be among the top 10 percent of listings in the market.

» **Occupancy rates:** *Occupancy rates* are the percentage of available nights that are booked. For example, an Airbnb listing that is made available for rental for 100 days out of the year and is booked 65 days has an occupancy rate of 65 percent (65 divided by 100). Just knowing the daily occupancy rate isn't enough if you don't know how many nights are being booked in the market. Similarly, obtaining a range of occupancy rates rather than just an average is more useful.

Take an honest assessment of your listing compared to the existing listings on the platform that are your competitors. Compare your listing to this entire set of direct competitor listings, ideally at least ten. Is your listing in a more attractive location versus the others? Does your listing look newer, more modern, or luxurious? Does your listing have more appealing amenities? Where does your listing place among this set? For an older property farther away from points of interest than competition, you may need to use the 25th percentile figure for your estimate because your listing will likely attract fewer guests. Alternatively, for an attractive new listing located immediately adjacent to the top performing listings in the market, you may use the 75th or 90th percentile figures instead because you can reasonably expect similar levels of performance to the top performers.

» **Rental revenue:** The top data providers will calculate the rental revenue figures for you and often present them in the same way they've presented the daily rates and occupancy rates data. Again, looking at the range is more helpful than the simple average. Brace yourself when you look at these figures the first time because many prospective hosts often have mismatched expectations from reality. For example, prospective hosts whose expectations are colored by the news articles covering the new breed of six-figure Airbnb hosts may be sorely disappointed to discover they'll likely earn far less than six figures in their market. Better to know the truth early even if disappointing than to find out later after investing significant time and resources.

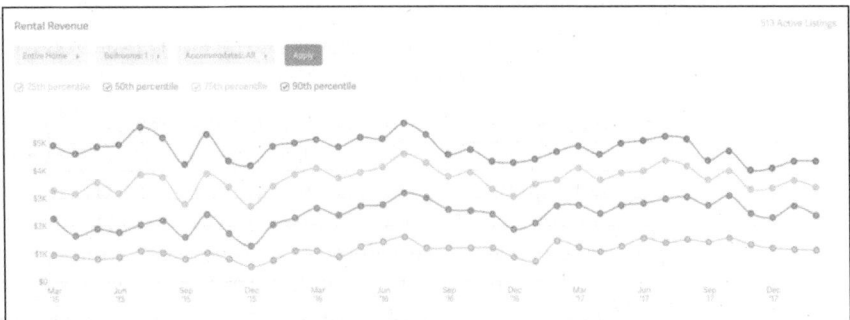

**FIGURE 2-3:**
Average monthly
rental revenue.

TIP

Although getting annualized figures are useful to understanding where your average daily rates, occupancy rates, and annual rental revenues may fall, you'll want to look at the monthly figures as well for the prior 12 months. Why? Some markets may have pronounced seasonality where the demand is much higher or lower during some months than others. Having this knowledge can better help you prepare for both the high and low travel seasons in your market. Refer to Chapter 4 in Book 5 for a detailed discussion of seasonality and how it impacts your pricing strategy.

## Understanding the market deeper

Each data provider will provide the three basic statistics for its users that are mentioned in the previous section. However, to stand out from their competition and to further entice their potential customers to choose them over others, the top listing data providers offer many additional statistics about the market.

Here are some other useful things you may find:

>> **Market mix:** The *market mix* is basically a relative ratio of different types of Airbnb listings in a given market. For example, the market mix for Airbnb listings by a large lake may skew toward cabins, whereas in a downtown urban market it may skew toward one- and two-bedroom apartments. This information lets you determine what the current composition of active Airbnb listings is, including whether more studio and one-bedroom units are being reserved compared to larger units with three or more bedrooms.

REMEMBER

Knowing the respective performance of the different subsets of listings can tell you what the travelers to this market are demanding. For example, if the top-performing listings are all private room and studio listings whereas the few large big house listings are mostly unoccupied, you may want to explore turning your five-bedroom house into multiple private room listings instead — you can't rent what people don't want.

>> **Long-term trends:** Understanding recent statistics tells you where the market is today, but those stats don't tell you how the market got where it is. Is the market growing or shrinking? Only by looking at several years of data can you spot this trend. With Airbnb increasing in popularity, more listings are coming online in more markets. However, in some markets, the influx of supply without a complementary growth in demand means more hosts competing for the same number of guests, leading to higher competition, lower pricing and occupancy, and ultimately lower profits for hosts.

>> **Amenities statistics:** To understand how your property stacks up against your competition, you need to know what your competition is offering. By looking at the amenities that everyone else provides and what only the top-performing listings offer, you can determine exactly what amenities you need to compete and what you can aim to have to stand out.

>> **Future statistics:** Some data providers have a direct data feed of hundreds of thousands of listings that allow them to know future occupancy and rates of competing listings. With this information you can price your future available dates to remain competitive.

>> **Top listings:** Being able to see the performance of the top listings in your market based on actual performance data provides a target at which to aim your performance. With this information you can scrutinize every aspect of these top listings from their photos and title to their descriptions, pricing, and policies. You can't emulate the best without first being able to identify the best.

>> **Rating statistics:** How guest ratings are distributed across property types and among your direct competitors can tell you how competitive your market is. The higher the ratings for existing hosts, the more competitive the market and the less margin for you to make hosting errors with your guests.

>> **Granular seasonality:** Even though monthly figures help you spot broad seasonality trends in your market during the calendar year, having access to market performance for each day can help you spot and prepare for unusual spikes in travel demand. For example, an annual conference that brings in thousands of travelers can lead to overbooking during those specific dates. Refer to Figure 2-4 for an example to see the full year seasonality for a market. For a full discussion on planning for and adjusting your pricing strategy for special events, refer to Chapter 4 in Book 5.

REMEMBER

In some markets, Airbnb travel demand is seasonal and varies significantly depending on the month of year. In addition, certain recurring special events can also create unusually high demand during specific days of the year. Knowing when they occur and how much impact they have on demand allows you, the host, to price your listings appropriately.

>> **Traditional rental statistics:** For investors who want to purchase property for renting them on a short-term basis on Airbnb, comparing the traditional rental market statistics in that market to short-term rental statistics is crucial to making a sound investment decision.

>> **Other statistics:** If it's an attribute you must decide on for your listing, chances are the data providers are tracking and sharing the results to their users. This information includes how others are handling minimum stays, security deposits, cleaning fee rates, cancellation policies, and more.

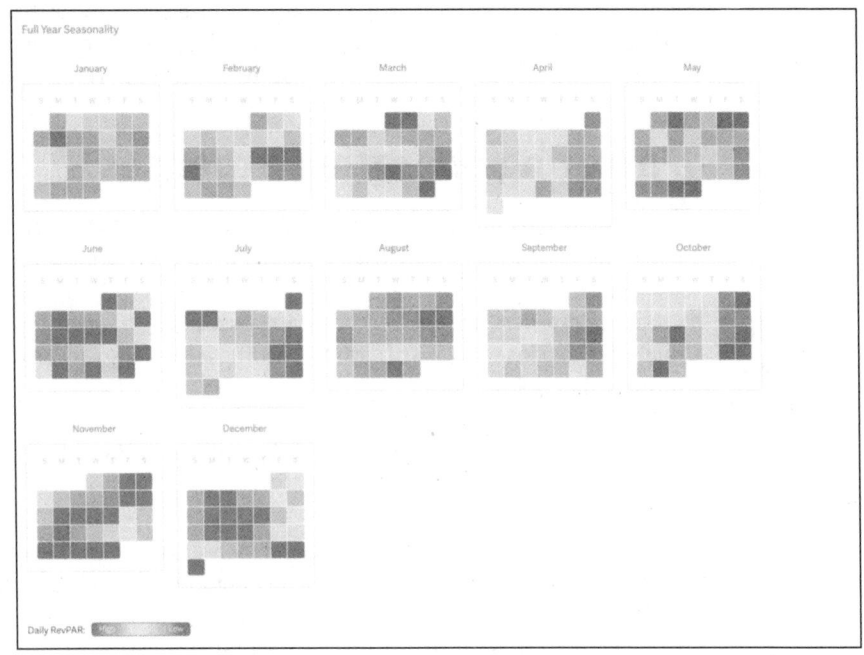

**FIGURE 2-4:** Seeing market seasonality.

Source: AirDNA.co

Hosts in different cities and countries find different data providers to be more or less accurate for them individually, so it's worth first exploring several options to see which will work best for you.

**TIP**

Each data provider presents its own data, and none will have all the metrics you want. So, take advantage of the free trials and then purchase a subscription for the one you find most useful for your goals. For the latest list of recommended data providers, go to www.learnbnb.com/airbnbfordummies.

# Determining the Size of Your Pie

Getting the market statistics can help you form realistic expectations for rental revenue, but you won't get to keep that amount of money. Unlike owning a traditional rental property, operating an Airbnb listing involves higher operating costs so for every dollar that you collect through Airbnb, you'll only get to keep a fraction of that.

Knowing what data and metrics to gather is the first step. Turning those findings into a profit estimate require additional work — for every dollar in booking revenue, you'll only get to keep a part of it because you'll incur expenses while operating your Airbnb listing. Additionally, it's important to compare your projected earnings against the expected time commitment required to host successfully.

## Factoring operating expenses

To estimate how much profit you'll get to take home, you need to understand and estimate the operating expenses involved in running your Airbnb rental.

REMEMBER

*Operating expenses* are the recurring expenses that happen monthly and exclude one-time expenses such as fixtures, furniture, and appliances that you need to set up your listing initially.

Although each Airbnb listing may differ, here are the most common operating expense items to factor into your analysis:

>> **Rent:** If you're renting a property and then subletting the entire unit on Airbnb during the full calendar year, then the rent that you pay is a rental expense. However, if you're renting a portion of the property on Airbnb, like a spare bedroom, or if you're only making the property available for rent for some of the days, then you'll need to divide the total rental expense between the parts of the property used for Airbnb and those for personal uses. You'll need to prorate the rental expenses by the percentage of the property used for Airbnb (by area or by the number of rooms) and by the ratio of days made available as an Airbnb rental out of total available days. Prorating expenses can get tricky depending on your jurisdiction and situation, so be sure to consult with your accountant.

>> **Management fees:** Management fees include commissions paid to others to take over the day-to-day operations for your Airbnb listing. For the many property owners who want to profit from Airbnb without hosting themselves, they'll need to set aside a portion of their rental revenue to pay a property manager or co-host to manage their Airbnb listing on their behalf.

- » **Utilities:** Guests staying in your property will want lights to see, running water to bathe, heat when it's cold, and air conditioning when it's hot. As a result, you need to pay the gas, water, and electricity bills. You also need to add any other regular fees paid to the city, including sanitation or sewage fees here. And due to the higher usage typical for short-term renters, these bills will be higher compared to that for long-term renters.

- » **Internet/cable/satellite:** High-speed wireless Internet is a required amenity in practically all Airbnb listings. Some hosts may even elect to provide cable or satellite television. These services aren't free.

- » **Cleaning:** For the many hosts who elect not to do the cleaning themselves, they hire outside cleaners. Although most of the cleaning fees are passed directly to guests, some hosts may subsidize the cost to charge a lower cleaning fee to their guests to encourage more bookings. Don't have a washer and dryer on the unit? Add laundromat fees.

- » **Repair and maintenance:** Operating an Airbnb listing means having more people come in and out of your property, adding more wear and tear on your property. Plumbing can leak or clog, furniture can become damaged, and appliances can break. And it's your job to make the repairs needed to keep your listing in pristine shape for the next guests.

- » **Permits:** More and more cities are requiring Airbnb hosts to obtain and maintain valid permits to operating their listings. Unfortunately for hosts, these permits aren't free, and more than likely they're an annual expense.

- » **Third-party tools:** From automated pricing to automated messaging and scheduling, third-party tools can help hosts simplify their operations and save them hours of manual work every week. But these tools come with monthly subscription costs.

- » **Consumables:** You need to keep your listing well stocked with items like toilet paper, soap, shampoo, and snacks and beverages. Although these items make up a small fraction of the operating expenses, you'll need to replenish them after each stay so the expenses do add up over the course of a year.

- » **Other supplies:** Some items don't need replenishment after each stay, but they still need regular replenishment over the course of a year. You may need to replace towels, linens, and sheets every three to six months due to wear or stains. Even the gas needed to make all the supply runs is an operating expense.

REMEMBER

This list isn't exhaustive or applicable to all hosts. Your specific operating expenses depend on factors specific to you such as whether you own or rent your property and how you ultimately choose to run your listing.

# Estimating time commitment

To determine whether hosting on Airbnb is worthwhile economically for you, just knowing the likely profit dollars you can make isn't enough. You also need to estimate the number of hours it'll likely require of you to earn that level of profits.

**REMEMBER**

How attractive it is to earn $1,000 in profits during the month are entirely different stories between putting in 20 versus 200 hours of work where you'll earn $50 per hour versus $5 per hour. How much time will it take to host? It depends on several factors:

>> **DIY versus outsourced cleaning:** Cleaning is one of the most time-consuming and physically draining aspects of Airbnb hosting. Whether you do it yourself or outsource drastically determines your hours of input as a host. The larger the property, the larger the group size, and the longer the stay, the longer it'll take to clean and turn the space for the next guest.

>> **Number of units you're hosting:** The more units you have, the more hours you must put into fielding inquiries, communicating with guests, making supply runs, coordinating with cleaners, updating listing pricing and calendars, and monitoring your performance.

>> **Manual versus automation:** The more tools and technology you use to automate operations and remove yourself from manual work, the more time you'll save. This includes decisions such as setting up remote check-ins and check-outs rather than doing them in person and using automation tools for pricing, messages, and scheduling.

>> **Self-managing versus outsourcing:** The biggest factor in time commitment depends on whether you'll manage your listing by yourself or hire someone else to do it for you. Whether you self-manage or outsource your Airbnb operations largely determines both the up-front commitment, the time it takes initially to set up your property and put together a winning listing, and the ongoing commitment, the time it takes to run your listing on a day-to-day basis.

Figure 2-5 shows the estimated hours per week a host can expect to spend on hosting-related activities. These estimated time commitments assume a listing that gets approximately eight to ten bookings a month with guests staying on average two to three nights. During the initial months of ramping up, hosts may spend more time adjusting and improving their listing and operations.

As you can see in this figure, the time commitment required for each host is different, depending on the property and the property management choices that get made.

| | Self Manage Self Cleaning | Self Manage Outsource Cleaning | Outsource Hosting |
|---|---|---|---|
| Room | 4–6 | 1–2 | <1 |
| Studio/1 bedroom | 6–10 | 1–2 | <1 |
| 2–3 bedroom | 8–12 | 2–3 | <1 |
| 4–5 bedroom | 12–16 | 2–3 | <1 |
| 6+ bedroom | 16+ | 2–4 | <1 |

FIGURE 2-5: Estimated time commitment required per week for hosting.

© John Wiley & Sons, Inc.

# USING THE AIRBNB POTENTIAL PROFIT CALCULATOR

To determine your overall profit potential and your profit potential for the hours you can expect to put into hosting, run a financial analysis with assumptions for rental revenue, operating expenses, and time commitment.

To make it easier for you, you can access a companion calculator online to make your own analysis. Go to www.learnbnb.com/airbnbfordummies. Look for the Airbnb Potential Profit Calculator and follow the instructions to download the file and access the video demonstration to complete your own analysis.

We provide this calculator as a free online resource you can use to make all your assumptions and get an accurate estimate of the profit potential for your future Airbnb listing.

The calculator can help you estimate your startup costs, rental revenue, operating expenses, and your time commitment as a host. By going through the exercise, you can gain an intimate and more realistic understanding of your Airbnb market and what you can expect to achieve with your listing.

# Comparing the Big City versus Rural Markets

If you live outside a large city away from the epicenters of Airbnb travel, you can still profit as a host. Although the local travel demand largely determines the profit potential of your listing, you can increase your profit potential even in less popular Airbnb travel destinations with the strategies in the following sections.

**REMEMBER**

In more remote markets, the revenue potential for one Airbnb listing is probably lower than for an equivalent listing in or near the city. However, this doesn't mean you can't make a profit in these areas.

## Earning a profit in any market

When the limited travel demand reduces the revenue potential of a single Airbnb listing in an area, the cost to acquire the properties and operate them as Airbnb listings will also be lower, making the path to Airbnb profits simple: Operate more units.

For example, a one-bedroom property in a very high-demand part of Los Angeles may average $200 per night and achieve 85 percent occupancy, helping it achieve rental revenue of $5,100 a month. But an equivalent listing an hour outside of downtown may only average $100 a night and a 60 percent occupancy, achieving only about $1,800 a month. However, the first unit likely requires a monthly rent of $2,500 or more a month whereas a host may be able to lease the second unit for about $750.

The city listing may achieve a gross profit of $5,100 – $2,500 = $2,600. After additional operating expenses, the final profit to the host may be closer to $1,500. For the more remote listing, it may achieve a gross profit of $1,800 – $750 = $1,050. After additional operating expenses, it may pocket only $500 in profits, one third of the city listing. Figure 2-6 breaks down the economics between the urban and remote listing.

**REMEMBER**

Even though the remote listing likely earns a lower overall profit compared to its urban counterpart due to the lower Airbnb travel demand in the remote market, it nonetheless can still be profitable for a host. But if you want to make the same dollar profit, you'll need to operate more listings.

|  | Urban Listing | Remote Listing |
|---|---|---|
| Occupancy Rate | 85% | 60% |
| Avg Nightly Rate | $200/night | $100/night |
| Monthly Revenue | $5,100 | $1,800 |
| Cost to Rent | ($2,500) | ($750) |
| Operating Expense | ($1,100) | ($550) |
| Monthly Profit | $1,500 | $500 |

**FIGURE 2-6:** Comparing an urban versus a remote listing.

© John Wiley & Sons, Inc.

## Adding more Airbnb listings without purchasing property

TIP

To list more properties, you must first get the permission to do so. Although you could purchase more properties, doing so is a time-consuming and cost-prohibitive strategy for most hosts. Instead of having to put tens of thousands of dollars toward a down payment in a purchase, here are two easier strategies if you want to add more Airbnb listings:

>> **Rental arbitrage:** Rent the property at the long-term rental rate from the owner, get explicit permission to sublet on Airbnb, and then earn your profit from the difference. Often, just one month's rent and a security deposit are often enough to secure the unit. This is the Airbnb equivalent of "buying low and selling high." However, most landlords are still wary of subletting to an Airbnb host, because it may expose them to neighbor complaints and additional liability risk. Refer to Chapter 3 in Book 5 for additional discussion on managing landlord relations.

>> **Co-hosting:** More and more property owners wish to reap the benefits (profits) of Airbnb hosting without hosting themselves. To do so, they either must hire a property management company or partner with a local Airbnb host to co-host their listing on their behalf. As a co-host, you can earn a percentage of the booking revenue from a property without having to purchase or lease the property.

# Determining the Legality of Hosting in Your Market

As the regulatory landscape for Airbnb and short-term rentals continue to evolve, one city at a time, you need to identify and understand the local regulations in your city that may impact your Airbnb operation if you're thinking of creating a listing.

Being aware of the short-term rental laws, whether current or just on the horizon, can help you avoid costly fines from your city and consider how they may impact your earning potential.

## Being aware of the potential risks of Airbnb hosting

Increasingly, new and pending local regulations move toward requiring licensing or permitting and adding limitations to short-term rentals. Cities around the world are implementing or contemplating more severe punishments for hosts of illegal short-term rental listings. To avoid facing potentially hefty fines, we encourage all prospective hosts to find out the local short-term regulations in their market.

Here's how local regulations affect your profit potential:

» **Permitting or licensing:** You may need to apply and pay for a license or permit to operate an Airbnb listing in your city legally. Many cities permit only properties in certain parts of the city and set a maximum number of permits they issue.

» **Fines:** Operating an illegal listing without a proper permit or license could subject you to hefty fines. In 2018, for example, Paris fined hosts more than $1.5 million over illegal listings. That same year, San Francisco fined a couple for $2.25 million for operating 14 illegal Airbnb listings.

» **Revenue potential:** Ultimately, the local laws regulating Airbnb hosting could significantly reduce your Airbnb revenue potential. For example, if there is a 120-day limit for using your property as a short-term rental, then you need to decide whether that's long enough to still make Airbnb hosting a worthwhile effort.

**REMEMBER**

It's not a question of *if or when* your city will regulate short-term rentals, but a matter of *how* your city is regulating or will regulate short-term rentals. The specific regulations that govern your market will have a significant impact on the overall profit potential and hurdles to getting started for your Airbnb listing.

## Finding out what laws or restrictions apply to you

Although cities have historically struggled to enforce their restrictions, things are changing as cities step up their enforcement efforts. For example, San Francisco forced Airbnb to remove 50 percent of its listings in the city as new laws came into effect in 2018.

TIP

To find out where your city stands regarding short-term rentals today, you can try the following methods:

>> **Airbnb Help Center:** Airbnb is continually adding more resources to help both prospective and current hosts stay in the know about their cities. To see the latest materials from Airbnb about your city, go to www.airbnb.com/help/home. Then type the name of your city into the search bar titled "Search help articles."

>> **Search engines:** A simple search engine query for "Airbnb law [your city name]" will produce results in most cities that have recently passed or working to pass new short-term rental regulation. If you live in a major city anywhere in the world, start here. You can also try combinations with "home-sharing," "short-term rental," "ordinances," and "regulations."

>> **Local hosting groups:** Find a local Airbnb or short-term rental hosting group on Facebook or Meetup and ask current hosts in the city where you can find the latest information on local regulations. Many hosts are eager to help fellow hosts. Just be sure to consult group posting rules or seek permission from group administrators before posting questions to the group profile pages.

>> **City hall website:** Go to your city's .org website and make the same query because municipal web pages often rank low on search engine results.

>> **City hall offices:** If you still have trouble getting the information, call your city hall's offices and ask them to direct you to the latest information. As a last resort, you can pay them a visit during normal visiting hours to get help.

WARNING

Given the potential for significant fines and operating limitations, don't start hosting your property on Airbnb, or on any other short-term rental platform, until you fully understand how to operate legally in your city.

IN THIS CHAPTER

» Maximizing your listing's profit potential

» Determining which amenities your guests want (and what's required)

» Deciding what space to list

» Managing your relationships with neighbors and your landlord

» Protecting your property with the right insurance

» Understanding hosting better by being a guest first

Chapter **3**

# Preparing Your Property

M aking sure your property is set up and ready to host guests on Airbnb is more than just putting a bed in a spare room. This chapter walks through everything you need to do to set up your space for success. Maximizing your space creates an exponential impact on your overall results. Consider that by increasing the value of your property by just $10 per night, you'll have the potential to earn an additional $3,650 every single year.

The first step is making sure your property is ready for guests, and second is making sure you as the host are ready for this new commitment. This chapter also talks about taking your property from its current state to where it needs to be in order to be successful on the Airbnb platform. Whether your property is furnished or unfurnished or has the required amenities, this chapter is here to help you get it ready for guests.

Figuring out what you want to list, whether it's your whole space or just an extra room, is another important decision that this chapter examines with simple instructions on all factors you need to consider.

Equally important is making sure you maintain good relations with your neighbors and your landlord when hosting. Here, you get the lowdown on maintaining good relationships with your neighbors and landlord. You find out just what you need to know so you can be an Airbnb host and avoid upsetting anyone or breaking any rules.

# Creating Profit Potential with Your Property

Your property ultimately dictates your maximum profit potential. There's a ceiling on what any given property can earn. However, most hosts don't reach that maximum potential for their property for a wide variety of reasons. The following sections help you figure out what that number is for you and how you can make sure your space is optimized so you actually hit that ceiling. You disover how you can increase your property's monthly maximum potential through a number of different methods.

For example, a one-bedroom apartment in Boise, Idaho, doesn't have the potential to earn $50,000 per month. No matter what you do to optimize your pricing or how much you spruce up the space, not enough people are seeking a one-bedroom apartment in Boise to generate that much income. Although you won't reach $50,000 per month, you do have the potential to turn a $1,500-per-month property into a $2,000-per-month property.

## Maximizing the potential of your listing by optimizing your space

Maximizing the potential of your listing is all about taking advantage of all your property's current features to provide the highest value. Consider your property as it currently exists, whether it has furniture, amenities, or nothing at all. It has a current maximum potential, and our goal is to show you all the ways that you can maximize that potential. This way, you aren't wasting any opportunities but instead taking advantage of all the potential your space offers. Taking the necessary steps to maximize the potential of your space allows you to earn much more money in the long run and have much more satisfied guests.

For example, an addition on your house would include more bedrooms and therefore increase your listing's earning potential. On a lesser extreme, maybe you could renovate or decorate your space and make it nicer. If done correctly, it's likely to lead to happier guests and more bookings.

Here are a few things to consider when looking for easy ways to further maximize your listing's potential:

>> **Don't block off any rooms.** The whole place should be accessible to guests. If you have a whole house listing and one bedroom is blocked off, you want to unblock that room. If you have a one-bedroom listing that's in your personal home, then make sure the closet in that space isn't being used by you. Guests should be able to use that space for their clothing and belongings.

>> **Make sure your sleeping arrangements are maximized.** Have properly sized beds in every bedroom and ensure your property is equipped to sleep as many people as it comfortably can. If you have a bedroom big enough for a king bed but you have a twin, then you can sleep one more person by upgrading to a king size. As long as the rest of your property can comfortably accommodate the extra person, making that investment is a no-brainer.

>> **Keep your property properly decorated so it looks inviting in your listing photos.** Your space needs to include more than just a bed with sheets and a mattress. Make your space feel like home for the people staying there.

If you can't take action right now, save some of your Airbnb earnings so you can upgrade and get a better return on your investment. How exactly you can optimize your space differs for each individual host. Take inventory of all opportunities you may be missing out on to maximize your potential even further. Make a list and execute the ones that make the most sense for your own situation.

## Starting your listing off strong

You always have room to improve your listing by further upgrading your space and offering more and better amenities to your guests. When you're first starting, the goal is not to invest as much time and energy as possible into your listing, but simply to grab all the low-hanging fruit. This way, you'll maximize your returns while minimizing your upfront investment. Consider the following sections when starting.

### Ensuring the maximum is as high as possible right now

You first want to ensure that the maximum nightly rate you're able to charge is as high as possible for right now. Although you want to do as much as possible to maximize your listing's potential before you welcome your first guest, you can also do other things to continually improve and increase your listing's potential all throughout your hosting journey. At some point, however, you may find that the return on your investment isn't necessarily there.

For example, consider if right now you aren't in a place to upgrade your single bed to a queen bed. Don't stress about it. You don't need to perform that upgrade right away. However, it makes sense to make note of that upgrade and keep it on a to-do list. Then, after you reach X amount of income from your listing, you can make the investment into the queen bed.

## Having the appropriate amenities

You want to make sure you have the important amenities for your listing that guests are going to expect. If your property can sleep eight people but only three of them can stay there comfortably, then you're wasting a big opportunity.

Consider if you have a pullout couch in the living room but lack bedding for that pullout couch. In this case, guests can't use the pullout couch so including it in the listing doesn't make sense. Cover your bases and make sure any additions or amenities are properly set up and ready for use by your guests. Find out more about amenities later in this chapter.

## Steering clear of money wasters

REMEMBER

A mistake that hosts tend to make is buying more things or nicer things haphazardly in an attempt to raise their prices and generate more income. Consider buying a nice TV or similar amenity. If your listing tends to attract business travelers who rarely watch TV during their stay, that investment is unlikely to yield a good return. Keep your guests' needs and wants at the forefront and start by focusing on the items that are sure to bring in higher returns.

# Determining the Amenities Guests Want in Your Market

When guests stay in your listing, they expect basic amenities. When you set up your Airbnb listing, you need a clear idea of which amenities to include. A great way to determine what amenities your guests want to have is by looking at other listings in your area that have great reviews. Look at what amenities they have that stand out or frequently get mentioned in reviews, and then make sure you add those similar amenities to your property. Doing so will increase your listing's desirability and overall potential. Offering guests the amenities they need for a comfortable and enjoyable stay is essential if you want to be a responsible Airbnb host and ultimately get great reviews.

The following sections discuss how you can make your listing competitive with the types of amenities you offer while also giving your guests a pleasant stay.

## Identifying the types of amenities to include in your listing

Some amenities are basic and you need to include them, no matter what, whereas other amenities are upgrades that improve the quality of guest stays and their reviews. These amenities increase your listing's potential. The basic must-haves are discussed in the later section "Focusing on the must-have amenities."

To provide more value to your guests, you can include more amenities that guests want that make your listing shine above your competition. Here are a few examples of upgrade amenities that can wow your guests:

>> Fireplace

>> Hot tub

>> Board games

>> Local touches

These examples of amenities attract more guests depending on your market. They are the above-and-beyond amenities that tie into maximizing the potential of your listing. Local touches that are quintessential to your area can also provide a more authentic experience to guests, which is sure to delight them. Specific types of amenities you should include in your listing are covered in the later section "Deciding Which Amenities, Furniture, and Appliances to Include."

Each market has different types of guests staying at your property. Consider whether your listing is in downtown Toronto and specifically appeals to business travelers. In this case, adding a gaming console probably doesn't make a big difference in your bookings. However, if your listing appeals to families, then a gaming console may be a drawing factor. Hence, you need to understand who your guests are and what kind of experience they want; keep reading for the scoop.

## Looking at your competition to better gauge what guests want

By understanding your market and your ideal guests, you can decide how best to move the needle forward on your listing's potential. Examine similar listings on Airbnb and determine which are performing best and what they offer. With that information, you can discover how to improve your own listing.

Focus on the listings with higher nightly rates and the best reviews and see what types of amenities those listing have. For example, if you have a ski chalet, you may discover that all the best-performing properties have a fireplace and a sauna, so you may want to consider adding a fireplace or sauna in your listing.

Here are a few other examples of amenities to give you an idea:

>> If you're in a family-friendly market, look for a gaming console or other types of games, like a dartboard, foosball, billiards, or ping pong.

>> If you're catering to larger groups, search for a big dining room table so everyone can sit and eat together.

Make note of the properties most similar to yours and see what amenities they have, which can give you a better glimpse at what guests in your market want.

Make sure to compare your property with properties that are your direct competition and comparable in the same level of luxury, size, and amenities. Comparing your cozy one-bedroom listing that prices around $80 a night to a luxury three-bedroom apartment that lists at $250 a night won't give you the types of results you're looking for.

# Deciding Which Amenities, Furniture, and Appliances to Include

Features that really impact a guest's stay are your furniture and appliances. Determine what furniture, appliances, and other amenities you want to include and then make sure you maintain them so your guests can utilize them.

Different items provide different levels of value for your guests. As a host, you want to determine which items deliver the greatest return on your investment (ROI). Pay attention to your reviews and the ways your guests respond to the amenities you provide so you can offer even greater value. Items like the fridge, beds, and Wi-Fi offer a much greater ROI because those are the must-haves for every guest's stay.

With furniture, appliances, and other amenities, certain items are must-haves, others are nice to have, others are outstanding to have, and others still are a waste of your money. Within these groups, you want to identify which is which for your property. It varies a bit from property to property, but generally the must-haves are quite similar. The following sections go through each category so you know how you can avoid wasting time, money, and effort on unnecessary amenities and pour more into the must-have and nice-to-have features.

**REMEMBER**

Issues that may not be a concern for you can really affect your guests' stay. To offer the best experience for your guests, make sure that everything in your space is in top condition, and if not fix it or replace it. For example, when your oven breaks, even if you rarely use it, you need to fix that promptly. If your guest's bed is lumpy and outdated, then replace the mattress or invest in a new bed altogether. If you don't take care of them, you risk guests having a poor stay and those misgivings later appearing in their reviews. And if something is showing wear and tear, replace it.

## Focusing on the must-have amenities

**REMEMBER**

Here is our list of must-have furniture, appliances, and other amenities. If you want to list a property on Airbnb, then make sure you have these items:

>> **Bed:** Your guests need something to sleep on. It can be a mattress with box springs, a sleeper sofa, or an air mattress.

>> **Nice towels and sheets:** Both make a huge difference on your guests' stay. When your guests arrive to your property and get into a scratchy bed, they won't feel good about the quality of the bedsheets. Furthermore, provide more than one towel per guest, especially if your guests are staying longer than a day.

>> **Coffee maker:** Most people consider a basic coffee maker as a must-have. Along with this, include some fresh coffee available that will last at least the first morning of your guests' stay.

>> **Fully stocked kitchen:** Make sure your kitchen is ready to use and fully stocked with a frying pan, utensils, proper cutlery, plates, and cups. The greatest area where hosts miss the mark is in the kitchen by not having the necessary amenities.

Coauthor James was once in a property that had a frying pan without a spatula. Unfortunately, he didn't realize the lack of a spatula until he was cooking eggs and couldn't flip them. He had to go buy a spatula in order to make breakfast, which was a pain and super inconvenient. At another property, hosts only provided two glasses and two plates, so guests had to wash their dishes after every meal. For vacations and holidays, guests don't want to be forced to do dishes after every meal or leave the property to purchase cookware.

>> **Refrigerator:** Most listings also need a working fridge, whether it's shared or not.

>> **Oven, stovetop, or microwave:** You generally need to offer a way to cook food by including an oven, stovetop, or microwave.

>> **Water:** You need drinkable water. If you're hosting in an area where you can't drink the tap water, you must offer bottled water or a water cooler for your guests so that when they arrive, they have something to drink.

During a trip to Thailand, coauthor James arrived at his Airbnb late at night with no water to drink. The host didn't provide a water cooler or any bottled water. In Thailand the tap water isn't safe to drink, so he had to go to a convenience store in the middle of the night and carry a bunch of water back. He was thirsty and just wanted to go to bed, but instead he had to schlep to get water. To not have access to a glass of water was a miserable way to start his stay, and it set a bad first impression: "Oh, I don't have water." As a basic necessity, you need drinkable water at your space for guests.

>> **Wi-Fi:** Your space should include an Internet router that reaches your entire house with no dead spots. Your guests should get a signal from anywhere in your space so that they aren't in their bedroom unable to access the Internet. Unless your listing is a remote cabin in the woods with the allure of being off grid, it needs Wi-Fi.

International guests rely on Wi-Fi. They often don't have cell service, so the only way they can keep connected is through reliable Internet. Furthermore, make sure your Wi-Fi speed is fast enough so multiple devices can stream. If you have 25 Mbps speed, you can tout that in your listing.

>> **Toilet paper, paper towels, and tissues:** Be sure to leave enough toilet paper for all your guests and for the duration of their stay. Leaving just enough to get them through the first couple of hours is simply poor hosting. If your guests are forced to leave the property to resupply the toilet paper, that's a hassle and overall a failure to meet a basic requirement.

A lot of hosts get stingy and think guests will steal the toilet paper. The reality is that some may, but you must accept it. What you stand to lose if you overstock the place is a couple of dollars. However, you stand to lose hundreds of potential dollars in income when you get poor reviews for only leaving one roll of toilet paper in the space.

>> **A shower curtain, bathmat, properly working sinks, and running hot water:** These items may seem basic, but depending on your situation, you may overlook them.

Sometimes people list a spare space in their own home and they neglect certain amenities that they themselves don't often use. For example, your oven may be broken and you don't care because you're always eating out. That doesn't mean your guests will be okay with your broken oven. You need to get it fixed. This issue is more evident to people who are hosting their entire space. They realize they need to get their oven fixed whereas when people live in the place, it may not occur to them.

For example, coauthor James stayed at a listing where the oven was broken. The host told him that she never used it. Instead she was storing boxes inside. Using it as an oven just wasn't part of her life, whereas James thought it odd to have boxes stored in the broken oven.

REMEMBER

Take inventory of all your basic appliances and ensure they're usable, accessible, and functioning so that you have all the basic amenities people need. Monitor furniture and if it starts to show wear and tear, consider replacing it. Just as important, make sure you don't overlook anything relatively obvious that your guests will need.

## Remembering the often forgotten

TIP

Hosts often forget a few important amenities that impact their guests' stay. Remembering these items sets you apart quite a bit from your competition:

>> **Bedside table with a lamp:** You'd be surprised at how many hosts forget the bedside table when setting up their listing, which is essential to have. When your guests get into bed, a bedside table is the ideal spot for their phone charging, eyeglasses, or glass of water.

>> **Plants:** Including plants in your space is important. Any homey space has some kind of greenery or plant. Even a faux plant is okay.

>> **Sharp knives:** Many people keep the typical butter knives in their homes but forget to include steak knives or a paring knife. If your guests prepare a meal and require a sharp knife, not having one is a huge inconvenience.

>> **Salt, pepper, and basic condiments:** Oils, salt and pepper, and a couple of condiments are essentials for most guests. If you're someone who eats out for most meals and doesn't cook at home, you still need to provide these cooking essentials for your guests. You risk leaving a bad taste in their mouths if they can't properly season their food.

## Stuck between a must-have and a nice-to-have

Some scenarios fall in what we call the ambiguous zone between a must-have and a nice-to-have, depending on your area and type of property. Here are those items you may have to figure out whether they're must-have or nice-to-have, based on your competition:

>> **Dishwasher:** A dishwasher, for many properties, is a nice-to-have. As long as you have a sink to clean the dishes, you're fine. However, if you have a higher-end property, then a dishwasher is widely considered a must-have.

>> **Air conditioning:** In some locations, AC isn't negotiable. It's a must-have, whether it's central air or a window unit. (Imagine staying in a stuffy New York City apartment in July or an Atlanta bungalow in September with no AC.) And if you're trying to attract a higher-caliber guest, then AC is a no-brainer.

However, AC may be nice-to-have but not essential in other types of listings. Take a city like Toronto that has a ton of old homes without central air. They may just have fans. Or a nontraditional listing such as a yurt may have no AC at all.

**REMEMBER**

Be conscious of your own property and your competition and the type of guests booking your listing so you can better determine what items are nice-to-have and what items are must-haves.

## Providing a bonus: The nice-to-haves

Sometimes nice-to-haves become must-haves, especially if you want to stay in line with what your competition is offering. Here are some examples of nice-to-haves:

>> **Smart TVs:** Smart TVs with some type of Internet connection to allow for streaming are generally always nice-to-have and often not a must-have. Maybe you don't have a cable to connect their computers to your TV, but your guests can still access features like Netflix or other online shows with your Wi-Fi.

>> **Higher-end coffee maker:** Although a basic coffee maker is a must-have, a higher-end coffee maker is a nice-to-have.

>> **Wine glasses:** Even if you aren't a wine drinker, the odds are high that one of your guests will want to enjoy a glass at some point.

**TIP**

If you try to think about hosting from your guests' perspectives rather than from your own perspective, you'll have a much easier time including all desired amenities.

>> **Water filter:** As long as tap water is potable and people can drink it, tap water is a must-have. A water filter is a nice-to-have.

>> **Toaster oven:** Although a toaster is a must-have, a toaster oven is a nice-to-have in most cases.

Check out your competition and identify the nice-to-haves in your own area. Depending on how high end the market is for your listing and your listing's competition, a gas range stove may be considered a standard nice-to-have. For most properties, investing in an expensive gas range oven doesn't make sense, but many high-end properties probably have them, so it makes sense to invest in one.

## Surprising with the outstanding

**TIP**

This is where you get the opportunity to go above and beyond for your guests. When the above-and-beyond elements are performed well, you see the guests' satisfaction reflected in their reviews. To determine what these are for your listing, note things that aren't expectations but are really nice for guests to have. These are the elements that surprise and delight your guests and leaves them with a great feeling. As a guest, this is the experience that makes you go "Wow, that's so smart" and "Why would someone not have that?" Consider the following:

>> **Universal phone chargers:** Having a universal phone charger in each bedroom and in the main living space is key. How many times have you gotten to a space and haven't had your phone charger out and ready to go? If there's a phone charger that's both compatible and convenient that goes a long way for people. It's an unusual thing that's not very common but goes a long way for your guests.

>> **Speakers:** Another amenity that's unusual but goes far with guests is having a speaker on your property that people can easily connect to and use. Most people want to play music. It may not be a baseline expectation and they won't come in and expect that it's there. However, it makes quite the difference when people have access to that amenity.

>> **Games:** If you're welcoming groups or families into your space, then having some games to play is a great way to win them over. Whether you're providing cards or board games, guests are often delighted to have those options. Especially if your market is heavy in groups, it's yet another way to set yourself apart from your competition.

A common concern with items such as the ones mentioned is theft. However, guests stealing your universal phone charger or board game happens rarely. Here are a few reasons why you shouldn't worry about your guests taking advantage of you as host:

>> **When you maximize the property potential, you appeal to the upper tier of guests who aren't looking for a cheap stay.** These are the guests with the highest income and who don't see the value in stealing a phone charger or bottle of soap.

- **As a host, you go above and beyond, which creates reciprocity.** The guests don't want to take from you. Instead, they're super grateful to be staying there. It's highly unlikely that you lose your phone charger, speaker, or rolls of toilet paper.

- **You have a security deposit and you can use that security deposit if a guest does take something more substantial in value.** If a phone charger or speaker gets taken, then you can present a claim against your guests and be compensated for anything high in value.

What you're really doing when you opt out of providing these types of amenities for fear of having them stolen is stepping over dollars to pick up pennies. You save $15 on a phone charger and then lose out on bookings at your property to the tune of several hundred dollars. Furthermore, you can't be skimpy on filling up your soap dispensers and body care products. Nothing is worse than having some cheap host who only fills them a little bit because they don't want guests taking it with them. The reality is that they likely won't. Even if your guests do snag a bottle of your shampoo, it's a $1 or $2 risk you must be willing to take as a host.

## Avoiding the wastes of money

**WARNING**

Determine your must-have and nice-to-have amenities and avoid these complete and total wastes of money:

- For example, spending $15,000 on a massage chair is a complete waste. Even if you get the odd guest who books your property for that reason, the likelihood that the stay adds $15,000 to your bottom line is very low.

- Another example of an unnecessary cost is having the highest-end satellite TV. In many cases, the satellite TV package is a waste of money. In reality even if you have basic cable, which is often still unnecessary, people typically prefer a smart TV or HDMI cable that they can use to connect their computer to the TV and stream their favorite shows. Overall those alternatives are more than enough. Most guests booking an Airbnb want to connect their computers or Netflix account if they're going to watch TV at all. Generally, they're still fine with local television or basic cable if those are the only options.

  Very few people are going to stream a sports event happening halfway across the world. And if they do, they usually have the ability to do so online if it matters that much to them. Investing in a top-of-the-line satellite package is more often than not a total waste of money.

- In terms of furniture and appliances, obscure items that are a complete waste include anything from a panini press to a pancake griddle. Having a frying pan and stove is sufficient.

# Figuring Out What Space Is Accessible to Guests in Your Listing

**REMEMBER**

Determining what areas of your space are accessible to guests is an important decision, depending on the type of listing you have. Keep these points in mind:

>> **If you're listing bedrooms in your personal home:** Be specific about the bedrooms and bathrooms your guests can use. You need to figure out whether they have access to all the bathrooms in the house or just one as well as whether they have access to the kitchen or the living room. If the answer is yes, you must maintain those spaces and keep them ready for guests.

>> **If you're listing a whole house:** Figuring out what space is accessible to guests is simple — keep all areas in your house available to guests. Ideally, you don't block off any space other than maybe a closet if you want to lock something away.

>> **If you're listing an auxiliary space such as a guesthouse:** Be intentional about only listing the parts of the space that are actually available to guests. Be clear in your listing about the areas that guests have access to and which areas are private versus shared.

Make a conscious decision on which spaces you're maintaining and keeping in guest-ready condition and then list only those spaces that you're willing to share with guests at any time. These sections give you more details, room by room.

## Bedroom and bathroom

Especially in shared spaces, be clear on which bedrooms guests have access to and which bedrooms aren't available to them. Determine whether they have access to all the closets in their bedrooms. Be crystal clear in your listing so there is no room for confusion.

Be just as specific with bathroom usage. If you have one bathroom that you specifically use to get ready in the morning and you don't want to give guests access to it or don't want to keep it guest-ready, then don't list it.

For both bedrooms and bathrooms, make sure that any locking doors don't require a key. It will only be a matter of time before guests lose a key or lock themselves out of one of the rooms, so avoid the issue entirely by using manual interior locks rather than keyed locks.

## Kitchen

If you offer access to the kitchen, leave space in the fridge for guests to use. If you aren't sharing the kitchen, then you can't list that space on Airbnb. If you want to allow access to your kitchen but don't plan on leaving any room in your fridge, then you can't list that guests have access to a full kitchen. More than likely, a guest at some point will want to put something in the fridge and be upset when there isn't room.

If guests don't have access to your kitchen in its entirety, be clear on whether they can use any of your kitchen materials such as the fridge, microwave, dishware, or blender.

## Access to living room, outdoor spaces, and other rooms

Concerning other common areas inside or outside your house, communicate what you want from your guests so they know your expectations, which can cause fewer problems down the line. If your guests have access to your living room, game room, or other common room, be specific in your listing.

If you have a guesthouse in your backyard, be clear on which parts of your backyard your guests can access as well as whether they can use your kitchen inside the main house. If your guesthouse doesn't include a kitchen but you plan on providing access to your kitchen in the main house, specify in your listing that the kitchen is in a separate building.

# Managing Neighbors' Relations

Hosting on Airbnb can potentially impact your neighbors, so communicating with them is important. You want to inform your neighbors that they'll see different people coming and going from your property.

Furthermore, maintaining a good relationship with your neighbors is important because you want them as allies. You want your neighbors to be friendly toward your guests if they pass them rather than treating them rudely. The last thing you want is for your guests to disrupt your neighbors or your neighbors to disrupt your guests.

**REMEMBER**

Most importantly, you want to avoid a situation where your neighbors are angry and hostile toward your Airbnb guests, which can lead to complaints and issues with your landlord or the city. In order to avoid any such situation, communicate clearly with your neighbors from the start. These sections help ensure you're a good neighbor when you're an Airbnb host.

## Being a good neighbor: Why doing so is profitable

Having a positive relationship with your neighbors can be profitable to you. In any situation, your neighbor either adds or subtracts value for your guests. More than likely, an unhappy neighbor may have a conflict with your guests, which can lead to a poor review. If a neighbor is adamantly opposed to your hosting, that neighbor can also cause issues with the city. On the opposite end of the spectrum, if your neighbor is thrilled with your hosting, that neighbor can be exceptionally warm and inviting toward your guests and add to their overall experience when they encounter each other.

**REMEMBER**

What you're providing to guests is more than just a place to sleep. You're providing your guests with an experience, and your neighbors can play a large role in determining whether that experience is positive or negative.

For example, if your neighbor passes your guests on the street and acts super welcoming and offers directions or recommendations to a local coffee shop, that's very helpful for your guests. Those are the comments that often come up in 5-star reviews. Guests write that they had a great time because everyone was so friendly.

Consider the alternative: unhappy neighbors who look for any reason to complain about you, whether it's to the city, your landlord, or whomever else. There's the potential to have your listing shut down if your neighbors are persistent enough. Overall, they can do a lot of damage to your hosting business.

## Investing in neighbor relations before you start

As soon as you start thinking about hosting on Airbnb, you want to run the decision by your neighbors. The more advance notice you give, the better for your relationship. Ask them whether you can provide them anything to keep them updated and to make the experience better. Your neighbors may not be impacted by every single one of your guests, but they will be affected sometimes. Explain to your neighbors how your Airbnb listing will bring guests to the neighborhood and that you want to make sure they're on board with having Airbnb guests as their neighbors.

Preparing Your Property

Keeping your neighbors updated can set the tone for your relationship, so do what you can to be a great neighbor. Generally, people love hosting because they like meeting new people, and many people enjoy having Airbnb guests as neighbors. They reap all the benefits without doing any work. They get to meet new people without having to do any of the grunt work. If you come in with the right attitude and start as early as possible, your neighbors more than likely will be much more receptive.

**WARNING**

On the flip side, if you wait to receive a complaint before informing your neighbors that you're hosting on Airbnb, more than likely they'll be unreceptive to your hosting. From your neighbors' point of view, your hosting will be nothing but a nuisance to them. Waiting to tell your neighbors after your hosting becomes an issue is never the right call.

## Communicating with your neighbors

The best way to be a good neighbor is to treat others the way you want to be treated. Treat your neighbor in line with what you would want if your neighbor started hosting their space on Airbnb. Take your neighbor into consideration in everything you do as a host. In order to put this into practice effectively, the most important thing to do is communicate clearly with your neighbor about what's going on at your property and why.

**REMEMBER**

Maintaining an open line of communication is ideal. When you do this, you have someone with whom you have a good relationship and who lives next to your property at all times. If you've ever had bad guests at your property, you can understand why that's so appealing. Your neighbor can let you know what's going on at your property and you can avoid potential damage from your property being abused. Here are some important points to remember when communicating with your neighbors:

>> **Give them your contact information and let them know the best way to get in touch with you.** Inform them whether you have a preferred mode of communication, such as text, phone call, or email. By sharing your contact details, your neighbors have a clear and easy way to get in touch with you whenever a question or concern arises.

>> **Set clear expectations on when and how you like to communicate.** Tell your neighbors how to most effectively contact you for different situations so that nothing gets missed or forgotten.

The greatest issues concerning your relationship with your neighbors aren't when something happens at your property but rather when something happens that doesn't get promptly and effectively handled by you or someone on your team. For example, if your cleaners forget to take the trash out to the curb, your neighbors won't care that they forgot as long as you let them know and get it taken care of another way. It won't cause an issue unless the trash remains out at the side of your house for a week or two and starts smelling and attracting animals. Then it's a big issue.

If your neighbors complain about noise at the property, but you deal with it immediately and the noise goes down, it's not an issue. However, consider if your neighbors try communicating with you and don't hear back. Then they aren't able to sleep and wind up having a miserable next day at work. Now, it's an issue. Instead, having that open line of communication is the best way to both prevent any negative situation and to make sure your neighbors' needs are fully met.

# Managing Landlord Relations

You have a few considerations when managing a relationship with your landlord if you rent the property you plan to list on Airbnb. The following sections touch on how to manage this relationship, how to get permission to host your property, and why that permission is important. Dealing with your landlord is an ongoing process. Effectively navigating the relationship makes hosting your space that much easier.

## Being aware of the risks of hosting without consent

The bottom line when planning to host an Airbnb listing out of your rented property is to get permission from your landlord. We can't stress this enough. Most standard lease agreements prohibit you from subletting. Many contracts now explicitly prohibit renters from hosting on Airbnb unless they reach an agreement with their landlord.

WARNING

The risk of hosting without explicit permission is that you violate the terms of your lease agreement. When your landlord finds out that you're hosting, your landlord has the authority and grounds to evict you from the property. Depending on your area and the specific laws, the landlord also can impose different fines on you for violating the terms of that agreement. Hosting without the consent of your landlord causes more headache than it's worth.

## Asking your landlord whether you can host on Airbnb

The process of requesting permission to host isn't always as simple as just asking your landlord. The best time to have the conversation is before you sign the lease agreement. At this point, you have more leverage than after you sign.

Landlords or property owners who rent their properties on the long-term rental market typically desire security and consistency. If they already have you as a tenant who's locked into a 12-month lease, when you ask about hosting, they'll less likely say yes. Essentially, there's no real benefit to them. You're already signed on for a year.

REMEMBER

If you ask before signing your lease, you tend to get better results due to the higher leverage you have. The change is a change in initial terms, before an agreement has been reached. If you try to negotiate after signing a lease, your landlord is likely to feel as though the initial agreement is being violated and that you're making an unreasonable request. However, no matter when you ask, ultimately landlords want to know what benefit hosting on Airbnb offers them, which is discussed in the next section.

## Seeing what landlords want to know when it comes to hosting

Landlords want to know what's in it for them to allow tenants to list their property on Airbnb. The best way to go about this is to just ask. After you find out how your hosting can benefit your landlord, you can ask about hesitancies or worries your landlord has. It could be any number of things, depending on your landlord and your landlord's specific needs.

Your landlord may wonder what types of guests are coming in and what risks that presents. Your landlord may ask what protections are in place in the event of any damage. The questions are wide and far ranging.

TIP

When you answer her questions, keep the following in mind:

>> **Show landlords what's in it for them.** If you make a simple request without showing the benefits, landlords have no reason to change or loosen the terms. Most people continue to do things the same way unless they see a reason for change. After landlords know the reason, they may be more open to the idea. The next section discusses these different benefits during your pitch.

>> **Ask what would be reasonable or desirable for your landlord.** Discuss your landlord's concerns so you can better address the specifics.

## Pitching your landlord

TIP

You have a few ways to show the benefits when pitching your landlord. Tell your landlord any combination of the following during this conversation:

>> **Be transparent and offer to share a link to your listing so your landlord can see how you're maintaining it.** You'll clean the place more often because it must be in pristine condition for your guests. Plus, the landlord doesn't have to worry about tenants trashing the place or using it for something illicit because you want to be a responsible Airbnb host. Your landlord can even check your guest reviews to see how you're cleaning and maintaining the property.

>> **Explain that hosting can financially help you so you're able to rent the space for longer.** Now you're a more reliable tenant.

>> **Offer to personally take care of any minor maintenance at the property.** If you have money from hosting that affords you the ability to fix the clogged toilet, for instance, you won't call the landlord anymore, which can be a huge benefit and take some burden off the landlord or property manager. You call your own maintenance person for the small stuff.

>> **Mention Airbnb's $1 million host protection.** This reassures that your landlord doesn't need to worry about potential damages because the property will likely be even better protected than with another tenant.

>> **Offer to pay rent further in advance, pay more rent overall, or pay a bigger security deposit for any potential damages.** This option is the last and least ideal one for you.

On the note of paying more rent, the amount doesn't have to be a lot. Typically, the value of a property is based on the rental rate. Increasing the rent payment by even $50 per month makes a difference because the landlord can sell the property for more money down the road. People are willing to pay more to buy a property because it can earn them more money. In other words, the rent increase doesn't have to be a lot to make it financially worthwhile to the landlord.

# Getting Proper Insurance Protection

You want to protect yourself from any potential liabilities because you don't want the scenario where you aren't insured and the worst possible scenario occurs. Although Airbnb provides its own insurance, we recommend multiple channels for protecting yourself and your property, which are discussed in the following sections.

# Grasping the importance of being properly insured

Buying insurance is about protecting yourself in the case something happens at your property. You can take a few actions to minimize or eliminate your risks of issues such as property damage or personal injury. However, you still want a backup plan in the event that an issue does occur so you're always fully protected against the worst-case scenario.

**WARNING**

Be aware that if you don't get the proper insurance specifically covering you for short-term rentals, you risk paying out of pocket for any issues or damages. What's important is that you're protected.

# Understanding Airbnb's liability protection and not relying on it alone

Airbnb does have a $1 million host protection policy that protects you as a host and covers any damages that occur on your property as the result of a guest staying there. It's a great policy, essentially offering third-party insurance from Airbnb to you for damages caused by a guest. Plus, it's good for up to $1 million. As an added layer of protection, Airbnb's host protection policy works.

**WARNING**

However, you shouldn't rely solely on it for the following couple of reasons:

>> **You don't have control.** If you go the route of only using Airbnb's policy, then you rely on Airbnb to submit those claims successfully and get you paid. To have full control over protecting your property, you want to steer the car and maneuver where it goes. However, consider the fact that Airbnb is balancing a couple of conflicting incentives when using that insurance policy to protect its hosts:

  • Whenever a guest causes damage that hurts the company's reputation, Airbnb wants to make sure the host is protected. The company has the incentive to show that the liability policy does pay out and the host gets covered so that the hosting community at large feels safe and protected.

  • However, Airbnb also knows that if the company uses the policy too much, then the premiums will increase. The company has a financial incentive to use that policy as little as possible.

>> **It only covers damages that are caused by guests during their stay.** This means that personal injury or any issues that occur outside of a guest's actual period of stay aren't covered. Such issues may be unlikely, but you'll want to be covered against them, nonetheless.

Hence, you want to make sure you have full control over your insurance.

# Buying your own insurance to ensure you're fully protected

REMEMBER

To ensure you have full control over your insurance coverage, you should purchase your own liability insurance policy that covers your property for damages. Your policy should clearly specify that it covers you for use of the property for short-term rentals. Then, if a guest does cause damage, you have three lines of defense:

>> The first line of defense is your guest's security deposit.

>> The second line of defense is Airbnb's liability policy.

>> The third line of defense is your own personal insurance plan.

This way, you know you're fully protected because you hold an insurance policy that protects your property from all damages. If you have all three of those pieces to protect yourself, more than likely you're covered for even the worst-case scenario.

TIP

To purchase your policy, start with a broker who is the most qualified person to help you get the right insurance policy. A broker looks at different options for you, given your property, the level of protection you need for your area, and the use of your property.

The price of an insurance policy and the level of protection varies, depending on if you're insuring your home up to $100,000 or $1 million as well as where your property is located and which company you choose.

Other pertinent issues are how often you host and whether you live in an urban area with high rates of crime or a small-town suburban neighborhood. Your broker evaluates all the options and has access to several different companies and plans.

Brokers receive a commission from the insurance company for selling the policy so as the consumer you won't pay anything extra to use an insurance broker. Your broker also helps you understand the plans and break down the policies to show you exactly what coverage you receive in different scenarios. Make sure to ask as many questions as needed to fully understand your plan.

Preparing Your Property

To find a broker in your area, ask around for referrals. The best people to help guide you in this matter are other hosts in your area, especially hosts with similar properties. If you're unable to find a broker through referrals, a quick online search for "short-term rental insurance [your city]" should yield some good recommendations. You can also consider joining an Airbnb host Facebook group for your city and post the question there.

# Being a Guest First to Better Understand Hosting: Walk in Your Guests' Shoes

"Walk a mile in your guests' shoes to understand them," said some wise Airbnb host. The best way to understand Airbnb and your competition is to experience it for yourself, so book an Airbnb listing or two in your locale and consider each component of the stay: from browsing to booking to checking in and checking out and to the actual visit. This practice takes you from being a mediocre host to a truly great host who knows what your guests want and who can deliver on it.

To truly appreciate the entire experience that guests go through to search, choose, book, check into, check out of, and rate Airbnb listings for their travel, you must become a guest first at an Airbnb. Here's how to get the most out of your educational Airbnb stays:

>> **Book at different levels of listing.** You can discover a lot from the pros by staying at the most popular and best performing listings in the markets hosted by Superhosts. You can also discover just as much from average or even underperforming listings. Your goal is to gather as much about what to do and what not to do.

>> **Take notes of every high and low point.** Pay attention to how you feel, especially whenever you're either stressed or grateful during your stay. Note the moments when you had questions, when you felt unsure or uncomfortable, or where something could have made the experience better. Keep track of the moments where you were pleasantly surprised by a thoughtful amenity or interaction with the hosts.

We strongly suggest you stay with a Superhost during one of your stays. If you have the ambition to become a Superhost, then staying with one will give you an idea of how a Superhost differs from a host who isn't.

During your research, ask yourself these following questions:

» What captures your eye to make you click on the listing: the cover photo, the price, or the listing headline?

» Why did you select that specific property?

» When you clicked what did you do next?

» Why did you not select a listing? Maybe it had great photos and a great description, but there was one bad review. Maybe you still booked anyways because there were other good reviews. Maybe it had two or three bad reviews. If the description didn't answer specific questions you had, such as parking situation, would that have mattered?

» When you finally booked the Airbnb, how was the experience?

» Did the host message you right away or wait awhile?

» Did the host get back to you in a reasonable time if you asked any questions?

» When it was time to check in, did you feel stressed out because you didn't receive check-in instructions or did the host send instructions well in advance?

» How easy was getting into the property?

» Is there anything you wished you had at the property?

» How attentive was the host during your stay? For example, did your host touch base with you to see if you needed anything? How quickly did the host respond to your questions?

» Did the host have a house manual with detailed instructions about commonly asked questions?

» Were any basic amenities missing that you needed?

» Was the listing description accurate to the property?

» What would have made your stay more pleasant?

» Did the host provide check-out instructions?

» When you write your review, what review are you writing and why are you writing it?

» At what point did you decide to give the host a 5-star review if you decided to do so? Or, at what point did you decide you wouldn't give more than 4 stars? What was it that triggered those decisions? What would have caused it to be a higher or lower review?

**TIP**

After you've been a host for a few months, go through this process again and treat yourself by booking a weekend getaway or staycation at an Airbnb and experience different levels of hosts, properties, and approaches to hosting, which can do wonders for your own hosting style. Again, take notes and find the areas you can improve and do differently. Experiencing different approaches to hosting and using them to figure out how to continue adding value for your guests is an effective hosting practice.

IN THIS CHAPTER

» **Understanding the factors in pricing**

» **Creating a ramp-up strategy**

» **Factoring in seasonality**

» **Monitoring temporality and special events**

» **Utilizing dynamic pricing**

» **Comprehending and setting various fees**

# Chapter **4**

# Setting Your Listing Pricing

A lot goes into setting the right pricing for your Airbnb, much more, in fact, than meets the eye. Many new hosts choose pricing haphazardly and resort to a "set it and forget it" mentality with pricing, often leading to suboptimal listing performance.

Setting the right pricing requires understanding the different factors that impact Airbnb pricing. Neglecting even just one of these factors in your pricing strategy can lead to fewer bookings and lower profits.

This chapter is navigates the process of staying on top of pricing so your listing can both get off to a great start and stay competitive on Airbnb. It examines each of the important components of pricing and shows you the tools and methodology to setting your own optimal pricing for your listing.

# Focusing on Baseline Pricing

**REMEMBER**

Determining a *baseline pricing* is finding the optimal amount you charge for your Airbnb listing under typical market conditions with average demand. Any adjustments you make to your pricing start from this baseline level.

To establish the baseline pricing, you analyze comparable listings on Airbnb to create a pricing strategy that works for you. The following sections help you start pricing your listing so it's competitive wherever you live.

## Studying your competition: Gather comparable market data

The best way to establish your baseline pricing is by looking at what your competition is charging in your market. You can think of your *market* as the tightest geographic radius that allows you to gather data for at least a dozen comparable and competitive listings. For example, in an ultra-high-density urban market, this could be just a one block or even a minute walking radius. In the sparse countryside, it could mean more than 10 miles or a 30-minute drive radius. In a typical suburban neighborhood, a safe starting point is three blocks or a 15-minute walking radius. You'll need to adjust as needed for your specific area.

**REMEMBER**

Your *competition* includes the most similar Airbnb listings in your market — those similar in size (beds, bedrooms, bathrooms), amenities, and overall positioning in terms of pricing and target audience. For example, if your Airbnb listing is a one-bedroom unit targeting the budget-friendly traveler who doesn't mind being a bit farther out from the main attractions, then your competition is similar, economy-focused one-bedroom Airbnb listings. However, if your Airbnb listing is a two-bedroom luxury condominium in a downtown luxury high-rise residence, your competition includes other two-bedroom luxury Airbnb listings.

When studying the competition, gather at least six (preferable a dozen or more) similar Airbnb listings and record the following information:

>> **Weekday rates:** For each comparable Airbnb listing and hotel listing, collect the average weekday rates (Sundays to Thursdays) for 4 weeks, 8 weeks, and 12 weeks into the future. Take the average of those 5 days for each of the 3 weeks for each comparable listing.

>> **Weekend rates:** For each comparable Airbnb listings and hotel listings, collect the average weekend rates (Fridays and Saturdays only) for 4 weeks, 8 weeks, and 12 weeks into the future. Take the average of those 2 days for each of the 3 weeks for each comparable listing.

TIP

If you're unable to find enough (at least six) comparable Airbnb listings in your market for your baseline pricing analysis, you can substitute with comparable hotel listings. For most hosts, comparing to economy and midrange hotel offerings makes the most sense. Identify the nearest 2- and 3-star hotels to your property and compare your studio or one-bedroom listing to their lowest priced offering. For larger properties of two or three bedrooms, compare to the lowest priced hotel suites. However, you may need to adjust your findings down by 15 to 30 percent because average hotel listings are often priced higher than their Airbnb counterparts in the same market.

When you're done collecting this information, you'll have six data points for each of the listings you've identified for your comparison — three weekday averages and three weekend averages — resulting from 21 daily prices for each of the comps.

Taking the average again of the average weekday and weekend rates for these similar listings gives you a good baseline pricing for your Airbnb listing in your market. Figure 4-1 shows an example with 12 comparable Airbnb listings and their corresponding data points for their weekday and weekend pricing.

| Comp # | Comp URL | Prop Type | Beds | Rooms | Baths | WD 1 | WD 2 | WD 3 | WE 1 | WE 2 | WE 3 | Averages Weekday | Weekend |
|---|---|---|---|---|---|---|---|---|---|---|---|---|---|
| 1 | www.airbnb.com/room | Entire place | 1 | 1 | 1 | $70 | $85 | $74 | $104 | $115 | $114 | $76 | $111 |
| 2 | www.airbnb.com/room | Entire place | 1 | 1 | 1 | $76 | $95 | $71 | $112 | $117 | $108 | $81 | $112 |
| 3 | www.airbnb.com/room | Entire place | 2 | 1 | 1 | $66 | $92 | $79 | $94 | $135 | $110 | $79 | $113 |
| 4 | www.airbnb.com/room | Entire place | 1 | 1 | 1 | $69 | $89 | $77 | $119 | $125 | $115 | $78 | $120 |
| 5 | www.airbnb.com/room | Entire place | 1 | 1 | 1 | $68 | $86 | $81 | $108 | $131 | $106 | $78 | $115 |
| 6 | www.airbnb.com/room | Entire place | 2 | 1 | 1 | $75 | $95 | $80 | $111 | $136 | $103 | $83 | $117 |
| 7 | www.airbnb.com/room | Entire place | 2 | 1 | 1 | $67 | $88 | $75 | $106 | $113 | $117 | $77 | $112 |
| 8 | www.airbnb.com/room | Entire place | 1 | 1 | 1 | $76 | $93 | $81 | $124 | $141 | $106 | $83 | $124 |
| 9 | www.airbnb.com/room | Entire place | 1 | 1 | 1 | $71 | $93 | $71 | $111 | $123 | $107 | $78 | $114 |
| 10 | www.airbnb.com/room | Entire place | 2 | 1 | 1 | $67 | $92 | $79 | $114 | $114 | $101 | $79 | $110 |
| 11 | www.airbnb.com/room | Entire place | 1 | 1 | 1 | $78 | $83 | $75 | $103 | $110 | $110 | $79 | $108 |
| 12 | www.airbnb.com/room | Entire place | 1 | 1 | 1 | $69 | $83 | $76 | $101 | $126 | $104 | $76 | $110 |

Above *Prices* header spans WD1–WE3.

**Overall average**     $79     $114

**FIGURE 4-1:** Baseline pricing exercise.

TIP

Tracking additional information for the comparable listings can help you understand the pricing dynamic in your market even better. Tracking additional information such as the listing URLs, property type, number of bedrooms, and number of bathrooms can assist you to fine-tune your baseline pricing analysis. If you want to track many factors for your comparable listings, download a spreadsheet template at www.learnbnb.com/airbnbfordummies.

## Choosing a baseline pricing strategy

REMEMBER

After you gather your data and have a baseline weekday and weekend pricing rate that you feel comfortable with, you need to figure out how to use that information. Here are three primary pricing strategies you can consider adopting to price your listing:

>> **Match market offering and charge less.** If you intend to match the amenities and overall offering of your competition, you can gain an edge by charging slightly less than your competition. By offering the same amenities at a discount, you'll be able to secure more bookings.

>> **Beat market offering and charge the same.** If you intend to clearly beat the offering of your competition, you can gain an edge by charging the same overall pricing as your competition. By offering better amenities at the same price, you'll also be able to secure more bookings.

>> **Make unique offering and charge premium.** If your Airbnb listing offers something unique that guests value and the competition in your market can't match, then you may be able to charge a premium. By offering something unique and valuable, you'll be able to charge more than your competition.

Depending on which strategy you find most fitting for your Airbnb listing, your baseline pricing will be lower than, about the same, or greater than the baseline pricing you found from the comparable listings.

However, settling on your baseline pricing doesn't mean you just set your pricing to these levels for the entire availability of your listing. At various times you want to purposely price lower or higher than your baseline pricing. Later sections explore each of those moments.

# Ramping Up to Baseline Pricing

The first such scenario where you price differently from your baseline pricing is during your ramping-up period, typically the first two to four months after an Airbnb listing first goes live on the platform. During these first months on the platform, your objective is to build momentum for your listing as quickly as possible, not to maximize the profits of any individual bookings.

TIP

To do so, get as many bookings and as many 5-star guest reviews as fast as possible. When a listing is fresh on the platform, it has no bookings and no reviews. All things equal, potential guests almost always book with listings that have more reviews than similar listings with no reviews.

**REMEMBER**

During your ramping-up period, follow this pricing schedule to build momentum for your listing.

1. **Start at 20 percent lower than your baseline pricing.**

   Doing so underprices your listing relative to your competition right out of the gate.

2. **Wait for one week and check to see whether your listing is mostly booked two weeks out.**

   - If mostly booked for next two weeks, then stay the course until your listing is mostly booked four weeks out — aim for 80 percent plus occupancy.

   - If not booked out, drop pricing by another 10 percent every week until you're booked four weeks out.

   - If more than four weeks are booked within the first week, then raise prices by 10 percent every week until you're fully booked for the next four weeks or until reaching baseline pricing.

3. **After you reach the baseline pricing, sign up for third-party dynamic pricing software to monitor and adjust pricing going forward automatically.**

   For more on dynamic pricing, check out the later section "Using Dynamic Pricing: Yes or No?"

**TIP**

Be sure to note in your listing profile title and description that your listing is "NEW." Doing so can help potential guests get comfortable with your lack of reviews and help them understand why your listing is priced so favorably versus competition — that it's due to your newness and not some defect.

# Understanding and Adjusting for Seasonality

When setting your pricing, sometimes you need to adjust for seasonality. *Seasonality* means the overall Airbnb demand — the occupancy and average nightly rates for Airbnb listings in the market — may be much higher or lower than their typical rates when travel is correspondingly much higher or lower than average.

For example, Airbnb cabins by a popular ski resort may be booked almost every evening, even at much higher than average nightly rates during the high demand skiing season. However, these same cabins may have a hard time booking nights even at significantly discounted rates during low season when the snow has melted and far fewer guests want to spend their hot summer on these dry barren ski slopes.

For some Airbnb markets with well-defined seasonal attractions, you can easily know whether there is seasonality in the market. But for many markets without obvious seasonal factors for travel demand, you can verify seasonality by obtaining the relevant market data for the prior 12 months (a full calendar year). Check out Chapter 2 in Book 5 for details on how to obtain earning statistics for your market.

The seasonality of your Airbnb market falls into one of these four categories:

>> **Flat seasonality:** If the demand is the same all year around, then there is flat seasonality. In these rare markets, you can expect the occupancy and average nightly rates to stay about the same throughout the year. Often, flat seasonality is associated with low overall Airbnb travel demand for the market.

>> **High season only:** If the demand spikes high for a part of the year but stays flat the rest of the year, then the seasonality is said to have a high season. In these markets, you can expect the occupancy and average nightly rates to spike higher only during the high season but stay relatively flat the rest of the time.

>> **Low season only:** If the demand drops lower for a part of the year but stays flat the rest of the year, then the seasonality is said to have a low season. In these markets, you can expect the occupancy and average nightly rates to fall noticeably lower only during the low season but stay relatively flat the rest of the time.

>> **High low seasons:** If the demand drops lower for a part of the year and spikes higher for a different part of the year compared to a middle level the rest of the year, then the seasonality has both a high and low season. In these markets, you can expect occupancy and average night rates both to drop during low season and spike during high season.

Figure 4-2 shows what each of these four seasonality scenarios may look like if you plotted the average occupancy rates in these markets by month where 100 represents the annualized average occupancy rate. When you obtain the market data for a full calendar year for your market, you can notice that the average occupancy or nightly rates in your market will look like one of these scenarios.

Figure 4-2a shows a flat seasonality market, Figure 4-2b a high-season-only seasonality market, Figure 4-2c a low-season-only seasonality market, and Figure 4-2d a high and low seasonality market. For all examples, the average occupancy rate during normal season is at 70 percent.

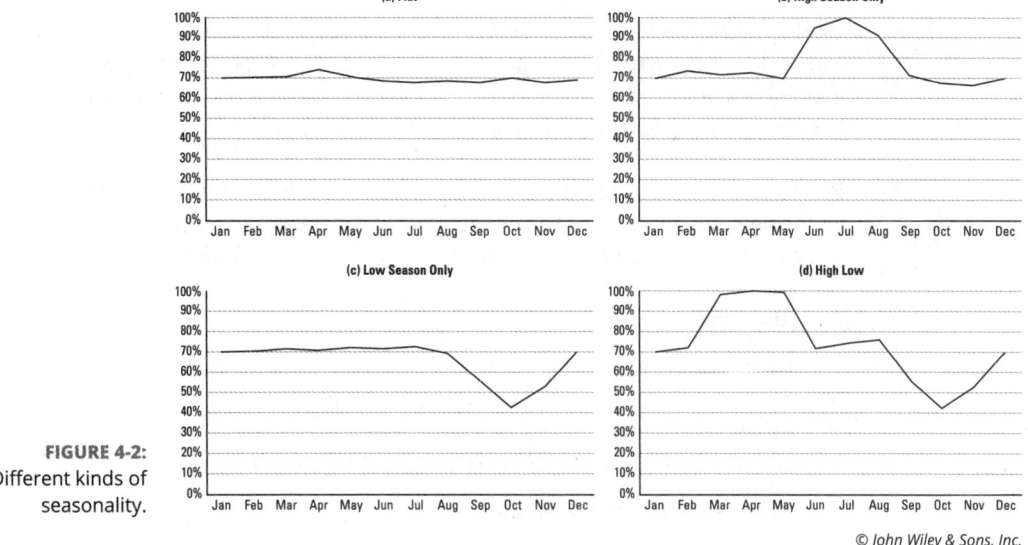

FIGURE 4-2:
Different kinds of
seasonality.

© John Wiley & Sons, Inc.

# Factoring in Temporality and Special Events: Going from High to Low

When pricing your Airbnb listing, you need to consider *temporality*, or how far out in advance the guest is booking. Having a guest book your listing six months out may feel good, but not if you allowed a guest to book it at a far lower rate than you could have achieved.

Consider an example from the airline industry. The prime booking window for airline tickets is somewhere between 20 to 120 days, with the best rates occurring around the 80 to 90 days from the flight. Booking earlier or later means paying higher prices for the consumers, but higher profits for the airlines.

Airbnb pricing has a similar dynamic when you optimize for temporality during dates with unusually high travel demand, such as when your city or nearby area has a special event that draws a sudden influx of travelers.

For example, the largest trade shows or conventions can draw hundreds of thousands of attendees, leading to booked hotels and Airbnb listings months in advance. Hosts who misprice their listings for these events by not increasing their prices can miss out on significant profits while hosts who appropriately price for the high demand by raising prices can achieve additional profits.

TIP

Unlike the airline industry, however, you won't typically see a large price hike for Airbnb bookings within the final two weeks prior to a special event. As the event approaches, you should reduce your pricing to ensure a booking rather than risk having an empty listing during an otherwise busy weekend.

REMEMBER

For pricing your Airbnb during special events, start high and then steadily reduce your pricing as the date of the event approaches. By using the following protocol, you can maximize your chances of earning more profits during special events:

1.  **Start high.**

    For two months or further out from the date of the event, price your listing at the highest price you can justify from one to two nights prior to the final night of event. Finding the right price to start with takes some guesswork, because it can vary from being only 20 percent higher to more than 400 percent higher.

2.  **Reduce weekly until booked.**

    Reduce the average nightly rates for those nights by an even amount such that by the final week prior to the event, you'd reach your normal rate. More than likely, you won't reach this pricing because your listing will most likely book beforehand. For example, if you're charging a premium of an additional $100/night for the event with eight weeks to go, reduce the premium by $12/night every week until it's booked.

3.  **Reduce aggressively if within two weeks.**

    If you've overpriced your listing and still not booked within two weeks of the special event, reduce your pricing more aggressively to ensure a booking rather than sitting empty. Pricing 10 to 20 percent lower than your remaining competition is typically enough to ensure booking at this stage.

# Using Dynamic Pricing: Yes or No?

Although manual pricing is useful for establishing your baseline pricing and understanding adjustments for seasonality and special events, it's woefully inadequate to account for a major factor in *optimal pricing* — the current available supply and pricing of your direct competition.

REMEMBER

That is, your pricing for any given available night for your listing should consider the overall availability of your competitors and their pricing for the same night. For example, if most of your competitors are also available the same night and their current pricing is low, you'd have a difficult time pricing your comparable listing at a premium. Similarly, if most of your competition is already booked, leaving few alternatives for the potential guests, you're more likely to be able to charge a premium for that night.

For a typical listing mostly available two months out, that's approximately 300 available nights to track the occupancy and pricing of competitive listings. Doing so manually just isn't possible to do, let alone keeping it updated. That's why we highly recommend you use *dynamic pricing tools* that track the competitive market supply and pricing and automatically update their Airbnb listing prices in near real time.

The following sections explore why you should opt out of Airbnb's own automated Smart Pricing tool and why a third-party provider is your best option.

## Underperforming with Airbnb's Smart Pricing tool

Airbnb's Smart Pricing optimizes pricing to maximize the number of bookings across the platform, not to maximize the profits for any individual listing, including yours. After all, Airbnb is a business, and it's in business to make money by charging service fees from both the guests and hosts of all bookings made through the platform. But it doesn't charge both sides equally.

At the time of writing, Airbnb currently charges most hosts a flat 3 percent of the gross bookings and most guests about 13 percent of the subtotal (the nightly rate plus cleaning fee and any additional fees) in North America. In other parts of the world, the host and guest fees range from 3 to 5 percent and up to 20 percent, respectively.

Here's how that works out for a three-night booking for an average listing priced at $150/night:

>> $150 per night times three nights = $450 total nightly rate

>> 13 percent of $450 is $58.50 guest service fee

>> 3 percent of $450 is $13.50 host service fee

>> $58.50 divided by $13.50 = 4.33

Airbnb makes more than four times more from guests than from hosts. In order to maximize its earnings from fees, Airbnb has incentive to get guests to book as many nights as possible by encouraging the listings to be priced as low as possible. And that's exactly what Airbnb's automated Smart Pricing does with its recommendations: It consistently recommends prices that are well below what the listings could often justify in their market.

Through interactions with thousands of hosts from around the world, we've seen many hosts who tried but eventually stopped using Airbnb's Smart Pricing after they discovered that their listings were at times charging 40 percent lower than their optimal prices. That's a quite a bit of profits to leave on the table!

## Aligning incentives with third-party dynamic pricing tool

Unlike Airbnb's Smart Pricing tool, third-party dynamic pricing tools don't earn a service fee from the guests. These tools only earn a fee as a small percentage of what their clients earn. The more that they help you earn, the more they earn. Their incentive is aligned with yours: Maximize profits for both.

At the time of writing, the typical fee for a third-party pricing provider is 1 percent of gross bookings. For example, for a two-night booking at $150 per night with total gross bookings at $300, the total fee for the booking will be $3. The fee is often even lower for hosts with multiple listings.

Here are some advantages of using a third-party dynamic pricing tool to help you see why they're a smarter choice:

>> **Dynamic pricing for every availability:** Without an automated service, a host can't evaluate the large number of data points every single day and set the optimal pricing for every available night over the next 12 months. A dynamic pricing tool ensures low demand nights are filled with lower pricing and high demand nights are booked at highest profit nightly rates, often resulting in both higher occupancy and higher overall profits for hosts.

>> **Positive return on investment:** Although the top third-party pricing providers tout that their clients can see revenue boosts of up to 40 percent (perhaps the host was coming from Airbnb's Smart Pricing), many hosts who have switched to third-party dynamic pricing typically saw revenue increases around 10 to 20 percent, which is still many times the payback on the nominal fee paid by the hosts.

>> **Market insight gain:** In addition to helping you set dynamic prices for your listing, the third-party pricing tools almost always include access to market statistics by letting you compare against similar listings in your market across the full calendar year. These insights can help you make manual adjustments in addition to the dynamic prices to account for factors not captured, such as major new events in the market.

>> **Cross-platform compatibility:** For hosts who want to list their property on other popular platforms in addition to Airbnb, most dynamic pricing providers

provide full integration with other top platforms and hosting management and scheduling tools.

» **Tools for other advanced tactics:** Besides options to fine-tune your pricing strategies to be more aggressive or conservative to suit your preferences, the top third-party dynamic pricing tools are constantly adding new feature sets to distinguish themselves from competition. For example, Wheelhouse (www. usewheelhouse.com/) added features that allow hosts to make fine manual adjustments for last-minute discounts, weekend rate adjustments, seasonality adjustments, and dynamic minimum nights requirements.

Here are the disadvantages of using a third-party pricing tool:

» **Initial setup required:** Although the process has become easier over the years, the early setup can be a steep learning curve for some hosts. Be sure to research your market to establish your baseline pricing and understand any seasonality before setting up third-party dynamic pricing.

» **Ongoing cost:** The fee is just 1 percent, but 1 percent of every booking made through the booking tool can still add up. However, even a modest gain more than makes up for it. By doing your own research and setting your own prices manually for several months and then signing up and for a third-party dynamic pricing provider, you can quickly see just how much a boost your listing will get.

» **Better functionality in major cities:** The pricing tool's recommendations are only as good as the data the provider gets to feed into its pricing recommendation engines. For listings that are well outside the popular markets in and around the major metros, the pricing recommendations can be less reliable. If you're in a less-populated area, establishing your own pricing first as a basis for comparison is vital.

» **24-hours updates:** Although the third-party pricing tool is far better than the weekly, monthly, or never updates from hosts manually managing pricing, it still isn't frequent enough. Supply and demand for certain travel dates can change significantly within 24 hours. Some providers allow manual update requests, but until tools start providing real-time updates, these tools have yet to reach their full potential.

Figure 4-3 shows a hypothetical Airbnb listing that averages 15 nights booked per month at an average nightly rate of $150 per night. Thus, its average monthly booking revenue, before any other fees collected, is $2,250. If this host signed up for a dynamic pricing provider, the host's revenue increases can range between 0 and 40 percent.

| Revenue Increase | New Revenue | 1% Fee | Net Gain |
|---|---|---|---|
| 0% | $ 2,250.00 | $ 22.50 | $ (22.50) |
| 5% | $ 2,362.50 | $ 23.63 | $ 88.88 |
| 10% | $ 2,475.00 | $ 24.75 | $ 200.25 |
| 15% | $ 2,587.50 | $ 25.88 | $ 311.63 |
| 20% | $ 2,700.00 | $ 27.00 | $ 423.00 |
| 25% | $ 2,812.50 | $ 28.13 | $ 534.38 |
| 30% | $ 2,925.00 | $ 29.25 | $ 645.75 |
| 35% | $ 3,037.50 | $ 30.38 | $ 757.13 |
| 40% | $ 3,150.00 | $ 31.50 | $ 868.50 |

**FIGURE 4-3:**
Example of how a third-party pricing tool could benefit a listing.

© John Wiley & Sons, Inc.

As you can see from Figure 4-3, if this host sees a revenue increase between 10 to 20 percent, which is common among hosts that switch to third-party dynamic pricing, the hosts can expect to gain $200 to $400 per month in additional revenue. If the listing was severely underpriced due to Smart Pricing and saw a 40 percent increase, the host would have nearly $900 more per month in revenue!

TIP

For a current list of recommended third-party pricing providers, go to www. learnbnb.com/airbnbfordummies.

# Setting Other Types of Fees

As an Airbnb host, you need to be aware of many other fees that you can set and charge guests. Get them right, and you could have more consistent bookings and profits. Get them wrong, and you could undo all the work you've put into your listing and pricing.

The following sections explore the important additional fees you can charge guests and how to use the right strategy for each.

## Setting the cleaning fee

The cleaning fee is often the biggest fee charged to guests and can range from nothing when hosts decide not to charge for cleaning to several hundred dollars for larger and higher-end listings.

When starting out, price at or slightly below the median rate of your competitors. As your listing gains momentum and as you build a competitive advantage versus your competition, you can adjust your cleaning fees higher.

TIP

During the ramping-up period, when you want to price very competitively, set your cleaning rate to match the rate of the lowest rates charged by any of your competition. As you ramp up your nightly rates, you can also adjust your cleaning fee.

These sections explore the different options you have as a host for pricing your cleaning fee.

## Charge nothing

Few hosts choose this option because guests are generally used to paying a cleaning fee and the standard for cleaning an Airbnb listing is higher than ever before. This option removes the barrier to booking as the price that guests see is what they pay (outside of Airbnb's service fee, of course), but not charging a cleaning fee means you lose out on profits.

The only hosts this option could potentially work for are

>> Hosts who operate small listings (rooms and small one-bedroom listings only) who enjoy doing the cleaning and turnaround themselves

>> Hosts whose listings allow them to charge a premium over their competition and thus pricing some portion of the cleaning fee into their nightly rate

## Charge in line with competition

TIP

For most hosts, this option is the recommended starting point. It allows you to pass most if not all the cleaning cost to your guests while still presenting a cleaning fee that is in line with market rates. If you want to go with this option, identify a dozen of the most comparable competitive listings in your market and charge slightly less than the median fee.

Charging in line with your competition creates no additional barriers versus competition. However, a cleaning fee may not always cover your cost, especially if you're hiring outside cleaners. Some listings with competitive amenities and great reviews could pass that onto slightly higher nightly rates.

## Charge for average length of stay

For many markets, the average booking is around three to four nights. Price your cleaning fee such that guests who are booking the most frequent length of stay in your market aren't turned off by the fee. This option is ideal for listings that tend to cater to longer stay bookings of five or more nights.

On one hand, this option discourages shorter stays because the cleaning fee often makes one- or two-night stays quite expensive. On the other hand, it may not always cover your cost to clean, especially if you're hiring outside cleaners.

## Charge based on your cost to clean

You could also charge based on your desired minimum hourly rate times the number of hours it takes you to clean or the actual cleaning fee that you pay to hire an outside cleaner. This option works for established listings that have solid reviews in a strong market where their potentially higher cleaning fees aren't enough to significantly impact overall bookings.

**WARNING**

Guests pay for the entire cost of cleaning for each booking — no out-of-pocket cost to you. However, using this option often prices you above your competition, especially for smaller listings, creating a barrier to booking.

# Setting the extra person fee

Airbnb lets you set a nightly rate for your initial occupancy and then set a fee for additional guests above and beyond the initial figure you set. Of course, you can still cap at the maximum occupancy number your property can legally accommodate. For example, by setting a $15 extra person fee, a three-night reservation with an extra guest will collect an extra $45 in rent (3 nights times $15 extra per guest per night).

Although many hotel chains charge an extra person fee, few enforce this rule at check-in. Most hotel travelers aren't even aware of this fee. For Airbnb travelers, even more aren't aware.

Airbnb used to ask potential guests for their number of guests at the end of the search, which led to surprises when the guests saw the extra person fees added. However, Airbnb now asks potential guests to input their number of guests at the start of their search, so the extra person fees are added to the totals of the search results, thus eliminating that unpleasant surprise at check-out.

## Why you should set an extra person fee

Here are some reasons you may want to include the extra person fee in your listing:

>> **Extra body means extra costs.** Having an additional guest often means higher utility costs, higher consumption of snacks and toiletries, more mess, and more wear and tear of furniture and appliances. The fee can help offset those extra costs.

>> **You get extra profit.** With Airbnb making it easier than ever to charge for extra person fees, it could mean extra profits left on the table if you don't charge that fee. For an average listing available year-round, that could mean $500 to $1,000 in additional annual profits.

## Why you shouldn't set an extra person fee

WARNING

You may not want to add an extra person fee for these reasons:

>> **Guests still see the charge before booking.** Although the extra person fee is less of a surprise now than before, guests still see the extra person charge as an added fee at check-out. In very competitive markets, even a little barrier for booking can mean fewer bookings and thus less profits.

>> **Average occupancy is max occupancy.** If the average occupancy of your bookings for your listing is the maximum occupancy for your property, then you can't add an extra guest fee because you have no physical space to accommodate the extra guest.

## How to calculate the extra person fee

You want to make sure your extra person fee isn't on the high side compared to your competition. Identify a dozen of the most comparable competitive listings in your market and charge slightly less than the median fee. If half of your competition isn't charging a fee at all, you shouldn't charge a fee.

If you don't have enough comparable listings to establish a starting point, start low with the following recommendations and then adjust by $5 increments as needed:

>> **Listings under $150 per night:** Start at $10.

>> **Listings between $150 per night and $300 per night:** Start at $15.

>> **Listings over $300 per night:** Start at $20.

TIP

During the ramping-up period, don't charge this fee to minimize barriers to booking. As your listing stabilizes and reaches your baseline pricing, then add the extra person fee.

# Setting the security deposit

Whether intentional or not, valuables can disappear from your listing and guests can inadvertently damage your things. A travel companion could decide to take the coffeemaker. A child may spill food and drink on the couch or mattress, requiring costly cleaning or replacement.

REMEMBER

To protect hosts and to discourage theft and careless behavior from guests, Airbnb lets hosts set a security deposit amount. Unlike traditional security deposits, it's more of a credit hold than an actual deposit of cash or credit. Guests aren't charged the value of the fee at booking.

Essentially, guests agree to place a hold on their credit card, in the amount of the security deposit, until the hold is released. In most cases, hosts never make a claim, and the hold is released 14 days after the guest checks out.

## Charging the security deposit: Why it's a good idea

Here are a couple of reasons why charging a security deposit is a wise idea:

>> **Most hosts require security deposits.** Guests are used to this and charging one won't create a barrier to booking unless the amount is glaringly outrageous. According to iGMS, a leading vacation rental software, 59 percent of Airbnb listings (at the time of writing) have a security deposit.

>> **It offers quick added protection.** Although the odds of you making a claim against the security deposit are extremely low, more than likely you'll need to do so at some point. Accidents happen. And if you host long enough, you'll eventually encounter a guest from hell. And for most incidents where the security deposit is enough, it's also the quickest way to get payment compared to making insurance claims or getting mediation through Airbnb support.

## Calculating the security deposit

Just as with other fees, you want to set your security deposit fee in a way that doesn't cause a potential guest to pause before booking.

TIP

Identify a dozen of the most comparable listings in your market and note the security deposit levels they've set. Don't be the highest. Start with, at most, the median rate. If you don't have enough comparable listings to base your security deposit level on, use the 25 percent rule. Keep your security deposit at no more than 25 percent of your average total booking. For example, if the average booking for your listing is three evenings at $150, then 25 percent of $450 is $112.50.

For most listings, the ideal level is generally between $100 to $600 per booking, where the $600 levels are typically reserved for listings with average bookings well over $2,000.

**TIP**

Keep these two other considerations in mind:

>> **Set the fee lower than your average booking value.** For example, if your listing is a $150-per-night listing and your average stay is three nights, then you'd want to keep your security deposit below $450. A $450 security deposit for a large listing with an average booking value of $2,500 is much more palatable than the same $450 fee for a $450 booking.

>> **Move unnecessary valuables.** If you have very expensive items like art or custom furniture that guests aren't likely to appreciate but may damage instead, remove those items from your property. Having fewer things that require costly cleaning, repairs, or replacement means you'll be able to get away with a lower security deposit fee.

**REMEMBER**

Yes, any incident that requires a claim against the security deposit likely will be time consuming and annoying. But incidents that require a claim are rare. So, don't let your fear of rare incidents influence your decision that impacts your listing's appeal to potential guests daily. The peace of mind that comes with setting a high security deposit could lead to costly missed bookings. For some hosts, getting additional insurance coverage is an option. Check out Chapter 3 in Book 5 for more on insurance.

## Lowering the barrier to booking

When deciding on appropriate fees, your goal is not necessarily to maximize additional revenue, but to lower the barrier to booking as much as possible. Sometimes, asking for too high of fees can backfire and lead potential guests to book with your competitors instead.

Airbnb already has a challenge with respect to short guest stays where the total cost after adding fees is often more than double that of the advertised nightly rate. Figure 4-4 highlights what booking a one-night stay on Airbnb often looks like for guests — irritating!

Although this mock-up example is extreme because the fees are only spread across one night, we can't overstate the impact of the fees on guests during the check-out process. Before making the final reservation, guests will decide based on looking at the final cost per night after adding in all the additional fees.

**FIGURE 4-4:**
The fees can add up.

REMEMBER

The bigger the gap between the final price and the subtotal from just the nightly rates, the less likely the guest will end up booking. In setting your fees, you want to make sure your fees are no more than the middle ground of your competition.

# 6

# It's All Over: Selling Your House

# Contents at a Glance

# Chapter **1**

# Deciding to Sell

S elling your house and moving can be an enjoyable (not to mention profitable) experience. Unfortunately, for most people, it isn't. Selling a house not only introduces financial turmoil into most people's lives but also causes them stress.

The reasons people want to sell their houses are almost as varied as the houses themselves. Here are some of the common, not-so-common, and downright bizarre reasons:

» Additional debt burden because of layoff, medical expenses, disability, or overspending

» Bad vibes or bad luck associated with the house

» Better job opportunities elsewhere

» Diminished space requirements now that children are grown

» House located in a flood, earthquake, or other disaster zone

» Increased space requirements for expanding family

» Lack of garage

» Neighborhood conditions incompatible with socioeconomic status

- » Noisy neighborhood
- » Noisy/messy/obnoxious family or business moved next door
- » Recent death of spouse
- » Recent marriage or divorce
- » Serious house defects (such as radon or termites) that owners don't want to or can't afford to fix
- » Unfriendly neighbors
- » Unsafe neighborhood
- » Unsatisfactory neighborhood shopping
- » Unsatisfactory school district
- » Unsuitable climate

As you can see from this partial list, most of the reasons why people have a desire to sell their houses are based on *wants*, not *needs*. You don't *need* to move because your neighborhood is too noisy or because your house seems too small. You don't *need* to move because the weather in your area isn't nice enough. You don't *need* to live on quieter, tree-lined streets.

All these features are things people desire or *want*, not things they *need*. And people who think they can afford to pay for such things usually get more of what they *want*. Sometimes, however, people spend money moving and, ironically, still don't get what they want. The weather in the new locale may not be terrific, the neighbors may not be friendly and quiet, and the schools may not turn children into stellar students. You may move to get away from particular problems and then find yourself facing a new set of problems.

How and where to spend your money is your choice. However, we definitely want you to make the most of your money. Unless you're one of the few who has far more money than you can ever possibly spend, you should prioritize the demands on your money to accomplish your most important financial goals.

REMEMBER

Nothing's wrong with spending money to trade in one house for another, but *before* you set those wheels in motion, think about the impact of that kind of spending on other aspects of your life. The more you spend on housing, the less you'll have for your other goals, such as saving for retirement or taking annual vacations, and the more time you may be forced to spend working.

# Figuring Out Whether You Really Need to Sell

Although spending your entire life in the first home you buy is an unlikely prospect, some people do end up living in the same home for 10, 20, even 30 or more years. Coauthor Ray, for example, lived in his home nearly 30 years. Ray's no fool; staying put must have its advantages.

If, like most prospective house sellers, you have a choice between staying put and selling, *not* selling has clear advantages. Selling your house and then buying another one takes a great deal of legwork and research time on your part. Whether you sell your house yourself or hire an agent, you're going to be heavily involved in getting your house ready for sale and keeping it pristine while it's on the market.

**WARNING**

In addition to time, selling your house and buying another one can cost serious money. Between real estate commissions, loan fees, title insurance, transfer tax, and myriad other costs of selling your house and then buying another one, you can easily spend 15 percent or more of the value of the property that you're selling (see the bar on the left in Figure 1-1).

Fifteen percent sounds like a lot, doesn't it? Well, consider this: Unless you own your house free and clear of any mortgage debt, your transaction costs are going to gobble up an even larger percentage of the money you've invested in your home.

Check out this scenario: You're thinking about selling your $240,000 house. If selling your house and buying another one costs you about 15 percent of the first house's value, then you're taking $36,000 out of your sale proceeds. However, if you happen to owe $180,000 on your mortgage, your *equity* in the home — the difference between the amount the house is worth ($240,000) and the amount you owe ($180,000) — is $60,000. Therefore, the $36,000 in transaction costs devours a huge 60 percent of your equity (see the bar on the right in Figure 1-1). Ouch!

**REMEMBER**

Before spending that much of your hard-earned money, make sure you give careful thought and consideration to why you want to sell, the financial consequences of selling, and the alternatives to selling. But before you get to the numbers, consider the qualitative issues in the following sections.

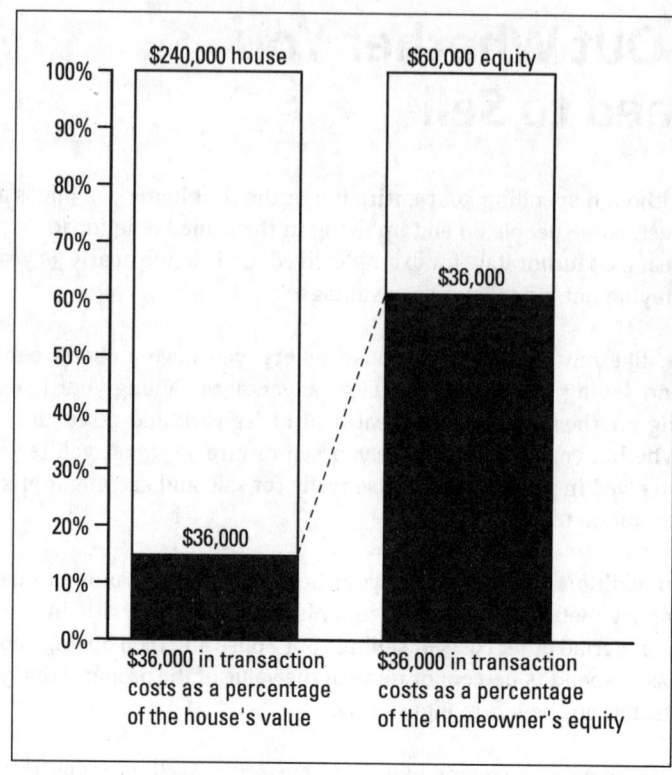

FIGURE 1-1:
Trading homes
can cost you
big bucks.

## Good reasons to stay

Whereas some people have clear and compelling reasons for selling their homes, others do so for the wrong reasons. You don't want to make the financially painful mistake of selling if you don't have to or can't afford to. The following sections offer reasons why you may be better off staying right where you are.

### You're already having trouble living within your means

TIP

If you're having difficulty making ends meet and you use high-interest consumer credit, such as credit cards or auto loans, to maintain your desired standard of living, you shouldn't spend more money on housing. Even if you're planning to trade your current house for one of comparable value, you may not be able to afford all the transaction costs of selling and buying.

Even if you aren't a consumer-debt user and you're saving a comfortable portion (10 percent or more) of your current earnings, *don't* assume you can afford to trade up to a more expensive home. In addition to a higher mortgage payment, you may also face increased property taxes, insurance rates, and home maintenance costs.

**REMEMBER**

A mortgage lender may be willing to finance a loan that enables you to trade up to a more expensive home, but qualifying for a loan doesn't mean you can *afford* that home. Mortgage lenders use simplistic formulas, based primarily on your income, to determine the amount they're willing to lend you. Mortgage lenders don't know (or care) how far behind you are in saving for your retirement, how many children you must help with college costs, or how much assistance you want or need to give to elderly parents.

Mortgage lenders are concerned about protecting their interests in the event that you default on your mortgage. As long as you meet a few minimal financial requirements (you make a sufficient down payment, and your housing expenses are less than a certain percentage of your income), the mortgage lenders can sell your loan with the backing of a government mortgage agency, effectively wiping their hands clean of you and your problems.

**WARNING**

If you're thinking about trading in your current house for another one, especially for a more expensive one, you absolutely, positively must consider the financial repercussions of changed housing expenses in addition to the costs of buying and selling.

## The problems are more in your perceptions

Everybody, at some point, leaps to conclusions based on faulty assumptions or incomplete research in virtually all aspects of his or her life. Peter, for example, was a single parent living with his son in a nice neighborhood in an urban environment. When his son started junior high school, Peter grew increasingly concerned with the possibility that his son would become involved with drugs, which seemed to be prevalent in their city.

Despite working in the city, Peter decided to move to an easygoing, suburban community about 45 minutes outside the city. Shortly after the move, Peter's son got mixed up with drugs anyway.

In addition to ignoring lifestyle issues (such as the length of his commute), Peter made a common human mistake — he assumed things were a particular way without getting the facts. The reality was that the suburban community to which Peter moved had as many problems with teenagers on drugs as the good neighborhoods in his former city.

**TIP**

Crime and safety make up another common realm where people have misconceptions. Some communities often make the evening news with graphic stories and film footage of crimes. Statistically, however, most crimes committed in a given city or town occur in fairly small geographic areas. Local police departments tabulate neighborhood crime rates. If you're concerned about crime and safety, don't guess; get the facts by contacting your local police department and asking them how to obtain the data.

Schools are another hot-button issue. In some areas, people make blanket statements condemning all public schools. They also insist that if you live in such-and-such town or city, you must send your children to private school if you want them to get a good education. The reality, as education experts (and good old-fashioned common sense) suggest, is that you can find good and bad public schools and good and bad private schools. You also need to evaluate if you're spending too many hours working and commuting just so you can make expensive tuition payments.

## Selling won't solve the problem(s)

Avoiding problems is another human tendency. That's what Fred and Ethel tried to do. Much to their chagrin, Fred and Ethel discovered that their home had two not-so-visible but, unfortunately, costly-to-fix problems. The new roof they needed was going to cost big bucks because local ordinances required the removal of several layers of existing roofing material when a new roof was installed. Fred and Ethel also had recently found out that their house contained asbestos, a known carcinogen.

Rather than research and deal with these problems, Fred and Ethel decided that the easiest solution was to sell their house and buy another one in a nearby town where they thought they'd be happy. They then attempted to sell their home without disclosing these known defects — a major legal no-no — but were tripped up by smart buyers who found out about the problems from inspectors they hired to check out the property.

Actually, the prospective buyers did Fred and Ethel two big favors:

» By uncovering the problems early, the buyers saved Fred and Ethel from a costly lawsuit that could easily have resulted if the flaws were discovered after the house was sold.

» By ultimately deciding to hold onto their home, which they otherwise were content with, Fred and Ethel saved themselves thousands of dollars in selling and buying transaction costs. Those savings more than paid for the cost of a new roof. And Fred and Ethel discovered that, because the asbestos was in good condition and properly contained, it was best left alone.

## You can fix some or all of the problems

When they realized that they couldn't run from their home's problems, Fred and Ethel, discussed in the preceding section, discovered how to get those problems fixed. You can address quite a number of possible shortcomings in your home less expensively than buying a new home.

If you think that home improvement projects are going to be too expensive, do some rough calculations to determine the cost of selling your current house and then buying another. Keep in mind that you can easily spend 15 percent of the house's value on all the transaction costs of selling and then buying again.

Instead of trading houses, why not spend those transaction dollars on improving the home you currently own? Do you hate the carpeting and paint job? Get new carpets and repaint. If your home is a tad too small, consider adding on a room or two. Just be careful not to turn your home into a castle if all the surrounding houses are shacks. Overimproving your property can be an expensive mistake. *Overimproving* means that after the improvements to your house, you'll own the most expensive house on the block, and you'll have difficulty recouping the cost of the improvements in the form of a higher house sale price.

**WARNING**

Some people are seduced by the seemingly better attributes of other houses on the market. If your house is small, larger ones seem more appealing. If you don't like your carpeting, houses that have hardwood floors may attract you. However, as is true of long-term friends or spouses, you know your current home's defects all too well because you've probably lived with them for years. Unless you're incredibly observant, you surely didn't know half of your home's faults and shortcomings before you moved in. The same is true of new homes you may be lusting after.

Some problems and defects are more easily fixed and more worth fixing than others. When you're deciding whether to fix problems or move away from them, consider these important issues:

>> **What's the payback?** Some home remodeling projects may actually pay for or come close to paying for themselves. We're not suggesting that you can have the work done for free. However, certain remodeling projects do increase your home's value by enough to make up for most or even all the cost of the improvement(s).

**TIP**

Generally speaking, projects that increase the cosmetic appeal or usability of living space tend to be more financially worthwhile than projects that don't. For example, consider painting and recarpeting a home versus fixing its foundation. The former projects are visible and, if done well, enhance a home's value; the latter project doesn't add to the visible appeal of the home or usability of living space. If, however, you *must* do foundation repairs or the house will collapse, spend your money on the foundation.

If you decide to stay put and renovate or improve your current home, you're going to need to find a way to pay for all that work. If you head down the renovation path, don't forget that contracting work often ends up costing more than you (and your contractor) originally expected.

>> **How intrusive will the work be?** As you surely know, money isn't everything. Six months into a home remodeling project that moves you out of your bedroom, spreads sawdust all over your kitchen table, and has you wanting to flee the country, the "payback" on the project doesn't seem so important anymore. In addition to costing more than most parties expect, contracting work almost always takes longer than everyone expects.

TIP

Ask yourself and others who've endured similar projects: How much will this project disrupt my life? Your contract with the contractor should include financial penalties for not finishing on time.

Some problems or shortcomings of your current house simply can't be fixed. If you're tired of shoveling snow in the winter and dripping sweat in the summer, you're not going to be able to change your local weather. If crime is indeed a big problem, you aren't going to be able to cut your area's crime rate anytime soon. Moving may be the best solution.

## PATIENCE — NOT MONEY — SOLVES SOME PROBLEMS

Some problems may solve themselves if you're patient and willing to wait things out. For example, coauthor Eric once lived a block away from a busy California freeway. Although adequate fencing and safety barriers separated the speeding cars on the highway from the neighborhood, the noise was a bit of a nuisance, especially during peak commute hours.

The longer Eric, who was raised in a quiet non-urban environment, lived in the home, the more the noise bugged him. Within several years of having bought the home, however, the problem was solved. Expansion of the freeway forced the state to add sound walls, which greatly dampened the noise and enhanced home values in the area.

# Reasons to consider selling

If you're in a situation where you really *need* to sell, as opposed to wanting to sell, by all means put your house on the market. And if you *want* to sell, and can *afford* to do so, you should go for it as well. The following sections offer some solid reasons for selling.

## You can afford to trade homes

Your desire to sell your current house and buy another one may be driven by a force as frivolous as sheer boredom. But if you can afford to sell and buy again, and you know what you're getting into, why not?

Now, defining *afford* is important. By *afford,* we mean that you've identified your personal and financial goals and you've calculated that the cost of trading houses won't compromise those goals.

**REMEMBER**

Everyone has unique goals, but if you're like most people, you probably don't want to spend the rest of your life working full time. To retire or semi-retire, you're going to need to save quite a bit of money during your working years. If you haven't yet crunched any numbers to see where you stand in terms of retirement saving, postpone major real estate decisions until you explore your financial future.

## You need to move for your job

Some people find that at particular points in their lives, they need to move to take advantage of a career opportunity. For example, if you want to be involved with technology companies, certain regions of the country offer far greater opportunities than others.

When you lack employment, paying bills is difficult, especially the costs involved in home ownership. If you've lost your job or your employer demands that you relocate to keep your job, you may feel a real need to move, especially in a sluggish economy.

**REMEMBER**

Moving for a better job (or simply for *a* job) is a fine thing to do. However, some people fool themselves into believing that a higher-paying job or a move to an area with lower housing costs will put them on an easier financial street. You must consider all the costs of living in a new area versus your current area before deciding that moving to a new community is financially wise.

And you should consider that you may be overlooking opportunities right in your own backyard. Just because your employer offers you a better job to get you to relocate doesn't mean you can't bargain for a promotion and stay put geographically.

Likewise, during an economic slowdown, if your employer says you must relocate or face downsizing, explore other employment options in your area, especially if you want to stay in the local area.

## You're having (or will have) financial trouble

Sometimes, people fall on difficult financial times because of an unexpected event. Check out these two scenarios:

» After Ryan graduated from college, he landed a good marketing job and seemed financially secure. So he bought a home. After a few years in the home, Ryan discovered that he had a chronic medical problem.

Ultimately, Ryan decided to go into a lower-stress job and work part time. As a result, his income significantly decreased while his medical expenses increased. He no longer could afford his home. It made sense for Ryan to sell his house and move into lower-cost housing that better addressed his reduced mobility.

» When Teri and her husband bought a home, they were both holding down high-paying jobs. Unfortunately, their marriage had problems. After much marital counseling and many attempts to get their marriage on a better track, Teri and her husband divorced. Because neither of them alone could afford the costs of the house, Teri and her husband needed to sell.

In addition to unexpected events, some people simply live beyond their means and can't keep their heads above the financial water of large mortgage payments and associated housing costs. Sometimes people get bogged down with additional consumer debt because they stretched themselves too much when buying their home.

TIP

Selling your house and moving to a lower-cost housing option may be just what the financial doctor ordered. On the other hand, if you can bring your spending under control and pay off those consumer debts, maybe you can afford to remain in your present home. Be sure you're being honest with yourself and realistic about your ability to accomplish your goals given your continuing housing expenses.

## You're retiring

If you decide to call it quits on the full-time working life, you may find yourself with more house than you need or you may want to move to a less costly area. Instead of trading up, you may consider trading down.

You can free up some of the cash you've tied up in your current house and use that money to help finance your retirement by moving to a less expensive home. If you're otherwise happy where you're currently living, don't think you must trade down to a less expensive home simply to tap the equity in your current property. You can tap your home's equity through other methods, such as taking out a reverse mortgage.

### Your house is associated with bad feelings

As with other financial decisions, choosing to sell or buy a home isn't only about money. Human emotions and memories can be just as powerful and just as real factors to consider.

If your spouse or child has passed away, you divorced, or your house was badly burglarized, the property may be a constant source of bad feelings. Although selling your house and moving won't make your troubles go away, being in a new home in a different area or neighborhood may help you get on with your life and not dwell excessively on your recent unpleasant experiences. Just be sure to temper your emotions with a realistic look at your financial situation.

# Knowing the Health of Your Housing Market

Your personal financial situation clearly is an important factor in deciding whether and when to sell your house, but the state of your local housing market may also influence your decision. Check out the following sections for the lowdown on the housing market and how it affects your sale.

## Selling in a depressed housing market

No one likes to lose money. If you scraped and saved for years for the down payment to buy a home, finding out your house is worth less than the amount you paid for it can be quite a blow. Between the decline in the market value of your home and the selling costs, you may possibly even lose your entire invested down payment. And you thought the stock market was risky!

Some homeowners even find themselves *upside down*, which simply means the mortgage on the house exceeds the amount for which the house can be sold. In other words, upside-down homeowners literally have to pay money to sell their houses because they've lost more than their original down payment. Ouch! (This happened to more folks during the severe financial crisis of 2008, which clobbered home values in many parts of the country.)

When deciding whether to sell in a depressed market, consider the factors discussed in the following sections.

## If you still have adequate equity

Although your local real estate market may have recently declined, if you've owned your house long enough or made a large enough down payment, you still may be able to net a good deal of cash by selling. If you can make enough money to enable yourself to buy another home, we say don't sweat the fact that your local real estate market may currently be depressed. As long as the sale fits in with your overall financial situation, sell your house and get on with your life!

**REMEMBER**

All real estate markets go through up cycles and down cycles. Over the long term, however, housing prices tend to increase. So, if you sell a house or two during a down market, odds are you'll also sell a house or two during better market conditions. And if you're staying in the same area or moving to another depressed housing market, you're simply trading one reduced-price house for another. If you're moving to a more expensive market or a market currently doing better than the one you're leaving, be sure that spending more on housing doesn't compromise your long-term personal and financial goals.

## If you lack enough money to buy your next home

Sometimes homeowners find themselves in a situation where, if they sell, they won't have enough money to buy their next home. If you find yourself in such a circumstance, first clarify whether you *want* or *need* to sell:

>> If you *want* to sell but don't *need* to and can avoid selling for a while, wait it out. Otherwise, if you sell and then don't have adequate money to buy your next home, you may find yourself in the unfortunate position of being a renter when the local real estate market turns the corner and starts improving again. So you'll have sold low and later be forced to buy high. You'll need to have an even greater down payment to get back into the market, or you'll be forced to buy a more modest house.

>> If you *need* to sell, you have a tougher road ahead of you. You must hope that the real estate market where you buy won't rocket ahead while you're trying to accumulate a larger down payment. However, you may also want to look into methods for buying a home with a smaller down payment. For example, a benevolent family member may help you out, the person selling you your new home may lend you some money, or you may decide to take out one of the low-down-payment loans that some mortgage lenders offer. If prices do

rise at a fast rate, you can either set your sights on a different market or lower your expectations for the kind of home you're going to buy.

If you must move or relocate and don't want to sell in a depressed market, you can rent out your home until the market turns around. Be sure you understand the tax consequences of this arrangement. Before becoming a landlord, consider your ability to deal with the hassles that come with the territory. You must also educate yourself on local rent-control ordinances and compare your property's monthly expenses with the rental income that you'll collect. (Find out how to calculate the difference between a property's income and expenses in the nearby sidebar "Figuring the cash flow on rental property.") If you're going to lose money each month, the constant cash drain may handicap your future ability to save, in addition to increasing your total losses on the property.

# FIGURING THE CASH FLOW ON RENTAL PROPERTY

*Cash flow* is the difference between the amount of money that a property brings in and the amount you have to pay out for expenses. Some homeowners-turned-rental-property-owners can't cover all the costs associated with rental property. In the worst cases, such property owners end up in personal bankruptcy from the drain of negative cash flow (that is, expenses exceed income). In other cases, the negative cash flow hampers the property owners' ability to accomplish important financial goals such as saving for retirement or helping with their children's college expenses.

Before you consider becoming a landlord, make some projections about what you expect your property's monthly income and expenses to be.

### Income

On the income side, determine the amount of rent you're able to charge:

- Take a look at what comparable properties currently are renting for in your local market.
- Check out the classified ads in your local paper(s).
- Speak with some leasing agents at real estate rental companies.

Be sure to allow for some portion (around 5 percent per year) of the time for your property to be vacant — finding good tenants takes time.

*(continued)*

*(continued)*

**Expenses**

On the expense side, you have your monthly mortgage payment (of which you're already painfully aware). And, of course, you have property taxes. Because you probably pay them only once or twice yearly, divide the annual amount by 12 to arrive at your monthly property tax bill.

You may end up paying some or all of your renter's utility bills, such as garbage, water, or gas. Estimate from your own usage what the monthly tab will be. Expect most utility bills to increase a bit because tenants will probably waste more when you're picking up the bill.

Be sure to ask your insurance company about how your property insurance premium changes if you convert the property into a rental. As is true with your property taxes, divide the annual total by 12 to get a monthly amount.

Don't forget repairs and maintenance. Expect to spend about 1 percent of the property's value per year on maintenance, repairs, and cleaning. Again, divide by 12 to get a monthly figure.

Finding good tenants takes time and promotion. If you choose to list through them, rental brokers normally take one month's rent as their cut. If you advertise, estimate at least $100 to $200 in advertising expenses, not to mention the cost of your time in showing the property to prospective tenants. You must also plan on running credit checks on prospective tenants.

**Estimated cash flow**

Now, total all the monthly expenses and subtract that number from your estimated monthly income after allowing for some vacancy time. Voilà! You've just calculated your property's cash flow.

If you have a negative cash flow, you may actually be close to breaking even when you factor in a rental property tax write-off known as *depreciation*. You break down the purchase of your property between the building, which is depreciable, and land, which isn't depreciable. You can make this allocation based on the assessed value for the land and the building or on a real estate appraisal. Residential property is depreciated over 27½ years at a rate of 3.64 percent of the building value per year. For example, if you buy a residential rental property for $250,000, and $175,000 of that amount is allocated to the building, that allocation means you can take $6,370 per year as a depreciation tax deduction ($175,000 multiplied by 0.0364).

After you've crunched all these numbers, if you find that you're still interested in renting your property, be sure to read Chapter 5 in Book 1, which introduces the basics of managing residential rentals.

# Selling during a strong market

What could be better than selling your house during a time of rising or already elevated home prices? If you can afford the transaction costs of selling your current house and buying another home, and if the costs of the new home fit within your budget and financial goals, go for it.

Just be careful of a few things:

>> Don't get greedy and grossly overprice your house. You may end up getting less from the sale than you expected, and the sale is likely to take much longer than if you'd priced the property fairly. If you price your house too high, when you finally drop the price to the right range, you may face lower offers because your house has the stigma of being old on the market. Chapter 3 in Book 6 details how to price your house for a quick sale that gets you top dollar.

>> Necessity being the mother of invention, the housing recovery, beginning in 2010, fostered a potentially risky but sometimes profitable pricing strategy. But beware, this strategy will only work during a sustained period of very low supply and very high demand. It entails pricing the home well below the apparent market value. The purpose is to create an auction atmosphere and attract so many buyers that they will bid the price well above the low list price and, hopefully, above the price you'd hoped to obtain. The danger with this strategy is that it doesn't always work. You may only receive one offer at or even below the listed price. If so, then this is likely the actual market value of your home. While you are never obligated to accept an offer, whether at list price or even well above, you can create hard feelings and, therefore, troubled negotiations by turning down offers at the asking price.

>> If you're staying in your current strong market or moving to another strong market, be careful about timing the sale of your current house and the purchase of your next one. For example, you probably don't want to sell and then spend months bidding unsuccessfully on other homes. You may get stuck renting for a while and need to make an additional move; such costs can eat up the cash from your recent sale and interfere with your ability to afford your next home. Chapter 2 in Book 6 explains how to time the sale of your house and the subsequent purchase of your new home.

# Chapter **2**

# Timing Is Everything

Thomas Edison, one of the United States' foremost inventors, was often called a genius. He modestly said genius was 1 percent inspiration and 99 percent perspiration. He should know. It took him years of hard work to invent the phonograph. Edison tested more than 4,000 different filaments before discovering the one he ultimately used in the first practical electric light bulb. Insight helps, but there's no substitute for hard work and planning.

You don't have to be a genius to get top dollar for your house when you sell it. Nor do you have to be lucky, although a little luck here and there never hurts. To paraphrase Edison, lucky sales are 1 percent good fortune and 99 percent planning and perspiration.

If you follow the right steps *before* you put your house on the market, good fortune may come your way throughout the transaction. You can control the selling process instead of reacting to it on a crisis-by-crisis basis. You can create your own luck. This chapter shows you how to make time your best pal.

## Timing the Sale of Your House

Time is your most precious gift. When it's gone, you can never get it back. Some people spend their time wisely; others foolishly fritter it away. Depending on how well or how poorly you use it, time can either be an ally or a ruthless enemy during the sale.

In most communities, choosing the date you put your house on the market is an important decision. Certain periods of each year are predictably advantageous for sellers. Others are just as predictably less than stellar.

Real estate marketing activity isn't flat throughout the year. No matter where you live in the United States, the real estate marketing calendar generally has two distinct peaks and valleys created by ebbs and flows of activity in your local real estate market (see Figure 2-1).

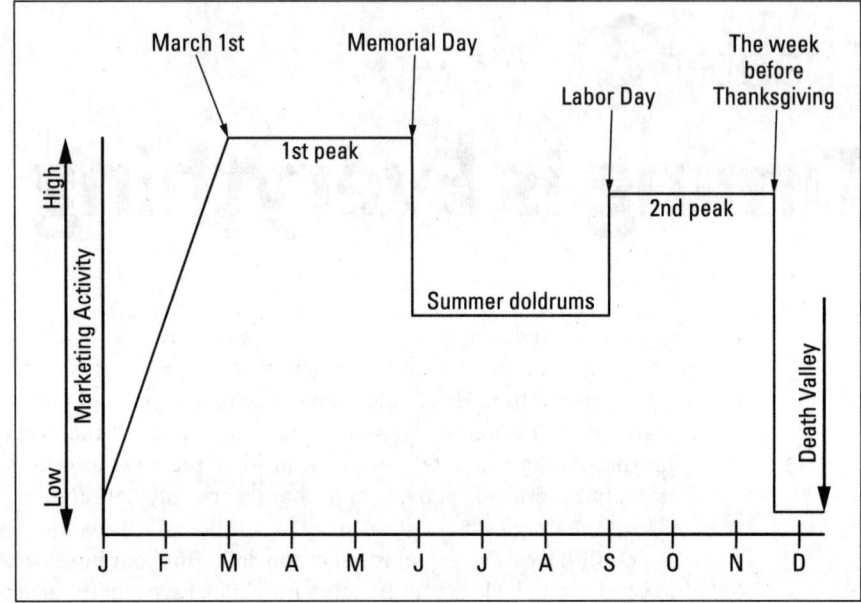

FIGURE 2-1: A real estate marketing calendar usually has predictable peaks and valleys in housing sales activity.

© John Wiley & Sons, Inc.

The sales peaks are higher and longer in good years, and the valleys are deeper and longer in bad years, but the marketing calendar's relentless rhythm never changes. These seasonal cycles are heartless. They don't care about birth, death, divorce, job loss, or any other life changes that force you to sell. You can't alter the rise and fall of market cycles any more than you can stop the tides. You can, however, use the predictability of these cycles to your advantage. The following sections help you identify when the best times are to put your house on the market and which are the worst.

424  BOOK 6  It's All Over: Selling Your House

## First peak season: Spring flowers and For Sale signs bloom

Calendar years begin January 1, but real estate years don't. Depending where you live, the longer and stronger of two annual peak seasons begins somewhere between late January and early March. If you live in a temperate area, such as Florida or California, the market kicks into gear sooner. If you're still digging out from under ten feet of snow on March 1, your market may take longer to heat up.

Weather aside, most folks don't bound out of bed on New Year's Day to buy a house. They need several weeks to adjust to the daily grind after that happy whirl of holiday parties and vacations. The buy-now, pay-later monster also rears its ugly head; people need time to recover from the trauma of paying all their holiday bills. As a result, many January buyers are extremely price conscious.

February through May normally is the most active selling time for residential real estate. Families with children want to get their purchase or sale out of the way by late spring so moving (which typically occurs 30 to 60 days after the ink dries on the contract of sale) won't disrupt the kids' schooling for the next academic year. Other people buy or sell early in the year for tax purposes or to avoid interference with their summer vacations. The annual outpouring of new listings pulls buyers out of the woodwork. Sellers are drawn into the market by all the buying activity.

TIP

The first peak season is usually the best time to put your house on the market. High sale prices result from spirited buyer competition. Because more buyers are in the market now than at any other time of the year, your best chance of getting a fast, top-dollar sale is during the first season. If you intend to buy another home after yours is sold, this time period offers the best selection of homes to purchase.

## First valley: Summer doldrums

Memorial Day generally marks the beginning of the first valley. Sales activity usually slows during June, July, and August. People who bought or sold in the spring move in the summer. Buyers, sellers, and agents often take summer vacations, which reduces market activity. Many folks spend their weekends having fun in the sun instead of looking at houses. Who wants to be cooped up inside on a sumptuous summer day?

Houses ordinarily take somewhat longer to sell in the summer because of a lower level of buyer activity. Unless you have to sell now (or if property values are declining), wait until the fall to put your house on the market. You're likely to get a higher price after people return from vacation.

TIP

If you're selling your house to buy another one, keep in mind that summer is your first opportunity to go bargain shopping. Summer is a good time to find motivated sellers who bought a new home and *must* sell their old one fast before the ownership expenses of two properties put them in the poorhouse. Less property is available to choose from in the summer than in the spring, but plenty is still on the market.

## Second peak season: Autumn leaves and houses of every color

Labor Day usually starts the second peak season. This peak normally rolls through September and October, and into November. Don't let the beautiful autumn leaves fool you, however. Just as fall brings a chill to the air, an icy edge of desperation develops in the second season for some sellers.

People who sell during late autumn tend to be *strongly* motivated. Some bought new homes in the spring before selling their old ones. Now they're slashing their asking prices — finally getting realistic after wasting months marketing overpriced properties.

Others are calendar-year taxpayers who sold houses earlier in the year and want to buy their new home before December 31. Why? So they can pay tax-deductible expenses (such as the loan origination fee, mortgage interest, and property taxes) prior to the end of the year to reduce the impact of federal and state income tax. Either way, calendar-year taxpayers are under pressure to buy.

TIP

If you're a bit of a gambler, the second peak season may be the most rewarding time to sell. Given that you correctly apply the pricing techniques in Chapter 3 of Book 6, your house should sell quickly and profitably. Unless prices are rapidly increasing in your area, wait until activity slows in mid-November and then buy your next home at a discount price. You get the best of both worlds — "sell high and buy low."

WARNING

Deciding to sell during the second peak season can be a risky gambit. If you inadvertently overprice your house, it won't sell. If you need to sell, carefully monitor buyer response to your property. Be prepared to drop your asking price as soon as you identify the danger signs (noted in Chapter 3 of Book 6). Don't wait until Thanksgiving to reduce your price. You may end up attempting to sell your house during the dreaded dead season (see the next section).

Another problem with waiting until the second valley in the real estate marketing calendar to sell your house and buy your next home is that you'll probably have a very small selection of houses to choose from. What good is a fantastically low price on a house you hate?

## Death Valley: Real estate activity hibernates until spring

The second peak season usually drops dead a week or two before Thanksgiving. With the exception of a few, mostly desperate, sellers and bargain-hunting or relocating buyers who stay in the market until the bitter end of December, residential real estate sales activity ordinarily slows significantly by mid-November. Folks stop buying property and start buying gifts. Would-be sellers take their houses off the market while their kids are out of school and their guests are visiting for the holidays. Ski slopes and sunny beaches beckon.

**WARNING**

This real estate Death Valley is generally the worst time of year to sell a house. Even the brilliant pricing techniques in this book may not be able to save you from getting your financial bones picked clean by bargain-hunting vultures if you're forced to sell at this time of the year. The weather is miserable, and very few buyers are in the market. Time will show you no mercy if you wait until this point to get realistic about pricing your house to sell. Don't put your house on the market during Death Valley days unless you have absolutely no other alternative.

### "NEVER TRY TO CATCH A FALLING SAFE"

"Never try to catch a falling safe" is an expression that describes the crushing financial burden of folks who compound their losses because they refuse to accept the reality of falling house prices in a declining market.

One of those safes smashed into Carlos and Jody, who bought a new home before selling their old one. Their tale began one Sunday about six months *after* prices peaked in one of San Francisco's real estate booms. A Victorian house they'd always admired had just come on the market. They decided to attend the open house and have a peek. The Victorian had high ceilings, great architectural details, and a gourmet kitchen. The

*(continued)*

(continued)

master bedroom contained a working fireplace, and the extra bedroom would make a perfect home office. It was love at first peek.

- "Can you believe our luck, Carlos? It's a steal at $895,000. They're practically *giving* it away. If we don't buy it today, someone else will."

- "I like it, too, Jody. But how can we buy it? Our money is tied up in our house."

- "Don't worry. Our house will sell fast. It's worth enough for us to afford this one. We'll get a long close of escrow, so we have plenty of time to sell our house. What can go wrong?"

Fortified by those comforting thoughts, they made a full-asking-price offer, which the sellers accepted.

Jody and Carlos then spent three weeks selecting an agent and spiffing up their house before putting it on the market. They asked $799,500, a price wishfully based on what they needed to net from the sale to buy their dream home.

Carlos and Jody were underwhelmed with offers. After five frustrating weeks with not even a nibble, they cut their asking price to $749,500 and pulled money out of their old house with a home equity loan to increase the deposit on their dream home. That "long" escrow was quickly nearing an end.

Jody and Carlos had a few showings after the price cut, but no offers. They finally got another home equity loan to close escrow. To their dismay, they'd inadvertently joined the elite ranks of people who own two homes. Their agent advised them to cut their asking price to $699,500 to prove that they were serious about selling.

At that price, they wouldn't clear enough from the sale to pay off the mortgage and home equity loans, but they had no alternative. They now had two mortgage payments, two insurance payments, two property tax payments, and two sets of utility bills each month. They unhappily lowered the asking price and covered the shortfall by selling some bonds that they'd been saving for their kids' college expenses. (That swooshing sound you hear is a falling safe.)

Knowing that the longer they kept the house, the more bonds they'd ultimately have to sell to make ends meet, Jody and Carlos sold their house for $675,000 six weeks after their final price reduction. This financial debacle wouldn't have happened if Jody and Carlos had used the techniques described in this chapter.

# The Seller's Quandary: Timing the Purchase of Your Home

So which comes first, selling your house before buying a new one, or buying first and then selling? Neither course of action is risk free. The adverse consequences of buying a new home before selling your present house, however, can be far more dire. At worst, buying your dream house before selling your present house may put you in the poorhouse.

If you read the sad tale of Carlos and Jody in the nearby sidebar "Never try to catch a falling safe," you may think that selling first is the only correct answer. Believe it or not, you can make a compelling case for either course of action:

>> **Selling before you buy eliminates financial risk.** When you sell first, you know precisely how much money you have from your sale to put toward your next home. No sleepless nights worrying about how you'll come up with the cash you need for a down payment on your new home or how much longer you'll have to make mortgage, property tax, and insurance payments on two houses. Your fiscal future is clear.

>> **Selling first, however, introduces uncertainties and problems.** If you sell first, you may be forced out of your old house before you have somewhere else to go. Where will you live? Where will your kids go to school? Where will you store your grand piano and your bowling ball collection if you're forced to rent an apartment while looking for another home? Do you really want to move twice? What if you can't find a home you like as much as the one you just sold? Putting your life on hold indefinitely while searching for a new home is emotionally draining and insomnia producing.

TIP

Given a choice between either selling your present house first *or* buying your next home first, we strongly recommend that you sell your present house before purchasing a new home. Even in good real estate markets, sales frequently drag on much longer than you expect. Selling in a weak market usually compounds the problem. Homeowners tend to overestimate their house's resale value and underestimate the length of the selling process — a fiscally deadly one-two punch.

# Consolidating Your Sale and Purchase

Suppose you don't want to sell your house first and then buy a new one. Nor do you want to buy a new home before selling the old one. What then? You can use a third option to sell your old house and buy your dream home without terror, chaos, pain, or privation. Your best alternative is to consolidate the sale and purchase into a seamless whole. The following sections describe how.

## Determine your house's current value

**REMEMBER**

The ultimate success or failure of your transaction depends on *accurately* determining your house's present fair market value. Don't kid yourself. This isn't a place for wishful thinking. Overpricing is bad in any real estate market — in a weak market, overpricing is a sure prescription for disaster. You must be realistic when pricing your house, or the sale of your present property and the purchase of your new home may flounder.

In a nutshell, you can either pay to have your house appraised or get a written opinion of its fair market value (called a *comparable market analysis*) from several real estate agents who fervently want to represent you during your sale. Chapter 2 in Book 2 covers everything you need to know about establishing a house's value.

## Check your buying power

*Buying power* is a function of the amount of cash you put down on your new home and the size of the mortgage you get. Both numbers are easy to figure out. Here's how:

>> **Calculate your cash position by subtracting the probable expenses of sale from your house's estimated resale value.** Probable expenses of sale include mortgage payoffs, corrective work credits, real estate agent's commissions, and property tax prorations. There are also relocation traps, such as higher housing costs associated with buying a more expensive home than the one you own now. You must figure your proceeds of sale *before* putting your house on the market.

>> **Have a lender evaluate your creditworthiness.** Find out the size of the mortgage you can get based on current interest rates, your income, and the probable down payment you can make on a new home if your present house sells at its estimated resale value. If you're nearly ready to sell your current house and buy another, now is a perfect time to get prequalified or, better yet, preapproved for a loan.

Lenders can't tell you how much money *you can afford to borrow* — just how much money *they're willing to loan you* based on their assessment of your ability to repay the mortgage. Lenders don't know or care about your other financial goals and objectives, such as providing for your retirement or socking away money to help your kids through college.

# Familiarize yourself with the market

Harry S. Truman, the 33rd president of the United States, was a renowned skeptic. He was fond of saying, "I'm from Missouri. You'll have to show me." Folks from the "show me" state don't value silver-tongued talkers. They live by the doctrine that seeing is believing.

When buying or selling houses, everyone needs to adopt Missouri's principle. To properly educate yourself about property values, you must tour comparable houses. No amount of book smarts beats good old shoe leather and eyeballing.

You have to wear two different hats during your property tours:

>> **Seller's hat:** A good comparable market analysis (CMA) prepared by a real estate agent to determine your house's current value contains two lists:

- One documents houses comparable to yours in condition, size, age, and location (called *comps*) that have sold within the past six months.

  - The other shows comps that are currently on the market. You probably won't be able to get into properties that have already sold, but you should make a point of touring each comp currently on the market to verify your house's resale value.

  If you're working with an agent, have them tag along when you tour properties. As you walk through a house, ask the agent to point out similarities and differences between it and recently sold properties that you haven't seen. This "show and tell" greatly speeds up your discovery process. After visiting a few comps, you start to *see* which houses are priced to sell and which houses are overpriced.

>> **Buyer's hat:** The house you intend to sell and the home you want to buy may be different — different neighborhoods, styles, sizes, ages, conditions, and prices. Your new home may not even be in the same city or state. You won't, however, have to reinvent the wheel as a buyer because most principles of valuing property apply whether you're a buyer or a seller. Smart buyers also use CMAs. Seeing is still believing, and nothing beats touring property currently on the market so you know what's available when the time is right.

TIP

For more information on finding your way through the purchasing maze, check out Book 2 as well as the latest edition of *Home Buying Kit For Dummies* by Eric Tyson, MBA, and Ray Brown (Wiley).

# Take action

Now you're ready to start the action phase — selling your old house and buying a new one. Timing is critical. If you structure your transactions properly from inception, you'll be in firm control of the process instead of the process controlling you.

## Putting your house on the market

First things first: Let the world know that your house is for sale. You must, however, continue looking at any new comps that come on the market after yours *as well as* other new homes being offered for sale. The market constantly changes. New property becomes available. Houses currently on the market sell. A good real estate agent can keep you posted regarding important changes that may affect your situation.

TIP

Push your hands deeply into your pockets whenever you tour prospective dream homes. Untimely dreams have a way of turning into nightmares. As long as your hands are safely out of harm's way, you can't sign any purchase offers.

REMEMBER

Don't make an offer to purchase your next home yet, for the following reasons:

>> **Your asking price may be too high.** Even though you try your best to price your property to sell, you may inadvertently overprice it. You know that you've overpriced your property if purchase offers fail to appear. Because the amount you can afford to spend for your next home probably depends on the amount you net from the sale of your current house, knowing how much money you'll have available may be critical. If your budget provides little wiggle room and you're forced to reduce your asking price, you can simply make a commensurate adjustment in the amount you eventually pay for your new home.

>> **You aren't a real buyer until you have a solid contract on the house you're selling.** Trust us; any offer you make on a new home that depends on first selling your present house (if your house isn't in contract yet) won't be taken seriously. Real sellers refuse to tie up their property indefinitely while you attempt to sell your house.

## Structuring your terms of sale

Concentrate on one extremely important aspect of the deal you make — structuring your terms of sale to provide enough time to purchase your new home. You shouldn't need a ton of time because you're already familiar with prospective new homes currently on the market, and you're probably either preapproved or, at least, prequalified for a mortgage.

**TIP**

Here's how you can give yourself the time you need to make a well-planned and executed purchase:

>> **Schedule close of escrow on your old house to occur 30 days after the buyers remove all their conditions of purchase and increase their deposit.** Buyers may take three or four weeks to remove the two most common conditions of nearly all house purchases — mortgage approval and property inspections. Getting loan approval usually takes somewhat longer than completing the various property inspections. Thirty days is your magic number, because lenders normally won't hold their loan commitment more than 30 days after they approve a mortgage.

Some lenders may be willing to hold mortgage commitments more than 30 days. One quick call to the buyers' loan officer is necessary to determine the lender's policy on this issue. If, for example, the buyers' lender guarantees a loan commitment 45 days after the loan is approved, schedule your close of escrow accordingly. The more time you give yourself to close your other transaction, the better.

>> **You can get even more time by putting a "rent-back" clause in your counteroffer to the buyers' purchase offer.** This clause lets you rent your house back from the buyers after escrow closes. It can buy you an extra month or two (or more) *if* the buyers agree to a rent-back. Sellers usually pay rent equal to their buyers' actual cost for principle, interest, taxes, and insurance. For example, if the buyers pay $1,500 a month for mortgage payments plus their prorated property tax and insurance payments, that amount is your rent. Although the rent may be more than you currently pay to live in your house, the amount is probably less than it would cost you to move into a motel for a month or two and much more convenient. Sellers are wise to prepare a formal lease agreement that covers the rent-back.

No standard rent-back clause exists. Check with your real estate agent or a lawyer to determine how rent-backs are best handled where you live.

## Timing the offer to buy your new home

**REMEMBER**

You may be tempted to rush out and make an offer on your dream home while the ink is still drying on the contract you just signed to sell your present house. Don't. Give yourself time to shake out deal-killing glitches in your sale before you make any offers on a new home.

>> **Don't present an offer to buy your next home until the contract on your present house resembles the Rock of Gibraltar.** If you want the sellers of your new home to treat your offer with respect, delay making an offer until your buyers remove all their conditions of purchase and increase their deposit on the house you're selling. Until you know the buyers' mortgage is approved and you resolve questions related to handling corrective work discovered during the property inspections, your contract is as solid as a bowl of pudding.

You may think that we're overly cautious when we urge you to wait until the contract for the sale of your house is rock solid before making an offer to buy your new home. We've seen seemingly solid deals blown apart out of the blue. The real estate gods can be cruel and fickle.

>> **Make the offer to purchase your new home subject to the sale of your present house.** This step protects you from being forced to buy a second home. Your offer should specify that if the escrow for the sale of your house doesn't close within the time specified in your contract of sale, you have the right to cancel the contract to purchase the new property. If for some utterly unforeseen reason the sale of your house falls apart, at least you can get out of the contract to buy the new home.

**REMEMBER**

Combining a 30-day close of escrow with a two-month rent-back clause gives you a three-month comfort zone in which to close the purchase of your new home. Ideally, you can simultaneously close the sale of your present house and the purchase of your new home. If you can't, however, then sell before you buy. You'll sleep better.

# Chapter **3**

# Price It Right and Buyers Will Come

I f you *really* want to be a successful seller, think like a buyer. You probably didn't buy the first house you looked at. Few folks do. On the contrary, most people spend months industriously inspecting many houses on the market. To avoid overpaying for the home they ultimately purchase, buyers are forced to become experts on property values.

You can ask any price you want for your house. But your house won't sell until you find a buyer who agrees that it's worth the price you're willing to accept. Smart sellers know that although only *one* person sets a price, *two* people — a seller and a buyer — make a sale.

Adverse factors outside your control (such as a flood of houses on the market, high mortgage interest rates, or dismal consumer confidence) may negatively affect your sale price. Even so, you don't have to passively let the real estate gods crush you. This chapter offers proven ideas you can use to create demand for your house no matter how poor prevailing market conditions are.

# Getting a Grasp on Pricing Methods

Chapter 2 in Book 2 explains how to use the asking prices and sale prices of *comps* (houses comparable to your house) to *factually* determine your house's value. This information puts you light-years ahead of sellers who either don't know about using comps or, worse yet, choose to ignore comps when pricing property.

You can pick a price for your house in a hundred different ways — visit an astrologer, poll your friends for their guesses about its worth, roll dice, pay for a professional appraisal, grab a number out of your hat, interview dozens of real estate agents until you find one with a suitably elevated opinion of your house's value, and so on. In the final analysis, however, they're all variations of the two pricing methods in the following sections.

## Four-phase pricing: Prevalent but ineffective

The consequences of pulling an unsubstantiated asking price out of the air are unacceptable for a smart seller. You may undervalue your house and risk leaving money on the table when you sell. Or, more likely, you may overprice your house, which results in an exhaustingly slow marketing process that ultimately lowers your sale price. Houses marketed by unrealistic sellers usually go through the following four distinct pricing phases prior to sale:

>> **Phase one:** Sellers start by blithely disregarding any factual pricing method, such as checking comparable property sales. Why? Some sellers don't know any better or get lousy advice from their real estate agents. Other sellers think their house is infinitely superior to those ticky-tacky comps. They're sure their house's inherent superiority will quickly attract a buyer with more money than good sense. Either way, this misguided method generally results in grotesque overpricing.

>> **Phase two:** After several months of total market rejection, the sellers grudgingly make a tiny price reduction, which brings their asking price down from the grotesque level to merely absurdly overpriced. Fantasy moderated is, however, still abject fantasy.

>> **Phase three:** More lonely months pass, and then two things happen:

- First, the sellers typically get a new agent — poetic justice for an agent who either didn't know property values or who intentionally misled the sellers about pricing to get the listing.

- Second, the sellers reduce their asking price to one that "leaves room to negotiate." Even though the revised price still is moderately higher than the house's probable sale price based on sales of comparable property, at least the new asking price has some basis in market reality.

>> **Phase four:** The sellers ultimately accept the validity of comps and reduce their asking price accordingly to a "let's sell it" level. After the sellers establish a good correlation between asking price and fair market value (FMV), their house *finally* sells.

Ironically, instead of getting more money with this method, four-phase pricing usually stigmatizes a property and reduces the eventual sale price to *less* than it would've been with more realistic pricing. Here's why:

>> **The listing agent can't justify an indefensible asking price.** If the asking price has no factual basis, the agent can't provide a good answer to buyers who ask, "Why hasn't the house sold after all this time on the market? What's *wrong* with it?" In degree of difficulty, this situation ranks right up there with "Just what do you think you're doing?" when your mom caught you with your hand deeply buried in the cookie jar.

>> **The property is slowly but surely buried by new listings that come on the market.** After several months, most buyers and agents either forget that your house still is on the market or belittle the house by saying, "That old thing. It'll never sell." In desperation, sellers are forced to slash their asking price to the bone to attract buyers.

Four-phase pricing creates a self-fulfilling prophecy. Folks who use this pricing method expect it will take a long time to sell their house. In a strong market, they're correct because the market will ultimately rise to their price level. In a weak market, they're disastrously correct as they chase the market ever lower.

## Pleasure-pleasure-panic pricing: Fast, top-dollar sales

If the four-phase pricing plan is a flop, what's your alternative? The smart way to sell your property is the pleasure-pleasure-panic pricing method. You can sell your house quickly *and* get the highest possible price by using this method. The secret of success is establishing a realistic asking price for your house when you first place it on the market.

**REMEMBER**

As Chapter 2 in Book 2 notes, the correct way to establish your house's value is to analyze houses comparable to yours in size, age, condition, and location — houses that currently are on the market and those that have sold within the past six months. Don't be misled by asking prices; many sellers use four-phase pricing. *Sale prices*, not asking prices, determine FMV.

Here's how the pleasure-pleasure-panic pricing method works. Milt and Judy have spent the last three months looking at houses on the market in their price range. They're educated buyers; they know how to distinguish between a well-priced house and an OPT (overpriced turkey).

Judy and Milt nearly bought a great house a couple of months ago. It had all the features they wanted and was fairly priced to boot. However, Milt didn't realize how well priced it was because he'd just started the education process. While Milt was haggling over the price and terms of sale, the seller accepted a better offer. Judy still blames Milt for losing their dream house.

They're spending today the same way they've spent the previous 11 Sundays, touring what seems like an endless series of newly listed OPTs with their agent. Then Judy and Milt trudge into your *first* open house and pleasure-pleasure-panic kicks into gear.

>> **Pleasure Number 1:** Judy and Milt love your property. It's the best place they've seen in the past three months. They could live in your house happily ever after. Their eyes start to sparkle.

>> **Pleasure Number 2:** Milt and Judy can't believe their eyes when they look at the asking price on your listing statement. By now, they know property values every bit as well as their agent. Your house is definitely priced to sell. Their hands start to tremble.

>> **Panic:** Judy and Milt see another couple entering your house. They've seen these folks at many other open houses during the past couple of months. That familiarity isn't a coincidence. The other couple obviously wants to buy a house in the same neighborhood and price range.

Judy and Milt stare at each other in horror. If they love your house and know it's well priced, so will the other couple. Their deodorants fail when they realize that if they don't act quickly, the other couple will snap up the house. Milt tells their agent to write up a full-asking-price offer. Judy kicks Milt in the shin and instructs the agent to go $10,000 above your asking price just to be safe. Milt agrees. He doesn't want to be a two-time loser.

That scenario explains how pleasure-pleasure-panic pricing creates a sellers' market even in the midst of a buyers' market. This approach puts intense pressure on buyers to perform quickly.

# FIRST OFFERS ARE WORTH A SECOND LOOK

No law guarantees that the first purchase offer you get will be the best one. However, as the following example illustrates, it often is.

Elaine decided to sell her house shortly after her husband died. The house was tough to price. It was in mint condition, had a great view, and was located on a large lot. It was far-and-away the best house on the block. No homes of equal quality had sold in her neighborhood in well over a year. Elaine's agent analyzed recent sales of similar properties that sold in comparable neighborhoods to determine an approximate value per square foot for Elaine's house. Based on these sales, her agent recommended asking $499,500. Neither Elaine nor the agent expected a fast sale because the highest previous sale in the neighborhood was $425,000.

Fortune smiled on Elaine. She got a $450,000 offer only two days after the For Sale sign went up. The people who made the offer were educated buyers who'd been looking at houses in her neighborhood for several months and were primed to pounce on any new listing that fit their needs. When their agent presented the offer, he told Elaine that the contract's terms and conditions of sale were flexible, but that the buyers were at their absolute upper limit financially.

Elaine's lawyer reviewed the offer. He found no legal flaws, but told Elaine he thought she was giving the house away. He reasoned that if she could get a $450,000 offer so quickly, she'd probably get a full-price offer soon.

Based on her lawyer's gratuitous advice, Elaine made a full-price counteroffer to the buyers. They rejected the counteroffer and moved on. Elaine's house had many showings the first month, but no other offers. After six weeks, her agent called the agent of the couple who'd offered $450,000 to see if they would submit another offer. No such luck. They had bought another house.

The real estate market went down the drain a couple of months later because of a severe economic slowdown. Elaine's house finally sold for $435,000 almost a year later. Had she taken the first offer she received, she would've made $15,000 more and spared herself a year of aggravation.

With 20/20 hindsight, blaming the lawyer for this fiasco is easy. However, blaming the lawyer is unfair. His advice was logical and compelling. When he gave it, no one could've said with certainty that a full-asking-price offer wouldn't be forthcoming.

That's the problem — uncertainty. Whether your house is the most expensive one on the block or the cheapest, no one knows what it's worth until it sells. FMV is established by the amount buyers pay and sellers accept.

*(continued)*

(continued)

When a house hits the market, uncertainty about FMV favors sellers. Therefore, the first offer is often the best one. If the property is priced close to the amount it's worth, educated buyers take their best shot at it. They want to get the house before someone else does. The fear of losing the house to another buyer works to the seller's advantage.

The longer a house sits on the market unsold, however, the more uncertainty about FMV favors buyers. Prospective buyers logically reason that the house can't be worth the asking price because, if it were, it would have already sold. The more buyers who see the property and don't make an offer, the more discredited the asking price becomes.

Fast first offers frighten sellers and buyers. Neither has the benefit of lengthy market exposure to confirm FMV. Sellers who reject a speedy first offer because it isn't full asking price take a calculated risk. A better offer may come along — but, then again, maybe not.

Don't be surprised if you get several purchase offers, including some that are equal to or more than full asking price, as soon as your house hits the market — if your house is priced right. After your property has been given broad, immediate market exposure, spirited competition forces buyers to pay top dollar for your house. This method works almost every time.

## Quantum pricing: An effective technique

Put yourself in the buyer's shoes for a moment and imagine that you're buying, not selling, your house. If you're like most people, one of the first things you do is decide how much you want to spend. For example, you set your upper limit of affordability at $250,000. If you're working with a real estate agent, you probably tell the agent, "I don't want to spend more than $250,000," or "Don't show me anything that costs more than $250,000." Why waste time looking at property you can't afford to buy?

Buyers use price limits, called *quantums*, to simplify house hunting. Pricing quantums are initially expressed in nice, round, easy-to-work-with numbers, such as $100,000 and $50,000, and then fine-tuned to $25,000 and $10,000 quantums.

Think of buyers as fish swimming in an ocean of houses for sale. At any given time, huge schools of buyer-fish usually are swimming in this sea. However, the buyer-fish swim at many different levels; one school swims at the $150,000-to-$200,000 price quantum level, another swims at the $200,000-to-$250,000 price quantum level, and so on.

Buyer-fish from higher-price quantums occasionally swim down to a lower quantum in their searches for a house. However, buyer-fish rarely swim up to a higher quantum (if they establish realistic affordability limits). When a buyer-fish can't afford to swim *up*, the price must drop *down* to the buyer-fish's price quantum for the house to sell.

## Establishing price quantums

**REMEMBER**

Follow these steps to use price quantums to hone your initial asking price to razor sharp, pleasure-pleasure-panic perfection:

1.  **Determine your house's market value within the appropriate $100,000 quantum, unless you happen to live in an area where no house ever has sold for more than $99,999.99.**

    Use the comparable market analysis (CMA) method described in Chapter 2 of Book 2 to define a general price range for your property. For example, if a CMA shows that five houses similar to yours in size, age, condition, and location sold within the past six months for $310,000 to $335,000, your house clearly belongs in the $300,000 to $400,000 quantum. So far, so easy.

2.  **Adjust the price within the correct $50,000 quantum.**

    Continuing with the same example, decide whether your asking price should be over or under $350,000. Because not one of the comps sold for more than $335,000, your price belongs in the $300,000 to $350,000 quantum. As problems go, still no head-scratcher.

3.  **Fine-tune your price to the closest $25,000 quantum.**

    The more accurate your pricing, the more exacting your scrutiny. Deciding whether the price should be in the $300,000 to $325,000 quantum or the $325,000 to $350,000 quantum requires careful analysis. If, for example, four of the five comps sold between $310,000 and $325,000 and the fifth went for $335,000, you'd be wise keeping the asking price under $325,000.

4.  **Ultrafine-tune your price to the nearest $10,000 quantum.**

    This is the moment of truth. Now you must decide on the *precise* point between $310,000 and $325,000 to put your price. If the actual prices of comparable houses that sold under $325,000 were $310,000, $317,500, $319,500, and $322,000, three out of four sales point toward an asking price under $320,000.

## Recognizing quantum-pricing finesse points

If you seriously want to sell quickly for top dollar, don't put your asking price in the next higher quantum to give yourself "room to negotiate." Here's why:

>> **Excitement:** It takes courage to price your house a hair *below* the nearest price quantum (rather than above the quantum, so you have room to negotiate downward). For example, suppose the comps indicate a probable sale near $250,000. A $249,500 asking price may create enough buyer excitement to generate multiple purchase offers that push your sale price higher than the asking price. Price your property at $269,500 to give yourself a $20,000 negotiating cushion, and your house is just another yawner.

>> **Computers:** All agents use computers tied to their multiple listing service's (MLS) database to perform property searches. For example, a buyer decides on a neighborhood and asks the agent for a list of homes with the following features: three bedrooms, two-and-a-half baths, a two-car garage, and an asking price of $250,000 or less. Per the agent's request, the MLS computer spews out listings that meet these conditions. The computer isn't smart enough to make allowances for properties with negotiating room in their prices. If your house is listed at $269,500 or even $251,500, it won't be on the printout, and buyers won't know it exists.

True, some agents show buyers higher-priced houses they think will sell in the buyers' price range because the asking prices are "soft." Smart agents, however, know that buyers are deeply concerned about being manipulated into purchasing a more costly house. These agents won't show buyers property over the stated price limit until the buyers have seen every house on the market in their specified price range and request to see more expensive homes.

REMEMBER

Less buyer exposure to your house means less buyer competition for it. Less competition translates into a longer time on the market — and usually a lower sale price, to boot. High sale prices come from spirited buyer competition.

>> **Conditioning:** Whether people are buying houses or blouses, everyone loves a bargain. Believe it or not, *$9.95 advertising* is mighty effective. A nickel ain't much, but most folks are well-conditioned to think that $9.95 is much cheaper than $10. Subconsciously, $249,500 is more exciting than $250,000, and $299,950 sounds like a much better deal than $300,000. Don't try to buck a lifetime of Pavlovian conditioning; smart pricing makes buyers drool.

WARNING

Don't price your property to dazzle your pals. You may impress people at a party by telling them you're asking $300,000 for your house, but that's a foolish price compared to $299,950. Price your house to sell, not to feed your ego.

# Identifying Incentives and Gimmicks

In strong real estate markets with many ready, willing, and able buyers clamoring to purchase good houses, property priced near its market value typically sells quickly. You don't need additional inducements in a red-hot market.

But when the tables are turned, and sellers far outnumber buyers, even pleasure-pleasure-panic pricing (covered earlier in this chapter) may not do the trick. If that's the case, you may have to offer buyers additional enticements to make a deal. In a buyers' market, the key to success is using incentives that help put a sale together instead of fancy gimmicks that tarnish your property and make it harder to sell. This section highlights a few incentives and gimmicks you may encounter when selling your house.

## Deal-making incentives

In a really rotten market, you can sweeten the deal by offering buyers money in the form of special financial concessions. One or more of the following incentives may be the key to putting a deal together:

>> **Credits in escrow:** One effective financial inducement is offering to pay a portion of your buyer's nonrecurring closing costs for such expenses as loan origination fees, title insurance, and property inspections. You may also graciously offer to pay for some or all of the repairs found by the property inspections. These payments usually are made as a credit in escrow from sellers to buyers.

>> **Seller financing:** On the plus side, financing some or all of the buyer's mortgage may get you a higher sale price, a faster sale, an attractive return on your money, and possibly some tax savings. Doing seller financing, however, ties up money you may need for the down payment on your new home. Worse yet, if the buyer defaults on your loan, you must foreclose on the mortgage to protect your money.

**WARNING**

## Deceptive gimmicks

Smart financial incentives make deals happen. Improper inducements (you can call them *gimmicks*) waste time and usually result in lower sale prices. Impractical sellers sometimes resort to subterfuge in a futile attempt to disguise how ridiculously overpriced their property actually is. Instead of reducing the asking price to a realistic level, they try in vain to enhance their house's value with gimmicks that fall into one of the following three categories:

>> **Buyer baubles:** "Buy our house, and we'll give you a free week in Paris for two (or a diamond ring, a brand new motorcycle, whatever) to sweeten the deal." Occasionally, sellers make this type of offer in phase one or two of four-phase pricing (explained earlier in this chapter). Sellers erroneously assume that buyers will be so dazzled by the "free" goodies that they won't notice the house's asking price is outrageously high.

TIP

Buyers usually know that the asking price includes a gimmick's cost. They aren't about to add the price of a trip to Paris, for example, into their 30-year mortgage. Opportunities to fly now and pay forever won't sell a house. Neither will drive-now-and-pay-forever deals, or wear-now-and-pay-forever gimmicks. *Buyers aren't stupid.*

>> **Agent payola:** Some sellers offer special inducements, such as trips or double commissions, to the agent who sells their property. These gimmicks are nothing more than blatant bribes for agents to sell their buyers down the river. Good agents categorically reject this kind of sleazy offer.

>> **Contests:** As the California real estate market hit bottom in the mid-1990s, a few desperate sellers decided that, if they couldn't sell their houses, they would give them away in contests. Owners of a $150,000 house, for example, put an ad in the local paper inviting folks who wanted to enter their contest to write a 250-word essay explaining why they wanted to live in the house. Each contestant had to submit a $100 money-order entry fee with the essay. If 1,500 people entered the contest at $100 a pop, the property owners got their asking price. If, however, not enough people entered to make the contest worthwhile, owners reserved the right to cancel the contest and return all entry fees.

WARNING

At least a dozen different California property owners tried variations of the contest gimmick. The ploy was a resounding flop. These contests uniformly drew far too little attention from contestants and far too much attention from state law enforcement personnel concerned about possible violation of California's antigambling statutes. The name of the game is *selling your house, not going to jail!*

REMEMBER

Even if you can find buyers gullible enough to overpay for your house, lenders can't consider the value of gimmicks when appraising property; the mortgage won't be approved if the property is overpriced. The bottom line: Don't waste time and money on gimmicks.

# Overpricing Your House

In a perfect world, your house will sell quickly for top dollar if you faithfully follow our sage advice. By now, however, you've probably discovered that the world is frequently far from perfect, and things don't always go according to plan.

What if you can't sell your house even though you've done everything recommended in this chapter? Did you waste the money you paid for this book? Should you abandon all hope of making a sale? Is it the end of the world as we know it? No. This section can help you understand why no one may have made an acceptable offer for your house.

## Can't sell versus won't sell

The *San Francisco Chronicle* ran a front-page story about a Bay Area house that was sliding down a muddy ridge that had been weakened by torrential rains. Battered by a series of severe storms, the house was slowly cracking in half. Mother Nature was putting the finishing touches on a remodeling job the ill-fated homeowner had started only a few months earlier.

"Can't," used in the context of selling a house, means the property is impossible to sell. Unlike most people who claim they *can't* sell their houses, the poor guy who owned this property really *couldn't* sell it. There's no market for unintentional mobile homes.

Fortunately, the vast majority of homeowners who claim they "can't" sell their houses are exaggerating. They aren't disaster victims whose property values have been abruptly reduced to zero. Usually, plenty of purchasers are willing to buy their houses, and many lenders are ready to make loans to those buyers.

If nothing is physically wrong with their properties, what's the problem? Most of the time, the predicament is because of overpricing camouflaged by denial. A more accurate statement of the situation, for most would-be house sellers, is "We are unwilling to accept the price the market tells us our house is currently worth."

These homeowners *can* sell. They simply *won't* sell. As long as you *choose* not to take the amount that buyers will pay for your house, it will continue to languish unsold on the market. Saying you can't sell your house is a self-fulfilling prophecy.

**REMEMBER**

If your house is under 6 feet of water, has been carried away by a tornado, is now a pile of rubble because of an earthquake, or was ravaged by some other natural disaster, you have a valid reason for saying you can't sell. If not, don't let denial blind you to the truth. You control your fate. You *can* sell your house after you correct the problem that's driving away prospective buyers. Perhaps you didn't follow the advice elsewhere in this book; you may have overimproved your property for the neighborhood, done a poor job of selecting an agent, or failed to properly prepare your house for sale. More often than not, however, the problem is overpricing.

## Three factors all buyers consider

Sooner or later, all buyers hear that the three most important things to consider when buying a home are *location, location, location.* Because you've been through the purchasing process (see Book 2), you know this cliché is a gross oversimplification. Here are the three factors buyers actually consider when selecting a home:

>> **Where the property is:** Okay. The old "location, location, location" adage is one-third true. Urban, suburban, or rural; high in the mountains, smack in the middle of the Great Plains, or by a shining sea; you can't get around the fact that a house's location greatly affects its value. People pay dearly to buy into "good" neighborhoods. Folks buy location every bit as much as houses.

>> **What the property is:** A house's value depends on many factors such as its size, age, condition, and architectural style. The quality of construction materials and interior appointments also enter into property valuation.

>> **How much the property costs:** Whether they're buying the most expensive house on the block or the cheapest, smart buyers try to get the biggest possible bang for their bucks. Furthermore, most people do a heck of a lot of comparison-shopping before they buy just to make sure they don't overpay.

**REMEMBER**

If you're having trouble selling your house, look at it in the same way buyers do. What can you change to bring your house's price in line with a buyer's perception of its value? Analyze your property with these three crucial factors in mind:

>> **Can you change *where* the property is?** Nope. Even if you *could* move the house, the land under it stays put.

>> **Can you change *what* the property is?** Possibly. For example, if a rusted-out car is the focal point of your front yard, hauling the car away will probably improve your prospects for making a sale. Reinspect your property inside and out. Make sure everything is in tip-top condition.

>> **Can you change *how much* the property costs?** Bingo. If you can't change the property's location, and you've done everything you can to prepare your house for sale, what's left to change? The price! Don't feel bad if you unintentionally overprice the property. Anyone can make that mistake. Pricing isn't an exact science.

# Danger signs of overpricing

When you price property correctly, it sells. Conversely, even if your property is in exquisite condition and actively marketed (open houses, classified ads, MLS, website, and so on, as Chapter 4 in Book 6 describes), a dearth of offers indicates it's overpriced. The warning signs of overpricing may include any or all of the following:

>> **No second showings:** Well priced or not, agents and buyers rush to see new listings. Watch out for a precipitous decline in showings after the initial flurry of activity when your house first hits the market. If nobody returns for a second look, you have a problem.

>> **Many showings, but no offers:** Switch hats — suppose you're a buyer. Your agent shows you a three-bedroom, two-bath house for $249,500. Then the agent takes you to a newer four-bedroom, three-bath home just two blocks away — *with the same asking price.* The agent doesn't have to say anything; the difference between price and value is starkly obvious. The first house helps sell the second one.

**TIP**

Your listing agent (if you're selling through a real estate agent) should help other agents route house tours by pointing out overpriced properties the agents can show their buyers *before* bringing them to your well-priced house. Successful agents show buyers OPTs (overpriced turkeys) to sell well-priced houses.

# The foolproof way to correct overpricing

During coauthor Ray's 22 years as an active real estate broker, he managed hundreds of real estate agents and participated directly or indirectly in thousands of sales. Having studied the correlation between asking prices and sale prices through all those years, he made an amazing discovery: Good market or bad, more than 97 percent of all property sells within 10 percent of its final asking price.

Ray's observation doesn't mean that every house starts out with the correct asking price — quite the contrary. Many properties go through a needless series of ineffective price reductions before ultimately arriving at the correct asking price. However, after owners finally reduce their houses' asking prices to within 10 percent of FMV, their properties sell.

**TIP**

If your house hasn't generated any offers, even though it shows wonderfully and is aggressively marketed, update your CMA. You may discover that your house is overpriced by 5 percent, or by 20 percent, or, gasp, by even more. When you update your CMA, consider the following:

>> **It's tough to precisely establish the value of attributes such as proximity to bus lines, wonderful landscaping, and views.** Your listing agent, if you're using one, or you may have given your house's amenities a much higher value than buyers do.

>> **You (or your listing agent) may have put too much emphasis on asking prices or used inaccurate sales data.** Perhaps houses that were on the market when you prepared the CMA ultimately sold for much less than their asking prices. Maybe some sale prices of comparable houses didn't reflect big credits in escrow from sellers to buyers for corrective work or nonrecurring closing costs.

>> **The local real estate market may have gone down the drain.** Did mortgage interest rates skyrocket, or did consumer confidence plummet since the CMA was prepared? Adverse market conditions drag prices down. Find out how many properties similar to yours have sold since your house came on the market. Maybe *nothing* is selling. On the other hand, if comparable houses are selling and yours isn't, put on your hard hat — falling price zone ahead.

>> **You may have missed the prime selling time.** As Chapter 2 in Book 6 discusses, every real estate market has peaks and valleys of sales activity. For example, suppose you base your price on sales made during September and October, when more buyers were active in your area. However, your house went on the market the day after Thanksgiving, after most buyers had vanished. Your timing is awful. To make a sale, you either have to cut your price to the bone or take your house off the market until buyers return in the spring.

**TIP**

Whatever the problem, don't compound it with excessive tenacity. If you haven't gotten any offers after approximately six weeks on the market, and other houses similar to yours are selling all around you, the odds are high that your asking price is *at least* 10 percent more than your house's FMV. Under these circumstances, correct the problem by cutting the price 10 percent. Here's how to maximize the impact of your price reduction:

>> **Bite the bullet and make a full 10 percent cut.** Making a series of smaller price reductions only prolongs the agony. Your property will be forgotten as more and more new listings come on the market. Don't turn your house into "That old thing? Something must be terribly wrong with it. It's been on the market forever."

>> **Use quantum pricing to fine-tune the new price.** Suppose your asking price is $279,500. A 10 percent reduction ($27,950) cuts the price to $251,550, which isn't a smart price. Never leave your asking price dangling just *above* the next quantum. You lose exposure to all the buyers who, for instance, instruct their agents not to show them anything over $250,000. As explained in the earlier section "Quantum pricing: An effective technique," a smarter price is $249,950.

>> **If you still haven't gotten an offer after another six weeks or so of active marketing at the new price, make another 10 percent reduction.** You may have been 20 percent or more over FMV when you put your house on the market. Perhaps you're in a market where prices are declining. If that's the case, the longer you delay a price cut, the greater the gap between your asking price and actual market value.

**TIP**

Six weeks isn't carved in stone. In a hot market, three or four weeks may be more than enough time to give your house maximum buyer exposure. In a slower market (such as the long, hot summer when kids are out of school and many buyers and agents take vacations), you may be wise to wait seven or eight weeks before a price cut. Let local market activity be your guide when you time price reductions.

## Placing the blame where it belongs

Telling sellers that they must cut their asking price if they want to sell is extremely difficult for agents. Many agents can't do it. They're afraid sellers will respond by saying, "This mess is all your fault. We relied on your advice to set the price. A halfway competent agent could've sold our magnificent house months ago. We don't need a price cut; we need a new agent. Get out of our house. Never darken our doorway again. We rue the day we ever met you. Curse you and all your offspring forevermore." Or words to that effect.

Firing the agent may be the correct thing to do. An agent who intentionally overstates your house's value to get the listing deserves to be dumped. By the same token, a likable but inept agent is utterly worthless. You need a good agent, not a fraud or a friendly fool.

Sometimes, however, dumping your agent is like throwing the baby out with the bath water. Perhaps your house is tough to price because it's unique or because no recent comparable sales have occurred in the neighborhood. Maybe the local economy took a nosedive right after your house went on the market. Venting your frustration on the agent for telling the truth won't get your house sold.

# CONCENTRATE ON REAL MONEY

Coauthor Ray had lunch a while ago at Perry's (his favorite San Francisco restaurant) with a friend who was trying to sell her house. Jeannine had a good agent, her house showed well, and the property was being aggressively marketed. But, after more than three months on the market, she had nary a nibble.

"Why hasn't my house sold, Ray? Is my problem the lousy real estate market?"

"Lousy is a matter of opinion, Jeannine. Compared to the hot market several years ago, sellers hate this market. Buyers, on the other hand, love it."

"What can we do? You know that my husband and I paid $425,000 for our house at the height of the boom market, and then spent $50,000 more remodeling it. We put it on the market in January at $495,000. Even though we dropped our asking price to $449,500 in March, we still haven't had even one offer."

"If you can't change what the house is or where it is, what's left to change, Jeannine?"

"Don't say the price, Ray. We're already losing money at $449,500."

"Property values in your neighborhood are nearly 20 percent lower today than they were three years ago when you bought the house, Jeannine. That's a hard, cold fact. Your chances of a break-even sale are no better than my chances of winning the Pulitzer Prize."

"All I can think about is the money we've lost."

"That's the problem, Jeannine. You're concentrating on money you've lost rather than money you still have."

"I don't understand."

"The money you lost when property values fell is gone. You can't get it back. Don't waste time thinking about it. Instead, focus on the money you've still got in the bank. Real money is money you haven't spent yet."

"What do you mean, Ray?"

"You told me how much money you'll save if you move to a community with less expensive housing and public schools to your liking."

"True."

"So every month the house doesn't sell means another raid on the real money in your savings account to pay high housing costs and private school expenses."

"Correct on both counts."

"That's real money you don't have to spend. You can't control the past. You can, however, control your future housing and school costs. Selling the house puts a tourniquet on the money bleeding out of your savings account. You know what you have to do to end this misery. The choice is yours."

Jeannine and her husband tried two more weeks to sell at $449,500, and then cut their asking price to $399,995. They accepted an offer of $395,000 within five days after the price reduction, and closed their sale 30 days later. They recovered the amount they lost as sellers by paying a lower price for their new home in a town with an outstanding public school system.

# Chapter **4**

# Marketing Your House

C urb appeal and staging are important aspects of showing your house off to its best advantage. But, by themselves, curb appeal and staging won't sell your house. Even adding the sophisticated pricing techniques from Chapter 3 in Book 6 to the package still won't do the trick. Regardless of how realistic your asking price may be, you lack one essential ingredient to make a sale.

Face it. Without a buyer, you're nothing more than the owner of a well-priced, bewitchingly staged property with loads of curb appeal. You need a buyer to convert you into a seller, and the best way to do so is to market your house. This chapter can help.

## Advertising That Works

In a red-hot seller's market, just sticking a For Sale sign in your front yard produces all the buyers you need. When you have five buyers for every good property on the market, advertising isn't so critical.

Unfortunately for sellers, the market isn't always hot. In fact, it sometimes gets downright chilly. When your neighborhood is a forest of For Sale signs and buyers are few and exceedingly far between, merely getting a buyer's attention is a major victory. The key to selling your house for top dollar — even in a dismal market — is simple: Implement a broad-based advertising campaign to generate spirited buyer competition for your property.

# INEFFECTIVE ADVERTISING

More than 99 percent of all residential property sold in the United States is marketed using the advertising techniques in this chapter. True, you may need special marketing to sell highly unusual properties, such as a 250-year-old historic house in Olde Cape Cod or an authentic castle that was disassembled stone-by-stone in Ireland and painstakingly reassembled lock, stock, and drawbridge on the vast plains of Texas. However, ordinary advertising techniques work just fine for the rest of us.

It's flattering to hear agents say your house is so special that only a fancy four-color brochure can do it justice. Furthermore, those same agents may say that to get top dollar, your property must be advertised in their international affiliate's glitzy magazine that ends up on coffee tables in Paris, London, Rome, Rio, and other exotic spots around the world. And as soon as you sign on the dotted line to list your house with them, they'll be delighted to get started on the brochure and international advertising program.

You know what's happening. The agents are trying to buy your listing. Before succumbing to their blandishments, ask yourself how often you see people from Paris, London, Rome, and Rio buying houses in your neighborhood. The world's best brochure coupled with a worldwide marketing effort won't sell overpriced property. Nor should you waste your time and money on deceptive marketing gimmicks. As noted in Chapter 3 of Book 6, essay contests don't work. Neither do bribes, such as trips to Tahiti or expensive cars for the buyers of your house or their agent. Stick to the basics; they work.

**REMEMBER**

Advertising isn't a cure-all. Glitzy advertising won't sell a house that's in terrible condition, poorly marketed, and overpriced to boot. Give buyers and agents credit for having a snippet of knowledge about property values and a smidgen of discernment. Think of advertising as the setting for an engagement ring. The world's most beautiful setting can't transform a cheap zircon into a priceless diamond. A stunning setting will, on the other hand, heighten the appeal of an appropriately exquisite diamond.

Whether you list your property with a real estate broker who handles all your advertising or you're selling on your own, the same rules apply. Certain types of advertising are *extremely* effective. Others, while popular, are big wastes of time and money. The following sections describe types of advertising that get our seal of approval.

## For Sale sign

A humble, low-tech For Sale sign stuck in your front yard or nailed to your house is, without a doubt, one of the most effective ways to tell folks looking for a home in your area that your property is on the market.

Real estate brokers know *sign calls* (people calling to get more information about a house after they see the For Sale sign) are far more likely to result in a sale than *ad calls* (people calling about property they read about in an ad). Why? When ad callers find out the location of the advertised property, the style of the house, the age of the house, or some other basic fact they'd already know if they'd actually seen the property from the street, they more often than not reject it. Sign callers, on the other hand, obviously like the neighborhood and at least the property's exterior, or they wouldn't have called; they have a higher probability of being serious buyers.

TIP

Good signs are simple and large enough for people to read easily. They include these elements:

>> The words "For Sale"

>> A phone number to call

>> The phrase "shown by appointment only" (unless you want people dropping in on you unexpectedly at all hours of the day and night)

>> Website link

>> The listing broker's company name (if you're using an agent)

This information is all you need on a sign. To attract folks driving by your house, use a two-sided sign placed perpendicular to the road so people can read it from either direction. If you have a corner lot, use two signs so both streets fronting your house have signs.

Be sure your sign makes a good first impression. Recycling is fine, but don't let your agent reuse someone else's old, beaten-up For Sale sign on your wonderful property; get a spiffy new one. A worn, dented, faded sign makes your property look equally tired. Don't put up the sign before you're 100 percent ready to sell, because after the sign goes up, you *will* start receiving calls.

## Classified ads

The classified section of your local newspaper is a cost-effective way to reach prospective buyers. Because most house hunters look at property on weekends, run an ad in your paper's Sunday real estate section or its weekend edition. If you're handling your own advertising because you're selling your house without a broker, get some tips from the pros. Study real estate brokers' ads for ideas on phrasing your ad. People who work in the classified-ad department usually can help you draft an ad and suggest standard abbreviations — such as "br" for bedroom, "ba" for bathroom, and "fp" for fireplace — so you can save money without confusing readers.

# TROUBLEMAKERS TO AVOID WHEN MARKETING YOUR HOUSE

If you're writing your own ads because you aren't using an agent, don't put *everything* about your property in the ad. For one thing, running a big ad every week is expensive. In addition, describing your property in too much detail isn't smart; good ads always leave out one essential bit of information — such as the address or number of bedrooms — so buyers have to call whomever placed the ad. Real estate agents use ad calls to make showing appointments. If you tell buyers *everything* in your ad, they won't have a reason to call, and you lose the opportunity to convince them to tour your wonderful property.

When you describe your house, failing to disclose information won't get you in trouble as long as you aren't withholding material facts that affect your property's value or desirability. What you do say, however, can turn out to be legally expensive if ever you cross the line between puffery and misrepresentation.

*Puffery* is the exorbitant use of high-sounding adjectives to extol the virtues of otherwise ordinary products. Everything from cars to cleaners is praised as being newer, bigger, faster, better, tastier, smoother, gentler, and, of course, brighter. Fine. Today's consumers are wise enough to make allowances for advertisers' excessive enthusiasm.

As bad as puffery is, misrepresentation is far worse. Folks can, after all, defend themselves against puffery because they can see reality with their own eyes. People know the difference between spacious and tiny no matter what the ad says.

*Misrepresentation* deals with factors that aren't readily apparent. For example, suppose you're selling a house that appears to be in excellent shape. The buyer asks you if the roof leaks. If you say it doesn't leak when you know for a fact the roof *does* leak, that's out-and-out intentional misrepresentation — fraud. If the buyers don't have the roof inspected because they rely on your statement about the roof, they'll probably do two things after the first big rainstorm hits their new home — buy a new roof and sue you. *Never assume anything.* "I don't know" is a perfectly acceptable and absolutely safe response to any question you can't answer with complete certainty — *never, never guess.*

How can you protect yourself from inadvertent misrepresentation? Here are ten troublemakers to avoid when writing your ad:

- **All:** Absolutes such as *completely, totally, perfect, none, entirely,* and *fully* are equally naughty. They should be avoided because they leave no room for exceptions, errors, or discrepancies. "All hardwood floors," "completely remodeled," and "totally renovated" are phrases that can lead to a lawsuit if the buyer finds *one thing* that disproves your all-inclusive language. When that happens, your property isn't as advertised.

- **Custom-built:** The *American Heritage Dictionary* defines this as "built according to the specifications of the buyer." Was your house built to your specifications? This term doesn't apply to a home where the developer created a plan and reproduced it multiple times. Custom-built is only applicable to a made-to-order, one-of-a-kind home.

- **Fixed:** When used to describe corrective work done over the years, "fixed" leads many buyers to incorrectly believe a problem was *permanently* rectified. A leaky roof, for example, is never "fixed." Trust us, the roof *will* leak again sooner or later, and when it does, the buyer will sue. Instead of saying the leak was fixed, say it was "repaired."

- **Never:** Just as dangerous as being too expansive is the tendency to deny that something can ever occur. "There has never been a problem with (fill in the blank)" has come back to haunt many a seller when the friendly next-door neighbor tells the new owner about that one time there was a problem with the sewer overflowing, flooding, high winds, elephant stampedes, and so on.

- **New:** What's new? Cars technically stop being new the moment they're driven away from the car dealership. There isn't such a fine dividing line in real estate, but there's logic you can apply. After appliances have been used, they're no longer new. A roof is only new for a brief time after installation. Trying to be cute by saying "newer" begs the question "Newer than what?" It's best to truthfully state when appliances were installed or a repair took place. Rather than saying "new roof," use the phrase "new roof installed (date of installation)."

- **Panoramic:** Although views from a house may be great, they're seldom an unlimited view in all directions, which is the true definition of panoramic. Unless the house is located at the top of a hill with a 360-degree view of everything around it, this term should be avoided. Words like *breathtaking, sweeping, grand,* and *awesome* are preferable.

- **People:** Avoid describing the neighbors or the "ideal" future owner. Just because you get along wonderfully with your neighbors doesn't mean the next owner will. Your idea of the ideal future owner is subjective. Litigation lurks.

- **Quiet:** This seemingly innocuous word has triggered considerable litigation. In one case, the cul de sac in which a house was located was always quiet in the winter when the real estate agent saw the property. It was anything but quiet in the spring after escrow closed when the marching band began practicing in the football field behind the house. Quiet is subjective. For some people, hearing *any* noise at all means the area isn't quiet.

*(continued)*

*(continued)*

- **Safe:** Make no promise of safety or security. No matter how safe you think the neighborhood is or how secure the "child-safe pool cover" is supposed to be, bad things can and do happen. There's no guarantee of safety or security.

- **Square footage:** Three appraisers can measure a house and get three completely different square footages. Always preface any mention of square footage with a word such as *approximately, nearly, about,* or *around* to allow for error or lack of precision. Approximately 2,300 square feet is safer than 2,320 square feet. If you must use a precise number, cite the source of your information (per tax records, assessor's records, and so on).

  Kip Oxman, an attorney, suggests using the following disclaimer when stating square footage: "If actual square footage is material to Buyer's decision to offer to purchase the subject property, Buyer should verify the square footage before making the offer. Although approximate square footage measurements according to tax records, or reported in previous appraisals, are sometimes available and are useful as informational guidelines, such numbers are frequently inaccurate. Seller can't guarantee the measurements of others."

  The best ads are masterpieces of understatement. Ideally, you want to describe your property in such a way that it actually delivers more — not less — than the ads promise. No one ever complains about that.

**TIP**

Thanks to the ubiquitous Internet, you may get an even bigger bang for your classified advertising buck. Most newspapers automatically put classified ads on their websites, so potential buyers from all around the world can look for a house with the click of a mouse. Check to see whether your local paper offers this benefit.

## Multiple listing service (MLS)

A multiple listing service (MLS) is composed of and operated by local real estate brokers and agents who pool their listings so information about property listed by any MLS member is immediately available to all participating members. Brokers and agents enter new listings into their computerized MLS database as soon as the listing contract is signed. Price changes and sales also are same-day entries. In most places, nonmembers (that is, the public) can't put property into an MLS.

**TIP**

If your property is listed with a real estate broker, insist that it be put into the MLS. An MLS listing gives your property wide exposure to a potent pool of market-educated buyers currently working with all other MLS members. If you're selling without an agent, consider paying a discount broker to put your property into the MLS. If you use the MLS, you *must* offer a commission to a cooperating broker who procures a buyer for your property.

# Listing statement

The *listing statement*, also called a *property statement*, is a data sheet and is given to people who tour your property on Sunday open houses or people who are shown through your house by appointment. Listing statements are effective point-of-purchase ads containing more information than you can put into a newspaper ad or an MLS listing (see Figure 4-1). This sheet offers you a chance to wax poetic about the special features of your property.

---

## PIONEER REALTY

**One Main Street, Yourtown**

**Serving the area since 1776**

Abstract: Lovingly maintained three bedroom, two bath home close to excellent schools, #4 bus line, shopping & just one block from Mountain Lake Park. Living room with fireplace, formal dining room, cook's kitchen, den, two car garage & garden. Built 1952.

Address: 1415 Poplar Lane                          Lot Size: 25' X 120'

List Price: $349,500                               Lot: 24    Block: 5724

### Gardener's Delight

Spacious master bedroom with walk-in closet and adjoining master bath. Two smaller bedrooms have been recently painted. Bathrooms are older, in good shape & waiting for new owner's special touch.

Gracious living room has working fireplace with gas starter. Large formal dining room features a built-in curio cabinet & hardwood floors. Adjoining the dining room is a cheery den with windows that overlook the patio & garden.

Kitchen has a chef-efficient layout with ample cabinets and counterspace. Refrigerator, gas range & dishwasher are included in the sale. Adjacent to the kitchen is a nook currently being used as a computer work space.

Directly outside the kitchen is an herb garden that leads to the meticulously maintained, fenced garden. Plantings include: oak & apple trees, roses, numerous perennial plantings, daffodil & tulip bulbs, which provide a riot of color in the spring & summer.

Full basement and insulated attic provide additional storage space. The two-car garage has overhead storage, bicycle & ski racks as well as a work bench & intercom to the kitchen.

To Show: By appointment with Listing Agent
Roland Jadryev                777. 777. 7777
E-Mail:                       Roland@wagontrain.net

*The information contained herein has either been given to us by the owner of the property or obtained from sources that we deem reliable. We have no reason to doubt its accuracy, but we do not guarantee it. The prospective buyer should carefully verify all information contained herein. Taxes will be reassessed upon sale. Prospective purchasers are advised to review the "Real Estate Transfer Disclosure Statement" on file with this office prior to making an offer.*

**FIGURE 4-1:** Here's what a good listing statement looks like.

**TIP**

To satisfy buyers with short attention spans and too much to do, include an abstract to *briefly* give basic facts about your property. The headline, "Gardener's Delight" in the listing statement in Figure 4-1, emphasizes the property's hot button. A good listing statement takes people through your house room-by-room, pointing out special features they may not notice, such as the working fireplace with gas starter, the built-in curio cabinet, personal property such as fireplace tools included in the sale, garden plantings, and the intercom system. A few other tips to remember when writing your listing statement include the following:

>> Don't use fancy 17-syllable words when simple ones will do.

>> Avoid rhetorical overstatement, such as "world's most fantastic view" or "extraordinarily enormous living room."

>> Keep the write-up short — one page maximum.

>> *Always* include a disclaimer similar to the one included at the bottom of the sample listing statement in Figure 4-1.

**REMEMBER**

The best way to avoid getting sued because your house is smaller than you claimed it was is to avoid giving *any* personal opinions about square footages unless you're absolutely, positively, 100 percent certain sure about the measurements. If you're inadvertently a few square feet shy of the square footage you stated, you could end up being sued by a nit-picky buyer with a tape measure and too much spare time. Actual square footage is less important than your buyers' conclusion that your house is big enough based on *their* visual inspection.

## Computers

In addition to the computerized MLS, brokers have websites they use to advertise their listings. As previously noted in the earlier section "Classified ads," most newspapers put classified ads on the Internet so computer users can access them without having to dirty their fingers with newsprint.

## Word of mouth

Word-of-mouth advice sounds so darn primitive coming right after "Computers" in the preceding section, but networking is an extremely effective form of targeted advertising. Tell people you know — friends, business associates, folks who go to your church, club members, and especially your neighbors, that your house is for sale. Make a point of inviting your friends and neighbors to your first open house. Who knows? One of them may have a pal who'd love to buy your house. Stranger things happen every day.

# HOT BUTTONS

If you want to be a successful seller, figure out exactly what you have to sell *before* you start advertising. People don't buy houses. They buy hot buttons and the house tags along.

Hot buttons vary from one house to the next. Gourmet kitchens, luxurious bathrooms, sensuous bedrooms, working fireplaces, panoramic views, and lovely gardens are turn-ons. So are huge walk-in closets — no one ever has enough closet space. In densely populated metropolitan areas like New York, Boston, and San Francisco, where parking spaces are slightly scarcer than Hope diamonds, garages can help sell houses. Location is a hot button if folks will buy a mediocre house to live in a superb neighborhood or to get their kids into a good school system.

Good agents see houses through the eyes of their owners. If you're working with an agent to sell your house, the agent will want to know about the property features that most appealed to you when you bought it. Whatever you liked when you first saw the house will most likely also be the next buyer's hot button.

For example, suppose your favorite part of the house is the master bedroom with a charming little fireplace. You love watching the firelight dance on the walls and hearing the fire snap and pop as you nod off to sleep on cold winter nights. If that's your house's strongest feature, then guess which attribute is emphasized in the listing statement, the MLS write-up, and your weekly newspaper ads.

For Sunday open houses and broker tours, the master bedroom is filled with fresh flowers and a small fire crackles in the fireplace. Private showings of your house to prospective buyers always end, not by coincidence, in the master bedroom because that room has the greatest emotional impact on buyers. In fact, the master bedroom is the closing room where agents working with motivated buyers first suggest writing up an offer on the house.

This approach doesn't mean that the listing agent ignores the rest of your house. Everything is, of course, staged to show beautifully. But smart sellers and agents push the hot button because that feature is probably the reason the next owners will buy the property.

# Arranging Open Houses

If a picture is worth a thousand words, personally touring property must be worth at least a couple of encyclopedias. That's why, in a touchy-feely business like residential real estate sales, open houses are an invaluable sales tool.

You can hold two distinctly different types of open houses to sell your property. Even though each type of open house targets a different market segment, they share a common objective — to sell your property. This section focuses on your two options.

## Brokers' opens

If you hire a broker to sell your house, one of the first things your listing agent does after you've signed the listing contract is tell the local brokerage community about your property. One extremely effective way to get the word out is scheduling a *brokers' open* — a special open house exclusively for local real estate agents.

Agents generally work with at least four or five *serious* buyers at any given time. After these buyers have, for one reason or another, seen and rejected all the houses of interest to them that currently are on the market, they go into a holding pattern waiting for a listing of just the right property. One primary mission of agents working with buyers is to scout out new property.

A brokers' open is amazingly targeted marketing. No guarantees, of course, but don't be surprised if the first brokers' open leads to a sale. After all, having 50 agents tour your house is the equivalent of showing it to 200 or 250 *motivated* buyers.

Although your house obviously won't appeal to every one of the agents' buyers, you can bet it'll press hot buttons for a few of them. Well-priced, attractive property almost always generates immediate showing requests. With the advent of cellphones, agents don't even have to wait until they get back to the office to call their clients about the fantastic property (yours, we hope) that they just saw on a brokers' tour.

**TIP**

Most areas designate one particular day each week as Brokers' Tour Day, the day on which agents and brokers tour newly listed properties. If many new listings enter the market the week of your first brokers' open, some agents won't see your property because of scheduling conflicts with brokers' opens on other houses. Even if only a few new listings are available when your property hits the market, some agents won't see your house because they're on vacation, have offers to present, have escrows to close, or are holding other houses open themselves. Whatever the reason, the way around scheduling conflicts is to be sure that your listing agent schedules at least two brokers' opens.

# Weekend open houses

Folks usually think of public open houses as *Sunday* open houses. That idea is prevalent because most houses are held open on Sundays. However, no law says you can't hold a Saturday open house every now and then to scoop up people who can't come to a Sunday open house. For that matter, you might also hold an open house on a Monday or Thursday evening after people get home from work. There are no rules here. Don't be afraid to get creative. Having planted that thought in your mind, we refer to all public open houses from now on as Sunday open houses for simplicity's sake.

Compared to brokers' opens (see the preceding section), you have lower odds of making a sale directly by holding a Sunday open house. But if you're trying to sell your house without an agent, you won't have access to brokers' opens.

After you open your house to the world at large, not everyone who walks through the front door is a legitimate buyer. You get Lookie Lou types who are trying to pick up some decorating hints and curious neighbors who always wanted to know how your house looks on the inside. You also get real buyers who were attracted by your open house sign but need a home in a different size or price range. Unfortunately, other than an address, open house signs don't contain a wealth of specific information to help qualify prospective buyers.

The incidental traffic isn't necessarily bad for you. Unless your visitors are terribly antisocial, people who come to your Sunday open houses probably have friends or neighbors who want to buy in the neighborhood. Word of mouth *is* powerful advertising (as noted earlier in this chapter).

**WARNING**

In a perfect world, nobody steals. Unfortunately, the world isn't perfect. Leaving small, easily portable valuables lying around during open houses is an open invitation to thieves. Either put expensive jewelry, precious coins, rare stamps, and your other small valuable items into a safe deposit box or figure out another place to put them so they are out of harm's way. Go through your medicine cabinets. Remove any medications that may be of interest to a thief. If you expect a great many visitors, see whether your listing agent can get another agent to help with your open house. One agent can show people through your house while the other stays at the front door to greet visitors, get names, answer basic questions, and, last but not least, watch for folks leaving the house with suspicious bulges.

# Showing Your Property

No one will buy your property sight unseen. Luscious listing statements, appealing ads, and inviting photographs of your house's interior and exterior fan the flames of buyer curiosity. To satisfy the inquisitiveness that you arouse, you must let prospective buyers wander through your house.

If you list your house with a real estate agent, showings are an inconvenience rather than a problem because a good agent handles the actual buyer and broker showings for you. Your job is simple. Make sure the property is staged to show well — no dirty dishes in the dishwasher, toilet lids closed, lights on — and make yourself scarce while the property is being shown.

## Preshowing preparations

If you don't know exactly how to generate property curb appeal and subtly stage your house, turn to Chapter 4 in Book 3 for the details. This section covers a few final things you must do to maximize the showing process:

**TIP**

>> **Make showing your property easy for agents:** The easier your house is to show, the more often agents will show it, and, most likely, the more you'll get for your house and the faster it'll sell. If you force agents to get a house key from you before each showing, you'll have fewer showings because some agents are too busy to get the key and others are too lazy. Instead of personally doling out your key each time there's a showing, you have two options:

- Give the listing agent a key if your house is only shown by appointment.

- Have your agent put a house key in a lockbox that agents open by using a special lockbox key or electronically coded lockbox card.

**REMEMBER**

From an agent's perspective, nothing is more embarrassing or frustrating than trying to explain to an antsy buyer the reason the front door can't be unlocked. Before you give the listing agent keys to your house, make sure that the keys actually unlock the door and that the lock works smoothly. (This is your chance to make a good first impression on the buyer.) Lastly, if the house has an alarm, make sure it's disarmed or that the showing agent knows how to turn off the alarm.

>> **Make yourself scarce during showings:** If you have a listing agent, leave the property while your agent shows it. Some buyers are too polite to say so, but having you hover over them as they tour your house is *very* inhibiting. Serious buyers want to look into all your closets and cabinets, look under all your

sinks, and explore every nook and cranny of the house — but they won't if you're hanging around.

By the same token, as long as you're around, buyers won't make derogatory comments. Sometimes, the most important information you get from a showing is the reason why someone *doesn't* like the property. Correcting a problem or overcoming an objection starts by finding out about the problem or objection. Your agent should follow up *every* showing by calling the buyer's agent to find out whether the buyer intends to make an offer and, if not, why not.

**TIP**

You can't vanish during showings or open houses if you're selling without an agent. Try, however, to be as unobtrusive as possible when buyers tour your property. For example, don't walk them through the house pointing out the obvious: "This is the kitchen. Here's the bathroom. This bedroom is where the kids sleep." Instead, point out special things they may not notice, such as the high ceiling in your dining room or the fact that a hardwood floor is under the wall-to-wall carpet in the family room. Make your points selectively and remember the quality of your guidance is more important than the quantity.

>> **Get used to living in a fishbowl:** If you follow the sage advice in this book, your house will sell quickly for top dollar. However, the sale probably won't *seem* quick. The best proof of the relativity of time is living in a house that's for sale and may be shown any time of the day or, within reasonable limits, night. You can't ever leave the bathtub dirty or dishes in the sink or clothes on the bedroom floor or cook liver and onions or lounge around in your bathrobe on Sunday morning. Be of good faith. This, too, shall pass.

## The final showing

You may think you've been put out of your misery after you accept an offer to purchase your property. "Goody," you say, "no more showings — I can have my life back."

Not quite. Inspections by the buyer's property inspectors aside, one extremely important showing remains: the inspection an appraiser makes as a condition of your buyer's loan approval.

This final showing to the appraiser is *critically* important. If the buyer's loan isn't approved because the appraiser thinks your property isn't worth the amount the buyer is willing to pay for it, your deal falls through, and you're back in the fishbowl again.

TIP

Take these two steps to prevent an appraiser from undervaluing your house:

>> **Shower the appraiser with attention and comps.** Your agent (or you, if you're selling your house yourself) should be present during the appraiser's property inspection to "sell" your house one last time. In addition to pointing out to the appraiser each and every valuable feature of your house and the neighborhood, your agent can give the appraiser an *updated* copy of the comparable market analysis (see Chapter 2 in Book 2) originally used to establish your asking price. The appraiser can use the comparable sales data to justify the sale price.

>> **Spiff up your house one more time.** Appraisers are *supposedly* above being influenced by a house's appearance. *Theoretically,* appraisers won't get a bad impression if your property looks lived in. Sure. No matter what appraisers say, they are human. Perfectly staging your house one last time almost certainly makes a favorable impression on the appraiser. And if you're going for a record sale price in your neighborhood, every little bit helps. One thing's for sure — it certainly can't hurt.

## LOCKBOXES VERSUS SHOWN-BY-APPOINTMENT ARRANGEMENTS

Depending on the location of your property, you may have to use a lockbox. If, for example, your property is 50 miles from the nearest town or located in a scenic but remote area, you may not have a viable alternative to a lockbox.

From the standpoint of making your property easy to show, lockboxes are great. Newer, electronic lockboxes contain a computer chip that maintains a record of which agent's lockbox card was used to open the box as well as the date and time the property was shown. Some lockboxes also have a lockout feature that limits key access to certain hours so that you can have some privacy every now and then. Super-sophisticated lockboxes can even be programmed with a call-before-showing code that forces agents to call the listing agent to get an additional code to enter the property.

But even the most sophisticated lockbox in the world still has drawbacks. Lockboxes can't straighten up your house before a showing; tell you which agent let Duke, the wonder cat, out of the house; point a finger at the agent who forgot to lock your front door after a showing; or, most important of all, help sell your house to buyers.

Houses can't speak for themselves. That's why, if humanly possible, your listing agent should be present every time your house is shown — to answer buyer questions, point out special features about your property and the neighborhood, and keep an eye on your pet and your valuables.

# 7

# Gone Global: Investing in International Real Estate

# Contents at a Glance

# Chapter **1**

# Introducing International Investment Strategies

R eal estate is an asset that pretty much anyone can understand. Unlike the more complex worlds of stocks, bonds, retirement savings, and the like, real estate is a rare type of investment because it's something you have an inherent basic understanding of. It's what you live in and vacation in, day in and day out. You already know what makes a home attractive, inviting, and desirable. You already have a good understanding of your local real estate market, because you've already bought or rented in that market. In other words, you get it.

Real estate is the natural choice for many investors. They're initially attracted by

» Relatively fewer market fluctuations compared to, say, twitchy and volatile stock exchanges

» Healthy cash flow with regular income coming your way

>> The ability to achieve capital growth (by selling a property and pocketing the profit) on top of a steady income

>> The potential to be fairly hands off and earn "passive" income

However, just because you understand real estate doesn't mean you'll be a successful real estate investor, especially on the international stage. You won't achieve financial security and real wealth by renting out one property; to be successful and secure, you need to build a diverse portfolio of real estate investments and develop an understanding of the full range of real estate strategies on offer. This chapter explains what that means in practice.

# Taking Your Real Estate Investments to the Next Level

Many books out there show you how to rent a property and become a landlord, including the latest edition of *Landlord's Legal Kit For Dummies* by Lawrence C. Harmon, JD, and Robert S. Griswold, MBA, MSBA (Wiley). That's not the goal in this chapter. (You can flip to Chapter 5 in Book 1 for an introduction, though.)

This chapter is designed to help you go beyond the basics so that you can progress as an investor and grow your real estate portfolio — wherever you are in the world and wherever you want to invest.

## Comparing property to other asset classes

**REMEMBER**

Lots of folks believe that real estate is a much better, much more achievable route to wealth than, say, stocks or bonds. That's because property is

>> **Tangible:** You can literally touch bricks and mortar, which, for many people, makes it easier to understand.

>> **Highly controllable:** You have total control over your strategy, the properties you buy, the location you buy in, and the types of tenants you decide to target. With other asset classes, you may not get the same level of control (for example, in the case of a fund investment, someone else will be making the investment decisions for you).

>> **More accessible in terms of knowledge:** Most people have a pretty good basic understanding of property.

>> **More accessible in terms of money:** You need serious capital if you want to make serious money with stocks. But with property, you can deploy a variety of strategies with little upfront capital, and leverage is available (in the form of mortgages and loans) to help you gear up.

>> **Less vulnerable to short-term market risk:** Because you're in control, you can shift your strategy and make different investment decisions in line with what's happening in the market. If you take a longer-term view (which is sensible in property investment), then the market fluctuations are more likely to iron themselves out over time with the inherent underlying asset still holding significant value even in "bad times."

But even though property is, for many people, head and shoulders above other types of investments, the comparison is useful because it reminds you that property is, above all, an *asset*. Real estate investments should be selected with all the care and attention that a stock investor uses when assessing which companies to invest in — and should be managed extremely carefully, like a diligent trader keeping a watchful eye on the markets.

**REMEMBER**

An asset is only an asset if it makes you money. If it's not making you money, it's a drain on your finances, time, and energy — in other words, it's a liability. Just like any other asset class, if you neglect your investment, take your eye off the ball, and become complacent, a property can become a liability pretty quickly. In practice, that means if you mismanage a property or neglect it to a point where people no longer want to live in it, you'll have a liability on your hands.

## Going beyond fixer-uppers and straightforward buy-to-rents

So, what's wrong with fixing up and flipping a property (see Book 4) or owning one rental property as a retirement nest egg? Absolutely nothing at all. Done well, flipping is a decent way to make some short-term profit, and renting out a property as a standard single rental (rented to one tenant or one family) will bring in a regular monthly income with little effort required.

But if you want to become a serious real estate investor, perhaps to the point where you can afford to give up your day job and concentrate on your real estate business, owning one rental property or flipping a house once in a while isn't going to cut it. You're going to have to dream bigger.

## Introducing multi-tenant strategies

You can grow your portfolio by having 12 properties that you rent out to 12 families or individuals. That's certainly one way to grow. But is it the smartest way? Maybe not. If you instead rented out your property on a room-by-room basis to young professionals or students, you'd earn significantly more rental income than you would on a standard single rental. Multiply that by multiple properties and you're really cooking.

For example, say you have a three-bedroom house that you rent to a nice young couple. You're earning $1,000 per month from your rental, and it requires little effort from you to keep the income coming in.

Now, imagine that same house is turned into a four-bedroom house for young professionals to share (four bedrooms because you've turned the dining room into an extra rental bedroom to maximize income). And each tenant is paying you $500 a month for a room. Now you have $2,000 per month coming in.

Sure, it's a little more work to find and manage four tenants than it is to deal with one nice young couple, but in return for that little bit of extra effort, you've doubled your rental income. And that's without making expensive upgrades to the property.

## Exploring other high-earning strategies

Multi-tenant strategies are a great way to turbo-boost your income, which allows you to grow your portfolio more quickly. But there are also plenty of other strategies on the table to maximize your income.

For example, you could invest in apartments that are rented as serviced accommodation by the night (like an Airbnb; see Book 5). You'll earn significantly more in rental income than renting out the same apartments on standard 12-month contracts (albeit it with higher costs and a higher risk of *void periods*, where the property sits empty).

Some of the strategies in this chapter will be more appealing to you than others. Some will play to your strengths. And some will work better in your chosen location than others. The critical thing is to be aware of the wide range of options available to you as a real estate investor, so that you give yourself the best chance of building a successful real estate portfolio and achieving your goals. This chapter gives you that grounding, so that you can build a portfolio that's right for you and your needs.

# Focusing on Investment Strategies That You Can Use Internationally

The vast majority of real estate books are entirely focused on one country's real estate market, typically the United States or the United Kingdom. They go into great detail on filing your tax return and understanding local property management regulations to the point that the guidance is unusable outside that market and the book is out of date within a year as the tax rules and property regulations evolve.

**TECHNICAL STUFF**

This approach has always puzzled coauthor Nicholas. As someone who runs his real estate portfolio as a serious business, he's not going to be poring over tax guidelines and filing his own tax returns. That's not the best use of his time as a business owner. Instead, he works with an awesome accountant and tax advisor who can help him manage his tax position and finances in the most efficient way.

What's more, most real estate strategies can be used successfully in a huge range of countries around the world, and in fact, lots of investors are actively drawn to the idea of investing overseas. Whether it's the thought of more affordable house prices, exciting returns delivered by emerging markets, or just a passion for a particular country or region, real estate markets around the world have been attracting overseas buyers for years.

Chapter 2 in Book 7 helps you decide whether you should invest in your home country or internationally. As part of this decision-making process, you may

>> Start with a real estate strategy that appeals to you and then investigate the best market for you to deploy that strategy (not forgetting the fact that the best market may well be your domestic one).

>> Start from a passion or personal interest in a specific country (again, your passion may lie close to home), and then spend time getting to know that market to find the most suitable strategy or strategies for that area.

If, after careful consideration, you do decide to invest in property overseas, expert local help will be vital. You'll need to build a network of trustworthy, reliable experts who can help you manage your portfolio and individual properties. The real estate–focused experts that you'll need to call upon may include the following:

>> **Mortgage broker:** A mortgage broker can help you find the right financing when you're ready to buy a new property.

>> **Tax advisor:** Real estate investments can have tax implications, and a good tax advisor will be able to explain the impact for you.

>> **Independent financial advisor:** This person can offer unbiased financial guidance, looking at the big picture of your finances, not just your real estate investments.

>> **Real estate lawyer:** You need someone who specializes in real estate to handle all the legal aspects of buying and selling properties.

>> **Real estate agent:** A real estate agent can help you find the right property opportunities when you're looking to buy, as well as help you sell the property when you're ready to unload it.

>> **Property manager:** If you're renting the property, a property manager can take care of finding tenants and managing the property on your behalf (collecting rent, handling repairs, and so on).

>> **Insurance agent:** Find an agent who specializes in real estate insurance to make sure you're properly covered.

>> **Architect:** If you're looking to renovate your properties, an architect will help with floor plans and elevation design drawings.

>> **Planning consultant:** A planning consultant can advise you on local planning laws and building codes and explain where you need permission or permits for building work or alterations.

>> **General building contractors and tradespeople (plumbers, electricians, and so on):** These experts will help you build, convert, develop, and maintain your properties. Your own team will scale up as your portfolio grows.

>> **Translator:** You'll need a translator for overseas investments where you aren't fluent in the local language.

Check out the nearby sidebar "Getting the most out of your dream team" for details on working effectively with experts, even when they're in a different country.

## GETTING THE MOST OUT OF YOUR DREAM TEAM

When you find the right people for your dream team, you want to keep them. So you need to maintain and nurture those working relationships and ensure things run as smoothly as possible. This means the following:

- **Keep in touch regularly.** This oils the wheels of communication and helps to build rapport.

- **Be absolutely clear about your expectations.** Agree upfront what work you want done and to what standard.

- **Review your arrangement regularly (at least every six months, more regularly in the early days).** If anything isn't working for you, address it head on and try to find a solution.

- **Treat your team members' time as carefully as your own.** That means not wasting people's time or calling them at 10 p.m. to ask something that can easily wait until the next day.

- **Talk about your future plans for growth.** This helps build trust and rapport, but it also serves a more practical purpose. If your dream teamers have an idea of your future aspirations, they'll be more invested in the success of your portfolio and can keep you informed on potential opportunities they've heard about on the grapevine.

- **Promote your contacts around your network.** Providing there's no conflict of interest, why not recommend your dream teamers to others in your network? Referrals work both ways. So, if you're happily recommending your tax advisor to your contacts, they'll be more likely to do the same for you among their own networks.

- **Always say thank you for a job well done.** Showing your appreciation provides a welcome boost to motivation and morale.

# Running Your Property Portfolio as a Business

The fact that you've turned to this chapter says that your ambitions go beyond holding one or two investment properties as a little retirement nest egg. You're looking to build a serious real estate portfolio — potentially including international investments — and generate real wealth and financial independence.

That means you need to think of yourself as a professional real estate investor and run your portfolio as a proper business. It's not a side project. It's not something you dabble in. It's a professionally run operation, and you're the entrepreneur at the helm.

Some of the key aspects of running your portfolio as a business include

>> **Focusing on passive income, wherever possible:** If you're doing this to escape the rat race and be free to live life your way, the last thing you want is to be working 14 hours a day managing your properties. So, as your portfolio grows, you may want to think about automating and delegating tasks when you can, just as the CEO of a company does.

>> **Having the right people (you can call it your "dream team" of experts), business processes, and tools in place:** This enables you to make sure your business runs like a well-oiled machine. You can find a list of needed experts in the earlier section "Focusing on Investment Strategies That You Can Use Internationally."

>> **Future-proofing and protecting your business against market changes:** You can do this by building a varied, robust portfolio of investments. There's more on this coming up later in this chapter.

>> **Cultivating the right habits for success:** If you create the right mindset for success, through positive habits like networking, educating yourself, thinking positive thoughts, setting goals, meditating, and so on, you've got a strong foundation that'll serve you well on your entrepreneurial journey.

You'll also need to manage your finances (both everyday cash flow and ways to finance your investments) as strictly as any business.

# Getting Your Financial Ducks in a Row

Your real estate portfolio may not really take off until you begin to fully grasp and take advantage of the full range of financing options and products that are available to investors. The following sections give you the scoop.

## Understanding financing options and valuation

Chapter 4 in Book 1 explores traditional financing options, like mortgages. These are typically the first considerations for most investors, but there are other, much more creative routes to financing your investments.

For example, if you have little upfront capital for a deposit on a mortgage, or you're investing in a nonstandard project that main-street lenders won't touch, you need to be able to think outside the box and find other means of financing your projects if you don't want to miss out on great opportunities. What's more, being fully aware of the wide range of financing options can enable you to move faster and secure financing quicker than other buyers — which is handy in a fast-moving market or when you're up against other investor buyers.

Less traditional, yet still entirely achievable, financing options include joint ventures, private lending, and crowdfunding. All these options are about investing with other people's money (OPM). Technically, even a regular mortgage is just another form of OPM, but with these more creative options, you're generally approaching partners and private lenders directly, rather than going to the bank. This creative route is about building win-win partnerships with fellow investors that will hopefully lead to many other successful projects in the future.

TIP

Whatever financing route you choose, it's really important to get a good handle on property valuation or real estate appraisals. Knowing which valuation method a particular lender is using can make all the difference when you're searching for the most appropriate financing. Head to Chapter 2 in Book 2 for more on determining a house's worth.

## Getting the expert help you need

Whenever you're considering your finance options, you should work with an expert, independent broker. Having a great broker on your side will save you time, money, and many, many headaches over the years — a good broker will not only help you evaluate financing options and narrow down the field of lenders, but also help you pull together and file the necessary paperwork. A good broker is worth their weight in gold.

So, too, is an accountant and/or tax advisor who specializes in real estate investments and who understands your goals. They'll be able to help you stay on top of your cash flow, manage costs, and ensure that your real estate portfolio is as financially efficient as possible — a lean, mean, profit-producing machine, if you will.

# Blending Real Estate Strategies to Create a More Robust Portfolio

Real estate is generally seen as a safe bet, investment-wise ("safe as houses" as the saying goes), but property markets are subject to change and fluctuations, just as any market is. Sure, the fluctuations in the real estate market may be less pronounced and unpredictable than, say, stock exchanges, but they can still hit an investor hard.

REMEMBER

That's why, over the course of your real estate career, you'll ideally look to build a varied real estate portfolio that isn't reliant on one strategy alone. Why? Because a varied portfolio is more robust and better able to withstand market blips or changes.

If a local bubble bursts, for example, and you're not able to sell a property that you've refurbished, your immediate cash flow will suffer enormously. But if you have some income-generating rental properties as part of your portfolio, you'll be able to keep the lights on (quite literally) until the market for sales recovers.

REMEMBER

Broadly speaking, real estate investment strategies can be broken down into two categories. Ultimately, both categories may form part of your portfolio:

>> **Shorter-term strategies that are designed to deliver periodic capital growth:** Property development, assuming the property is sold for a profit after the development is finished, is an ideal example of this.

>> **Longer-term strategies that center on owning or controlling a property for the long haul so that you can earn a regular income from it:** Residential rental properties are the prime example of this.

The following sections give you a brief overview of specific real estate strategies, from developing properties to running vacation rentals. These strategies are best for maximizing returns and creating a varied, healthy portfolio.

## Keeping an open mind about different strategies

REMEMBER

Before you get to the strategies themselves, here's a pro tip: Even if a strategy isn't right for you at this point in your investment career, don't discard it from your memory altogether. Successful real estate investing is often a case of pairing the right strategy with certain scenarios or potential clients (or buyers or investors) as they come your way. So, just knowing that a strategy exists can be valuable to you — you never know when an opportunity to use that knowledge will arise.

Here's a great example of what this means: Say you've been sourcing development opportunities to turn into luxury family homes. As part of your search, you come across some properties that perhaps aren't right for your needs, but the sellers are motivated so you file them and their properties away in your brain under "could be useful for the future."

Two weeks later, you're chatting with a fellow investor at one of your regular networking events, and discover this investor is interested in a certain type of property — and, thanks to your recent research, you have just the right sort of properties in mind. You can potentially act as a buyer's agent (subject to licensing rules that may apply in your country), and help pair this buyer with the right property, for a fee.

If you hadn't been aware of the buyer's agent strategy, in this case, you may have missed out on an opportunity to deepen your relationship with your fellow investor (which can, in turn, lead to other projects in the future) and earn a commission in the process.

So, be sure to keep an open mind about the various strategies as you read this chapter. Just because something isn't suitable for your portfolio right now doesn't mean it won't work for you in future.

## Incorporating shorter-term strategies into your portfolio

A large part of becoming a successful, profitable real estate entrepreneur is the ability to *add value* to a property. Property development is a great way to add value.

### Developing for success

*Property development* can mean many things, but it commonly refers to physically improving a property by renovating it so that it's worth more or adding value to a plot of land by building a property or properties on it.

However, property development can also cover changing the use of a property, such as turning an office block into luxury apartments, or simply changing the way a regular house is used (for example, making structural changes or changing the layout so that you can rent the property to more tenants).

TIP

Turning commercial property into residential property has proven a particularly lucrative strategy for coauthor Nicholas in recent years, although it does require a certain level of experience and expertise to successfully manage larger developments like this. If you're new to development, small projects make a better starting point.

**REMEMBER**

If property development appeals to you, it's vital you start by thinking about your end goal or exit strategy. Are you going to sell the property to a family or keep it and rent it out to young professionals? Is it going to be rented as a vacation home? Everything about the development process — from what kind of property you buy, to how you finance it, to how you physically develop it — will depend on your end strategy.

Another key ingredient for success as a developer is being able to source the right kind of properties — in fact, sourcing properties directly, properties that aren't yet on the market, is a particularly valuable technique and something you may like to try. You also need to be a master at project management and communication if your development projects are to be completed on time, on budget, and without any major hiccups.

### Low-capital, shorter-term strategies

But what if you don't have the capital to develop property, but you still want to build a career in real estate? If that sounds like you, then consider sourcing property leads and acting as a retained buyer's agent.

Whether you're sourcing property or acting as a buyer's agent, you're effectively trading in information or leads by bringing together people who have a property to sell and investors who are looking to buy that exact type of property. In a way, it's a bit like being a niche real estate agent who specializes in a particular type of property for investor buyers only. And like a real estate agent, you earn commission for each sale you facilitate.

Meanwhile, you're learning the market from the inside and constantly developing your own network of buyers and sellers — all of which will pay dividends if you one day want to take on your own investment projects.

## Exploring longer-term strategies for earning a regular income

The thing that really drew coauthor Nicholas to property (apart from all those addictive property shows on TV) was the ability to earn a regular income from renting out property, so that he could quit the rat race and work for himself. Indeed, the ability to earn a steady income is what draws most investors into the real estate game.

Investing for rental income is a smart move because it gives you a certain amount of security and freedom to live life your way. Each of the strategies in the following sections is designed to help you achieve that financial security and freedom by delivering steady returns, now and for many years to come.

## Low-capital rental strategies for cash-strapped investors

The obvious barrier to entry for real estate investors is capital, or rather, lack of it. If you haven't got the money to buy a property, how on earth can you earn money by renting it out?

REMEMBER

But actually, ownership isn't as important as you may think. What matters is *control* of a property. If you're managing a property that someone else owns, there's still money to be made.

Rent-to-rent is a prime example of how controlling or managing a property that you don't own can deliver a healthy monthly income. With this strategy, you rent a property from a landlord and (with the landlord's permission) sublet the property to your own tenants, typically on a room-by-room basis for maximum returns.

You earn profit by managing the property more intensively, and your landlord no longer has to manage the property, which keeps the landlord happy. Creating win-win scenarios like this is one of the things many people love most about real estate.

Alternatively, you may consider negotiating a lease option. This is very similar to rent-to-rent in that you sublet the property to your own tenants, but as part of the deal with the landlord, you also negotiate the option to buy the property in the future. That gives you income in your pocket now, and the potential for capital growth in the future. However, finding an open-minded landlord and negotiating the terms of the lease option can be complex.

WARNING

Rent-to-rent and lease options can have a bit of an unsavory reputation; rent-to-rent because it implies slum landlords squeezing far too many people into a crappy property, and lease option because it implies taking advantage of distressed sellers who are unable to sell through other means. It's important you establish yourself as an ethical, professional operator and conduct your business accordingly.

## Adding value by changing how the property is used

Rather like developing properties, income-producing rental strategies are all about *adding value* to a property so that you can optimize your rental income. Two awesome ways to add value to a rental property are

>> **Changing the use so that instead of renting to one tenant or household as in the standard single-tenant model, you rent to multiple tenants in the same property, on a room-by-room basis:** Why should you consider renting to multiple tenants in one property? Two reasons spring immediately to mind:

- You'll earn more.

- There's enormous demand for this type of accommodation these days, and from different types of tenants, too.

You could, for example, be renting to young professionals in expensive, desirable cities who couldn't dream of having a place of their own at this stage in their lives. Or you could be renting to students, who generally embrace the house-sharing model as a way to get the most out of college life. Or you could be renting to low-income-housing tenants and satisfying a local need for comfortable housing on a tight budget.

REMEMBER

With multi-tenant strategies like these, there's definitely more work for you (or your team) in terms of proactively managing tenants (after all, there are more of them). And you need to be on your game when it comes to keeping up with regulations, such as health and safety, and planning/zoning restrictions. But the reward is significantly higher monthly returns.

>> **Changing the use so that instead of renting on a standard 12-month lease, you rent the property on a nightly or weekly basis as serviced accommodation or a vacation rental:** Both of these options involve renting on a short-term basis, typically by the night or week, which will earn you much more in rental income than a standard 12-month rental agreement.

REMEMBER

There's a lot of work involved in setting up and running these two types of hospitality businesses. More guests means more wear and tear on the property, for example. What's more, whether you're running a large apart-hotel, a small Airbnb apartment (see Book 5), or a luxury beachside villa, you absolutely need to be committed to delivering an outstanding service to each and every guest.

## Avoiding spreading yourself too thin

As you can tell, there are many different real estate strategies out there, and a varied real estate portfolio that doesn't rely on one single strategy is recommended.

**WARNING**

The potential downside of this is that investors can take a scattershot approach to their portfolios, dipping their toes into multiple strategies at once without really mastering any of them, thereby never really maximizing their potential for returns — and, at worst, losing money because of lack of research or poor decisions.

**REMEMBER**

It takes time and effort to really learn and master any real estate strategy, and it's important to focus that learning on one strategy at a time, instead of trying to take on three different strategies at once. Take your time to learn one strategy, establish yourself in that field, and make a success of your investments in that strategy before you even *think* about exploring another strategy.

# So Which Strategies Are Right for You?

Done well, all the strategies mentioned in this chapter have the potential to make you money. But some strategies deliver higher returns than others, some are more work than others, some will be better suited to your individual skills than others, and some will be better suited to current market conditions than others. In other words, not all investment strategies are created equal. So, how can you tell which strategies are right for you and where you should you focus your initial efforts?

**TIP**

A good starting point is to think about your passions, interests, and goals (both from an investment sense and your personal goals). Chapter 2 in Book 7 talks more about these factors, especially in the context of international real estate investing, but before you head there, take a moment now to ask yourself this: Why are you drawn to property? What is it about real estate that excites you?

For example, is it the creative aspect of visualizing something and bringing that vision to life? If so, property development sounds like your bag. Is it that your kid is going off to college and you've been introduced to the potentially very lucrative world of student housing? With your direct knowledge, you're well placed to rent to students. Or is it just that you want to be more entrepreneurial and quit your 9-to-5 job? If that's the case, high-income (and high-effort) strategies like serviced accommodation or vacation rentals may be for you.

It doesn't really matter what your initial reasons are. What matters is that you're driven by an underlying passion or goal, and that will inform your choices as you get better acquainted with the various strategies.

Another question to ask yourself is: What sort of tenants, buyers, or clients do you honestly want to do business with? Renting to students or low-income-housing tenants can be a good earner, or you may be like Coauthor Nicholas, for example, who prefers to rent to professionals, so that's where he focuses the majority of his rental properties.

Budget constraints are another important factor to consider at this early stage. If you're short on capital but you have plenty of time and energy, then a rent-to-rent or lease-option strategy may be a good starting point for you.

**REMEMBER**

The beauty of real estate is that there are so many options, you're bound to find at least one that works for your interests, goals, and passions — and your budget.

**IN THIS CHAPTER**

» **Deciding whether investing internationally is right for you**

» **Factoring in your finances and weighing risks**

» **Considering how you'll manage your property**

» **Identifying the best market for you**

» **Narrowing your focus**

Chapter **2**

# Investing at Home or Abroad: Which Is Right for You?

One of the decisions you'll face when first developing your real estate port-folio is which market, or markets, to invest in. Many people take their first step into property investing in their local market — an area they know well and feel comfortable in. But that's not always the case. Sometimes, budget, curiosity, or personal aspirations lead people to invest farther afield.

**REMEMBER**

Depending on the market and strategy you choose, investing abroad can deliver attractive returns on your investment, particularly in property markets that are less established or expensive than back home.

We all love those property shows about buying a place in the sun. You know the ones: A couple jets off to where the sun shines brighter and the beer is always colder to view beautiful properties that seem as cheap as chips. Those TV shows provide a wonderful bit of escapism, but when you go beyond buying a holiday home or retiring to the south of France, investing in international markets is hard, serious work and something that needs careful thought. This chapter is designed to help you decide whether it's the right step for you.

# Deciding Whether to Invest Abroad: It's Not All about the Numbers

When choosing whether to invest abroad, consider two simple questions:

» Do you have a passion or affinity for a particular country?

» If so, how much do you know about that market?

These questions often surprise people, because they're not about money, specific investment strategies, real estate expertise, or experience. Other important factors, such as your budget, will obviously impact your decision, and they are covered later in this chapter. But we're addressing these two basic questions first because they get right to the heart of why some people succeed in overseas real estate investments where others fail spectacularly.

The following sections cover these two facets — passion and accessibility — in more detail.

## Playing on your passion

This chapter isn't about whether to buy a vacation home for your family, or a retirement spot in the sun. The considerations for purchasing a vacation or retirement home are quite different from the ones outlined here. (Of course, if you occasionally want to use an investment property for your family vacation, that's great!)

Instead, this chapter is talking about whether you want to build a robust real estate portfolio, using the strategies outlined in Chapter 1 of Book 7, in an overseas market — or whether you'd actually be better off investing closer to home.

Building a robust real estate portfolio, whether at home or abroad, means treating your investment(s) as a business. This is why it's so important to find your passion.

Passion is what fuels successful businesses. Passion brings out the best in people and gives them the drive to succeed. After all, every business venture hits the odd bump in the road, and it's passion that keeps your enthusiasm alive when you get that call about a burst water pipe in Berlin at 6 a.m.

That's why budding investors should consider whether they have an affinity with a particular country. Have you always jaunted to Jamaica, for example? Are you fanatical about all things French? Do you dream of Denmark?

One of coauthor Nicholas's passions is the Netherlands. His wife is Dutch, his kids are half-Dutch, they have family there, and he loves the country. He's definitely eager to develop a portfolio in that country. And when he does, he knows that his passion for the country will help make that learning curve easier and more enjoyable.

Bottom line is, when you like what you're doing, you do it better. So, although crunching the numbers and doing the research are important (and we get to those later in the chapter), don't be afraid to let your personal passion inform your decision making. And if your passion lies closer to home, go for that instead!

## Tapping into available knowledge

Just because a country appeals to you or looks great on paper (in terms of growth prospects, return on investment, and so on) doesn't mean it's accessible for you personally as an investor. If you have no prior experience or knowledge of that country and no contacts there, you may struggle to set up and manage your investment.

After you've identified where your passion lies, you need to realistically assess how accessible that country is for you as a first-time investor in that market.

If your own knowledge and experience of a particular country is limited, don't be shy about hitting up your friends, family, and acquaintances for advice. Make a list of your contacts who have some experience of your chosen market, whether it's your colleague's brother who has a holiday home or the local barista who grew up there. Most people are happy to help by answering questions and recommending useful contacts.

Ultimately, it's not all about the numbers. Some countries, no matter how attractive they look financially, just won't stack up for you personally. Be realistic about what's achievable for you at this point in your property journey.

## UNCOVERING YOUR REAL PASSION

Anita Roddick, founder of The Body Shop, once said, "To succeed, you have to believe in something with such a passion that it becomes a reality." That was exactly the attitude coauthor Nicholas adopted when he first started his property business. He lived and breathed his business, literally willing it into life. Without that passion and belief, he doesn't think he would have been able to create the real estate portfolio and multiple businesses that he now owns.

Property was definitely his passion from the get-go, but maybe it's not yours. Maybe your passion is building a portfolio of investments that allows you to quit your job and spend more time with your family. Maybe *that's* what really lights a fire in your belly. Or maybe your passion is building financial security for you and your loved ones. Maybe your passion is simply becoming your own boss, and property provides the best way for you to achieve that goal.

It genuinely doesn't matter whether property is your prime passion, or whether your passion lies in becoming more entrepreneurial, securing a comfortable retirement, or whatever. The important thing is that you feel that overwhelming drive and passion to achieve your goals. If you're thinking of investing in Tuscany (or Tulsa, for that matter) because Bob from IT told you it was a good idea, then alarm bells should be ringing. After all, it's not Bob from IT who'll be dealing with the research, the bureaucracy, the phone calls, and so on.

Passion and drive are critical parts of real estate investing because they link to goal-setting, positivity (including maintaining a positive attitude when things don't go according to plan), and attracting success. In other words, getting into the mindset of a successful real estate investor is an important part of the journey.

# Considering Your Budget

Passion aside, unless you've got plenty of funds to play with, your budget will absolutely impact your decision on whether to invest at home or abroad.

Simple budget constraints have driven many real estate investors into exciting foreign markets. For example, the London real estate market is so buoyant that beginner investors are often priced out altogether. So, if you're renting an apartment in South London and looking to get into property investing, chances are, you'll have to look farther afield. You'll certainly get a lot more for your money in Bulgaria than you will in Balham!

When you're deciding which country to invest in, budget is an important factor. You may well have a passion for Monaco, but if your budget is more slot machine than high roller, the world's most expensive property market will be way out of your reach.

TIP

It's fun to see what you can get for your money around the world. On sites like www.rightmove.co.uk and www.primelocation.com, you can get a feel for average property prices all over the world.

REMEMBER

Your budget may not be your own cash. Taking out a mortgage or other form of finance means you need less upfront capital to purchase a property. However, if you plan to buy your investment property with a mortgage, availability of financing in a given country is another factor to consider.

Some of the more mainstream investment countries like Portugal, France, and Spain will do mortgages for overseas buyers, which makes those countries more accessible to investors with limited capital. In less developed markets, however, obtaining a mortgage may not be an option.

REMEMBER

In addition to getting a mortgage in your chosen investment country, other financing options include the following:

>> **Taking out a mortgage in your home country:** Some specialist providers offer mortgages for overseas properties, although these mortgages tend to be more expensive and difficult to obtain.

>> **Releasing equity from your home or another property you own:** This approach is a great low-barrier way to purchase affordable property overseas because it means you can pay cash and avoid any overseas financing. On the downside, it ties your investment to your home and can put your home at risk.

>> **Taking out a personal loan:** For investors on a budget who have no equity to release and limited access to mortgage funds, a personal loan can provide a relatively quick and easy way to raise funds.

>> **Buying with friends and family:** Pooling your resources with like-minded friends and family can be a great way to boost your budget. However, you should always have a legal agreement in place that sets out who owns what proportion of the property and be clear from the outset who will be responsible for managing the property.

The low property prices in many overseas markets means you can be a bit more creative with financing options. One couple purchased a ridiculously cheap property in Eastern Europe by borrowing on their credit card!

**REMEMBER**

Taking on additional mortgage debt or a personal loan isn't for everyone, and whether it's right for you will depend on your tolerance for risk (discussed in the next section). A risk-averse investor may only be comfortable with a small mortgage of, say, 30 percent of the value of the property — or even no mortgage at all — while someone who's more comfortable with risk may be willing to stretch to an 80 percent or 90 percent mortgage.

**WARNING**

Never borrow more than you can afford to repay, no matter how mouthwatering the investment opportunity. And always talk to an independent financial advisor before making any decision. They'll be able to help you decide what you can afford and which financing option, if any, is right for you.

# Assessing Your Risk Profile

Every investment is different, and the success of each investment depends on a wide range of factors or risks. In an overseas market, there are even more factors to consider. So, before you dive into the cool, sparkling waters of overseas property, you need to understand your personal risk profile. Why? Because your attitude to risk in general should inform any investment decision, especially whether investing overseas is the right move for you.

**REMEMBER**

Your *risk profile* can best be defined as how much risk you're willing to accept, or how much risk you're comfortable with, as you work toward your real estate goals.

Of course, you should be concerned about any risk that may affect your ability to make money on a property, but some people have a greater tolerance for risk than others. Understanding your attitude to risk is an important step in deciding whether to invest overseas or closer to home.

## Identifying where you sit on the risk spectrum

Consider someone purchasing an apartment in the Algarve, Portugal. Let's call this fictional investor Dave. Dave doesn't know the Algarve well, and this is his first overseas investment. So, in addition to getting up to speed on running a property as a vacation rental, Dave also has many other specific barriers to overcome:

>> The language barrier

>> Lack of local contacts

>> No knowledge of local laws

>> Currency risk (Portugal being in the eurozone)

>> Limited ability to manage the property himself (because he lives 2,000 miles away)

All these factors make the investment a higher risk than, say, a buy-to-rent apartment in Dave's hometown. Understanding Dave's risk profile essentially means understanding how concerned he is about these factors.

**REMEMBER**

No investment is absolutely risk free, so there's always an element of risk to contend with. The key is to work out what you're comfortable with and not push yourself beyond that point.

If Dave were very risk averse, this investment may be too high a risk. If Dave were a very adventurous investor, he may see the Algarve's stable real estate market, which is a favorite among foreign investors, as too "safe," not delivering high enough returns. Dave sits somewhere in the middle: He's comfortable with the risks associated with investing in Portugal, but he wouldn't be comfortable venturing into markets that are relatively untested for overseas investors.

In this way, risk tolerance is a spectrum, not a black-or-white issue. Are you the sort of person who likes jumping out of planes, bungee jumping, and climbing mountains? Then, in general, you have a greater tolerance for risk than coauthor Nicholas does (he's a guy who enjoys fishing, playing guitar, and taking his family on vacation in their vintage camper van). But having started his own business in his twenties, Nicholas has a greater tolerance for risk than, say, someone who has worked for the same company, in the same job, for 30 years.

Even if your general attitude to risk is pretty gutsy, and you do enjoy jumping out of planes in your spare time, that doesn't mean you'll feel comfortable with high-risk real estate investments. The goal isn't to push yourself into one form of investing over another — it's to figure out what you're comfortable with.

## Considering country-specific risk factors

You've got a passion for a particular country. You've got a base level of local knowledge, either through your own experience or existing contacts. It's within your budget. Now, how can you tell whether that country suits your risk profile?

Assessing countries for risk is kind of like assessing companies when investing in the stock market. Do you go for a newer company with huge potential for growth (and, let's be honest, utter failure), or do you go for an established blue-chip company that's expected to deliver steady returns over many years?

It's the same with international real estate. If you want a safer investment (as "safe" or reliable as any investment can get), you'll probably opt for a country that

>> Has a stable economy (steady economic growth, minimal fluctuations in exchanges rates and interest rates, and so on)

>> Enjoys political stability

>> You understand and know well (or have the ability to access and gain knowledge more easily)

>> Has an established real estate market that's already welcoming lots of international investors

With a fairly low-risk country like this, you may see smaller gains in terms of capital growth than you would in a higher-risk real estate market, but you'll also probably experience fewer crazy swings in terms of income and costs.

Like stocks and shares, as a rule of thumb, higher-risk real estate markets tend to offer higher returns. Someone with the foresight to purchase a two-bedroom apartment in East Berlin in the early 1990s, just after the fall of the Berlin Wall, would have paid as little as $9,000. Now, it would be worth easily $300,000. But investing early in untested markets like this may mean weathering years of political and financial uncertainty before you see real gains.

Even a country with an established real estate market that attracts thousands of foreign buyers each year isn't immune to risk. If the economy isn't stable, you can still get burned. Take Greece, for example. After years of political and economic uncertainty and a crippling financial crisis, property prices in Greece fell drastically starting in 2008, while property taxes and rental taxes increased multiple times. For the gung-ho investor, these low prices in Greece may represent an opportunity for a bargain. But if the country were to be ejected from (or opt to leave) the eurozone, prices would likely plummet further. Depending on your ultimate goal (see the next section), this risk may not be a deal breaker for you, but for many people, it would be a huge concern.

## Factoring your goals into the equation

When weighing the risks of overseas investments, you need to understand your ultimate goals, because your goals will affect your risk tolerance.

REMEMBER

Consider the following:

>> **How long you intend to hold the investment:** If you're planning to hold the property as a long-term investment, short- and medium-term fluctuations will be less of a concern. In the context of decades, housing bubbles will pass and political landscapes will (often, but not always) smooth out. However, if you're planning to turn the property around as a short-term investment, perhaps as a development project, then political and economic fluctuations can have a huge impact on the success of your investment.

>> **Whether you're looking for capital growth (an increase in the property's value) or regular income (for example, as a rental property):** If you want to be earning income immediately and consistently, you need to invest in an established market with a ready-and-waiting target audience. You can't afford to wait for an emerging market to catch up to your vision.

>> **What strategy you intend to employ:** This ties in closely to the previous point. An ongoing income strategy like houses in multiple occupation or vacation lets likewise requires an established market.

One of coauthor Nicholas's investments very much falls into the emerging market field: an apartment in Egypt. In the short and medium term, financial and political instability (compared to, say, Europe or the United States) means returns are, for now, small. But his goal for this investment was to get into the market early, buy cheap, hold the investment for ten years (maybe longer), and get a great return. In the context of this goal, short–term fluctuations and uncertainties aren't such a concern. He's also spread his risk by creating a real estate portfolio that's as diverse as possible.

# Figuring Out How You'll Manage Your Property

Managing a property that's farther away is more difficult than managing one down the street. (You didn't need to buy this book to figure that out.) In the early stages, when you're looking for a place to buy, it's harder to learn about the local market. Later on, after you've purchased the property, it's harder to manage relationships with tenants and other people when you can't have a face-to-face conversation and perhaps don't even speak the language.

This challenge is another reason why passion is so important in real estate investing. One real estate investor lives in the south of England and owns an investment property in France. Particularly in the early days, he was traveling to France regularly for meetings with local experts and tradespeople. Sometimes this involved a 16-hour day — flying over in the morning, spending the day there, and getting home late at night. Without passion, this sort of commitment gets old fast!

REMEMBER

Even if you have outstanding local contacts from the outset, be prepared to spend time in your chosen country, getting to know the local market, setting up and managing your investments, and developing those all-important relationships that will make your life easier when you're back home.

If your chosen market is a local town, it's obviously easier to build that knowledge (you know a lot about the market already) and manage your investments. If you have ten rental properties where you live, you could potentially manage them yourself, particularly in the early days if you want to save on costs. You could, for example, inspect all of them in one day and check in new tenants yourself when necessary. But if you have ten rental properties spread across the Algarve (our friend Dave has been busy!), it would be nearly impossible to manage them yourself if you didn't live there. You'd inevitably need local contacts to manage certain or all aspects for you.

This is where your "dream team" comes into play. Your dream team is made up of the people who will help you manage your investments and take care of things personally in your absence. This includes everyone from a good lawyer to a trustworthy plumber. Whether you're investing at home or abroad, you always need reliable people you can trust, but you'll certainly rely on them more for an overseas investment. Turn to Chapter 1 in Book 7 for a list of folks you need on your dream team.

REMEMBER

Local help comes with additional cost, so you'll need to factor this into your budget and cash flow. As an absent owner, you'll undoubtedly have higher maintenance and management costs than if you were managing the property locally yourself.

**REMEMBER**

None of this should put you off investing in international property. If it suits your aims, your passion and your risk profile, it's well worth that investment of your time and money to carefully establish and run your investment.

# Drilling Down to the Right Market for You

The goal in this chapter isn't to identify one catch-all international market that works for everyone. The truth is, no single choice is ideal for all investors. The best place for you as an individual to invest — whether it's in your home country or overseas — will depend on the factors outlined in this chapter.

**REMEMBER**

Start the decision-making process by identifying countries that you're passionate about rather than focusing solely on cold, hard facts and figures. After you've identified your passion, you can get more analytical and assess that country in terms of your budget, your risk profile, and so on.

But what if you're certain you want to invest abroad, but you don't have a passion for a particular country? Or your passion pulls you in two different directions? Or the country you love doesn't match your budget or risk profile? That's where the following sections can help.

## Looking at the cold, hard facts and figures

If you're in a position where you need to narrow down your international options, the Internet will fast become your best friend (as if it isn't already). Online you can find a raft of information about real estate markets all over the world.

**REMEMBER**

In addition to researching the real estate market in a given country, you should also carefully weigh practical considerations such as the following:

>> **If you don't speak the local language, how widely is English (or your native language) spoken?** Will you struggle to find a certified translator or deal with local tradespeople for instance?

>> **How easy is it for you to physically get to the country?** After you're established, and with your dream team in place, you shouldn't need to be on the ground often. But you never know when something unforeseen may crop up that requires your physical presence (especially in countries with a love of

bureaucracy). Owning property that's an expensive 12-hour flight away may not be ideal if you're new to overseas investments.

>> **Will you be able to build a trusted dream team in that country?** In many countries, there are still elements of corruption and horror stories of investors getting ripped off, so don't scrimp on your research and due diligence. You absolutely need to be able to trust the people who will be looking after your property on your behalf.

>> **Will your preferred strategy apply in that country?** As Chapter 1 in Book 7 explains, multiple strategies can be successfully deployed abroad, and your preferred strategy will influence your country choice.

You then need to drill down further from the overall country level to pinpoint your chosen town or region within that country. Again, that involves assessing specific regions in relation to the points outlined in the preceding list, as well as the following:

>> **What are the hot locations and property sectors in that country?** In Germany, for instance, student rental apartments in major cities like Berlin and Hamburg are currently performing well.

>> **What is the best geographical location for your chosen strategy or strategies?** If you want to run the property as a vacation rental, proximity to a beach or a ski or lake resort may be your preferred choice.

**REMEMBER**

If you want to market the property to tourists, you'll also need to consider factors like local infrastructure (such as highway access), facilities (shops, restaurants, and so on), whether English or other languages are widely spoken, and other potential barriers to attracting international visitors or out-of-towners.

## Developing your knowledge of that country and region

After you've settled on a country and a specific region within that country, you need to start developing your knowledge and understanding of that market.

**TIP**

When you're investing in a new market, you can never spend too much time on the three Rs: *research, research, research.* As a starting point, here's what you can do when you're getting to know a new area:

>> **Read up on investing in that country.** Devour any information you can get your hands on regarding your chosen country, including property blogs and websites, economic forecast data, and political news.

>> **Research local agents before you set foot in the country.** Are there multiple agents to choose from or, if it's a less-developed market, is there just one local agent? Do they have a professional website? Are they certified by that country's accreditation body? (Read more about finding and vetting local experts in the nearby sidebar "Finding and vetting experts, at home and overseas.") If it's a less developed market, are you going to have to do the legwork and source your own opportunities by talking to local property owners?

>> **Spend time in the place.** Internet research is great, but there's no substitute for spending time there, getting to know the lay of the land, immersing yourself in the local properties, demographics, infrastructure, facilities, and the like.

>> **Meet with local agents face to face.** No one knows the local market like the local agents, so invest time in establishing, developing, and nurturing those relationships. It will pay dividends in the long run.

>> **Get to know the local property ownership laws, planning regulations, tax issues, and other rules that are relevant to your particular strategy.** In some countries, the bureaucracy is both legendary and mind-boggling. Even the locals struggle! So source a reliable local lawyer, financial advisor, and other relevant experts (an architect, for example) as early as you can. Turn to Chapter 1 in Book 7 for a list of experts you'll need on your dream team.

**WARNING**

Don't take one agent's opinion on face value. There are lots of great agents out there — and there are lots of cowboys out there, too, looking to make a fast buck off naïve buyers. You always need to do your own due diligence and build a thorough picture of the facts by talking to multiple experts.

As you can tell, you need to go through several layers of thought processes and research. The lists in this section are by no means exhaustive — the specifics will depend on your chosen country and investment strategy (or strategies).

**REMEMBER**

Ultimately, whether a country, region, and investment opportunity is right for you will depend on you as an individual: what's accessible for you, what appeals to your interests, what suits your risk tolerance, and so on.

# FINDING AND VETTING EXPERTS, AT HOME AND OVERSEAS

Whether you're investing in your local town or overseas, the same general approach to finding and vetting your "dream teamers" applies. Thanks to the Internet and online platforms like Upwork, it's never been easier to tap into additional resources and support whenever and wherever you need it. Here are some tried-and-tested methods for finding the right support:

- **Network, network, network.** Join your local general business networking group and seek out any property-specific networking groups in your area.

- **Don't forget online networking opportunities.** With sites like Property Forum (www.propertyforum.com), you can network with property experts and tap into their knowledge.

- **Ask your contacts for recommendations.** Many of coauthor Nicholas's support team members have come to him via recommendations from people he knows and trusts.

- **Search via the accrediting organization, where appropriate.** For certified professionals, like lawyers and real estate agents, the certifying body will often provide a listing of professionals in your area. If you're based in a different country from the expert in question, it's a good idea to search for professionals who have direct experience working with international clients.

- **For more general business tasks, online platforms like Upwork (www.upwork.com) and Fiverr (www.fiverr.com) can connect you with skilled freelancers from all over the world.** If you prefer to work with someone local to you, seek out a local virtual assistant or business support agency. (Again, your local networking group will be a great resource for this.) Many business support agencies can handle anything from admin and research to marketing and web support.

When you find your potential dream teamers, research them thoroughly before meeting with them and certainly before you enter into any sort of agreement. You wouldn't employ a contractor to renovate your house without getting references, would you? It's exactly the same with your dream team. Vetting your experts and freelancers can be as simple as answering the following questions:

- **Are they doing the job full time and getting paid for it, or is it a side project or hobby for them?** Your next-door neighbor's brother may be handy with a wrench, but that's no substitute for a qualified, full-time plumber!

- **Do they have a professional website?** The website should clearly outline their skills, experience, and expertise, and show testimonials from previous clients.

- **Where appropriate, are they licensed or certified?** They must also be fully insured for the work you're hiring them to do.

- **What experience do they have with your specific type of property investment?** A commercial real estate lawyer might not be the best expert for you if you're purchasing a vacation rental.

- **What do previous and existing clients have to say about them?** Always ask to speak to two or three of their clients for a reference. For a building contractor, ask to visit properties the contractor has worked on recently.

- **Are there online reviews of their services?** Reviews aren't just for hotels and restaurants anymore. These days, just about any business can be reviewed online. Check out Yelp (www.yelp.com), Trustpilot (www.trustpilot.com), and other review platforms to see what people have to say about the business.

- **Do they respond to your emails and calls quickly?** Are they easy to get a hold of? If you have to work hard to get their attention, that's not a great sign.

You can do a lot of this research and vetting online and over the phone, but if possible, it's always a good idea to meet with members of your dream team, particularly the real estate agents. Even if you're investing overseas, you should definitely go and meet potential agents face to face; in-person meetings like this are crucial for establishing trust and building those all-important relationships.

Especially if you're investing overseas and don't know the local area that well, the real estate agent will be probably be the first person on your dream team. You can then leverage the real estate agent's contacts to start building your dream team in that region. Your agent's recommendations for builders, lawyers, and so on will be invaluable in the early days. Tapping into your agent's network is a great way to get started when you're new to an area.

Of course you should be wary of relying solely on your agent's recommendations. "Backhanders" aren't uncommon, so you want to make sure you're getting a genuine recommendation, not helping your agent scratch someone else's back. It's your back the agent should be scratching! Always do your due diligence on any company that your agent recommends.

# Focusing Your Attention on One or Two Key Markets

So you've decided that investing overseas is the right step for you. Awesome! However, as with any investment, it's important not to get carried away and spread yourself too thin.

**WARNING**

No matter how mouthwatering the investment potential of multiple countries, spreading your investments across many diverse international markets can end up costing you a lot in terms of time, money, and stress.

**REMEMBER**

If you do want to invest in international property, you're better off really developing your knowledge of one international market — and ideally focusing on a specific region of that country, at least at first. By focusing your efforts in one specific region, you can develop a strong foothold in that area, getting to know the market and local experts in great detail. You also benefit from economies of scale.

In other words, when you're ready to add other investments in that region, you already have your dream team of advisors and experts in place. Your second investment in that area will be a heck of a lot easier to establish than your first investment was. The third investment should be even easier than the second, and so on.

Then, having mastered that market, with your investments well established and your dream team running everything like a tight ship, you may feel ready to take advantage of the opportunities available in a different international market. That's fine — great even — but keep in mind that you'll be starting from scratch in terms of getting to know a new market and establishing your local dream team.

**TIP**

Even as your real estate portfolio becomes more developed and your confidence grows, you should still limit yourself to no more than three different international markets. Investing in more than three countries at the same time is best left to advanced real estate investors who have deep pockets full of capital and an army of advisors.

# 8

# The Next Level: Investing in Commercial Real Estate

# Contents at a Glance

IN THIS CHAPTER

» **Understanding the basics of commercial real estate**

» **Surveying the types of investments available**

» **Discovering the tools you need to get started**

» **Debunking the myths of investing in commercial real estate**

» **Keeping timing in mind when selling, buying, and holding**

Chapter **1**

# A Crash Course in Commercial Real Estate Investing

W hat comes to mind when you think of commercial real estate? Downtown skyscrapers? Corner strip malls? Apartment complexes? Okay, that's a good start. But have you thought about being the owner of one? You may assume it'd be too complex or too expensive, but jumping into commercial real estate investing could be the wisest and most lucrative investment you ever make. To us, the benefits outweigh the risks. But find out for yourself.

In this chapter, you find out what commercial real estate is, and you discover the different types available. It breaks down the big world of commercial investing into easy-to-follow categories so that you can pick and choose your favorites. It also uncovers the five biggest myths that stop people from investing and understanding commercial real estate. Because the value of commercial real estate depends on the cash flow that it produces, you find out how cash flow is made on a monthly basis, and you discover the steps to building long-term wealth. This chapter also tells you when it's the most profitable time to buy, hold, sell, or bail. By the end of this chapter, you're sure to be convinced that commercial real estate is, by far, the best way to produce true and lasting wealth.

# Comparing Commercial Real Estate and Residential Real Estate

**REMEMBER**

Here's our definition of commercial real estate: It's any piece of real estate that's bigger than one house on one lot. So, commercial real estate includes everything from small apartment buildings (five or more units) and large office buildings to shopping centers, to industrial parks, and even land development.

The three biggest differences between commercial real estate and residential real estate include the following:

>> **Commercial real estate projects are passive investments only after they're up and running.** Unless you have a ton of money and don't care about getting huge returns, commercial real estate will take a lot of your time and effort to get started. After all, you have to deal with many things, including the learning process, finding the right mentors or teachers, searching for the right deal, financing your investment, picking management teams, protecting it from lawsuits, and overseeing the project.

**REMEMBER**

The good news is that after you have a commercial project off the ground, it's usually big enough that it allows you to pay other people to take care of it. So, it won't take much of your time at all — and that's why it's called a *passive investment*. Compare this to a single-family home that may require collecting rents and making repairs for many years to come.

>> **All it takes is one big commercial deal for you to be set for life.** Doing one commercial deal the right way can generate you a profit several times your yearly salary in addition to providing you sizable monthly income as long as you own the property. Residential real estate can produce a sizable profit as well, but it will not generate anywhere near the cash flow that a commercial property will. You'll receive one check per month from a single-family residence, but you can receive several hundred checks per month from a commercial property.

Consider this: Some investors shared how they got started in commercial real estate. One of them is in a project that already has a profit of $10 million or more. Another one bought a piece of land near their home for $1.5 million, and it has jumped in value over the past two years to $9 million (and they didn't even have to use their own money).

>> **The people you meet who invest in commercial real estate are all big thinkers.** They're people who have decided that they want to think big, live big, and hang around other people who are just as passionate about life as they are. Until you get involved, it's difficult to really understand just what your life could look like. Investors of residential real estate think of one monthly check and one tenant; they wait for appreciation (which may never come); and they're limited in ways of creating massive value for their property.

# Deciding to Invest in Commercial Real Estate

We think commercial real estate investing is a great way to generate wealth, and the main reason we like it so much can be boiled down to one word: leverage. Leverage is what allows you to use a small amount of your time and money to bring you a magnified return. Commercial properties are usually bigger and more valuable than other types of real estate, such as houses. What this means to you is that after you figure out how to find, negotiate, and buy commercial property without using much of your own money, you'll be able to sit back and watch the magic of leverage work wonders for your financial future. Your family will thank you for generations to come.

When people get started with their investing, most of them dream of creating a six-figure annual income stream so that they can quit the rat race. However, deep down many of them have doubts that they can actually make it happen. But never fear. The goal of Book 8 is to give you the starting steps and specific know-how to help you realize that you really can live the life of your dreams.

Understand that there are still going to be naysayers out there who say you can't invest in commercial real estate in today's market, in today's economy, or in today's cosmic layering of celestial occurrences. But you have a choice. You can either buy into what these financially stressed-out individuals are desperately clinging to, or you can let go of everything that's been holding you back and go after the future that you want and deserve.

**REMEMBER**

To be clear: Commercial real estate allows you to make whopping piles of money. With commercial real estate you can make anywhere from $20,000 to $100,000 on a little deal. And you can make $10 million or more from a bigger property. Sound interesting? Does it take work? Sure, it does. But a $1,000,000 commercial deal doesn't take anywhere near ten times the work that a $100,000 residential deal takes. So, what you're doing is working at a higher level that rewards you with the opportunity to make a lot more money with just a little more effort.

## HOW A COLLEGE DROPOUT TURNED $4,000 INTO A $120,000 PROFIT IN 60 DAYS

Morgan was the kind of teenager who struggled in high school. He didn't get good grades, and he didn't earn a college degree. He worked a variety of jobs until he found himself working as a bouncer in a bar and surviving on 69-cent cans of beans. Financially, he had a pretty bleak-looking future.

For some reason, Morgan had the wild idea that he could somehow make money investing in real estate. So, he drove around town talking to agents and looking at properties. One day he saw a sign on an empty lot that said, "Exxon Corporation Land for Sale." Morgan didn't know much about land, but after looking at the county records, he figured that the property might be worth about $200,000.

After calling and meeting with the agent, he was able to put a contract in place to buy the land for $160,000. But now Morgan had a big problem because the agent was calling about the $4,000 earnest money deposit that Morgan had promised to give to them. So, he went down to the bank and talked them into lending him the $4,000 based on the value of his car, which was the only real asset that he had.

Now Morgan was faced with the problem of having to close the deal in 120 days, or he would lose his deposit and perhaps his car, too. So, he went back to the county office and looked at all the other parcels of land around his piece that he had under contract. He saw that there was a larger lot behind his property that could have its access restricted depending on how he developed his property.

With the help of an architect, Morgan put together two sets of plans. One set showed a larger commercial shopping center that restricted access to the lot behind it. He also put together another set of plans with another smaller building designed as a gateway to the property behind it. Morgan's next step took a straight face. He marched into a meeting with the owner of the property that was behind his property and dropped both sets of plans down. Morgan told the owner (in a nice way) that they had a choice: The owner could either accept a wholesale assignment of Morgan's purchase contract for

$320,000 so the owner could develop it with the gateway, or (if the owner didn't want to buy it) Morgan was going to develop the property himself and restrict the other property owner's access.

Morgan was scared stiff at this point because he knew that he didn't have any way to close the deal himself. Fortunately, the owner agreed to the wholesale assignment of Morgan's property for a total price of $320,000 — and after they went through the due diligence, the price dropped down to $290,000. The seller got the $160,000 they were expecting, and Morgan walked away with $130,000 in profit by assigning his purchase contract. This happened because of two reasons: One was that Morgan found himself in a place in life where he didn't have a lot of choices. Either he was going to go for it and make it in life, or he wasn't. The second reason that Morgan was successful is because he had guts. Guts boil down to a willingness to move ahead, even though you've never done it before and even though you're scared to death.

# Exploring the Available Types of Investments

Most people think commercial real estate is all about apartment rentals. Even though residential properties *are* a big part of commercial real estate investing, other types of properties make for excellent investment opportunities as well. For instance, commercial real estate includes offices and warehouses, retail centers, and even undeveloped land.

We define commercial real estate as any real estate that's bigger than one house on one lot. So even if people live in the property, it's still commercial as long as it's bigger than one house. Some people would argue that a little property like a duplex or a four-unit isn't really commercial. That's okay. We like keeping our definitions simple. Actually, five or more units in an apartment building is considered commercial, but who's counting? The following sections explain each of the different types of commercial property.

## Apartment buildings (also known as residential properties)

The commercial properties that are in the residential category include everything from small apartment properties (five or more units) to huge apartment building projects that cover several city blocks. You drive by thousands of commercial properties like this every day (or you may even live in one). Every single building you see is owned by a commercial investor who's in the game to make money. (Now anytime you see a nice apartment building, you won't be able to stop thinking about getting into commercial real estate investing.) What's great about investing in apartments is that they're easy to find, banks love to lend on them, and they're great cash flow generators.

The advantage of starting off with residential properties is that they're a great way to jump into the exciting world of commercial real estate investing. Coauthors Peter Conti and Peter Harris both started off investing in small- to medium-sized multi-unit properties. This was a great experience because it allowed them to make the jump to get started. For most people, getting started is the hardest part. However, after you've started investing in commercial real estate, you'll have a difficult time going back to the old grind of the rat race that so many others find themselves trapped in.

## Office buildings

After you get the itch to invest in commercial real estate, you'll never walk into an office building again without thinking, "Somebody owns this building. Why couldn't it be me?"

As populations expand, more and more office buildings are being constructed. Offices are great for investing because they have what are called *triple net leases*. This type of lease is one in which the tenants in the property pay you the rent plus they pay for the following:

>> All maintenance and repairs

>> The insurance on the property

>> The real estate taxes

Bingo! It's called *passive income* for a reason. After you get your office building rented out, you can sit back and watch the cash flow come rolling in. Heck, you can even hire a property management company to lease it out for you. Then your only obligation is to sit on the beach.

REMEMBER

Triple net leases are so called because the tenants in your office building pay for all three categories of expenses. Tenants pay all three of these costs so that the rent you get is a net amount from which you don't have to pay expenses. So, after the tenants pay for all the expenses and you pay the mortgage, the rest goes into your pocket. It's quite typical for a triple net lease to be 5 to 20 years in duration with rent increases every couple of years. But that can be a disadvantage as well, and here's why: Say that the lease is for ten years. If your neighborhood experiences explosive growth over the next three to five years, you won't be able to charge higher rents or capitalize on what's happening because you're locked into a ten-year lease agreement. But overall, triple net lease investments are very much sought after.

## Retail centers

Retail centers, also known as shopping centers or malls, are at the heart of most of the towns and cities in the United States. These are the places where people come to shop, eat, and meet with friends. And retail centers are one of the commercial property asset types that you can invest in. Most investors like retail centers because, like office and warehouse properties, many retail properties are leased out on a long-term triple net lease basis where the tenants pay for all the expenses. The upside to this as an investor is that your rates of return won't go down over time as the taxes and expenses go up. In fact, as rents go up over time, your returns just keep getting better and better. And as in most triple net lease agreements, rent increases are built into the agreement with the tenant.

**REMEMBER**

Office buildings and retail properties have gone through massive changes as a result of the COVID-19 pandemic. Thousands of office workers got the chance to become remote workers and discover they (most of the time anyway) like working from home. Big national companies have closed their stores at shopping malls with some of them going completely out of business. Other stores have transitioned over to doing a large portion of their business online. This change creates opportunities as investors. Office buildings are being converted into apartments. Some apartment buildings now include separate "work at home" areas. Department stores have been converted into warehouses for online companies that ship out their products.

## Warehouses or industrial properties

With the advent and growth of online shopping or e-commerce, companies that ship to customers need a place to store their goods. These buildings, known as warehouses, are pretty simple — large structures, four walls, multiple doors, and centrally located for shipping purposes. Warehouses tend to be relatively low-maintenance properties, focusing on storage more than aesthetics. Also, warehouse tenants may be more inclined to sign longer-term leases in the coming years as e-commerce grows.

## Self-storage facilities

Just like everyone needs a place to sleep at night, nearly everyone needs a place to store their stuff — old things, recently purchased things, and treasured personal things.

Why is it so popular amongst investors? Compelling reasons include

>> No toilets to clean

>> Low cost of operations

>> Low building costs

>> Operations can be automated

>> Low down-payment loans

The various types of self-storage facilities to consider are

>> Self-storage

>> Warehouses

>> Cold storage

>> Climate-controlled storage

>> Vehicle storage (including RVs, boats, and cars)

TIP

For you, the average investor, we recommend you begin your acquisition search for mom-and-pop self-storage facilities. Avoid the "big boys," such as U-Haul and Public Storage, and all other franchise-types, because they are too expensive for the beginning investor.

TIP

One of the most important things to consider is your facility's location. Ideally, it should be located where there's demand for storage, where it's easy to drive to, and where there's high visibility. If there are a lot of small houses in a town, it's good sign that there is an opportunity for a self-storage investment. Small houses mean a large percentage of people in that town require extra storage spaces for their stuff.

## Hotels and resorts

This asset type isn't recommended as the place to get started, but many experienced investors have found it to be a fun and highly profitable area to focus on. Of course, other investors have also lost their shirts (and sometimes their trousers, too), so make sure that you know what you're doing before jumping in. Most of the deals coauthors Peter Conti and Peter Harris have run into have been smaller hotels or motels rather than the larger nationally branded, or as they're referred to, "Flagged" hotels.

One investor used a commercial master lease, a form of creative financing to get a 40-unit motel outside of Springfield, Missouri. They changed the name of the motel, hired new staff, and upgraded the units. Six months later they sold it for almost twice as much, making almost $500,000. Another investor has a 135-unit hotel under contract with plans to convert it into apartments.

**REMEMBER**

The success of any hotel or resort is composed of two parts, the property itself and the business of marketing, managing, and operating the property. If you're going to invest in this niche, you should invest in the property and then lease it out to another company that will operate the hotel or resort.

# Getting Started

What's the secret ingredient that allows someone to make it big in commercial real estate? If we told you, how long would it take for you to jump up, bolt out the door, and go find your first commercial deal? Well, you're about to find out, so put on your running shoes. The secret ingredient is none other than motivation. If you were expecting some fancy formula, we're really sorry. But in the end, it really boils down to how bad you want it and what you are willing to do to get it.

If you are truly motivated, you'll find a way. But now that you know the secret, you still need to be familiar with the tools, techniques, and guidance that help you along the way. The following sections explain them.

**REMEMBER**

Investing in commercial real estate requires a handful of skills. You don't need to understand differential equations or know how to rebuild a transmission. However, the skills in the following sections are a must.

## Easily meeting people and making new friends

If you connect with people easily and like meeting new friends, you'll do well at creating a stash of contacts. It's important to network with the people who will be investing in your commercial real estate deals because they hold the "pot of gold." People that you meet will eventually be your advisors, investors, and partners, and they'll send deals to you and connect you with wealth-building resources.

If you're the shy type, we're betting that you'll sooner or later get over your shyness after you see all the money that's being made by other investors who love having a network of colleagues and friends. If you really want to succeed as commercial real estate investor, you'll have to gradually come out of your shell.

## Doing simple math

You'll need to be able to look at property information online, properly enter numbers into a simple spreadsheet, and use a calculator. These skills help you determine what a commercial property is worth, what you should pay for it, and what your payday will be.

**TIP**

If you need some pointers and guidance when it comes to numbers, a course in business math is sure to get you up to speed.

## Accounting and collecting

If you're going to be in business, you're going to need to be comfortable asking other people to pay you the money that they owe you (in rents). The neat part is that you can hire a property management company to do all the collecting for you. And if you're starting small, you need to get a good handle on accounting and other business essentials. Why? Because investing in commercial real estate is like investing in a real business where you have to pay bills, hire employees, deal with contractors, and know how to read simple financial reports.

**TIP**

When coauthor Peter Conti started his first business more than three decades ago, he read the book *Small Time Operator* by Bernard B. Kamoroff (Lyons Press) so he could understand the basics of accounting, setting up a business, paying various taxes, and staying out of trouble.

# Recognizing Myths and Questions about Investing in Commercial Real Estate

Like any complicated business, commercial real estate investing has its share of myths and questions. Knowing this information brings forth some valuable truths that will rescue you from the trappings of confusion.

The following are some pretty common misconceptions about investing in commercial real estate:

>> **You must start off in residential real estate to get into commercial real estate.** There's no rule, rhyme, or reason stating that you must first invest in residential real estate in order to make the leap into commercial real estate investing. These fields are two different animals, two different languages, and two different consumers. It's like comparing apples to oranges.

>> **Only the rich need apply.** As you can probably imagine, this myth is just that: a myth. It isn't true that you have to be rich to get involved with commercial real estate investing. You can be as creative in your financing here as you can be when investing in homes.

Here's an example: Donald recently purchased a 24-unit apartment building. The purchase price was $750,000. The owner carried a second mortgage of $100,000 for Donald. That left him $50,000 for a down payment. Donald negotiated $30,000 for repair credits at closing. That left him with an out-of-pocket cost of $20,000, which he funded from a refinance from another property. Donald proves you only need to be rich in motivation and creativity.

>> **This game is only for big-time players.** In commercial real estate it doesn't matter where you start, and it doesn't matter if you only want to devote part of your time to do it. Having a full-time job or being a single parent doesn't matter either.

Coauthor Peter Harris started his career by buying small commercial properties. His first was a cheap seven-unit apartment building. His second was a small and quaint self-storage building used by the plumbers in town. He did this part time while holding a full-time day job and raising a small family. It all started from there and grew to owning and operating large community properties around the country.

>> **You need a real estate license.** A lot of investors don't have a real estate license, and they often wonder if not having a license poses a problem. Our answer is no. Not having a license will not hinder you, nor has it hindered many successful investors who invest full time or part time. Even one of your humble coauthors doesn't currently have a license. The fact is that as long as you're a principal in the transaction, you don't need to be licensed. (A *principal* is someone who buys property to make a profit.)

*Agents* and *brokers,* on the other hand, are those who help an investor buy or sell, and they're the ones who get a commission as compensation. The duties they perform require a license. As long you don't receive compensation or represent yourself or someone else in the transaction, you don't need one.

>> **Commercial real estate investing is riskier.** To this we say, "Compared to what?" If you compare it to stocks, do you have control over the companies you own stock in — in areas such as income, expense, debt, management, and insurance? Probably not. However, you do have these five controls in commercial real estate investing. If you compare it to residential real estate investing, what happens if you rent out your single-family home and the tenant moves out? What's your monthly income then? The answer: Zilch. If, on the other hand, you own a 24-unit apartment building and one tenant moves out, what's your monthly income? Answer: 23 paying tenants worth of rent! What's riskier? We rest our case.

>> **Commercial real estate is too complex for simple folks.** Again, this isn't true. Remember when you started using some new software? You had no idea how to use it. It seemed too complicated, and it had entirely too many features. But there was a help section or YouTube tutorial to get you started. After that, through repetition and practice, what seemed much like a puzzle is now fully understood and appropriately used. Getting to know commercial real estate investing is the same concept. You have quite a few things to master, but it isn't rocket science.

REMEMBER

Real estate, like the rest of life, does have risks. If it didn't, it probably wouldn't be as fun. And it surely wouldn't pay off with the incredibly strong rates of return that it does.

# Timing the Commercial Real Estate Market

Wouldn't it be great if you could time the commercial real estate market precisely? For instance, what if you could predict what the office building market would do five years from now in your town? Imagine if you had a process and procedure for knowing the perfect time to buy in a certain market. Well, here's a secret: None of this exists. Sorry for bursting your bubble! But if we could predict such things, we'd be living on our own islands off of Tahiti.

But here's the good news. Remember the old adage, "Buy low and sell high?" Believe it or not, this truly is how you get wealthy in real estate over time. It's a tried-and-true method. And here's another secret (and this time we're serious): A tool exists that helps you buy low and sell high in any market anywhere in the United States. That tool is the *real estate cycle*. And when you pair this cycle with some knowledge of trends, you're sure to be successful.

## Knowing whether to buy, hold, or bottom-fish

Real estate cycles are like traffic lights. When you see a green light, you go. When you see a yellow light, you might go, but if so, you proceed with caution. When you see a red light, you stop. The trick, however, is knowing when you're facing green, yellow, or red lights. Here are some examples:

>> A green light in commercial real estate investing may be spotted when you notice upcoming job growth due to a factory expansion. Or when the demand

to build exceeds the supply of available properties. Most likely, you'll also see a lot of undeveloped land sales activity.

>> A yellow light may be indicated by interest rates creeping up suddenly and causing you to examine your costs of new money to borrow. Or it could be when you see vacancies and "lease specials" increase. What if your newsfeed reveals many struggling businesses in an area? That has yellow light written all over it.

>> A red light may be revealed by a halt in new construction, which may be caused by overbuilding in the area. An increase in foreclosures and a decrease in property values is a sure red light.

REMEMBER

Making big money in commercial real estate is all about managing risks. Understanding and gaining knowledge of real estate cycles helps you lower your risk. Even though predicting real estate cycles is largely a game of luck, it gets downright dangerous if you know nothing about the trends in the market in which you're investing. The following is an outline of the typical commercial real estate cycle. This cycle can help you determine the best time to buy, sell, or go bottomfishing. Here are the phases of the cycle, which are depicted in Figure 1-1:

>> **Expansion phase:** During this phase, population increases, incomes rise, employment is good, vacancies are decreasing, and rents are rising. New buildings are planned. The human emotion here is excitement.

>> **Peak phase:** This is the time to sell for maximum profit. This is a seller's market, and in this phase, you see new building projects increasing and bidding wars between investors. Listings are on the market for only a short period of time. The human emotion here is sheer confidence.

>> **Contraction phase:** Most likely, you'll see a bunch of new projects on the market now, and you may see evidence of overbuilding. Inflation is up, interest rates are increasing, vacancy rates begin to creep up, and prices begin to level. Foreclosures generally grow during this time. The human emotion here ranges from mere concern and denial to utter shock.

>> **Recession phase:** Real estate in this phase is becoming more difficult to sell, and so properties stay on the market for longer periods of time. Property values decrease, interest rates are high, and landlords are competing for tenants because of overbuilding. Foreclosures are usually rampant. The human emotion here is complete panic.

>> **Bottom phase:** This is the best time to buy. However, this is the scariest phase there is: Unemployment and inflation are high, and the demand for apartments is decreasing. This phase separates the men from the boys, the women from the girls, and the true investor from the stock market refugee. The human emotion here is plain old depression for most folks.

>> **Recovery phase:** This phase is the breath of fresh air. The local economy shows signs of life, vacancies decrease, rents level off and start to trickle upward, speculation starts again, and money begins to flow back into market. The human emotion here is pride, because you've waited out the storm.

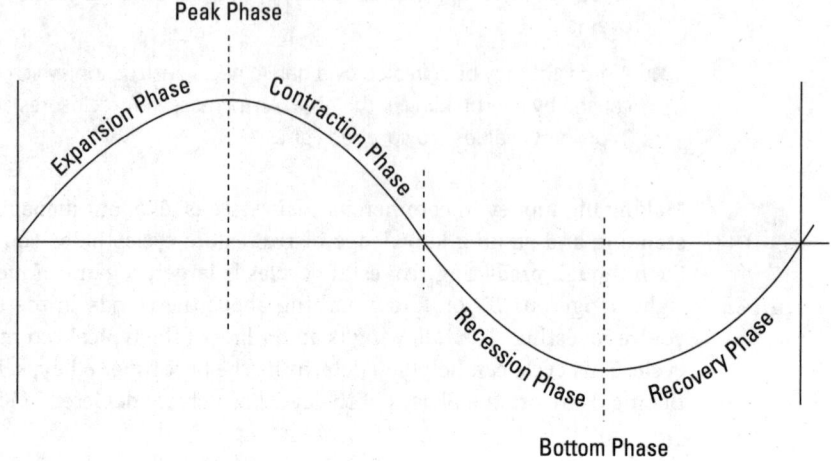

© John Wiley & Sons, Inc.

FIGURE 1-1: The real estate cycle.

REMEMBER

If you can recognize the cycles of your local economy, three obvious questions come to mind, and answering them will determine whether or not you're a successful investor:

>> **When is the best time to buy?** The truthful answer is that it depends. If you're a smart investor, you should buy in the bottom or middle of the expansion cycle. That way, you're buying on trends and following the market and other investors. You'll likely feel safe because you're following what everyone else is doing.

>> **When is it the best time to sell?** The best time to sell is at the peak phase, right at the top of the market. And the biggest problem with selling here is knowing exactly where the top is. Here are two clues that have never failed us yet: Watch the rents and vacancy rates separately. After rents level off and become flat for three straight months or more, you've reached the top. Or for another indication you've reached the top: After vacancy rates are at a three- to five-year low, you've reached the top. It's that simple.

>> **When is it the best time to go bottom-fishing?** If you aren't a bold risk taker, you may find this advice uncomfortable (so consider yourself forewarned!). Maverick investors buy at the bottom phase or at the front end of the recovery phase. This is called "bottom-fishing" for deals. This is where the

big, big money is made. Maverick investors are brave and courageous trendsetters. They're usually the first investors in the worst part of town, and they're usually banking on the area to come back big time. If they play their cards right, they come out on top, and if they don't, they simply walk away with an "aw, shucks." Now that's bravery!

# Following trends

True friends are always around when you call on them, and they won't ever let you down. And economic and demographic trends are your true friends in commercial real estate investing. And best of all, these trends aren't terribly complex or difficult to determine. Here are the three trends that are plainly fundamental when investing in any commercial real estate:

**TIP**

>> **Job growth:** This trend makes perfect sense: Where the jobs are, people are. And where the people are, demand exists for apartment rentals, office space, and consumer goods. Job growth is an excellent indicator of a healthy real estate market.

The best place to start in researching job growth is to contact your local economic development department or chamber of commerce and ask for historical and current job growth data.

>> **Development:** This trend is all about supply and demand. After all, if a shortage of office space or apartment housing is evident, you clearly have a demand for new development. On the other hand, if you see that the city is overbuilding, it's an indication for you hold off and reassess.

>> **In the path of progress:** It isn't too difficult to spot this trend with your own eyes. Whenever new building and development is either coming your way or surrounds your property, you're in the thankful path of economic development. You can feel the "buzz" of prosperity around you.

Chapter **2**

# Evaluating Commercial Real Estate

There's a rumor around town that you need to be an accountant with an Ivy League degree to evaluate and analyze office buildings, retail centers, and apartment complexes. Don't believe the hype. You can count and do some basic math, so you'll have no problem figuring out what your cash flow and return on investment are for any piece of commercial property.

In this chapter, you'll get the inside scoop on the Commercial Property Evaluator. This tool will help you figure out what a commercial property is worth without any fancy calculations or spreadsheets. You'll discover a super quick method to analyze an apartment building and a shopping center like a pro. This chapter also explains how to know a good deal from a bad deal and provides invaluable guiding principles of investment that will keep bad properties out of your portfolio — guaranteed.

# Talking the Talk: Terms You Need to Know

**REMEMBER**

This chapter uses some terminology that you need to be familiar with. Having these terms under your belt is crucial on two fronts:

>> We presume you're reading Book 8 because you want to invest in commercial real estate. Most likely, you'll be using a real estate broker to help you locate and close the deal. Real estate brokers know — and use — most of the terms mentioned here. Gaining a thorough understanding of the terms levels the playing field. If you can speak their language, you gain instant credibility and a relationship advantage over someone without your knowledge and understanding.

>> Just by increasing your word power, you gain increased confidence, which enables you to make sound, efficient investment decisions, and gives you an increased ability to hold your position, especially in negotiations.

Here are the words you need to know to navigate this chapter and talk the talk:

>> **Capitalization rate:** Your *capitalization rate* is your net operating income divided by the sales price. Also known as the *cap rate,* it's the measure of profitability of an investment. Cap rates tell you how much you'd make on an investment if you paid all cash for it; financing and taxation aren't included:

- Cap rate = net operating income ÷ sales price

>> **Cash flow:** Your *annual cash flow* is net operating income minus debt service. You also can figure *monthly cash flow* by dividing your annual cash flow by 12:

- Annual cash flow = net operating income – debt service
- Monthly cash flow = annual cash flow ÷ 12

>> **Cash-on-cash return:** To find your *cash-on-cash return,* divide your annual cash flow by the down payment amount:

- Cash-on-cash return = annual cash flow ÷ down payment

>> **Debt service:** *Debt service* is calculated by multiplying your monthly mortgage amount by 12 months:

- Debt service = monthly mortgage amount × 12

>> **Effective gross income:** You can find your *effective gross income* by subtracting vacancy from gross income:

- Effective gross income = income – (vacancy rate % × income)

>> **Gross income:** *Gross income* is all of your income, including rents, laundry, or vending machine income, and late fees. It can be monthly or annual.

>> **Net operating income (NOI):** Your *net operating income* is your effective gross income minus operating expenses:

- Net operating income = effective gross income − operating expenses

>> **Mix:** When a commercial investor says "What's the *mix?*" they're asking how many studios, one-bedroom, or two-bedroom units the property has.

>> **Operating expenses:** Your *annual operating expenses* for the property typically include taxes, insurance, utilities, management fees, payroll, landscaping, maintenance, supplies, and repairs. This category doesn't include mortgage payments or interest expense.

>> **Vacancy:** A *vacancy* is any unit that's left unoccupied and isn't producing income. *Note:* A unit that's vacated and re-rented in the same month isn't considered a vacancy; it's considered a *turnover.*

>> **Vacancy rate:** Your *vacancy rate* is the number of vacancies divided by the number of units:

- Vacancy rate = number of vacancies ÷ number of units

# THE TECHNICAL MEANING BEHIND THE NUMBERS

*Cap rate, cash flow, cash-on-cash return,* and *net operating income* are investment terms that are explored in this chapter, but what do they really *mean* to you as an investor? Here's the in-depth explanation:

- **Capitalization rate:** A *cap rate* is used as a measure of a property's performance without considering the mortgage financing. If you paid all cash for the investment, how much money would it make? What's the return on your cash outlay? Cap rate is a standard used industrywide, and it's used many different ways. For example, a high cap rate usually typifies a higher risk investment and a low sales price. High cap rate investments typically are found in low-income regions. A low cap rate usually typifies a lower risk investment and a high sales price. Low cap rates typically are found in middle-class to upper income regions. Therefore, neighborhoods within cities have their assigned cap rates "stamped" on them.

  That said, if you know what the NOI is, and you know the given cap rate, you can estimate what the sales price should be: sales price = NOI ÷ cap rate. For example, if the NOI is $57,230 and you want to make investments into 7 percent cap properties, the price you'll offer will be $817,571 (57,230 ÷ 7%). This is a good way to come up with your first offer price — at the very least, it's a starting point.

*(continued)*

*(continued)*

- **Cash flow:** Positive *cash flow* is king, and it's one of your primary objectives in investing. Positive cash flow creates and maintains your investments' momentum. When purchasing an apartment building containing more than five units (considered commercial), a bank's basis for lending is the property's cash-flow capabilities. Your credit score is a lower priority than the cash-flow potential. An apartment building with poor cash flow almost always will appraise much lower than its comparables for the area. Finally, positive cash flow keeps you sleeping at night when property values drop, because your bills and mortgage will still be paid.

- **Cash-on-cash return:** This is the velocity of your money. In other words, how long does it take for your down payment to come back to you? If your down payment were $20,000, how soon would your monthly cash flow add up to $20,000? If your cash flow added up to $20,000 in one year, your cash-on-cash return would be 100 percent. If it takes two years, your cash-on-cash would be 50 percent. If it takes three years, it would be 33 percent.

  Commercial real estate investing can produce phenomenal returns. Cash-on-cash returns of more than 100 percent aren't uncommon. Now, if you were to go to your local bank and deposit $20,000 into its most aggressive CD investment for one to three years, what type of cash-on-cash return could you expect? Maybe 1 percent or if you're really lucky 4 percent? You need to put an emphasis on cash-on-cash return when you invest simply because you need to know how fast you and your investors can get the down payment back so everyone can invest it again — and again into future deals that you find.

- **Net operating income (NOI):** This term is one of the most important ones when analyzing any deal. The net operating income is the dollar amount that's left over after you collect all your income and pay out your operating expenses. This amount is what's used to pay the mortgage. And what's left after you pay the mortgage is what goes into your pocket — your cash flow.

  Always keep your eye on the NOI and look for ways to increase it by either raising rents or reducing expenses. As the NOI increases, so will the value of your property. In fact, if you're in an 8 percent cap neighborhood, for every $100 that the NOI increases, your property value will increase by $1,250. Is that a good return for your efforts or what?

  You know that cap rate = NOI ÷ sales price, but you also can flip the calculation: sales price (or value) = NOI ÷ cap rate. Therefore, you can figure a new value by dividing your new NOI or increase of NOI by the going cap rate. So, $100 ÷ 8 percent = $1,250. Now, if you can increase your NOI by $20,000, your property value will have gone up by $250,000 ($20,000 ÷ 8 percent = $250,000).

# The Commercial Property Evaluator

When you first hear the word *analysis*, you may freak out — especially if you aren't a spreadsheet guru. Coauthors Peter Conti and Peter Harris were intimidated by that word when they first started out, too. But through the years, they've come to look at property analysis more simply.

**TIP**

You got more than you bargained for when you picked up this book. You also get free access to a five-part Masterclass — How to Find, Analyze, and Make Offers on Commercial Properties That Get Accepted. You also get access to the Commercial Property Evaluator. You can let this tool do the math for you so you can quickly determine the value of commercial properties. The Evaluator helps to keep things simple and get new investors past "paralysis of analysis." You can attend the Masterclass and get the Commercial Property Evaluator by going to CommercialQuickStart.com.

## Why a seller's numbers can't be trusted

One of the biggest lessons to learn when you start looking at commercial properties to invest in is that sellers tend to under report their expenses. The reason for this is simple. If the expenses are lower, this increases the net operating income, which results in a higher property valuation.

In some situations, a seller's expenses are lower for a valid reason. For example, the owner may personally manage the property and do the maintenance and repairs themselves. In this case, although the owner might be providing "real" numbers, your costs to run the property would be higher assuming that you're going to hire professional management and maintenance staff.

**TIP**

It's recommended that you hire professional management and a maintenance staff to take care of your property. You won't get wealthy doing low-level work that you can hire specialists to do for you.

To see how this issue could affect you, take a look at this example: If the expenses are under reported by just $10,000, and you're using a .07 cap rate, then the property valuation is going to be off by $142,857 (in the seller's favor). That's quite a difference.

# How the Commercial Property Evaluator works

You can make copies of the Commercial Property Evaluator (as seen in Figure 2-1) and fill in the blanks to use some algorithms developed over the years to tell you the estimated property value.

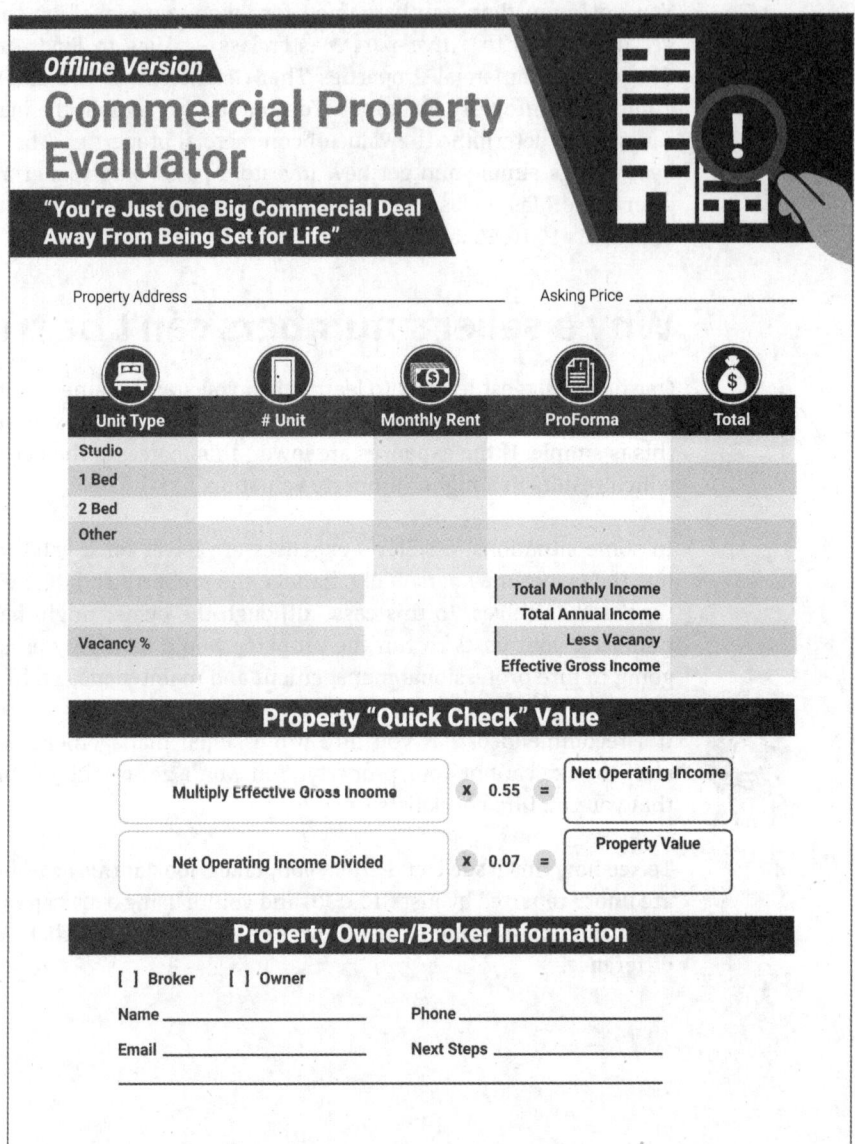

FIGURE 2-1:
The Commercial Property Evaluator is a tool that helps you evaluate a property's worth. It's available on Commercial QuickStart.com.

The online version provides even more information, telling you if the deal is worth pursuing and, if so, an appropriate purchase price and a suggestion initial offer price.

The Commercial Property Evaluator helps you determine whether a deal is worth pursuing by comparing the actual value to the asking price. If the property is way overpriced, the online version provides a red light telling you not to waste your time. A yellow light indicates maybe there's a deal here. When you see a green light, that means go! You've come across a great deal and need to move quickly to get it before someone else does.

Here's the data you need to enter into the Commercial Property Evaluator:

>> The number of units

>> The asking price

>> The unit mix (how many studios, one-bed, and two-bed units)

>> The average rent per unit type

REMEMBER

To keep this super simple, the Commercial Property Evaluator is for apartment buildings only, got it? While the quick valuation provided by the Commercial Property Evaluator isn't perfect for every situation, it's close enough to help you sort deals into red, yellow, and green light piles so that you can avoid the biggest mistake that most new commercial investors make, like getting stuck over analyzing properties and never making any offers. Here's what you can ignore when using the Commercial Property Evaluator:

>> The claimed expenses (because they are highly suspect)

>> The cap rate shown in the listing (since it's not likely to be accurate)

>> Any "proforma" information (which includes projected claims about future income)

Because cap rates are higher or lower depending where you are investing, and can change over time, you can adjust the cap rate you prefer to use in your market. Any good commercial broker can help you determine which cap rate to use for your market. After you decide on this, make sure to use the same cap rate to value every property in the same class. You can fill in the cap rates for your market in Table 2-1.

TIP

Try out using the Commercial Property Evaluator and get the free Masterclass by going to CommercialQuickStart.com.

TABLE 2-1

## Cap Rates

| Property Class | Typical Cap Rate | Cap Rate for Your Market |
|---|---|---|
| Class A | 3.5 to 4.5 | |
| Class B | 5.0 to 6.0 | |
| Class C | 6.5 to 7.5 | |

The Commercial Property Evaluator will determine the leased up, stabilized value of the property for you using the following default settings, which is what we are currently using for most Class C apartment buildings:

» 5% vacancy

» 45% expenses

» .07 cap rate

If you'd like a look under the hood, Table 2-2 displays the formulas used by the Commercial Property Evaluator along with some actual numbers from the 50-unit "Courtside Apartments" so you can see how this works.

**TABLE 2-2** ## Courtside Apartments Example

| Step | Description | Courtside Apartments | Shortcut to Next Step |
|---|---|---|---|
| One | Total Monthly Income | $80,000 | Get Annual Income (Multiply × 12) |
| Two (Multiply × .95) | Total Annual Income | $960,000 | Remove 5% Vacancies |
| Three (Multiply × .55) | Effective Gross Income | $912,000 | Remove 45% Expenses |
| Four (Divide by .07) | Net Operating Income (NOI) | $501,600 | Apply Cap Rate |
| Five | Property Value | $7,165,714 | |

Using the online version, investors also enter the market rents to come up with a "Proforma" value so they know what the property will be worth when they increase the rents up to market value. To do this yourself with the Commercial Property Evaluator here in this chapter, take an extra step and enter the market rents instead of the actual rents. This will give you the proforma value of the property.

You then compare these three values to give an indication of what the upside looks like and whether it's worth your time to pursue the deal:

>> Asking price from the seller

>> Actual property value

>> Proforma value

You can use the Commercial Property Evaluator to quickly separate deals into three piles so that you don't waste your time on properties where the seller is simply asking way too much for the property. In most cases this is a pretty good clue that they aren't motivated. They're hoping that someone comes along who's willing to pay more for the property than it's actually worth.

WARNING

Because you're calculating the leased-up stabilized value of the property using a 5 percent vacancy rate, you'll obviously have to make further adjustments with a property that has a high vacancy rate or that needs to have rehab work done.

# Diving Deeper into Property Valuation

The dictionary definition of the word *analysis* is "a separation of the whole into its component parts." So, during this deep dive you break down *any* property analysis into its component parts:

>> Income

>> Expense

>> Debt

That's it. You take a look at the income information. Then you take a look at the expenses. And finally, you add a loan or mortgage to the overall picture. You combine them to come to a conclusion as to whether this deal makes money. Analysis made simple.

REMEMBER

The size or complexity of the deal doesn't matter. Separate the deal into its three component parts:

>> Analyze and compile the income part.

>> Analyze and compile the expense part.

>> Analyze and compile the debt part.

Any deal can be broken up into these parts. When you have these parts, you can calculate the net operating income, cash flow, cash-on-cash return, and cap rate. It's easy-peasy once you've done it a few times!

## Not-so-obvious tips on analyzing

When you're analyzing any property, keep the following in mind:

>> **Be leery of broker proformas.** *Proformas* are brokers' presentations of data on the property that reflect a best-case scenario or even a perfect-world situation. For example, even though the property may have eight unrentable vacant units, the broker proforma will reflect those units as if they were producing income. So, be careful in your analysis when you see the word *proforma*. It isn't how the property is actually performing.

   Here's the bottom line: Never make offers based on proforma data.

>> **Look deeper into the price.** When analyzing apartments, always look at sales price per door or price per unit. Get information on what local apartments have sold for recently on a price-per-unit basis. For example, if you know for a fact that the last three sales of comparable apartments on the same street sold for $45,000 per unit, then you know in your analysis that paying $65,000 per unit may be too much. Knowing your price per unit allows you to make quick decisions if the real estate agent is asking too much or if you're getting a steal of a deal.

>> **Not knowing expenses can cost you.** One of the most understated and misunderstood aspects of property analysis is expenses. Of course, plugging actual and true operating expenses into your analysis isn't easy because often that data isn't available.

   You'll get your most reliable expense data from your property manager or from a professional property manager who manages similar properties, not from the broker. Look at property expenses in three different ways:

   - Look at it in expenses per unit. Basically, divide the total expenses by the number of units.

   - Look at expenses as a percentage of the income. For example, as a general rule, for apartment sizes that are greater than 50 units, take expenses to be at least 45 percent of the income.

   - Look at expenses in the form of expenses per square foot. You get this number by dividing the total expenses by the total square footage of the living space.

**REMEMBER**

>> **Don't forget about the taxes.** Be wary of property taxes stated in your analysis or given to you by the broker. Brokers who present property data rarely have the *new* property taxes in their spreadsheets. *New taxes* refer to what your new tax bill would be upon transfer of ownership. For example, the current owner may have owned the property for 30 years, and his property taxes may have increased only slightly in those years. But when you take over, the tax assessor will reassess the property value, most times based on your sales price. Therefore, it's quite possible that your taxes may increase three to five times from what the previous owner paid. Do your research by calling the property tax assessor's office and ask how property taxes are reassessed upon transfer of ownership.

**TIP**

>> **Verify your analysis.** When coauthors Peter Conti and Peter Harris are analyzing a deal in which the broker feels that they can either raise the rents or decrease the expenses after they take over, they always verify the broker's projections. To verify whether raising the rent is possible, they use an online tool called Rentometer. They also call properties in the area to find out what they are getting for similar units; it only takes a few minutes to do, and the information is invaluable. To verify whether they can reduce expenses, they call their property manager or contact another professional property manager and run the expense scenario by them. It's easy to do — with results worth their weight in gold.

>> **Get a thumbs up from your lender.** When coauthors Peter Conti and Peter Harris get excited about a deal during their analysis, they send it to their lender. The lender looks at it from their point of view: Are the numbers good enough to get a good loan on it? Investors may run cash-flow projections based on a 15 percent down payment, but the lender may spot something in the financials that may qualify the property for only a 25 percent down payment. If your lender won't do this for you, get another lender.

**WARNING**

>> **Keep in mind that concessions may penalize your future.** When you're presented with information about the tenants, ask about any move-in specials given to the current tenants. Those specials are called *rent concessions,* and concessions are given when the market is weak and tenants need to be enticed to move in or renew their leases. Usually, the tenants are given one month rent free, and it's usually the 13th month of a 12-month lease. The problem with this is that if you're acquiring the property, you won't receive rent from that tenant on the 13th month of the lease. And this gets worse if 50 percent of your tenants have this concession, especially if their 13th month is the same month — this means that 50 percent of the tenants will not be paying you rent that month. Ouch!

## Breakeven analysis

When analyzing property, you always want to know what the breakeven point is. The *breakeven point* is the point at which occupancy income is equal to your mortgage payments. In other words, if you know that your breakeven point is 70 percent occupancy, you know you're able to at least pay your expenses plus mortgage without going into a negative cash-flow position. For a property that's highly leveraged or has a large mortgage payment, its breakeven point is higher than usual — meaning that you have more risk if you're negative in cash flow.

**REMEMBER**

To calculate your breakeven point, add up all your property's operating expenses and annual mortgage payments and divide by the gross potential income. *Gross potential income* is what the income of the property would be if it were 100 percent occupied with paying tenants. Here's the equation you'll need to calculate the breakeven point:

Breakeven point (%) = operating expenses + annual mortgage payments ÷ gross potential income

For example, say that your operating expenses are $75,000, your annual mortgage payments are $35,000, and your gross potential income is $200,000. To find your breakeven point percentage, use this calculation:

$75,000 + $35,000 ÷ $200,000 = 55%

This means that at 55 percent occupancy, you're breaking even when it comes to cash flow (see Figure 2-2). Anything greater than 55 percent occupancy sends you to cash-flow positive. Conversely, if you drop below 55 percent occupancy, you're in negative cash flow.

## Establishing and following guiding principles

When you're looking at many types of income properties and analyzing them, you need to have a set of guiding principles for investment. Without them, you'd probably wander aimlessly in the real estate investment game.

Coauthors Peter Conti and Peter Harris have established some starting guiding principles for you. These principles will set the standards for your investments and help you set working goals moving forward. They've used the following standards for years themselves and with their clients, which has saved many people from passing up that great once-in-a-lifetime deal or buying that deal that really stunk. Your guiding principles are basically fail-safe measures to guide you into cash-flowing, wealth-building investments and to keep you out of negative cash-flowing ones.

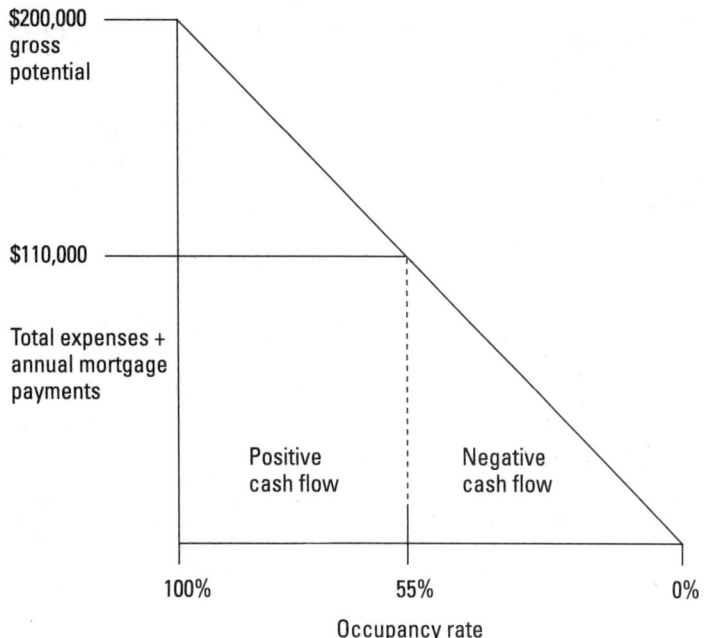

**FIGURE 2-2:**
The breakeven
point in this
example is
55 percent.

**REMEMBER**

Here are the guiding principles:

>> **Make sure that you have a positive cash flow.** Having positive cash flow
keeps your momentum going. Positive cash flow allows you to leave your day
job if that's your goal. Positive cash flow allows you to invest more money, and
it opens doors for the next investment to flow right in.

>> **Have a cash-on-cash return of 8 percent or greater.** A good cash-on-cash
return puts velocity on your money. It keeps your cash flow positive when you
have those not-so-good months. A good cash-on-cash return allows you to
brag to your investor buddies about what a well-run property you have.

>> **Have a cap rate of 7 percent or greater.** A great cap rate means your NOI is
healthy. A healthy NOI is stable and growing, which means your property
value is doing the same. A great cap rate also gets you the best loan terms.

These are only *starting* guiding principles of investment. You have to start some-
place, right? You may be thinking, "But you won't find any 7 caps in my city!" And
you may even believe that it's impossible to find higher cash-on-cash returns. Or
you may be convinced that it's impossible to cash flow positively unless you put
down 50 percent. Well, sooner or later, you'll be convinced and support the theory
that at any one time, great deals are out there waiting for you.

# Running the Numbers on Some Properties

After you have some basic commercial property investment terms and principles under your belt, it's time to walk through analyzing two properties. This is where it gets fun!

**TIP**

Be sure to follow these tips when analyzing your own retail property deal:

>> **Look at the price per square foot.** When analyzing retail, one of the first things to look at is the price per square foot. It's an easy way to compare apples to apples and oranges to oranges. It's also a way to get a reality check to see whether you're paying too much for the property compared to other recent sales.

>> **Be conservative in your number crunching.** What you'll find when you own a few retail centers is that incomes given to you by either the broker or seller are overstated, and expenses are understated. Really take a hard look at each item given and then take a conservative approach when running your numbers.

>> **Replace your reserves.** One of the most overlooked expenses when analyzing retail is the replacement reserve. *Replacement reserve* is an amount set aside every month to pay for property items that wear out and need to be replaced, such as roofs, siding, sidewalks, parking lots, heating/air-conditioning equipment, and so on. When these items come up for repair or replacement three to five years after you take ownership, the money has to come from somewhere — refinancing, your pockets, your partner's pockets, or a reserve account you cleverly set up ahead of time.

>> **Look at the parking ratio.** The parking ratio for your retail center is more important than you think. The standard to begin with is four spaces per 1,000 square feet. If you don't have enough parking, it can create a problem down the road.

>> **Consider class.** All commercial properties fall under classifications — A, B, C, or maybe even D. Class A properties are newer, have top-of-the-line features, are in the best locations, and attract the highest-quality tenants. As you go into the lower classes, location, age, and construction become less desirable. Pay attention to what class property you're evaluating because as classes differ, so do location, price, rent, and occupancy.

>> **Match rent rolls to estoppels.** The *rent roll* is a list of tenant names showing what they pay in rent, in addition to when the lease agreement expires. *Estoppels* are letters sent to the tenant by someone other than the landlord to confirm in writing the terms of the lease, including rent amount, lease expirations, and any other options they have agreed on.

Estoppels are used because the tenant may not be paying the landlord the appropriate rent (for whatever reason), or the landlord may have made a side agreement with the tenant that can't be confirmed or enforced by new owners. When the tenant-signed estoppels are received, you can compare them to the rent rolls and actual signed leases for income verification.

>> **Check in with your lender early.** Before digging too deeply into your analysis, call up your lender and present the rent roll, the type of tenants, and financials to them. Have the lender review this deal from their perspective. Some lenders may not like certain businesses. For example, securing a loan for a shopping center with a dry cleaner or automotive repair place has been more difficult lately because of environmental concerns. Even movie theater chains and office buildings have come under scrutiny because of recent changes in the marketplace.

# Analyzing an apartment deal

Apartments are a great place to start practicing since they're easy to analyze and everyone needs a place to live. Looking at a sample deal together means you can follow along with the process.

Cool Heights Apartments is offered at $1,650,000. It's a well-maintained 20-unit (all 2-bed/1-bath) complex located in an up-and-coming area one block from City Hall. Each unit is rented for $1,575 per month, and the building is currently 100 percent occupied. The owner has spent more than $100,000 in rehab and upgrades in the last 12 months. All new furnaces and air conditioners were installed. The owner is retiring to Florida, which is the reason for selling. Professional property management is in place, and the building is managed very well. It has a good rental history. Covered parking is included. Tenants are responsible for their own electric and heat utility bills; the owner pays for the property's water and garbage removal. The total building square footage is 22,160 square feet.

The following financial data was given for yearly operating expenses:

>> Insurance: $13,500

>> Real estate taxes: $28,830

>> Maintenance: $44,700

>> Electrical (common area): $3,900

>> Water/sewer: $28,200

>> Property management (5 percent): $18,630

>> Garbage removal: $3,450

>> Supplies: $8,100

>> Reserves: $18,000

>> Accounting: $4,200

So, adding that up, the total operating expenses are $171,510.

Now, separate this whole deal into its three simple components of income, expenses, and debt. Here's the income breakdown:

>> Gross income = $1,575 × 20 units × 12 months = $378,000 per year

>> Vacancy rate = $378,000 per year × 10 percent (assumption) = $37,800

>> Effective gross income = $378,000 – $37,800 = $359,100 per year

Here's the expense breakdown:

Total operating expenses = $171,510

To figure out the debt breakdown, assume that the interest rate is 5.5 percent today with a 25-year amortization period:

>> Asking price = $1,650,000

>> Down payment = 20 percent of asking price, which is $330,000

>> Loan amount (principal) = $1,650,000 – $330,000 = $1,320,000

>> Loan payment per month = $18,106 (we used a mortgage calculator for this figure)

>> Loan payments per year (debt service) = $8,106 × 12 months = $97,272

Now you have everything you need to figure out whether this deal makes money or not, using these four easy steps:

**1.** **Calculate the net operating income (NOI).**

Net operating income = effective gross income – operating expenses

$359,100 – $171,510 = $187,590

**2.** **Calculate the annual cash flow.**

Annual cash flow = net operating income – debt service

$187,590 – $97,272 = $90,318

3. **Calculate the cash-on-cash return.**

   Cash-on-cash return = annual cash flow ÷ down payment

   $90,318 ÷ $330,000 = 27.41 percent

4. **Calculate the cap rate.**

   Cap rate = net operating income ÷ sales price

   $187,590 ÷ $1,650,000= 11.4 percent

So, in a nutshell, you're putting down $330,000 to earn $90,318 per year in cash flow, or approximately 27 percent return on your $330,000. That's pretty darn good.

# Analyzing a retail shopping center

One of the most important items to understand when analyzing retail investments is the lease. A *lease* is a written legal agreement between the landlord (called the *lessor*) and the tenant (called the *lessee*) that establishes how much the tenant will pay in rent; how long the tenant is legally committed to stay; any additional payments by the tenant for taxes, insurance, or maintenance; rent increases; renewal clauses and options; and all rights, privileges, and responsibilities of the tenant and landlord.

Following are types of leases you'll run into in the course of looking into investing in retail shopping centers. Each has its own wrinkles and stipulations, so pay attention to the small differences:

- » **Gross lease:** The landlord agrees to pay all operating expenses and charges the tenant a rent that's over and above the operating expenses. The types of expenses covered include taxes, insurance, management, maintenance, and any other costs associated with operating the property.

- » **Modified gross lease:** This lease is slightly different from the standard gross lease in that some of the operating expenses — such as maintenance, insurance, or utilities — aren't paid for by the landlord and are passed on to the tenant. These expenses are called *pass-through expenses* because they're passed through to the tenant. Many office-type buildings use a modified gross lease.

- » **Net lease:** In a net lease, the tenants pay the operating expenses of the property, and the landlord gets to net a certain amount every month by charging rent over and above the total operating expenses. This lease is favorable in many ways: It's favorable to landlords because they aren't responsible for any operational expenses of the property. It's favorable to tenants because they get to fix up their stores as they see fit and do their own maintenance and cleaning. Net leases typically are customized to fit tenant needs.

This type of lease is used mainly by retailers. The landlord takes care of the common area maintenance, and the expense of that is spread among the tenants and billed back to them.

Here are the several different levels and types of net leases:

- **Single net lease (N):** In a *single net lease,* the tenant agrees to pay property taxes. The landlord pays for all other expenses in the operation.

- **Double net lease (NN):** In a *double net lease,* the tenant agrees to pay property taxes and insurance. The landlord pays for all other expenses in the operation.

- **Triple net lease (NNN):** A *triple net lease* is most favorable for landlords and is one of the most popular today. The tenants agree to pay the landlord rent plus all other property-related expenses including taxes, insurance, and maintenance. The landlord gets a true net payment. Banks, fast-food restaurants, and *anchor tenants* typically use triple net leases.

Anchor tenants are major tenants, usually the tenant occupying the most space. Anchor tenants are critical in giving value and security to a retail shopping center investor. Their signs are usually the largest and stand out. Major retail chain stores typically are anchor tenants and are called so because they attract other businesses to the shopping center location. They "anchor" the shopping center so to speak.

A common clause used in net leases is the *expense stop clause,* which states that any amount over a certain fixed expense will be charged to the tenant. The fixed expense is a dollar amount agreed on by the tenant and landlord.

**TIP**

A great income generator for landlords is to build a *percentage of sales* clause into the lease. With this clause, the landlord gets an additional payment from the tenant if and when the tenant reaches a certain sales volume or profitability. For example, say a burger restaurant has agreed to pay an additional 3 percent of its gross sales after its sales reach a certain level. The landlord would be paid the 3 percent in addition to the normal lease payment.

Even though retail leases are long term — say, 5 to 15 years in length — it's common for leases to have rental increases or rent escalations in the middle of the leasing years. For example, you could have a rent escalation of 5 percent once every five years until the lease expires.

After you have all that info on leases down, it's time to analyze a deal. Here's the deal: Kimo's Landing, a 36,000-square-foot retail center anchored by a major chain pharmacy is in the center of town, right in the path of progress. It's on 3 acres of land. The retail center is composed of eight stores of various types, ranging from a bagel shop to a U.S. post office. Table 2-3 provides the square footage and yearly rent of each unit.

**TABLE 2-3**

## Square Footage and Yearly Rent for Kimo's Landing

| Lessees | Square Footage | Rent Per Square Foot | Yearly Rent |
|---|---|---|---|
| Pharmacy | 10,000 | $10 | $100,000 |
| Bank | 8,000 | $8 | $64,000 |
| Bagel shop | 1,500 | $5 | $7,500 |
| Express photo shop | 1,500 | $5 | $7,500 |
| Electronics shop | 1,000 | $6 | $6,000 |
| Beauty store | 2,000 | $6 | $12,000 |
| Clothing store | 6,000 | $7 | $42,000 |
| U.S. post office | 6,000 | $8 | $48,000 |
| **Total** | **36,000** | — | **$287,000** |

All leases are triple net (NNN), with the owner charging the tenants for common area maintenance (CAM). The CAM expense for the owner is $3,000 per month and includes landscaping, parking lot, hallways, and restrooms.

Now you need to separate this whole deal into its three simple components of income, expenses, and debt. Here's the income breakdown:

Gross income = $287,000

For the expense breakdown, because this is a triple net lease, the tenants pay all property operating expenses. The landlord initially pays for all common area maintenance (CAM) expenses, but then the CAM expense is billed back to and divided among the tenants. That's why there's no expense listed here as a cost to the landlord.

To figure the debt breakdown, you need to figure out what the yearly loan payments would be. Assume that the interest rate is 6.5 percent today with a 30-year amortization period:

>> Asking price = $3,100,000

>> Down payment = 20 percent of asking price, which is $620,000

>> Loan amount (principal) = $3,100,000 – $620,000 = $2,480,000

>> Loan payment per month = $15,675 (we used a mortgage calculator for this figure)

>> Loan payments per year (debt service) = $15,675 × 12 months = $188,100

Now you have everything you need to figure out whether this deal makes money, using these four easy steps:

1. **Calculate the net operating income (NOI).**

   Net operating income = effective gross income – operating expenses

   $287,000 – $0 = $287,000

2. **Calculate the cash flow.**

   Annual cash flow = net operating income – debt service

   $287,000 – $188,100 = $98,900

3. **Calculate the cash-on-cash return.**

   Cash-on-cash return = annual cash flow ÷ down payment

   $98,900 ÷ $620,000 = 16 percent

4. **Calculate the cap rate.**

   Cap rate = net operating income ÷ sales price

   $287,000 ÷ $3,100,000 = 9.3 percent

That's a pretty decent return on your investment, and it's pretty hands-off compared to being involved with managing a property every day.

# Valuing Properties like a Professional

Professional property evaluators, commonly called *real estate appraisers,* have the awesome responsibility of estimating or giving an opinion of a value on commercial properties. It makes sense for you to understand how appraisers value commercial real estate so you can apply their techniques to our methods of estimating value.

# Approach #1: Comparable sales

The first and easiest method in commercial property evaluation is called the *comparable sales approach.* If you've bought a house before, you may remember the bank had an appraiser go out and give the property a value that you hoped at least equaled your purchase price. Well, the same applies here for commercial property. The commercial appraiser goes out and compares prices of recently sold local properties that are similar in form and function to the property they're appraising. The comparison will produce an average price, and that price is what your property will be valued at. But in commercial comparables, instead of looking at just overall sales price, the sales price per square foot of the building is also considered one of the main factors.

Here's a quick example:

>> **Property A,** a 10,000-square-foot building, sold last spring for $65 per square foot. Doing the simple math to compute the sales price, you calculate 10,000 square feet × $65 per square foot = $650,000.

>> **Property B,** a 9,000-square-foot building, sold three months ago for $68 per square foot. Again, doing the math, 9,000 square feet × $68 per square foot = $712,000.

>> **Property C,** the property you want to figure a price for, is similar to Property A and Property B and is 11,000 square feet in size. If you average out the price per square foot on both Property A and Property B, the average comes out to $66.50 per square foot. Use that price per square foot as your number to evaluate Property C. Doing the math, you get 11,000 square feet × $66.50 = $731,500 as the value for Property C.

TIP

When attempting to value apartment complexes, price per unit or price per door is used more often than price per square foot. Much like the preceding example, price per unit is calculated from previous apartment sales. When you have an average of price per unit for several complexes, you can estimate a value of another complex.

WARNING

Even though the comparable sales approach is the easiest method for figuring out a value for a commercial property, it can be flawed. When a market isn't stabilized, or values go up or down, this can nullify the use of the comparable sales approach. In some small-town markets, there are no comparable sales because of the lack of overall sales.

# Approach #2: Income

When you get out into the real world of commercial real estate, you'll discover that commercial properties are chiefly valued by the amount of income they bring in. (That's why they're called income properties!) To be more precise, it's the net operating income that's most important.

The *income approach* of valuing a property can be used when accurate financial and operating data are available on the property. This approach is based on the capitalization rate being calculated for a property. To calculate the cap rate, you must know the property's net operating income and sales price.

After you calculate the cap rate of a property, the next step is to compare the cap rate to similar properties' cap rates. Every area in your city that has commercial properties has a cap rate stamped on it. Your job is to find those other properties and their cap rates and get the average. That average cap rate percentage is what you use in calculating property value when you know the net operating income.

Take a look at this example: You want to value a 50-unit apartment building. You calculate the net operating income to be $180,000. Your research from previous apartment sales tells you that the going cap rate for the neighborhood in which the property is located is 8 percent. Now, if you know the net operating income and the cap rate, you can figure out the sales price. Here's how:

>> Cap rate = net operating income ÷ sale price

>> 7 percent = $180,000 ÷ sale price

>> Sale price = 180,000 ÷ 7 percent = $2,571,428

Now you know that the property should be valued at or estimated to be $2,571,428, based on average cap rates in the area and the property's net operating income. We love dealing with numbers in the millions. At times it feels like we're playing Monopoly!

REMEMBER

Every investor who wants to find out how to estimate values of income-producing properties should know and understand the basics of the income approach. It's an indispensable tool that investors, real estate agents, and lenders use often.

# Approach #3: Cost to replace the property

The third approach to figuring out what a property is worth is the *cost approach*, which appraisers seldom use these days. The theory behind it is this: The value of a property is whatever it costs to construct a new one in addition to the cost of the land.

**REMEMBER**

The cost approach is best when the property is new or almost new. For older properties, because you can buy properties for much less than it costs to build a new property, appraisers are likely to use this approach.

To apply the cost approach in valuing a building, you must first figure out what the value of its land would be. This is typically done via a sales comparison approach (see the earlier section "Approach #1: Comparable sales"). Then you have to determine what it will cost to construct, reproduce, or replace the building in question as if you were doing it from scratch. Be sure to allow for accrued depreciation and obsolescence of the building.

You end up with a property value calculation of the following:

Land value + building cost – depreciation = estimated property value

# Understanding What Creates Value

What is it that really creates value in commercial real estate? Well, in residential real estate, such as single-family homes, what creates value is location. "Location, location, location!" Sound familiar? The most expensive homes are in the best of neighborhoods, right? But location isn't the only factor that creates value in commercial real estate. In fact, two factors are actually *more* important than location: use and the lease. They're covered in the following sections.

## Use: How the property is used gives value

How a property is used is probably the most important factor in understanding values in commercial real estate. Here's why: Say that you have a 5-acre lot directly across the street from a brand-new luxury apartment complex that has a three-month waiting list for new tenants. Common sense says that you should develop it into another apartment complex because there's great demand. It appears big money awaits you.

But upon further research, you find out that the city says that your 5-acre lot can be used for only agricultural purposes. Where is there greater investment value — in a high-rent luxury apartment complex or a tomato farm? Unless you are also in the sauce business, the luxury apartment complex is the winner. Use determines value.

Sorry, friend, but you can't always use your property however you want. The city's local planning department determines how a piece of land or property can be used. The planning department keeps control of this through zoning. *Zoning* specifies which type of property may be built in specific areas. Zoning is a governmental system for regulating land use and is typically master planned by the city. In the preceding example, the city has zoned that particular piece of land, the 5 acres, as agricultural use. This means that it can be used for only agricultural purposes and can't be used to build apartments, retail centers, office buildings, or industrial parks. The 5 acres would achieve its highest investment value if it were zoned for apartments or even retail — but the planning department may have other development plans for the area.

Here's a quick example showing how use can have a significant impact on property value: Say you go ahead and decide to farm and grow tomatoes on your 5 acres. You can produce a thousand 25-pound cartons of tomatoes per 5 acres. You can sell them for $2 per pound, which produces an income of $50,000. After you deduct a production cost of 30 percent, you're left with $35,000 of income over 5 acres. So, you end up with $7,000 per acre. If you were to capitalize that at 8 percent, here's what it would look like: $7,000 ÷ 8 percent = $87,500 per acre. And here's how to get the estimated value over the 5 acres: 5 acres × $87,500 = $437,500.

Now, say that the 5 acres were approved for use as an apartment building. On your 5-acre lot, you can fit 2 acres of living space. Each acre is 43,560 square feet. So, 2 acres equals 87,120 total square feet of living space. It's reasonable to say that apartment sales are going for $50 per square foot. Therefore, 87,120 square feet × $50 per square foot = $4,356,000, which is the estimated value for the apartment building.

Wow, how exciting! This is what commercial real estate is all about — finding opportunity, creating a product that betters humankind, and then reaping the rewards. The challenge in front of you in this example is to get the zoning changed on the 5 acres to allow an apartment building.

## Leases: As the lease goes, so goes the value

A *lease* is a written legal agreement between the lessor (the landlord) and the lessee (the tenant) whereby the lessee compensates the lessor (by paying rent) for the use of the property for a specific time period. There's no such thing as a typical commercial lease, but here are a few main differences between a lease for a commercial property and a residential property (an apartment unit, for example):

>> A commercial lease is a lot tougher to get out of than a residential lease.

>> A commercial lease tends to last a lot longer, sometimes for 20 years.

>> Because no standard commercial lease exists, parties can be as flexible and creative as they want.

>> A commercial lease has significantly less consumer protection (for the tenant) than a residential lease does. Many tenant/landlord laws such as rent control don't apply.

REMEMBER

When you buy a commercial property, you're buying the leases, and the property comes for free. That's how important the actual lease is to the value of the property. Simply put, if the lease is weak, your property value is weak. And conversely, if the property has a strong lease, the property value is going to be strong.

As you may imagine, leases are the number-one killer of deals. They're the lifelines of income to the property. If the lifeline is tethered and weak, then your income is weak as well. And who wants to invest big dollars in a not-so-sure income stream? The lender won't, and you shouldn't either. In fact, if a business in one of the shopping center's stores has a lease agreement with one year left, the income from that store isn't even counted by the lender when making a loan decision — maybe you shouldn't count it in your initial analysis either.

Here's how you, the investor, or a lender would look at a property's lease in connection to the value it creates for the property: Say you've been sent a great deal from your broker. It's for a 5,000-square-foot, single-tenant property that's occupied by the successful family-run and family-owned Grandma's Corner Groceries. The rent is $7 per square foot, or $35,000 per year and that includes taxes, insurance, and maintenance. The current lease has five years remaining.

Say also that you've been sent another deal for a 5,000-square-foot property that has a Starbucks as its tenant. Starbucks pays $6 per square foot, or $30,000 per year, which also includes taxes, insurance, and maintenance. The current lease has five years remaining.

The question is this: Which is the better investment? Grandma's Corner Groceries or Starbucks? Which one is a lower risk? Which one allows you to predict that you'll be paid every month for the next five years? Which one is less likely to go out of business? Which one will enable you to sleep at night knowing that your investment dollars are in good hands?

Starbucks is the obvious answer, even though you have higher income on the grocery store. Starbucks is a highly rated company and is publicly traded on the NASDAQ. Its financials are open to the public. It has a responsibility to its shareholders to make a profit. Even if it decides to close up shop there and abandon the property, it must make good on the lease and pay the lease off in its entirety. On the other hand, Grandma's Corner Groceries is backed by who knows what. Grandpa? If it goes out of business for some reason — fire, theft, infighting, divorce — your options for financial recourse don't favor your breaking even. So, the property with the Starbucks lease will command a greater value because of its lower risk.

Here are a handful of things to watch for when reviewing a lease agreement as an investor:

>> Rent amount

>> Lease term or how long the lease is for

>> Additional costs that the landlord and tenant may be responsible for

>> Subleasing

>> Whether you need to do any improvements to the property before you move tenants in

>> Is it a gross lease where the landlord pays expenses or a net lease with the tenant paying their share of the expenses?

Read the leases thoroughly many times so that you don't miss a thing. Check out this example about some investors who missed a very important clause in the lease: They purchased a shopping center and the largest tenant, which took up one-third of the total space, had a clause in the lease that said if the store didn't produce $600,000 in gross sales per year, it could back out of the lease. Two years into the lease, the sales volume dropped below $600,000, and the tenant opted out of the lease.

## Location: The unchangeable factor

As mentioned earlier, location is a key factor in understanding what creates value in commercial real estate. How does location create value? One way is job growth. If a city has gone out of its way to attract and entice employers to open up businesses there, that causes economic growth to occur. And economic growth affects real estate value in a positive way, just as a city with negative economic growth causes real estate values to fall.

Certain neighborhoods or districts are better bets than others for commercial real estate, especially if they're in the path of progress. New construction and revitalization including changes such as trendy shops or new restaurants are all associated with instilling new life into a neighborhood or district. If you witness an area undergoing any of these, you can bet the real estate values there will be impacted positively.

# SUPPLY AND DEMAND: TIMING THE MARKET JUST RIGHT

When demand is high for certain commercial real estate, value goes up. Your job as the investor is to find out why. Why is demand high? What's driving the demand? Is it the influx of companies moving in or expanding in the area? Is it the explosion of retail shopping due to the influx of young families and professionals? Find out what's going on.

See where you are in the real estate cycle. Are you in a rising market, at the top of the market, or in a down market? If you're in a rising market, values will increase. Ride it to the top, and then make a decision to sell or wait for the inevitable downward trend. The downward trend is absolutely okay if the property sustains itself and cash flows well. If you find yourself on the downward trend, get out before you lose too much value or weather the storm and think long term.

Keep in mind that supply and demand come in cycles. And because of this, property values will be cyclical as well. (Study the real estate cycle in Chapter 1 of Book 8, which will help you see where your market is currently and how values are affected by supply-and-demand situations.) Here's how you can time the market to ride the wave of increasing value:

- **Watch prices.** If the downward trend has stopped, you've reached bottom or almost bottom. It's time to buy and ride the wave back up.

- **Watch job reports.** When job growth is positive, it's time to ride the wave.

- **Watch investors.** When you see other investors come in and start investing heavily early, it's time to jump in with them.

However, there are pitfalls to valuing the market by watching rising prices, positive job growth, and outside investors. Here are some of those pitfalls:

- **You waited too long.** Determining exactly when the upward wave starts isn't easy. If you wait for signs that are too obvious, you can miss the wave entirely. You have to start paddling at some point or you'll have to wave that wave goodbye.

- **You misjudged the wave.** What you thought was a wave was just a ripple. Oops.

- **You got greedy.** People tend to get overly confident when the market just keeps going up and up and up. But what goes up must come down at some point. So, if you wait too long, you may miss your run at the profits.

**REMEMBER**

The success of a shopping center, for example, largely depends on its location. You can fix parking lots and physical appearance, but you can't fix poor location. A great location combined with well-selected stores equals long-term success and a superb investment.

# Differentiating a Good Deal from a Bad Deal

If you get stuck trying to figure out what's a good deal or how to you define a bad deal, you're not alone. Unfortunately, the answers can be a bit squishy. After all, what's good for one investor may be bad for you, and vice versa. It really depends on the purpose of your investment buys. The purpose behind your investment could be for cash flow, long-term hold, or short-term hold. The following sections examine all three.

## Cash-flow investors

Cash-flow investors invest to produce cash-in-your-pocket-every-month income. For the cash-flow investor, any of these would be a good deal:

>> A 95 percent to 100 percent occupied, well-maintained apartment complex with excellent professional property management

>> An apartment complex that has a breakeven occupancy point of 70 percent or less

>> A retail shopping center with a highly rated, credited tenant on a ten-year triple net lease with rent escalations every year

>> A multistory office building that you own debt free and that's filled with great long-term tenants

**WARNING**

For the cash-flow investor, any of these would be a bad deal:

>> Any type of property with lots of deferred maintenance

>> Any property that's so highly leveraged with debt that if 10 percent of the tenants moved out, you'd be in a negative cash-flow situation

>> An apartment complex in an apartment-filled neighborhood in a soft rental market

# Long-term investors

Long-term investors hold their investments over time and build wealth through appreciation and paying down the loan principal.

For the long-term investor, here are some good deals:

>> A shopping center with a long-term triple net lease in a medium-sized town with an aggressive economy

>> An apartment complex built in the path of new construction and job growth

>> Any commercial investment in an area that has had decreasing cap rates for the past few years

**WARNING**

For the long-term investor, here are some bad deals:

>> Overpaying in an area where cap rates are increasing

>> Buying in an area where the economy has been sustained by one large employer

>> An office building that's functionally obsolete today with new building projects underway nearby

# Short-term investors

Short-term investors hold their investments two years or less. Their goal is to buy, fix up, stabilize, and sell.

For the short-term investor, here are a couple of good deals:

>> Buying at a really low price by using ultraconservative resale figures

>> Acquiring an "easy-fix" rehab property with little down payment and owner financing in a seller's market

**WARNING**

For the short-term investor, these are some bad deals:

>> Buying a rehab in a market that starts to decline right after your purchase

>> Not doing a thorough enough analysis and due diligence and finding out that your rehab budget is actually off by double the amount

>> Assuming a loan with a large prepay (early payoff) penalty over the next few years

# Chapter **3**

# Property Management: Who's Minding Your Ship?

ommercial properties are similar to cruise ships in some ways. If you have a successful, well-informed captain steering the ship to your destination, you'll get there and have lots of fun doing it. You may even relax a little. However, if your captain takes you off course and into choppy waters, you could get seasick and end up on a deserted island. Well, the same applies to your commercial property investment: You have to make sure that your "captain" is a good one, or else your investment may receive a burial at sea.

In this chapter, you get down to the business of discovering the essential skills of navigating and managing your property. You get tips on how to do it a few different ways. You can do it yourself or hire and manage a property manager. You get an inside look into the day-to-day responsibilities of a property manager. You also discover the world of absentee owners. Knowing how to successfully manage a property from afar is a critical navigational skill to possess. It allows you to put the pieces together in owning and operating a commercial property successfully and profitably.

# Being the Boss: Manage Your Commercial Property Yourself

So, you want to manage your own commercial properties? Well, here's a little secret about making nice profits, growing your real estate business, and making smart investment decisions: It's not about the property. That's right, being successful in managing your own property has little to do with the property. So, if it isn't about the property, who or what is it really about? The answer is you! It's about you, the investor; you, the property owner; and you, the property manager. The following sections give you all that you need to know in order to successfully manage your real estate.

**REMEMBER**

Your property's success will *never* go beyond your own personal business development. So, go forth and spend money and time educating yourself on how to successfully manage a property and improve your overall business skills. Your future depends on it!

## Improving your management skills with a few basic tips

**TIP**

When managing the property yourself, keep the following time-tested advice in mind:

>> **Never be friends with your tenants.** Instead, make sure your relationship is a business-friendly one. The last thing you want to do is take your friend to court for an eviction (which means that you probably won't, and you'll be the one to lose out).

>> **Know that people (not properties) cause problems.** Properties don't pay late, cause damage, or cause high vacancy. People cause these problems. So, make it a point to lease to good tenants and good companies. Having no tenant is better than having a bad one.

>> **Get everything in writing.** As manager of any real estate, words *spoken* are like sticks and stones — not worth very much. So, make sure that you write everything down, including rent increases, promises to pay, renewals, or improvements or repairs that the tenant has agreed to do.

>> **Know your market like the back of your hand.** Always know what your competitors down the block are doing with their properties. Know what they're offering to their tenants, know what sells, and know what the tenant-landlord laws are in your area. To find out how to best become familiar with your market, check out Chapter 2 in Book 8.

>> **Have nothing in your name.** Protect yourself and your personal assets from lawsuits by having your properties and businesses legally detached from you personally. First of all, the property should be in an LLC (a limited liability company) or in another type of legal entity that you and your real estate attorney and tax advisor agree on. That way if a tenant files a lawsuit, he can only go after what's in the LLC or entity, not after your home and personal belongings. Also, don't commingle the finances between the property and your personal expenses in any way because, in most cases, that will negate the protection an LLC or entity provides you.

**REMEMBER**

The success and profitability of your commercial real estate investing business also depends a lot on your management techniques and how you implement them. Here are a few tips to help you get the ball rolling:

>> **Work on your people-handling skills.** When managing commercial real estate, you're responsible for managing people of many different types: your tenants, employees, contractors, vendors, government employees, and the list goes on. The key to success is patience and tact (and it doesn't hurt to be nice either).

>> **Know your lease agreements inside and out before they're signed by either side.** It's often said that when you buy a commercial property, you're buying the lease and the building comes for free. In other words, if your lease is legally "weak," then your investment is financially weak in the eyes of other investors, lenders, and appraisers.

>> **No matter how busy you get, write a business plan for the property.** Remember, commercial properties are businesses. Treating them that way allows you to sleep at night because you know exactly what needs to be done and when. A good and well-thought-out business plan has a property summary, a market analysis, a sales and marketing plan, a management summary, and a financial plan.

>> **Know your strengths and weaknesses in managing the property.** After you assess your strengths and weaknesses, be sure to build on your strengths. Take on those tasks that you do well and that give you joy. Hire out those that you don't do well or that you don't like to do.

>> **Do it right the first time.** Pay for good help. The lowest bid may not be the best choice. Focus on quality, thoroughness, and attention to detail in everything you do concerning the property. After all, it's your property (and it's what pays the bills!).

**TIP**

Set a benchmark for your own personal cash flow. When you get right down to it, you're in this business to make money, right? After setting up a budget that takes into account the income and expenses of the property, set an amount that you'll collect as a payment for yourself as the owner and operator. Treat that amount as you would any other expense on the property.

# Developing basic business systems

**REMEMBER**

When you're about to purchase a commercial property, remember that what you're really about to own is a full-blown business. You're making a huge financial commitment, no matter how much of a down payment you make. Just as with any other business, you have *customers* — the tenants that you lease to — and you have *inventory* — the spaces or apartments that you're renting. There's also a sizable exchange of money between you and the tenants. Having said that, remember that every well-operated business develops basic systems to help it run efficiently. Commercial properties are no different.

For instance, you need to develop the following basic business systems in order to successfully manage your own property:

>> **An accounting system:** This type of system will help you handle the cash flowing in and the cash flowing out. Accounting systems are getting better and better as new software is developed.

**REMEMBER**

Because the lifeblood of a business is cash, you always need to be conscientious of your accounts. Take every measure to ensure that all the cash is accounted for every day — not just once per month.

>> **A sales and marketing system:** Whether you know it or not, you're a sales person when managing your own property. You're selling units of space, apartments, or entire floors to a customer, your tenant. So, smile and close that sale. Your sales and marketing system may include various means of advertising, ways of tracking the effectiveness of your advertising, training of staff to show prospective tenants the property, and market studies about competition.

>> **An operations system:** When managing your own property, you have to keep track of all the legal requirements of operating a property, such as enforcement of leases, building codes, local ordinances, building security, and hiring and managing contractors and vendors. And don't forget to track lease renewals.

>> **A maintenance system:** Say that a tenant notices water streaming down into the workspace. Do you simply get your tenant a cup or bucket? No, of course not. You need to have a system for tenants to report such things, so that you can fix them quickly. Also, you need to implement a preventive maintenance plan for every moving part on your property, such as air conditioners, furnaces, fans, elevators, escalators, and whatever else has moving parts. (The later section "Training your tenants to respect you and the property" provides some examples.)

# Doing it yourself: A checklist

Especially when first starting out in managing your own property, you may end up doing everything yourself (if you want to). You'll take care of advertising, showings, leasing, credit checks, some of the maintenance, hiring help, keeping the books, and the rehab, if required. Look at it as a way to learn the business from the inside out, earning your stripes, while at the same time cutting costs by doing those things yourself. If you're going it alone, all the many details can be pretty overwhelming. But if you follow our lead, you'll be just fine. Here are a few helpful questions to sort through as you get started:

>> **Is the commercial space ready to be leased?** Make sure it is clean and presentable, meets building codes, and is approved for its intended use.

>> **Who are you intending to lease to?** Decide who your ideal tenants would be and market to them specifically. Focus on your target market.

**REMEMBER**

Don't try to be a "be-all" to everyone because it's impossible to make everyone happy.

>> **How much are you leasing the unit or space for?** Pick up the phone and do a market survey and find out what your competitors in the area are charging for similar space. Commercial spaces that are kept full are priced just right.

>> **Do you have a solid lease agreement?** Make sure your lease agreement is from a reputable source and is lawyer approved. A commonly heard phrase in this line of work is "Your property is only worth the strength of the lease." So, if this lease is your first ever, definitely get some help from a local real estate attorney.

**REMEMBER**

There's no such thing as a standard lease agreement. Office building, retail center, and apartment leases are way different from each other.

>> **Do you have the means to do a background and credit check on the prospective tenant?** Again, whether you're leasing to a person or company, both need to be creditworthy and qualified with solid financial strength. Many online sources are available to perform credit and background checks on individuals. They charge a fee each time, but these costs are passed on to the applicant. In order to have a quick check of a business's credit, obtain a Dun and Bradstreet report (www.dnb.com/).

>> **Is your support team in place?** Your support team, which includes a contractor, an electrician, a plumber, a janitor, a landscaper, a bookkeeper, and an attorney, needs to be on hand at all times in case you need them. And, believe us, you *will* need them.

>> **What's your CPA's name?** That's right, you need a CPA, and you need to know their name. You need a CPA to do your tax planning and strategies. Come on, you can't do *everything* yourself.

# Training your tenants to respect you and the property

When you think about it, tenants are sort of like kids (but please don't tell them so). For instance, if you raise and train kids properly, they'll behave most times. When they misbehave, however, you have to show them who's boss, or else your house will be a mess. The same theory applies for your tenants: If you don't train them consistently and according to the rules you've established, your property will be a mess. Guaranteed.

**REMEMBER**

Training tenants and expecting them to conform goes both ways. Don't expect the tenants to pick up trash if your maintenance staff doesn't do this as well. Also, don't expect them to pay on time 100 percent of the time if you allow them to sometimes pay late without being penalized.

The following list provides some training ideas for your tenants. However, due to the different natures of tenants in each property type, you'll have to make them fit into your own plan of management. Here are some of the things you can do to run a tidy and successful ship:

>> **Allow peaceful enjoyment of the premises.** Allowing loud noises, loud parties, and rowdy gatherings is a surefire way for things to get out of hand in a jiffy. Put yourself in the shoes of a tenant who just wants to come to work (or come home) and get things done but is disturbed by loud noises down the hall every day. Is your tenant going to renew when the lease is up for renewal? It's doubtful. To avoid an exodus of tenants, give everyone strict guidelines on what's permitted and what isn't by providing a written set of rules.

>> **Implement a system to report maintenance issues.** To avoid cranky tenants, make sure that everyone is well informed on how to report any maintenance or repair issue with their particular unit or with any safety issues they notice on the property. Give the tenants a very simple and convenient method of reporting such things. With some properties tenants can use an app on their phone to request repairs; with other properties tenants can call a central number to report a maintenance issue. In addition, you can have an emergency service available 24/7 for late at night, weekends, and holidays.

>> **Conduct routine physical inspections.** As a preventive measure that's sure to create happy tenants, perform routine physical inspections of the units or space on a regular basis such as every 6 to 12 months. This gives you the opportunity to see whether any property abuses are occurring. If so, you can address them right away with the tenant. The proper way to make these inspections is to give the tenants advance notice that you'll be conducting an inspection of their units or space on a certain day and time.

>> **Provide a feeling of order within the property.** Believe it or not, no matter how free-spirited tenants may think they are, they all desire order and consistency in their place of stay or business. To create a feeling of order, make sure signs are well cared for and clean. Make sure any posted notices are in good shape and are up-to-date. Make sure gates are closed when and where they should be. Make sure the landscape is regularly maintained. Even make sure that your company stationery is professional and consistent. There's nothing like professionalism to set the tone.

>> **Present written tenant policies and procedures.** Providing a list of policies and procedures is important because it provides a road map as to how you will operate the property. You can have each tenant read, acknowledge, and sign your policy and procedures form as part of their lease package. In this form, you can include your operational policies and procedures on how you expect tenants to perform their part of the lease agreement. For instance, you can include expectations regarding payment, parking, environmental disturbances, maintenance, pets (if allowed), and so on.

>> **Don't accept late payments.** Cash-flow problems start with tenants not paying on time. Properties with a lot of delinquent payments and outstanding balances usually fell into that trap by allowing only one tenant to pay late. Then the word spread like wildfire to the rest of the tenants because your "iron fist" wasn't laid down. Properties with a history of late payments are absolutely a property management problem. As mentioned before, cash is the lifeblood of your operation, and so the life of your property will be drastically affected if you don't take ownership of the cash owed to you by the tenants.

**REMEMBER**

Your tenants' profiles will reflect the way you run your property. If you have a run-down property, you'll attract run-down tenants. On the other hand, if you own a property that shows pride of ownership, you'll attract tenants that are in tip-top shape themselves.

# Operating successfully day-to-day with the proper people and tools

**REMEMBER**

Managing your own property requires you to have certain things right within your reach. So, what tools do you need to get the job done as a property manager? What skilled people do you need to hire? What type of data or research do you always need to have on hand? Here's a list of things you need to have or know to manage your property:

>> **Property management software:** A couple of years into his real estate investing career, coauthor Peter Harris found himself pushing the envelope in keeping track of all the properties he owned. Soon, he was forced to start using property management software that allowed him to keep track of tenant information, tenant payments, vacancies, delinquencies, lease rates and renewals, maintenance records, and vendor information. This type of software is a wise investment and will likely enable you to expand your business.

>> **Advertising:** You must have a means of advertising your property's vacant spaces or units. To do so, use one or more of the many methods available:

- The tried and true "For Rent" or "For Lease" signs are amazingly effective and inexpensive. Your lowest cost and most effective advertising is typically the signs you have on the property. Banners and lawn signs are also popular.

- Referrals by tenants are quite helpful. They're cheap; the only money you have to pay is the amount that you offer a tenant for a referral. Also, it's always a compliment to your property when a tenant feels obliged to recruit for you.

- Online advertising is probably the most-used method of getting the word out these days. You can sign up with numerous websites, some of which are free; others require you to pay a fee to use their services.

- You can hire someone to do the advertising for you. Consider hiring a *leasing specialist,* a person who specializes in finding tenants for your property.

>> **Accounting software:** There's a wide range of accounting software programs that you can use to keep track of your property's finances, including QuickBooks by Intuit. When coauthor Peter Harris first started, he managed his property's finances with the spreadsheet software that came with his computer. He soon outgrew it and upgraded to a more professional program. It was worth its weight in gold. You can take this task to the next level by combining your accounting software with property management software.

>> **Vendors:** You're going to need to contract with skilled people to do such things as electrical, plumbing, carpentry, landscaping, or anything that you're unable to do yourself due to your lack of skill or time. The best way to find these types of vendors is by word of mouth. Ask for a referral from a fellow investor or from one of your other vendors. Always check references and ask to see a sample of their work, if available.

>> **Onsite maintenance:** A good handyperson is invaluable in the commercial real estate business. These people are the operation behind the operation. They can do routine and preventive maintenance and small repairs around or on the property. In the apartment business, you need one maintenance person for every 50 apartment units. For shopping centers and offices, property needs vary too greatly to estimate.

>> **A maintenance reporting system:** If a window is broken in an entryway, who tells who to fix it? How does the new window get purchased? Who makes sure it's fixed quickly? How does the property manager know when the work is done? All these questions are answered when you have an internal system of maintenance reporting. When a tenant reports a problem, it needs to be taken care of swiftly, cost-effectively, and correctly, and the boss must be notified when it's done. Maintenance should focus on curb appeal, daily and routine maintenance, and capital improvements.

>> **An attorney:** Evictions and tenant disputes are bound to occur at some time. It's just part of the business you're in. Unless you stay up-to-date and familiar with the local laws involving tenant-landlord matters, hire a real estate attorney to handle these types of things. You can go ahead and handle some of the more routine evictions, but consult a real estate attorney for the more complex matters. Forms and notices that are improperly drawn up can be thrown out of court and can send you back to square one with the problem tenant.

>> **A market survey:** One sure way of increasing the value of your property is to raise the rents or lease rates. In commercial real estate, don't rely on appreciation. Focus on the bottom line: the net operating income. So, one way of knowing if you can increase your rents is if your property consistently stays 100 percent occupied. When your space is constantly full, it usually means that your rates are below the top market rents for the area.

How do you know for sure if your rents are low? The answer is to perform a rent- and lease-rate survey or a competitive analysis of neighboring properties. You do this by researching and asking those property managers what their rates are. It's that simple. Compare their rates to yours. If your rates are lower than theirs and your property is 100 percent occupied, this indicates that there's room for you to increase your rates to at least the competitor's level. Another way of getting this important information is to call a local real estate broker.

# Letting Go: Using Professional Property Management Companies

After several years of purchasing properties locally, coauthor Peter Harris came to a time in his career where he had to make the decision to step away from the captain's seat to allow a professional property management company to manage his properties. As his area matured in pricing and his returns on investment started to decrease with each new purchase, he decided to look outside of his area. As he analyzed deals outside of his area, they looked quite attractive and he began to invest more there.

He had definitely begun reaping the benefits of higher returns when something started to happen: Because he owned and operated more properties, locally and out of the area, his whole business life became managing the properties. He had virtually no time to search for, analyze, and invest in new and exciting projects because nearly all of his time was spent on operating the properties. It even began to weigh in on his personal and family life as well. In essence, his management duties had taken over his life. And luckily, he knew there was more to life than just real estate.

So, he had to make a decision: Keep on trucking at a mile a minute or let go? He decided to let go and hire professional property management companies to oversee his properties. He soon got his life back. We don't want you to get sucked in like Peter did, so the following sections discuss how to successfully hire and manage property management companies.

## Understanding the ins and outs of professional property management

**REMEMBER**

Professional property managers are a special breed. They have to be extremely effective organizers, and they must be masters of the day planner. Frankly, we don't know how they can keep track of thousands of apartment units and millions of square feet of space at any one time. But the successful ones do this quite well. And thankfully so. Here's a typical list of the day-to-day responsibilities of a professional property manager. They must do the following:

>> Collect and deposit rents

>> Oversee maintenance of the property

>> Handle day-to-day operations

>> Contract in the name of the owner for utilities

>> Enforce leases

>> Hire and supervise all employees and independent contractors

>> Keep accounting books and records

>> Pay all bills in a timely fashion

>> Furnish the owner with financial reports

>> Prepare and execute annual operating budget and capital expenditures

>> Write a sales and marketing plan

>> Monitor effectiveness of the sales and marketing plan

>> Handle legal matters, such as evictions

>> Handle emergencies

>> Work with local officials, such as police and code enforcement

What the previous list does is help you define the role of the professional property manager or property management company. It's always helpful to know what to expect out of a person or company that you hire. Be clear and concise up front and have everything in writing before signing on the dotted line.

## Deciding to hire a professional property management company

Think of your million-dollar investment as a suitcase full of money. Now imagine that due to your busy schedule, you need to find someone to look after your suitcase when you can't be around. You can imagine how scrutinizing you would be of the person or company you chose to guard your suitcase full of money. You'd check that person's or company's background, credibility and capability, and integrity to the utmost with tough questions.

Treat hiring and managing of a property management company for your property with the same care. After all, your investment is worth a lot of money!

**REMEMBER**

Determining whether you want to hire a property management company to look after your investment can be a difficult and frustrating decision. However, there are some instances in which you're almost sure to hire someone. Here are those four instances:

>> **The property isn't local, or it's too far away.** For instance, performing the following duties can be difficult if you're operating properties that aren't in your area:

- Overseeing maintenance and repairs

- Taking care of evictions

- Handling emergencies

>> **The property is too large.** Here are two questions to ask yourself if you aren't sure whether your property is too large:

- How will I manage 100 apartment units myself and still have a daytime job?

- Can my current self-managed apartment business handle double or triple the number of units efficiently?

>> **You want to have a life or get your life back.** Let's face it, managing property profitably takes time — your time. How is your time best used? Are you spending too much time on your apartments and not enough on the other parts of your life? If so, hiring a property management company may be the right decision for you.

>> **You aren't good at managing property.** You know you're leaving money on the table each month due to your lack of skills. If that's the case, hire someone who has these skills and has a system and passion for managing property. This way, you get to do what you do (and enjoy!) best.

## Searching for property management candidates

When you're trying to round up property manager candidates, start by asking for referrals. For instance, use commercial real estate brokers as a resource for referrals. Hopefully, they have done enough deals where their clients are using management companies that they can speak on their experiences. You can also ask fellow investors who own properties like yours. Inquire about their experiences with certain companies that you're looking into. If one of your referrals doesn't pan out, ask *that referral* for a referral. Because property management selection is such a hit-or-miss process, it's best to start off interviewing someone who has already used that particular management company.

**TIP**

Here are some search-related tips to keep in mind:

>> It's helpful to drive around the neighborhood looking for "For Rent" or "Now Leasing" signs. Most times, the phone numbers listed are from property managers. Call those companies and start "feeling them out" as possible interview candidates. Just be honest and straightforward and tell them the reason for the call is to find property management for yourself.

>> It's best to gather a minimum of three property managers to interview. Obviously, the more you interview, the better your chances are of hiring the best suitor for the property.

>> If you're unable to find a reputable property management company, don't purchase the property — no matter how good of a deal it is. Remember the suitcase of money?

# Interviewing your prospective managers

Okay, so now it's time to pick up the phone and start the initial interview process. Keep in mind that this is just a "feeling out" process, in which you're looking for professionalism, prompt return of your phone call, and good rapport. There's no way you can judge the quality of the candidates' management skills just yet. In fact, you can go through all the interview situations and assessments and still not have a full grasp on a candidate's skills. You don't find out who your new manager really is until they are hired and put into action.

REMEMBER

This interview isn't for telling every candidate everything you expect. It's merely to gather information in order to make a decision regarding who you want to conduct a full interview with.

Here are a few questions to ask during your initial phone calls:

>> **What is the general vacancy rate in your area?** "Your area" could be a city, town, neighborhood, district, or street. This information is crucial when studying the feasibility of owning property in this area.

>> **How many units and/or square feet of space do you currently have under management? What type?** Make sure that the company has experience with your type of property. After all, a property management company that manages 400 single-family homes isn't the same as one that manages 400 units of apartment buildings.

>> **How long have you been in business?** If a candidate has less than a year of experience, don't use them. A candidate really needs to complete at least one cycle (spring, summer, fall, winter) to know what's going on. We personally wouldn't use anyone with less than three years of actual experience.

>> **What are your percentage management fees?** Plug these fees into your property cash-flow analysis. Compare fees and services with other companies.

>> **Do you have your own maintenance staff or do you use independent contractors?**

>> **What is the cost for an eviction process from start to finish?** Have the candidates review the whole process.

>> **What are the costs of new leases to the new owner?** You may have to compensate your property manager with 50 to 100 percent of the first month's rent in some markets.

>> **How do you advertise your vacancies?** Some properties get by with their sign and a few banners along a busy street. Other properties pay someone to manage a social media marketing campaign. Ask the property manager whether any advertising is included as part of their regular fees.

>> **What are your business hours?** This can make a difference especially if you're trying to fill up a property with empty units. You don't want prospective tenants coming by on a Saturday who aren't able to view your units for rent.

>> **How are tenant emergencies and weekend calls handled?** Find out how this works. Is it a phone call or an app that tenant can use? Are you paying double time after hours or does the property manager have a staff person on call?

>> **What monthly reports do you typically send owners?** Make sure to ask *when* these go out. If there's a problem, the sooner you know about it the better.

TIP

After hanging up from a phone interview, it helps to sit back and ask yourself this important question: "What does my gut feeling tell me about this person and their company?" Gut feeling and instinct are an important part of this process, so honor your perception. If you feel that there wasn't a connection between the two of you, move on to the next candidate. Whatever you do, don't continue with a candidate just because they were really nice. Nice doesn't cut it in property management.

## Checking credibility and capability

TIP

After conducting your initial phone interviews, you have to narrow your choices. To do so, ask those companies that you're interested in whether they're interested in managing your property. If the answer is yes, the next step is to invite them to the property for a face-to-face meeting and walk-through. During this meeting, you have to gauge their credibility and capability. Asking yourself the following three questions can help:

>> **Is this company a mom-and-pop operation?** Smaller-sized operations don't have the manpower to get the job done. They're just too small to consistently deliver what they promise. You'll likely need to hire a medium-sized property management company. Medium-sized companies have more structure, more employees, and have a "company feel" to them. On the other hand, hiring a very large property management company may be a bit too expensive.

>> **Does the company's management style match yours?** Is your preference to work with a very aggressive "in your face" manager or one that's more diplomatic? Both styles can be effective in their own ways. Choose a type that settles with what you've been exposed to in your own life.

>> **Is the company local?** Find out whether the company operates in the same city as your property. If it doesn't, how far away is it and does it currently manage property in the vicinity? If the company is not local and has no presence, you'll have to question how well they know the area, the market, and potential tenants.

REMEMBER

You need to make sure that you and the manager have a complete understanding of each side's expectations. So, be sure to express, in detail, as much about your expectations as you can to the property manager. In general, and from an owner's point of view, here are your likely expectations plainly put:

>> Maximize potential rental income and reduce operating costs.

>> Strengthen tenant retention and relations.

>> Enhance visual appeal of property and increase property value.

These are ultimate goals for a property when you get right down to it.

WARNING

Inquire whether any of the property management companies you're considering hiring owns and manages properties they personally own. This is a huge potential conflict of interest. The property they manage for you may be in direct competition with theirs.

## Drafting the property management agreement

After you've selected a property management company, you need to create a legally binding agreement, called a *property management agreement,* between the both of you. This agreement should describe the duties and responsibilities of both the owner and the manager. Before you sign one of these agreements, make sure that you have certain clauses in the contract. In our experiences, property managers want to get away with as little as possible that's written into the agreement. The following are basic "must-have" clauses of a property management agreement:

>> **Leasing clause:** This clause says that the manager must use their best efforts to keep the property rented and leased by procuring tenants for the property and negotiating and executing on behalf of the owner.

>> **Rents clause:** Under this clause, the manager is required to collect and deposit the rents and any revenues from the property and serve all notices for the collection of rent and other charges. The manager is also required to initiate actions for evictions and when necessary, to settle, compromise, or release actions or suits and reinstate tenancy.

>> **Service contracts clause:** A service contract clause requires the manager to execute in the owner's name for utilities and services for the operation and maintenance of the property.

>> **Accounting clause:** This clause says that the manager must keep proper books of account for the property and that these books need to be open for inspection by the owner. Also, the property manager must give the owner a monthly statement of financial status and operations on a specified date of each month.

>> **Owner approval dollar amount clause:** This clause states that the property management shall seek the written approval of the owner before spending an amount of money that exceeds a previously established amount.

>> **Reserve account clause:** Under this clause, the owner must maintain a specific amount of money in their account as a reserve amount. If the balance falls below this amount, the owner shall replenish it within 30 days.

>> **Compensation to property manager clause:** Under this clause, the owner agrees to pay the property manager on a monthly basis for the services that the manager provides. Compensation can be a percentage of collected revenues or a fixed fee. The percentage typically ranges from 4 percent to 10 percent of collected income.

TIP

Before signing your contract, find out whether there's a *per new lease fee.* A per new lease fee is a dollar amount charged to the owner every time a new lease is signed. In some cases, this fee can be as much as one month's rent. Find out who keeps the late fees, and determine whether there's an extra charge at any time during the eviction process. Will the property manager charge you every time they go to court? All these fees can quickly add up and erase your cash flow.

>> **Obligations of owner clause:** This clause states that the owner's require-ments include providing direction, specifications, and plans to the property management, reimbursing the property management for expenses occurred, and maintaining proper insurance levels.

>> **Terms of agreement clause:** This clause obviously provides information on the terms of the agreement. Initial terms are usually for 12 months. Never sign on for more than 12 months at any time because the property manager

may not be a good fit for you after all. Either party may terminate the agreement by giving a 30-day written notice to the other party.

>> **Default clause:** This clause states that if either party fails to perform his obligations per the agreement, the performing party may terminate the agreement. Legal action on either side is discussed in this clause as well.

>> **Terminations clause:** According to this clause, immediately upon termination, the property manager must provide the owner with all originals or copies of leases and all agreements and related documents. All property financial records in possession of the property manager must be delivered to the owner. A 30-day notice is required for termination.

>> **Fiduciary responsibility/statutory of compliance clause:** This is the code of ethics clause. It states that the property manager will perform all duties in the agreement. It also states the following:

- That the property manager's main obligation is to obey and abide by the law

- That the property manager will notify the owner of professional opinion matters

- That the property manager shall keep the owner's information strictly confidential and shall not share it with the public

**WARNING**

Be wary of fine print embedded in the agreement. For instance, if you ever see a "hold harmless" clause, have it removed from the agreement. This type of clause grants the property management company immunity from any harm and liability it causes on your property whether it's the company's fault or not. If it's a professional company and you're taking a risk on hiring them, they must take some of the responsibility. That's only fair, right? Also, be sure to delete any clauses stating that the property manager will act as real estate agent or broker or will receive commission if and when the owner sells the property. Hire a real estate agent to market and sell your property and let the property managers do what they do best — manage.

**TIP**

When working with property management companies on either capital improvement projects (such as replacing a roof or repaving the parking lot) or on rehabilitation projects, never pay for the whole project upfront and never put all the money into an account that the property management has access to. It's human nature to spend, rather than save, when money is readily available — especially if the money being used isn't theirs. Instead, have the money available on an "as-needed" or "draw" basis.

# Getting your reports: Monthly and weekly accountability

Remember getting report cards from school? They showed how well you were doing in each subject and what you needed help with. Your property receives a similar report from the property management company. Property management will likely send you status reports on different parts of the property. For example, it will send you reports regarding the income, the delinquent income or late payments, the expenses in detail, how many vacant apartments or spaces you have, and what maintenance was performed on the property during the month, just to name a few. The following sections explain the two different types of reports that you're likely to receive: monthly and weekly reports.

TIP

Weekly reports are rarely used, but they are just as important as monthly reports. To get the most out of reporting, make sure you incorporate weekly reporting. Later in this chapter, you find out what weekly reports are composed of and, more important, why you should use them.

## Typical monthly reports

Certain property management reports are sent to you once a month. These reports are sent monthly to give you the "big picture" of how the property is performing both financially and operationally. See Table 3-1 for a list of the typical reports that you're likely to receive each month.

**TABLE 3-1** **Typical Monthly Reports**

| Monthly Report | Details within the Report |
| --- | --- |
| Accounts receivable report | Detailed rent rolls of tenants with gross potential rent included |
| | Vacancy report showing empty units or space |
| | Vacancy report showing if empty units or space are preleased |
| Accounts payable report | Check register showing who each check was paid to |
| | Expense distribution breaking down the expenses into sections |
| General ledger report | Balance sheet |
| | Profit/loss (operating statement) — monthly |
| | Profit/loss (operating statement) — year-to-date |
| Maintenance and work order activity report | Requests for maintenance (by tenants) and status of the repairs |
| Budget and capital improvements report | A list of work that's scheduled, in progress, and completed |

**WARNING**

Don't stand for late reporting. If you were promised a set of reports on the first of every month and the reports are late, contact your property manager. Ask why the reports are late and be adamant about getting them immediately. If you don't hold the property manager accountable for this now, other important duties may start slipping as well. After all, it's human nature for folks to procrastinate when they can.

## Weekly reports

This section describes a weekly accountability system that's simple and easy to follow and understand, but most important, that's very effective. First of all, this system is designed to be easy for the property manager to follow, fill out, and report on. Because there's nothing complex about it, your property manager can't come up with any excuses why they can't turn it in on time. You should ask to receive this report every Monday morning.

**REMEMBER**

The idea of accountability is to focus weekly on key items such as occupancy, marketing, rent collection, rent delinquencies, and maintenance items. Why ask for a weekly rather than a monthly report? Well, think of it this way: Normally, owners speak with their property managers once per month (or once every 30 days) on the status of their properties. So, what happens if a vacancy issue occurs on the fifth of the month? You probably wouldn't find out until the first of next month, right? So, almost a month goes by before you can even address this vacancy issue. However, if you get a weekly accountability report, you would know about this issue and could promptly set forth on resolving it on the same day that it's reported. In this case, you have the ability to be *proactive* rather than *reactive.*

You can describe this accountability system with a sports metaphor. For example, when you're playing a game and you want to look at the score quickly, what do you do? You look at the scoreboard, of course! The scoreboard lets you know how you're doing — how many points you're ahead or behind, who has the ball, who's up next, how much time is on the clock, and so on. Figure 3-1 shows an example of a one-page property scoreboard.

**TIP**

This report is an exact copy of what coauthors Peter Conti and Peter Harris get on a weekly basis. Show this to your current or to-be-hired property manager as an example of what you require. The key to making it not overbearing to your property manager is to keep it to a single page in length. From this report you can see critical information that gives you a "scoreboard" view of how your property is performing from week to week. You'll be able to see upward or downward trends in income, vacancies, and maintenance issues — all important accountability items.

The _____ Apartments (Your Property)
To: _____ (Property Owner -- You)
From: _____ (Management Company)

Date: 10/21/05

Re: weekly report as of 10/21/05

Pages: 1

Property: _____ Apartments          Total Units: 94

**Occupancy Status:**

| Type | # of units | Rate | Sq. Ft. | Vacants | Leased | Notices to move out |
|------|-----------|------|---------|---------|--------|---------------------|
| 1 beds | 26 | $499 | 650 | 4 | 2 | 1 |
| 2 beds | 60 | $599 | 850 | 2 | 2 | |
| 3 beds | 8 | $699 | 1050 | 0 | 0 | |
| | | Total Available | | 6 | | |

**Current move-in bonus:** one month free stopped as of 10/1

**Vacants:** 6          **Leased:** 4          **Move Ins:** 2          **Total Made Ready Units:** 5

**Traffic Generated From:** resident referral, drive by, local paper

**Potential Income (if 100% rented):** $54,506

**Collected Income:** $48,730 as of 10/10

**Delinquent Amount:** $2582

**Maintenance Calls:**

| Appliance | AC | Plumbing | Electrical | Key | Other |
|-----------|----|----------|-----------|-----|-------|
| 2 | 6 | 1 | | 3 | 3 |

**FIGURE 3-1:**
A weekly property report.

# Knowing How to Be an Effective Absentee Owner

An *absentee owner* is an owner of a property that doesn't personally manage or reside on the property owned. An out-of-state owner could fall into that category. These types of owners often get a bad rap. Why? Because absentee owners have been known to ruin properties and cause decay in the neighborhoods where the properties are located. This weakening happens not only because the owner is physically absent from the property, but because they're emotionally absent as well. Their lack of involvement in the care and operation of the property causes the property to head in a downward spiral. This in turn affects the quality of the tenants that the property attracts as well as the overall neighborhood feel.

Here are signs and symptoms that you may be turning into an absentee owner:

>> You never visit the property.

>> You're in denial that the property is in financial trouble.

>> The city officials don't like you.

>> Your property has become or is located in what people refer to as a "war zone."

>> Nobody wants to live on the property.

>> You don't spend money on preventive maintenance and capital improvements.

>> Your maintenance solution for everything is to place temporary bandages on much-needed fixes.

However, don't worry; it is possible to be a positive, well-respected, and successful absentee owner. The first step is to turn the previous list of negative symptoms into positives. For instance, simply visit your property more often and see what's going on and what needs fixed. Second, give thoughtful attention to the way the property looks. Also, be sure to get (positively) involved with the city officials — they can help you out more than you'd think. And don't allow criminals on the property.

TIP

Here are some other ways that you can put your best foot forward:

>> **Have a precise management plan.** Before you buy the property, know who the property management will be. Hire a well-known and battle-proven property management company that knows exactly what it's going to take to successfully run the property. As one of our mentors once said, "If you fail to plan, plan to fail." A good and well-thought-out business plan has a property summary, a market analysis, a sales and marketing plan, a management summary, and a financial plan.

>> **Understand the infrastructure.** A successful property infrastructure means having an accounting system, a sales and marketing system, an operations system, and a maintenance system. When considering a property, make sure

that it has an infrastructure and determine how well it's working. If it isn't working, can it be fixed without breaking the bank? Know exactly what you're buying.

>> **Know the market.** Before you buy a property, understand the market conditions and know what's going on. Be sure to consider lease rates, rental rates, move-in bonuses, vacancy rates, job growth, population growth, and any upcoming economic development in the city.

>> **Have an exit strategy in place.** Know upfront, before you even make any offers, why you're purchasing the property. Are you buying it for cash flow, to refinance later, as a tax shelter, or for long-term growth? In fact, knowing your reasoning upfront may even cause you to pass on the deal altogether. It may even stop you from purchasing a property that's hundreds or thousands of miles from your area.

>> **Be ready to commit.** Be ready to commit time, money, and management to the property to ensure its success. And note that not all properties — even those of the same type — are the same. Some properties may take years to stabilize the income and occupancy, while others may take months. So, always plan for longer than you expect.

>> **Buy a large enough property.** Purchase a property that allows you to afford a staff for operation. The smaller the property, the smaller the income. And the smaller the income, the less hired help you can afford. In your analysis of the property, make sure that you can afford a property management company and its staff.

>> **Plan for a rainy day.** Rainy days are bound to happen in the commercial real estate business. Roof failure, water damage, and broken boilers are all common problems that you may come across. Have money saved up for these issues, and be sure to have reputable vendors lined up for when the problems strike.

>> **Visit the property routinely.** No matter how far away you are from the property, plan on paying a visit to the property at a minimum of once per year although twice or three times is recommended. However, during the first year of ownership, quarterly visits are recommended. Throw in a surprise visit every now and then too.

# Index

credits in escrow

about, 443

negotiating, 181–184

crime rates, low, as a characteristic of good neighborhoods, 104

curable defects, 107–108

curb appeal

about, 277

assessing potential, 279–280

'custom-built,' in advertising, 457

# D

daily rates, market statistics for Airbnb hosting, 349–350

date recorded, on mortgage/note, 226

days-on-market (DOM) statistics, 106

deals

"cash back at closing," 246

closing, 247–248

finding, 127–137

Death Valley, for selling, 427

debt service, 520

decision-making, for mortgages, 72–75

Declaration of Covenants, Conditions, and Restrictions (CC&Rs), 121, 123, 125

decluttering, for showings, 241–242

deductible expenses, as a tax advantage, 13–14

deed in lieu of foreclosure, 194

deed recording fee, 296

deed warranty names, on property title, 225

deeded (fee simple) ownership, 34

deeds

about, 329

preparation of, as marketing and selling costs, 300

default clause, in property management agreements, 565

deferred taxes, with installment sales, 14

delegating duties, 309–311

delinquent water or sewer bills, as marketing and selling costs, 300

delivering on expectations, 337

demand, supply and, 545

Department of Justice, 53

dependability, establishing trust through, 336

depreciation

land investing and, 43

as a tax advantage, 13–14

depressed housing market, selling in a, 417–420

detached residences, 111–117

detached single-family dwelling, 112

determining

current value of house, 430

home value, 139–158

need to sell, 409–417

profit potential for Airbnb hosting, 345–361

what Airbnb guests want, 366–368

which amenities to include in Airbnb listings, 368–374

developing

an eye for home improvements, 304–305

business systems, 552

disability insurance, 22

discount points, 296

dishwashers, as an amenity in Airbnb, 372

distressed property sales

about, 150

as a flaw of CMAs, 152

estimating
  rehab costs, 273–290
  resale value, 294–295
  time commitment for Airbnb hosting, 356–357
estoppel certificate, 330
estoppels, 532–533
evaluating
  apartment deals, 533–535
  commercial real estate, 519–547
  competition with Airbnb, 367–368
  potential curb appeal, 279–280
  real estate as an investment, 7–24
  retail shopping center deals, 535–538
  risk profile, 490–493
eviction, 197
excess liability (umbrella) insurance, 22
excitement, quantum pricing and, 442
expansion phase, of commercial real estate investing, 515
expectations
  awareness of hidden, 338–339
  delivering on, 337
expenses
  accounting for, 295–302
  for vacation homes, 30
extension cords, 284
exterior lighting, 95
external factors, 141
extra person fee, for Airbnb hosting, 400–401
eyeballing, 153

**F**

fact, opinion vs., 166
Fair Housing Act, 86–87

fair housing laws, 86–88
fair market value (FMV)
  about, 143–144
  calculating, 146–153
  median home prices vs., 145–146
  need-based pricing, 144–145
fake sellers, 176–179
faucets, 284
Federal Emergency Management Agency (FEMA), 106
fee simple (deeded) ownership, 34
fees
  setting for Airbnb hosting, 398–404
  types, 70–72
FEMA (Federal Emergency Management Agency), 106
fiduciary responsibility/statutory of compliance clause, in property management agreements, 565
filing for bankruptcy, 193–194
final showings, 465–466
finalizing foreclosures, 196–197
financial advisors, 48
financial health, ensuring, 21–22
financial issues
  as a disadvantage of condominiums, 121–122
  with foreclosures, 133
financial risk, accepting, 73
financing
  about, 63
  borrowing against home equity, 75–76
  buybacks through insurance-policy proceeds, 253
  buyer's, 320–321
  co-operative apartments, 126–127
  fees, 70–72

## H

Hamilton, Gene (author)
 *Bathroom Remodeling For Dummies,* 305
Hamilton, Katie (author)
 *Bathroom Remodeling For Dummies,* 305
hardwood floors, 286
Harmon, Lawrence C. (author)
 *Landlord's Legal Kit For Dummies,* 470
health, of housing market, 417–421
health insurance, 22
HELOCs (home equity loans), 75–76
HGTV (website), 304
hidden expectations, awareness of, 338–339
hiring professional management companies, 559–560
holding costs, 270, 298–299
*Home Buying Kit For Dummies* (Tyson and Brown), 432
home equity loans (HELOCs), 75–76
*Home Improvement For Dummies* (Carey and Carey, Jr.), 305
home improvements, developing an eye for, 304–305
home value
 about, 139–140
 appraisals *vs.* CMAs, 153–154
 buyers, sellers and, 154–158
 comparable market analysis, 146–153
 components of worth, 140–142
 determining, 139–158
 factors affecting, 102–103
 fair market value, 143–146
home warranty, as marketing and selling costs, 300
home-and-garden shows, 304

HomeInfoMax, 224
homeowners
 guiding during foreclosures, 201–202
 telephone number of, 229
homeowners' association fees
 about, 114
 as a holding cost, 299
homeowners associations, 126
homeowner's insurance
 about, 22
 as a holding cost, 298
homes
 buying, 26–27
 converting to rentals, 27–28
 new, 112–115
 used, 115–117
homestead exemption update, 330
honesty, for brokers/agents, 59
hospitality mindset, 333–338
hot tub safety, 95
hot water, as an amenity in Airbnb, 370
hotels, as investments, 510–511
housing market, health of, 417–421
HUD homes
 niche markets and, 268
 repos, 211
HUD/FHA 90-day rule, 271
HUD/FHA 91-to-180-day rule, 271
hybrid loans, 74

## I

icons, explained, 2
identifying
 amenities to include in Airbnb listings, 367
 do-it-yourself projects, 309

offering prices, 142

offers

  comparing, 320–324

  negotiating, 245–247

  power of multiple, 327–328

office buildings, as investments, 508–509

online advertising, 556

online listings, 244

onsite maintenance, 557

open houses

  about, 304, 462

  brokers' open, 462–463

  weekend, 463

opening bid, 229

operating expenses

  Airbnb hosting and, 354–355

  defined, 521

  of new homes, 114

operations system, 552

opinion, fact vs., 166

opportunities to add value, real estate investing compared with other investing, 14

opportunity costs, land investing and, 42–43

OPTs (overpriced turkeys), 158

ordering

  dumpsters for renovations, 314

  materials for renovations, 314

OREO (Other Real Estate Owned) opportunities, 210–211

other charges and fees, as marketing and selling costs, 300

Other Real Estate Owned (OREO) opportunities, 210–211

outdoor spaces, in an Airbnb, 376

outlets, 285

out-of-neighborhood comps, as a flaw of CMAs, 152

outsourcing, self-managing vs., 356

oven, as an amenity in Airbnb, 370

overpriced turkeys (OPTs), 158

overpricing homes, 445–449

owner approval dollar amount clause, in property management agreements, 564

owners, absentee, 568–570

ownership, taking of rental properties, 84–85

ownership investment, 12

Oxman, Kip (attorney), 458

# P

page numbers, on mortgage/note, 226

'panoramic,' in advertising, 457

paper towels, as an amenity in Airbnb, 370

parking, as a disadvantage of condominiums, 123

parking ratio, 532

partial recourse loan, 81

passion, investing and, 486–487, 488

pass-through entities, Qualified Business Income (QBI) deduction for, 16–17

patience, for brokers/agents, 59

payment of closing costs, as a buyer request, 322–323

payment policies, setting, 89

peak phase, of commercial real estate investing, 515

'people,' in advertising, 457

per new lease fee, 564

percentage of sales clause, 536

performance statistics, 348

performing due diligence, 215–235

permits

  for Airbnb hosting, 360

  as an operating expense for Airbnb hosting, 355

*Personal Finance For Dummies* (Tyson), 22

perspective, negotiating and, 163

phase I, 71

photos, for property inspection, 232–233

physical problems, with foreclosures, 133

pipes, 284

planned unit developments (PUDs), 38–39

planning consultants, for international investments, 474

plants, as an amenity in Airbnb, 371

pleasure-pleasure-panic pricing, 437–440

plumbing, 284

PMI (private mortgage insurance), 182

points, 65–66

poker face, for foreclosure auctions, 209–210

pool safety, 95

portfolios, running as businesses, 475–476

positive absorption, 42

possession at closing, as a buyer request, 322

possession problems, with foreclosures, 133

preapproval, 321

pre-auction stage, for foreclosures, 200–204

preparing

  for closing, 329

  properties for Airbnb hosting, 363–386

  for showings, 464–465

prepayment penalty, 75

prequalification, 321

price

  for comparing offers, 245

  as a components of worth, 142

  paid, on property title, 225

  previous, on property title, 225

price per square foot, 532

price relativity, 145

price trends, 145

pricing, for sales

  about, 435

  four-phase, 436–437

  methods for, 436–442

  pleasure-pleasure-panic, 437–440

  quantum, 440–442

pride of ownership, as a characteristic of good neighborhoods, 105

principle of conformity, 110–111

principle of progression, 107–109

principle of regression, 109–110

prioritizing

  needs, 105

  renovation projects, 305–308

privacy, as a disadvantage of condominiums, 121

private mortgage insurance (PMI), 182

probate, niche markets and, 268

professional help
  home *vs.* overseas, 498–499
  for international investments, 477
  for renovations, 310–311
professional management companies,
    558–568
professional valuations, 538–541
profit, calculating, 291–302
profit potential, of Airbnb hosting
  creating, 364–366
  determining, 345–361
  effect of location on, 346–348
  national averages, 346
projects, prioritizing for renovation,
    305–308
properties. *See also specific types*
  acquiring after foreclosure auctions,
    210–212
  bidding for at foreclosure auctions,
    207–210
  buying from other investors, 212
  checklist for, 233–234
  class of, 532
  collecting information about, 216–229
  comparing to other asset classes,
    470–471
  determining current value of, 430
  finding, 223–224, 277–278
  leasing to foreclosed-on
    homeowners, 253
  managing, 493–495
  preparing for Airbnb hosting, 363–386
  reselling to previous owners/families,
    250–251
  tax ID number for, 228
  taxable value of, 228

property development, 479–480
property inspection contingency, 171
property inspections
  about, 230–233, 273–274
  air conditioner, 285
  assessing potential curb appeal, 279–280
  big-ticket items, 281–286
  for condominiums, 120
  electrical system, 284–285
  estimating repair/renovation costs,
    289–290
  finding properties for, 277–278
  floors, 282
  foundations, 281–282
  furnace, 285
  gutters, 283
  lighting, 285–286
  odors, 280–281
  plumbing, 284
  promising features, 286–298
  roof, 283
  siding, 282
  tools for, 274–276
  walls, 282
  windows, 283
property management
  about, 549
  being effective absentee owners,
    568–570
  DIY, 550–557
  professional companies for, 558–568
  software for, 556
  for vacation homes, 30
property management agreements,
    drafting, 563–565

risks
  of Airbnb hosting, 360
  of Airbnb hosting without consent, 379
  of commercial real estate investing, 513
  real estate investing compared with
    other investing, 12–13
Roberts, Ralph R. (author)
  *Flipping Houses For Dummies*, 212, 241
roles, in flipping strategies, 262
roof, 283
rural market, for Airbnb hosting, 358–359

# S

'safe,' in advertising, 458
safety obligations, 94–97
sales
  foreclosure, 190–191
  negotiating, 319–330
sales and marketing system, 552
sales price
  about, 435
  four-phase, 436–437
  methods for, 436–442
  pleasure-pleasure-panic, 437–440
  quantum, 440–442
satellite, as an operating expense for
  Airbnb hosting, 355
schools, quality, as a characteristic of good
  neighborhoods, 104
screening applicants, 89–90
searching, for property management
  companies, 560–561
seasonality, adjusting to for Airbnb
  hosting, 391–393
second mortgage, 75, 207, 329

second peak season, for selling, 426–427
second-rate showings, 278
security deposits
  for Airbnb hosting, 402–403
  managing, 91–92
seized homes, niche markets and, 268
selecting
  baseline pricing strategies for Airbnb
    hosting, 390
  homes for purchase, 107–111
  neighborhoods, 105–107
  seller's agents, 239–240
  short-term or long-term mortgages, 74
self-managing, outsourcing *vs.*, 356
self-storage facilities, as investments,
  509–510
seller financing, 443
seller-financed loans, 75–78
sellers
  buyers compared with, 154–158
  cooperative, 179
  fake, 176–179
  forthright, 179
  motivated, 177
  time frames for, 177–178
  unrealistic, 157
seller's agents, choosing, 239–240
seller's market, 174
selling
  about, 407–408, 423, 435, 453
  advertising, 453–461
  checking buying power, 430–431
  consolidating sale and purchase, 430–434
  co-operative apartments, 127

special events, with Airbnb hosting, 393–394

special tax credits, for low-income housing and old buildings, 14–15

'square footage,' in advertising, 458

stability, as a characteristic of good neighborhoods, 105

staging, for showings, 240–243

start rate
  about, 69
  on ARMs, 66–67

state department of transportation, 211

state drug enforcement agencies, 211

state laws, 87–88

stopping foreclosure process, 191–195

storage, as a disadvantage of condominiums, 123

stovetop, as an amenity in Airbnb, 370

strong market, selling in a, 421

structural repairs, for fixer-uppers, 129

style, principle of conformity and, 111

subdivision, from foreclosure notice, 218

sublets, 97

submitting counteroffers, 326–327

supply and demand, 545

switching on utilities, 313–314

# T

tax advantages, real estate investing compared with other investing, 14–18

tax advisors
  about, 47–48
  for international investments, 474

Tax Cuts and Jobs Act (2017), 15

tax ID number, for property, 228

tax liens, 207, 227

taxable value, of properties, 228

tax-deferred compounding of value, 8

tax-free rollovers, of rental property profits, 14

T-bills (Treasury bills), 68

team-building
  about, 45–46
  agents, 52–59
  appraisers, 59–60
  attorneys, 61
  avoiding financial conflicts of interest, 49–50
  brokers, 52–59
  financial advisors, 48
  lenders, 50–52
  mortgage brokers, 50–52
  tax advisors, 47–48
  timing for establishing your team, 46–47

teardowns, niche markets and, 268

teaser rate, on ARMs, 66

Technical Stuff icon, 2

technology, Airbnb hosting and, 341–342

temporality, with Airbnb hosting, 393–394

1099-S report, 330

tenants
  moving in/out, 92–94
  protecting from criminal activity, 96–97
  training, 554–555

terminating rental contracts, 98

terminations clause, in property management agreements, 565

termite inspection report, 329

terms and conditions, in lease-option agreements, 255

Upwork, 498

U.S. Department of Commerce's Bureau of Economic Analysis, 107

U.S. Department of Housing and Urban Development (HUD), 107

U.S. Securities and Exchange Commission, 197

use, as a factor creating value, 541–542

used homes, 115–117

USPAP (Uniform Standards of Professional Appraisal Practice), 60

utilities

as an operating expense for Airbnb hosting, 355

as a holding cost, 299

switching on, 313–314

# V

VA foreclosures, niche markets and, 268

VA repos, 211

vacancy, 521

vacancy rate, 521

vacation homes, 29–31

valuations

options for, 476–477

professional, 538–541

value

about, 139–140

appraisals *vs.* CMAs, 153–154

buyers, sellers and, 154–158

comparable market analysis, 146–153

components of worth, 140–142

defined, 104

determining, 139–158

factors affecting, 102–103

factors creating, 541–546

fair market value, 143–146

as a moving target, 141

variable building costs, in purchase agreements, 267

vendors, 557

verifying

buying power, 430–431

capability of property managers, 562–563

credibility of property managers, 562–563

# W

walls, 281, 282

warehouses, as investments, 509

Warning icon, 2

water, as an amenity in Airbnb, 370

water bills, unpaid, 295

water filter, as an amenity in Airbnb, 372

water heater, 284

water pressure, 284

wealth-producing potential, of real estate, 8–10

wear and tear, as a flaw of CMAs, 151

websites

Airbnb Help Center, 361

American Society of Home Inspectors (ASHI), 107

Better Homes and Gardens, 304

Cheat Sheet, 3

Commercial Multiple Listing Service (CMLS), 54

Commercial Property Evaluator, 523, 525

Contractors.com, 297

CoStar, 54

# About the Authors

**Ray Brown** is a veteran of the real estate profession with over four decades of hands-on experience. A former manager for Coldwell Banker Residential Brokerage Company, McGuire Real Estate, and Pacific Union GMAC Real Estate, as well as a founder of his own real estate firm, the Raymond Brown Company, Ray is currently a writer, consultant, and public speaker on residential real estate topics. On his way to becoming a real estate guru, Ray worked as the real estate analyst for KGO-TV (ABC's affiliate in San Francisco) and was a syndicated real estate columnist for *The San Francisco Examiner*. For 16 years he hosted a weekly radio program, *Ray Brown on Real Estate,* for KNBR. In addition to his work for ABC, Ray has appeared as a real estate expert on CNN, NBC, CBS, and in *The Wall Street Journal* and *Time*. He is the coauthor of *Home Buying Kit For Dummies* and *Selling Your House For Dummies.*

**Peter Conti** is the CEO of RealEstate101.com. For many years he ran a large company with hundreds of mentoring clients and traveled across the country teaching seminars. He now leads a small team of investors who are buying commercial properties across the country. He is the coauthor of *Commercial Real Estate Investing For Dummies.*

**Robert S. Griswold, MSBA,** is a successful real estate investor, expert witness, and hands-on landlord/property manager with a large portfolio of residential and commercial rental income properties. He uses print and broadcast journalism to bring his many years of experience to his readers, listeners, and viewers. He is the author of *Property Management For Dummies* and *Property Management Kit For Dummies* and for 15 years was the real estate expert for NBC San Diego, with a regular on-air live-caller segment. Robert was the host of a live weekly radio talk show, *Real Estate Today!,* for nearly 15 years, and he's also the columnist for the syndicated "Rental Roundtable" and "Rental Forum" columns. These popular features are published in dozens of major newspapers throughout the country, and Robert has been recognized twice as the number-one real estate broadcast journalist in the nation by the National Association of Real Estate Editors. He is the coauthor of *Real Estate Investing For Dummies* and *Landlord's Legal Kit For Dummies.*

**Laurence C. Harmon,** president of Harmon Law LLC, specializes in real estate law and provides extensive teaching, market research, and consulting on subjects related to multifamily housing, marketing, and management, with concentration in federal and state fair housing law. He earned his bachelor's degree in history and marketing, *cum laude,* from Pomona College, Juris Doctorate (JD) with honors from the Stanford University School of Law, and the Certified Property Manager (CPM) designation from the Institute of Real Estate Management (IREM). He is the coauthor of *Landlord's Legal Kit For Dummies.*

**Peter Harris** is the CEO of Commercial Property Advisors. He has purchased and put together commercial and residential real estate deals across the country for years. He also sits on the board of advisors on several private and national real estate investment and development companies. He is the coauthor of *Commercial Real Estate Investing For Dummies*.

**Symon He** is a co-founder of LearnBNB.com, a leading online educational destination for all things Airbnb hosting. His research and works have been cited in the *Wall Street Journal* and *Forbes* and on Reuters, CNBC, and SKIFT. Through his training and coaching programs, he has worked directly with thousands of aspiring Airbnb hosts beginning their hosting journeys. He is the coauthor of *Airbnb For Dummies*.

**Joe Kraynak** is a freelance writer who has authored and coauthored dozens of books on topics ranging from slam poetry to computer basics. You can find Joe on the web at JoeKraynak.com. He is the coauthor of *Foreclosure Investing For Dummies* and *Flipping Houses For Dummies*.

**Kyle Roberts** is a human resources professional who has supported teams such as field operations, talent management, and talent development. Like his father, Ralph R. Roberts, he also has a passion for flipping houses. He is the coauthor of *Foreclosure Investing For Dummies* and *Flipping Houses For Dummies*.

**Ralph R. Roberts**'s success in real estate sales is legendary. He has been profiled by the Associated Press, CNN, and *Time* magazine and has done hundreds of radio interviews. Ralph is a seasoned professional in all areas of house flipping, including buying, rehabbing, and reselling homes quickly and at a handsome profit. For more about Ralph, visit RalphRoberts.com. He is the coauthor of *Foreclosure Investing For Dummies* and *Flipping Houses For Dummies*.

**James Svetec** is the creator and founder of BNB Mastery Program, where he helps people to earn a full-time income managing other people's properties on Airbnb. He is also the co-owner of LearnBNB.com, the No. 1 resource for people from all over the world to learn about the world of Airbnb hosting. Having successfully built a short-term rental management company in record time, James now teaches fellow Airbnb hosts and managers how to achieve success on Airbnb. He is the coauthor of *Airbnb For Dummies*.

**Eric Tyson, MBA,** is a bestselling author and syndicated columnist. Through his counseling, writing, and teaching, he equips people to manage their personal finances better. An accomplished freelance personal finance writer, Eric is the author of the national bestsellers *Personal Finance For Dummies* and *Investing For Dummies,* and was an award-winning columnist for the *San Francisco Examiner*. His work has been featured and quoted in hundreds of national and local publications, including *Newsweek,* the *Wall Street Journal, Forbes, Kiplinger's Personal Finance Magazine,* the *Los Angeles Times,* and *Bottom Line/Personal;* and on Fox, NBC's *Today Show,* ABC, CNBC, PBS's *Nightly Business Report,* CNN, CBS national radio, Bloomberg Business Radio, and Business Radio Network. He's on the web at www.erictyson.com. Eric is the coauthor of *Real Estate Investing For Dummies, Home Buying Kit For Dummies,* and *Selling Your House For Dummies.*

**Nicholas Wallwork** is a leading international real estate market commentator, entrepreneur, investor, and developer. Nicholas heads up several real estate and investment companies and has produced and presented a number of real estate TV shows on Sky TV in the United Kingdom. As an author, he writes a multitude of educational content dedicated to supporting landlords, real estate professionals, and investors across the industry through www.propertyforum.com (a real estate chat forum, educational hub, and news portal) and www.bullmarketboard.com (a stock market investing chat forum, hub, and news portal). He is the author of *Investing in International Real Estate For Dummies.*

## Publisher's Acknowledgments

**Senior Acquisitions Editor:** Tracy Boggier
**Senior Managing Editor:** Kristie Pyles
**Compilation Editor:** Georgette Beatty
**Project Manager:** Tracy Brown Hamilton
**Copy Editor:** Jennifer Connolly

**Production Editor:** Saikarthick Kumarasamy
**Cover Image:** © MicroStockHub/Getty Images